Lecture Notes in Computer Science 7387

Commenced Publication in 1973
Founding and Former Series Editors:
Gerhard Goos, Juris Hartmanis, and Jan van Leeuwen

Marco Brambilla   Takehiro Tokuda
Robert Tolksdorf (Eds.)

Web Engineering

12th International Conference, ICWE 2012
Berlin, Germany, July 23-27, 2012
Proceedings

 Springer

Volume Editors

Marco Brambilla
Politecnico di Milano, Dipartimento di Elettronica e Informazione
Via Ponzio 34/5, 20133, Milano, Italy
E-mail: marco.brambilla@polimi.it

Takehiro Tokuda
Tokyo Institute of Technology, Department of Computer Science
2-12-1 Oookayama, Tokyo 152-8552, Japan
E-mail: tokuda@cs.titech.ac.jp

Robert Tolksdorf
Freie Universität Berlin, Institut für Informatik
Königin-Luise-Strasse 24-26, 14195 Berlin, Germany
E-mail: tolk@ag-nbi.de

ISSN 0302-9743   e-ISSN 1611-3349
ISBN 978-3-642-31752-1   e-ISBN 978-3-642-31753-8
DOI 10.1007/978-3-642-31753-8
Springer Heidelberg Dordrecht London New York

Library of Congress Control Number: 2012941612

CR Subject Classification (1998): H.3.5, H.3.3, H.3, H.4, D.2.1, D.2, J.1, H.5.3, H.5,
H.2.8, I.2.6, I.2.4, C.2

LNCS Sublibrary: SL 3 – Information Systems and Application, incl. Internet/Web
and HCI

Typesetting: Camera-ready by author, data conversion by Scientific Publishing Services, Chennai, India

Printed on acid-free paper

Springer is part of Springer Science+Business Media (www.springer.com)

Preface

The crucial role of the Web in every aspect of contemporary societies and of everyday life is clearly visible at a global scale. Web engineering strives to accomplish the wish of an accessible, universal and affordable virtual platform where people and applications can smoothly interact. To this end, Web engineering systematically applies the knowledge and techniques of a large range of disciplines, spanning from computer science to social sciences.

This volume contains the proceedings of the 12th International Conference on Web Engineering (ICWE2012), which was held in Berlin, Germany, in July 2012. Berlin has an outstanding research landscape in computer science. The Freie Universität Berlin and three large universities in and surrounding Berlin offer computer science and information systems degrees. Berlin and Potsdam host various world-renown research institutions. The upcoming EU Knowledge Innovation Center on ICT as part of the European Institute of Technology will be located in Berlin. This makes Berlin a perfect place for researchers and practitioners to meet and discuss innovation in ICT in general and on the Web in particular. The ICWE conferences represent first-class forums for the Web engineering community. ICWE is endorsed by the International World Wide Web Conference Committee (IW3C2) and the International Society for Web Engineering (ISWE). Previous editions took place at Paphos (Cyprus), Vienna (Austria), San Sebastian (Spain), Yorktown Heights, NY (USA), Como (Italy), Palo Alto, CA (USA), Sydney (Australia), Munich (Germany), Oviedo (Spain), Santa Fe (Argentina), and Cáceres (Spain).

This year's call for papers attracted 98 submissions from 37 countries. Paper topics cover a broad range of areas, namely, Web modeling, linked data management, Web services, mashups, AJAX, user interfaces, personalization, search, social networks and so on. Submitted papers were reviewed by at least three reviewers from the Program Committee comprising 69 experts in Web engineering. Based on their reviews, 20 submissions were accepted as full papers (acceptance rate of 20%) and 15 submissions were accepted as short papers (acceptance rate of 15%). In addition, six posters, 12 demos, and five tutorials were also part of the conference program. The conference hosted a keynote by Richard Soley, president of OMG, on the impact of standardization on the Web and Web engineering activities. Several co-hosted workshops offered a venue for specialists to discuss on-going research and devise future research agendas.

Such an eventful program would not have been possible without the involvement of a large number of people and institutions. We would like to express our deep gratitude to Freie Universität Berlin as the local organizer. We are also indebted to Geert-Jan Houben, who acted as liaison to ISWE and ICWE Steering Committee, and to Bebo White, who acted as liaison to the IW3C2.

Berlin   Marco Brambilla
Summer 2012   Takehiro Tokuda
                                                           Robert Tolksdorf

Organization

General Chair

Robert Tolksdorf — Freie Universität Berlin

Program Chairs

Marco Brambilla — Politecnico di Milano
Takehiro Tokuda — Tokyo Institute of Technology

ICWE Steering Committee Liaison

Geert-Jan Houben — TU Delft

Workshop Chairs

Michael Grossniklaus — Portland State University
Manuel Wimmer — TU Wien

Tutorial Chairs

Maria Bielikova — Slovak University of Technology
Fabian Abel — TU Delft

Demo and Poster Chairs

Stefan Pietschmann — TU Dresden
Sven Casteleyn — Universidad Politecnica de Valencia

PhD Mentoring

Irene Garrigs — University of Alicante
Oscar Pastor — Universidad Politécnica de Valencia

Local Chair

Markus Luczak-Rösch — Freie Universität Berlin

Program Committee

Silvia Abrahao	Universidad Politecnica de Valencia
Sören Auer	Universität Leipzig
Fernando Bellas	Titular Professor of University
Boualem Benatallah	University of New South Wales
Davide Bolchini	Indiana University
Alessandro Bozzon	Politecnico di Milano
Marco Brambilla	Politecnico di Milano
Jordi Cabot	INRIA-École des Mines de Nantes
Coral Calero	Universidad de Castilla-La Mancha
Fabio Casati	University of Trento
Key-Sun Choi	KAIST
Richard Cyganiak	Digital Enterprise Research Institute, NUI Galway
Florian Daniel	University of Trento
Olga De Troyer	Vrije Universiteit Brussel
Damiano Distante	Unitelma Sapienza University
Peter Dolog	Aalborg University
Suzanne Embury	University of Manchester
Flavius Frasincar	Erasmus University Rotterdam
Piero Fraternali	Politecnico di Milano
Martin Gaedke	Chemnitz University of Technology
Irene Garrigos	University of Alicante
Dragan Gasevic	Athabasca University
Athula Ginige	University of Western Sydney
Michael Grossniklaus	Portland State University
Volker Gruhn	Universität Duisburg-Essen
Hao Han	National Institute of Informatics
Simon Harper	University of Manchester
Andreas Harth	AIFB, Karlsruhe Institute of Technology
Olaf Hartig	Humboldt-Universität zu Berlin
Bernhard Haslhofer	Cornell University Information Science
Martin Hepp	Bundeswehr University Munich, Germany
Geert-Jan Houben	TU Delft
Gerti Kappel	Vienna University of Technology
In-Young Ko	Korea Advanced Institute of Science and Technology
Nora Koch	Ludwig Maximilians University of Munich
Frank Leymann	Institute of Architecture of Application Systems
Steffen Lohmann	Universidad Carlos III de Madrid
Markus Luczak-Rösch	Freie Universität Berlin
Maristella Matera	Politecnico di Milano

Santiago Meliá	University of Alicante
Hamid Motahari	HP Labs
Wolfgang Nejdl	L3S and University of Hannover
Axel-Cyrille Ngonga Ngomo	University of Leipzig
Luis Olsina	GIDIS and National University of La Pampa
Satoshi Oyama	Hokkaido University
George Pallis	University of Cyprus
Oscar Pastor Lopez	Valencia
Cesare Pautasso	University of Lugano, Switzerland
Vicente Pelechano	Universidad Politecnica de Valencia
Alfonso Pierantonio	University of L'Aquila
Matthias Quasthoff	Hasso-Plattner-Institut
I.V. Ramakrishnan	SUNY Stony Brook
Gustavo Rossi	LIFIA-F. Informatica, UNLP
Fernando Sanchez-Figueroa	Universidad de Extremadura
Felix Sasaki	FH Potsdam / W3C German-Austrian Office
Fumiko Satoh	IBM Tokyo Research Laboratory
Daniel Schwabe	PUC-Rio
Juan F. Sequeda	The University of Texas at Austin
Michael Sheng	University of Adelaide
Weisong Shi	Wayne State University
Tetsuya Suzuki	Shibaura Institute of Technology, Saitama, Japan
Takehiro Tokuda	Tokyo Institute of Technology
Robert Tolksdorf	Freie Universität Berlin
Riccardo Torlone	Roma Tre University
Jean Vanderdonckt	Université catholique de Louvain
Erik Wilde	UC Berkeley
Marco Winckler	ICS-IRIT, Université Paul Sabtier
Bin Xu	DCST, Tsinghua University
Ying Zhang	The University of New South Wales, Sydney

Poster and Demo Track Program Committee

Fabian Abel	Web Information Systems, TU Delft
Sören Auer	Universität Leipzig
Devis Bianchini	University of Brescia
Maria Bielikova	Slovak University of Technology in Bratislava
Alessandro Bozzon	Politecnico di Milano
Marco Brambilla	Politecnico di Milano
Sven Casteleyn	Universitat Politècnica de València
Richard Chbeir	LE2I-CNRS
Florian Daniel	University of Trento
Oscar Diaz	University of the Basque Country
Peter Dolog	Aalborg University
Flavius Frasincar	Erasmus University Rotterdam

Irene Garrigos	University of Alicante
Gerti Kappel	Vienna University of Technology
Nora Koch	Ludwig Maximilians University of Munich
Maristella Matera	Politecnico di Milano
Santiago Melia	University of Alicante
Cesare Pautasso	University of Lugano, Switzerland
Stefan Pietschmann	Technische Universität Dresden
Gustavo Rossi	LIFIA-F. Informatica, UNLP
Fernando Sánchez Figueroa	Universidad de Extremadura
Takehiro Tokuda	Tokyo Institute of Technology
Robert Tolksdorf	Freie Universität Berlin, Networked Information Systems
Antonio Vallecillo	University of Malaga
William Van Woensel	Vrije Universiteit Brussel
Marco Winckler	ICS-IRIT, Université Paul Sabtier
Jürgen Ziegler	University of Duisburg-Essen

Additional Reviewers

Aguilar, Jose Alfonso
Ahmed, Faisal
Asadi, Mohsen
Becker, Pablo
Benner, Marian
Bislimovka, Bojana
Blanco Bueno, Carlos
Book, Matthias
Brosch, Petra
Busch, Marianne
Bühmann, Lorenz
Caballero, Ismael
Chen, Alex
Clemente, Pedro J.
Conejero, Jose Maria
Danylevych, Olha
Di Ruscio, Davide
Diez, David
Eramo, Romina
Feng, Song
Fernandez, Adrian
Fons, Joan
Garcia, Felix
Ge, Mouzhi
Grapenthin, Simon
Haag, Florian
Haupt, Florian

Hellmann, Sebastian
Imran, Muhammad
Iovino, Ludovico
Islam, Asiful
Janusz, Daniel
Kovanovic, Vitomir
Kovatsch, Matthias
Kuznetsova, Polina
Langer, Philip
Lew, Philip
Linaje, Marino
Ma, Jiangang
Mathew, Sujith Samuel
Mayrhofer, Dieter
Mazón, Jose-Norberto
Melnyk, Valentyn
Mohabbati, Bardia
Molina, Hernan
Morales-Chaparro, Rober
Noor, Talal
Nowak, Alexander
Oosterman, Jasper
Paulheim, Heiko
Peternier, Achille
Polo, Macario
Preciado, Juan Carlos

Qin, Yongrui
Rodriguez, Carlos
Rodriguez-Castro, Benedicto
Rodriguez-Echeverria, Roberto
Roy Chowdhury, Soudip
Satoh, Fumiko
Schleicher, Daniel
Serrano, Manuel
Shekarpour, Saeedeh
Soi, Stefano
Soviak, Andrii
Stadtmüller, Steffen
Trent, Scott
Valderas, Pedro
Vigo, Markel
Wagner, Sebastian
Weippl, Edgar
Wimmer, Manuel
Xie, Dong
Yao, Lina
Yu, Weiren
Zaveri, Amapali
Zhang, Chenyuan
Zor, Sema

Silver Sponsors

SparxSystems Software GmbH
Handelskai 340 Top 5 / Ecke Marathonweg
A-1020 Wien
Tel.: +43 (0)662 90 600 2041
Fax: +43 (0)662 90 333 3041
e-Mail: sales@sparxsystems.eu

WebRatio
Piazza Cadorna, 10
20123 Milano
Tel.: +39 02 3671 4280
Fax: +39 02 3671 4291
e-Mail: contact@webratio.com

Table of Contents

Social Networks and Collaboration

Tagging

Personalization and Personal Systems

Search

Web Modeling

AJAX and User Interfaces

Web Services

Web Crawling

Web and Linked Data Management

Posters

Demos

Tutorials

Reusable Awareness Widgets for Collaborative Web Applications – A Non-invasive Approach

Matthias Heinrich[1], Franz Josef Grüneberger[1],
Thomas Springer[2], and Martin Gaedke[3]

[1] SAP Research, Germany
{matthias.heinrich,franz.josef.grueneberger}@sap.com
[2] Department of Computer Science,
Dresden University of Technology, Germany
thomas.springer@tu-dresden.de
[3] Department of Computer Science,
Chemnitz University of Technology, Germany
martin.gaedke@cs.tu-chemnitz.de

Abstract. Creating awareness about other users' activities in a shared workspace is crucial to support efficient collaborative work. Even though the development of awareness widgets such as participant lists, telepointers or radar views is a costly and complex endeavor, awareness widget reuse is largely neglected. Collaborative applications either integrate specific awareness widgets or leverage existing awareness toolkits which require major source code adaptations and thus, are not suited to rapidly enrich existing web applications.

Therefore, we propose a generic awareness infrastructure promoting an accelerated, cost-efficient development of awareness widgets as well as a non-invasive integration of awareness support into existing web applications. To validate our approach, we demonstrate the integration of three developed awareness widgets in four collaborative web editors. Furthermore, we expose insights about the development of reusable awareness widgets and discuss the limitations of the devised awareness infrastructure.

1 Introduction

Collaborative web applications such as Google Docs have become pervasive in our daily lives since they expose a rich feature set, provide broad device support and offer instant accessibility without inducing time-consuming installation procedures. Commonly, those collaborative real-time applications allow multiple users to edit the same document concurrently which requires workspace awareness support. Workspace awareness is defined as the "up-to-the-moment understanding of another person's interaction with the shared space" [1] and in essence, it enables effective collaborative work [2] by answering the "who, what, and where" questions (e.g. who is in the workspace, what are the other participants doing, where are they working). Examples of widely adopted awareness

M. Brambilla, T. Tokuda, and R. Tolksdorf (Eds.): ICWE 2012, LNCS 7387, pp. 1–15, 2012.

Fig. 1. Screenshots of application-specific awareness widgets extracted from Google Docs, Codoxware and EtherPad

widgets supporting collaborative work are participant lists, telepointers, radar views, etc. (cf. Figure 1).

Even though multi-user applications largely offer the same set of awareness widgets (e.g. most collaborative applications provide some kind of participant list) and software reuse has been advocated for decades [3], there are no web frameworks accommodating out-of-the-box awareness support and promoting a non-invasive integration approach. Thus, developers re-implement awareness widgets for each collaborative web application or face massive source code changes adopting awareness toolkits, in particular, if existing applications are enriched. Both approaches entail major development efforts and costs.

Therefore, we devised a generic awareness infrastructure (GAI) that on the one hand side simplifies the development of awareness widgets by providing basic awareness services. On the other hand side, the GAI promotes the reuse of awareness widgets facilitating a non-invasive integration approach. The widget reuse is achieved by anchoring the GAI in various W3C specifications (e.g. CSS Object Model [4], DOM Core [5] or DOM Events specification [6]). Consequently, standards-based web applications are able to leverage the GAI including the library of reusable awareness widgets.

The main contributions of this paper are three-fold:

- We propose a generic awareness infrastructure facilitating non-invasive awareness support for standards-based web applications.
- We expose a development blueprint supporting developers to devise novel reusable awareness widgets for web applications.
- We evaluate the generic awareness infrastructure by incorporating three implemented awareness widgets into four collaborative web applications and discuss the limitations of the proposed approach.

The rest of this paper is organized as follows: Section 2 elaborates on the challenges devising reusable awareness widgets. Section 3 illustrates the GAI architecture and introduces the development blueprint for novel reusable awareness widgets. While Section 4 presents the validation of the GAI approach, Section 5 carves out strengths and limitations. Section 6 compares our work to the state-of-the-art and Section 7 exhibits conclusions.

2 Challenges

Devising a generic solution instead of an application-specific one imposes additional challenges since universal solutions have to abstract from certain specifics to aspects that hold for an entire class of applications. Characteristics that are especially challenging while developing generic awareness support for web-applications are

1. the diversity of collaborative web applications,
2. the multitude of available browsers, and
3. the proliferation of web-enabled devices.

The diversity of collaborative web applications embraces aspects like the targeted runtime engine (e.g. standards-based browser runtime or plug-in technology based one) and the addressed application domain (e.g. text editing, graphics editing, etc.). Considering the variety of plug-in technologies (e.g. Adobe Flash, Java Applets or Microsoft Silverlight) and their slipping importance with respect to web engineering, we will primarily try to tackle this challenge for W3C standards-based applications.

Another aspect that a generic awareness solution should take into account are the various browser implementations. Since the set of available browsers in its entirety also encompasses peculiar implementations such as text browsers (e.g. Lynx) we will focus on modern browsers (e.g. Apple Safari 5, Google Chrome 16, Mozilla Firefox 10) that cover a wide range of novel HTML5 features.

In the age of tablets and smartphones, the third challenge – supporting a myriad of web-enabled devices – becomes even more important since an ever increasing share of web traffic is generated by tablets and mobile devices. Because awareness widgets are part of the application's user interface, device aspects such as screen size and interaction mode (e.g. touch, mouse or keyboard interaction) are the crucial ones which have to be considered by a generic awareness solution.

3 Generic Awareness Infrastructure

In this section, we introduce an approach enabling application-agnostic awareness support which is materialized by the generic awareness infrastructure. Furthermore, we expose a specific development blueprint for developing reusable awareness widgets.

To devise an approach for generic awareness support, we set out to identify an abstract editor architecture and carved out the editor components depicted in Figure 2(a). All web-based editors, except plug-in based solutions, adhere to this architecture that divides the application stack in application-specific and application-agnostic artifacts. While the editor components (e.g. the user interface) and the associated editor APIs are specific to each editor, the standardized W3C APIs (e.g. DOM API [5]) and the underlying document object model (DOM) are application-agnostic. Awareness widgets using editor APIs directly (e.g. to keep track of document changes) turn out to be application-specific. In

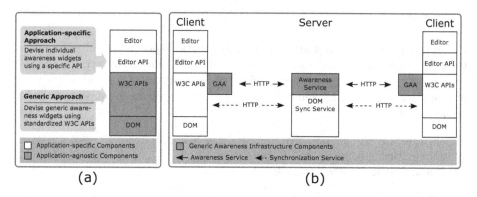

Fig. 2. a) Abstract architecture of web-based editors as well as approaches to anchor awareness support and b) Overview of the generic awareness infrastructure for web applications

contrast, awareness widgets leveraging the standardized W3C API layer (cf. Figure 2(a)) are application-agnostic and consequently capable of serving multiple web editors.

Therefore, we claim that anchoring awareness support at a standardized layer is the key to create an application-agnostic solution. Moreover, taking into account that W3C APIs are implemented in most modern browsers for PCs, tablets or even smartphones and that recently developed collaborative web-applications are predominantly standards-based, we conclude that the aforementioned challenges can be overcome.

The proposed approach to link awareness support to well-established W3C APIs is embodied in the generic awareness infrastructure illustrated in Figure 2(b). The distributed collaboration system consists of a server and an arbitrary number of clients. Clients comprise the very same application stack shown in Figure 2(a) associated with one additional component denoted as the generic awareness adapter (GAA). The GAA comprises registered awareness widgets and is devoted to execute three essential tasks:

1. Initializing registered awareness widgets.
2. Pushing collected awareness information from registered awareness widgets to the server.
3. Receiving, interpreting and eventually visualizing awareness information from other clients by means of registered awareness widgets.

To distribute awareness information among all clients, the central server propagates the respective data sets. Additionally, the server provides concurrency control services encompassing the synchronization of various DOM instances as well as a conflict resolution mechanism which is able to resolve potential conflicts arising if numerous participants change the same document artifacts (e.g. a graphic or a phrase) simultaneously. Even though the generic DOM synchronization service is a crucial part of the collaboration system, details which were specified in [7] are beyond the scope of the paper.

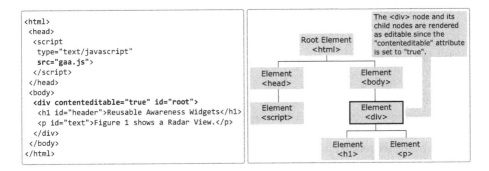

Fig. 3. HTML page of a minimal web editor and the corresponding DOM tree

3.1 Generic Awareness Adapter

The generic awareness adapter depicted in Figure 2(b) is the key component of the GAI and primarily in charge of accommodating awareness widgets as well as providing essential services to those widgets. Arbitrary widgets (e.g. telepointers, radar views) that adhere to a specific development blueprint (cf. Section 3.2) can be registered at the GAA. Once the registration is successful, awareness widgets have to be initialized before they actually capture and visualize awareness information.

In the following paragraphs, we illustrate the integration of the GAA into existing web applications and describe the setup as well as the operation's mode of the GAA.

Integration: The GAA pursues a lightweight integration approach to ease the process of converting existing editors to awareness-enabled editors. To accomplish the integration, a specific JavaScript file named "gaa.js" has to be embedded in the HTML code of the original web application (cf. Figure 3). The awareness integration process operates non-invasively meaning that the original JavaScript source code is not subject to changes. That implies that developers don't have to become familiar with the internal source code of the original application and can thus accomplish the integration of awareness support in a lightweight and rapid fashion.

Setup: Once the "gaa.js" is successfully embedded in the HTML application and the browser loaded the modified collaborative application, the GAA will be initialized. The initialization phase comprises the following tasks:

- Setup an HTTP communication channel connecting client and server to allow pushing and receiving awareness information.
- Establish session and user management (e.g. assign a color to each participant to create a color coding adoptable by telepointers and other widgets).

– Generate global identifiers for all relevant DOM nodes to have a uniform referencing mechanism (e.g. a newly inserted text node can therefore be addressed using the very same identifier at all sites).
– Initialize registered awareness widgets.

Operation: After the initialization, the GAA switches into its operation's mode where awareness information captured by different widgets is serialized and propagated to the server. Besides sending awareness messages, the reception of awareness-related data is also accomplished by the GAA. Received data is deserialized and forwarded to registered awareness widgets. All message exchanges are based on the JavaScript Object Notation (JSON) which is beneficial since it is a standardized format [8] with standardized methods for serialization (`JSON.stringify()`) and deserialization (`JSON.parse()`). Note that messages sent from the GAA are propagated by the server (cf. Figure 2(b)) to all clients except the sender client.

3.2 Awareness Widget Blueprint

The awareness widget blueprint serves as a guideline for awareness widget developers. We have adopted this blueprint for our widget development but it may also serve other web developers. The blueprint divides each widget in three components (initialization, capturing and visualization component) and reassures that implemented widgets are reusable. The widget implementation is illustrated providing a concrete example revisiting the minimal text editor shown in Figure 3. The text editor allows to modify the text of the `<h1>` and `<p>` elements because the `contenteditable` attribute of the embracing `<div>` element is set to `true`.

Initialization Component: As stated before, the blueprint divides each awareness widget into three building blocks whereas the initialization component is in charge of the following tasks:

– Visualization Setup: Create a visualization context for the awareness widget and render an initial visualization.[1]
– Event Listener Registration: Add event listeners to the awareness root (identified by the GAA) to record modifications in the shared workspace.

Setting up the initial visualization for awareness widgets demands the creation and positioning of an additional `<div>` container that acts as an encapsulated awareness model which is not interwoven with the actual document model. All

---

[1] The Separation of Concerns (SoC) principle [9] has to be enforced to prevent synchronization issues. The document model accommodating the content artifacts (e.g. text or graphical shapes) is subject to continuous synchronizations to assure all participants are working on a consistent document. In contrast, the visualization of awareness widgets is client-specific (e.g. the radar view depends on the local scrolling position) and therefore should be encapsulated and excluded from all sync processes.

awareness-related visualizations (e.g. the telepointer cursor, the input highlighting, etc.) are drawn onto this special overlay. Besides the creation of the visualization layer, additional tasks required by specific awareness widgets are executed upon request. For instance, a radar view widget might copy a DOM subtree into its visualization layer (i.e. the extra `<div>` element) to build a miniature view or a highlighting widget for SVG [10] tools might clone the SVG root element to build up a special SVG tree for shapes highlighting remotely created shapes.

To keep track of modifications in the shared workspace, awareness widgets have to register event listeners. As mentioned before, compatibility with the majority of web applications has to be ensured in order to devise a reusable solution. Therefore, awareness widgets directly leverage standardized DOM Events [6]. We identified three groups of DOM events (1) mouse events (e.g. `click`, `mouseover`), (2) keyboard events (e.g. `keydown`, `keyup`) and (3) mutation events (e.g. `DOMNodeInserted`, `DOMAttrModified`) that are relevant since they trigger important awareness-related application updates. For example, semantic cursors have to be adapted upon `DOMCharacterDataModified` events, telepointer positions have to be updated on `mousemove` events and document history widgets have to be refreshed if `DOMNodeInserted` events are fired. The setup of event handlers can be accomplished by means of the `element.addEventListener(...)` method.

Suppose we want to enrich the text editor depicted in Figure 3 with a primitive awareness widget that highlights newly entered characters at all remote clients. This entails the following implementation tasks. First, an additional `<div>` container encapsulating the visualization artifacts has to be created which is straightforward (`document.createElement("div")`). Second, the insertion of characters has to be monitored and therefore event handlers have to be attached to the `<div>` node which is illustrated in Figure 4(a). Note that the listener registration does not require to add listeners to each individual DOM node since installed event listeners also listen to changes of the respective child nodes. In our example, the attached event handler would also listen to modifications of the `<h1>` or `<p>` node.

Capturing Component: After the initialization, local changes are recorded by a capture component that gathers changes for dedicated awareness widgets. The main objectives of the capture component are:

- Awareness Information Filtering: Retrieve essential awareness information from the vast set of data provided by registered event handlers
- Data Preparation: Prepare relevant awareness information for the message transfer.

Gathering and filtering awareness-related information is accomplished by event handlers registered during the initialization. As soon as event handlers are called, awareness information is prepared according to the requirements of awareness widgets. In some cases, the information capturing is trivial since `Event` objects [6] directly expose the required properties. For example, a telepointer could capture

```
captureChanges = function() {
  range = document.getSelection().getRangeAt(0);
  //serialize range information into JSON
};

document.getElementById("root").addEventListener(
  "DOMCharacterDataModified", captureChanges, true);
```

(a) Initialize Implementation

```
{
  start : {
    parentNode : range.startContainer.parentNode.id,
    relPos : getRelativePos(parentNode, startContainer),
    offset : range.startOffset
  },
  end : {
    parentNode : range.endContainer.parentNode.id,
    relPos : getRelativePos(parentNode, endContainer),
    offset : range.endOffset
  }
}
```

(b) Capture Implementation

```
highlightChanges = function (json) {
  startContainer = resolveNode(json.start.parentNode, json.start.relPos);
  endContainer = resolveNode(json.end.parentNode, json.end.relPos);

  range = document.createRange();
  range.setStart(startContainer, json.start.offset);
  range.setEnd(endContainer, json.end.offset + 1);

  rect = range.getBoundingClientRect();

  div = document.createElement("div");
  style = {
    "top" : rect.top,
    "left" : rect.left,
    "height" : rect.height,
    "width" : rect.width,
    "background" : red,
    "pointer-events" : none
  }
  div.css(style);
  document.body.appendChild(div);
};
```

(c) Visualize Implementation

Fig. 4. Minimal awareness implementation capable of highlighting local text changes at all remote clients

the X- and Y-coordinates by retrieving the `screenX` and `screenY` attributes from the `MouseEvent` object. However, this is only appropriate for strict what you see is what I see (WYSIWIS) tools [11] where all clients share the same window size, viewport, etc. In relaxed WYSIWIS environments [11] where participants might have different viewports, zoom levels, etc., the information capturing is much more complex and cannot leverage window coordinates (e.g. highlighting a word at zoom level 100 covers a different screen area than highlighting the same word at a zoom level of 200 percent). Therefore, advanced mechanisms are required to calculate positions. A robust way to capture fine grained positioning values is offered by the HTML Editing API [12]. It defines selections in HTML documents that can be obtained using the `window.getSelection()` method. The call returns a `Selection` object that exposes either the caret position or the text selection potentially spanning across multiple elements. It can comprise one or more `Range` objects [13] (indicated by the `rangeCount` property). Each `Range` object represents a contiguous part of the selection. In order to reconstruct selections or caret positions, the start and end of every `Range` object have to be transmitted to other clients.

The preparation of update messages is the second important capture task. Awareness information has to be serialized before the data transmission can take place. Therefore, JSON-compliant objects are employed as data containers combining all relevant awareness information. These JSON objects are then passed to the GAA which eventually serializes these objects and sends out awareness update messages.

Regarding the example of the minimal text editor, the capture mechanism would be triggered upon text modifications affecting the `<h1>` or `<p>` node. This capture mechanism is defined in the `captureChanges` function depicted in Figure 4(a). First, the `getSelection` method retrieves a list of `Range` objects representing currently selected DOM elements. If the caret resides in the `<h1>` or `<p>` node, there is only one `Range` instance that is retrieved through getRangeAt(0). This Range instance is exploited to create a JSON object as illustrated in Figure 4(b). The JSON message contains information about the affected node (id), the caret position (offset), etc. After the message construction, the JSON string is transferred to the server.

Visualization Component: The third building block of the proposed blueprint is the visualization component which processes and eventually renders incoming awareness information. In detail, this component carries out the following tasks:

- – Awareness Information Processing: Distribute, interpret and render received awareness information.
- – Awareness Information Re-Rendering: Refresh UIs of awareness widgets upon local change events.

Awareness widgets receive its data via JSON-compliant data exchange objects that were created by the GAA during the deserialization of awareness messages. Data exchange objects contain awareness information collected by the capturing component. For example, a data object dedicated for an input highlighting widget might carry information about the captured range of newly inserted characters. If this information has been passed to the specific widget, the visualization process can start. First, a new Range object has to be created (document.createRange()). Second, the start and end of the range have to be set invoking range.setStart(startNode, startOffset) and range.setEnd (endNode, endOffset) respectively. The start and end nodes can be obtained via document.getElementById(...) using the identifiers stored in the data exchange object. After these two initial steps, the visualization engine can profit from the rich APIs specified in the CSS Object Model Standard [4]. It enriches existing DOM interfaces like Document, Window or Element with sophisticated functions like caretPositionFromPoint(), getClientRects(), etc. The range.getClientRects() method, for instance, returns a collection of ClientRect objects that serve as a representation for the range's occupied screen area. Each rectangle exposes read-only left, top, right and bottom properties. These properties and its assigned values are used as CSS properties for the established <div> overlay element. Note, that this <div> element can be styled according to your application's look and feel since solely CSS properties have to be changed. The defined procedure ensures the correct handling of relaxed WYSIWIS situations, because abstract awareness information is interpreted locally and therefore adapted to the local environment (e.g. zoom level, viewport, etc.). For graphics tools a rectangular highlighting of the modified DOM element might not be appropriate. In particular, inline SVG graphics embedded in the DOM tree require advanced highlighting mechanisms. A compelling way to highlight SVG elements is to first clone the affected SVG element to the <div> overlay container of the corresponding awareness widget. Afterwards the cloned SVG element can be styled, i.e. its properties (e.g. fill or stroke color) are cleared and then a new stroke is created. Setting the stroke-width and stroke-color properties completes the sophisticated SVG highlighting.

If local changes occur (e.g. window size modifications, scrolling, etc.) the awareness visualization has to be re-rendered to adapt to the updated environment. To keep track of those local changes, additional event listeners have to be registered while initializing the awareness widget.

In the introduced example, the simple awareness widget has to highlight the characters recently entered by the remote user. Figure 4(c) illustrates the required steps. In summary, a new rectangular `<div>` element is constructed that has the same dimensions and coordinates as the newly created characters. Dimensions and coordinates fetched from the deserialized `Range` object are applied to the created `<div>` by assigning a CSS style.

4   Validation

To assess the reusability of awareness widgets which were devised leveraging the GAI approach, we opted for a two-step validation. First, we implemented three example widgets according to the presented architecture blueprint (cf. Section 3). Second, we incorporated these awareness widgets bundled with the configured GAA into four collaborative web editors.

In the first step aiming to produce exemplary awareness widgets – due to resource restrictions – we had to choose three awareness widgets from the multitude of common widgets. Therefore, we based our selection on a classification dividing widgets in *extrinsic* and *intrinsic* ones. *Extrinsic awareness widgets* are encapsulated in a single UI container and do not intermingle with the UI representing the document content (e.g. participant list, radar view or document history). *Intrinsic awareness widgets* are intermingled with the UI representing the document content (e.g. input highlighting, semantic cursor or telepointer). Besides taking into account the classification, we also wanted to cover the prevalent application domains (i.e. shared editing and shared drawing). Therefore, we decided to build widgets exposing the following characteristics: (1) intrinsic for shared editing as well as (2) intrinsic for shared drawing and (3) extrinsic for arbitrary collaborative applications. Correspondingly, we developed (1) an input highlighting widget for text editors as well as (2) an input highlighting widget for graphics editors and (3) a generic participant list.

To test the three developed awareness widgets, we set out to find collaborative editors lacking awareness support. Existing multi-user editors were not appropriate since they already offer awareness features to some extent. Hence, we chose to convert available single-user applications into multi-user applications and leveraged the transformation approach described in [7] that produces shared editing tools featuring document synchronization and conflict resolution. The produced collaborative web editors were suitable test applications since they did not provide any awareness support. According to our proposition, we transformed editors from different application domains including two text editors and two graphics editors. In the following paragraph, we briefly introduce the four web applications that were successfully converted to collaborative applications.

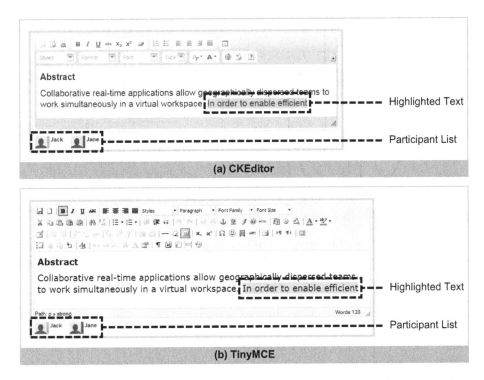

Fig. 5. User interfaces of the web-based text editors CKEditor [14] and TinyMCE [15] enriched with awareness support (changes by the remote user Jane are highlighted red)

CKEditor [14] and *TinyMCE* [15] are two popular web-based text editors offering common features such as text formatting, image insertion or text alignment. Both editors were enhanced with the very same participant list widget as well as an input highlighting widget (cf. Figure 5). Input highlighting is accomplished by adding a colored overlay to newly created characters for a certain period of time. The color overlay corresponds to the color coding established in the participant list. *SVG-edit* [16] and *FNISVGEditor* [17] are editors for scalable vector graphics providing common graphics tools to accomplish reoccurring drawing tasks such as create lines, ellipses or rectangles. Both editors incorporated a participant list widget and an input highlighting widget (cf. Figure 6). Note that the input highlighting widget differs from the text input highlighting. In contrast to emphasizing newly created characters, in this case, recently created shapes (e.g. circles, rectangles) are subject to highlighting.

Eventually, we could show that it is feasible to reuse awareness widgets by incorporating them non-invasively in four distinct collaborative applications. The editor screenshots depicted in Figure 5 and Figure 6 demo the achieved awareness support. Furthermore, the resulting collaborative editors are demonstrated on our GAI demo page `http://vsr.informatik.tu-chemnitz.de/demo/GAI/`. Note that during the widget integration some issues were encountered. One class

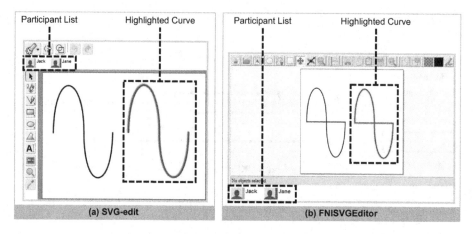

Fig. 6. User interfaces of the graphics editors SVG-edit [16] and FNISVGEditor [17] enriched with awareness support (changes by the remote user Jane are highlighted red)

of issues was related to the positioning of highlighted ranges. Since the document viewport establishes an extra coordinate system that is embedded in the browser window coordinate system, coordinate calculations have to take offsets into account. Another identified issue was discovered incorporating the participant list widget. The proposed approach to draw the participant list on an extra overlay layer requires an empty window portion which is not always the case. Therefore, the participant list has to be embedded directly into the application layer. The outlined issues could all be solved configuring the GAI accordingly.

5 Discussion

In our validation, we illustrated the strength of the GAI approach. A major advantage is the provisioning of awareness support at infrastructure level. Once implemented, the awareness features supported by our GAI are reusable by numerous applications from different domains. Moreover, the creation of awareness widgets is also simplified. Widgets can exploit awareness information supplied by the GAA and mediated by the GAI. Therefore, development effort and time for awareness widget implementations are significantly reduced in contrast to conventional approaches.

We also showed in our validation the non-invasive integration of awareness widgets into existing collaborative applications. Extrinsic as well as intrinsic widgets were successfully integrated without having to change the source code of the original application. Moreover, the devised awareness widgets were adopted in different applications of the same domain and even across domains which demonstrates the high reusability of GAA widgets.

However, the gained experience developing numerous GAA-compliant awareness widgets revealed two critical limitations that are immanent to the proposed GAI approach:

Application Model not Represented in the DOM: The defined GAI implementation and in particular the information capturing components rely on standardized DOM events that are fired if the DOM is manipulated. If this notification mechanism is somehow bypassed and not actively producing events anymore, the GAI information tracking cannot operate properly and eventually, registered awareness widgets are affected since required awareness information is not supplied. For example, if one part of the application is implemented using a plug-in technology (e.g. Adobe Flash or Microsoft Silverlight), changes affecting a plug-in internal data structure do not emanate DOM events and thus awareness information cannot be retrieved. Therefore, it is mandatory that the editor document and its content (e.g. the text of a text editor or the shapes of a graphics editor) are represented as a part of the DOM.

Cross-Browser Inconsistencies: Differing browser engines (e.g. Apple Safari, Google Chrome, etc.) are not fully consistent with respect to their model representation (i.e. the DOM) even though they request and render the very same serialized HTML file (e.g. an element is represented as one single node in one browser engine and as multiple nodes in another browser engine). This can break the global identification scheme and impair the awareness information association. For instance, adding a line break to a text embedded in an HTML `textarea` results in a `Text` node split. Removing this line break once again is handled differently by different browser engines. While some engines merge the text nodes, other browser engines keep two separate text nodes.

Even though the GAI approach entails some limitations, we argue that a standards-based solution such as the GAI can efficiently tackle the aforementioned challenges (cf. Section 2). In particular in the light of the HTML5 movement where standards are aggressively pushed and rapidly adopted.

6   Related Work

Our GAI approach is related to work in two major research domains, namely full-fledged collaboration frameworks and user interface (UI) toolkits accommodating also awareness support.

UI toolkits like the Multi-User Awareness UI Toolkit (MAUI Toolkit) [18], WatchMyPhone [19] or GroupKit [20] provide sets of awareness-ready UI components and also facilitate document synchronization. Most of the approaches are tailored to a particular runtime environment. While the MAUI Toolkit targets the Java runtime, WatchMyPhone is a solution dedicated for the Android platform. Even though some toolkits encapsulate functionality like the distribution of awareness information into generic components, there is a tight coupling between UI controls and awareness support. Thus, reusability of awareness widgets is achieved at the design phase rather than at the runtime phase. Developers have to become familiar with the applications' source code and eventually are asked to replace standard UI controls with their collaborative counterparts. In contrast, our non-invasive GAI approach allows to incorporate awareness features in a rapid and cost-efficient manner since it only involves the integration of an extra JavaScript file without requiring source code changes.

Advanced frameworks for the development of collaborative applications like Apache Wave [21], BeWeeVee [22] or CEFX [23] focus on the provisioning of concurrency control mechanisms but neglect the aspect of awareness support. In our approach the generic awareness support is embedded into the GAI which decouples the UI layer from the awareness support. This increases reusability of awareness support and results in reduced effort for developing awareness widgets on top of the GAI.

7   Conclusion

Workspace awareness is a key feature for collaborative real-time applications enabling effective collaborative work. At the present time, well-established and pervasively available collaborative web applications like Google Docs implement awareness features in an application-specific manner, even if the same set of awareness widgets could be shared among various applications. As a result, the time and resource consuming task of implementing and testing awareness widgets is repeated again and again.

In this paper, we presented an application-agnostic approach for the creation of out-of-the-box awareness widgets which are reusable in collaborative web applications. Our solution is based on the idea to anchor basic awareness support at the application-independent level of standardized W3C APIs. The proposed generic awareness infrastructure captures information about user interactions at this generic level and mediates it to all participating users via a server hosting the awareness service as well as the concurrency control service. As part of the generic awareness infrastructure, generic awareness adapters are able to incorporate arbitrary awareness widgets which have to be developed following a predefined development blueprint.

To validate our approach, we implemented a set of awareness widgets which have been integrated into four collaborative web editors for text and graphics. As demonstrated in our validation, created awareness widgets cannot only be used for the development of new collaborative web-applications; in particular, they are tailored for the incorporation into existing ones. Since awareness widgets can be adopted within several applications of the same domain (e.g. input highlighting widget) or even across application domains (e.g. generic participant list) our approach ensures reusability of awareness features to a large extent.

In future work, we will extend the set of available awareness widgets to create a base for performance and user studies. Especially, the quality/impact of provided awareness features will be explored in detail.

References

1. Gutwin, C., Greenberg, S.: A Descriptive Framework of Workspace Awareness for Real-Time Groupware. Computer Supported Cooperative Work 11(3-4), 411–446 (2002)

2. Gutwin, C., Stark, G., Greenberg, S.: Support for Workspace Awareness in Educational Groupware. In: CSCL, pp. 147–156 (1995)
3. Sommerville, I.: Software Engineering, 9th edn. Addison Wesley (2010)
4. van Kesteren, A.: CSSOM View Module, http://www.w3.org/TR/2011/WD-cssom-view-20110804/ (working draft August 4, 2011)
5. Hors, A.L., Hégaret, P.L.: Document Object Model (DOM) Level 3 Core Specification (2004), http://www.w3.org/TR/DOM-Level-3-Core/
6. Schepers, D., Rossi, J.: Document Object Model (DOM) Level 3 Events Specification (2011), http://www.w3.org/TR/DOM-Level-3-Events/
7. Heinrich, M., Lehmann, F., Springer, T., Gaedke, M.: Exploiting single-user web applications for shared editing: a generic transformation approach. In: WWW, pp. 1057–1066 (2012)
8. Crockford, D.: The application/json Media Type for JavaScript Object Notation (JSON). RFC 4627 (Informational) (July 2006)
9. Hürsch, W.L., Lopes, C.V.: Separation of Concerns. Technical report (1995)
10. Ferraiolo, J.: Scalable Vector Graphics (SVG) 1.0 Specification (2001), http://www.w3.org/TR/SVG10/
11. Stefik, M., Bobrow, D.G., Foster, G., Lanning, S., Tatar, D.: WYSIWIS Revised: Early Experiences with Multiuser Interfaces. ACM Trans. Inf. Syst. 5, 147–167 (1987)
12. Gregor, A.: HTML Editing APIs, Work in Progress. http://dvcs.w3.org/hg/editing/raw-file/tip/editing.html (last update January 19, 2012)
13. Kesselman, J., Robie, J., Champion, M., Sharpe, P., Apparao, V., Wood, L.: Document Object Model (DOM) Level 2 Traversal and Range Specification (2000), http://www.w3.org/TR/DOM-Level-2-Traversal-Range/
14. CKSource: CKEditor - WYSIWYG Text and HTML Editor for the Web (2011), http://ckeditor.com/
15. Moxiecode Systems: TinyMCE - JavaScript WYSIWYG Editor (2011), http://www.tinymce.com/
16. Schiller, J., Rusnak, P.: SVG-edit - A Complete Vector Graphics Editor in the Browser (2011), http://code.google.com/p/svg-edit/
17. Leppa, A.: FNISVGEditor - JavaScript-based Online Editor for SVG Graphics (2010), http://code.google.com/p/fnisvgeditor/
18. Hill, J., Gutwin, C.: The MAUI Toolkit: Groupware Widgets for Group Awareness. In: Computer-Supported Cooperative Work, pp. 5–6 (2004)
19. Bendel, S., Schuster, D.: Providing Developer Support for Implementing Collaborative Mobile Applications. In: Third International Workshop on Pervasive Collaboration and Social Networking, PerCol 2012 (2012)
20. Roseman, M., Greenberg, S.: Building Real-Time Groupware with GroupKit, a Groupware Toolkit. ACM Trans. Comput.-Hum. Interact. 3, 66–106 (1996)
21. Apache Software Foundation: Apache Wave (2011), http://incubator.apache.org/wave/
22. BeWeeVee: BeWeeVee - Life Collaboration Framework (2011), http://www.beweevee.com
23. Gerlicher, A.: Collaborative Editing Framework for XML (2009), http://sourceforge.net/projects/cefx/

News-Topic Oriented Hashtag Recommendation in Twitter Based on Characteristic Co-occurrence Word Detection

Feng Xiao, Tomoya Noro, and Takehiro Tokuda

Department of Computer Science, Tokyo Institute of Technology, Japan
Meguro, Tokyo 152-8552, Japan
{xiao,noro,tokuda}@tt.cs.titech.ac.jp

Abstract. Hashtags, which started to be widely used since 2007, are always utilized to mark keywords in tweets to categorize messages and form conversation for topics in Twitter. However, it is hard for users to use hashtags for sharing their opinions/interests/comments for their interesting topics. In this paper, we present a new approach for recommending news-topic oriented hashtags to help Twitter users easily join the conversation about news topics in Twitter. We first detect topic-specific informative words co-occurring with a given target word, which we call characteristic co-occurrence words, from news articles to form a vector for representing the news topic. Then by creating a hashtag vector based on tweets with the same hashtag, we calculate the similarity between these two vectors and recommend hashtags of high similarity scores with the news topic. Experimental results show that our approach could recommend hashtags which are highly relevant to the news topics, helping users share their tweets with others in Twitter.

Keywords: Social Media, hashtags, tweet, characteristic co-occurrence word, clustering, news topic, Twitter.

1 Introduction

News articles, as a traditional medium for distributing information all over the world, have been increasingly impacted by a new way of information delivery called social media. Social networking services, such as Twitter, Facebook, and Digg, provide plenty of ways for users to share information with others. For example, since Twitter was launched in July 2006, the number of users and messages, called tweets, increased dramatically. Most of tweets in Twitter often concern topics of headline news or persistent news [1], making Twitter a suitable and important data resource for posting/receiving breaking news and opinions.

Currently, a lot of tools/functions are provided to help news agencies/users easily share news information in Twitter. Most of news websites provide Tweet Button in their Web pages to help readers easily share news articles with their followers. Retweet function greatly accelerates the spreading speed of information and mention function using @username help Twitter users exchange information directly with

M. Brambilla, T. Tokuda, and R. Tolksdorf (Eds.): ICWE 2012, LNCS 7387, pp. 16–30, 2012.

others. Hashtags (the # symbol prefixed to a short character string) are widely used to categorize and joint tweets together based on a certain topic and make your tweets more easily searchable by other users with the same interest.

However, it is hard for Twitter users to use hashtags in their tweets properly when they want to share contents or their opinions/interests/comments for news topics. For many news websites, they do not provide any hashtag in tweets when users click the Tweet Button on their Web pages, which means users' sharing could only be seen by their followers and might not reach far to the others. Other news websites append hashtags automatically while most of them are not for the purpose of helping users share their tweets or too unique. Some of news websites use their formal name (such as "#CNN") as the hashtag in every tweet from the Tweet Button of their news Web page no matter what the topic the news article reports. Such a kind of hashtag could only help these sites watch the information spreading in Twitter or promote reputation for advertising. Other news websites like Yahoo! Japan News provide hashtags such as "#yjfc_wall_street_protest" when users post tweets from news Web pages reporting protest in Wall Street while such a kind of hashtags might only be used by Yahoo! Japan readers and is not widely used by other users.

It is also very hard for Twitter users to create/select proper hashtags by themselves. Users try to create hashtags which they took for granted that these hashtags should be widely used for topics while the truth might be just on the contrary. For example, "# Wall_Street_Protest" might be thought as a meaningful hashtag used in tweets talking about the protest in Wall Street, but we found that no one uses this hashtag in his tweets up to the point of writing this paper. Users could search for some topic-related keywords and read all those responded tweets to find hashtags that relate to the topic. However, there might be too many hashtags contained in those responded tweets, relating to more than one topic, that users may have no idea which hashtags should be chosen. If all else fails, users may have to add the # symbol prefixed to every word in their tweets; wishing one of these hashtags could be the one which is widely used by others for the topic in Twitter. However, such a behavior would make the tweets hard to read and impolite. The users may be taken as tweet spammers.

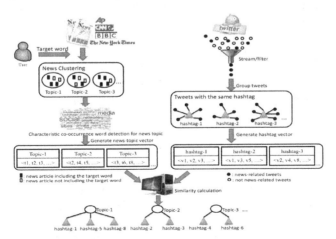

Fig. 1. System structure of the news-topic oriented hashtag recommendation

In this paper, we present a new approach for recommending hashtags to the user who wants to join the conversation for a news topic by using hashtags in Twitter after he/she searches for the news topic by a keyword (we refer to it as target word in this paper) but has no idea which hashtag could be used. The whole system structure is depicted in Figure 1. In our approach, we first collect news articles and news-related tweets published in a certain period of time concurrently. Then news articles are clustered into topics. News-related tweets including mentioned or tagged screen names of news agencies (e.g. @CNN, #CNN) are concatenated based on the hashtags and a vector for representing each hashtag is created. After the target word has been provided, news topics that relate to the target word are selected and a vector is created for representing each of the news topics. We calculate the similarity score between each news-topic vector and each hashtag vector, and hashtags with high similarity scores are recommended for the news topic.

To represent news topics that relate to the target word, we propose a new method named Probabilistic Inside-Outside Log (P-IOLog) method to detect characteristic co-occurrence words from news articles. Characteristic co-occurrence words are topic-specific words which provide information for news topics related to the target word and could be detected based on the assumption that characteristic co-occurrence words should often co-occur with the target word in news articles while they are less likely to appear when the target word is not contained. Words with their scores detected by our P-IOLog method are used to create news-topic vectors. We also extend this P-IOLog method for hashtags to detect informative words co-occurring with the hashtags in tweets and all these detected words with their scores are used to create hashtag vectors. We refer to the extended method as P-IOLogH method.

Notice that our approach is trying to recommend hashtags which have been created and used in tweets. New hashtag generation is not our goal. Also we are trying to help users who want to share their opinions/interests/comments and join conversations for news topics in Twitter. Other kinds of Twitter users, such as bots, are not considered.

The organization of the rest of this paper is as follows. We present related work in the next section. In Section 3, we describe our method for detecting characteristic co-occurrence words with the target word, named Probabilistic Inside-Outside Log (P-IOLog) method, and how to create news-topic vectors based on these detected words. In Section 4, we propose two methods (TF-IHF and P-IOLogH) to weight words co-occurring with hashtags for creating hashtag vectors and explain how to get recommended hashtags for news topics. Experimental results and evaluations are described in Section 5. In Section 6 we make the conclusion with directions for future research.

2   Related Work

Hashtags in Twitter are one special type of a more general concept, tag, which is an important feature for many social networking services. People could create tags with few taxonomic constraints to categorize resources for later browsing, or to describe resources for searching. Many approaches for tag recommendation in social networking services have been proposed recently. They are mainly classified into two classes.

One class of these approaches focuses on the relationship between tags and their associated resources, and recommends tags to a newly added resource. One application in this class is the tag recommendation system for weblog. Brooks et al. [2] try to select words in blog posts that have high TF-IDF scores to be used as tags, and find that those tags are more representative than human-assigned ones. Mishne G. [3] and TagAssist [4] recommend tags to a new blog post by providing tags in those old blog posts which have high TF-IDF similarity with the new one. These approaches recommend tags in similar resources by using techniques from Information Retrieval (e.g. TF-IDF). However, these methods are no longer effective for recommending hashtags in Twitter because TF-IDF reduces the chance of relevant tweets to be selected since the tweet length is limited and their contents have less information [5].

Other approaches exploit tag co-occurrence patterns through a history of tag assignments in a collaborative tagging environment when the resource with which the tag was associated is hard to retrieve such as audio, video, and image. Sigurbjornsson et al. [6] recommend tags for each user-defined tag for photos based on tag co-occurrence in Flickr. Wartena et al. [7] proposed another approach to calculate the similarity between tag co-occurrence distribution and the user profile. Tags with high similarity are recommended to the user. Belem et al. [8] extended tag co-occurrence exploiting and considered about terms extracted from other textual features such as title and description. All these approaches are based on two assumptions: tags are assigned to resources beforehand and most of resources have two or more tags[1]. However, most of tweets in Twitter only contain one or even no hashtag. For example, in all news-related tweets collected on December 20th 2011, 88.6% of tweets contain one or no hashtag. Exploiting tag co-occurrence in tweets becomes impossible due to the small number of tweets containing two or more hashtags.

Recently, researchers found out that hashtags in Twitter play a different role compared to tags in other social networking services. Huang et al. [9] compared user tagging behaviors between Twitter and Delicious. They found out that hashtags in Twitter are used to join discussions on existing topics while in Delicious tags are used to re-access resources. Our approach is based on the conversational nature of hashtags and tries to recommend hashtags to help users join the conversation about the news topic so that users do not need to be "exposed" to too many hashtags

Approaches for hashtag retrieval/recommendation in Twitter have been proposed while there are some problems still existed. Weng et al. [10] proposed methods for modeling the interestingness of hashtags by studying how hashtags are discussed within and across communities, but they do not correlate hashtags with topics in which users are interested. Correa et al. [11] proposed a new approach for recommending tags to other social networking services such as Flickr and YouTube, using hashtags and terms in tweets. Our approach is different because we correlate Twitter with traditional news media, not other social networking services. Efron M. [12] and Wagner C. et al. [13] proposed new approaches to retrieve useful hashtags after a keyword is given. However, one keyword may relate to more than one topic and all

---

[1] Flickr allows its users to add 75 tags per photo at most; In YouTube the total length of your tag list is limited to 500-character.

hashtags related to different topics would be mixed together. Also, ranking hashtags based on their in-degree in [13] would make some general hashtags (e.g. #tech) be ranked higher, which is still not helpful. Zangerle et al. [14] proposed a method to recommend hashtags to users' inputted contents by calculating similarities between newly inputted contents and old tweets based on TF-IDF. Hashtags which frequently appear in old tweets with high similarities are recommended. However, similarity among tweets is hard to decide by simply relying on those common words since semantics and synonyms are not considered. Also, due to the huge number of tweets, TFIDF is no longer a good choice because the IDF part would dominate the final score, assigning large score to the word which appears scarcely (e.g. misspelling).

Other approaches interweaving traditional news media with social networking services have also been proposed for Topic Detection and Tracking [15, 16], news recommendation [17], and user profile construction [18]. To the best of our knowledge, our approach is the first one trying to recommend hashtags for news topics in which users are interested.

3   Characteristic Co-occurrence Word for News Topic

A news topic is a group of news articles published in a period of time (for example: one day) reporting about the same recent event in the world. Traditional method for representing the news topic is to define a centroid vector which is calculated by averaging vectors of all news articles in this topic under the Vector Space Model [19]. Each vector dimension corresponds to a separate term in news articles and term weights are calculated by the TF-IDF. Although TF-IDF works well in many tasks such as Information Retrieval, it is no longer the best choice for our approach. Firstly, TF-IDF is a query-independent term weighting method, which means the term weight doesn't change no matter what the query is. Secondly, TF-IDF is a topic-independent method. The term which appears in most news articles of a news topic should be weighted higher while TF-IDF could not reflect this idea. At last, even news articles of the same news topic may share many common terms, a news topic may contain thousands of separate terms, which would greatly increase the computation.In order to solve these problems, we propose a new method for detecting characteristic co-occurrence words of news topics with the target word which is queried by users. Characteristic co-occurrence words are those words which provide important information for news topics related to the target word. Our method for detecting characteristic co-occurrence words is based on two assumptions:

- Characteristic co-occurrence word w should often co-occur with the target word t in news articles; we take it as the Inside part.
- Characteristic co-occurrence word w should not always appear in news articles without the target word t; we take it as the Outside part.

Based on these two assumptions, words often appearing in news articles including the target word while being less likely to appear in news articles without the target word are taken as the characteristic co-occurrence words. However, all of news articles containing the target word do not always deal with the same news topic and characteristic co-occurrence words related to different news topics will be mixed together. Also, some words which often co-occur with the target word regardless of the news topic (e.g. Obama and White House) should be excluded since those words provide little information for a specific news topic.

In order to solve these problems, we firstly clustered news articles and those articles which related to the same news topic are hopefully put into the same group while news articles related to different news topics would be partitioned into different ones. Then we can detect characteristic co-occurrence words for every news topic related to the target word separately without a mixture of words. The procedure is depicted in the Figure 2(a). When dealing with one news topic, all news articles containing the target word in this topic are taken as the Inside part while all the other news articles regardless of existence of the target word are taken as the Outside part. Words co-occurring with the target word regardless of the topic are excluded under this way.

To reflect our idea, we introduce Probabilistic Inside-Outside Log method to calculate the score of word w co-occurring with the target word t in topic c as follows.

$$\text{P-IOLog}(w,t,c) = \log \frac{(1-s_p)P(w|t \wedge c)+s_p}{(1-s_p)P(w|\neg(t \wedge c))+s_p} \qquad (1)$$

$$P(w|t \wedge c) = \frac{df(w \wedge t \wedge c)}{df(t \wedge c)} \qquad (2)$$

$$P\big(w|\neg(t \wedge c)\big) = \frac{df(w \wedge \neg(t \wedge c))}{df(\neg(t \wedge c))} = \frac{df(w) - df(w \wedge t \wedge c)}{N - df(t \wedge c)} \qquad (3)$$

where $df(w)$ is the number of news articles containing w. $df(w \wedge t \wedge c)$ is the number of news articles not only containing both w and t, but also belonging to the news topic c. $df(w \wedge \neg(t \wedge c))$ is the number of news articles containing w but not containing t or not being assigned to news topic c (Figure 2(b)). N is the total number of news articles and s_p is a smoothing parameter which ranges from 0 to 1. The P-IOLog score will vary from $\log(s_p)$ to $\log(1/s_p)$. The larger the score is, the more likely the word w is a characteristic co-occurrence word with the target word t for news topic c.

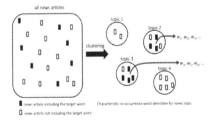

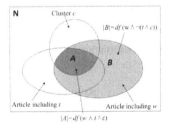

(a) Characteristic co-occurrence word detection for news topic   (b) Probabilistic Inside-Outside Log method

Fig. 2. Procedure of characteristic co-occurrence word detection for news-topic

For every news topic related to the target word, we select the target word t and top-$(n-1)$ words whose P-IOLog scores are larger than the others to create a news-topic vector. The news-topic vector's dimension is n and the term weight for every dimension is defined as the normalized P-IOLog score. They are created as follows.

$$\vec{nt}(t,c) = < ct_1, ct_2, ..., ct_n > \tag{4}$$

$$ct_i = \frac{\text{P-IOLog}(w_i, t, c)}{\sqrt{(\text{P-IOLog}(w_1, t, c))^2 + ... + (\text{P-IOLog}(w_n, t, c))^2}} \tag{5}$$

where ct_i is the normalized weight for word w_i. $\vec{nt}(t,c)$ is the vector for representing news topic c that relates to the target word t. The weight of the target word t is assigned as the maximum value of P-IOLog.

Compared with other methods for calculating co-occurrence coefficients, our P-IOLog method is an asymmetric method while some others are symmetric measures (e.g. Jaccard). However, for detecting characteristic co-occurrence words which are topic-specific, detected words should be query and topic-dependent while symmetric measures could not reflect this idea. Also, unlike other asymmetric methods such as DF-IDF, our method considers not the raw word co-occurrence frequency, but the co-occurrence probability in news articles with/without the target word. Detailed experiments of comparison could be found in [20].

4   News-Topic Oriented Hashtag Recommendation

In order to find news-topic oriented hashtags, one intuitive way is to retrieve tweets related to a news topic and recommend commonly used hashtags among these tweets. However, tweet content is limited within 140 characters, which means there is far not enough information in a single tweet to decide whether the tweet relates to the news topic. Also, traditional way as TF-IDF for weighting terms is no longer effective for short text which has been pointed out [5].

Our method to recommend news-topic oriented hashtags is based on two assumptions:

- Tweets containing recommended hashtags should relate to the news topic.
- Recommended hashtags should be widely used by Twitter users when they discuss the news topic.

For the first assumption, when Twitter users are discussing a news topic, some informative words of this news topic would be likely to be used in their tweets. The second assumption means that when one hashtag is widely used for a news topic in Twitter, users would use this hashtag to exchange information about the news topic from different perspectives, which means more informative words of the news topic are likely to be used in users' tweets.

Based on these two assumptions, we concatenate all tweets which contain the same hashtag and a hashtag vector is created based on concatenated contents of tweets. Each dimension of the hashtag vector corresponds to a separate term in the concatenated contents of tweets. We propose two different methods to calculate the term weight for the hashtag vector.

4.1   Term Frequency-Inverted Hashtag Frequency (TF-IHF)

Term Frequency-Inverted Hashtag Frequency (TF-IHF) is a variation of TF-IDF measure which considers not only the term frequency in a single document, but also the general importance of terms. TF-IHF score will be calculated as follows.

$$\text{TF} - \text{IHF}\left(w_i, ht_j\right) = \text{TF} \times \text{IHF} = \frac{n_i}{\sum_k n_k} \times \log \frac{|\text{HT}|}{|h_d : w_i \in h_d|} \tag{6}$$

where w_i is the term to which the TF-IHF score corresponds and ht_j is the hashtag. $|\text{HT}|$ gives the total number of hashtags in the dataset and h_d means the concatenated contents of tweets containing the same hashtag ht_d where $d \in \{1, \ldots, |\text{HT}|\}$. n_i is the number of times w_i appears in h_j and k is the total number of separate terms in h_j. TF-IHF value ranges from 0 to log$|\text{HT}|$ and high value would be reached when w_i frequently appears in the concatenated contents of tweets for hashtag ht_j and rarely co-occur with other hashtags.

However, TF-IHF does not consider about the number of tweets containing both term w_i and hashtag ht_j, which might cause a bias towards terms appearing many times in a few tweets with the hashtag. These terms might get higher TF-IHF scores compared to the others which appear in more tweets with the hashtag but only occur once in each tweet.

4.2   Probabilistic Inside-Outside Log Method for Hashtags (P-IOLogH)

To conquer the problem in TF-IHF method, we extend our idea in section 3 and apply those two assumptions for tweets. Our Probabilistic Inside-Outside Log method for hashtags (P-IOLogH) takes those tweets containing hashtag ht_j as the Inside part and tweets containing other hashtags as the Outside part. Terms which often co-occur with hashtag ht_j in tweets of the Inside part while not so often appear in tweets with other hashtags in the Outside part would be taken as the characteristic co-occurrence words with the hashtag and assigned a high term weight. P-IOLogH score will be calculated as follows.

$$\text{P-IOLogH}(w_i, ht_j) = \log \frac{(1-s_p)P(w_i|ht_j)+s_p}{(1-s_p)P(w_i|\neg ht_j)+s_p} \tag{7}$$

$$P\left(w_i|ht_j\right) = \frac{\text{TweetFrequency}(w_i \wedge ht_j)}{\text{TweetFrequency}(ht_j)} \tag{8}$$

$$P\left(w_i \middle| \neg ht_j\right) = \frac{\text{TweetFrequency}(w_i) - \text{TweetFrequency}(w_i \wedge ht_j)}{NT_{ht} - \text{TweetFrequency}(ht_j)} \tag{9}$$

where $\text{TweetFrequency}(w_i \wedge ht_j)$ gives the number of tweets containing both term w_i and hashtag ht_j. NT_{ht} means the total number of tweets containing hashtags in the database. The P-IOLogH score get a value ranging from $\log(s_p)$ to $\log(1/s_p)$ with s_p as the smoothing parameter. The larger the P-IOLogH score is, the more likely term w_i is the characteristic co-occurrence word with the hashtag and be more informative.

4.3   Hashtag Vector Creation and Similarity Calculation

For every hashtag, tweets which contain the same hashtag are concatenated to form contents. Term weight for each separate term in the concatenated contents would be calculated by TF-IHF and P-IOLogH. Top-n words whose term weights are larger than the others are selected to create the hashtag vector. Value in each dimension of the hashtag vector is normalized to make the norm of the vector equals to 1.

Our two assumptions for hashtag recommendation result in a high cosine similarity between the news-topic vector and the hashtag vector. Hashtags whose vectors have high similarity with the news-topic vector should be recommended to users who wish to join the conversation about the news topic in Twitter.

5   Experiment and Evaluation

5.1   Description of the Dataset

In order to validate the effectiveness of our approach on real-world data, news dataset and news-related tweet dataset are prepared for the experiment. News dataset contains 10,855 news articles crawled from 96 news sites (21 countries/regions) on December 20th, 2011. However, due to the huge number of tweets for different topics in Twitter, it is hard to retrieve all those tweets related to news topics. Our solution is to manually select 54 active Twitter accounts of news agencies and collect tweets which are posted by these accounts or contain mentioned/tagged screen names of these accounts (e.g. @CNN, #CNN) by using Twitter Streaming API [21]. At last we collected 124,481 tweets on December 20th, 2011 to create our news-related tweet dataset. Although there might be some other tweets related to news topics, collecting those tweets by formal Information Retrieval technologies is no longer effective due to the limited length of a tweet and a trade-off has to be made.

5.2   Experimental Setup

News articles in our news dataset are parsed by using TreeTagger [22] and Stanford Named Entity Recognizer (SNER) [23]. All nouns, proper nouns, foreign words, verbs and adjectives are picked up for representing each news article under Vector

Space Model as TF-IDF vector. Then all news articles are clustered based on their cosine similarities. News articles relating to the same news topic are hopefully grouped into the same cluster with a predefined similarity threshold of 0.22. To represent the news topic, traditional TF-IDF method and P-IOLog method in Section 3 are used to weight terms to create a news-topic vector. For the TF-IDF method, we calculated the centroid vector of all news article vectors for this topic and top-n words in the centroid vector which have higher TF-IDF scores were selected to create the news-topic vector, we refer to it as V_{TD-N}. We also selected top-n words whose term weights were calculated by the P-IOLog method of Equation 1 and the news-topic vector was created by these top-n words in Equation 4, we refer to it as V_{IO-N}. Words which are informative and tightly related to the news topic should be selected in these top-n words with larger term weight than the others.

Tweets in the news-related tweet dataset are also preprocessed. Firstly, tweets which contain no hashtag or are written in non-English languages are excluded by checking the main language in the publisher's profile as "en". Secondly we filtered out all formal retweets and include tweets which have been retweeted in the dataset because Twitter users are not allowed to modify tweet contents when they use formal "Retweet" function and hashtags in those retweets may not reflect the original idea of Twitter users. At last 20,094 tweets remain after this step. Thirdly, for every hashtag in those tweets, we concatenate contents of all tweets which contain the same hashtag while mention, URL, and hashtags are removed. Hashtags appearing in less than 10 tweets are considered un-valuable and excluded. Up to now, 433 hashtags and their corresponding concatenated tweet contents have been got. We also use TreeTagger and SNER to parse concatenated contents of tweets into terms and created hashtag vectors. Here TF-IHF and P-IOLogH which have been described in Section 4 are used to weight terms and top-n terms whose term weights are larger than the others are selected to create the hashtag vector. Smoothing parameter s_p in both P-IOLog and P-IOLogH are set as 0.05. Finally we got two vectors for every hashtag: V_{TH-N} is the vector whose term weight is calculated by the TF-IHF and V_{IH-N} is the vector whose term weight is the score of P-IOLogH.

We chose "Republican", "North Korea", "Syria", and "protester" as the target words. For each target word, news topics which contain more than half of news articles including the target word are selected and summaries of these news topics are described in Table 1.

For each news topic, we set four experiments with different combinations of term weighting methods to calculate similarities between news topics and hashtags.

- Exp. 1: $V_{TD-N} \cdot V_{TH-N}$; term weight for news-topic vector is the TF-IDF score and term weight for hashtag vector is the TF-IHF score.
- Exp. 2: $V_{TD-N} \cdot V_{IH-N}$; term weight for news-topic vector is the TF-IDF score and term weight for hashtag vector is the P-IOLogH score.
- Exp. 3: $V_{IO-N} \cdot V_{TH-N}$; term weight for news-topic vector is the P-IOLog score and term weight for hashtag vector is the TF-IHF score.
- Exp. 4: $V_{IO-N} \cdot V_{IH-N}$; term weight for news-topic vector is the P-IOLog score and term weight for hashtag vector is the P-IOLogH score.

Table 1. Summary of each news topic

ID	Summary
News topics for "Republican"	
R_1	Iowa Republican caucus
R_2	House Republicans refused to extend payroll tax cut bill.
News topics for "North Korea"	
NK_1	World worried about power transition after Kim Jong-il's death.
NK_2	World stock market affected by Kim Jong-il's death.
News topic for "Syria"	
S_1	Syria allowed Arab observers into the country to end crisis.
News topic for "protester"	
P_1	Egyptian army started to clear Tahrir Square with force.

In each experiment, top-n words whose term weights are larger than the others for news topics and hashtags are selected to create vectors with n taking the value of 50, 100, and 200. Methods which outperform others are considered ranking those topic-specific informative words higher and hashtags recommended by these methods are considered more proper for the news topic.

5.3   Assessments

To evaluate recommended hashtags from four experiments, we ask assessors to judge the relevance of the recommended hashtags to each news topic. To help our assessors better understand the news topic, they could scan/search for any information if they need to make a proper decision. The whole procedure is depicted as below.

1. Three assessors are asked to read at least ten news articles which are carefully selected for each news topic so that these news articles can cover the main contents of the news topic to make them understand the news topic.
2. Top-15 hashtags with largest similarities recommended by each of four experiments are mixed to form a hashtag list for each news topic. Assessors judge the relevance of each hashtag in this list to the news topic on a three-point scale: highly relevant, partially relevant and irrelevant. They can use any tool (e.g. TagDef, Google) to find definitions for hashtags.
3. For each news topic, hashtags which are judged as highly relevant by at least two assessors are defined as highly relevant hashtags. We also define relevant hashtags as they should not be judged as irrelevant by any of assessors. Notice that highly relevant hashtags are a sub-set of relevant hashtags.

Table 2. Recommended hashtags for R_1 using top-50 words, and evaluation results

Exp.1	Exp.2	Exp.3	Exp.4
teaparty	iacaucus	teaparty	iacaucus
teamfollowback	gop2012	trms	trms
tcot	ronpaul	iacaucus	gop2012
ronpaul	politics	ronpaul	gop
gop	gop	gop2012	ronpaul
politics	trms	gop	gingrich
trms	teaparty	tcot	politics
iacaucus	tlot	teamfollowback	fitn
gop2012	fitn	gingrich	teaparty
topnews	tcot	politics	tlot
snn	gingrich	tlot	huntsman
gingrich	teamfollowback	mittromney	tcot
tlot	p2	romney	romney
fitn	foxnews	nh	p2
iowa	nh	fitn	teamfollowback
Highly Relevant Hashtags (HR)	gop2012, gingrich, tcot, ronpaul, iacaucus		
Relevant Hashtags (R)	huntsman, gop2012, gingrich, newt, tcot, politics. gop,mittromney, fitn, iowa, ronpaul, iacaucus, teaparty		

For example, "#iacaucus" was judged as a highly relevant hashtag because tweets containing this hashtag mainly talked about the Iowa Caucus of Republicans. However, "#gop" which is often used to mark tweets about Republican was considered as relevant hashtags because it also relates to other Republican issues. Hashtags such as "#topnews" used for other purposes were judged as irrelevant. Finally we got 26 highly relevant hashtags and 59 relevant hashtags for six news topics.

To evaluate performances of four experiments for six news topics, we use Precision as the evaluation metric under two-levels:

- **Precision at highly relevance (P@HR):** P@HR is the fraction of top-N_{hr} recommended hashtags in each experiment that are highly relevant hashtags, where N_{hr} is the number of highly relevant hashtags for the news topic.
- **Precision at relevance (P@R):** P@R is the fraction of top-N_r recommended hashtags in the experiment that are judged as relevant hashtags, where N_r is the number of relevant hashtags for the news topic.

The experiment whose P@HR and P@R values are both larger than the others should be considered as the best one for recommending hashtags. If some experiments share the same value of P@HR, the experiment whose P@R value is larger outperforms. We only evaluate Precision here because Recall and F-measure share the same value in our experiments.

5.4 Experimental Result

We select top-n words ($n = 50, 100, 200$) whose term weights are larger than the others by using different term weighting methods to create vectors for representing news topics and hashtags. Four experiments described in Section 5.2 are evaluated based on precision metric under two-levels for six news topics (R_1, R_2, NK_1, NK_2, S_1, P_1).

Table 3. Experiment results of P@HR and P@R with their average precisions (Ave@HR, Ave@R) for six news topics (R_1, R_2, NK_1, NK_2, S_1, P_1) by four experiments (Exp.1 – Exp.4)

		P@HR				Ave@HR	P@R				Ave@R
		HR	top50	top100	top200		R	top50	top100	top200	
R_1	Exp.1	5	0.4	0.6	0.6	0.533	13	0.615	0.615	0.615	0.615
	Exp.2		0.6	0.8	0.8	**0.733**		0.692	0.769	0.692	0.7179
	Exp.3		0.6	0.4	0.4	0.466		0.692	0.692	0.615	0.6667
	Exp.4		0.6	0.6	0.8	0.666		0.769	0.846	0.692	**0.7692**
R_2	Exp.1	2	1	1	1	1	8	0.625	0.625	0.625	0.625
	Exp.2		1	1	1	1		0.75	0.75	0.625	0.7083
	Exp.3		1	1	1	1		0.625	0.75	0.625	0.6667
	Exp.4		1	1	1	1		0.75	0.75	0.75	**0.75**
NK_1	Exp.1	3	0.333	0.333	0.3333	0.333	11	0.454	0.636	0.636	0.5758
	Exp.2		0.666	0.666	0.666	0.666		0.636	0.727	0.727	0.697
	Exp.3		0.666	1	0.666	0.777		0.727	0.727	0.727	0.7273
	Exp.4		1	1	1	**1**		0.727	0.818	0.818	**0.7879**
NK_2	Exp.1	4	0.5	0.5	0.25	0.416	8	0.375	0.375	0.375	0.375
	Exp.2		0.5	0.5	0.5	0.5		0.375	0.5	0.5	0.4583
	Exp.3		0.25	0.5	0.75	0.5		0.5	0.75	0.75	0.6667
	Exp.4		0.75	0.75	0.75	**0.75**		0.625	0.75	0.875	**0.75**
S_1	Exp.1	4	0.75	0.75	0.75	0.75	9	0.666	0.556	0.556	0.5926
	Exp.2		0.5	0.5	0.5	0.5		0.666	0.667	0.556	0.6297
	Exp.3		0.75	0.75	0.75	0.75		0.666	0.667	0.778	0.7037
	Exp.4		0.75	0.75	0.75	0.75		0.777	0.778	0.778	**0.7778**
P_1	Exp.1	8	0.875	0.75	0.75	0.791	10	0.7	0.7	0.7	0.7
	Exp.2		0.875	0.875	0.875	0.875		0.7	0.7	0.8	0.7333
	Exp.3		0.875	0.875	0.75	0.833		0.9	0.9	0.9	**0.9**
	Exp.4		0.875	0.875	0.875	**0.875**		0.8	0.9	0.9	0.8667

Table 2 gives a detailed example about top-15 recommended hashtags for news topic R_1 from four experiments and assessors' judgment results. For example, there are 5 hashtags considered as highly relevant hashtags by assessors (N_{hr}). Among top-5 hashtags recommended by Exp. 4, 3 of them (iacaucus, gop2012, ronpaul) belong to the highly relevant hashtag and the precision at highly relevance (P@HR) is calculated as 3 divided by 5. Also, there are only 2 hashtags (tcot, ronpaul) out of top-5 hashtags recommended by Exp. 1 taken as highly relevant hashtags and the P@HR should be 2 divided by 5. Precision at relevance (P@R) is calculated in the same way. For each experiment, average precision values (Ave@HR, Ave@R) are calculated with different n values. Table 3 gives out final evaluation results for four experiments among six news topics. Bold numbers are the largest average precision values for highly relevant and relevant hashtags while columns of HR and R give out the number of highly relevant and relevant hashtags for each news topic.

Exp. 4 which applies our proposed methods based on Inside and Outside assumptions to both news topics (Section 3) and hashtags (Section 4.2) has a larger average precision value than the others in most cases, which means hashtags recommended by the Exp.4 are more meaningful than hashtags recommended by other experiments. Although Exp. 4 shares the same Ave@HR value with other experiments in R_2 and S_1, it outperforms others in Ave@R, which also means Exp. 4 performs better. By applying our proposed methods for hashtags or news topics in Exp. 2 and Exp. 3, results show an improvement, although they still perform not so well compared to Exp. 4. These improvements also prove that our Probabilistic Inside-Outside Log methods for both news-topics and hashtags have positive affection to the final results. By varying the value of n for top-n words which are used to build the vectors, we can also observe that Exp.4 outperforms others with different n values ranging from 50 to 200, which proves that our proposed methods are more likely to rank informative words higher than the others. Applying our proposed methods only for hashtags or news topics in Exp.2 and Exp.3 could also partially improve the results with different n values compared to the Exp.1 due to the outperformance of our methods.

6   Conclusion

In this paper, we presented an approach for recommending hashtags in Twitter on news topics searched for an input target word. As basic components of the approach, we also proposed a method for detecting/weighting characteristic words co-occurring with the target word in news articles and two methods for detecting/weighting characteristic words co-occurring with a hashtag in tweets. Experimental results shown that our proposed methods for both news-topics and hashtags could recommend more news-topic relevant hashtags than the other methods such as TF-IDF.

The current system could recommend existed hashtags only for news topics while other topics which have been discussed in Twitter without reported by news agencies are unable to get recommended hashtags. In the future, we are planning to deal with not only news topics, but also other topics discussed by Twitter users. Also, in some cases, the current system returns too many hashtags and it is difficult for us to select appropriate hashtags from them. We think that hashtags used by influential Twitter users in the topic of interest are more likely to be recognized by others and the hashtags should be ranked higher. Finding influential Twitter users for hashtag recommendation would be another research direction we are considering.

References

1. Kwak, H., Lee, C., Park, H., Moon, S.: What is Twitter, a social network or a news media? In: Proc. of the 19th Int. Conf. on World Wide Web, Raleigh, North Carolina, USA (2010)
2. Brooks, C.H., Montanez, N.: Improved Annotation of the Blogosphere via Autotagging and Hierarchical Clustering. In: Proc. of the 15th Int. Conf. on World Wide Web, Edinburgh, UK (2006)
3. Mishne, G.: AutoTag: A Collaborative Approach to Automated Tag Assignment for Weblog Posts. In: Proc. of the 15th Int. Conf. on World Wide Web, Edinburgh, UK (2006)
4. Sood, S.C., Owsley, S.H., Hammond, K.J., Birnbaum, L.: TagAssist: Automatic Tag Suggestion for Blog Posts. In: Int. Conf. on Weblogs and Social Media (2007)
5. Singhal, A., Buckley, C., Mitra, M.: Pivoted Document Length Normalization. In: 19th Annual International ACM SIGIR Conference on Research and Development in Information Retrieval (SIGIR 1996), pp. 21–29. ACM (1996)
6. Sigurbjornsson, B., van Zwol, R.: Flickr Tag Recommendation based on Collective Knowledge. In: Proc. of the 17th Int. Conf. on World Wide Web, Beijing, China (2008)

7. Wartena, C., Brussee, R., Wibbels, M.: Using Tag Co-Occurrence for Recommendation. In: Proc. of Int. Conf. on Intelligent System Design and Application (ISDA 2009), Pisa, Italy (November 2009)
8. Belem, F., Martins, E., Pontes, T., Almeida, J., Goncalces, M.: Associative Tag Recommendation Exploiting Multiple Textual Features. In: Proc. of the 34th Int. ACM SIGIR Conf. on Research and Development in Information Retrieval, Beijing, China (July 2011)
9. Huang, J., Thornton, K.M., Efthimiadis, E.N.: Conversational Tagging in Twitter. In: Proc. of the 21st ACM Conf. on Hypertext and Hypermedia, Toronto, Ontario, Canada (2010)
10. Weng, J., Lim, E.-P., He, Q., Leung, C.W.-K.: What Do People Want in Microblogs? Measuring Interestingness of Hashtags in Twitter. In: Proc. of the 2010 IEEE Int. Conf. on Data Mining, ICDM 2010, pp. 1121–1126 (2010)
11. Correa, D., Sureka, A.: Mining Tweets for Tag Recommendation on Social Media. In: Proc. of the 3rd Int. Workshop on Search and Mining User-Generated Contents, SMUC 2011, Glasgow, Scotland, UK (2011)
12. Efron, M.: Hashtag Retrieval in a Microblogging Environment. In: Proc. of the 33rd Int. ACM SIGIR Conf. on Research and Development in Information Retrieval, ACM SIGIR 2010, Geneva, Switzerland (2010)
13. Wagner, C., Strohmaier, M.: The Wisdom in Tweetonomies: Acquiring Latent Conceptual Structures from Social Awareness Streams. In: Proc. of the 3rd International Semantic Search Workshop, p. 6. ACM (2010)
14. Zangerle, E., Gassler, W., Specht, G.: Recommending #-Tags in Twitter. In: Proc. of the Workshop on Semantic Adaptive Social Web, UMAP 2011, Gerona, Spain (2011)
15. Phuvipadawat, S., Murata, T.: Detecting a Multi-Level Content Similarity from Microblogs Based on Community Structures and Named Entities. Journal of Emerging Technologies in Web Intelligence 3(1) (February 2011)
16. Sankaranarayanan, J., Samet, H., Heitler, B.E., Lieberman, M.D., Sperling, J.: TwitterStand: News in Tweets. In: Proc. of the 17th ACM SIGSPATIAL Int. Conf. on Advances in Geographic Information System, ACM GIS, Seattle, WA, USA (November 2009)
17. Phelan, O., McCarthy, K., Smyth, B.: Using Twitter to Recommend Real-Time Topical News. In: Proc. of the 3rd ACM Conf. on Recommender Systems, ACM RecSys, New York, NY, USA (October 2009)
18. Abel, F., Gao, Q., Houben, G.-J., Tao, K.: Semantic Enrichment of Twitter Posts for User Profile Construction on the Social Web. In: Antoniou, G., Grobelnik, M., Simperl, E., Parsia, B., Plexousakis, D., De Leenheer, P., Pan, J. (eds.) ESWC 2011, Part II. LNCS, vol. 6644, pp. 375–389. Springer, Heidelberg (2011)
19. Salton, G., Wong, A., Yang, C.S.: A Vector Space Model for Automatic Indexing. Communications of the ACM 18(11), 613–620 (1975)
20. Xiao, F., Noro, T., Tokuda, T.: Detection of Characteristic Co-Occurrence Words from News Articles on the Web. In: 21st European-Japanese Conference on Information Modelling and Knowledge Base, vol. 1, pp. 242–258 (June 2011)
21. Twitter Streaming API, https://dev.twitter.com/docs/streaming-api
22. Schmid, H.: Probabilistic Part-of-Speech Tagging Using Decision Trees. In: First International Conference on New Methods in Natural Language Processing, pp. 44–49 (1994)
23. Stanford Named Entity Recognizer, http://nlp.stanford.edu/software/CRF-NER.shtml

Crowdsourced Web Engineering and Design

Michael Nebeling, Stefania Leone, and Moira C. Norrie

Institute of Information Systems, ETH Zurich,
CH-8092 Zurich, Switzerland
{nebeling,leone,norrie}@inf.ethz.ch

Abstract. We present an approach for the lightweight development of web information systems based on the idea of involving crowds in the underlying engineering and design processes. Our approach is designed to support developers as well as non-technical end-users in composing data-driven web interfaces in a plug-n-play manner. To enable this, we introduce the notion of crowdsourced web site components whose design can gradually evolve as they get associated with more data and functionality contributed by the crowd. Hence, required components must not necessarily pre-exist or be developed by the application designer alone, but can also be created on-demand by publishing an open call to the crowd that may in response provide multiple alternative solutions. The potential of the approach is illustrated based on two initial experiments.

Keywords: Lightweight web engineering, end-user development, crowd-sourcing.

1 Introduction

Crowdsourcing is currently an important topic in both research and industry. The term was originally coined in an article by Jeff Howe [1] and refers to the idea of outsourcing some kind of task to a larger group of people in the form of an open call. In a software engineering context, it is typically used to refer to *crowdsourced systems* [2] which provide a kernel application that other developers, or even the increasingly larger community of end-users with programming experience, can complement and extend with new peripheral services and system functionality. Two popular examples in a web engineering context are Facebook[1] and WordPress[2] where many parts in the form of small applications, plugins and themes are developed by the community. However, there is currently no dedicated support in web engineering tools for making use of crowdsourcing.

By contrast, within the HCI community, recent work has been directed towards *crowd-powered systems* that aim to embed crowds directly into interfaces as a way of supporting collective problem solving through crowdsourcing und human computation [3]. Paid micro-task crowdsourcing markets such as Amazon Mechanical Turk[3] play an important role in enabling this research since

---

[1] http://www.facebook.com

[2] http://www.wordpress.org

[3] http://mturk.com

M. Brambilla, T. Tokuda, and R. Tolksdorf (Eds.): ICWE 2012, LNCS 7387, pp. 31–45, 2012.

studies established it as a viable platform for crowdsourcing experiments [4]. Hence, our goal is to build on these ideas and bring them to the web engineering community.

Given the proliferation of powerful Web 2.0 platforms such as WordPress and advanced mashup tools, e.g. [5,6], end-users are increasingly provided with support for building web information systems in a plug-n-play manner. However, there is relatively little support if the required web site components do not already exist somewhere on the web. Therefore, we decided to investigate a systematic approach to engineering web applications based on the mashup paradigm even if they are designed from scratch. At the same time, the goal is to support the whole range from less experienced end-users to expert web developers as well as the complete design-build-evaluate cycle by providing support for crowdsourcing at all stages of design. This work builds on previous research on a crowdsourced platform for information system development [7,8] and crowdsourced web site adaptation [9] and extends it towards our proposal for crowdsourced web engineering. In the same sense, it is also related to recent work on crowdsourcing web usability tests before and after deployment [10].

In this paper, we present a first platform and design environment as well as two possible crowdsourcing models for the lightweight composition and crowdsourced design of new web applications based on the proposed paradigm. To facilitate this, our approach also supports the plug-n-play style of composing web applications similar to WordPress and advanced mashup editors. In contrast to these approaches, however, we build on a new notion of crowdsourced web site components that support the evolution of content, presentation and behaviour by continuously refining their design with the help of the crowd. Similar to programmableweb.com or userscripts.org, this may work as a community-based design approach just by itself, but we also present an integration of our design environment with Mechanical Turk so that crowd workers can directly contribute. The requester can then review and choose from suggested design alternatives to be used in their own applications, as well as starting new iterations based on the best results so far.

Section 2 presents the background to this work. We introduce our crowdsourcing approach along with the platform in Section 3. We then present a first realisation of our proposal in Section 4, followed by the implementation in Section 5. Section 6 reports an initial evaluation of the approach for two simple examples, while concluding remarks are presented in Section 8.

2   Background

There are numerous frameworks and development environments for building web information systems. Early approaches have focused on supporting developers in the systematic engineering of web information systems by designing applications at a higher level of abstraction. For example, web methodologies such as WebML [11], UWE [12] and Hera [13] build on a set of different models to describe the structural, navigational and presentation aspects of web information systems. Models are typically defined graphically and most methodologies offer a platform for application generation and deployment according to the model definitions. However, while these model-driven approaches are generally very powerful, they follow a bottom-up development method that usually starts from the data model. The focus is therefore on modelling rather than designing which is less appropriate for web designers and non-technical end-users.

In contrast, other research has focused on end-user development of web-based information systems by providing application editors that are closer to a WYSI-WYG approach [14,15]. The WYSIWYG editor presented in [14] supports web information system development using a top-down approach, where a user starts by specifying the presentation layer and creating forms that represent domain entities, from which the underlying system is then generated. However, the presentation is restricted to forms and there is no support for rich UI controls. In [15], a more advanced WYSIWYG visualiser and editor for managing structured datasets based on an active document paradigm is presented. Here, data is stored alongside structure and presentation as an active document, which basically corresponds to a web page.

With the new proliferation of web platforms and services, there has been an increasing trend of building web mashups that integrate and visualise information aggregated from various distributed web data sources rather than designing applications from scratch. In a first response, visual mashup editors such as Yahoo Pipes[4], MashMaker [16] and Mash-o-matic [17] have been designed to enable general mashup creation, such as the aggregation of feeds and data visualisation on a map, through the graphical composition and integration of data from different sources. However, while most mashup editors help users integrate information from distributed sources, they do not provide the basic infrastructure to facilitate the design and composition of new applications for their own data, which is one of the scenarios supported by our approach. An exception is MashArt [5] which is a platform that combines the ideas of web information system development and mashups. MashArt enables advanced users to create their own applications through the composition of user interface, application and data components. The focus is on supporting the integration of existing presentation components based on event-based composition, where components can react to events of other components.

Recently, DashMash [6] was introduced as a graphical mashup editor for creating new components based on the same event-based approach, but with increased support for end-users. For example, while composing a system from existing services, DashMash can recommend other services that could also be useful in the current design context. However, it is not clear who defines and configures available services and how the approach can scale to supporting the development of complex web applications. To this end, the work presented in [18] may, in principle, provide an interesting solution based on Firecrow—a web site component extraction tool that can liberate selected interface controls from existing web sites while preserving their functionality. However, the focus of this work is on

---

[4] http://pipes.yahoo.com/pipes/

extraction rather than reuse and, due to the complexity and diversity of modern web interfaces, there are many critical edge cases, in particular when it comes to extracting relevant JavaScript code. This approach therefore provides no general solution. In addition, there is currently no specific tool support for reusing and embedding extracted components in existing web pages.

The focus of recent work has been on end-user development approaches and specifically the combination of existing web application components as well as the aggregation of web data from various existing sources. We build on this research, but also take some of the ideas further. The goal is to support *application designers* in general, which may be non-technical end-users, but also experienced developers, by leveraging crowdsourcing as part of the development process. On the one hand, we envision crowdsourcing scenarios that support end-users by asking the crowd to contribute new web site components with tailored functionality. On the other hand, the crowd may also provide alternative designs or iterate over existing ones, which can support developer creativity and increase quality. In both cases, the idea is that the underlying system functionality and application design can evolve and adapt with the help of crowdsourced contributions. This is in contrast to mashup editors, where the focus lies on service composition rather than refinement and evolution.

3   Crowdsourced Web Engineering and Design

Our approach to engineering web information systems with the help of crowdsourcing is based on two aspects. First, we support component-based composition of applications by associating user interface controls with data in a plug-n-play style. Second, we promote a crowdsourcing paradigm for the development, sharing and reuse of web site components. We will first introduce the crowdsourced component concept, followed by the design and composition processes it enables and the underlying crowdsourcing models.

Figure 1 illustrates the component concept. In our approach, we distinguish between the information component part and the user interface component part that together describe an application component. Information components define the data as well as the schema which consists of both structural and behavioural

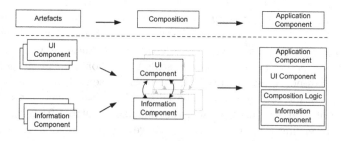

Fig. 1. Crowdsourced Web Site Components Concept

information. They can therefore be regarded as components that provide data as well as facilities to manage that data [7]. On the other hand, user interface components define static presentation aspects and dynamic user interface behaviour. They can hence be either basic templates for presenting content or more advanced form-based controls and widgets that allow a user to view, work with and manipulate the information.

Further, the processes of designing interface components and linking them to information components are supported from within a design environment that is directly embedded in the web site. As illustrated in Fig. 2a, the process of designing interface components is facilitated by allowing application designers to adapt, compose and group interface elements in order to build more complex ones. For example, in the first step, the designer may choose an image component and associate it with a label to build an image preview. The composition process illustrated in Fig. 2b then allows designers to associate the resulting interface components with information. This involves binding the data provided by information components to the interface component. Both processes along with other features of our design tool are described in detail in the next section.

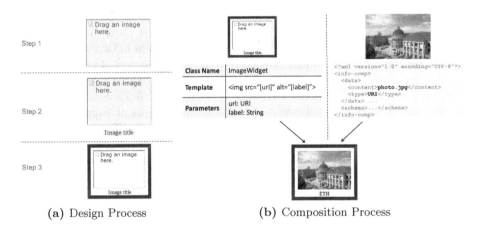

(a) Design Process   (b) Composition Process

Fig. 2. Development Processes based on Crowdsourced Web Site Components

Moreover, our component concept is designed to support the evolution of components in that both the interface and information component parts can be defined in multiple versions. Here, versions may be alternative solutions or refinements of previous ones [19]. Each of these versions in turn may either be created by the same application designer or be contributed from others through a form of crowdsourcing. Due to the way in which we defined the component concept, the resulting flexibility is reflected at both the information management and user interface levels. There are therefore several possibilities of making use of crowdsourcing based on the concept.

– **Crowdsourcing Information Components.** Application data as well as the schema that describes the data may be crowdsourced. For data crowdsourcing, it is possible to automatically generate a data input user interface based on the component schema to allow crowds to contribute data [20]. Crowdsourcing data is particularly useful for data that is not directly accessible over the web or if existing extraction algorithms are insufficient. These are also two cases where mashup solutions would fail since they require existing interfaces and data sources. Furthermore, it is also possible to crowdsource the schema. One way to do this is through the sharing of schemas from existing applications within a community and enabling their reuse in new applications. This is discussed in detail in [8] and therefore not the focus of this paper. However, since information components define schema and data, both crowdsourcing ideas are enabled by our concept.

- **Crowdsourcing Interface Components.** Crowdsourcing could also be used in several ways at the user interface design level. For example, non-technical end-users may not be able to develop their own web site components, but could build on those that have been contributed by more experienced developers. At the same time, experienced application developers could benefit from crowdsourcing by getting design feedback and specifically asking for new design proposals. The focus of our previous work in this respect was on increasing the adaptivity of user interfaces by asking end-users to contribute variations of the layout suitable to their particular use context [9]. We build on these techniques, but extend them in two ways. First, to allow for new design ideas that go beyond customisation of existing user interface parts, we developed more flexible tools that enable application designers to add new interface elements or change and replace existing ones with alternatives. Second, we designed a simple means of supporting the definition of new user interface components from scratch. To enable this, a placeholder component is provided that the application designer can specify up to a certain level and which may then be realised and refined through crowdsourcing. Note that placeholder components may be used at the presentation as well as the content level in order to let both aspects of an application component evolve. However, in the scope of this paper, we focus on the idea of crowdsourcing interface rather than information components.

As indicated in previous examples, our approach supports two different crowdsourcing models that complement each other.

- **Sharing and Reuse.** The first is based on the idea of building a common component library to enable the sharing and reuse of components within a community. Given the component concept, it is possible to share either information or interface components, or both, and this with or without data. This allows application designers to contribute as well as benefit from shared components within the community.
- **Active Crowdsourcing.** The second model is based on services provided by paid crowdsourcing markets like Mechanical Turk. This then turns the previous, indirect crowdsourcing model into an active request-response cycle that enables the application designer to directly call on the crowd by

publishing requests to the crowdsourcing service. Moreover, this model also gives control over additional parameters such as the number of workers to contribute to the design process as well as time and cost.

The two models are complementary since both can contribute to having a larger library of shared components. While this is obvious in the first case, also in the latter case it can be supported by sharing crowdsourced components again with the community. The models can therefore work independently, but may more effectively be combined by leveraging both the application developer community as well as involving paid, external crowds.

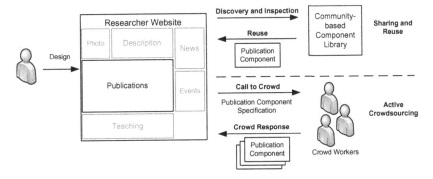

Fig. 3. Crowdsourcing Models illustrated for an Example Web Site

Figure 3 summarises the ideas behind our crowdsourced web engineering approach and illustrates them for the scenario of creating a researcher web page. In the example, the application designer decides to use the crowd for the design of a publications component and may choose from two complementary crowdsourcing models. On the one hand, the application designer may access the community-based component library and search for a suitable component to be reused. On the other hand, the designer may issue an open call to the crowd and select a component from the crowd response. Application designers are encouraged to combine the two models and share components received through the open call in the community-based component library.

4   Crowdsourcing Platform and CrowdDesign Prototype

For crowdsourced web application development based on the new component concept and the crowdsourcing models presented in the previous sections, we have developed a crowdsourcing platform and web-based design environment, CrowdDesign. The underlying architecture is illustrated in Fig. 4.

The platform is responsible for orchestrating the definition and sharing of both information and interface components. Likewise, two separate libraries of shared components, one for information components and one for interface components, are maintained by the platform. Application designers can access these

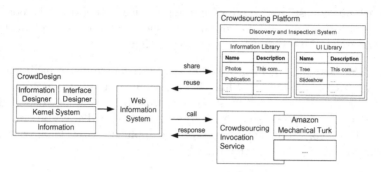

Fig. 4. Architecture

libraries either directly through the discovery and inspection system offered by the platform, or transparently through the development environment when designing applications. Each application designer contributing to the aforementioned crowdsourcing scenarios is provided with a local CrowdDesign instance running on the client machine. The platform services are exposed through the visual design environment of CrowdDesign that is composed of two parts. The first part is an information designer that supports the definition of information components as presented in [8]. The second is an interface designer for the customisation of existing components and the definition of new interface components. The design tools therefore enable the design process in terms of definition and maintenance of instances of each component type as well as their composition to application components. Web applications based on our approach are directly hosted by the platform and run from within CrowdDesign, but they can also be deployed separately as standalone web information systems using the same kernel system. The integration with Mechanical Turk is facilitated by the crowdsourcing invocation service as an intermediary which may be extended with support for other crowdsourcing markets.

The CrowdDesign prototype is divided into several different areas shown in Fig. 5. The client area in the centre is the workspace where application designers can design and compose applications. On the left, the designer has access to the library of user interface components shared within the community. As mentioned previously, these may include basic user interface form controls, such as lists and buttons, as well as more complex widgets such as image slideshows or video players. On the right, the application designer has access to their own or shared information components that are organised by type and can be browsed and accessed via a hierarchical navigation.

The application designer initiates the actual composition process by simply dragging components from the information library and dropping them on interface elements in the workspace. CrowdDesign then performs an automatic mapping between the user interface component and the information component depending on supported parameters and the data type. For example, a picture view component may define two parameters, namely a URL for the image and text for the label. The application designer can then associate text components

Fig. 5. CrowdDesign Tool

with the picture view in order to set the label as well as an image URL to link to the actual image. For some widgets such as the image slideshow from previous examples, it is also possible to associate a collection of images with the control in a single interaction if the underlying presentation template provides support for array parameters. Note that the application designer can also customise and edit the suggested mapping in a separate dialog (not shown here), which is usually optional, but may be required in the case of ambiguities.

In our current prototype, we use a rather simple representation of both interface and information components. Both types of components are identified by a component descriptor. Interface components are represented as a parametrised template that defines presentation as well as behaviour using a combination of HTML, CSS and JavaScript. Information components define the content in the form of semi-structured data in XML format. Application designers may simply add new information components by uploading corresponding XML files. New interface components can be defined programmatically and imported into the workspace. As shown in Fig. 6, this is supported by allowing application designers to specify supported parameters and the corresponding presentation template as well as uploading required resource files. On the other hand, interface components from the interface library can be added to the workspace via drag-n-drop. Workspace components can be resized and positioned freely as required. Alternatively, they may also be anchored at the edges of other components in the interface. The difference is that, in the first case, the position and size within the workspace are only defined in terms of CSS, while in the latter, CrowdDesign also manages the underlying HTML DOM tree to maintain a fully functional web interface. This is based on the techniques presented in [9].

In addition, the application designer can formulate an active crowdsourcing request by providing a description of the task and desired result for a new

Fig. 6. New Widget Dialog and Simple Crowdsourcing Interface

interface component. Alternatively, the designer may formulate a task based on an existing component. In both cases, a placeholder is first used in the workspace, while CrowdDesign can automatically submit requests to Mechanical Turk on behalf of the application designer and periodically check for responses. For the integration with Mechanical Turk, the application designer needs to specify additional parameters such as the number of tasks to be generated, maximum work time and the payment to be awarded for each response the application designer accepts after review.

On Mechanical Turk, workers interested in CrowdDesign tasks are then first shown the task description and any other information provided by the application designer. Should they choose to accept the task, they are forwarded to a CrowdDesign sandbox providing access to selected parts of the workspace and the tools necessary to contribute to the task. By default, CrowdDesign is configured to show both the interface and information components that are relevant and to allow for customisation of the existing parts as well as adding new components using the aforementioned CrowdDesign features. As shown in Fig. 7a, responses collected from workers can be previewed by the application designer who may accept or reject the results after exploring them in more detail. Each accepted contribution is automatically imported into the application designer's local CrowdDesign workspace and payment will be issued to the respective worker via the Mechanical Turk platform.

Note that workspace components can be removed simply by dragging them onto the trash bin shown in the top area of Fig. 5. This supports the idea of rapidly prototyping new components by building on relevant parts of existing ones. It is therefore also possible to merge and benefit from several crowd solutions. Likewise, components may again be recycled from the bin. Moreover, only the link between selected interface and information components may be revoked by clicking the unlink button.

Finally, application designers can save the state of the workspace so that it can be reaccessed in later sessions. Each workspace state is described by an additional XML manifest file and versioned separately together with the respective component descriptors. Further, the current workspace may also be exported as a new user interface component that will then appear in the interface library.

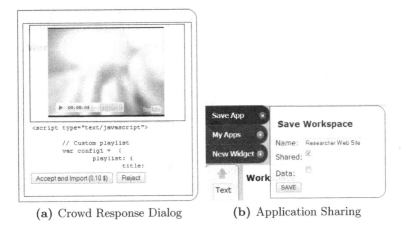

(a) Crowd Response Dialog   (b) Application Sharing

Fig. 7. Features for Reviewing and Sharing of Components

This can be done locally for the application designer to reuse the component in other applications or globally within the community [8]. As illustrated in Fig. 7b, we offer the possibility of exporting and sharing new user interface components either with or without data. In the case that data is shared, the user interface component is shared together with the associated information components as a snapshot so that all parts can be reused independent of how the source components may evolve as part of other operations.

5   Implementation

The community platform is implemented on the server-side using PHP based on the open-source CakePHP framework[5] in combination with a MySQL database. On the other hand, our web site design tool, CrowdDesign, is implemented using client-side technologies HTML, CSS3 and JavaScript based on the popular jQuery framework[6]. Much of the interface design functionality is based on the implementation of [9], while the information designer is currently simplified to a basic visual data explorer building on AJAX techniques to fetch data on demand as well as PHP's support for file uploads of new information components specified in XML.

   The integration with Mechanical Turk is based on the MTurk API to generate and submit new component-related tasks, retrieve completed work, and approve or deny that work. Instead of building on MTurk's in-built question-response API, we use an external question in order to wrap the developer's request. CrowdDesign can be configured to be either embedded into an HTML iframe or opened in a new window. To keep a record of workers that contributed

---

[5] http://cakephp.org
[6] http://jquery.com

new components, we use MTurk's internal task assignment code to identify each CrowdDesign sandbox as well as associating it with the corresponding component versions to coordinate the import into the respective CrowdDesign instance.

6   Evaluation

We evaluated the basic functionality of CrowdDesign in two smaller experiments. The first experiment was conducted with the help of members of our group and designed to simulate a community-based design approach. In this experiment, one of the members got the task of designing a web page featuring his research profile together with the help of others. The other members got the task of browsing web pages of researchers and extracting common components and sharing them in the library. To keep the experiment simple, screenshots rather than fully-functional components were sufficient.

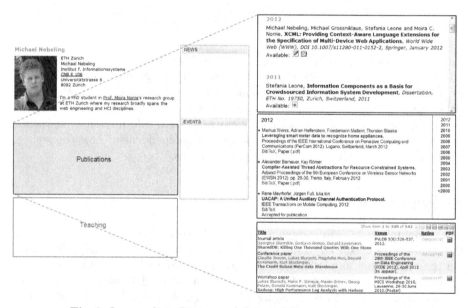

Fig. 8. Intermediate Design and Selected Community Answers

Figure 8 shows a screenshot of the workspace with an intermediary design of the researcher's homepage. At this stage, the application designer structured the page into several components. Some of the components were rapidly prototyped using his own data, such as the photo, biography and contact details, while others, such as the news and events components, have only been sketched using labelled placeholder components. In the centre, the application designer started to design a component for listing his publications. Five members of our group participated in this experiment and some of them contributed several components with different designs and functionality as input for developing such a publication component.

Also shown in the figure are three of the crowdsourced publication components originating from web sites of research groups in our institute. While all components list the publication details as well as a link to an electronic copy of each publication, there are also several differences that the designer may take into account for developing his own component. For example, the first crowdsourced publication component lists publications in reverse chronological order grouped by year and users can scroll through the list. In contrast, the solution in the middle displays publications only for a selected year and a bibtex entry is also provided. The last solution paginates the list of publications and provides navigation controls similar to database browsers. An additional functionality in this solution is that publications can also be rated.

In the second experiment, we used an active crowdsourcing model and instead built on Mechanical Turk. Here, the general task was to design a new search component for finding content within a web page. For this experiment, we issued a call for an interface component in which we specified that it should present a simple search interface and include the necessary JavaScript to run the query. The call was issued via Mechanical Turk with a 15 minute request for 5 workers at 50 cents each. Workers were presented a minimal CrowdDesign interface to upload the required resources and enter the necessary code. Figure 9 shows three of the answers we received in response. The first two are rather simple form interfaces making use of only HTML. While they both catered for basic search functionality using JavaScript, the code provided by the crowd only worked for certain browsers. The third is a solution that relies on an open-source JavaScript plugin that is cross-browser compatible. Moreover, the interface uses a more sophisticated popup-based design and also allows to search backwards.

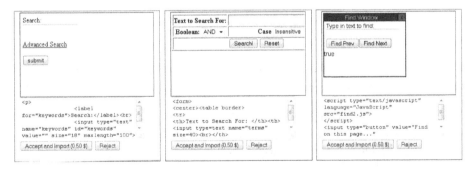

Fig. 9. Worker Responses for Simple Search Component Experiment

7   Discussion

Even though our evaluation is still preliminary, it already showed that our new idea of crowdsourced web engineering and design is generally fruitful and that a system like CrowdDesign could facilitate the task of crowdsourcing the design of new application components. While our first experiment targeted a community-based design approach, it still left a single developer in charge. However, with the ideas and tools presented in this paper, it is in principle possible to enable the co-development of components and to allow multiple application designers to work on and develop for the same web site. This would then provide a first basis for additional ideas of participatory design. The second experiment provided first insights into the different roles crowdsourcing could play for the proposed approach. As mentioned previously, it can be used both to support non-technical users to develop complex application components by building on the contributions provided by others. At the same time, it could allow even advanced developers to benefit from the design input of other users and generate new ideas. Generally, it is important to see how our use of crowdsourcing allows us to overcome some of the limitations of previous approaches. For example, content extraction is typically found to be difficult given that most existing components on the web are tightly woven into the hosting web sites and rely on a combination of HTML, CSS and JavaScript. While there are some tools such as Firecrow [18] that can be used to extract interface controls from existing web sites, it is still hard to fully automate the extraction process and also difficult to support the integration with new web sites. We argue that our approach based on crowdsourcing principles can provide a solution for such problems since experienced developers can do the extraction and package the components in such a way that they can easily be integrated with new web sites. Platforms such as programmableweb.com that are maintained by an active community show that this is not only feasible in principle, but also has the ability to scale in practice.

To enable future experiments with such ideas, we plan on making the tool and platform proposed in this paper available to the community. This would then also allow other researchers to explore the ideas of collaborative web design and to leverage crowdsourcing for hard problems such as component extraction from existing web sites.

8   Conclusion

We have presented an approach for crowdsourced web engineering and design as well as the enabling concept, platform and design environment. Our focus has so far been on the architectural and tool support. The supported crowdsourcing scenarios naturally make the approach dynamic and scalable. As a consequence, a number of issues may emerge, such as motivational incentives to contribute, quality control and security mechanisms as well as general questions of authorship and credit. These could be investigated based on our proposal and the first realisation presented in this paper. At the same time, we plan to extend and explore the presented techniques mainly along two directions. First, we plan to foster the engineering aspects of our approach and find ways of improving the technical quality of crowdsourced contributions. Second, we will investigate new possibilities enabled by our approach such as support for creativity and participatory design.

Acknowledgements. We would like to thank our IS Lab 2011 students and Kazuhiro Komoda for their help with the implementation of the prototype presented in this paper.

References

1. Howe, J.: The Rise of Crowdsourcing. Wired 14(6) (2006)
2. Kazman, R., Chen, H.M.: The Metropolis Model: A New Logic for Development of Crowdsourced Systems. CACM 52(7) (2009)
3. Quinn, A.J., Bederson, B.B.: Human Computation: A Survey and Taxonomy of a Growing Field. In: Proc. CHI (2011)
4. Kittur, A., Chi, E.H., Suh, B.: Crowdsourcing User Studies With Mechanical Turk. In: Proc. CHI (2008)
5. Daniel, F., Casati, F., Benatallah, B., Shan, M.-C.: Hosted Universal Composition: Models, Languages and Infrastructure in mashArt. In: Laender, A.H.F., Castano, S., Dayal, U., Casati, F., de Oliveira, J.P.M. (eds.) ER 2009. LNCS, vol. 5829, pp. 428–443. Springer, Heidelberg (2009)
6. Cappiello, C., Matera, M., Picozzi, M., Sprega, G., Barbagallo, D., Francalanci, C.: DashMash: A Mashup Environment for End User Development. In: Auer, S., Díaz, O., Papadopoulos, G.A. (eds.) ICWE 2011. LNCS, vol. 6757, pp. 152–166. Springer, Heidelberg (2011)
7. Leone, S., Geel, M., Norrie, M.C.: Managing Personal Information through Information Components. In: Soffer, P., Proper, E. (eds.) CAiSE Forum 2010. LNBIP, vol. 72, pp. 1–14. Springer, Heidelberg (2011)
8. Leone, S., Norrie, M.C.: Constructing eCommerce Systems from Shared Micro-Schemas. In: Proc. CoopIS (2011)
9. Nebeling, M., Norrie, M.C.: Tools and Architectural Support for Crowdsourced Adaptation of Web Interfaces. In: Auer, S., Díaz, O., Papadopoulos, G.A. (eds.) ICWE 2011. LNCS, vol. 6757, pp. 243–257. Springer, Heidelberg (2011)
10. Nebeling, M., Speicher, M., Grossniklaus, M., Norrie, M.C.: Crowdsourced Web Site Evaluation with CrowdStudy. In: Brambilla, M., Tokuda, T., Tolksdorf, R. (eds.) ICWE 2012. LNCS, vol. 7387, pp. 494–497. Springer, Heidelberg (2012)
11. Ceri, S., Fraternali, P., Bongio, A., Brambilla, M., Comai, S., Matera, M.: Designing Data-Intensive Web Applications. Morgan Kaufmann Publishers Inc. (2002)
12. Hennicker, R., Koch, N.: A UML-Based Methodology for Hypermedia Design. In: Evans, A., Caskurlu, B., Selic, B. (eds.) UML 2000. LNCS, vol. 1939, pp. 410–424. Springer, Heidelberg (2000)
13. Vdovják, R., Frăsincar, F., Houben, G.J., Barna, P.: Engineering Semantic Web Information Systems in Hera. JWE 1(1-2) (2003)
14. Yang, F., Gupta, N., Botev, C., Churchill, E.F., Levchenko, G., Shanmugasundaram, J.: WYSIWYG Development of Data Driven Web Applications. PVLDB 1(1) (2008)
15. Karger, D.R., Ostler, S., Lee, R.: The Web Page as a WYSIWYG End-User Customizable Database-backed Information Management Application. In: Proc. UIST (2009)
16. Ennals, R., Brewer, E., Garofalakis, M., Shadle, M., Gandhi, P.: Intel Mash Maker: join the web. SIGMOD 36(4) (2007)
17. Murthy, S., Maier, D., Delcambre, L.: Mash-o-Matic. In: Proc. DocEng. (2006)
18. Maras, J., Štula, M., Carlson, J.: Reusing Web Application User-Interface Controls. In: Auer, S., Díaz, O., Papadopoulos, G.A. (eds.) ICWE 2011. LNCS, vol. 6757, pp. 228–242. Springer, Heidelberg (2011)
19. Grossniklaus, M., Norrie, M.: An Object-Oriented Version Model for Context-Aware Data Management. In: Benatallah, B., Casati, F., Georgakopoulos, D., Bartolini, C., Sadiq, W., Godart, C. (eds.) WISE 2007. LNCS, vol. 4831, pp. 398–409. Springer, Heidelberg (2007)
20. Franklin, M.J., Kossmann, D., Kraska, T., Ramesh, S., Xin, R.: CrowdDB: Answering Queries with Crowdsourcing. In: Proc. SIGMOD (2011)

Scaling Pair-Wise Similarity-Based Algorithms in Tagging Spaces

Damir Vandic, Flavius Frasincar, and Frederik Hogenboom

Erasmus University Rotterdam,
P.O. Box 1738, NL-3000 DR, Rotterdam, The Netherlands
{vandic,frasincar,fhogenboom}@ese.eur.nl

Abstract. Users of Web tag spaces, e.g., Flickr, find it difficult to get adequate search results due to syntactic and semantic tag variations. In most approaches that address this problem, the cosine similarity between tags plays a major role. However, the use of this similarity introduces a scalability problem as the number of similarities that need to be computed grows quadratically with the number of tags. In this paper, we propose a novel algorithm that filters insignificant cosine similarities in linear time complexity with respect to the number of tags. Our approach shows a significant reduction in the number of calculations, which makes it possible to process larger tag data sets than ever before. To evaluate our approach, we used a data set containing 51 million pictures and 112 million tag annotations from Flickr.

1 Introduction

Due to the ever increasing amount of data readily available on the Web, the development of applications exploiting this data flourishes as never before. However, because of the data abundance, an increasing number of these Web applications suffers from scalability issues. These developments have caused the focus of recent Web research to shift to scalability aspects. Social Web applications (e.g., in the area of products, photos, videos, links, etc.) also face these scalability issues. The reason why these systems do not scale well is because they often use pair-wise similarity measures (e.g., cosine similarity, Dice coefficient, Jaccard coefficient, etc.) [9,10]. This introduces scalability problems as the number of pair-wise similarities that have to be computed (i.e., the number of unique pairs) grows quadratically with the number of vectors. As a result of this, the algorithms that use these pair-wise similarities have at least $O(n^2)$ time complexity, where n is the number of input vectors.

The fact that an algorithm has $O(n^2)$ complexity makes it difficult to apply it on large data sets. An area where this becomes evident are the social tagging systems, where users can assign tags to Web resources. These Web resources can be for example URLs (e.g., Delicious), images (e.g., Flickr), and videos (e.g., YouTube). Because users can use any tag they want, the number of distinct tags is enormous. Besides the number of unique tags, the number of resources is also growing fast. For example, let us consider Flickr, which is a Web site where

M. Brambilla, T. Tokuda, and R. Tolksdorf (Eds.): ICWE 2012, LNCS 7387, pp. 46–60, 2012.

users can upload pictures and assign tags to them. In 2011, Flickr had 6 billion pictures in their database [11]. Now imagine that Flickr needs to compute the similarity between all (unique) pairs of pictures. Let us assume that Flickr is able to compute 100 billion pairs per second. Even at this speed, it would take a little less than 6 years to compute all combinations[1]. From this computation, we can see that there is a need to deal with pair-wise similarity computations for such large amounts of high-dimensional data.

In this paper, we focus on the scalability issue that arises with the computation of pair-wise similarities in tagging spaces (e.g., Flickr). We present an algorithm that approximately filters insignificant similarity pairs (i.e., similarities that are relatively low). The proposed algorithm is not exact but it has linear time complexity with respect to the number of input vectors and is therefore applicable to large amounts of input vectors. We report the results for the cosine similarity applied on a large Flickr data set, but our approach is applicable to any similarity measure that uses the dot product between two vectors.

The structure of this paper is as follows. We present the related work in Section 2. In Section 3, we define the problem in more detail and present our algorithm using a synthetic data set and the cosine similarity used as similarity measure. We evaluate our approach on a real data set and present the results in Section 4. Last, in Section 5, we draw conclusions and present future work.

2   Related Work

The cosine similarity is a popular similarity measure that is widely used across different domains. In particular, we can find many approaches in the tagging spaces domain that are that are making use of this similarity [5,7,9,10]. The reason for this is that the cosine similarity has proven to give stable results for tagging data sets. The drawback of using the cosine similarity is that it introduces scalability issues, as nowadays the number of tags and resources is growing fast. Because all similarity pairs have to be computed, the approaches that use the cosine similarity have at least $O(n^2)$ time complexity, where n is the number of tags of resources.

In the literature we can find several approaches that aim to address the scalability issue of computing pair-wise similarities. A technique that is related to our approach is the Locality Sensitive Hashing (LSH) technique, presented in [6]. LSH is a well-known approximate algorithm that is used to find clusters of similar objects. For example, it can be used to perform approximate nearest neighbour search. LSH generates n projections of the data on randomly chosen dimensions. After that, for each vector in the data set and each previously computed projection, a hash is determined using the vector features that are presented in that particular projection. The similarity pairs are constructed by finding all vector pairs that have a matching hash along the same projection.

---

[1] If $C = ((6 \times 10^9)^2 - (6 \times 10^9)) \times 0.5 \approx 1.8 \times 10^{19}$ unique combinations, and we can process 100×10^9 combinations per second, then it takes approximately $C/(100 \times 10^9)/(60 \times 60 \times 24 \times 365) \approx 5.71$ years to compute all similarities.

The key difference between LSH and our approach is that our approach has guaranteed linear time complexity with respect to the number of input vectors, while LSH has a polynomial pre-processing time.

The authors of [2] take a different approach to the similarity search problem. They propose an exact technique which is able to precisely find all pairs that have a similarity above some threshold. This approach uses an inverted index where the inverted indices are dynamically built and a score accumulation method is used to collect the similarity values. The difference between our approach and this approach is that we propose an approximate algorithm that gives good results with the focus on reducing the computational effort, while the authors of [2] propose an exact algorithm that works with a given threshold. Furthermore, the approach in [2] has not been evaluated on data sets obtained from tagging spaces.

Although not directly related to our research, there are approaches from the database community that address a similar problem, which are worth mentioning. For example, the authors of [3] depart from traditional database design to more flexible database design that is more suited for parallel algorithms. These parallel algorithms are used for the purpose of speeding up the computation of pair-wise similarities (e.g., cosine similarity). In this paper we focus on efficient the computation of similarities in a sequential execution.

3 Algorithm

In this section, we explain in detail the proposed algorithm, which aims at reducing the number of cosine computations. The proposed algorithm has some similar characteristics to LSH, as it also uses a hash function to cluster potentially similar objects, but differs on many aspects. For example, we use only one hash function, which results in a binary encoding of the vector that indicates where the significant parts of the vector reside. Furthermore, we have only one corresponding hash value for each vector.

As already mentioned, our algorithm is tailored and evaluated for tag spaces. Algorithms and applications for tag spaces often use a so-called tag co-occurrence matrix. A tag co-occurrence matrix is a $n \times n$ matrix C, where n is the number of tags, and C_{ij} denotes how often tag i and tag j have co-occurred in the data set (e.g., on pictures). Note that co-occurrences matrices are symmetrical, i.e., $C_{ij} = C_{ji}$.

Let us consider the tag co-occurrence matrix shown in Table 1(a). From the table, we can see for example that tag 0 and 3 occur together in total 3 times. The character "-" represents 0 as we define the co-occurrence of a tag with itself to be 0. We used the symbol "-" to differentiate from the case where two tags (not identical) do not co-occur with each other (co-occurrence labelled with 0). The total number of similarity pairs, given n tags, is $(n^2 - n) \times 0.5$. For the co-occurrence matrix in Table 1(a), we have to compute $(6 \times 6 - 6)/2 = 15$ cosine similarities.

Table 1. An example of a tag co-occurrence matrix, shown in (a). The co-occurrence matrix is split in two equally sized parts, shown in (b) and (c).

(a)			(b)		(c)	
Tag	0 1 2 3 4 5		Tag	1 2 3	Tag	0 4 5
0	- 2 1 5 2 0		0	2 1 5	0	- 2 0
1	2 - 7 1 1 0		1	- 7 1	1	2 1 0
2	1 7 - 3 0 2		2	7 - 3	2	1 0 2
3	5 1 3 - 1 0		3	1 3 -	3	5 1 0
4	2 1 0 1 - 6		4	1 0 1	4	2 - 6
5	0 0 2 0 6 -		5	0 2 0	5	0 6 -

In practice, a tag co-occurrence matrix is sparse, i.e., it contains many zero values. This is because a tag on average only co-occurs with a small subset of the total set of tags. We can make use of this sparsity property in order to improve the scalability of any pair-wise similarity measure that is dependent on the dot product between two vectors. For example, the dot product between vectors **a** and **b** gives the cosine similarity, assuming the data is normalized to unit length vectors. This makes the cosine similarity a candidate for our algorithm. In the rest of this section, we explain our algorithm in the context of tag spaces, where input vectors are tag co-occurrence vectors.

The basic idea of our algorithm is to construct clusters of tag vectors from the original matrix, based on the position of the non-zero values. Because the matrix is symmetrical, it does not matter whether we cluster the columns or rows of the matrix, but for sake of clarity we assume that we cluster the columns. Tables 1(b) and 1(c) show two possible partitions (i.e., clusters) that could be obtained from the co-occurrence matrix that is shown in Table 1(a). For these two smaller matrices, we calculate the similarity only for the pairs within a cluster. For example, we do not compute the similarity between tag 3 and tag 4, as they appear in different clusters. Using this approach, the number of similarity computations that have to performed is $((3 \times 3 - 3)/2) \times 2 = 6$. This is a reduction of 60% on the total number of computations, as we have to compute the similarity only for 6 pairs instead of 15 pairs.

In order to cluster each column (i.e., tag vector) from the co-occurrence matrix, we compute a hash value for each column. This is done by first splitting each column in a predefined number of equally sized parts. Then, for each column, the relative weight of each part is computed. This is done by dividing the sum of the values in a part by the sum of the values for the whole column. After that, the columns are clustered based on the most important parts. The most important parts are defined by the smallest set of parts for which the sum of values in the parts is larger than some predefined percentage of the total column sum. This process is best explained with an example. Suppose we have the tag vector $[0, 6, 4, 0, 0, 0, 1, 0]^T$. Now, consider we choose to split this column representation in 4 parts. For each of these 4 parts, we compute the sum of the values in that part, as shown in Table 2(a). The next step is to calculate the

Table 2. Table (a) shows the part scores and (b) the part statistics for vector $[0, 6, 4, 0, 0, 0, 1, 0]^T$. We can see that the first and second part are the most important parts of this vector.

	(a)			(b)	
Part	Sum	Indices	Part	Score	Hash
1	6	0, 1	1	0.545	1
2	4	2, 3	2	0.364	1
3	0	4, 5	3	0	0
4	1	6, 7	4	0.091	0

total sum of the vector values and represent the previously determined sums as percentages of the total sum, which we call the relative score. In our example, the total sum is found by taking the sum of the values in the parts $6 + 4 + 0 + 1 = 11$. After dividing the computed sum for each part by the total sum, we obtain the relative scores, as shown in column 2 of Table 2(b).

The goal of the proposed algorithm is to cluster columns that have the same distribution of important parts, i.e., parts that have a large relative score. The algorithm pursues this goal because the similarity between two vectors will be high if the two vectors have the same important parts, assuming that the similarity measure depends on the dot product between two vectors (such as the cosine similarity). If two vectors do not share the same important parts, i.e., there are not many indices for which the vectors both have non-zero values, the similarity will be low. In order to cluster the tag columns based on this criteria, we compute a hash value based on the distribution of the relative scores of the parts. This is performed by creating a binary representation of each column of relative scores, where each part in the column is represented by a bit.

We define the parameter α as the minimum sum of relative scores for each column. We select the minimum number of parts for which the sum of the scores is larger than α. First, we sort the relative scores of each vector parts. In the previous example, if $\alpha = 0.75$ (75%), we first add part 1 (with a score of 0.545) to our list. As we do not reach 0.75 yet, we add the next largest part to our list, which is part 2 in this example. Now, we have selected $0.545 + 0.364 = 0.909$, which is larger than α. We can set the bits for parts 1 and 2 to 1, Table 2(b) shows the binary representation for our example in the third column. Again, we can observe that for this vector the most important parts are at the top, as the value for the top two parts is 1 and for the two bottom parts it is 0.

Algorithm 1 gives the previously described process in pseudo-code. The algorithm defines the function $s(t, k)$, which computes the relative part scores for a tag t using k parts, and the function $h(sc, \alpha)$, which is used to compute the binary hash for a vector with scores sc and using a threshold α. For the $h(sc, \alpha)$ function, we currently use the quick sort algorithm to sort the k part scores after which we select the top scores based on the α threshold. Because quick sort has an average $O(p \log(p))$ time complexity, with p being the size of the sorted list, one can verify that our algorithm has time complexity $O(n(k \log k))$, where n is

---

Algorithm 1. Hash-based clustering algorithm

Require: The input: a tag co-occurrence matrix T
Require: The algorithm parameters:

- k, in how many parts the vector should be splitted,
- α, the minimum percentage of the total column sum required to compute the binary representation.

Require: The algorithm functions:

- $s(t, k)$, computes the relative part scores for a tag t, using k parts,
- $h(sc, \alpha)$, computes the hash for a vector with relative scores sc, using threshold α.

1: **for** each tag column $t \in T$ **do**
2:    $C = \{\}$ $\{C$ is a set of (cluster,hash) pairs$\}$
3:    $score_t = s(t, k)$ $\{$vector with part scores of tag $t\}$
4:    $hash_t = h(score_t, \alpha)$ $\{$binary encoding of tag $t\}$
5:    **if** $\exists c$ s.t. $(c, hash) \in C \wedge hash_t = hash$ **then**
6:       $c = c \cup \{t\}$ $\{$add t to existing cluster$\}$
7:    **else**
8:       $c' = \{t\}$ $\{$otherwise, a new cluster is created$\}$
9:       $C = C \cup \{(c', hash_t)\}$ $\{$add to set of clusters the newly created cluster$\}$
10:   **end if**
11: **end for**

---

the number of tags and k is the number of parts. This means that our algorithm performs linear in time with respect to the number of tags.

There is a trade-off between the number of clusters and the accuracy of the algorithm. If we have a low number of clusters, the number of skipped high cosines will be relatively small but the reduction in the number of computations would be also small. For a small data set, splitting the matrix in 2 will give sufficient discriminant power, while a large matrix might need a split into 10 or even 20 parts. An important aspect of the algorithm is the parameter k, i.e., the number of parts a column is split into. For a given k, one can show that there are $2^k - 1$ possible binary hash representations. Because the number of clusters is dependant on the number of possible binary representations, the parameter k can be used to control the trade-off between the number of clusters and the accuracy of the algorithm.

The idea of the algorithm is to find clusters of columns such that the similarity between two tags located in different clusters is minimized. In this way, the algorithm indirectly selects column pairs for which one has to compute the similarity (intra-cluster tags) and column pairs for which the similarity is set to zero, i.e., pairs that are skipped (inter-cluster tags). The distribution of the number of columns in the clusters is important for the number of similarity pairs that are skipped. Ideally, one would like to have clusters that contain an equal number of tag columns. In this way, the number of similarity pairs that are skipped is maximized. One can show that for $n \to \infty$, the reduction $\to 1/m$, assuming that the clusters are equally sized[2]. The maximal number of clusters is $2^k - 1$, where k is the number of parts.

In order to improve the 'recall' of the algorithm (i.e., not skipping high similarity pairs), we experiment with a heuristic that identifies clusters that potentially may have many high cosines and are difficult to be processed by our algorithm. One approach would be to remove the columns from our algorithm that have a value sum greater than some threshold. The idea behind this is that the higher the sum, the more the tag is co-occurring with other tags. For this group of tags that are removed from the data set, we have to compute all pair-wise similarities with all other tags. The advantage of this approach is that less high similarities are skipped. The downside of this approach is that the number of computations that has to be performed increases. There is a clear trade-off between the number of computations and the number of skipped high similarities, as will become more clear in the evaluation.

4   Evaluation

For our experiments, we used a Flickr data set that has been gathered by the authors of [4]. The original data set contains 319,686 users, 1,607,879 tags, 28,153,045 pictures, and 112,900,000 annotations. We have selected a threshold on the number of times a tag is used. In the end, we selected the top occurring 50,000 tags. The reason for selecting the frequently occurring tags is that we want to eliminate the low-end outliers, which seldom co-occur with other tags and thus pollute the clustering process. At the same time we want to keep the data set size small enough in order to perform a brute force evaluation of all cosines for reference purposes. To be able to evaluate the performance of our algorithm, we needed to compute all cosines for this subset, which is in total 1,249,975,000 cosine computations. The used data set contains approximately 10 times more cosines between 0 and 0.1 than cosines between 0.1 and 0.2. This shows that there are many tags that are not similar to each other, which is common for data sets obtained from tagging spaces.

4.1   Experiments

In order to evaluate our algorithm, we have designed an experimental setup that covers a broad range of parameter combinations. Table 3 shows the ranges for different parameters that were used in the experiments. The total number of experiments is the number of unique combinations of the parameters, as shown in Table 3. For the parameter k, i.e., the number of parts a vector is split into, we chose a range of 3 to 50, with a step size of 1. For α, we chose the range 0.05 to 0.95, with a step size of 0.05. For the filter type (excluding a number

---

[2] With n being the number of input vectors and m the number of clusters, we have
$$reduction(n, m) = \frac{((n/m)^2 - (n/m)) \times 0.5}{(n^2 - n) \times 0.5} \times m = \frac{(n-m)}{m(n-1)}, \lim_{n \to \infty} \frac{(n-m)}{m(n-1)} = \frac{1}{m}.$$

Table 3. Experimental setup

Parameter	Range
k (parts count)	min: 3, max: 50, step size: 1
α (hash threshold)	min: 0.05, max: 0.95, step size: 0.05
filter type	magnitude / sum
filter threshold	min: 50,000, max: 200,000, step size: 10,000

of tags from the algorithm), we have experimented with two approaches. In the first filter type approach we left out all tags that have a magnitude larger than a certain threshold and in the second approach we left out all tags that have a sum larger than a certain threshold. The last row of Table 3, the filter threshold, indicates the threshold used in the filter type. We varied the threshold for both the magnitude filter and the sum filter, from 50,0000 to 200,000 with a step size of 10,000.

In total, we performed 30,720 experiment runs (this is the total amount of unique parameter combinations). For each experiment run, we execute our clustering algorithm and store the resulting clusters. Using the clusters, we determine which tag pairs should be skipped, i.e., the similarity should be assumed to be 0. After determining which tag pair similarities are set to 0, we record the actual similarity values of these tag pairs for reference purposes. We also compute the average similarity of pairs of tags in the same cluster, which usually results in high similarities.

4.2   Results

Figure 1 gives an overview of the results. The figure shows, for different skipped cosine thresholds, the trade-off between the percentage of similarity pairs that has to be computed and the percentage of cosines that is higher than the threshold. So if a point is located on $(0.4, 0.1)$ then this means that 40% of the original number of computations has to be done (60% is skipped in total), but you skip 10% of the important cosines. The 'important' cosines are defined to be higher than the threshold used in the evaluation (0.4, 0.5, 0.6, 0.7, 0.8, and 0.9). For the tags that passed the magnitude/sum filter, we compute all pair-wise similarities to the other tags, as we do not use these tags in our clustering algorithm. The values that are reported for the x-axis include these combinations. Each point in a sub-plot of Figure 1 represents a parameter combination obtained from the experimental setup shown in Table 3. The ideal situation would be to have low values for both the x-axis as the y-axis (as close as possible to the origin), because then one has to compute relatively a small amount of the original computations while a low amount of the important cosine similarities is skipped.

We can make the two important observations from the results presented in Figure 1. First, it is clear that as the percentage of total similarity pairs that has to be computed increases, the percentage of skipped high cosines decreases. This is as expected because the probability of skipping important cosines trivially becomes smaller when more similarity pairs are computed. Second, we observe that

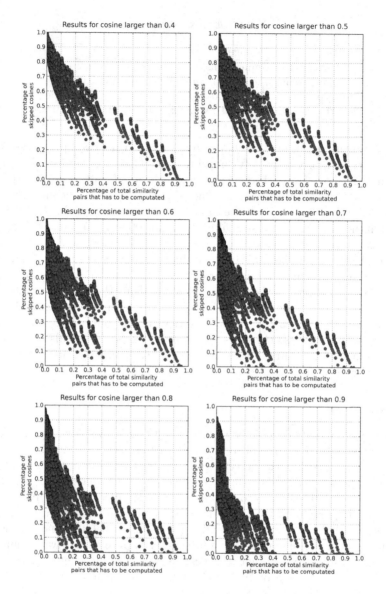

Fig. 1. In this figure we see a scatter plot of parameter combinations for different thresholds, with the x-axis showing the reduction of the total number of computations and the y-axis the percentage of skipped high cosines

for cosine similarities ranging from 0.5 and higher, the algorithm is capable of just computing approximately 30% of the total number of computations while skipping a relatively low number of high cosines, i.e., approximately 18%. For the cases when 'high' cosines are considered to be 0.6 and higher, the results are even better. The algorithm is able to compute the significant cosines by just computing approximately 18% of the total number of combinations while just skipping 10% of the high ones. We find this already to be useful in computationally-intensive Web applications based on pair-wise similarities. When we consider higher thresholds we observe that the percentage of skipped high cosines further decreases. For example, for the case when cosines are considered to be high from 0.7 and onwards, the percentage of skipped high cosines is below 3% when computing 18% of the total number of combinations.

Although it is a bit difficult to see from Figure 1, the results show that if the user allows for less freedom in skipping high cosines (i.e., cosines higher than 0.6), the algorithm can be tuned to achieve a high cosine skipping percentage of approximately 5%, while having to compute around 30% of the original number of cosine similarities. As one can notice here, our algorithm can be tuned to meet various conditions. This shows the flexibility of our algorithm and its applicability to a wide range of Web applications (e.g., applications where a good trade-off between speed and quality is necessary, applications where speed is more important than quality, applications where similarity quality is more important than speed, etc.).

In order to understand how the parameters of our clustering algorithm influence the results, we have performed parameter sensitivity analysis. Table 4 shows information on some points (i.e., parameter combinations) from the plots given in Figure 1. We have chosen a few points that are interesting and need further explanation. The first part of Table 4 shows for each threshold the point that is closest to the origin. These points are the 'optimal' points when one gives equal weight to the percentage of computed cosines and to the percentage of skipped high cosines. For the thresholds 0.5 and 0.6, we notice that the optimal value for parameter k is 7 and the optimal value for parameter α is 0.2. The number

Table 4. This table shows a few interesting parameter combinations and their performance (e.g., the points that are closest to the origin) for each considered threshold. The first part of the table shows for each threshold the point that is closest to the origin. The second part of the table shows some points that might be useful in an application context where quality is more important than speed.

Threshold	Computations to be done	Skipped high cosines	Number of clusters	k	α	Filter type "sum >"	Filtered count
0.4	27.5%	27.1%	6	5	0.2	40,000	3.87%
0.5	17.5%	22.9%	29	7	0.2	40,000	3.87%
0.6	17.5%	11.3%	29	7	0.2	40,000	3.87%
0.7	14.2%	8.8%	37	8	0.2	40,000	3.87%
0.8	11.5%	5.6%	56	10	0.2	40,000	3.87%
0.9	8.0%	1.0%	1309	14	0.3	40,000	3.87%
0.4	76.9%	9.5%	7	3	0.85	40,000	3.87%
0.5	40.8%	14.3%	4	3	0.3	40,000	3.87%
0.6	22.5%	9.3%	6	5	0.2	40,000	3.87%
0.7	17.5%	2.7%	29	7	0.2	40,000	3.87%
0.8	17.5%	0.0%	29	7	0.2	40,000	3.87%
0.9	8.2%	0.0%	2803	22	0.2	40,000	3.87%

of clusters that is obtained using these parameter values is 29. The theoretical reduction (with the percentage of computations that have to be performed) is therefore $1/29 \approx 0.03$ for these two cases. For both the thresholds 0.5 and 0.6, we can also see that the observed reduction resulted in having to perform 17.5% of the total number of computations, which is approximately 6 times higher than the theoretical number of computations that could have been performed. This is probably due to the fact that there is still a large number of 'popular' tags present in the data set. The presence of these often occurring tags results in one or more large clusters. This makes the total reduction in the number of computations lower, as the tags are unequally distributed among the clusters.

The second part of Table 4 shows some points that might be useful in an application context. The reason for choosing these points is that they give a good trade-off between the number of computations and the skipping of high cosines, giving more weight to the latter. We can observe, for example, that for an application where high cosines are the ones that are higher than 0.4, it is necessary to compute approximately 76% of the cosines (and to have less than 10% skipped high cosines). The parameters for this situation are $k = 3$ and $\alpha = 0.85$. If we consider a different situation, where high cosines are the ones that are higher than 0.7, the optimal parameters change. With $k = 7$ and $\alpha = 0.2$ the algorithm is able to skip a relatively small amount (i.e., 2.7%) of the high cosines while computing just 17.5% of the cosines. In this way we retain most of the high cosines while performing a minimal amount of computations.

From the table we can also immediately notice that there is one filter that seems to give the best results, as for all rows this filter is found to be the optimal one. For this data set, this filtering is achieved by leaving out all tags of which the sum is greater than 40,000. The other filter, a threshold on the magnitude of a vector, seemed to give worse results. One final observation we can make is that the k parameter is more important and influential than the α parameter when considering the optimal points shown in the upper part of Table 4. The α parameter only seems to play an important role when considering a low threshold for high cosines. For the other situations, the parameter k determines the performance of the algorithm. A possible explanation of this is that the k determines the number of possible binary hash representations, and thus is the most influential parameter for the performance of the algorithm.

In order to understand in more detail how the parameters affect the performance of our algorithm, we also visualize a part of the sensitivity results. First, we focus on the reduction aspect of the algorithm, i.e., the factors that determine how many computations are skipped. Figure 2 shows a plot on the x-axis the considered values for the parameter k and on the y-axis the reduction of the number of computations as percentages. The different series in the plot each represent a value for the α parameter, as indicated by the legend. What we can observe from this figure is that in general the percentage of total combinations that has to be computed exponentially decreases as the number of parts (k) increases. We should note that an asymptotic behaviour seems to be present in this plot, i.e., when k is larger than 10, the percentage of total combinations

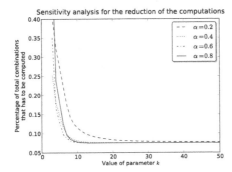

Fig. 2. A plot that shows the relationship between the values for parameters k and α and the reduction of the number of computations

that has to be computed in general does not increase nor decrease. This can be explained by the fact that for $k > 10$ the number of possible binary hash representations becomes so large, that the upper bound of the actual number of unique hash representation for our data set is achieved.

We can further notice that $\alpha = 0.2$ converges the slowest. In Table 4 we already saw that 0.2 was the optimal setting for α in most cases. This stresses again the trade-off between the computation reduction power of the algorithm and the quality of the results. Figure 2 shows that even though the line $\alpha = 0.2$ is the slowest one converging, the overall reduction on the number of computations is relatively large and not much different from the other settings. One can note that for low values of k (less than 10), medium values of α (0.4 and 0.6) tend to provide for a better reduction in the number of cosines to be computed. Figure 2 also confirms our findings that the α parameter is not the ultimate determining factor of the performance of our algorithm.

Last, we have analysed how the parameters of the clustering algorithm influence the percentage of skipped high cosines, where we again consider different thresholds for the definition of a 'high' cosine similarity. Figure 3 shows 6 plots, one for each threshold, where the plots are similar to the plot in Figure 2, with the exception that the y-axis is now the percentage of skipped cosines for a particular threshold. From the figure we can observe that the percentage of skipped cosines grows with respect to the number of splits of a vector (parameter k). This is because of the number of clusters increases with k and thus the probability of skipping a high similarity increases. As a result of this, in general it is desirable to choose low values for k when it is more important not to skip high similarity pairs than to reduce the computational effort. When we consider the different α values, one can notice that a value of 0.2 gives the lowest amount of skipped high cosines, across all k values and considered cosine threshold values, something we already noticed in Table 4. Another observation is that for a threshold value of 0.7 or larger there are parameter combinations for which no high cosines are skipped. Although the number of computations is probably

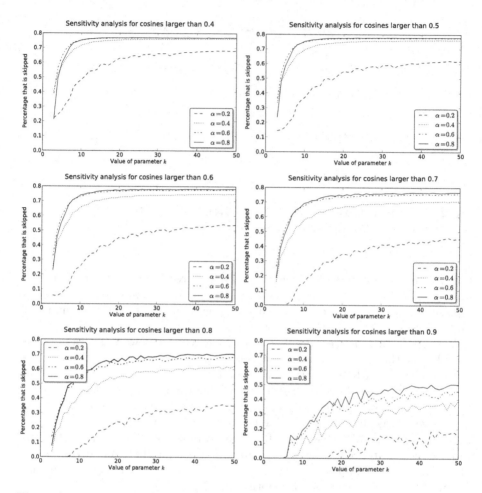

Fig. 3. An overview of how the parameters k (number of parts) and α (hash threshold), for different thresholds, influence the skipped high cosines

high for these parameter combination, we still find it useful as it does decrease the computation time. Last, we can also observe that the asymptotic behaviour becomes less visible as we increase the threshold that defines what a 'high' cosine similarity is.

We have chosen to implement our algorithm and the experiments in Python. In order to efficiently deal with matrix algebra, we have made heavily use of the NumPy library [8]. For efficiently storing and querying large amounts of data, we have used PyTables [1]. PyTables provides an easy to use Python interface to the HDF5 file format, which is a data model for flexible and efficient input/output operations. The experiments were run on a cluster with nodes that had CPUs equivalent to a 2.5-3.5 GHz 2007 Xeon with 8 GB RAM. Each node was assigned to perform experiments for a set of parameter combinations. By running our code on 120 nodes, we cut down the computing time for the experiments and the computation of the cosine similarity for all pairs (our reference) from approximately 40 days to 5 hours.

5   Conclusions

In this paper we focused on the scalability issue that arises with the computation of pair-wise similarities in large tag spaces, such as Flickr. The main problem is that the number of similarity computations grows quadratically with the number of input vectors. Besides being large, the data sets in tagging space problems are usually sparse.

We have presented an algorithm that intelligently makes use of the sparsity of the data in order to cluster similar input vectors. In order to filter insignificant similarity pairs (i.e., similarities that are relatively low) we only compute the similarities between vectors that are located in the same cluster. The proposed algorithm performs the clustering of the input vectors in linear time with respect to the number of input vectors. This allows our approach to be applicable to large and sparse data sets.

For the evaluation of our solution we report the results for the cosine similarity on a large Flickr data set, although our approach is applicable to any similarity measures that are based on the dot product between two vectors. We have used an experimental setup that covers a broad range of parameter combinations. The results presented in this paper show that our algorithm can be valuable for many approaches that use pair-wise similarities based on the dot product (e.g., cosine similarity). The algorithm is, for example, capable of reducing the computational effort with more than 70% while not skipping more than 18% of the cosines that are larger than 0.5.

In order to gain more insight in how exactly the algorithm can be tuned, we performed an in-depth sensitivity analysis. From the results of this sensitivity analysis we can conclude that our proposed clustering algorithm is tunable and therefore applicable in many contexts. We have found that with respect to parameter k, the percentage of similarities that have to be computed is a decreasing function and the percentage of skipped high similarities is an increasing function. This means that if a high value for k is chosen, the algorithm produces better results with respect to the percentage of total similarities that have to be computed. When a low value for k is chosen, the algorithm skips a smaller number of high similarities. As for the parameter α, we have found that the effect on the performance of the algorithm is smaller than that of the parameter k. In general, there exists an optimal pair of values for k and α. The optimal values tend to be on the lower side of the considered values scale. Also, we find that increasing these values does not yield better results as the clustering algorithm performance seems to saturate at some point.

As future work one can consider the use of a clustering algorithm (e.g., 1-NN using kd-trees) for the binary hash representations of vectors as an extra step in our approach. We would first like to investigate whether the overall performance of the algorithm is increased, and second, how the time complexity of the algorithm is changed by this extra step.

Acknowledgment. The authors are partially sponsored by the NWO Mozaiek project 017.007.142: Semantic Web Enhanced Product Search (SWEPS) and NWO Physical Sciences Free Competition project 612.001.009: Financial Events Recognition in News for Algorithmic Trading (FERNAT).

References

1. Alted, F., Vilata, I., et al.: PyTables: Hierarchical Datasets in Python (2012), http://www.pytables.org
2. Bayardo, R.J., Ma, Y., Srikant, R.: Scaling Up All Pairs Similarity Search. In: 16th International Conference on World Wide Web (WWW 2007), pp. 131–140. ACM Press (2007)
3. Cohen, J., Dolan, B., Dunlap, M., Hellerstein, J.M., Welton, C.: MAD Skills: New Analysis Practices for Big Data. VLDB Endowment 2(2), 1481–1492 (2009)
4. Görlitz, O., Sizov, S., Staab, S.: Pints: Peer-to-peer Infrastructure for Tagging Systems. In: 7th International Conference on Peer-to-Peer Systems (IPTPS 2008), pp. 19–19 (2008)
5. Halpin, H., Robu, V., Shepherd, H.: The Complex Dynamics of Collaborative Tagging. In: 16th International Conference on World Wide Web (WWW 2007), pp. 211–220 (2007)
6. Indyk, P., Motwani, R.: Approximate Nearest Neighbors. In: 13th Annual ACM Symposium on Theory of Computing (STOC 1998), pp. 604–613. ACM Press (1998)
7. Li, X., Guo, L., Zhao, Y.E.: Tag-Based Social Interest Discovery. In: 17th International Conference on World Wide Web (WWW 2008), pp. 675–684. ACM Press (2008)
8. Oliphant, T.E.: Python for Scientific Computing. Science & Engineering 9(3), 10–20 (2007)
9. Radelaar, J., Boor, A.-J., Vandic, D., van Dam, J.-W., Hogenboom, F., Frasincar, F.: Improving the Exploration of Tag Spaces Using Automated Tag Clustering. In: Auer, S., Díaz, O., Papadopoulos, G.A. (eds.) ICWE 2011. LNCS, vol. 6757, pp. 274–288. Springer, Heidelberg (2011)
10. Specia, L., Motta, E.: Integrating Folksonomies with the Semantic Web. In: Franconi, E., Kifer, M., May, W. (eds.) ESWC 2007. LNCS, vol. 4519, pp. 624–639. Springer, Heidelberg (2007)
11. TechRadar: Flickr reaches 6 billion photo uploads (2012), http://www.techradar.com/news/internet/web/flickr-reaches-6-billion-photo-uploads-988294

Methodologies for Improved Tag Cloud Generation with Clustering

Martin Leginus, Peter Dolog, Ricardo Lage, and Frederico Durao

Department of Computer Science, Aalborg University,
Selma Lagerlofs Vej 300
{mleginus,dolog,riclage}@cs.aau.dk, freddurao@gmail.com
http://iwis.cs.aau.dk/

Abstract. Tag clouds are useful means for navigation in the social web systems. Usually the systems implement the tag cloud generation based on tag popularity which is not always the best method. In this paper we propose methodologies on how to combine clustering into the tag cloud generation to improve coverage and overlap. We study several clustering algorithms to generate tag clouds. We show that by extending cloud generation based on tag popularity with clustering we slightly improve coverage. We also show that if the cloud is generated by clustering independently of the tag popularity baseline we minimize overlap and increase coverage. In the first case we therefore provide more items for a user to explore. In the second case we provide more diverse items for a user to explore. We experiment with the methodologies on two different datasets: Delicious and Bibsonomy. The methodologies perform slightly better on bibsonomy due to its specific focus. The best performing is the hierarchical clustering.

1 Introduction

Tags are textual labels users use in social web sites, such as *Flickr*, *Technorati* and *del.icio.us*, for annotating information resources. They can be assigned freely to these resources to help remind a user of the intended meaning to him or her. Tags are also typically aggregated by social web sites into tag clouds. These are visual elements that highlight certain tags by different users, assisting them in the navigation of the web site [14, 19]. However, the tags in the tag clouds are mostly presented alphabetically, with their font size weighted according to their frequency. These popularity based tag clouds [21,19,6] have at least the following limitations:

- First, syntactical variations of tags i.e., typos, singular and plural forms and compounded tags that share the same semantical meaning are not addressed. Therefore, the coverage of a tag cloud is lower as syntactically different tags are not aggregated.
- Moreover, a tag cloud can contain syntactical variations of the same tag which leads to redundancy.

M. Brambilla, T. Tokuda, and R. Tolksdorf (Eds.): ICWE 2012, LNCS 7387, pp. 61–75, 2012.

– Finally, the most popular tags typically have a broader meaning, covering
  redundantly a certain set of documents which results into a low diversity
  of tags.

To address these limitations and attempt to improve the quality of tag clouds, we
experiment with different clustering techniques. Due to the resource demanding
nature of quality assessment of tag clouds performed by users, [23] introduced
synthetic measures of quality based on tag cloud properties, such as coverage and
overlap. Coverage measures a proportion of documents tagged with a particular
tag with respect to the all considered documents. The overlap is a measure which
captures to which extent different tags considered in comparison are associated
the same resources and what is the proportion of the same resources with respect
to all considered resources. In our previous paper [4] we have already shown
that a specific kind of clustering, spectral clustering, has an effect on tag cloud
generation and on its properties such as coverage, relevance, and overlap.

The contributions of this paper can be summarized as follows:

– We propose two new methodologies on how to integrate clustering into tag
  cloud generation methods, further improving coverage and overlap.
– Within the second methodology, we compare four different clustering algorithms and show that the hierarchical clustering performs the best.
– We introduce a new synthetic metric - chained coverage - which combines
  coverage and overlap together.

We experiment on two different datasets, Delicious and Bibsonomy. The first one
is a general purpose collaborative resource tagging system. The second one is a
specific tagging system for scientific literature. We show that on the Delicious
dataset, the hierarchical clustering algorithm obtained a 12.4% improvement on
coverage over the second best performing algorithm we tested.

The remainder of this paper is organized as follows. Section 2 positions our
work with respect to related findings in the literature. Section 3 provides a background on clustering techniques we are embedding in the studied methodologies.
Section 4 describes our contribution in two methodologies we have designed for
the generation of tag clouds. Section 5 describes experimental set up and results which we gained from the experiments. Section 6 summarizes the paper
achievements and roadmap to future work.

2   Related Work

Research on tag clouds has concentrated on methods for rendering and presentation aspects [2, 19]. In [19], the authors perform a number of experiments to
assess the effects of semantic versus alphabetical and random arrangements of
tags in tag clouds. The outcome shows that clustered tag clouds can provide
improvements over random layouts in specific search tasks and that they tend
to increase the attention toward tags in small fonts compared to other layouts.
They also claim that tag cloud layout does not seem to influence the ability

to remember tags. Our focus is different. We decouple the presentation aspects from the selection of tags for the tag clouds generation. We study and apply clustering but we experiment with methodologies on how to combine clustering into the process of selection and generation of the tag cloud and not only in its rendering process. By doing so we enable a combination of different methods for tag selection generation and tag cloud rendering.

Random and alphabetical ordering of tags in a tag cloud was tested in [6]. Hierarchical browsing [15] looks at how to structure the layout of a tag cloud. Studies on the font size, weight, intensity and position of tags in the cloud are studied in [3, 11, 18]. In this paper we study the selection of tags for tag cloud generation. We implement a popularity and coverage based visualization method which renders the tag cloud as one approach and not as a main goal of research. However, the aforementioned approaches can be utilized for presentation of tags selected for a tag cloud in our approach as well.

Sinclair et al. [21] consider tag clouds as useful retrieval interface when a user's searching task is not specific. In order to build the tag cloud, their approach results in displaying the top 70 most-used tags in the database. The size of each tag in the cloud is proportional to the log of its frequency, which follow a power law distribution. In our work, 8 tag clouds varying in number of tags enclosed are tested. We try to find out which number of tags in the tag cloud improved the tag cloud properties the most, which is a new findings in comparison to [21]. Further, although the size of each tag is not considered for rendering purposes, the tag relevancy is calculated and determined by its popularity in the corpus, i.e. the most frequent tags are more relevant over the less popular ones. We extend the popularity/usage based approaches for tag selection with clustering and as we also show in experiments with improvements.

[20] the authors deal with tag redundancy and ambiguity through a hierarchical agglomerative clustering of tags for recommendations. Hierarchical clustering is studied in our work as well as is the tag redundancy in the syntactical pre-clustering using the Levenhstein distance. However, the focus and end product is different from the work of [20], as is the methodology where we apply the clustering.

[23] proposes different tags selection algorithms for tag clouds. Our method differ in the way the selection is performed. [23] do not apply clustering. Our objective function for computing clusters and representative tags for the tag clouds in the second methodology also differ. As a result, our generated tag clouds result in a more diverse tags thus a user can explore and browse more topics from the generated tag cloud.

[7,4] propose to group semantically related tags and depict them in a tag cloud near by with similar color. Such approach provides better orientation in the tag cloud as related tags can be easier identified by users. Tags are clustered based on their co-occurrences. Similarly, our proposed tag cloud generation method also groups similar tags. However, our approach is more robust as syntactically similar tags are firstly pre-clustered (grouping singular, plural or misspellings of tags) similarly as proposed in [22]. It leads to tag space reduction as resulted tag

cloud does not contain syntactically similar tags. In the second phase, tags are similarly clustered based on tags co-occurrences but our proposed approach also considers retrieved semantic distances from WordNet dictionary if available.

[12] benefit from "syntagmatic" relations based on co-occurrences similarity and subsequent clustering to generate semantically enhanced tag cloud. The elementary tasks of their approach are the calculation of tag similarities and subsequent clustering. Our work differs, first methodologically as a combination of clustering and popularity, and second as a study to find out which clustering approach performs the best.

3   Clustering Techniques

In the following section, we present several clustering techniques that are utilized in the process of tag cloud generation. Firstly, we introduce syntactical pre-clustering based on Levenhstein distance. Then, we present three different clustering techniques. The first two proposed approaches(Correlated Feature Hashing and Complete linkage hierarchical clustering) cluster tags according to their co-occurrence based similarities. The third (K-means) algorithm considers each tag from a tag space as feature vector. These techniques were proposed and described in [16].

3.1   Syntactical Pre-clustering

Syntactical pre-clustering filters out items with typographical misspellings unnecessary plural and singular forms of the same item and also compounded items from two different terms connected with some separator. These redundant items would occupy an item set unnecessarily as they would have the same semantical meaning. Levenhstein distance is first computed for each term pair from the initial term space. The distance between two terms measures the number of required changes (substitution, insertion and deletion of a character are allowed operations) to transform one term into another. We justify its use because it attains significantly better results than Hamming distance as shown in [5].

3.2   Correlated Feature Hashing

We propose to reduce a tag space with hashing function that is similar to the proposed technique in [1] where authors successfully reduced dictionary size by utilizing hashing. The idea is to share and group tags with similar meaning.

We sort the tags used within the system according to the frequency of usage such that t_1 is the most frequent tag and t_T is the least frequent. For each tag $t_i \in 1, \ldots, T$ is calculated $DICE$ coefficient with respect to each tag $t_j \in 1, \ldots, K$ among the top K most frequent tags. The $DICE$ coefficient is defined as:

$$\text{DICE}(t_i, t_j) = \frac{2.\text{cocr}(t_i, t_j)}{\text{ocr}(t_i) + \text{ocr}(t_j)} \tag{1}$$

where $\mathrm{cocr}(t_i, t_j)$ denotes the number of co-occurrences for tags t_i and t_j, $\mathrm{ocr}(t_i)$ and $\mathrm{ocr}(t_j)$ is the total number of tag t_i and t_j assignments respectively. For each tag t_i, we sort the K scores in descending order such that $S_p(t_i) \in 1, \ldots, K$ represents the tag of the p-th largest DICE score $\mathrm{DICE}(t_i, S_p(t_i))$. We can then use hash kernel approximation defined as:

$$\bar{\Phi}_{t_j}(x) = \sum_{t_i \in T : h(t_i) = t_j} \Phi_{t_i}(x) \tag{2}$$

and given by a hash function:

$$h(t_i) = S_1(t_i) \tag{3}$$

The described approach is replacing each tag t_i with the tag $S_1(t_i)$. We have reduced tag space from all T tags to the K most frequent tags.

3.3   Complete Linkage Hierarchical Clustering

In the second approach we utilize Complete linkage agglomerative hierarchical clustering technique [10]. In the beginning, each entry that should be clustered is considered as single cluster. For each cluster is computed Dice similarity (see Formula 1) with all other clusters. The cluster with the highest similarity to the considered cluster is merged with the cluster. When clusters contain more tags, the lowest similarity between two tags from those clusters is considered for the merging step. The aggregation of clusters repeats until the single cluster is obtained. The final clustering structure is denoted also as dendrogram. The required number of clusters is obtained by cutting a dendrogram at a certain level such that a given number of clusters is obtained.

3.4   K-means

The following clustering technique differs from the previous in such a way that each tag is expressed in n-dimensional vector space where the i-th dimension corresponds to the i-th item res_i (in a similar way as in [17,9]).

We denote $T = \{t_1, t_2 \ldots, t_{|T|}\}$ as the set of all distinct tags that are clustered and $R = \{res_1, res_2 \ldots res_n\}$ the set of all items that are tagged with tags from T. Let $f(t, res_i)$ be equal to a frequency of a tag t assigned to item res_i otherwise it is equal to 0. Then, the vector representation of tag t is:

$$t = (f(t, res_1), f(t, res_2), \ldots, f(t, res_n)) \tag{4}$$

Once, tags from T are expressed as n-dimensional vectors, we proceed with the cluster analysis. The K-means is a simple well known clustering technique that groups objects from a given set into k clusters (given a priori). The clustering of a tag space with the K-means algorithm is computed as follows:

1. Each tag from a tag space T is expressed as n-dimensional vector. According to the size of the tag space and user requirements an amount of clusters is set to k.
2. It randomly places k centroids such that a distance from each other is maximized.
3. Each tag from the tag space is bound to the nearest centroid.
4. New centroids are computed as the mean value of tags vectors grouped with a given centroid. It continues with the step 3, until new centroids are identical with the centroids from the previous iteration.

We obtained k disjoint clusters of tags so we can proceed with the selection of tags for the tag cloud generation. The results of K-means algorithm depend on used distance measure - we exploit only Cosine distance as it attains the best results [16].

4   Methodologies for Improved Tag Cloud Generation with Clustering

In this section, we present common metrics that measure different aspects of a tag cloud. Next, we introduce our two methodologies for tag cloud generation that attempts to improve the tag clouds according to the presented metrics.

4.1   Tag Cloud Metrics

The quality of tag clouds is usually assessed by the users that subjectively rate the structure and arrangement of tags in the cloud. However, such users based assessments are expensive and hardly available. To overcome this limitation, we use synthetic metrics for evaluation of different aspects of a generated tag cloud. Such metrics allow to measure the quality of tag clouds and, as a consequence, various tag selection algorithms can be utilized to maximize considered metrics. In this work, we consider 2 well-known metrics, *coverage* and *overlap*, introduced in [23]. Furthermore, we introduce a new metric *chained coverage* which is utilized in the proposed methodologies. For the following definitions consider D as a set of exiting documents, T as the whole set of existing tags and D_t as the set of documents assigned to a tag $t \in T$.

The first metric is *coverage*, defined as:

$$\text{Coverage}(t) = \frac{|D_t|}{|D_a|}, \tag{5}$$

where $|D_t|$ is the number of documents assigned to a tag t and $|D_a|$ is the number of all documents that are considered during a tag cloud generation process. The metric ranges between 0 and 1. When a coverage for a particular tag t is close to 1, the majority of considered documents was annotated with a tag t. We utilize this metric during the selection process to maximize number of documents that can be accessed directly by exploring a tag cloud.

Overlap of T_c: Different tags in T_c may be assigned with the same item in D_{T_c}. The overlap metric captures the extent of such redundancy. Thus, given $t_i \in T_c$ and $t_j \in T_c$, we define the overlap $over(T_c)$ of T_c as:

$$\text{Overlap}(T_c) = avg_{t_i \neq t_j} \frac{|D_{t_i} \cap D_{t_j}|}{\min\{|D_{t_i}|, |D_{t_j}|\}}, \tag{6}$$

If $over(T_c)$ is close to 0, then the intersections of documents annotated by depicted tags are small and such tag clouds are more diverse.

There exist different selection techniques that try to optimize a given metrics which result into enriched tag clouds. In this work, we propose two new methodologies that improve introduced metrics. Furthermore, we introduce a new metric *chained coverage* that captures how many documents are covered by a considered tag given that documents covered by previously selected tags are not considered. This metric combines coverage and overlap altogether and provides simpler decision-making during the tag selection for the tag cloud. *Chained coverage* is given as:

$$\text{Chained coverage}(t|T_s) = \frac{|D_t \setminus D_{T_s}|}{|D_a|}, \tag{7}$$

where D_{T_s} is a set of documents covered by previously selected tags T_s. The proposed metric can be understood as combination of the classical coverage with the zero overlap with the respect to the previously selected tags. We assume that the diversity of the tag cloud is desired property as users are not interested in retrieving redundant documents covered by different tags. Therefore, the goal is to maximize a chained coverage of each tag used for the tag cloud generation. The metric simplifies a selection process of tags as instead of optimizing two independent metrics i.e., coverage and overlap we maximize only the chained coverage.

4.2 Syntactical Pre-clustering of Tags

Social tagging systems collect heterogeneous tags assigned by the users to the resources of the system. Tags in these systems can have the same semantical meaning however they are syntactically different i.e., typos, singular and plural forms and compounded tags. For example, when we look at the 20 most frequent tags of Delicious dataset (introduced in Section 5) and identified that they have at least 6 and at most 20 different syntactical alternatives in the whole tag space are present. Tags like *Web_design*, *web-design*, *webDesign* or **webdesign* can be aggregated and represented only with the most frequent tag *webdesign*.

To remove from the tag cloud syntactically different tags with the same semantical meaning, we propose a methodology that aggregates syntactically similar tags into clusters. In the tag cloud generation process, obtained clusters can be represented only with the most frequent tag which can have the following benefits:

- The coverage of the depicted tag in the tag cloud improve as it covers all documents annotated with the syntactically different tags from the given cluster
- Generated tag cloud does not contain syntactical variations of the same term as only the most frequent tag from each cluster is considered. Therefore, it allows to create a more diverse tag cloud, i.e., lower overlap between depicted tags.

In our method, syntactical pre-clustering introduced in Section 3.1 is used in the following manner. Levenhstein distance is first computed for each tag pair from the initial tag space. The edit distance between two tags measures the number of required changes (substitution, insertion and deletion of a character are allowed operations) to transform one tag into another. We justify its use because it attains significantly better results than Hamming distance as shown in [5].

Once, an edit distance is calculated, the tag space is divided into clusters. Each group contains only tags where the Levenhstein distance is equal or lower than a defined threshold (a number of maximum changes to transform a tag from the tag pair into a second tag). Then, the most frequent tag for each cluster is selected and is used in all further computations. It represents all other tags from a considered cluster.

In the end, our goal is that syntactical pre-clustering will affect the structure of the generated tag cloud in the sense that depicted tags are semantically more diverse.

4.3   Improving Coverage and Diversity of Tag Clouds with Clustering

The second methodology aggregates semantically related tags into a disjoint group. Each cluster can be perceived as a latent topic described with the related tags. The goal of cluster analysis is to cover all available topics in the tag space and as a consequence map it into a generated tag cloud to achieve maximal diversity of depicted tags. The methodology is motivated due to the drawback of the usual approach (denoted also as a baseline approach) where only the most frequent tags are considered. The selection of the most popular tags results into a tag cloud with terms that have too broad meaning. Therefore, depicted tags cover redundantly a certain set of documents i.e, the overlap of such tag cloud is unnecessary high. For instance a tag cloud generated from the top-25 most frequent tags from Bibsonomy dataset [13] contains tags as *public*, *video*, *Media*, *books*, *blog* or *search*. Obviously, such tags have general meaning or no information value for users. Moreover, often are assigned to the documents in combination with other frequent tags. The possible solution is to minimize a number of tags with the general meaning and additionally select popular but more specific tags as the objective is to preserve the coverage and minimize overlap of the tag cloud.

The aforementioned drawbacks of tag clouds generated from the most popular tags are addressed with the combination of cluster analysis of tags and maximization of the introduced metric – chained coverage. The former one provides basis for a diversity of a generated tag cloud by assuring that all latent topics within the tag space are captured. The latter one suppresses tags with the general meaning and instead selects popular but specific tags. The maximization of the chained coverage promotes (specific) tags with the high coverage of not yet covered documents by previously selected tags. On the other hand frequent tags with low chained coverage (general meaning) are omitted.

We explore different approaches of tags selection from the created clusters. The method based on selecting one tag with the highest coverage from each cluster generates more diverse tag clouds. However, the coverage is lower or comparable to the baseline approach as the chained coverage of generated clusters follows a power law distribution. Thus, majority of clusters belong to the long tail of such distribution.

Therefore, we propose a technique (see Algorithm 1) that selects tags proportionaly from each cluster. The provided tags are syntactically grouped and subsequently semantically clustered by one of the introduced clustering technique. The number of clusters is equal to the tag cloud size. The obtained clusters are sorted by chained coverage in descending order. The chained coverage of each cluster is given by previously explored clusters starting from cluster with the highest coverage. The method computes the number of tags to be selected from the cluster based on the chained coverage of a given cluster given the tag cloud size. From each cluster is selected a number of tags with the highest chained coverage. The goal is to cover a given cluster as good as possible in terms of coverage and overlap. The selection based on maximization of chained coverage satisfies such requirements. The method terminates when the number of selected tags is equal to the tag cloud size.

4.4   Tag Cloud Generation

Once, the tags are selected according to our proposed methodologies, they are depicted in the tag cloud. Semantically related tags from the same cluster are displayed with the same color which is specific for each cluster. Such tags are also located near each other and it allows to explore tags in more convenient way. Location and particular color of tags from the identical cluster results into a tag cloud which is semantically structured and as was shown in [8]. This presentation structure differs from the most common visualization of tag clouds where tags are alphabetically sorted. It allows to differentiate main topics in the tag cloud and also users can perceive and notice semantic relations between tags in neighbourhood [8]. Moreover, it helps to understand connections between tags, for example, tags cucumber and Spain are hardly interpretable in alphabetically sorted tag cloud. However, if they are depicted together with the tag E.coli a user can easily assume that these tags are related to E.coli outbreak.

Personalized Tag Cloud Generation: Another benefit of performed cluster analysis is a possibility to generate personalized tag clouds. Such tag cloud is an

Input: tags, tagCloudSize
Output: selectedTags
1 tags ← syntacticalClustering(tags);
2 clusters ← semanticalClustering(tags,tagCloudSize);
3 clusters ← sortClustersByChainedCoverage(clusters);
4 **foreach** *cluster in clusters* **do**
5 | tagsToSelect ← cluster.chainedCoverage(exploredClusters) · tagCloudSize
6 | **for** *i=1* **to** *tagsToSelect* **do**
7 | | **foreach** *tag in cluster* **do**
8 | | | **if** *tag.chainedCoverage(selectedTags) is highest in the cluster* **then**
9 | | | | **if** *tag.chainedCoverage(selectedTags) > threshold* **then**
10 | | | | | selectedTags ← selectedTags + tag;
11 | | | | **end**
12 | | | **end**
13 | | **end**
14 | **if** *size of selectedTags > tagCloudSize* **then**
15 | | **return** *[selectedTags]*
16 | **end**
17 | exploredClusters ← exploredClusters + cluster;
18 **end**

Algorithm 1. The methodology for tag cloud generation

adapted version of the above-mentioned general tag cloud model. User's preferences are incorporated into the tag cloud such that tags related to user's tags are preferred over others. The selection of similar tags is performed by retrieving tags from the clusters that contain at least one of the user's tags. However, in this work we do not evaluate proposed methodologies on the personalized tag clouds.

5   Experiments

We investigate the improvements of the proposed methodologies in terms of coverage and overlap of generated tag clouds. The proposed techniques are evaluated on the BibSonomy dataset [13] and the snapshot of Delicious dataset which consists of bookmarking activity on www.delicious.com from 8th till 16th of September 2009. Bibsonomy dataset contains 5794 distinct users, 802045 items and 204850 tags. The total number of tagging posts is 2555080. The snapshot of Delicious dataset contains 187359 users, 185401 unique tags and 355525 bookmarks. The total number of tagging posts is 2046868. The evaluation is conducted on the above-described datasets as they represent the most popular collaborative tagging systems of Web nowadays.

All the experiments are conducted on Ubuntu Server 11.10 64-bit operating system running on Intel Xeon X3460 CPU 2.8GHz with 8 GB RAM. The tag cloud generation methodologies and clustering techniques are implemented in Java 6 and source code and all results are available on our website[1].

---
[1] http://people.cs.aau.dk/~mleginus/icwe2012/

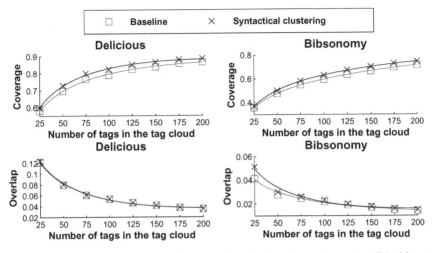

Fig. 1. Coverage and overlap results for baseline (red) and pre-clustering (black) methods and their corresponding logarithmic fit

5.1 Syntactical Pre-clustering of Tags

Table 1 summarizes the mean values of both methods in both datasets in terms of coverage and overlap. Results show that the coverage of the syntactical pre-clustering of tags is better than the baseline on the two datasets we tested. Coverage had a 5% (5079 documents) increase on BiSonomy dataset and 3.5% (3072 documents) increase on Delicious. Overlap, on the other hand, had similar results. Pre-clustering on BibSonomy had slightly higher mean but the values were practically the same on Delicious. One explanation but the higher means on

Table 1. Mean values of coverage and overlap for the baseline and syntactical pre-clustering methods on BibSonomy and Delicious datasets

Dataset	Coverage		Overlap	
	Baseline	Pre-Clustering	Baseline	Pre-Clustering
BibSonomy	0.586	0.616	0.022	0.025
Delicious	0.776	0.803	0.059	0.060

Delicious is the different nature of both datasets. BibSonomy is a more specific dataset, containing domain-specific tags. Delicious, on the other hand, is used by a wider variety of users on different domains.

Next, we looked at how the two methodologies perform as a function of the number of tags in the tag cloud. Figure 1 shows these results. In both methods, as number of tags increases, coverage and overlap improves in a logarithmic fashion. In fact, the logarithmic curve fits almost perfectly (R-square > 0.98, p-value < 0.001) in all cases. That means that coverage and overlap improve significantly after tag clouds with 75 tags but then stabilizes. Note that coverage of the syntactical pre-clustering improves over the baseline as the number of tags increase. This is specially the case in the BibSonomy dataset. In the case of overlap, the values stay almost identical on the Delicious dataset. On BibSonomy, overlap is worse with the pre-clustering method for tag clouds with few tags but improves as the number of tags increase.

Overall, these results indicate that by using the pre-clustering method, coverage of tag clouds improve. We consider it positive to note that overlap remains similar to the baseline as the number of tags in the tag cloud increases. This indicates a solid improvement of the coverage of the tag clouds generated.

5.2   Improving Coverage and Diversity of Tag Clouds with Clustering

We compare the proposed methodology with the baseline algorithm on both datasets. In this work, the tag cloud generation considers the whole tag space and all available resources of the social tagging systems. However, the generated tag cloud consists from at most 200 tags and not frequent tags can be omitted. Therefore, without loss of generality, we prune considered datasets. The evaluated methods utilize tags that were assigned by users at least 50 times and related documents that were annotated at least 5 times. For both techniques, we iteratively increase a number of tags in the tag cloud starting with 25 till 200 tags with the step 25. The results are presented in the following Figure. 2. The proposed methodology improves the coverage on both datasets. Similarly, the overlap of generated tag clouds is decreased. The best performing clustering technique is hierarchical clustering which computes a tag pairs co-occurrences. The obtained clusters consist of semantically related tags and as consequence

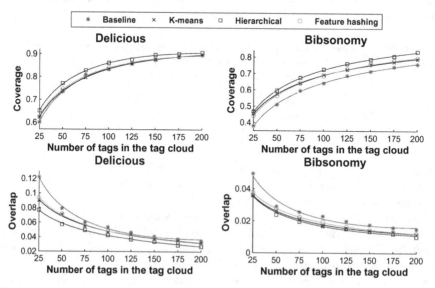

Fig. 2. Improvements of coverage and overlap on Bibsonomy and Delicious datasets with different clustering techniques and their corresponding logarithmic fit

a tag space is uniformly covered by these clusters. Feature hashing improves metrics insignificantly in comparison to the baseline method. The drawback of this clustering method is that aggregates all tags to the top-k most frequent tags which can be considered as centroids of generated clusters. The most frequent tags are often semantically similar and it negatively affects the structure of obtained clusters. K-means clustering represents each tag as a feature vector. and the size of features is number of documents. As the number of features is enormous, the computation of distances between tags results into a creation of clusters with semantically not related tags. Another drawback is the random placement of the initial centroids of clusters that significantly affects a final structure of clusters.

In average, the proposed methodology improves the coverage with 12.4% on Delicious and 3.01% on Bibsonomy dataset. The improvements of coverage can be expressed also with the number of additionally covered documents. The tag clouds generated by the methodology cover additional 2794 documents on Delicious and 56508 documents on Bibsonomy. The diversity of tag clouds is also improved which can be observed by decreased overlap

The average improvements are presented in the following Tables 2 and 3. The main reason of improvements is the introduced maximization of chained

Table 2. Mean values of coverage for the baseline and different clustering methods on BibSonomy and Delicious datasets

Dataset	Coverage			
	Baseline	K-means	Hierarchical	Feature hashing
BibSonomy	0.6285	0.6756	0.7064	0.6741
Delicious	0.8112	0.8139	0.8362	0.8171

Table 3. Mean values of overlap for the baseline and different clustering methods on BibSonomy and Delicious datasets

Dataset	Overlap			
	Baseline	K-means	Hierarchical	Feature hashing
BibSonomy	0.0245	0.0194	0.0185	0.0204
Delicious	0.0731	0.0543	0.0637	0.0631

coverage. The metric significantly simplifies the selection process of tags for the tag cloud as it maximizes coverage and minimizes overlap of generated tag cloud altogether. The overall coverage is equal to the chained coverage of the whole tag cloud. Therefore, the presentation of the chained coverage is unnecessary however, it is a core factor of achieved improvements.

Although the experiments were carried out using the Delicious and Bibsonomy dataset, other datasets should be also evaluated. Statistical properties of each dataset differ therefore, we assume that our methods could be succesfully aplied on other folksonomy based datasets. However, this needs to be empirically proved.

6   Conclusion and Future Work

In this work, we propose two different methodologies for an enhanced tag cloud generation. The former one improves the coverage of the tag clouds by aggregation of syntactically similar tags. Moreover, it prohibits a depiction of the syntactically similar tags and as a consequence additional tags can be selected for the generated tag cloud. It results into more diverse structure of the tag clouds. The latter methodology improves coverage and decreases overlap of tag clouds. Introduced metric – chained coverage simplifies a selection process and the optimization of coverage and overlap is straightforward. The utilization of clustering techniques allow to divide the tag space into disjoint groups which allows to select more diverse tags from the obtained clusters. The best improvements are attained with hierarchical clustering that computes tag pairs co-occurrences and produces the most reasonable clusters. The proposed methodology produces tag clouds that cover As a future work we intend to explore possible new metrics that would incorporate well-known metrics altogether and in a such way simplify a selection process of tags.

Acknowledgements. This work has been supported by FP7 ICT project M-Eco: Medical Ecosystem Personalized Event-Based Surveillance under grant No. 247829.

References

1. Bai, B., Weston, J., Grangier, D., Collobert, R., Sadamasa, K., Qi, Y., Chapelle, O., Weinberger, K.: Learning to rank with (a lot of) word features. Information Retrieval 13(3), 291–314 (2010)
2. Bateman, S., Gutwin, C., Nacenta, M.: Seeing things in the clouds: the effect of visual features on tag cloud selections. In: Proceedings of the Nineteenth ACM Conference on Hypertext and Hypermedia, HT 2008, pp. 193–202. ACM, New York (2008)
3. Bateman, S., Gutwin, C., Nacenta, M.: Seeing things in the clouds: the effect of visual features on tag cloud selections. In: Proceedings of the Nineteenth ACM Conference on Hypertext and Hypermedia, HT 2008, pp. 193–202. ACM, New York (2008)
4. Durao, F., Dolog, P., Leginus, M., Lage, R.: SimSpectrum: A Similarity Based Spectral Clustering Approach to Generate a Tag Cloud. In: Harth, A., Koch, N. (eds.) ICWE 2011. LNCS, vol. 7059, pp. 145–154. Springer, Heidelberg (2012)
5. Echarte, F., Astrain, J.J., Córdoba, A., Villadangos, J.: Pattern Matching Techniques to Identify Syntactic Variations of Tags in Folksonomies. In: Lytras, M.D., Damiani, E., Tennyson, R.D. (eds.) WSKS 2008. LNCS (LNAI), vol. 5288, pp. 557–564. Springer, Heidelberg (2008)
6. Halvey, M.J., Keane, M.T.: An assessment of tag presentation techniques. In: Proceedings of the 16th International Conference on World Wide Web, WWW 2007, pp. 1313–1314. ACM, New York (2007)
7. Hassan-Montero, Y., Herrero-Solana, V.: Improving tag-clouds as visual information retrieval interfaces. In: INSCIT 2006 Conference, Merída (2006)

8. Hassan-Montero, Y., Herrero-Solana, V.: Improving tag-clouds as visual information retrieval interfaces. In: International Conference on Multidisciplinary Information Sciences and Technologies, Citeseer, pp. 25–28 (2006)
9. Huang, A.: Similarity measures for text document clustering. In: Proceedings of the Sixth New Zealand Computer Science Research Student Conference (NZCSRSC 2008), Christchurch, New Zealand, pp. 49–56 (2008)
10. Johnson, S.: Hierarchical clustering schemes. Psychometrika 32(3), 241–254 (1967)
11. Kaser, O., Lemire, D.: Tag-cloud drawing: Algorithms for cloud visualization. CoRR, abs/cs/0703109 (2007)
12. Knautz, K., Soubusta, S., Stock, W.G.: Tag clusters as information retrieval interfaces. In: HICSS, pp. 1–10 (2010)
13. Knowledge and U. o. K. Data Engineering Group: Benchmark folksonomy data from bibsonomy, version of January 1 (2010)
14. Kuo, B.Y.-L., Hentrich, T., Good, B.M., Wilkinson, M.D.: Tag clouds for summarizing web search results. In: Proceedings of the 16th International Conference on World Wide Web, WWW 2007, pp. 1203–1204. ACM, New York (2007)
15. Kuo, B.Y.-L., Hentrich, T., Good, B.M., Wilkinson, M.D.: Tag clouds for summarizing web search results. In: Proceedings of the 16th International Conference on World Wide Web, WWW 2007, pp. 1203–1204. ACM, New York (2007)
16. Leginus, M., Zemaitis, V.: Speeding up tensor based recommenders with clustered tag space and improving quality of recommendations with non-negative tensor factorization. Master's thesis, Aalborg University (2011)
17. Ramage, D., Heymann, P., Manning, C., Garcia-Molina, H.: Clustering the tagged web. In: Proceedings of the Second ACM International Conference on Web Search and Data Mining, pp. 54–63. ACM (2009)
18. Rivadeneira, A.W., Gruen, D.M., Muller, M.J., Millen, D.R.: Getting our head in the clouds: toward evaluation studies of tagclouds. In: Proceedings of the SIGCHI Conference on Human factors in Computing Systems, CHI 2007, pp. 995–998. ACM, New York (2007)
19. Schrammel, J., Leitner, M., Tscheligi, M.: Semantically structured tag clouds: an empirical evaluation of clustered presentation approaches. In: Proceedings of the 27th International Conference on Human Factors in Computing Systems, CHI 2009, pp. 2037–2040. ACM, New York (2009)
20. Shepitsen, A., Gemmell, J., Mobasher, B., Burke, R.: Personalized recommendation in social tagging systems using hierarchical clustering. In: Proceedings of the 2008 ACM Conference on Recommender Systems, RecSys 2008, pp. 259–266. ACM, New York (2008)
21. Sinclair, J., Cardew-Hall, M.: The folksonomy tag cloud: when is it useful? J. Inf. Sci. 34, 15–29 (2008)
22. van Dam, J., Vandic, D., Hogenboom, F., Frasincar, F.: Searching and browsing tag spaces using the semantic tag clustering search framework. In: 2010 IEEE Fourth International Conference on Semantic Computing (ICSC), pp. 436–439. IEEE (2010)
23. Venetis, P., Koutrika, G., Garcia-Molina, H.: On the selection of tags for tag clouds. In: Proceedings of the Fourth ACM International Conference on Web Search and Data Mining, WSDM 2011, pp. 835–844 (2011)

Semantic Collaborative Tagging
for Web APIs Sharing and Reuse

Devis Bianchini, Valeria De Antonellis, and Michele Melchiori

Dept. of Information Engineering University of Brescia
Via Branze, 38 - 25123 Brescia, Italy
{bianchin,deantone,melchior}@ing.unibs.it

Abstract. Sharing and reuse of Web APIs for fast development of Web applications require advanced searching facilities to enable Web designers to find the Web APIs they need. In this paper we describe a Web API semantic collaborative tagging system to be implemented on top of the public ProgrammableWeb Web API repository. The system is designed to be used in a social context: the designers can take actively part in the semantic tagging of Web APIs, thus sharing their experience in developing their own Web applications. Moreover, they can exploit new searching facilities to find out relevant Web APIs according to different search scenarios and reuse them for fast deployment of new applications. To this aim, they rely in an hybrid fashion on the semantic tags and on the collective knowledge derived from past designers' experiences. Proper matching and ranking metrics are defined and applied during Web API searching.

1 Introduction

Sharing and reuse of Web APIs is becoming a very popular way to quickly develop Web mashups, that is, low-cost, personalized Web applications, designed and implemented to be used for short periods of time (also referred as *situational applications*). To this aim, the ProgrammableWeb API public repository has been made available, where Web API providers share their own components and Web designers can look for Web APIs they need to compose new Web applications without implementing them from scratch. The repository registers almost 5,800 Web APIs (a number that is continuously growing[1]) and presents methods to programmatically retrieve the registered Web APIs and also to track all the mashups which have been developed starting from them. Currently, the repository contains more than 6,600 Web mashups.

In this context, enabling Web designers to effectively find Web APIs they need is becoming a more and more crucial asset. Some solutions propose the definition of component models [1,2] to support fast Web application development. Other solutions suggest the introduction of a Web API semantic characterization to

---

[1] See http://www.programmableweb.com/: the last access on April 30th, 2012 counts 5,792 Web APIs.

M. Brambilla, T. Tokuda, and R. Tolksdorf (Eds.): ICWE 2012, LNCS 7387, pp. 76–90, 2012.
© Springer-Verlag Berlin Heidelberg 2012

face issues such as the heterogeneity across Web API descriptions [3]. However, the use of new Web API models on top of the ProgrammableWeb repository, although improves Web API retrieval and composition, introduces an additional learning effort for Web API providers who must adopt the models. Such an additional requirement is often not feasible in a social scenario, where the average skill of Web designers prevents from using complex models other than common Web programming technologies. In this paper we propose a lightweight semantic tagging system to be deployed on top of the ProgrammableWeb repository to be used in a social context. Web designers can take actively part in the semantic tagging of Web APIs, thus sharing their experience in developing their own Web applications, going beyond the limitations of traditional tags, which lack in facing ambiguities such as polisemy and omonyms. Moreover, Web designers can also exploit the search facilities of the system to find out relevant Web APIs according to different search scenarios and reuse them for fast deployment of new applications. To this aim, they rely in an hybrid fashion on the semantic tags and on the collective knowledge derived from past designers' experiences in developing mashups.

In the next section we describe the scenarios which motivated our work. Section 3 contains a formalization of proper matching and ranking metrics based on the Web API semantic tags and collective knowledge to be applied during search. In Section 4 we describe the implementation of the proposed system. Section 5 shows a preliminary validation of the system and a comparison with the state of the art. Section 6 closes the paper.

2   Motivations and Open Issues

Consider a simple example. Danielle is a designer who aims at building a Web application for her friends, to share pictures by posting photos on the Web site and showing with marks on a map the locations where photos have been taken. Danielle does not want to implement the Web application from scratch, since, for instance, the design of a Web interface for displaying points on a map is a time-consuming task and Danielle does not have time and the required advanced skills. Nevertheless, already available Web APIs, such as the Google Maps APIs, have been implemented for this purpose. She has to search for existing Web APIs to post pictures and personalize maps and has to properly wire them in the mashup. She inspects the ProgrammableWeb repository (see Figure 1), where she can: (i) find Web APIs by specifying keywords that will be matched against the descriptions associated with available Web APIs in the repository; (ii) filter available Web APIs according to their category, the company which proposed the APIs, the adopted protocols and data formats; (iii) find mashups composed of the available Web APIs. On ProgrammableWeb Danielle can not:

1. specify both the features of the Web APIs to search for and of the Web mashups which the Web APIs will be used in, to perform more advanced search; for instance, Danielle can not specify that she needs a mapping Web

Fig. 1. An example of Web API search on ProgrammableWeb.com

API to be used in combination with a Web API for posting pictures; if she looks for a mapping Web API, the system returns about 210 results, which can be restricted to 11 results by selecting the most famous Google company (see Figure 1), but not all the returned APIs enable the definition of markers for displaying points on a map;

2. avoid limitations of traditional tag-based search, specifically false positives and false negatives due to the tag polisemy (that is, the same tag refers to different concepts) and tag omonyms (i.e., the same concept is pointed out using different tags); false positives are APIs incorrectly included among the search results, they are affected by polisemy; false negatives are APIs incorrectly excluded from search results, they are affected by omonyms;

3. be assisted in more articulated developing scenarios, where Danielle needs a proactive support for her search; for instance, let us suppose that Danielle already has at her disposal a Web mashup which combines a Web API for searching sightseeing locations and a Web API to display them on a map; ProgrammableWeb is neither able to proactively suggest different APIs that can be substituted to the sightseeing search API and properly wired with the map API (thus minimizing the efforts required to adapt the new Web API into the existing mashup) nor can suggest other Web APIs (e.g., a Twitter API) to be added to the mashup, because of many existing mashups where Web designers put together such kinds of Web APIs.

3   Semantic and Social Characterization of Web APIs

Given the open issues highlighted above, we inferred the need of both a semantic characterization of Web APIs, to face polisemy and omonyms problems, and a social characterization of Web APIs, to rely on the past experiences of Web designers and enable the support for more articulated developing scenarios (see point 3 in Section 2). Formally, we denote a Web API description $\mathcal{W}$ as $\langle \mathcal{W}_{Sem}, \mathcal{W}_{Soc} \rangle$, where $\mathcal{W}_{Sem}$ and $\mathcal{W}_{Soc}$ are the semantic and social characterization of $\mathcal{W}$, respectively.

3.1 Semantic Characterization

The semantic characterization of a Web API $\mathcal{W}$ is defined as follows:

$$\mathcal{W}_{Sem} = \langle c_{\mathcal{W}}, \{t_{\mathcal{W}}\}, \{m_{\mathcal{W}}\} \rangle \tag{1}$$

The elements of such a characterization are discussed in the following and are extracted both from the contents of the ProgrammableWeb repository and from the information provided by the designers.

Web API category $c_{\mathcal{W}}$. It is used to provide a high level classification of the Web API. We rely on the classification of Web APIs provided by ProgrammableWeb, composed of 67 categories such as mapping, payment, search.

Web API semantic tags $t_{\mathcal{W}}$. Tags are used to provide a fine-grained semantic characterization of the Web API. To this purpose, we rely on tags defined by the designers who adopted the Web API. During the assignment of such tags, sense disambiguation techniques based on the WordNet [4] lexical system are applied. In WordNet the meaning of terms is defined by means of *synsets*. Each synset has a human readable definition and a set of synonyms. In our model, a Web API semantic tag $t_{\mathcal{W}}$ is a triple, composed of: (i) the term itself (namely, $t_{\mathcal{W}}^0$) extracted from WordNet; (ii) the set $t_{\mathcal{W}}^{syn}$ of all the terms in the same synset of $t_{\mathcal{W}}^0$; (iii) the human readable definition $t_{\mathcal{W}}^d$ associated with the synset. The designer is supported in the selection of the synset to better specify the meaning of a tag as shown in Section 4.

Web mashup semantic tags $m_{\mathcal{W}}$. When the Web API is tagged, the designer is also required to add a set of semantic tags $m_{\mathcal{W}}$ that describe the Web mashup where the Web API has been used. The semantic tags $m_{\mathcal{W}}$ has the same structure of semantic tags in $\{t_{\mathcal{W}}\}$.

An example of semantic characterization of the Flickr Web API to be used in a file sharing application could be the following:

$Flickr_{Sem} = \langle$ Photos, $\{\langle$ photo, $\{$ photograph, exposure, picture, pic $\}$, "a representation of a person or scene in the form of a print or transparent slide or in digital format" $\rangle\}$,

$\{\langle$ file, $\{$ date_file $\}$, "a set of related records (either written or electronic) kept together" $\rangle$,

$\langle$ sharing, $\{\}$, "using or enjoying something jointly with others" $\rangle\}$

Web API category, semantic tags in $\{t_{\mathcal{W}}\}$ and Web mashup semantic tags in $\{m_{\mathcal{W}}\}$ will be used to empower the Web API search by applying advanced matching techniques described in Section 3.4.

3.2   Social Characterization

In a Web 2.0 context, the suggestion of a Web API to be used in a mashup should also consider as relevant past experiences of the designers who adopted the Web APIs in their mashups. We denote these aspects as the social characterization of the Web API $\mathcal{W}$:

$$\mathcal{W}_{Soc} = \{d \in \mathcal{D}_\mathcal{W} | d = \langle \sigma, \mu, \{\mathcal{W}_k\} \rangle\} \tag{2}$$

where, for each designer $d \in \mathcal{D}_\mathcal{W}$, who used the Web API $\mathcal{W}$, σ is the designer's skill for developing Web applications and μ is a quantitative rating (within the range [0,1]) given by the designer to the Web API $\mathcal{W}$. Social characterization of the Web API $\mathcal{W}$ is further refined by asking the designer, during semantic tagging, to specify other Web APIs $\mathcal{W}_k$ that he/she used together with $\mathcal{W}$ in the same Web mashup. It is worth mentioning that if a Web API has been adopted by designers with high skill, the system should better rank such Web API with respect to the other ones among the search results. The skill σ is collected during designer's registration to the system (see Section 4). A set of options are proposed to be selected by the designer, ranging from unexperienced to expert, and are uniformly mapped into the [0,1] range, with unexperienced=0 and expert=1. The capability of the system to automatically update the designers' skills on the basis of the number of developed mashups and their complexity (for instance, based on the size of developed mashups as the number of included APIs) will be investigated as future work. Also the set $\{\mathcal{W}_k\}$ could be loaded directly from the mashups stored on ProgrammableWeb if the Web designer is registered on the repository Web site.

The value of μ is selected by the designer according to the 9-point Scoring System[2]. This scoring system has few rating options (only nine) to increase potential reliability and consistency and with sufficient range and appropriate anchors to encourage designers to use the full scale. During the rating, we provided the designer with the set of options that are mapped into the [0,1] range, as shown in Table 1.

Table 1. The 9-point Scoring System for the classification of designers' Web API rating

Rating (additional guidance on strengths/weaknesses)	Score
POOR (*completely useless and wrong*)	0.2
MARGINAL (*several problems during execution*)	0.3
FAIR (*slow and cumbersome*)	0.4
SATISFACTORY (*small performance penalty*)	0.5
GOOD (*minimum application requirements are satisfied*)	0.6
VERY GOOD (*good performance and minimum application requirements are satisfied*)	0.7
EXCELLENT (*discreet performance and satisfying functionalities*)	0.8
OUTSTANDING (*very good performances and functionalities*)	0.9
EXCEPTIONAL (*very good performances and functionalities and easy to use*)	1.0

---

[2] http://www.nhlbi.nih.gov/funding/policies/nine_point_scoring_system_and_program_project_review.htm.

An example of social characterization of two photo sharing Web APIs, `Flickr` and `23hq.com`, used in Web applications like the one described in the motivating scenarios, is the following:

Flickr	$d_1 = \langle 1$ (expert), 0.7 (excellent), $\{$GoogleMaps, del.icio.us$\}\rangle$
	$d_2 = \langle 1$ (expert), 0.6 (very good), $\{$GoogleMaps$\}\rangle$
23hq.com	$d_3 = \langle 1$ (expert), 0.4 (satisfactory), $\{$GoogleMaps, SilverlightStreaming, YouTube$\}\rangle$
	$d_4 = \langle 0.5$ (medium), 0.6 (very good), $\{$YouTube, Twitter, GoogleMaps, del.icio.us, Amazon$\}\rangle$

In the example, `Flickr` has been rated as excellent and very good by two experts, while `23hq.com` as satisfactory by an expert and very good by a medium-skilled designer. All the designers used these Web APIs in past applications together with the Google Maps API. Social characterization of the available Web APIs in the ProgrammableWeb repository is exploited for ranking purposes after search. Given a set of Web APIs among search results, they are ranked according to the ratings of other designers that used such APIs in the past, taking into account their skills. Ranking metrics will be detailed in Section 3.4.

3.3 Web APIs Search Scenarios

The semantic and social characterization of Web APIs described above enable to match a request $\mathcal{W}^r$ against the $\mathcal{W}_{Sem}$ and $\mathcal{W}_{Soc}$ of available Web APIs in the repository and to rank the search results with respect to designers' skills and ratings. Formally, we define a request $\mathcal{W}^r$ for a Web API as follows:

$$\mathcal{W}^r = \langle c^r_{\mathcal{W}}, \{t^r_{\mathcal{W}}\}, \{m^r_{\mathcal{W}}\}, \{\mathcal{W}_h\}\rangle \tag{3}$$

where $c^r_{\mathcal{W}}$ is the requested category, $\{t^r_{\mathcal{W}}\}$ is a set of semantic tags specified for the Web API to search for, $\{m^r_{\mathcal{W}}\}$ is a set of semantic tags featuring the Web mashup in which the Web API to search for should be used, if any, $\{\mathcal{W}_h\}$ is the set of Web APIs already included in such a mashup, if any, which the Web API to search for should be wired with. We distinguish two different search scenarios:

- in the first scenario, Danielle is looking for a Web API to start the development of a new Web mashup; to this aim, she specifies a category $c^r_{\mathcal{W}}$ and a set of semantic tags $\{t^r_{\mathcal{W}}\}$; Danielle has not in mind any mashup where the Web API to search for should be used; the request is formalized as $\mathcal{W}^r_1 = \langle c^r_{\mathcal{W}}, \{t^r_{\mathcal{W}}\}\rangle$; we denote this scenario as *simple search*; a variant of this scenario is the one where Danielle has already in mind a set of semantic tags $\{m^r_{\mathcal{W}}\}$ which denote the mashup where the Web API to search for should be used; the request is formalized as $\mathcal{W}^r_2 = \langle c^r_{\mathcal{W}}, \{t^r_{\mathcal{W}}\}, \{m^r_{\mathcal{W}}\}\rangle$ and we denote this variant as *advanced search*;
- in a second scenario, Danielle has already built or started the construction of a Web mashup, composed of a set of Web APIs $\{\mathcal{W}_h\}$, but she has to complete it and the system could suggest the best Web API that can be wired with the other Web APIs already within the mashup; the request is formalized as $\mathcal{W}^r_3 = \langle c^r_{\mathcal{W}}, \{t^r_{\mathcal{W}}\}, \{m^r_{\mathcal{W}}\}, \{\mathcal{W}_h\}\rangle$ and we denote it as *completion search*; in a variant of this scenario, Danielle has no preferences on the Web

API to search for (i.e., $\{t^r_{\mathcal{W}}\}$ is empty) and she totally relies on the system that should proactively suggest to Danielle which APIs could be added on the basis of the semantic tags $\{m^r_{\mathcal{W}}\}$ on the mashup that is being developed, the set $\{\mathcal{W}_h\}$ of Web APIs already included in the mashup and past experiences of mashups, registered within the repository; in this case, the request is formalized as $\mathcal{W}^r_4 = \langle \{m^r_{\mathcal{W}}\}, \{\mathcal{W}_h\} \rangle$ and we denote it as *proactive completion search*.

For instance, an example of request formulated in the *completion search* scenario to find a Web API in the category Photos to be used for picture sharing together with the Google Maps Web API can be represented as follows:

$\mathcal{W}^r = \langle$ Photos, $\{\langle$ picture, $\{$photograph, photo, exposure, pic$\}$, "a representation of a person

or scene in the form of a print or transparent slide or in digital format"$)\}$,

$\{\langle$ picture, $\{$photograph, photo, exposure, pic$\}$, "a representation of a person

or scene in the form of a print or transparent slide or in digital format"$\rangle$,

$\langle$ sharing, $\{\}$, "using or enjoying something jointly with others"$\rangle)\}$, $\{$GoogleMaps$\}\rangle$

where $\{t^r_{\mathcal{W}}\} = \{$picture$\}$ and $\{m^r_{\mathcal{W}}\} = \{$picture, sharing$\}$. The designer is supported in the formulation of the request by the same sense disambiguation techniques used during semantic tagging, as explained in Section 4.

3.4 Web APIs Matching and Ranking

The search scenarios introduced above can be satisfied by applying a set of metrics that are used to compare the affinity between categories, semantic tags and mashups in which the Web APIs must be included. The matching and ranking model we adopted in our system is defined by the following elements:

$$\Gamma = \langle \mathcal{W}^r, \{\mathcal{W}\}, \texttt{target}, Sim(), \rho \rangle \tag{4}$$

where $\mathcal{W}^r$ is the request, $\{\mathcal{W}\}$ is the set of semantic and social characterization of available Web APIs $\mathcal{W}$ in the repository ($\mathcal{W} = \langle \mathcal{W}_{Sem}, \mathcal{W}_{Soc} \rangle$), target is the kind of search (*simple, advanced, completion, proactive completion*), $Sim(\mathcal{W}^r, \mathcal{W})$ is the similarity measure used to evaluate candidate Web APIs as search results and ρ is the ranking function for search results. The **matching** measure $Sim(\mathcal{W}^r, \mathcal{W})$ is based on the semantic characterization $\mathcal{W}_{Sem}$ of $\mathcal{W}$ and is composed of the following elements.

Category similarity. The similarity between the category $c^r_{\mathcal{W}}$ of $\mathcal{W}^r$ and the category $c_{\mathcal{W}}$ of $\mathcal{W}_{Sem}$ is inferred from the ProgrammableWeb repository; since no hierarchies are defined among the available categories, advanced semantic-driven techniques (such as category subsumption checking) can not be used; nevertheless, we consider the two categories as more similar as the number of Web APIs that are categorized in both the categories, denoted with $|c^r_{\mathcal{W}} \cap c_{\mathcal{W}}|$, increases with respect to the overall number of Web APIs classified in $c^r_{\mathcal{W}}$, denoted with $|c^r_W|$, and in c_W, denoted with $|c_W|$; formally, the category similarity is defined as follows:

$$Sim_c(c^r_W, c_W) = \frac{2 \cdot |c^r_W \cap c_W|}{|c^r_W| + |c_W|} \qquad (5)$$

Semantic tag affinity. Semantic tag affinity applied between two tags t_1 and t_2, denoted with $TagSim(t_1, t_2) \in [0, 1]$, is used to state how much similar they are with respect to the WordNet lexical system. In WordNet the synsets used to define the meaning of terms are related by eighteen different kinds of relationships. Some relationships have been designed to refine search capabilities and enhance the navigation of the net of terms in the lexical system. In particular, *hyponymy/hypernymy relations* are used to represent the specialization/generalization relationship between two terms: for instance, `station wagon` is a more specific term with respect to `automobile`; this means that there is a semantic affinity between `station wagon` and `automobile`, that is, if a user is looking for an automobile, also those resources that have been tagged with the station wagon term can be considered relevant. According to this viewpoint, we state that the affinity between two tags t_1 and t_2 is maximum if the tags belong to the same synset; otherwise, if they belong to different synsets, a path of hyponymy/hypernymy relations which connects the two synsets is searched: the highest the number of relationships in this path, the lowest is semantic tag affinity, that is:

$$TagSim(t_1, t_2) = \begin{cases} 1 & \text{if } t_1 \text{ and } t_2 \text{ belong to the same synset} \\ 0.8^L & \text{if there are } L \text{ hyponymy/hypernymy relations between } t_1 \text{ and } t_2 \\ 0 & \text{otherwise} \end{cases}$$
$$(6)$$

The value 0.8 has been proved to be optimal in our experiments on WordNet terms affinity [5]. Nevertheless, it can be parameterized (within the range [0,1]) and set by the designer. The affinity between two semantic tags t_1 and t_2 is evaluated considering t^0_1 and t^0_2, while the list of synonyms and the human readable description in the t_1 and t_2 definitions are used to speed up $TagSim$ evaluation and to enable the identification of the synsets within WordNet. The tag affinity between two sets of semantic tags $\mathcal{T}_1$ and $\mathcal{T}_2$ is evaluated by computing the semantic tag affinity between each pairs of tags, one from $\mathcal{T}_1$ and one from $\mathcal{T}_2$ by applying the Dice formula [6]:

$$Sim_t(\mathcal{T}_1, \mathcal{T}_2) = \frac{2 \cdot \sum_{t_1 \in \mathcal{T}_1, t_2 \in \mathcal{T}_2} TagSim(t_1, t_2)}{|\mathcal{T}_1| + |\mathcal{T}_2|} \qquad (7)$$

This is used to evaluate the total affinity $Sim_t(\{t^r_W\}, \{t_W\})$ between semantic tags used to annotate the Web APIs and $Sim_t(\{m^r_W\}, \{m_W\})$ between semantic tags used to annotate the mashups. Pairs to be considered for the Sim_t computation are selected according to a maximization function that relies on the assignment in bipartite graphs. For instance, there exists a path of length $L = 2$ between terms `picture` and `file` in WordNet, therefore $Sim_t(\{$`picture`, `sharing`$\}, \{$`file`, `sharing`$\})$ is evaluated as $[2 \cdot (0.8^2 + 1.0)]/4 = 0.82$.

The final matching measure $Sim(\mathcal{W}^r, \mathcal{W})$ is computed as:

$$Sim(\mathcal{W}^r, \mathcal{W}) = \omega_1 \cdot Sim_c(c_{\mathcal{W}}^r, c_{\mathcal{W}}) + \omega_2 \cdot Sim_t(\{t_{\mathcal{W}}^r\}, \{t_{\mathcal{W}}\})$$
$$+\omega_3 \cdot Sim_t(\{m_{\mathcal{W}}^r\}, \{m_{\mathcal{W}}\}) \in [0, 1] \tag{8}$$

where $0 \leq \omega_i \leq 1$, with $i = 1, 2, 3$, and $\sum_{i=1}^3 \omega_i = 1$ are weights set according to the target, as shown in Table 2. Setup experiments showed that the category is only a coarse-grained entry point to look for Web APIs in the repository (this explains the low values for ω_1 weight). For instance, the $Sim(\mathcal{W}^r, \text{Flickr})$ between the sample request $\mathcal{W}^r$ shown in Section 3.3 and the $Flickr_{Sem}$ characterization shown in Section 3.1 is computed as follows:

$$Sim(\mathcal{W}^r, \text{Flickr}) = 0.2 \cdot 1.0 + 0.4 \cdot 0.82 + 0.4 \cdot \frac{2 \cdot 1.0}{2} = 0.928 \tag{9}$$

Table 2. The setup of ω_i weights for computation of matching measure $Sim(\mathcal{W}^r, \mathcal{W})$

Target	Request $\mathcal{W}^r$	Weights setup
Simple	$\mathcal{W}_1^r = \langle c_{\mathcal{W}}^r, \{t_{\mathcal{W}}^r\} \rangle$	$\omega_1 = 0.4$, $\omega_2 = 0.6$, $\omega_3 = 0.0$
Advanced	$\mathcal{W}_2^r = \langle c_{\mathcal{W}}^r, \{t_{\mathcal{W}}^r\}, \{m_{\mathcal{W}}^r\} \rangle$	$\omega_1 = 0.2$, $\omega_2 = \omega_3 = 0.4$
Completion	$\mathcal{W}_3^r = \langle c_{\mathcal{W}}^r, \{t_{\mathcal{W}}^r\}, \{m_{\mathcal{W}}^r\}, \{\mathcal{W}_h\} \rangle$	$\omega_1 = 0.2$, $\omega_2 = \omega_3 = 0.4$
Proactive completion	$\mathcal{W}_4^r = \langle \{m_{\mathcal{W}}^r\}, \{\mathcal{W}_h\} \rangle$	$\omega_1 = \omega_2 = 0.0$, $\omega_3 = 1.0$

The Web APIs included in the search results (which we denote with $\{\mathcal{W}'\} \subseteq \{\mathcal{W}\}$) are those whose overall similarity is equal or greater than a threshold γ experimentally set. The Web APIs $\{\mathcal{W}'\}$ are ranked according to the social characterization of each $\mathcal{W}'$. In particular, the **ranking** function $\rho : \{\mathcal{W}'\} \mapsto [0, 1]$ takes into account the past experiences of designers in using the $\mathcal{W}'$ Web API ($\rho_1(\mathcal{W}')$) and the ratings given by the designers to $\mathcal{W}'$ ($\rho_2(\mathcal{W}')$). Depending on the declared skills, past experiences and ratings of more expert designers are considered as more relevant for ranking search results. In particular, we define $\rho(\mathcal{W}') = \alpha \cdot \rho_1(\mathcal{W}') + \beta \cdot \rho_2(\mathcal{W}')$. In the performed preliminary experiments, the weights α and β are both set to 0.5 to give the same relevance to the two aspects.

The computation of $\rho_1(\mathcal{W}')$ is different if the request $\mathcal{W}^r$ contains the set $\{\mathcal{W}_h\}$ of the Web APIs already included in the mashup in which the Web API to search for should be used (completion or proactive completion search scenarios) or not (simple/advanced search scenarios). In the first case, let be $\{\mathcal{W}_k^i\}$ the Web APIs included by the i-th designer $d^i \in \mathcal{D}_{\mathcal{W}'}$ in the same mashup where he/she used $\mathcal{W}'$. We use the degree of overlapping between $\{\mathcal{W}_h\}$ and $\{\mathcal{W}_k^i\}$, to quantify the closeness of mashup in which $\mathcal{W}'$ has been used and the mashup where $\mathcal{W}'$ will be used, through the same rationale applied to category similarity in formula (5), that is:

$$Sim_m(\{\mathcal{W}_h\}, \{\mathcal{W}_k^i\}) = \frac{2 \cdot |\{\mathcal{W}_h\} \cap \{\mathcal{W}_k^i\}|}{|\{\mathcal{W}_h\}| + |\{\mathcal{W}_k^i\}|} \in [0, 1] \tag{10}$$

where $|\cdot|$ denotes the number of Web APIs in the set and $|\{\mathcal{W}_h\}\cap\{\mathcal{W}_k^i\}|$ denotes the number of common Web APIs in the two sets. The computation of $\rho_1(\mathcal{W}')$ is then performed as follows:

$$\rho_1(\mathcal{W}') = 1 - \frac{\sum_i(1 - \sigma_i \cdot Sim_m(\{\mathcal{W}_h\},\{\mathcal{W}_k^i\}))}{|\mathcal{D}_{\mathcal{W}'}|} \in [0,1] \qquad (11)$$

where σ_i is the declared skill of designer $d^i \in \mathcal{D}_{\mathcal{W}'}$. The formula above ensures that the past experiences of more expert designers have a higher impact on the $\rho_1(\mathcal{W}')$ computation. Intuitively, the closest the σ_i and $Sim_m(\{\mathcal{W}_h\},\{\mathcal{W}_k^i\})$ values to 1 (maximum value) for all the designers d^i, the closest the second member in formula (11) to zero, that is, the ranking $\rho_1(\mathcal{W}')$ assumes the best value. For instance:

$$\rho_1(\texttt{Flickr}) = 1 - \frac{(1 - 1.0 \cdot \frac{2\cdot1.0}{3}) + (1 - 1.0 \cdot \frac{2\cdot1.0}{2})}{2} = 0.833 \qquad (12)$$

The value $\rho_1(\texttt{23hq.com})$ is computed in the same way and is equal to 0.334. If we consider the simple or advanced search scenario, where $\{\mathcal{W}_h\} = \emptyset$, we simplify formula (11) by putting $Sim_m(\{\mathcal{W}_h\},\{\mathcal{W}_k^i\})$ to 1, that is, $\rho_1(\mathcal{W}') = 1 - [\sum_i(1 - \sigma_i)]/|\mathcal{D}_{\mathcal{W}'}|$. The Web API $\mathcal{W}'$ is ranked better if all the designers who adopted it have high development skill.

The computation of $\rho_2(\mathcal{W}')$ follows the same rationale, considering in this case the rating μ_i given by the designer d^i to the Web API $\mathcal{W}'$, that is:

$$\rho_2(\mathcal{W}') = 1 - \frac{\sum_i(1 - \sigma_i \cdot \mu_i)}{|\mathcal{D}_{\mathcal{W}'}|} \in [0,1] \qquad (13)$$

For instance, $\rho_2(\texttt{Flickr}) = 1 - [(1 - 0.7) + (1 - 0.6)]/2 = 0.65$.

4   The System Implementation

A designer can access our system using the *search facilities* to find out relevant Web APIs according to the search scenarios introduced above. Alternatively, he/she can *register himself/herself* in the system and he/she can take actively part in the semantic and social characterization of Web APIs he/she used. The architectural overview of our system is shown in Figure 2. The *Web API Semantic Tagging* and *Search interfaces* are PHP pages accessed through the Web browser and interact with: (i) the *ProgrammableWeb APIs* for retrieving basic information on Web APIs and Web mashups from the repository[3]; (ii) the *Web API Storage module*, where semantic and social characterization of Web APIs are stored together with designers' development skills and ratings and matching and ranking routines are implemented; (iii) the WordNet lexical system for sense disambiguation. We rely on a WordNet version made available for J2EE

---

[3] api.programmableweb.com/.

platform, therefore we implemented the sense disambiguation module as a Web service to enable communication between PHP pages and Java classes. Interactions with the other modules are managed with the AJAX technology to ensure good performances of the Web interfaces.

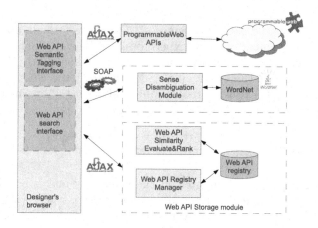

Fig. 2. Architecture of the Web API semantic collaborative tagging system

4.1   The Web API Semantic Collaborative Tagging

The *Web API Semantic Tagging interface* is implemented to manage the interaction of the designer during the semantic and social characterization of Web APIs after registration and authentication. Designer's registration is required to setup the development skill, authentication enables the system to associate the characterization of the Web API with the designer's profile. The designer is guided in a set of steps in the semantic and social characterization of the Web API (see Figure 3). On the top, the details of the Web API extracted from ProgrammableWeb are shown, together with the category which the Web API belongs to. On the bottom, four tabs which correspond to the four steps of the Web API semantic and social characterization are shown: the specification of semantic tags on the Web API; the optional specification of semantic tags on the Web mashup which the Web API has been used in; the optional specification of other Web APIs, among the ones registered in ProgrammableWeb, which have been used together with the current one in the Web mashup; the rating of the Web API, mapped into the numeric scores as shown in Table 1. In particular, the figure shows the first step. A text field is provided to enter the tag. As the designer inputs the characters of the term he/she wants to specify for tagging, the system provides an automatic completion mechanism based on the set of terms contained in WordNet. Starting from the tag specified by the designer, the Sense Disambiguation Module queries WordNet and retrieves all the synsets that contain that term and shows the semantic tags list.

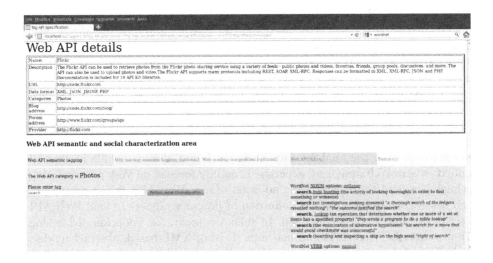

Fig. 3. The Web API Semantic Tagging interface

4.2 The Web API Search Interface

The *Web API Search interface* presents the same steps described for the Web API Semantic Tagging interface (except for the rating step) to specify the request $\mathcal{W}^r$. The designer can be either authenticated in the system or not, to execute a semantic tagging-based search. The designer's authentication could be explored to provide targeted search results, adapted to the skill and past Web mashups developed by the designer. This functionality has not been developed yet, but we plan to introduce it into future versions of the system. Different search modalities (*basic, advanced, completion, proactive completion*) can be chosen by the designer to enable/disable the tabs for specifying the $\mathcal{W}^r$ elements.

5   Related Work and Evaluation Issues

Some authors proposed the use of models to define Web APIs and the way they are composed in a Web mashup to empower their reuse and sharing. In [7] an abstract component model and a composition model are proposed, expressed by means of an XML-based language, for the construction of dashboards. In particular, components abstract the descriptions of enterprise internal services, public APIs and Web resources from technical details. Other efforts based their recommendations upon models. In [8] the formal model based on Datalog rules defined in [1] is proposed to capture all the aspects of a mashup component (called *mashlet*). In this model authors also consider the mashups that have been implemented using the Web API which is being modeled, but do not rely on other social aspects such as ratings and designers' expertise: when the designer selects a mashlet, the system suggests other mashlets to be connected on the basis of recurrent patterns of components in the existing mashups. In [3] semantic annotations have been proposed to enrich Web API modeling in presence of high heterogeneity and proper metrics based on such annotations have been defined to improve recommendations on Web API retrieval and aggregation. This model has been extended in [9] with traditional API tagging to exploit *collective knowledge* for Web API recommendation, but also in this case ratings and designers' expertise are not taken into account. Although such models enable more precise metrics for Web API retrieval and the (semi)automatic generation of the glue code for deploying the final mashup, their use is not always feasible in a social context, where Web designers' expertise is mainly focused on Web programming technologies, and the ever growing addition of new Web APIs which present an high heterogeneity hampers the definition of proper wrappers to load Web API descriptions inside the model itself. In such a context, the adoption of Datalog rules to describe Web APIs and mashups [1] or of XML-based, abstract models for Web API description and composition [3,7] should be further investigated. In [10], a faceted classification of unstructured Web APIs and a ranking algorithm to improve their retrieval are proposed. The classification and searching solutions are based on IR techniques. The proposal provides a coarse-grained discovery mechanism and adopts components descriptions as published on ProgrammableWeb, without any further semantic characterization of components. In this paper, we also rely on the information stored on ProgrammableWeb, but we extend Web API descriptions with additional facets based on semantic tagging and on the past experiences of designers who adopted the Web APIs in their own mashups. With respect to approaches on semantic tagging of Web pages [11] and social search engines, such as Yahoo My Web 2.0, the semantic and social characterization of Web APIs on top of ProgrammableWeb must take into account not only each single resource (i.e., Web API) to be recommended, but also the way they are wired together within Web applications or mashups, thus raising additional aspects also related to the Web 3.0 context.

Preliminary evaluation. We performed an initial evaluation on the precision of the semantic tagging system in retrieving relevant Web APIs and on the ranking procedure. We focused on the application domain of the running example: we considered a subset of 395 Web APIs grouped in the Entertainment, File Sharing, Mapping and Photos categories of ProgrammableWeb repository; we collected a subset of mashups from the same repository, among the ones built with the selected Web APIs, and the corresponding developers (for example, the Flickr Web API has been used in about 602 mashups owned by 302 developers, while 23hq.com has been used by 4 developers in 8 mashups); we performed semantic tagging starting from the keywords extracted from the Web APIs and Web mashups descriptions; finally, we classified developers' skills on the basis of the number of mashups and APIs they own. After semantic and social characterization, we performed four different kinds of search, corresponding to the four search scenarios. We manually built twelve requests $\mathcal{W}^r$ like the sample one

Table 3. Search results collected during the preliminary evaluation of the system (PW = ProgrammableWeb)

Search tags	# of retrieved APIs	Precision	Recall	Relevant APIs in the first 20 results
photo, sharing	83 APIs (233 on PW)	85% (33% on PW)	79% (40% on PW)	15 (9 on PW)
picture, sharing	83 APIs (30 on PW)	85% (22.5% on PW)	79% (19% on PW)	15 (6 on PW)

shown in Section 3.3 and we manually classified relevant Web APIs by carefully analyzing Web API descriptions in the ProgrammableWeb repository and the mashups where Web APIs have been used. We performed search experiments on our systems and directly on ProgrammableWeb, using the first elements in $\{t^r_W\}$ and $\{m^r_W\}$ as normal keywords without considering synonyms and human-readable descriptions. The obtained results are like the ones presented in Table 3, where we showed the output for the request W^r used in Section 3.3.

We evaluated the precision (number of relevant results among the retrieved ones) and the recall (number of relevant results that are retrieved). Experiments showed as our system presents better search results and, in particular, presents relevant results in the first positions of the search outcome. Increased precision is due to the adoption of sense disambiguation techniques, that enable to discard not relevant Web APIs, while increased recall is obtained thanks to the inclusion among search results of those Web APIs that have been annotated with tags that are synonyms of the ones specified during search. For example, it is interesting to underline that, if we change the search tag `photo` with `picture`, the performances of our system do not change due to the exploitation of synsets, while ProgrammableWeb returns worse search results (e.g., it does not return `Flickr` Web API). More in-depth tests with designers will be performed in future work, after a long-term interactions of designers with the system.

6 Conclusions

In this paper we described the functional architecture of a Web API semantic tagging system to be deployed on top of the public ProgrammableWeb API repository. The system is designed to be used in a social context: the designers can take actively part into the semantic tagging of Web APIs, thus sharing their experience in developing their own Web applications. Moreover, they can exploit the search facilities of the system to find out relevant Web APIs according to different search scenarios and reuse them for fast deployment of new applications. To this aim, they rely in an hybrid fashion on the semantic tags and on the collective knowledge derived from past designers' experiences. The proposed system does not require the application of complex models for Web API description, while ensuring extensibility, for example by adding further features beyond the semantic ones (such as the one defined in [10]) or additional sources for sense disambiguation (such as DBPedia), thus improving the precision and recall of the searching procedure. The final product will be a Web API and Web mashup sharing and reuse system, built on top of common social applications, in Web 2.0 and Web 3.0 contexts.

References

1. Abiteboul, S., Greenshpan, O., Milo, T.: Modeling the Mashup Space. In: Proc. of the Workshop on Web Information and Data Management, pp. 87–94 (2008)
2. Bislimovska, B., Bozzon, A., Brambilla, M., Fraternali, P.: Graph-Based Search over Web Application Model Repositories. In: Auer, S., Díaz, O., Papadopoulos, G.A. (eds.) ICWE 2011. LNCS, vol. 6757, pp. 90–104. Springer, Heidelberg (2011)
3. Bianchini, D., De Antonellis, V., Melchiori, M.: Semantics-Enabled Web API Organization and Recommendation. In: De Troyer, O., Bauzer Medeiros, C., Billen, R., Hallot, P., Simitsis, A., Van Mingroot, H. (eds.) ER Workshops 2011. LNCS, vol. 6999, pp. 34–43. Springer, Heidelberg (2011)
4. Fellbaum, C.: Wordnet: An Electronic Lexical Database. MIT Press, Cambridge (1998)
5. Bianchini, D., De Antonellis, V., Melchiori, M.: Flexible Semantic-based Service Matchmaking and Discovery. World Wide Web Journal 11(2), 227–251 (2008)
6. van Rijsbergen, C.J.: Information Retrieval. Butterworth (1979)
7. Cappiello, C., Matera, M., Picozzi, M., Sprega, G., Barbagallo, D., Francalanci, C.: DashMash: A Mashup Environment for End User Development. In: Auer, S., Díaz, O., Papadopoulos, G.A. (eds.) ICWE 2011. LNCS, vol. 6757, pp. 152–166. Springer, Heidelberg (2011)
8. Greenshpan, O., Milo, T., Polyzotis, N.: Autocompletion for Mashups. In: Proc. of the 35th Int. Conference on Very Large DataBases (VLDB 2009), Lyon, France, pp. 538–549 (2009)
9. Melchiori, M.: Hybrid techniques for Web APIs recommendation. In: Proceedings of the 1st International Workshop on Linked Web Data Management, pp. 17–23 (2011)
10. Gomadam, K., Ranabahu, A., Nagarajan, M., Sheth, A., Verma, K.: A Faceted Classification Based Approach to Search and Rank Web APIs. In: Proc. of International Conference on Web Services (ICWS 2008), Beijing, China, pp. 177–184 (2008)
11. Marchetti, A., Tesconi, M., Ronzano, F., Rosella, M., Minutoli, S.: SemKey: A Semantic Collaborative Tagging System. In: Proc. of WWW 2007 Workshop on Tagging and Metadata for Social Information Organization, Banff, Canada (2007)

Opening Personalization to Partners:
An Architecture of Participation for Websites

Cristóbal Arellano, Oscar Díaz, and Jon Iturrioz

ONEKIN Research Group, University of the Basque Country (UPV/EHU),
San Sebastián, Spain
{cristobal.arellano,oscar.diaz,jon.iturrioz}@ehu.es
http://www.onekin.org/

Abstract. Open innovation and collaborative development are
attracting considerable attention as new software construction models.
Traditionally, website code is a "wall garden" hidden from partners. In
the other extreme, you can move to open source where the entirety
of the code is disclosed. A middle way is to expose just those parts
where collaboration might report the highest benefits. Personalization
can be one of those parts. Partners might be better positioned to
foresee new ways to adapt/extend your website based on their own
resources and knowledge of their customer base. We coin the term
"Open Personalization" to refer to those practises and architectures that
permit partners to inject their own personalization rules. We identify
four main requirements for OP architectures, namely, resilience (i.e.
partner rules should be sheltered from website upgrades, and vice
versa), affordability (easy contribution), hot deployment (anytime rule
addition), and scalability. The paper shows the approach's feasibility
using *.NET*.

Keywords: Personalization, Open Development, .NET, MEF.

1 Introduction

Web personalization refers to making a Web site more responsive to the unique
and individual needs of each user [4]. It accounts for important usability
and productivity gains, specifically for organizational websites. Here, it is
important to notice that organizations seldom work in isolation. Organizations
establish (contractual) relationships with their partners to achieve their goals.
Suppliers, collaborators, associates and the like are common terms to reflect
these ecosystems. Hence, it is just natural that these relationships commonly
surface the website of these organizations. Corporate websites tend to include
data about the logistics, payment or providers, which do not represent the kernel
of the corporate activity but collaborate to fulfil the corporate's objectives.
Even an ephemeral activity such as a conference organization includes in its
website, data about hotel partners, proceeding publishers or sponsors which
might all be subject to contractual agreements. In this setting, this work

M. Brambilla, T. Tokuda, and R. Tolksdorf (Eds.): ICWE 2012, LNCS 7387, pp. 91–105, 2012.
© Springer-Verlag Berlin Heidelberg 2012

addresses the following research question: *How is Web personalization affected by the collaborative nature of the organization activities to which the website gives support to?*

Traditional personalization assumes a centralized approach. The website master (the "who") decides the personalization rules (the "what"), normally at the inception of the website (the "when"). In this context, partners tend to be mere stakeholders who do not actively participate in the *development* of the website. However, personalization opportunities might be difficult to foresee by the website master. Indeed, as documented in [2], a large rate of interesting innovations comes from the users/partners once the system is in operation. This scenario is also akin to *open innovation* [8], and the *client-shared-source software model* where vendors let partners access the source code through a common platform [14]. By its very nature, personalization is a perfect candidate for being subject to "open innovation". In addition, resource scarcity makes the website master only incorporate major enhancements while a more active participation of the partners could also serve the long tail.

Therefore, we want custom extensions to be built by any partner instead of being left only to the web master. We introduce the notion of *Open Personalization (OP)* as a means for partners to collaborate in the personalization of the website. The premise is that owners might be willing to open their websites provided (1) minimal additional burden is required and (2), ability of partners to contribute with valuable and up-to-date content for the website users (even if outside the website business model). OP might lead to new business models where openness might be subject to agreements on how to split potential revenues similar to the way *Google AdWords* works. This model can be of interest when partner relationships surface the website of the host. This includes online portals that offer third-party products such as travel agencies (with partnership with resorts and air carriers) or department stores (with partnership with logistic companies).

This paper's main contribution rests on proving the technical feasibility of such approach by introducing an OP architecture for *.NET*. First, we identify a set of quality criteria for OP architectures (Section 3). Next, we address the realization of OP from the partners' perspective (i.e. definition of their own personalization strategies) and the host viewpoint (i.e. how to safely disclose code) in Sections 4 and 5, respectively. Section 6 revises the OP architecture along the requirements previously set. We start by confronting "closed personalization" versus "open personalization".

2   "Closed Personalization" *versus* "Open Personalization"

Typically, Web design methods define three main models: the *Domain Model*, in which the structure of the domain data is defined; the *Navigation Model*, in which the structure and behaviour of the navigation view over the domain data is defined, and finally, the *Presentation Model*, in which the layout of the generated hypermedia presentation is defined. On these grounds, *personalization rules* are defined that adapt any of the three models based on the characteristics of the current user. This implies the introduction of two additional models: the *User Model* (e.g. demographic data, relevant behaviour while interacting with the site, etc.) and the *Personalization Model*. Broadly, the *Personalization Model* commonly resembles that of condition-action rules. The condition basically checks the state of the *Domain Model* and the current *User Model*. The action impacts the navigation structure and presentation, and might also update the user information specified in the *User Model*.

Distinct commercial tools (e.g. ILog JRules, LikeMinds, WebSphere, Rainbow, Infusionsoft) help to define and manage the personalization strategy. These tools might play the role of frameworks (providing an enhanced container where to run your code) or IDEs (helping in generating the code). No matter the approach, the generated code commonly follows the *Model-View-Controller* pattern. For the case of .NET, the mapping goes as follows: (1) the Domain Model is realized as a set of C# classes, (2) the User Model is kept in a special class known as the *ProfileBase*; (3) the Navigation Model is supported through *Controller* classes which can check the Model classes (including *ProfileBase*) and decide which content to pass to the View through *ViewData*, a system-defined variable for Controller-View data passing; (4) the Presentation Model is realized as a set of Web Forms which provide the appropriate renderings for the data kept in *ViewData*. In this setting, a personalization rule commonly ends up being realized as part of the Controller, and impacting the View.

As an example, consider the ICWE'09 conference website. The website basically contains standard information for conferences, i.e. papers, keynotes, accommodations, etc. It is a one-size-fits-all solution where all attendees get the very same content. We have extended the original site with login so that role-based personalization is now possible based on whether the current user is a PC member, a session chair or an author. For instance, additional banquet information can be displayed when login as an attendee with a full passport. This example illustrates "closed personalization": the Web administrator (the "who") decides the personalization rules (the "what"), normally at the inception of the website (the "when"). More sophisticated approaches such as those based on configurations or detection of access patterns (i.e. adaptive and adaptable techniques [3]) are a step ahead but they are still centrally foreseen and developed by the host designer. Of course, partners can participate as stakeholders, and contribute with some personalization scenarios. Some examples follow for the ICWE website:

- Barceló Resorts FACILITATES a 50% discount on room booking over the weekend, PROVIDED the attendee holds a full passport,
- Springer-Verlag FACILITATES a 10% discount on books authored by the seminars' speakers, PROVIDED the attendee is registered for this seminar,
- The Tourism Information Office FACILITATES information about cultural activities on the city during the free slots left by the conference program.

Supporting (and maintaining) these scenarios still rests on the host's shoulders. This setting is not without bumps. First, owner's lack of motivation. The website owner might regard previous scenarios as not aligned with its business model (e.g. room offers might not attract more conference attendees) and hence, not paying-off the effort. Second, partnership might be dynamic, being set once the website is in operation (e.g. pending agreements with the publisher). For instance, the aforementioned rule by Springer-Verlag might require updating not just the View but also the Controller, and even the User Model if seminar attendance is not recorded. As a result, partner rules might end up not being supported by the website. This is not good for any of the actors. End users lose: they will not get the discounts or overlook interesting data. Partners lose: they miss an opportunity to drive more customers to their services. Website owners lose: the website reduces its "stickiness", missing the chance to become a true data hub for the subject at hand (e.g. the ICWE conference).

Open Personalization (OP) pursuits to engage external partners in the personalization endeavour: partners introduce their rules on their own with minimal impact on the owner side. This arrangement makes more economical sense. Partners might regard OP as a chance to increase their own revenues by personalizing their offerings in those websites that serve as a conduit for their products/services (e.g. room offers when booked through the conference website). On the other side, the owner can be willing to facilitate (rather than develop) such initiatives for the good of its customers as long as its involvement is limited. However, OP should not be viewed only as a way to share the maintenance cost but as an enabler of and means for truly collaborative solutions and lasting partner relationships. In this paper however, we focus on the technical feasibility of OP.

3   Open Personalization: Requirements

Open APIs are one of the hallmarks of the Web2.0 whereby Web applications disclosure their data silos. However, "opening data" is not the same that "opening personalization". Personalization requires not only access to the data but also adaptation in the content/navigation/layout of the website. OP would then mean to offer (controlled) access to the *User/Domain Model* (better said, their implementation counterparts) and the (regulated) introduction of the partners' personalization rules (hereafter referred to as *"mods"*). This basically calls for "an architecture of participation". This term was coined by Tim O'Reilly "to describe the nature of systems that are designed for user contribution" [12]. O'Reilly writes that "those that have built large development communities have done so because they have a modular architecture that allows easy participation by independent or loosely coordinated developers". OP is then about creating a community with your partners.

Based on these observations, we introduce the following quality criteria (and driven requirements) for "an architecture of participation" for OP:

- **Resilience.** *Mods* should be shelter from changes in the underlying website, and vice versa, partners' code should not make the website break apart.

- **Extensibility**. OP departs from some model-driven approaches where personalization is decided at design time and captured through models. Mods can be added/deleted as partnership agreements change throughout the lifetime of the website.
- **Scalability**. Growing amount of *mods* should be handled in a capable manner.
- **Affordability**. Partner effort should be minimized. Designs based on widely adopted programming paradigms stand the best chance of success. Intricate and elaborated programming practices might payoff when used internally, but the advantage can be diluted when partners face a steep learning curve. The more partners you expect to attract, the simpler it must be and the more universal the required tools should be.

As a proof of concept, next section introduces "an architecture of participation" for .NET driven by the aforementioned requirements.

4   Open Personalization: Specification

OP is about disclosing code for partners to inlay their *mods*. Therefore, we risk existing *mods* to fall apart when the underlying website is upgraded (i.e. the code changes), hence putting an additional maintenance cost on partners. Isolation solutions should be sought to ensure that the evolution of the website has minimal impact on the existing *mods*. Among *.NET* artefacts (i.e. the Model classes, the Web Forms and the Controller classes), Model classes are certainly the most stable part of a Web application. Therefore, *mods* pivot around Model classes. Those classes that are amenable to participate in a *mod* are said to support a **Modding Concept**.

> *A Modding Concept is a Model Class whose rendering realization (i.e. Web Forms) is amenable to be leveraged by a partner through a **mod**,* i.e. *an HTML fragment to be injected into the appropriate Web Forms.*

The latter still suggests that *mods* might be affected by changes in Web Forms. To ensure decoupling, all interactions between Web Forms and *mods* are conducted through events. Model classes are manipulated through traditional set/get methods. In addition, those classes playing the role of Modding Concepts have an additional interface, the **Modding Interface**, which holds[1]:

- **Publishing Events**, which notify about instances of Modding Concepts (e.g. *Accommodation*) being rendered by the website. For instance, the event *LoadAccommodation* is produced by the host everytime an accommodation is rendered. This event can be consumed by a *mod* through a handler (a.k.a. listener).

---

[1] The terminology of "processing events" and "publishing events" is widely used for event-based components such as portlets [10].

```
1    using System.Collections.Generic;
2    [ModdingConcept(PublishingEventType.Load)]
3    [ModdingConcept(ProcessingEventType.AddViewMod,"HTMLTableCellElement")]
4  ⊟public class Accommodation : IAccommodation {
5       [ModdingProperty]
6       public string Name { get; set; }
7       public string Url { get; set; }
8       [ModdingProperty]
9       public int Stars { get; set; }
10      [ModdingProperty]
11      public double SinglePrice { get; set; }
12      [ModdingProperty]
13      public double DoublePrice { get; set; }
14      public double Distance { get; set; }
15      public bool Breakfast { get; set; }
16   }
17   [ModdingConcept(PublishingEventType.Load)]
18  ⊟public class Profile : IProfile {
19      [ModdingProperty]
20      public string UserName { get { /*...*/ } }
21      public string FirstName { get { /*...*/ } }
22      public string FamilyName { get { /*...*/} }
23      public string Email { get { /*...*/ } }
24      [ModdingProperty]
25      public string RegistrationType { get { /*...*/ } }
26      [ModdingProperty]
27      public IEnumerable<ITutorial> PlansToAttendTutorial { get { /*...*/ } }
28      [ModdingProperty]
29      public IEnumerable<IRole> HasRoles { get { /*...*/ } }
30   }
```

Fig. 1. Domain classes annotated to become *Modding Concepts*

– **Processing Events** (a.k.a. actions), which are those that output an HTML
fragment. For instance, the event *AddViewModAccommodation* provides
a HTML fragment to be injected in those places where *Accommodation*
instances are rendered. Therefore, *mods* can decide *what* to add but
not *where* to add it. The latter is up to the host. For instance, the
AddViewModAccommodation event is produced by a *mod* but it is let to
the host decide where to handle it.

This notion of Modding Concept aims at minimizing the impact of OP for owners
and partners alike. This is the topic of the next subsections.

4.1   Impact on the Host: Making a Website Mod-Aware

The additional effort required for a traditional website to become mod-aware
is: (1) annotating the Model classes and (2), introducing place holders to locate
mod output in Views (i.e. Web Forms).

Annotating Model Classes. Model classes can be decorated with the
annotation *[ModdingConcept]*. Figure 1 shows the case for the ICWE website:
the class *Accommodation* becomes a Modding Concept. *[ModdingConcept]*

```
1    <%@ Page Language="C#" MasterPageFile="~/Views/Shared/ICWE.master" %>
2    <asp:Content ContentPlaceHolderID="contentPlaceholder" Runat="Server">
3    ...
4    <% foreach (Accommodation acc in (IList<Accommodation>)ViewData["Accommodations"]) { %>
5    <tr>
6        <td class="text"><%:acc.Name%> <%:acc.Stars%>*<br/>...</td>
7    ...
8        =(((Dictionary<Accommodation, String>)ViewData["AddViewModAccommodation"])[acc])
9    </tr>
10   <%} %>
11   ...
12   </asp:Content>
```

Fig. 2. Mod-aware Views: the ASPX includes a place holder that accesses the *AccommodationMod* (line 8)

annotations produce Modding Interfaces. These interfaces are termed after the annotated class (e.g. the *Accommodation* class will generate the *IModdingConceptAccommodation* interface). This interface collects all the events to mod *Accommodation*. Event names are obtained from the event type (*Load*) plus the class name as a suffix (e.g. *LoadAccommodation*, *AddViewModAccommodation*). Each annotation introduces an event type. So far, publishing events are limited to *"Load"* whereas processing events include *"AddViewMod"*. The latter outputs an HTML fragment hence, its payload is HTML-typed [15]. For instance, modding an *"Accommodation"* is set to be of type *HTMLTableCellElement*, meaning that mods to *Accommodation* need to be compliant with this type. This introduces a type-like mechanism for modding regulation. It can then be checked whether this *payloadType* is fulfilled, and if not so, ignores the mod but still renders the rest of the page. If *Accommodation* is rendered in different Views with different HTML requirements then, different *AddViewModAccommodation* events can be defined associated with distinct HTML types. It is also worth noticing that *not* all properties of a modding class might be visible. Properties available for *mods* are annotated as *[ModdingProperty]*.

Introducing Place Holders in Views. A View is mod-aware if it foresees the existence of mods that can produce additional HTML fragments to be inlayed in the View. This is so achieved using place holders. Commonly, Views that render Modding Concepts should cater for this situation, though this is up to the host. Figure 2 provides a View that renders *Accommodation* data. Since *Accommodation* is a Modding Concept, this View introduces a place holder (line 8). In *.NET*, data passing between the Controller and the View is achieved through the system variable *ViewData*. This variable holds an array for each possible type of data that can be passed. By convention, this array is indexed based on the type of the variable (e.g. *ViewData["Accommodations"]* conveys accommodations). Likewise, we use the convention of adding the prefix *"AddViewMod"* to the concept (e.g. *AddViewModAccommodation*) to refer to the information passed from the mod to the View (through the Controller). In this case, the content is an HTML fragment. The View retrieves this fragment, and

```
1   using System; using System.Collections.Generic; using System.Linq; using System.Text; using S
2   [InheritedExport]
3   public interface IPlugin {}
4   public class HotelPlugin : IPlugin {
5       IProfile profile; IList<IAccommodation> accommodations; bool done;
6       IModdingConceptProfile Profile; IModdingConceptAccommodation Accommodation;
7       [ImportingConstructor]
8       public HotelPlugin(IModdingConceptProfile i1, IModdingConceptAccommodation i2) {
9           Profile = i1; Accommodation = i2;
10          accommodations = new List<IAccommodation>(); done = false;
11          Profile.load += new EventHandler<LoadProfileEvent>(loadProfileHandler);
12          Accommodation.load += new EventHandler<LoadAccommodationEvent>(loadAccomodationHandler);
13      }
14      void loadProfileHandler(object sender, LoadProfileEvent loadProfileEvent) {
15          profile = loadProfileEvent.getCurrentTarget();
16          barceloPersonalization();
17      }
18      void loadAccomodationHandler(object sender, LoadAccommodationEvent loadAccomodationEvent) {
19          accommodations.Add(loadAccomodationEvent.getCurrentTarget());
20          barceloPersonalization();
21      }
22      void barceloPersonalization() {
23          foreach(IAccommodation accommodation in accommodations) {
24              if (!done && profile != null &&
25                  profile.RegistrationType.Equals("Passport") &&
26                  accommodation.Name.Equals("Barceló Costa Vasca")) {
27                  AddViewModAccommodationEvent ev =
28                          new AddViewModAccommodationEvent(accommodation, "<td class=\"text\"><a href=\"\
29                  Accommodation.OnSignal(ev); done = true;
30      }}
31  }}
```

Fig. 3. *Mods* as plugins that import Modding Interfaces (line 8)

places it as appropriate. The only aspect known in advance is the type of the
HTML fragment as indicated in the event payload when annotating the Modding
Concepts.

4.2 Impact on Partners: Defining Mods

Unlike the open-source approach, OP restricts code access through the Modding
Interfaces. Mod expressiveness is that of monotonic additions to the content of
the host. Deletions are not permitted. Implementation wise, this means *mods*
can extend the content of existing Views, and add new Views & Controllers.

Extending Existing Views. The programming model for *mods* is event-based.
First, a mod subscribes to publishing events to collect data about the User Model
and the Domain Model that is going to be rendered. Second, a mod signals
processing events to indicate the availability of an HTML fragment ready to
be injected in the current View. Therefore, the mod is totally unaware of all,
the Model classes, the Controllers and the Web Forms that are in operation.
From the *mod* perspective, the website is wrapped as a set of *Modding Concepts*
and their corresponding events. Figure 3 shows the *mod* to be provided by the
hotel partner for the rule: *"a 50% discount on room booking over the weekend is
offered, provided the attendee holds a full passport"*:

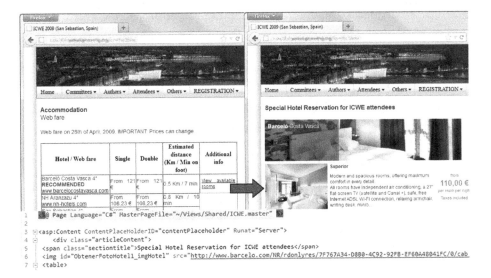

Fig. 4. A *mod* that introduces a new View & Controller. In the up side, the host's View links to the partner's View and the rendering of the partner's View. In the down side the partner's View code refers to the host template (i.e. MasterPageFile).

- a *mod* works upon Modding Concepts (e.g. *Accommodation* and *Profile*). This implies obtaining the classes for the corresponding interfaces (e.g. *IModdingConceptAccommodation* and *IModdingConceptProfile,* line 6). These classes' instances are obtained dynamically using dependency injection (see next section). This explains the *[ImportingConstructor]* annotation.
- a   *mod*   can   subscribe   to   Publishing   Events (e.g. *LoadProfile, LoadAccommodation*). This entails associating a handler to each Publishing Event of interest (lines 11, 12).
- a *mod* can signal Processing Events (e.g. *AddViewModAccommodation*). This signal is enacted in the context of a personalization rule. This rule is just a method (e.g. *barceloPersonalization*) which proceeds along three stages: (1) checks the pertinent aspects of the User Model and Domain Model as obtained from the Publishing Events (e.g. variables "*profile*" and "*accommodation*"); (2) constructs the event payload (i.e. an HTML fragment) and creates the event at hand; and finally (3), signals the Processing Event.

Adding New Views and Controllers. In the previous example, the output of the *mod* could have contained links to Views with additional information (e.g. room pictures). Figure 4 provides an example. These Views are kept as part of the ICWE website but they are provided by the partners. This requires the partner not only to extend host Views with "hooks" (i.e. a link to the partner View), but also to facilitate his own View and Controller. Partners' Controllers are like host Controllers. Partners' Views are like any other View except that they refer to the (rendering) template of the host so that the look&feel and non-contextual links of the hosting site are preserved (see Figure 4). This permits the partner's Views to link back to the rest of the website.

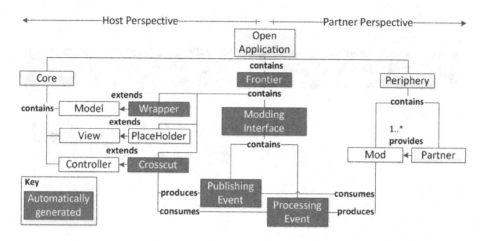

Fig. 5. Decoupling the *Core* from the *Periphery*: a model of the involved concepts

5   Open Personalization: Architecture

This section introduces the main architectural elements that ground the semantics of the *[ModdingConcept]* annotation. That is, the artefacts and associations to be generated as a result of a Domain Concept being turned into a Modding Concept. *Specifically, each annotation automatically outputs the following types of artefacts: Wrappers, Crosscuts and Modding Interfaces.*

Figure 5 outlines the main artefacts and conceptual relationships of our architecture. An **Open Application** contains a **Core**, a **Frontier** and a **Periphery.** The Core stands for the traditional architecture along the Model-View-Controller pattern. The Periphery includes the **Mods** provided by the **Partners.** Finally, the Frontier mediates between the Core and the Periphery through **Modding Interfaces.** Modding Interfaces encapsulates Model classes through events. **Publishing Events** are <*consumed*> by the Mods but <*produced*> by the Core. Alternatively, **Processing Events** are <*produced*> by Mods but <*consumed*> by the Core.

Mods impact on the Core. This impact is supported by different means depending on the nature of the artefact at hand. For Model class, the impact is in terms of a **Wrapper**: a class that becomes a Modding Concept is encapsulated so that only modding properties can become event payloads. For Controller classes, the impact is supported as a **Crosscut** for each of the class methods. Each method handles a Web Form (i.e. denoted in the code as *"return View(webFormName)"*). The Crosscut is "an aspect" that extends the base method with an "after advice" with two duties: (1) raising a Publishing event for each concept instance to be loaded by the Web Form (e.g. hotel Barceló), and (2), handling the Processing Events raised by the *mods*. Finally, the View (i.e. the Web Forms) requires the introduction of **PlaceHolders** where the mod output is to be injected.

So far, the description seems to suggest that the Core knows in advance the mods to be instantiated. However, this is not the case: mods can be added at anytime. This implies hot deployment, i.e. the ability of adding new *mods* to a running Web server without causing any downtime or without restarting the server. The Core cannot have an explicit dependency on *mods*. Inversion of Control and Dependency Injection are two related ways to break apart dependencies in your applications [6]. Inversion of Control (IoC) means that objects do not create other objects on which they rely to do their work. Instead, they get the objects that they need from an outside source. Dependency Injection (DI) means that this is done without the object intervention, usually by the "assembler" that passes constructor parameters and set properties. The assembler is a lightweight object that assembles different components in the system, in order to produce a cohesive and useful service.

In our architecture, Controllers are the component in charge of instantiating the *mods*. However, these instantiation are not achieved directly by the Controllers but through an assembler. That is, Controllers become IoC compliant components (a.k.a. parts), i.e. they do not go off and get other components that they need in order to do their job. Instead, a Controller declares these dependencies, and the assembler supplies them. Hence, the name Hollywood Principle: *"do not call us, we will call you"*. The control of the dependencies for a given Controller is inverted. It is no longer the Controller itself that establishes its own dependencies on the mods, but the assembler.

6   Revising the OP Requirements

Resilience. *Mods* should be resilient to View upgrades. This is the rationale of the Modding Interface: changes in the content or layout of a View should not impact the *mod*. Even if a concept (e.g. *Accommodation*) is no longer rendered, the mod will still raise the event, but no View will care for it. No dangling references come up. The mod becomes redundant but not faulty. And vice versa, new Views can be introduced where *Accommodation* data is rendered. This has no impact in the *mod*. Just the payload of the signalled event (i.e. the HTML fragment) will now start being injected in the place holder of the new View. This place holder should accept HTML fragments of the type being outputted by the *mod*. Otherwise, some disruption might occur that might eventually impact the rendering.

Extensibility. *Mods* can dynamically be added/deleted as partnership agreements change. Existing Model classes left outside partner agreements in the first round, might become Modding Concepts by just adding the corresponding annotations. However, this will require stopping the website to update the annotations and re-compile the code. This also raises the need for authorization mechanism so that not all partners will have access to all modding events. Grant and revoke privileges would be issued by the owner based on agreements with his partners. This is not yet available.

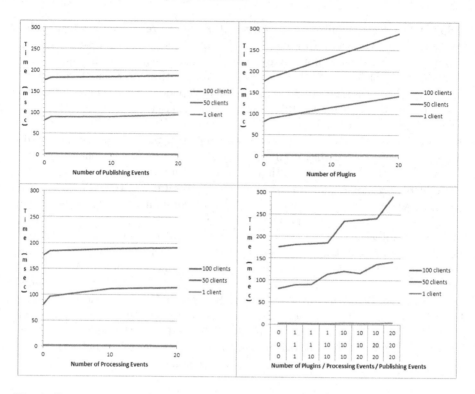

Fig. 6. Latency introduced by distinct OP factors (clockwise from bottom left): #Processing Events, #Publishing Events, #Plugins, and finally, the combined effect of all three

Scalability. *Mods* should not deteriorate the site performance. OP rests on a flexible architecture where (1) mods are installed dynamically and (2), mods interact with the Core through events. Both mechanisms trade flexibility for efficiency. Specifically, satisfying a URL request for a particular page now requires four additional steps: (1) instantiating the mod plugins at hand, (2) generating a publishing event for each Modding Concept in this page, (3) issuing a processing event for each mod that wants to contribute, and (4), capturing such processing events by the Controller at hand. As a general rule, end users should not pay a performance penalty for mods that are installed but not used during the current request. This section describes the results of a stress testing (a.k.a. load testing) of the OP architecture. The study evaluates the additional latency introduced when the ICWE site becomes mod-aware.

Stress testing entails a process of creating a demand on service, and measuring its response. Specifically, we measure the service that outputs the "Accommodation" page. The ICWE application has been deployed in an IIS 7.0 on Intel Core2 Duo T7500 2.2 GHz CPU with 4GB of memory. The test is conducted through Microsoft Web Capacity Analysis Tool (WCAT), a free lightweight HTTP load generation tool which is used to test performance and scalability of IIS and ASP.NET applications [7]. WCAT is configured as follows: 30 seconds to *warmup* (no data collection)[2], 120 seconds of *duration* of simultaneous requests, 10 seconds to *cooldown* (no data collection), range of {1, 50, 100} *virtual clients* (concurrent clients over the same page), and finally, *request* stands for the petition of the *"Accommodation"* page.

The experiment is parameterized along the number of *mods*, the number of publishing event occurrences and the number of processing event occurrences for the request at hand. Figure 6 depicts the "time to last byte" metric for these three factors. For the ICWE-with-*no*-modding, the "Accommodation" request accounts for 2 msec. On top of it, OP introduces some affordable overheads. As suggested by the bottom right chart about the combined effect of the three factors, the event-based mechanism has minimal impact (i.e. the plateau in the charts stands for increases in the *#events* but keeping the *#plugins* constant). By contrast, the *#plugins* reveals itself as the factor with larger impact. Along the lines of IoC, each request implies to instantiate the involved plugins for the Controller at hand. For a hundred simultaneous requests, the impact of 1, 10, 20 plugins account for an increase of 5%, 33% and 64%, respectively. To be perfectly honest, we seldom envisage a scenario where a page is subject to over 20 plugins. We do not foresee more than 3/4 plugins per page on average, and this would represent a 15% penalty. Notice, that this number is just for satisfying the request, not to be confused to the elapsed time that the end user experiments. If normalized with the elapsed time (typically around 1300 msec.), the OP architecture represents around a 2% of increment for the most common envisaged scenarios.

Affordability. *Mods* should be easy to develop and maintain. *Mods* follow an event-driven style of programming. That is, the logic is split between event handlers and event producers. This is particularly helpful in our context where these event roles can be naturally split between partners and owners: partners focus on what should be the custom reaction (i.e. processing events) for the rendering of Modding Concepts, while owners focus on signalling when Modding Concepts are displayed (i.e. the Publishing events). This certainly leads to cleaner code. On the downside, the flow of the program is usually less obvious.

7   Related Work

Extensible architectures are a long-standing aim in software [11,5]. As a first requirement for in-house development, extensibility is becoming a must to integrate code from third parties. The motivation here is *"to integrate and build on existing work, by writing only the specialized code that differentiates them from their competition"* [1]. The ability to respond quickly to rapid changes

---

[2] WCAT uses a "warm-up" period in order to allow the Web Server to achieve steady state before taking measurements of throughput, response time and performance counters. For instance there is a slight delay on first request on ASP.NET sites when Just-In-Time (JIT) compilation is performed.

in requirements, upgradeability, and support for integrating other vendors' components at any time, all create an additional push for flexible and extensible applications, and grounds the work of Web architectures such as PLUX .NET [9], that resembles MEF, the .NET library we utilize to support OP. In the Java realm, the Open Services Gateway Initiative (OSGI) [16] framework propose a dynamic component model for Java, i.e. a way for components (known as bundles) to be started, stopped, updated and uninstalled without the need to reboot the system. OSGI also includes a way to define dependencies between bundles but it does not preclude any communication mechanism between components. Compared with an OSGI-like architecture, our approach rests on a "core component" (i.e. the website) and a set of "satellite components" where the interaction is only permitted from the core to the satellites. From this perspective, our approach is more rigid but it reflects the asymmetric relationship between the website owner and the third parties.

More akin with the OP vision is SAFE [13] an architecture of Web Application extensibility aimed at permitting users to personalize websites. SAFE is based on a hierarchical programming model based on f-units (the component model). An f-unit clusters all code fragments for a specific functionality within a web page, including the business logic, the visual appearance, and the interaction with users or other f-units. A web page is modelled as a so-called "activation tree" in which f-units are organized hierarchically, and activation flows top-down (naturally corresponding to the hierarchical DOM structure of an HTML page). Thus, a user who would like to personalize an application simply has to replace an existing f-unit with a new f-unit of her choice. Such customizations are dynamic in that f-units are registered and activated without stopping the running system. F-units contain SQL statements and this serves to support an implicit interaction between f-units sharing the same data. The bottom line is that SAFE proposes a more innovative mean for open participation by introducing a hierarchical model to web programming. This is simultaneously the main benefit, but also jeopardy, of SAFE. By contrast, we advocate for a more *evolutionary* approach. OP only makes the assumption of the MVC pattern and code annotation, and uses the well-known event-based programming model as the interaction mechanism. Capitalizing on existing techniques and programming models will certainly facilitate partner participation. The challenge is not only on *pluggable* components/f-units/mods but also *affordable*, *risk-controlled* technology that facilitates partner engagement. We use an existing technology (*.NET*) and use annotations to leverage from the general-purpose technology to domain-specific concepts. This motivates the conceptual leveragement of Model Classes into Modding Concepts. The notion of Modding Concept attempts to reduce the conceptual gap for partners and owners to understand each other while maximising decoupling by using events as the interaction mean.

8   Conclusions

Fostering a win-win relationship between website owners and partners, substantiates the efforts of Open Personalization (OP). This paper's goal was to demonstrate that OP is feasible with existing technologies such as *.NET*. Though proving feasibility requires focusing on a specific platform, the approach is easily generalizable to any framework that supports "Inversion of Control". As future development, we plan to look into ways for partners to extend the User Model (i.e. the profile base). The profile base as designed by the host, might be insufficient to conduct some *mods*. Permitting partners to seamless define and collect additional user information through the website is certainly a challenge. Besides the technical challenges, OP also introduces new business models that need to be investigated.

Acknowledgements. This work is co-supported by the Spanish Ministry of Education, and the European Social Fund under contract TIN2011-23839 *(Scriptongue)*.

References

1. Birsan, D.: On Plug-ins and Extensible Architectures. ACM Queue 3, 40–46 (2005)
2. Bloomberg, J.: Events vs. services. ZapThink white paper (2004)
3. Brusilovsky, P.: Methods and Techniques of Adaptive Hypermedia. User Modeling and User Adapted Interaction 6, 87–129 (1996)
4. Cingil, I., Dogac, A., Azgin, A.: A Broader Approach to Personalization. Communications of the ACM 43, 136–141 (2000)
5. Erl, T.: A Comparison of Goals - Increased Extensibility. In: SOA Principles of Service Design, p. 451. Prentice Hall (2007)
6. Fowler, M.: Inversion of Control Containers and the Dependency Injection pattern (January 2004), `http://martinfowler.com/articles/injection.html`
7. Friedman, E.M., Rosenberg, J.L.: Web Load Testing Made Easy: Testing with WCAT and WAST for Windows Applications. In: Proceesings of the 29th International CMG Conference, Dallas, Texas, USA, pp. 57–82 (December 2003)
8. Hippel, E.V.: Open source software projects as user innovation networks. In: Proceedings of the Open Source Software: Economics, Law and Policy, Toulouse, France (June 2002)
9. Jahn, M., Wolfinger, R., Mössenböck, H.: Extending Web Applications with Client and Server Plug-ins. In: Software Engineering, pp. 33–44 (2010)
10. JCP: JSR 168: Portlet Specification Version 1.0 (2003), `http://www.jcp.org/en/jsr/detail?id=168`
11. Oberndorf, P.: Community-wide Reuse of Architectural Assets. In: Software Architecture in Practice. Addison-Wesley (1997)
12. O'Reilly, T.: The Architecture of Participation (June 2004), `http://oreilly.com/pub/a/oreilly/tim/articles/architecture_of_participation.html`
13. Reischuk, R.M., Backes, M., Gehrke, J.: SAFE Extensibility for Data-Driven Web Applications. In: Proceedings of the 21st World Wide Web Conference, Lyon, France, pp. 799–808 (April 2012)
14. Riepula, M.: Sharing Source Code with Clients: A Hybrid Business and Development Model. IEEE Software 28, 36–41 (2011)
15. Robie, J., Hors, A.L., Nicol, G., Hégaret, P.L., Champion, M., Wood, L., Byrne, S.: Document Object Model (DOM) Level 2 Core Specification. Tech. rep., W3C (2000)
16. The OSGi Alliance: OSGi Service Platform Core Specification, Release 4.3 (2011)

Role-Based Access Control
for Model-Driven Web Applications

Mairon Belchior[1], Daniel Schwabe[1], and Fernando Silva Parreiras[2]

[1] Department of Informatics, PUC-Rio.,
Rua Marques de Sao Vicente, 225. Rio de Janeiro, RJ 22453-900, Brazil
[2] Faculty of Business Sciences – FACE, FUMEC University,
Av. Afonso Pena 3880, 30130-009, Belo Horizonte, Brazil
mbelchior,dschwabe@inf.puc-rio.br,fernando.parreiras@fumec.br

Abstract. The Role-based Access Control (RBAC) model provides a safe and efficient way to manage access to information of an organization, while reducing the complexity and cost of security administration in large networked applications. However, Web Engineering frameworks that treat access control models as first-class citizens are still lacking so far. In this paper, we integrate the RBAC model in the design method of Semantic Web applications. More specifically, this work presents an extension of the SHDM method (Semantic Hypermedia Design Method), where these access control models were included and seamlessly integrated with the other models of this method. The proposed model allows the specification of semantic access control policies. SHDM is a model-driven approach to design Web applications for the Semantic Web. This extension was implemented in the Synth environment, which is an application development environment that supports designs using SHDM

Keywords: SHDM, Access Control Model, RBAC, Semantic Web, Ontology.

1 Introduction

Web engineering is a discipline that promotes systematic approaches for dealing with multiple aspects of the process of developing Web applications. Over the years, frameworks like, WebML (Web Modeling Language) [2], UWE (UML-based Web Engineering) [7], OOHDM (Object-Oriented Hypermedia Design Method) [10], Hera [11], and SHDM (Semantic Hypermedia Design Method) [9] have been incrementally improved for dealing with challenges inherent in Web applications.

Access control has long been identified as a necessary feature in applications, notably using models such as Role-based Access Control model (RBAC) [12,3]. Such access control models aim at simplifying security management and at providing constructs for specifying policies.

Although access control models have been investigated over the years, the seamless integration of access control models with Web Engineering frameworks has not gained as much attention as the integration of other models within Web Engineering like domain, navigation and interface models. In this scenario, the question that arises is: What are the connection points of a seamless integration between access control modeling and Web application modeling languages?

M. Brambilla, T. Tokuda, and R. Tolksdorf (Eds.): ICWE 2012, LNCS 7387, pp. 106–120, 2012.

This seamless integration enables Web engineers to handle access control elements such as users, resources and rights as first-class citizens. It provides a mechanism for specifying and validating user access to resources in a declarative matter.

The challenge of integrating access control modeling and Web application modeling languages lies in the differences between underlying formalisms of each aspect. Access control models typically rely on formalisms such as the Web ontology language (OWL) as underlying formalism. In contrast, Web application modeling approaches cannot commit to such an expressive language and often rely on RDF to define concepts, properties and relations.

Proposed solutions like [4, 5, 6] use OWL to represent the role-based access control model and, thus, to describe resources. The problem with these approaches arises when a resource in the RBAC model requires the reification of many objects in the domain model. This problem hampers integrated reasoning with both RBAC models and Web application models.

We extend current work by proposing an approach for connecting RBAC models with RDF-based Web application models, such as the Semantic Hypermedia Design Method (SHDM). We treat access control concepts as first-class citizens in the SHDM approach, which enables users to specify, validate and implement access control models seamlessly integrated with domain and business logic models.

We present our approach in this paper as follows. After describing the example we are going to use through the paper in Section 2, we present our approach for integrating access control modeling and Web application modeling in Section 3. We discuss the implementation and proof of concept in Section 4[1]. Section 5 presents the related work and with Section 6 we draw some conclusions and discuss future work.

2   Running Example

To help illustrate the concepts discussed in the paper, we use a running example of a simplified Conference Review Management System, which provides a set of services to run a conference. Activities are carried out by roles, as follows:

a)   Conference Chairs (CC) – create a conference, providing name, place, dates, and nominating one or more PC Chairs;

b)   PC Chairs (PCC) – responsible for assembling the Program Committee; invite Senior and regular PC Members; assign/de-assign papers for review by PC members; assign/de-assign papers for Senior Reviewers to coordinate reviews from regular reviewers; accept/reject papers;

c)   Senior reviewer (SR)– Responsible for overseeing the reviews of assigned papers by regular reviewers; summarize reviews making recommendation to PC Chairs for acceptance/rejection;

d)   Reviewer (R) – Responsible for producing a review for each paper assigned to him/her;

e)   Author (A) – Responsible for creating/removing submissions; producing final copy of paper if accepted; queries the acceptance status of her/his paper.

---

[1] A demo of Synth with Access Control, with the running example can be found in http://www.tecweb.inf.puc-rio.br/navigation/context/o_e1a8b079@0?p=

A snippet of the Domain Model for this application is shown in Fig. 1.

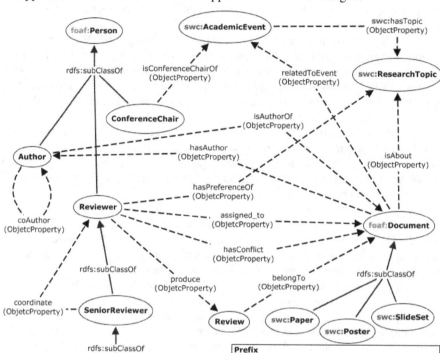

Fig. 1. A Domain Model for the Conference Management System

There are many policies applicable in this domain. In the following, we illustrate some that incorporate semantic concepts of the domain, such as "conflict of interest".

1. Reviewers and Senior Reviewers may also be Authors.
2. Nobody is allowed to see any information about a paper for which there is a conflict of interest.
3. A conflict of interest for a reviewer R with respect to a given paper occurs if
   - R is an author of the paper;
   - R is in the same Department/Lab/Group/Project as co-author S of the paper;
   - R and S have co-authored another paper submitted to the same conference.
4. A Reviewer can only see other reviews of a paper assigned to her/him if she/he has already entered his/her own review for that paper.

Next we present our proposed RBAC model, and then discuss how it has been integrated with the SHDM design method.

3   Integrating SHDM and Role-Based Access Control

An access control mechanism is usually composed of two parts: *authentication*, responsible for verifying user identity, and *authorization*, responsible for granting user access to system objects.

Existing approaches for modeling access control share a core set of concepts: they essentially refer to a *User* in the role of *Subject*, having some kind of *Permission* to execute an *Operation* on an *Object*. A well-known approach for modeling access control rules is the Role-based Access Control (RBAC) [12] model, which allows defining policies based on the subject like competence, interest and privilege.

With the rise of the Semantic Web, several techniques like [4, 6, 5] have investigated the usage of OWL for representing RBAC models, which has led to multiple alternatives for creating a formal representation of RBAC models. In this section, we describe the modeling approach we propose for integration with a Web Engineering method. The reader might notice that the solution proposed for integrating RBAC models and a Web Engineering framework is independent of the approach used for the latter. Therefore, it is possible to apply the proposed technique in other configurations of RBAC and other Web Engineering frameworks.

3.1   The RBAC Model

An approach for modeling RBAC using OWL is proposed by [5], named RowlBAC. They develop two different approaches to represent the RBAC model using the OWL language, including the concepts of subject, role, object, actions and associations defined by roles. The first approach specifies roles as classes and subclasses, while the second approach, the roles are represented as properties. The model of access control implemented in this work is based on the second approach, as it is simpler and more concise.

Fig. 2 depicts a diagram with the main concepts and properties of the second approach. Roles are represented as instances of the class *Role*. A role hierarchy is defined by the property *subRole(Role, Role)*, which is an owl:TransitiveProperty. The property *supRole(Role, Role)* is the inverse of (owl:inverseOf) *subRoleOf(Role, Role)*. The relation between a *Subject* and a *Role* is defined by the property *role(Subject, Role)*. The binding between access permissions and roles is done by the properties rbac:permitted and rbac:prohibited, that connect a role (rbac:Role) to a permitted action (rbac:PermittedAction), and to a prohibited action (rbac:ProhibitedAction), respectively.

Not all components of the RBAC model can be specified using OWL DL. Rules in N3Logic were added to the RBAC ontology to define the hierarchy of roles, the static and dynamic constraints, activation and deactivation of roles and permissions associated with roles.

In this paper, we extend the SHDM method to include a new model, the Access Control Model as an addition to the existing Behavior Model.

The Access Control Model is composed of primitives responsible for the description of concepts related to access control, such as subject, the subject's role, permission, object and operation.

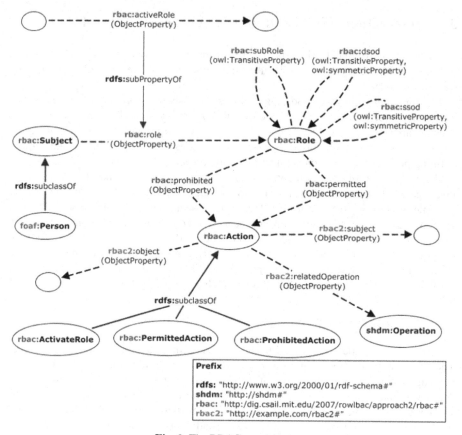

Fig. 2. The RBAC vocabulary

We have modified the ROWLBack model as follows:

- The property rbac:subject is no longer an owl:FunctionalProperty, because a certain action (rbac:Action) can be performed by more than one user (rbac: Subject) who has permission to perform this action. For example, the actions rbac:createReview, rbac:editReview, rbac:downloadPaper and rbac:context can be performed by myconference:DanielSchwabe. This property became rbac2:subject in our model;

- The property rbac:object also ceased to be an owl:FunctionalProperty because an action (rbac:Action) may be related to more than one object (rbac:Object). For example, the action rbac:createReview can be applied to rbac:paperA, rbac:paperD and rbac:paperM as objects of this action. This property became rbac2:object;

- The property rbac2:relatedOperation was added to the model to represent which operation (shdm:Operation) defined in the Operation Model of the SHDM is being controlled;

- Classes rbac:PermittedRoleActivation and rbac:ProhibitedRole Activation are not used by this model, therefore they have been removed;

The property rbac2:relatedOperation is used to represent which operation (shdm:Operation) defined in the SDHM Operation Model is being tracked. The code below shows an example of the definition of this property using N3.

rbac:createReview rbac2:relatedOperation shdm:createReview .

The property shdm:relatedAction was added to the SHDM Operation Model to represent that an shdm:Operation resource has a corresponding rbac:Action, which means that the shdm:Operation is controlled by the application using the primitives of the RBAC access control model.

The association between Roles in the RBAC model and the classes in the Domain Model of SHDM is achieved using the rdfs:subClassOf property, as illustrated in **Fig. 2** with the foaf:Person class.

3.2   Defining Rules

In order to identify the permission to execute a certain action (rbac:Action), we have used N3Logic rules following the same approach as Finin et al. N3Logic is a formalism that allows rules to be incorporated in RDF (Resource Description Framework) [13]. N3Logic uses the syntax Notation3 (or N3), and extends the RDF model to include a set of predicates, e.g., implications, quantified variables, nested graphs, functions and built-ins.

Our approach adds the rule shown below to check if an action (rbac:Action) has an object (rbac:Object). If so, this action is of type rbac:ActionWithObject. The N3Logic rules below, on the right check whether a subject has the permission to perform a certain action on a certain object.

```
#Check if action has object
{      ?A a ?RACTION ;
              rbac2:subject ?S ;
              rbac2:object ?O .

       ?RACTION a rbac:Action .
       ?S a rbac:Subject .
       ?O a rbac:Object .

} => { ?A a rbac:ActionWithObject } .
```

```
#Permission checking
{?A a ?RACTION ;
              rbac2:subject ?S ;
              rbac2:object ?O .
       ?RACTION a rbac:Action .
       ?S a rbac:Subject .
       ?O a rbac:Object .
       ?Role rbac:permitted ?RACTION .
       ?S rbac:activeRole ?ROLE .
       ?RACTION rbac2:object ?O
       ?A a rbac:ActionWithObject .

} => { ?A a rbac:PermittedAction;
       rbac2:subject ?S;
       rbac2:object ?O
       rbac2:action ?RACTION } .
```

3.3   Modeling Rules for Policies

An access policy is a set of rules that are evaluated to determine whether a user has the right to access a given object. The access policy specifies who is allowed to perform what action on which object depending on (i) properties of the user who made the request, (ii) object properties, (iii) parameters of the action, and (iv) background factors (such as time) [14].

The class rule:Rule reifies the concept of access control policies. It has properties of type DatatypeProperty such as rule: rule_name: defines the name of the rule; rule: rule_title: define a title for the rule; rule: rule_code: defines the specification of the rule; rule: rule_language: defines the language used to specify rules.

Besides these, we consider three additional properties: properties:rule_role, rule:rule_action and rule_object that are used to identify, respectively, the role (rbac:Role), action (rbac:Action) and the object of the action (rbac:Object) on which the rule applies. Examples of rules specifying access policies are shown in section 4.5.

4   Implementation Architecture

A modular software architecture for Access Control was designed as shown in **Fig. 3**. The architecture is divided into two parts: the Authentication Mechanism that is responsible for identifying the user to the system, and the Authorization Mechanism that determines what the user is allowed to do within the system. There are three modules: Authentication Module, Permission Module and Inference Module, represented as gray boxes; white boxes represent the components of the architecture.

The Authentication Module is responsible for performing an authentication protocol, such as FOAF + SSL[2] protocol or OpenID protocol[3]. The Permission

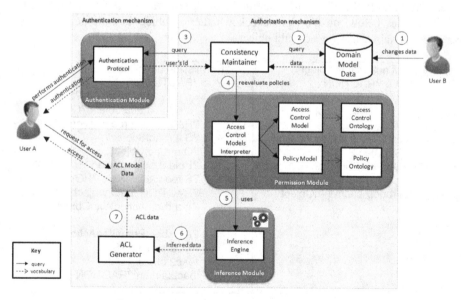

Fig. 3. Conceptual Architecture for Access Control

---

[2] See http:// www.w3.org/wiki/Foaf+ssl
[3] See http://openid.net

Module should be able to define all access control concepts and policies of the application. The Access Control Model Interpreter maintains and interprets the Access Control and Policy models described by their corresponding ontologies.

The inference module includes a rule inference engine responsible for inferring new facts from existing facts, which effectively evaluate the access control rules. We used the Euler proof engine[4] that supports N3 rules as the inference engine.

The proposed access control system implemented in this work computes the permissions specified in the policies to generate an Access Control List (ACL) [8], represented in the ACL model. This allows for efficient runtime execution, since permissions are read directly from the ACL to decide about authorization, which was previously generated running the reasoner only once.

To be authenticated, a user must provide her credentials to the Authentication Protocol. If the information given is correct, the user is authenticated and the URI representing this user is stored in the application session.

After authentication, the user may request permission to access some resource controlled by the application by providing what operation the user wants to perform on which object, if it exists. The application will check if a permission is present in the ACL model, and if so, the user is authorized to perform the operation. Otherwise, an error message will appear to the user. The ACL needs to be updated whenever a user changes any data. When this occurs, the Consistency Maintainer component of the architecture is triggered, to maintain the permission's consistency in the ACL Model, re-evaluating the policies applicable for that user, and the ACL is regenerated by the ACL Generator component, materializing new inferred permissions. The steps for policy reevaluation are shown in Fig. 3.

The OpenID protocol was used for Authentication. It was chosen because it has support for popular services such as MyOpenID, Google, Yahoo!, etc.

4.1   Integration in the Synth Development Environment

Synth is a development environment for building applications that are modeled according to SHDM. It provides a set of modules that receives, as input, models generated in each step of SHDM and produces, as output, the hypermedia application described by these models. Synth also provides an authoring environment that facilitates the adding and editing of these models through a GUI that can run on any Web browser [1]. Synth was implemented with Ruby on Rails, which is an MVC framework for Web applications development. With this work, the Synth architecture was extended to include the Access Control Module.

4.2   Software Architecture of Synth

The software architecture of Synth consists of five modular components: domain, navigation, behavior, interfaces, and persistence modules. They are responsible for

---

[4] See http://eulergui.svn.sourceforge.net/viewvc/
   eulergui/trunk/eulergui/ html/documentation.html

maintaining and interpreting each of the models generated in each phase of SHDM method. Each module is composed by a model described in a corresponding ontology in RDFS or OWL, and an interpreter that gives semantics to the models, in addition to the basic semantics of RDFS and OWL, in which they are represented [1]. These modules work together, interpreting their models and communicating with each other, in order to generate the application runtime in accordance with the definitions of each model.

The Access Control module was embodied in the Synth architecture and is responsible for generating the authorization decisions for the application. It maintains and interprets the Access Control and Policy models described by their corresponding ontologies. The Behavior Model Interpreter was extended to handle the Access Control List, checking the permissions in ACL Model whenever an operation is performed. The existing Behavior Model in SHDM, as implemented in Synth, already allows defining a pre-condition to activate an Operation; applying the ACL permissions was implemented simply as a pre-loaded pre-condition on all operations.

Fig. 4 shows a conceptual view of the extended Synth software architecture. The gray boxes represent the modules and the white boxes represent the components of each module. The light gray box is the Access Control Module included in the architecture.

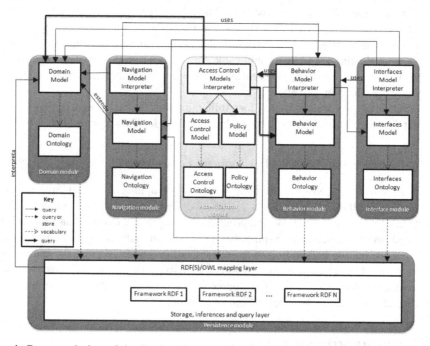

Fig. 4. Conceptual view of the Synth software architecture extended with the Access Control Module

The Behavior Module handles all business logic operations of the application. The Behavior Model Interpreter uses the Access Control Module to determine whether or not an operation can be executed, and the Access Control Model Interpreter queries the

Behavior Model to obtain a set of RDF resources related to the activated operation and its parameters. Similarly, the Access Control Model Interpreter queries the Domain Model to obtain application domain data on which the access control policies are applied.

4.3   Permissions Generation

The generation of access control list (ACL) is achieved in the following steps:

1. A set of possible authorization questions testing if a user has permission to perform an operation on a particular object is generated, by activating all possible roles assigned to this user;
2. Rules in N3Logic to create the ACL resources are generated;
3. The Euler proof engine is activated taking as input all application data and all rules in N3Logic defined in authoring environment.
4. The permissions returned by inference engine containing the RDF resources in the ACL model are added to Synth's database.

The ACL rules in step 2 are generated as follows:

For each access control rule defined in authoring environment with a consequent stating the action is an rbac:PermittedAction, an ACL rule is created with the code whose structure follows the example shown below. The statement "<Access_Control/rulesResult.n3> log:semantics F" associates the inferred triples to F, according to the N3Logic semantics [13].

The sentences (a) "A rbac:action RACTION." and (b) "A a rbac:PermittedActionRBAC." are added to assert that (a) the action is used by the ACL Model and that (b) this action must be permitted by the RBAC Model.

```
@forAll F, S, O, A, RACTION .
{ <Access_Control/rulesResult.n3> log:semantics F .
        F log:includes {
                A a rbac:Action ;
                        rbac2:subject S ;
                        rbac2:object O.

                A a rbac:createReview .
                S rbac:activeRole rbac:reviewer_role .
                O a foaf:Document .

                A a rbac:PermittedActionRBAC .
                A rbac:action RACTION .

                A a rbac:PermittedAction .
        } .
} => { [ a acl:Authorization ;
                acl:mode RACTION ;
                acl:agent S ;
                acl:accessTo O ] } .
```

Notice that if F doesn't include the statement "A a rbac:PermittedAction.", no ACL triples are generated. When accessing the ACL, the absence of authorization is taken as failure.

Occasionally an action can be inferred as permitted and prohibited at the same time. For example, suppose a person is assigned to both reviewer and author roles. Suppose also that there is a policy that defines that an author cannot view the navigational context that lists the papers a reviewer can review, and there is another policy that defines that reviewers can access all navigational contexts of the application. Therefore, when this reviewer is authenticated, all the roles assigned to him will be activated, and then when he tries to navigate to the context described above, whose navigation's semantic is given by the operation shdm:context, such action will be both an rbac:PermittedAction and an rbac:ProhibitedAction at the same time. There are two approaches – conservative and liberal - to deal with this situation to decide which permission should be given. The liberal approach chooses the prohibited action (i.e., everything is permitted unless explicitly stated otherwise) while the conservative approach (everything is denied unless explicitly stated otherwise) selects the permitted action. A parameter in the ACL generation module allows choosing one of these approaches.

4.4   Policy Examples

The policies stated in section 2 can be now defined using N3Logic rules, as used in the Synth environment.

The policy that a Reviewer is not allowed to review a paper by an author from the same institution (one kind of conflict of interest) is defined as follows (left column).

```
{   ?A a rbac:Action ;
        rbac2:subject ?S ;
        rbac2:object ?O .
    ?A a rbac:createReview .
    ?S rbac:activeRole
    rbac:reviewer_role .
    ?O a foaf:Document .

    ?S myconference:assigned_to ?O .

    ?AUTHOR rbac:role rbac:author_role
    .
    ?AUTHOR myconference:isAuthorOf
    ?O .

    ?AUTHOR myconference:memberOf
    ?I1 .
    ?S myconference:memberOf ?I2 .

    ?I1 log:uri ?URI1 .
    ?I2 log:uri ?URI2 .
    ?URI1 log:equalTo ?URI2 .

} => { ?A a rbac:ProhibitedAction } .
```

```
{ ?A a rbac:Action ;
        rbac2:subject ?S ;
        rbac2:object ?O .
    ?A a rbac:createReview .
    ?S rbac:activeRole rbac:reviewer_role
    .
    ?O a foaf:Document .

    ?S myconference:assigned_to ?O .
    ?AUTHOR rbac:role rbac:author_role .
    ?AUTHOR myconference:isAuthorOf
    ?O .
    ?AUTHOR myconference:isAuthorOf
    ?O2 .

    ?O log:uri ?URI1 .
    ?O2 log:uri ?URI2 .
    ?URI1 log:notequalTo ?URI2 .
    ?S myconference:isAuthorOf ?O2 .

} => { ?A a rbac:ProhibitedAction } .
```

The right column shows another similar policy regarding conflict of interest, which states that a reviewer cannot review a paper of a co-author of his/hers, would be very similar, looking at the myconference:isAuthorOf property for two different papers, O and O2.

A third example is the policy whereby a Reviewer can only see other reviews of a paper assigned to her/him if s/he has already entered his/her own review for that paper. This is stated as

{	?A a rbac:Action ;	?D a foaf:Document .
	rbac2:subject ?S ;	?O myconference:belongTo ?D .
	rbac2:object ?0 .	?S myconference:assigned_to ?D
	?A a rbac:context .	.
	?S rbac:activeRole	
rbac:reviewer_role .		
	?O a myconference:Review .	} => { ?A a rbac:PermittedAction } .
	?REV a myconference:Review .	
	?S myconference:produce ?REV .	
	?REV myconference:belongTo ?D .	

4.5   Evaluation

We carried out some preliminary evaluations to determine the overhead of Access Control in Synth. The performance tests were run on a Intel Core i5 CPU M 450 2.40 GHz with 4GB of RAM using Windows 7 Professional 64-bit. Fig. 5 depicts the performance time to query the ACL Model 100 times to access the permission for random access requests for 10 different contexts, where the ACL Model had 217 resources. The fluctuations in the beginning can be attributed to "start up" effects of the simulation as it was run in several separate runs.

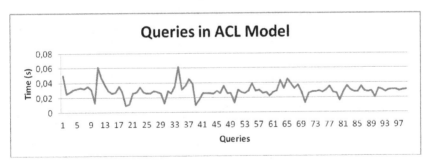

Fig. 5. Time to query the ACL Model

Fig. 6 shows the time to execute all policies (13 plus those used by the RBAC model and those used for ACL generation) access control rules in the example application 50 times by adding a constant number of resources in each run. As expected, the evaluation time grows with the number of data elements added to the database. Note that we currently use a naïve policy re-evaluation strategy.

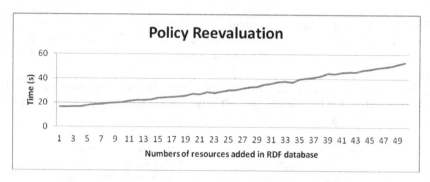

Fig. 6. Time to reevaluate all policies after a change in the database

5   Related Work

Several researchers have investigated the integration of access control with languages related to Web Engineering. In this section, we compare them with our proposal.

Mühleisen et al [15] developed an access control system that allows the use of rules defined in a language created by the authors based on SWRL (Semantic Web Rule Language). However, this language does not follow the RBAC principles and does not allow for modeling any further aspects of the system.

Hollenbach et al [16] developed a system to control access based on ACLs. Although it is possible to model domain aspects, this system does not support the formulation of access control policies.

Finin et all [5] presented two approaches to express the components of the RBAC model using OWL. The main disadvantage of this approach is that each change on the authorization requires a new execution of the inference rules, making the authorization process costly.

Ferrini et al [4] also modeled the RBAC model using OWL and access control policies using XACML in an integrated manner. However, both approaches commit to the principles of OWL, which restricts applications when the closed-world assumption is required.

Knechtel et al [6] show an approach to model an extension of the RBAC model called RBAC-CH, using OWL. RBAC-CH is an access control model that extends the RBAC model by adding a hierarchy of object classes. To evaluate policies using this approach, the inference engine based on OWL is executed once, and the inferred axioms are the available at runtime. However, the authors do not take into account the static and dynamic constraints of the RBAC model, nor do they allow rules for building policies.

Finally, it should be noted that none of the approaches above has been integrated with a Web Engineering method, and is supported by an authoring environment.

6   Conclusions

In this paper, we have presented a novel approach for handling the integration of role-based access control and Web Engineering frameworks. By providing the bridges between these two approaches, we enable Web engineers to specify access control policies at the same level of domain knowledge as well as navigation knowledge. Additionally, we allow for access control models and other Web Engineering models to evolve independently. Our contribution extends the body of knowledge in the field by identifying the links between RBAC and Web Engineering and providing mechanisms for representing the underlying constraints.

There are several extensions we continue to work on. First, extending the policy model to be able to handle dynamic policies, which cannot be evaluated at runtime; second, we want to investigate more opportunistic strategies for incremental policy re-evaluation, so that only affected policies are re-executed when data changes. A third extension can also optimize the ACL, by including the actual role in the ACL itself. Finally, we want to provide a better authoring environment for policies to help end users understand complex sets of policies.

Acknowledgments. Daniel Schwabe was partially supported by CNPq (WebScience INCT). Mairon Belchior was partially supported by a grant from CAPES. Fernando Silva Parreiras was partially funded by FP7-PEOPLE-2009-IRSES, under grant number 24761.

References

1. de Souza Bomfim, M.H., Schwabe, D.: Design and Implementation of Linked Data Applications Using SHDM and Synth. In: Auer, S., Díaz, O., Papadopoulos, G.A. (eds.) ICWE 2011. LNCS, vol. 6757, pp. 121–136. Springer, Heidelberg (2011)
2. Ceri, S., Fraternali, P., Bongio, A.: Web Modeling Language (WebML): a modeling language for designing Web sites. In: Procs of the WWW9 Conf., Amsterdam (May 2000)
3. Ferraiolo, D., Chandramouli, R., Kuhn, D.R.: Role-based access control, 2nd edn. Ebrary, INC., vol. xix, p. 381. Artech House, Boston (2007)
4. Ferrini, R., Bertino, E.: Supporting RBAC with XACML+OWL. In: Proceedings of the 14th ACM Symposium on Access Control Models and Technologies, SACMAT 2009, Stresa, Italy, June 03-05, pp. 145–154. ACM, New York (2009)
5. Finin, T., Joshi, A., Kagal, L., Niu, J., Sandhu, R., Winsborough, W., Thuraisingham, B.: Rowlbac: representing role based access control in OWL. In: Proceedings of the 13th ACM Symposium on Access Control Models and Technologies, SACMAT 2008, Estes Park, CO, USA, June 11-13, pp. 73–82. ACM, New York (2008)
6. Knechtel, M., Hladik, J.: RBAC authorization decision with DL reasoning. In: Proceedings of the IADIS International Conference WWW/Internet, pp. 169–176 (2008)
7. Koch, N., Kraus, A.: The Expressive Power of UML-based Web Engineering. In: Proceedings of the 2nd International Workshop on Web-Oriented Software Technology (IWOOST 2002), CYTED, pp. 105–119 (2002)
8. Lampson, B.W.: Dynamic Protection Structures. In: AFIPS Conference Proceedings, vol. 35 (1969)

9. Lima, F., Schwabe, D.: Application Modeling for the Semantic Web. In: Proceedings of LA-Web 2003, Santiago, Chile, pp. 93–102. IEEE Press (November 2003)
10. Schwabe, D., Rossi, G.: An object-oriented approach to Web-based application design. Theory and Practice of Object Systems (TAPOS), 207–225 (October 1998)
11. Vdovjak, R., Frasincar, F., Houben, G.J., Barna, P.: Engineering Semantic Web Information Systems in Hera. Journal of Web Engineering 2(1&2), 3–26 (2003)
12. Sandhu, R., Ferraiolo, D., Kuhn, R.: The NIST model for role-based access control: Towards a unified standard. In: Proceedings of the Fifth ACM Workshop on Role-Based Access Control, Berlin, pp. 47–63 (July 2000)
13. Berners-Lee, T., Connolly, D., Kagal, L., Hendler, J., Schraf, Y.: N3Logic: A Logical Framework for the World Wide Web. Journal of Theory and Practice of Logic Programming (TPLP), Special Issue on Logic Programming and the Web (2008)
14. Bonatti, P.A., De Coi, J.L., Olmedilla, D., Sauro, L.: Rule-Based Policy Representations and Reasoning. In: Bry, F., Małuszyński, J. (eds.) Semantic Techniques for the Web. LNCS, vol. 5500, pp. 201–232. Springer, Heidelberg (2009)
15. Mühleisen, H., Kost, M., Freytag, J.-C.: SWRL-based Access Policies for Linked Data. In: SPOT 2010 2nd Workshop on Trust and Privacy on the Social and Semantic Web, Heraklion, Greece (2010)
16. Hollenbach, J., Presbrey, J., Berners-Lee, T.: Using RDF Metadata To Enable Access Control on the Social Semantic Web. In: Workshop on Collaborative Construction, Management and Linking of Structured Knowledge (CK 2009) (ISWC 2009), Washington, DC (2009)

Recovering Role-Based Access Control Security Models from Dynamic Web Applications

Manar H. Alalfi, James R. Cordy, and Thomas R. Dean

School of Computing, Queens University,
Kingston, Ontario, Canada
{alalfi,cordy,dean}@cs.queensu.ca

Abstract. Security of dynamic web applications is a serious issue. While Model Driven Architecture (MDA) techniques can be used to generate applications with given access control security properties, analysis of existing web applications is more problematic. In this paper we present a model transformation technique to automatically construct a role-based access control (RBAC) security model of dynamic web applications from previously recovered structural and behavioral models. The SecureUML model generated by this technique can be used to check for security properties of the original application. We demonstrate our approach by constructing an RBAC security model of PhpBB, a popular internet bulletin board system.

1 Introduction

Models provide a formal basis to specify various properties of software, such as access control properties. When the application is later generated from the model, developers have a reasonable expectation that these properties will be implemented in the software. However, determining the access control properties of an existing software application is a non-trivial task. We can try to verify the properties directly on the source code, or we can recover a model from the code that is amenable to analysis. One particular area of interest is dynamic web applications, which are often designed to interact with the general public and thus are directly accessible to a wide variety of attackers. In many current web applications, access control policies are spread throughout the application, making understanding and maintaining them a difficult task [1].

Security and vulnerability analysis of dynamic web applications is not new. Pistoia et al. [2] survey a variety of techniques that check for vulnerabilities such as SQL injection and cross site scripting. Alafi et al. [3] present a comprehensive survey of models and methods for web application verification and testing. They found that while models were built to analyze static and dynamic properties of the system, none of the surveyed techniques were able to model or check the access control policies of dynamic web applications.

In this paper we use TXL [4], a source transformation tool, to transform previously recovered structural and behavioral models [5, 6, 7, 8] to a role-based access control (RBAC) [9] model. The target model, a SecureUML [10] model

M. Brambilla, T. Tokuda, and R. Tolksdorf (Eds.): ICWE 2012, LNCS 7387, pp. 121–136, 2012.
© Springer-Verlag Berlin Heidelberg 2012

expressed in XMI 2.1, can then be used to check that the desired access control properties are correctly implemented in the code. TXL is a source transformation language originally used at the source code level, but recently shown to be useful in transforming models [11, 12]. Such transformations are applicable to large models, including heterogeneous models that integrate components in a variety of languages. Using source transformation techniques allows us to integrate diverse models, to map platform-independent models to platform-specific ones, and to handle other tasks that involve dealing with multiple meta-models at once.

The key contributions of this paper are:

- An approach and tool to automatically recover security models from dynamic web applications using source transformation technology.
- A demonstration of the approach to recover a role-based security model from a widely used real world web application, PhpBB.

This paper is organized as follows: Section 2 introduces PhpBB as a running example used to demonstrate our technique and explains why it is an appropriate choice. We give an overview of our reverse engineering approach to recovering security models from a dynamic web applications in Section 3. The construction of a SecureUML security model from recovered structural and behavioral models is presented in Section 4. Section 5 highlights the advantages of the transformation-based approach in considering the correctness and completeness of the recovered models. Section 6 reviews related work, and Section 7 concludes the paper and presents directions for future work.

2   Running Example

We demonstrate our technique on PhpBB 2.0 [13], an internet bulletin board system used as a running example throughout the paper. Our focus is on recovering security models from production web applications, whose recovered models are much too large to show in a paper. Hence we show only snippets of the recovered models and concentrate on only three roles to illustrate our approach. In practice our method efficiently recovers complete RBAC models for multiple roles from production dynamic web applications of any size.

Our present implementation, or rather the front end that recovers the structural and behavioral models, is designed to handle web applications built using Apache, PHP and MySQL. Our choice of this combination is based on the popularity and predominance of these technologies on the web [14, 15, 16]. While we have thus far concentrated on these technologies, our overall approach is not technology dependent and can be extended to other choices as well. The security model construction approach of this paper is also not limited to automatically recovered models. It can be used to construct security models from any structural and behavioral models that conform to the meta-models provided in Figure 3, including those crafted by hand or using MDA authoring tools.

3   Overview

Figure 1 shows the general framework of our technique to convert the structural and behavioral models into a SecureUML security model. The work described in this paper is part of a larger toolset to analyze role-based access control which begins with automated recovery of structural and behavioral models described in detail elsewhere [5, 6, 7, 8]. The lower left (SQL2XMI) represents our automated recovery of the structural model (represented by an ER Data Model) from the application's schema source, while the upper left (PHP2XMI, WAFA, DWASTIC) represents the automated recovery of the application's behavioral model (represented by a sequence diagram) using a combination of static and dynamic analysis. In this section we give a brief overview of the reverse engineering of these models, which is described in full in other papers.

The remainder of Figure 1 describes the model transformation process which is the subject of this paper. We begin by building a dictionary of of the entities that will form the core of the security model. We use this dictionary of entities to identify the attributes, relations and constrained events affecting them in the recovered models. These are then mapped to a SecureUML security model, an example of which is shown in Figure 2. This transformation process is presented in detail in Section 4.

The model recovery process begins with a static analysis to recover a structural model of the application resources as they pertain to the user's use of systems, applications and business processes. While UML is considered the standard for application modelling, there is no corresponding open standard for data modeling. SQL2XMI [6] is the technique we use to automatically transform an SQL DDL schema to a UML 2.1 ER diagram. The top part of Figure 3 shows the meta-model for the recovered UML-ER data model representing the structure of the application.

The second part of the model recovery uses a combination of static and dynamic analysis to recover a behavioral model of the application (Figure 3). A set of three tools, PHP2XMI [5], WAFA [8] and DWASTIC [7] is used to recover this model. First, PHP2XMI uses source transformation to instrument the

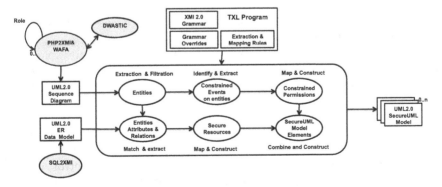

Fig. 1. PHP2SecureUML Framework

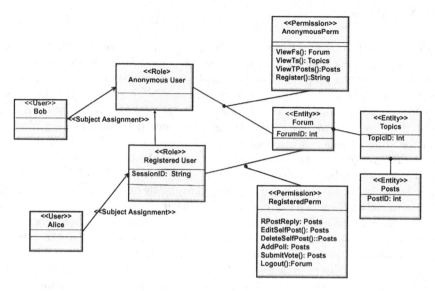

Fig. 2. An example SecureUML model

code and exercises it to recover the permissions associated with each user role, representing the result as a UML sequence diagram.

This sequence diagram is then extended by WAFA, which recovers a fine-grained interaction model from the application. From the point of view of user interaction, the secured resources are represented by lifelines for the web pages delivered by the application. The diagrams operations are used to map the different type of access allowable to the user over the applications secured resources. All aspects of this access are captured as either operations parameters or constraints. These include the accesss type, timestamp, condition, return value, and unique id. The unique id is to identify the accesss relation with the source code and the source page. Message names encode a combination of these values in a single string. The lower part of Figure 3 shows the recovered elements (shaded) based on the UML sequence diagram meta-model. The black dashed line represents the relation between the recovered sequence and ER diagrams, where each entity in the ER diagram (secure resource) is mapped to a class in the sequence diagram represented as a lifeline.

Because our behavioral model recovery uses dynamic analysis to explore the behavior of the application, a measure of completeness for the recovered behavioral model is required. For this purpose, we have developed DWASTIC, a tool that augments the dynamic analysis with additional code coverage instrumentation. DWASTIC uses several coverage criteria specialized for web applications to help ensure that all pages and potential interactions are explored. It provides a direct way to trace those parts of code that are not covered by test cases, and serves as a coverage measure for extraction of the access control security model. The accuracy of the results is both hand verified and robust since it is automatically back-checked at run time.

4   SecureUML Model Construction

In the previous section we briefly outlined how SQL2XMI, WAFA and PHP2XMI help us to recover UML-based structural and behavioral models from web applications, and how DWASTIC provides a measure of coverage. In this work we use the relevant elements of these two recovered models to construct a role-based (RBAC) security model that conforms to the SecureUML [10] meta-model (middle of Figure 3).

SecureUML is an implementation of the Model Driven Security approach, a specialization of Model Driven Architecture. It explicitly integrates security aspects into the application's models and provides support for model transformation. The approach has been proposed to bridge the representation gap between the graphical languages used for specifying application design models,

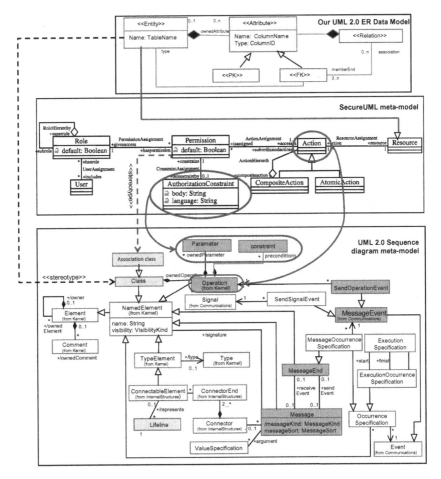

Fig. 3. UML2.0 Structural and behavioral meta-models and their mappings to the SecureUML [10] meta-model

such as UML, and the textual languages used to specify security models. It is built on a modular schema that comprises three basic elements: a language for security policy specification; a language for design model construction; and a dialect for defining integration points in these two languages. The abstract syntax for SecureUML is based on role-based access control (RBAC) [9]. It defines a meta-model that extends RBAC with authorization constraints to enable formal specification of access control policies that depend on dynamic aspects of the system, such as the access date or the values of the system's environment variables. The modeling notation for SecureUML is based on a UML profile that uses UML stereotypes and tagged values to represent the abstract syntax elements in the meta-model schema. Users, groups, and roles are represented as classes with stereotypes ≪ *User* ≫, ≪ *Group* ≫ and ≪ *Role* ≫ respectively, and permission is represented as an association class with a ≪ *Permission* ≫ stereotype.

Figure 2 shows an example of a SecureUML model for a web forum application. The diagram shows two users in different roles who are permitted different sets of actions based on their roles. Bob, who is an anonymous user, is permitted to access the forum entities using read operations. So, Bob can access a forum via *ViewForum()*, read a forums' topics via *ViewTopic()*, read topic posts via *ViewTPosts()*, and can register in a forum. Alice, who is a registered user of the forum, can not only perform all the operations available to Bob but is also permitted write access to the forum. Thus, she can also reply to posts via *RPostReply()*, edit her own posts using *EditSelfPost()*, and so on.

Our work defines a mapping from the recovered structural and behavioral meta-models to the target SecureUML meta-model which forms the basis of our transformation. Figure 3 shows the relationship between the UML-sequence diagram meta-model and our UML 2.0 data meta-model. The *Entity* element in the UML data meta-model corresponds to the *Class* element of the sequence diagram meta-model via a stereotype relationship, represented as a dotted line in the figure. Based on this relationship, the structural information for each entity in the sequence diagram can be pulled from the data model.

We implement this phase as a model transformation encoded as a sequence of source transformations in TXL [4]. Although the model transformation process accepts models as an input and generates models as output, where each of these conforms to a specific meta-model and reflects a particular view of the system, we can implement the transformation process between source and target models as a source-to-source transformation as long as they can be serialized into a text-based format. Fortunately, this can be easily done by most modeling tools, including ArgoUML and RSA, using the XMI export and import facility. While modeling tools often use different versions of XMI, TXL grammars can be adapted to accept and manipulate a range of XMI versions, and can generate multiple versions of the serialized models to match a range of modeling tools.

4.1   Entity Extraction and Filtration

The set of classes (entities) in the sequence diagram is the abstract representation of the diagram's lifelines and maps to the application's secure resources, which include the application server, browser session, and database-backend entities. In this first step these elements are identified and filtered to remove any redundancies, using source transformation.

We have developed a TXL grammar for XMI schemas which enables the manipulation of models that conform to the UML sequence diagram (SD), UML-based ER diagram and SecureUML meta-models. The process accepts as input a serialization of both the SD and ER models, and uses a rooted set of source transformation rules to enable the model's manipulation, integration and transformation to construct the target security model.

The transformation begins by searching for the set of secure resources that are engaged in the interaction behavior modeled by the SD. These elements are represented abstractly as a set of classes, and graphically as a set of lifelines. The corresponding source transformation rule (Figure 5) matches all SD class elements in the XMI representation and filters out any redundant ones. Redundancies can occur due to the fact that multiple secured resources receiving the same set of actions are represented as a single class and modeled using a single lifeline. The names of these resources are combined into a single string which represents the class name. Thus the transformation rule must refactor the combined string to identify the names of the corresponding secure resources.

Figure 4 presents a snippet of a recovered sequence diagram showing the results of the the first step of our approach, the list of entities engaged in the interaction. Some of the entities shown in the diagram snippet are: {*phbbb_forums,*

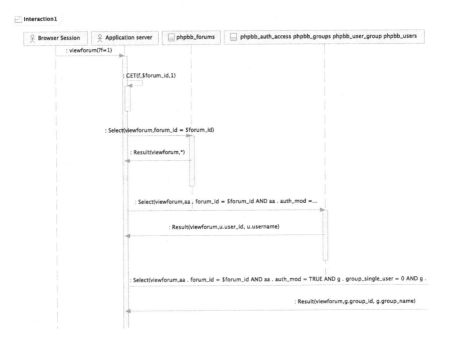

Fig. 4. A snippet of the UML2.0 Entity-level sequence diagram for PhpBB 2.0 generated by WAFA and PHP2XMI

```
% Search for class elements in the sequence diagram
deconstruct PackagedElement
    '< 'packagedElement 'xmi:type = XmiType [stringlit]
        'xmi: 'id =  ClassID [stringlit]
        'name = ClassName [stringlit] '>
        owndOp [repeat XMItoken]
    '</ 'packagedElement '>
where
    XmiType [= "uml:Class"] [= "uml:Actor"]
```

Fig. 5. A small part of the TXL rule to extract class elements from the behavioral model sequence diagram. This pattern matches all Class and Actor elements in the XMI 2.0 representation of the recovered sequence diagram for the web application.

```
% Search the structural model for a matching Entity description
% for the EntityName extracted from the behvioural model
match * [repeat XMItoken]
    '< 'packagedElement 'xmi:type = "uml:Class"
        'xmi: 'id = EntityName 'name '= ClassName [stringlit] '>
        owndAttrib [repeat XMItoken]
    '</ 'packagedElement '>
    More [repeat XMItoken]
% Extract the entity's owned attributes
construct OwnedAttribElements [repeat owned_Attribute]
    _ [^ owndAttrib]
% And its owned attribute relations
construct  OwnedAttribRelElements [repeat owned_AttributeRel]
    _ [^ owndAttrib]
```

Fig. 6. A small part of the TXL rule to extract the attributes and relations associated with each entity from the structural ER data model. This pattern matches the elements in the XMI 2.0 representation of the recovered structural diagram for the web application corresponding to the entities extracted from the behavioral model.

phpbb_auth_access, phpbb_user_group, phpbb_users, Browser Sessions, Application Server}. Note that the set of entities representing the third lifeline has been re-factored into separate entities.

4.2   Entity Attribute and Relation Extraction

Once the set of secure resource elements engaged in interaction behavior has been identified, another source transformation rule is applied to each of the identified elements (Figure 6). This subrule consults the UML ER diagram to search for structural information relevant to those elements, including attributes and relations with other resources.

Conceptually, the transformation rule searches for all class elements with the Entity stereotype in the ER model that matches one of the entities identified in the previous section. It extracts the entities' attribute elements and associations with other entities in the identified set. The result of this phase is an ER diagram of the secure resources engaged in interactions in a particular browsing session.

In our running example, the set of entities extracted in the previous step is used to extract the entities' attributes and relations from the recovered ER diagram of the system, a snippet of which is shown in Figure 7. This step is necessary so that Entities, attributes and relations not relevant to the target

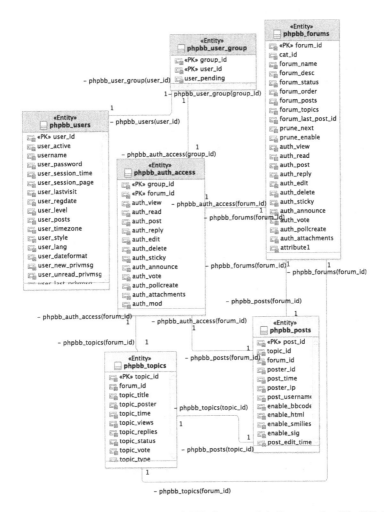

Fig. 7. A snippet of the recovered ER data model diagram for PhpBB 2.0

security model (i.e., not involved in the interactions) are filtered out and not extracted. Thus the {*Topic, Post*} entities, in the ER diagram (Figure 7) and their attributes and relations will not be included in the artifacts used to construct the diagram representing the secure resources.

As an example, some of the attributes and relations extracted by this step for the *phpbb_forums* entity are: {<< *PK* >> *forum_id, cat_id, forum_name*}, and the association attribute between *phpbb_forums* and *phpbb_auth_access*. Note that relations between *phpbb_forums* and *phpbb_ topics, phpbb_posts* are not recovered because they are not part of the interactions described in our example.

4.3   Constrained Event Extraction

The set of permissions allowed on each of the recovered entities (i.e., secure resources) is modeled as the message receive events of the corresponding lifeline. Each recipient event element in the sequence diagram meta-model is represented as an operation which may be associated with parameters and constraints. The next source transformation rule receives as a parameter the set of recovered resources, matches the elements of the serialized sequence diagram, and whenever a class with the same resource name is matched, identifies and extracts the set of all operation elements associated with the class, along with its parameters and constraints (Figure 8).

The rule then constructs the meta-model elements of SecureUML to represent the recovered permissions. Each operation element and its parameters is mapped to a *permission* action, and operation constraints are mapped to *authorization* constraints. The rule constructs an association class to represent the set of recovered operations for each specific resource. The association class is marked as a *permission* stereotype to reflect its security semantics.

For each entity in the resulting secure resources diagram of the previous step, the set of actions, action constraints and other relevant parameters are extracted. For instance, for the *phpbb_forum* entity, these artifacts are:

$Action : Select(allattributes)$.
$Constraint(forum\_id = \$forum\_id)$.
$Timestamp(1247604868)$.
$ActionIdInCode(viewForum, 366)$.

where *viewForum* is the page name and 366 the operation ID in the source code.

```
% Identify and extract operation elements corresponding to
% extracted secure resources
  deconstruct ownedOp
    '<'ownedRule 'xmi:type '= "uml:Constraint"
        'xmi:id '= ConsID [attvalue]
        'name '= AcName [attvalue]
        'constrainedElement '= ConstElm [attvalue] '>
    <'specification 'xmi:type '= "uml:OpaqueExpression"
        'xmi:id '= ConsExprID [attvalue]
        'name '= ConsExprName [attvalue] '/'>
    '</'ownedRule'>
    ownedOp2 [repeat XMItoken]
```

Fig. 8. A small part of the TXL rule to extract operation elements corresponding to identified resources from the recovered behavioral model sequence diagram. This pattern matches ownedRule elements in the XMI 2.0 representation of the recovered sequence diagram corresponding to each secure resource identified in the previous step.

4.4   SecureUML Model Element Construction

The previous steps have identified all the security elements necessary to construct the RBAC security model. In this step, we construct a security model that conforms to the SecureUML meta-model shown in Figure 3. A set of transformation rules is used to construct the security model, in which the extracted sequence

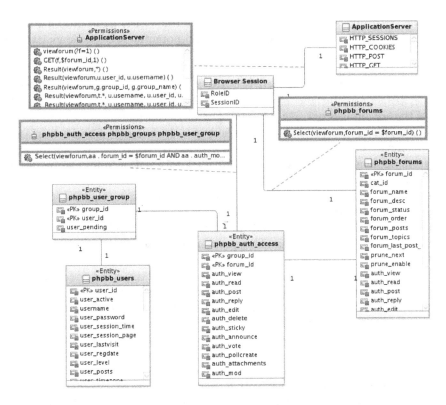

Fig. 9. An example generated SecureUML model instance for PhpBB 2.0

diagram's operations are mapped into permissions, operation constraints into authorization constraints, and the entities of the ER data model into resources.

In the SecureUML notation, the representation of resources is left open, so that developers can decide later which elements of the system they consider secure and to which they want to apply access constraints. These elements are defined using a dialect. In section 4.2, we identified the secure resources and represented them as an ER diagram. In section 4.3, we recovered the permission-action pairs and authorization constraints, and represented them as an association class with parameters and preconditions. Using a final TXL transformation rule, two association links are created: one that connects the association class, stereotyped by permissions, with the entity (resource) affected by the permission's actions; and a second that connects the acting role with the constructed association class.

In our running example, Figure 1 shows snippets of the resulting SecureUML model. For instance, an association class with name *phpbb_forum* is constructed with permission stereotype and attached to the entity *forum*, and the *browser session* entity represents the user role accessing the forum. The final result is a complete SecureUML model of the web application which can be checked for security properties using a standard model checker or custom analysis. In our

case, the resulting SecureUML model is transformed once again into a Prolog
formal model checked using Prolog rules to find potential access role violations.

5 Correctness and Completeness of the Recovered Model

One of the advantages of using a formal source transformation system for deriving and exploring security models from source code is that it is easier to reason
about completeness and correctness of the tools. By contrast with hand-coded
analyzers implemented in Java or C, source transformation rules can be tested
and verified piecewise.

Because source transformations are based on parsing technology, the well-
formedness of the results is guaranteed. TXL transformation rules are simply
incapable of producing a result that does not conform to the syntactic forms of
the target grammar/metamodel. The question of the semantic soundness of the
constructed security model is also made simpler using a source transformation
technique. Rather than having to reason about an entire hand-coded analysis
program all at once, each TXL source transformation rule can be considered
independently of the others. Whether the entire transformation is correct then
becomes just a question of whether the set of rules forms a complete transformation, which can be checked separately. In our system this question is addressed by
separating the process into a sequence of separate source transformation steps.
Because each step yields a concrete intermediate text file representation that the
next step parses as input, erroneous or incomplete results of a step are typically
caught immediately by the next step. For example, if the data model extracted
from the web application's schema is missing anything, there will be unresolved
links when integrating the models that will make this fact immediately evident
in the next transformation step.

Using source transformation rules to analyze the schema, source code and
behavioral models also assists in guaranteeing completeness. For example, the
TXL parser syntactically identifies all references to the SQL database in the
source code, and the transformation rule for analyzing them simply transforms
them to an instrumented form. The question of whether we have missed any
database interactions in the extracted model is therefore easy to evaluate, simply
by counting the number of SQL interactions in the model and comparing it to the
number identified by the parser in the source. Dynamic behavioral completeness
is handled by including coverage counters in the instrumentation, implemented
using the DWASTIC tool discussed in section 3.

Our approach has been validated in a case study to extract RBAC security
models from PhpBB 2.0. Table 1 presents some statistics on the size of the
recovered models for two roles: anonymous (guest) user and registered user.
The table presents results in terms of the number of resulting model elements as
described in Section 2. These results are based on an ER diagram consisting of 30
entities, 370 attributes, and 55 relations, and a sequence diagram with a partial
behavioural coverage of 50% of PhpBB 2.0 by page access and an average of %20
by back end access (to database and server environment variables). Even with

Table 1. Sizes of recovered SecureUML models for the anonymous and registered user roles in PhpBB 2.0

Anonymous (Guest User) Role						
Entities	Attributes	Relations	Operations	Permissions	Constraints	Parameters
12	191	36	321	14	1465	9567

Registered User Role						
Entities	Attributes	Relations	Operations	Permissions	Constraints	Parameters
15	249	62	59294	24	28304	177627

this relatively low percentage of coverage we can notice the variation in the size of the recovered SecureUML models, specifically for the number of operations, constraints and parameters, which reflects the fact that registered users have significantly more access than guest users.

A more detailed evaluation of the recovered models will be presented in [17], where the resulting models are transformed into a formal Prolog model and checked for security properties. We are also working on validating the approach using a larger case study, recovering RBAC security models for the educational support web application *Moodle*.

6   Related Work

Most of the early literature on web application security concentrates on the process of modeling the design of the web applications. It proposes forward engineering-based methods designed to simplify the process of building highly interactive web applications [18, 19, 20, 21]. Other research uses reverse engineering methods to extract models from existing web applications in order to support their maintenance and evolution [22, 23, 24], However, few approaches recover security models from web applications, and in particular access control security models. In Alalfi et al. [3] we survey the state of the art in these techniques.

The most relevant related approach in this domain is the Letarte and Merlo approach [25] which uses static analysis to extract a simple role model from PHP code, and more specifically from database statements. Changes in authorization level in the code are modeled using an inter-procedural control flow graph with three kinds of edges: positive-authorization (change to admin), negative-authorization (change to user), and generic (no change in security level). A predefined authorization pattern is used to identify transfer of control in the code and changes in authorization level in the extracted model. Unlike our approach, the Letarte and Merlo approach simplifies to only two roles (admin vs. user) for which access may or may not be granted to database statements. The model is based on an application-dependent authorization pattern and does not provide any link back to the source code.

Other approaches have been proposed to recover models and/or check for access control properties for domains other than web applications, with a focus on Java based applications. Koved et al. [26] use context sensitive data and control flow analysis to construct an Access Right Invocation graph, which represents the authorization model of the code. This enables identification of classes in each path that contain a call to the Java 2 security authorization subsystems. The approach is used to automatically compute the access rights requirements at each program point in mobile Java applications such as applets and servlets.

Pistoia et al. [2] statically construct a call graph to represent the flow of authorization in an application by over-approximating method calls and identifying access-restricted methods. The graph is used as the basis of several security analyses, including detecting if the application's RBAC security policy is restrictive or permissive. The authors generate reports on code locations that have inconsistencies and suggest a replacement policy to eliminate the vulnerabilities. The approach is implemented as a part of IBM's Enterprise Security Policy Evaluator and has been evaluated on a number of Java EE applications.

Mendling et al. [27] propose a meta-model integration approach to enhance the security features of Business Process Management Systems that operate using Web Services (BPEL). The meta-model elements of web services' BPEL are mapped to RBAC elements. Roles and partners in BPEL, which represent the sets of operations that are carried out during a business process, are mapped into RBAC roles. Activities, which provide a channel for an external party to send a message to a BPEL, are mapped into RBAC permissions. The authors develop an XSTL transformation script to extract an XML description of roles and permissions from a BPEL process definition which enables the definition and enforcement of RBAC polices and constraints.

There has been only a little work on UML-based security modeling [28, 29, 30, 31] . The focus of UMLsec [28] is on modeling security issues such as data confidentiality and integrity. Basin et al. propose Model Driven Security (MDS) and its tool SecureUML [30] to integrate security models into system models. The authors first specify a secure modeling language for modeling access control requirements and embed it as an extension of UML Class diagrams. The authors of authUML [29] take a step back and focus on analyzing access control requirements before proceeding to the design modeling to ensure consistent, conflict-free and complete requirements.

The Ahn and Hu method [31] differs from the above approaches in using standard UML to represent access control features of the security model. They provide policy validation based on Object constraint Language (OCL) and a role-based constraint language (RCL2000) [32], and then translate the security model to enforcement code. These efforts are forward engineering approaches, while the real need is for a reverse engineering approach that recovers and analyzes access control polices in existing applications. This is the focus of our work.

7   Conclusions and Future Work

In this paper we have presented an approach and a tool, PHP2SecureUML, to recover a role-based access control (RBAC) security model from automatically recovered structural and behavioral models of dynamic web applications. We use source transformation technology to implement the model-to-model transformation and composition. The resulting model can be used to check for RBAC security properties in the application under test. We demonstrated our approach on recovering RBAC security models for a medium-sized production web application, PhpBB 2.0. In our current work we are using the generated models to support web application security analysis, testing, maintenance and reengineering, using PhpBB 2.0 as an example, and we have recently begun a similar study of role-base security in the popular production educational support system Moodle. We are also planning to conduct a large scale evaluation to better test the effectiveness of our method, and to extend and adapt our approach to address other security analysis tasks.

References

[1] Project, O.W.A.S.: The Top Ten Most Critical Web Application Security Vulnerabilities, `https://www.owasp.org/index.php/Category:OWASP_Top_Ten_Project` (last access November 26, 2011)

[2] Pistoia, M., Flynn, R.J., Koved, L., Sreedhar, V.C.: Interprocedural Analysis for Privileged Code Placement and Tainted Variable Detection. In: Gao, X.-X. (ed.) ECOOP 2005. LNCS, vol. 3586, pp. 362–386. Springer, Heidelberg (2005)

[3] Alalfi, M., Cordy, J., Dean, T.: Modeling methods for web application verification and testing: State of the art. Softw. Test. Verif. Reliab. 19, 265–296 (2009)

[4] Cordy, J.R.: The TXL source transformation language. Science of Computer Programming 61, 190–210 (2006)

[5] Alalfi, M.H., Cordy, J.R., Dean, T.R.: Automated Reverse Engineering of UML Sequence Diagrams for Dynamic Web Applications. In: ICSTW, pp. 295–302 (2009)

[6] Alalfi, M.H., Cordy, J.R., Dean, T.R.: SQL2XMI: Reverse Engineering of UML-ER Diagrams from Relational Database Schemas. In: WCRE, pp. 187–191 (2008)

[7] Alalfi, M.H., Cordy, J.R., Dean, T.R.: Automating Coverage Metrics for Dynamic Web Applications. In: CSMR, pp. 51–60 (2010)

[8] Alalfi, M.H., Cordy, J.R., Dean, T.R.: WAFA: Fine-grained Dynamic Analysis of Web Applications. In: WSE, pp. 41–50 (2009)

[9] Sandhu, R., Coyne, E., Feinstein, H., Youman, C.: Role-based Access Control Models. IEEE Computer 29, 38–47 (1996)

[10] Basin, D.A.: Model Driven Security. In: ARES, p. 4 (2006)

[11] Paige, R., Radjenovic, A.: Towards Model Transformation with TXL. In: First Intl. Workshop on Metamodeling for MDA, pp. 163–177 (2003)

[12] Liang, H., Dingel, J.: A Practical Evaluation of Using TXL for Model Transformation. In: Gašević, D., Lämmel, R., Van Wyk, E. (eds.) SLE 2008. LNCS, vol. 5452, pp. 245–264. Springer, Heidelberg (2009)

[13] phpBB Group: PhpBB, `http://www.phpbb.com/` (last access November 27, 2011)

[14] Netcraft Ltd: web server survey (November 2011), `http://news.netcraft.com/archives/2011/01/12/january-2011-web-server-survey-4.html` (last access November 26, 2011)

[15] PHP Group: PHP usage Stats for (April 2007), `http://www.php.net/usage.php` (last access November 26, 2011)

[16] MySQL: MySQL Market Share, `http://www.mysql.com/why-mysql/marketshare/` (last access November 26, 2011)

[17] Alalfi, M., Cordy, J., Dean, T.: Automated Testing of Role-based Security Models Recovered from Dynamic Web Applications. In: WSE (2012) (submitted)

[18] Garzotto, F., Paolini, P., Schwabe, D.: HDM - A Model-Based Approach to Hypertext Application Design. ACM Trans. Inf. Syst. 11, 1–26 (1993)

[19] Schwabe, D., Rossi, G.: An object oriented approach to Web-based applications design. Theor. Pract. Object Syst. 4, 207–225 (1998)

[20] De Troyer, O., Leune, C.J.: WSDM: A User Centered Design Method for Web Sites. Computer Networks 30, 85–94 (1998)

[21] Ceri, S., Fraternali, P., Bongio, A.: Web Modeling Language (WebML): a modeling language for designing Web sites. In: WWW, pp. 137–157 (2000)

[22] Hassan, A.E., Holt, R.C.: Architecture recovery of web applications. In: ICSE, pp. 349–359 (2002)

[23] Antoniol, G., Penta, M.D., Zazzara, M.: Understanding Web Applications through Dynamic Analysis. In: IWPC, pp. 120–131 (2004)

[24] Di Lucca, G.A., Di Penta, M.: Integrating Static and Dynamic Analysis to improve the Comprehension of Existing Web Applications. In: WSE, pp. 87–94 (2005)

[25] Letarte, D., Merlo, E.: Extraction of Inter-procedural Simple Role Privilege Models from PHP Code. In: WCRE, pp. 187–191 (2009)

[26] Koved, L., Pistoia, M., Kershenbaum, A.: Access rights analysis for Java. In: OOPSLA, pp. 359–372 (2002)

[27] Mendling, J., Strembeck, M., Stermsek, G., Neumann, G.: An Approach to Extract RBAC Models from BPEL4WS Processes. In: WETICE, pp. 81–86 (2004)

[28] Jackson, D.: Software Abstractions: Logic, Language, and Analysis. MIT Press, Cambridge (2006)

[29] Alghathbar, K., Wijesekera, D.: authUML: a three-phased framework to analyze access control specifications in use cases. In: FMSE, pp. 77–86 (2003)

[30] Basin, D.A., Clavel, M., Egea, M.: A decade of model-driven security. In: SAC-MAT, pp. 1–10 (2011)

[31] Ahn, G.J., Hu, H.: Towards realizing a formal RBAC model in real systems. In: SACMAT, pp. 215–224 (2007)

[32] Ahn, G.J., Sandhu, R.S.: Role-based authorization constraints specification. ACM Trans. Inf. Syst. Secur. 3, 207–226 (2000)

Diversification for Multi-domain Result Sets

Alessandro Bozzon, Marco Brambilla, Piero Fraternali, and Marco Tagliasacchi

Politecnico di Milano, Piazza Leonardo Da Vinci, 32 - 20133 Milano, Italy
{bozzon,mbrambil,fraterna,tagliasa}@elet.polimi.it

Abstract. Multi-domain search answers to queries spanning multiple
entities, like "Find a hotel in Milan close to a concert venue, a museum
and a good restaurant", by producing ranked sets of entity combinations
that maximize relevance, measured by a function expressing the user's
preferences. Due to the combinatorial nature of results, good entity instances (e.g., five stars hotels) tend to appear repeatedly in top-ranked
combinations. To improve the quality of the result set, it is important
to balance relevance with diversity, which promotes different, yet almost
equally relevant, entities in the top-k combinations. This paper explores
two different notions of diversity for multi-domain result sets, compares
experimentally alternative algorithms for the trade-off between relevance
and diversity, and performs a user study for evaluating the utility of diversification in multi-domain queries.

1 Introduction

Multi-domain search tries to respond to queries that involve multiple correlated
concepts, like *"Find an affordable house in a city with low criminality index,
good schools and medical services"* . Multi-domain search has the potential of
bridging the gap between general purpose search engines, which are able to
retrieve instances of at most one entity at a time (e.g., cities, products), and
vertical search applications in specific domains (e.g., trip planning, real estate),
which can correlate only a fixed set of information sources. Formally, multi-
domain queries can be represented as rank-join queries over a set of relations,
representing the wrapped data sources [11][14]. Each item in the result set is
a combination of objects that satisfy the join and selection conditions, and the
result set is ranked according to a scoring function, which can be expressed as
a combination of local relevance criteria formulated on objects or associations
(e.g., price or rating for a hotel, distance between the conference venue, hotel,
and restaurant). Due to the combinatorial nature of multi-domain search, the
number of combinations in the result set is normally very high, and strongly
relevant objects tend to combine repeatedly with many other concepts, requiring
the user to scroll down the list of results deeply to see alternative, maybe only
slightly less relevant, objects.

As a running example, consider a multi-domain search scenarios where three
data sources are wrapped by the following relations: *Hotel*(HName, HLoc, HRating,
HPrice), *Restaurant*(RName, RLoc, RRating, RPrice), *Museum*(MName, MLoc,
MRating, MPrice).

M. Brambilla, T. Tokuda, and R. Tolksdorf (Eds.): ICWE 2012, LNCS 7387, pp. 137–152, 2012.

Table 1. Top-K result set based on relevance

	Hotel		Restaurant		Museum		$S^{(a)}(\tau, q)$
	HName	HPrice	RName	RPrice	MName	MPrice	Total price
τ_1	Hotel Amadeus	€35	Miyako	€25	Galleria d'Arte Moderna	€0	€60
τ_2	Hotel Amadeus	€35	Miyako	€25	Museo Civico di Milano	€0	€60
τ_3	Hotel Amadeus	€35	Miyako	€25	Museo di Storia Contemp.	€0	€60
τ_4	Hotel Amadeus	€35	Porca Vacca	€25	Galleria d'Arte Moderna	€0	€60
τ_5	Hotel Amadeus	€35	Porca Vacca	€25	Museo Civico di Milano	€0	€60
τ_6	Hotel Amadeus	€35	Porca Vacca	€25	Orto Botanico di Brera	€0	€60
τ_7	Hotel Amadeus	€35	Spontini 6	€25	Galleria d'Arte Moderna	€0	€60
τ_8	Hotel Amadeus	€35	Spontini 6	€25	Museo Civico di Milano	€0	€60
τ_9	Hotel Amadeus	€35	Spontini 6	€25	Orto Botanico di Brera	€0	€60
τ_{10}	Hotel Amadeus	€35	Spontini 6	€25	Museo di Storia Contemp.	€0	€60

A query issued with a mobile phone aims at finding combinations within a short distance from the user location and good ratings, to be returned in order of total price. If we suppose to find 100 hotels and restaurants and 20 events, and assume a 10% selectivity of the join and selection condition on distance and minimum rating, a total number of 20000 combinations can be used to build the top-K result set. Supposing to show only 10 combina-

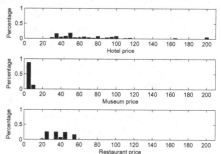

Fig. 1. Score distribution of Table 1 result set

tions disregarding the relevance of the constituent objects, up to 30 distinct objects out of 220 can be presented (14%). However, in real situations, the composition of the top-K results also depends on relevance, which decreases diversity.

For illustration, Table 1 shows a result set, which contains the top-10 combinations ranked according to total price. We observe that the result is rather poor in terms of diversity, as only 1 hotel, 3 restaurants and 4 museums are represented. Indeed, the number of distinct objects that appear in the top-K results is sensitive to the distribution of attribute values used to compute the score of the combination. In our case, the price range of good-rated hotels is larger than the price ranges of restaurants and events, as illustrated in Figure 1. Hence, budget hotels will appear repeatedly in the top-K list, lowering the number of distinct objects seen by the user. The same observation applies when, fixed an hotel, one considers the price range of restaurants compared to the price range of museums. This empirical observation is supported by Theorem 1 discussed later in this paper.

Improving the diversity of the result set is the aim of *diversification*, which can be defined in the context of multi-domain search as the selection of K elements out of a universe of N combinations, so to maximize a quality criterion that combines the *relevance* and the *diversity* of the objects of distinct types seen by the user. In this respect, Table 2 shows an example of result set with diversified combinations. We observe that the set does not necessarily contain the top-10

Table 2. Top-K result set based on relevance and diversity

	Hotel		Restaurant		Museum		$S^{(a)}(\tau,q)$
	HName	HPrice	RName	RPrice	MName	MPrice	Total price
τ_1	Hotel Amadeus	€35	Miyako	€25	Galleria d'Arte Moderna	€0	€60
τ_2	Hotel Amadeus	€35	Porca Vacca	€25	Museo di Storia Contemp.	€0	€60
τ_3	Hotel Amadeus	€35	Miyako	€25	Orto Botanico di Brera	€0	€60
τ_4	Hotel Nazioni	€36	Miyako	€25	Galleria d'Arte Moderna	€0	€61
τ_5	Hotel Nazioni	€36	The Dhaba	€25	Orto Botanico di Brera	€0	€61
τ_6	Hotel Nazioni	€36	Spontini 6	€25	Pad. d'Arte Contemp.	€2	€63
τ_7	Hotel Zefiro	€39	Matto Bacco	€25	Galleria d'Arte Moderna	€0	€64
τ_8	Hotel Zefiro	€39	Porca Vacca	€25	Museo Civico di Milano	€0	€64
τ_9	Hotel Nazioni	€36	Porca Vacca	€25	Museo della Perma.	€6	€67
τ_{10}	Hotel Zefiro	€39	Miyako	€25	Museo di Storia Naturale	€3	€67

combinations in terms of total price. Nevertheless, the result is much richer: 3 hotels, 5 restaurants and 7 museums are selected.

The contributions of the paper can be summarized as follows: (**a**) We discuss the problem of diversification in the context of multi-domain search, an area made quite interesting by the increasing availability of public "joinable" Web data sources. (**b**) We formalize multi-domain diversification and propose two criteria for comparing combinations (*categorical* and *quantitative* diversity). (**c**) Result diversification is NP-hard also in the multi-domain context; we therefore experimentally study the behavior of three known greedy algorithms, testing the hypothesis that the diversification algorithms improve the quality of the result set with respect to a baseline constituted by the selection of the most relevant K combinations. (**d**) We formally analyze under which conditions diversification can be potentially effective in improving the quality of the results. In particular, we consider the impact of the score distributions on the diversity of the result set which includes the top-K combinations based on relevance only. (**e**) We evaluate the perception and utility of diversification in multi-domain search with a user study that focuses on explicit comparison of result sets diversified according to different algorithms.

The organization of the paper is as follows: Section 2 presents the formalization of the problem and introduces different diversity measures for combinations; Section 3 illustrates the results of the experimental activity; Section 4 discusses previous work; Section 5 concludes and discusses future work.

2   Multi-domain Diversification

Consider a set of relations $R_1, R_2, \ldots, R_n$, where each R_i denotes the result set returned by invoking a search service σ_i over a Web data source. Each tuple $t_i \in R_i = < a_i^1, a_i^2, \ldots, a_i^{m_i} >$ has schema $R_i(\mathtt{A}_i^1 : \mathtt{D}_i^1, \ldots, \mathtt{A}_i^{m_i} : \mathtt{D}_i^{m_i})$, where $\mathtt{A}_i^{m_i}$ is an attribute of relation R_i and $\mathtt{D}_i^{m_i}$ is the associated domain. As usual in measurement theory, we distinguish the domains $\mathtt{D}_i^k$ into *categorical*, when values admit only equality test, and *quantitative*, when values can be organized in vectors embedded in a metric space.

A multi-domain query over the search services $\sigma_1, \ldots \sigma_n$ is defined as a join query $q = R_1 \bowtie \ldots \bowtie R_n$ over the relations $R_1, \ldots, R_n$, where the join predicate can be arbitrary. We call *combination* an element of the join $\tau = t_1 \bowtie \cdots \bowtie t_n =< a_1^1, a_1^2, \ldots, a_1^{m_1}, \ldots, a_n^1, a_n^2, \ldots, a_n^{m_n} >$, and *result set* $\mathcal{R}$ the set of combinations satisfying the query q.

2.1 Relevance

The goal of multi-domain search is to support the user in selecting one or more combinations from the result set of a multi-domain query, so to maximize the satisfaction of his information seeking task. To this end, combinations can be presented in order of relevance. The relevance of a combination with respect to the query q can be expressed quantitatively by means of a user-defined (possibly non-monotone) *relevance score function* $S(\tau, q)$, which can be assumed to be normalized in the $[0, 1]$ range, where 1 indicates the highest relevance. When the result set $\mathcal{R}$ is sorted, e.g. in descending order of relevance, τ_k indicates the k-th combination of $\mathcal{R}$.

Example 1. With respect to the relations introduced in Section 1, consider a function *city()*, which returns the city where the geographical coordinates of a location belong to, and the multi-domain query $q =$ select * from *Hotel, Restaurant, Museum* where *city*(HLoc) $=$ Milan $\wedge$ *city*(RLoc) $=$ *city*(HLoc) $\wedge$ *city*(MLoc) $=$ *city*(HLoc). The following relevance score functions could be used to rank hotel, restaurant and museum triples: **(a)** The overall price of the combination: $S^{(a)}(\tau, q) = sum($HPrice$[t_h],$ RPrice$[t_r],$ MPrice$[t_m])$. **(b)** The average rating for the hotel and the restaurant, $S^{(b)}(\tau, q) = avg($HRating$[t_h],$ RRating$[t_r])$. **(c)** The distance of the shortest path that connects the hotel, the restaurant and the museum: $S^{(c)}(\tau, q) = f_{distance}($HLoc$[t_h],$ RLoc$[t_r],$ MLoc$[t_m])$.

Note that $S^{(a)}$ and $S^{(b)}$ are simple linear (thus monotone) functions based solely on a subset of the attribute values of the constituent tuples, whereas $S^{(c)}$ uses a more complex function, not necessarily monotone, that might incorporate external knowledge (e.g. road maps).

2.2 Diversity

An implicit goal of multi-domain search is to present to the user a set of combinations that expresses a good coverage of the population of the constituent entities. Coverage can be improved by avoiding in the result set combinations that are too similar, according to some definition of similarity. Two different criteria can be employed to express the similarity (or symmetrically, the diversity) of combinations: **(a)** *Categorical diversity*: two combinations are compared based on the equality of the values of one or more categorical attributes of the tuples that constitute them. As a special case, categorical diversity can be based on the key attributes: this means evaluating if an object (or sub-combination of objects) is repeated in the two combinations. **(b)** *Quantitative diversity*: the diversity of two combinations is defined as their distance, expressed by some metric function.

In both cases, for each pair of combinations τ_u and τ_v, it is possible to define a diversity measure $\delta : \mathcal{R} \times \mathcal{R} \rightarrow [0,1]$, normalized in the $[0,1]$ interval, where 0 indicates maximum similarity.

Definition 1. *Let* $A_i^{j_i,1}, \ldots, A_i^{j_i,d_i}$ *be a subset of* d_i *attributes of relation* R_i *and* $\mathbf{v}_i(\tau) = [a_i^{j_i,1}, \ldots, a_i^{j_i,d_i}]^T$ *the projection of a combination* τ *on such attributes. Categorical diversity is defined as follows:*

$$\delta(\tau_u, \tau_v) = 1 - \frac{1}{n} \sum_{i=1}^{n} \mathbb{1}_{\mathbf{v}_i(\tau_u) = \mathbf{v}_i(\tau_v)} \tag{1}$$

where n *is the number of relations* R_i *and* $\mathbb{1}$ *is the indicator function, returning one when the predicate is satisfied.*

Intuitively, categorical diversity is the percentage of tuples in two combinations that do not coincide on the attributes $A_i^{j_i,1}, \ldots, A_i^{j_i,d_i}$. When these attributes are the key, categorical diversity can be interpreted as the percentage of objects that appear only in one of the two combinations.

Definition 2. *Let* $\mathbf{v}_i(\tau)$ *be as in Definition 1. Let* $\mathbf{v}(\tau) = [\mathbf{v}_1(\tau), \ldots, \mathbf{v}_n(\tau)]^T = [v_1(\tau), \ldots, v_d(\tau)]^T$ *denote the concatenation of length* $d = d_1 + \ldots + d_n$ *of such vectors. Given* d *user-defined weights* $w_1 \ldots, w_d$ *and a normalization constant* δ_{max}, *quantitative diversity is defined as:*

$$\delta(\tau_u, \tau_v) = \frac{1}{\delta_{max}} \sqrt[p]{\sum_{l=1}^{d} w_l |v_l(\tau_u) - v_l(\tau_v)|^p} \tag{2}$$

Quantitative diversity between combinations τ_u, τ_v is formalized as the (weighted) l_p-norm of the difference between the vectors $\mathbf{v}(\tau_u)$ and $\mathbf{v}(\tau_v)$. The normalization constant can be chosen, e.g., as the maximum distance value between pairs of combinations in the result set.

Example 2. A categorical diversity function can be computed by defining $\mathbf{v}_h(\tau) = [\text{HName}(\tau)]$, $\mathbf{v}_r(\tau) = [\text{RName}(\tau)]$ and $\mathbf{v}_m(\tau) = [\text{MName}(\tau)]$. As an example, consider the combinations of Table 2. Then, $\delta(\tau_1, \tau_2) = 2/3$, $\delta(\tau_1, \tau_3) = 1/3$ and $\delta(\tau_1, \tau_6) = 1$.

A quantitative diversity function based on the hotel, restaurant and museum rating attributes can be defined as follows: let $p = 1$, $w_l = 1$, and $\mathbf{v}_1(\tau) = [\text{HRating}(\tau)]$, $\mathbf{v}_2(\tau) = [\text{RRating}(\tau)]$ and $\mathbf{v}_3(\tau) = [\text{MRating}(\tau)]$. As an example, consider the combinations of Table 2. Then, $\mathbf{v}(\tau_1) = [35, 25, 0]$, $\mathbf{v}(\tau_3) = [36, 25, 0]$ and $\mathbf{v}(\tau_6) = [36, 25, 2]$. Then $\delta(\tau_1, \tau_3) = 1/\delta_{\max}$, $\delta(\tau_1, \tau_6) = 3/\delta_{\max}$ and $\delta(\tau_3, \tau_6) = 2/\delta_{\max}$.

2.3   Computing Relevant and Diverse Combinations

Based on the notion of diversity, it is possible to address the problem of extracting from the result set of a multi-domain query the top-K most relevant and diverse combinations. Let $N = |\mathcal{R}|$ denote the number of combinations in the result set and $\mathcal{R}_K \subseteq \mathcal{R}$ the subset of combinations that are presented to the user, where $K = |\mathcal{R}_K|$. We are interested in identifying a subset $\mathcal{R}_K$ which is both *relevant* and *diverse*. Fixing the relevance score $S(\cdot, q)$, the dissimilarity function $\delta(\cdot, \cdot)$, and a given integer K, we aim at selecting a set $\mathcal{R}_K \subseteq \mathcal{R}$ of combinations, which is the solution of the following optimization problem [8]:

$$\mathcal{R}_K^* = \operatorname*{argmax}_{\mathcal{R}_K \subseteq \mathcal{R}, |\mathcal{R}_K| = K} F(\mathcal{R}_K, S(\cdot, q), \delta(\cdot, \cdot)) \tag{3}$$

where $F(\cdot)$ is an objective function that takes into account both relevance and diversity. Two commonly used objective functions are MaxSum (Equation 4) and MaxMin (Equation 5), as defined in [8]

$$F(\mathcal{R}_K) = (K - 1) \sum_{\tau \in \mathcal{R}_K} S(\tau, q) + 2\lambda \sum_{\tau_u, \tau_v \in \mathcal{R}_K} \delta(\tau_u, \tau_v) \tag{4}$$

$$F(\mathcal{R}_K) = \min_{\tau \in \mathcal{R}_K} S(\tau, q) + \lambda \min_{\tau_u, \tau_v \in \mathcal{R}_K} \delta(\tau_u, \tau_v) \tag{5}$$

where $\lambda > 0$ is a parameter specifying the trade-off between relevance and diversity.

Solving problem (3) when the objective function is given in (4) or (5) is NP-hard, as it can be reduced to the minimum k-center problem [9]. Nevertheless, greedy algorithms exist [8], which give a 2-approximation solution in polynomial time. Algorithm 1 and Algorithm 2 give, respectively, the greedy algorithms for MaxSum and MaxMin. In both cases the underlying idea is to create an auxiliary function $\delta'(\cdot, \cdot)$ and iteratively construct the solution by incrementally adding combinations in such a way as to locally maximize the given objective function.

Algorithm 1. Greedy algorithm for MaxSum.

Input : Set of combinations $\mathcal{R}$, K
Output: Selected combinations $\mathcal{R}_K$

1 **begin**
2 | Define $\delta'(\tau_u, \tau_v) = S(\tau_u, q) + S(\tau_v, q) + 2\lambda\delta(\tau_u, \tau_v)$
3 | Initialize the set $\mathcal{R}_K = \emptyset$, $U = \mathcal{R}$
4 | **for** $c = 1 : \lfloor K/2 \rfloor$ **do**
5 | | Find $(\tau_u, \tau_v) = \operatorname*{argmax}_{x, y \in U} \delta'(x, y)$ Set $\mathcal{R}_K = \mathcal{R}_K \cup \{\tau_u, \tau_v\}$ Set $U = U \setminus \{\tau_u, \tau_v\}$
6 | **end**
7 | If K is odd, add an arbitrary combination to $\mathcal{R}_K$
8 **end**

Another objective function, closely related to the aforementioned ones, is *Maximal Marginal Relevance* (MMR), initially proposed in [1]. Indeed, MMR implicitly maximizes an hybrid objective function whereby relevance scores are summed together, while the minimum distance between pairs of objects is controlled.

The algorithm originally proposed in [1] is identical to Algorithm 2, where line 6 is replaced by

$$\tau^* = \operatorname*{argmax}_{\tau \in \mathcal{R} n \mathcal{R}_K} \left\{ S(\tau, q) + \lambda \min_{x \in \mathcal{R}_K} \delta(\tau, x) \right\} \qquad (6)$$

and at line 4 the set $\mathcal{R}_K$ is initialized with the most relevant combination.

Algorithm 2. Greedy algorithm for `MaxMin`.

Input   : Set of combinations $\mathcal{R}$, K
Output: Selected combinations $\mathcal{R}_K$

1 **begin**
2   Define $\delta'(\tau_u, \tau_v) = \frac{1}{2}\left(S(\tau_u, q) + S(\tau_v, q)\right) + \lambda\delta(\tau_u, \tau_v)$
3   Initialize the set $\mathcal{R}_K = \emptyset$
4   Find $(\tau_u, \tau_v) = \operatorname*{argmax}_{x,y \in \mathcal{R}} \delta'(x, y)$ and set $\mathcal{R}_K = \{\tau_u, \tau_v\}$
5   **while** $|\mathcal{R}_K| < K$ **do**
6           $\tau^* = \operatorname*{argmax}_{\tau \in \mathcal{R} \backslash \mathcal{R}_K} \min_{x \in \mathcal{R}_K} \delta'(\tau, x)$
7   Set $\mathcal{R}_K = \mathcal{R}_K \cup \{\tau^*\}$
8   **end**
9 **end**

Note that for $\lambda = 0$ all algorithms return a result set which consists of the top-K combinations with the highest score, thus neglecting diversity.

2.4   When Diversification Helps

The score function and the diversity function both work on the attribute values of tuples. The question arises about the circumstances in which the ranking function alone would already guarantee a sufficiently varied result set, thus lowering the utility of diversification. The intuition is that when the attributes used in the ranking function have values distributed with comparable variance in the input relations, then the relevance score performs better at sampling the population than when attribute values are distributed with large variance differences. The following result formalizes this intuition and provides a guideline for deciding if diversification is needed. For simplicity, we consider two relations R_1 and R_2, with a population of N_1 and N_2 tuples, respectively.

Theorem 1. *Given a positive integer $K \in \mathbb{N}^+$, a score function $S(\tau, q) = w_1 s_1(t_1) + w_2 s_2(t_2)$, a set $\mathcal{R}_K$ that contains the K combinations with the highest score $S(\tau, q)$. Let $D_1(K)$ (resp. $D_2(K)$) be the expected number of distinct tuples of relation R_1 (resp. R_2) represented in $\mathcal{R}_K$. If the values of the score functions $s_1(), s_2()$ are uniformly distributed in intervals of width Δ_1 (resp. Δ_2), then $D_1(K)/D_2(K) = (w_2 \Delta_2 N_1)/(w_1 \Delta_1 N_2)$.*

Proof. The value of the local score $s_i = s_i(t_i)$ can be regarded as sampled from a probability density function $p_{s_i}(s_i)$. We want to determine the and $D_1(K)/D_2(K)$ given the score distributions $p_{s_1}(s_1)$ and $p_{s_2}(s_2)$.

Let $n_i(s_i)$ denote the number of tuples in R_i that exceed the value of s_i. Note that, given a deterministically chosen score value $\tilde{s}_i$, $n_i(\tilde{s}_i)$ is a discrete random variable, whose expected value can be expressed as

$$E[n_i(\tilde{s}_i)] = \bar{n}_i(\tilde{s}_i) = N_i\left(1 - P_{s_i}(\tilde{s}_i)\right) \tag{7}$$

where $P_{s_i}(\tilde{s}_i)$ is the cumulative density function of the random variable s_i evaluated at $\tilde{s}_i$. The value of $D_i(\theta)$ (number of tuples of R_i contributing to the top combinations, i.e. those whose score $s_1 + s_2$ exceeds θ) can be determined as follows

$$D_i(\theta) = \sqrt{\beta}E\left[\bar{n}_i(s_i)|\, s_1 + s_2 > \theta\right]$$
$$= \sqrt{\beta} \int_{-\infty}^{+\infty} \bar{n}_i(s_i)p_{s_i}(s_i|s_1 + s_2 > \theta)ds_i \tag{8}$$

where $\beta \in [0,1]$ denotes the join selectivity, i.e. $|R_1 \bowtie R_2|/|R_1 \times R_2|$, assuming that the join predicate does not depend on the scores. In order to determine $p_{s_i}(s_i|s_1 + s_2 > \theta)$ we leverage Bayes's theorem

$$p_{s_i}(s_i|s_1 + s_2 > \theta) = \frac{p_{s_i}(s_1 + s_2 > \theta|s_i)p_{s_i}(s_i)}{\Pr\{s_1 + s_2 > \theta\}} \tag{9}$$

where

$$\Pr\{s_1 + s_2 > \theta\} = p(s_2 > \theta - s_1) = 1 - P_{s_2}(\theta - s_1)$$
$$= p(s_1 > \theta - s_2) = 1 - P_{s_1}(\theta - s_2) \tag{10}$$

and

$$p(s_1 + s_2 > \theta) = 1 - P_{s_1+s_2}(\theta) \tag{11}$$

Therefore

$$D_i(\theta) = \sqrt{\beta} \int_{-\infty}^{+\infty} N_i\left(1 - P_{s_i}(s_i)\right) \frac{\left(1 - P_{s_i}(\theta - s_i)\right)p_{s_i}(s_i)}{1 - P_{s_1+s_2}(\theta)} \tag{12}$$

Rewriting the previous expression, we obtain:

$$D_i(\theta) = \sqrt{\beta}\frac{N_i}{1 - P_{s_1+s_2}(\theta)} \int_{-\infty}^{+\infty} p_{s_i}(s_i)\left(1 - P_{s_i}(s_i)\right) \cdot$$
$$\cdot \left(1 - P_{s_{\bar{i}}}(\theta - s_i)\right)ds_i \tag{13}$$

where $\bar{P}_{s_i}(s_i) = 1 - P_{s_i}(s_i)$ and the integral can be compactly written in terms of a convolution product, that is, $[(\bar{P}_{s_i} \cdot p_{s_i}) * \bar{P}_{s_{\bar{i}}}](\theta)$.

The value of $D_i(\theta)$ can be readily evaluated for simple distributions, e.g. uniform distributions of the scores, i.e. $s_i \sim U[\underline{s}_i, \bar{s}_i]$. In this case, $\theta \in [\theta_{\min}, \theta_{\max}] = [\underline{s}_1 + \underline{s}_2, \bar{s}_1 + \bar{s}_2]$. Note that, for each value of θ, the expected number of combinations whose score exceeds θ is given by

$$K(\theta) = \frac{\beta}{N_1 N_2}\left(1 - P_{s_1+s_2}(\theta)\right) \tag{14}$$

We are interested to the case when K is small, thus $\theta \simeq \theta_{\max}$. Let $\Delta_i = \bar{s}_i - \underline{s}_i$. When $\theta \in [\max\{\theta_{\max} - \Delta_1, \theta_{\max} - \Delta_2\}, \theta_{\max}]$, the integral in (13) evaluates to

$$D_i(\theta) = \frac{\sqrt{\beta} N_i}{1 - P_{s_1+s_2}(\theta)} \frac{1}{24\Delta_i^2 \Delta_{\bar{i}}} (\bar{s}_1 + \bar{s}_2 + \theta)^3 \tag{15}$$

Therefore, the ratio $D_1(\theta)/D_2(\theta)$ simplyfies to

$$\frac{D_1(\theta)}{D_2(\theta)} = \frac{N_1}{N_2} \frac{\Delta_2}{\Delta_1} \tag{16}$$

Since there is a one-to-one mapping between K and θ,

$$\frac{D_1(K)}{D_2(K)} = \frac{D_1(\theta)}{D_2(\theta)} = \frac{N_1}{N_2} \frac{\Delta_2}{\Delta_1} \tag{17}$$

The case in which the scoring function is weighted, i.e. $w_1 s_1 + w_2 s_2$, can be reduced to the result above, by defining a new random variable $\hat{s}_i = w_i s_i$, such that $\hat{s}_i \sim U[w_i \underline{s}_i, w_i \bar{s}_i]$ and $\hat{\Delta}_i = w_i \Delta_i$. Therefore:

$$\frac{D_1(K)}{D_2(K)} = \frac{N_1}{N_2} \frac{w_2 \Delta_2}{w_1 \Delta_1} \tag{18}$$

According to Theorem 1 the ratio of the number of tuples from relation R_1 and R_2 in the top-K combinations is inversely proportional to the ratio of the score ranges. The result holds both when combinations are computed with the Cartesian product and with a join with arbitrary predicate. This observation can be used to determine the self-diversification power implicit in the distribution of data and in the ranking function and, indirectly, to assess the expected improvement that can be obtained with diversification, with respect to the case in which only the relevance score function is used to build the result set.

Say that $N_1 = N_2$ and $w_1 = w_2$; if if the variance of the scores is the same in both input relations (i.e. $\Delta_1 = \Delta_2$) then $D_1(K) = D_2(K)$, i.e. the number of distinct tuples extracted from R_1 and R_2 in the top combinations is the same, regardless the average score (i.e., even if $E[s_1] \neq E[s_2]$). Therefore, the result set computed based on relevance only already picks up tuples evenly from the input relations and, if the sizes of the populations are comparable, diversification is not expected to help much.

If, instead, the number of distinct tuples extracted from R_1 contributing to the top combinations is Δ_2/Δ_1 larger than the number of tuples extracted from R_2 (i.e. $\Delta_1 < \Delta_2$), then $D_1(K) > D_2(K)$, i.e. tuples coming from the distribution characterized by the largest variance tend to be under-represented in the top combinations. Hence, diversification is expected to help, especially when $\Delta_2 \gg \Delta_1$ or, viceversa, $\Delta_1 \gg \Delta_2$.

3 Experiments

Multi-domain search deals with *combinations* of objects; therefore, the evaluation of diversity in multi-domain result sets must assess the ability of a given algorithm to retrieve useful and diverse tuples within the first K results in the query answer. In this section we elaborate on the performance of the diversification algorithms described in Section 2 (MMR, MaxSum,MaxMin). We calculated a set of quantitative objective metrics, and we conducted a subjective user study. All the algorithms were evaluated using a $\lambda = 1$, thus giving equal importance to both diversity and ranking.

A well-known metrics for relevance in diversified result sets is the α-*Discounted Cumulative Gain* (α-DCG_K) [3], which measures the usefulness (gain) of a document based on its position in the result list and its novelty w.r.t. the previous results in the ranking. In the original formulation of α-DCG_K, documents are composed by a set of *information nuggets*. In the context of multi-domain resultsets, the α-DCG_K can be defined by assimilating an information nugget to a tuple $t_i \in R_i$, where $R_1, \ldots, R_n$ are the relations involved in a multi-domain query. Therefore, we define α-DCG_K as:

$$\alpha\text{-}DCG_K = \sum_{k=1}^{K} \frac{\sum_{i=1}^{n} J(\tau_k, t_i)(1 - \alpha)^{r_{t_i,k-1}}}{\log_2(1 + j)} \qquad (19)$$

where $J(\tau_k, t_i)$ returns 1 when tuple t_i appears in a combination τ_k at position k in the result set and 0 otherwise. J is defined as $J(\tau_k, t_i) = \mathbb{1}_{\pi_{R_i}(\tau_k)=t_i}$, where π_{R_i} denotes the projection over the attributes of R_i, and $r_{t_i,k-1} = \sum_{j=1}^{k-1} J(\tau_j, t_i)$ quantifies the number of combinations up to position $k-1$ that contain the tuple t_i. In our experiments, α is set to 0.5 to evaluate novelty and relevance equally.

Sub-topic recall at rank K (S-$Recall_K$) [16] is a recall measure for search results related to several sub-topics, often applied to evaluate diversification algorithms [4]. In multi-domain search, a tuple in a combination can be assimilated to a subtopic in a document. Therefore, multi-domain recall at rank K (MD-$Recall_K$), defined next, measures, for each relation R_i involved in a query (with $i = 1 \ldots n$) and for all rank positions k from 1 to K, the set of *distinct* tuples ($R_i^k = \{t_i \in R_i | \exists j \leq k . \pi_{R_i}(\tau_j) = t_i\}$) retrieved in the result set, with respect to the entire population of the relation ($|R_i|$).

$$MD\text{-}Recall_K = \prod_{i=1}^{n} \frac{|\cup_{k=1}^{K} R_i^k|}{|R_i|} \qquad (20)$$

3.1   Implementation and Datasets

We extended an existing architecture for multi-domain search application development [2] with a diversification component embedding the algorithms described in Section 2. Experiment has been performed on two usage scenarios. In the first scenario – Night Out *(NO)* – a user looks for a museum, a restaurant, and a hotel in Milan. We created a dataset consisting of the *Hotel* (50 tuples), *Restaurant* (50 tuples), and *Museum* (50 tuples) relations, where the initial 125,000 combinations have been pruned by removing all the triples for which the total walking distance from the Central Station in Milan is greater than 4 Km, which leaves

5000 combinations. We computed the mutual location distances, and we defined three quantitative relevance scores – the combination cost, the total walking distance, and the average ratings (see Example 1).

In the Study Abroad *(SA)* scenario, a user looks for a U.S. university, considering the rating of the university, the quality of life in the area, and the overall cost, including accommodation. The supporting dataset consists of three relations *University* (60 US universities with their academic quality score[1], walkability score of the surroundings[2], and average tuition fee), *State* (including their crime rate), and *Flat* (1200 flats). Joins were performed on the *state* attribute, yielding a dataset of 5100 combination. We defined three relevance scores: the overall yearly expenditure, a "quality" index[3], and the distance between the university and the flat.

3.2   Discussion

The evaluation covers both the *Night Out* and *Study Abroad* scenarios presented in Section 3.1. To avoid query-dependent bias, results are averaged over multiple experiments in each scenario. For the categorical case, 3 experiments have been performed, each of them applying one of the score functions described in Section 3.1, and diversification according to categorical distance. For the quantitative case, 6 experiments have been performed: for each score function in Section 3.1 the value computed by the remaining ones are, in turn, used to evaluate quantitative distance as in Equation 2.

Figure 2 shows $\alpha\text{-}DCG_K$ and $MD\text{-}Recall_K$ for the result sets obtained with no diversification and with the diversification algorithms MMR, MaxSum, and MaxMin, applying both categorical and quantitative distances. Each data point of the X-axis represents the k-th element in the result-set. The Y-axes represent, respectively, the values of $\alpha\text{-}DCG_K$ (Figure 2(a,b,e,f)) and of $MD\text{-}Recall_K$ (Figure 2(c,d,g,h)).

MMR and MaxMin always outperform the un-diversified baseline when used with the categorical diversity function both in terms of $\alpha\text{-}DCG_K$ and $MD\text{-}Recall_K$; MaxSum instead does not provide significant improvements with respect to the baseline. One can also notice that MMR and MaxMin offer similar performance: this is not surprising, as the greedy algorithms for the two objective functions are also very similar.

For quantitative distance, instead, all algorithms provide similar performance. In particular MMR and MaxMin degrade their performance with respect to categorical distance, and behave only slightly better than the baseline. This may also be influenced by the chosen quality measures ($\alpha\text{-}DCG_K$ and $MD\text{-}Recall_K$), that are based on diversity of extracted objects and therefore are more suited to evaluate

---

[1] Source:
   http://archive.ics.uci.edu/ml/machine-learning-databases/university/
[2] WalkScore - http://www.walkscore.com/
[3] A function of the academic quality score, the walkability index of a university and the crime rate in a state.

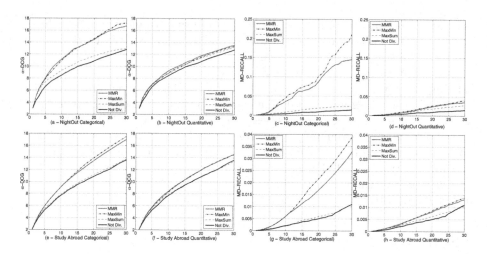

Fig. 2. Quantitative evaluation results. *Night Out* dataset: α-DCG_K for (a) categorical and (b) quantitative distances; MD-$Recall_K$ for (c) categorical and (d) quantitative distances. *Study Abroad* dataset: α-DCG_K for (e) categorical and (f) quantitative distances; MD-$Recall_K$ for (g) categorical and (h) quantitative distances.

categorical diversification. Nonetheless, we notice an overall coherent behavior of MMR and MaxMin in all settings; likewise, MaxSum consistently performs similarly to the un-diversified case. Overall, these results support the hypothesis that diversification algorithms can improve the quality of multi-domain result sets.

3.3 User Study

We conducted an (uncontrolled) user study focused on explicit comparison of result sets diversified according to the selected algorithms: users were asked to directly compare two alternative result sets (displaying 10 combinations each) and to select the one that, in their opinion, provided the best *quality* and *variety* of the items. As quantitative analysis provided evidence that MMR and MaxMin algorithms clearly outperformed the baseline when adopting categorical distance, we decided to consider only categorical distance for the user study; we also decided not to include MaxMin in the evaluation as its performance was comparable to MMR.

The study addressed both the scenarios *Night Out* and *Study Abroad* as described in Section 3.1. To avoid bias on the data instances, we generated 10 different subsets from the original result sets of each scenario, and then we applied separately the diversification algorithms to all of them. To avoid the effect of possible learning bias, the two scenarios were performed in random order; each user was shown two options among the three calculated result sets (un-diversified, MMR and MaxSum), in a round-robin fashion. The users could select their preferred result set in each scenario; they had unlimited time for completing the task. Each preference counted as a vote to the respective algorithm. The test was performed by 74 users, among which 25% were students and 75% were either search experts from industry or academia.

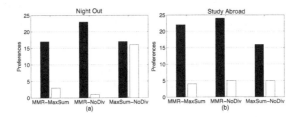

Fig. 3. *Direct comparison* user study: Preferences assigned to the different resultsets

Figure 3 shows the results of the voting. All the pairwise comparisons were subject to a binomial test, where the null hypothesis was that the preferences for both algorithms were equally likely to be expressed by the user. The perceived quality reflects quite well the quantitative results described in Section 3.2: result sets produced with the MMR algorithm were perceived to have higher quality and variety than both MaxSum and the un-diversified result (at significance level $\alpha = 0.01$). Conversely, the MaxSum algorithm was not significantly found better than the un-diversified result-set, as also suggested by the fact that the null hypothesis cannot be rejected.

The user experiment confirmed the considerations emerged from the quantitative evaluation, thus suggesting a user-perceivable benefit in the adoption of diversifications algorithm in multi-domain search applications.

4   Related Work

The evolution of search systems towards the extraction of structured information from Web content have been widely addressed in several recent works (e.g. *Concept search* [7]). Multi-domain search [2] focuses on processing queries involving several topics and domains on Web data sources. The present work explores diversification in this context, as a mean for improving the utility of result sets made of associated entity instances.

Result diversification is a well-investigated topic; [6] provides a survey of existing approaches, while [8] discusses a systematic axiomatization of the problem, that is the base of the formalization of multi-domain diversification in Section 2. A broad distinction can be done between the contributions that focus on diversifying search results for document collections (e.g. [12]) and those that concentrate instead on structured data sets [10,13,15].

Our work is mostly related to diversification applied to structured data. In this field, diversification in multiple dimensions is addressed in [5], where the problem is reduced to MMR by collapsing diversity dimensions in one composite similarity function. The work in [15] examines the diversification of structured results sets as produced by queries in online shopping applications. The paper shows how to solve *exactly* the problem of picking K out of N products so to minimize an attribute-based notion of similarity and discusses an efficient implementation technique based on tree traversal. Multi-domain diversification, as discussed in this paper, is a broader problem; it could be partially reduced to prefix-based diversification only in the case of categorical diversity, by choosing an arbitrary order for the categorical attributes used to measure combination diversity. Keyword search in structured databases is addressed in [4], where diversification is not applied to result sets, but to query interpretations, which are assumed to be available from the knowledge of the database content and query logs. The multi-domain search applications addressed in this paper assume for simplicity unambiguous queries and thus a fixed interpretation, but could reuse the interpretation diversification approach of [4] to cope for multi-domain searches with more than one possible interpretation. A recent related work is [13], which applies to the selection of Web services characterized by their non-functional properties. The authors introduced a novel diversification objective, MaxCov, which leads to the selection of items with high relevance score, such that the remaining ones are not too far from any of the elements of the diversified result set. We plan the testing of MaxCov as part of the future work.

Finally, the work [10] investigates the diversification of structured data from a different perspective: the selection of a limited number of features that can maximally highlight the differences among multiple result sets. Although the problem is apparently different from multi-domain search (the actual goal of [10] is to find a set of attribute values that maximally differentiates a number of input results set, respecting a size upper bound) identifying the best attributes to use for ranking and diversification is relevant to multi-domain search as well, and we have started addressing it by studying how the distribution of attribute values affects the capability of the ranking function to sample the population of the input relations evenly.

5   Conclusions

Multi-domain search is a promising trend in search applications; however, to preserve the current ability of search engines to squeeze in one page the most interesting results, the combinatorial explosion of result sets formed by several correlated entity instances must be tamed. In this paper, we have investigated the problem of multi-domain result set diversification, by showing how the diversification techniques well studied in the context of IR can be extended to support this class of applications. We experimentally tested three algorithms for the trade-off between relevance and diversity, and showing that they can introduced a significant degree of diversification in the result set; a user study demonstrated a positive perception of the utility of diversification by users.

In the future, we plan to extend this work in several directions. On the methodological side, we plan to better investigate the interplay between the score function and the similarity measure (beyond the simple case of uniform data distribution studied in Section 2), so to propose a methodology for the selection of the most promising scoring and diversity functions. On the architecture side, we will investigate issues like the design of appropriate data and index structures for efficient diversification, relevance and diversity-aware caching of results, and the thorough evaluation of the overhead of diversification. Finally, we plan a careful graphical user interface design and a novel round of user testing of the multi-domain search concept, this time using online data and real users.

Acknowledgments. This research is partially supported by the Search Computing (SeCo) project, funded by European Research Council, under the IDEAS Advanced Grants program; by the Cubrik Project, an IP funded within the EC 7FP; and by the BPM4People SME Capacities project. We wish to thank all the participants to the user study and all the projects contributors.

References

1. Carbonell, J., Goldstein, J.: The use of mmr, diversity-based reranking for reordering documents and producing summaries. In: SIGIR 1998: Proceedings of the 21st Annual International ACM SIGIR Conference on Research and Development in Information Retrieval, pp. 335–336. ACM, New York (1998)

2. Ceri, S., Brambilla, M.: Search Computing Systems. In: Pernici, B. (ed.) CAiSE 2010. LNCS, vol. 6051, pp. 1–6. Springer, Heidelberg (2010)

3. Clarke, C.L., Kolla, M., Cormack, G.V., Vechtomova, O., Ashkan, A., Büttcher, S., MacKinnon, I.: Novelty and diversity in information retrieval evaluation. In: SIGIR 2008: Proceedings of the 31st Annual International ACM SIGIR Conference on Research and Development in Information Retrieval, pp. 659–666. ACM, New York (2008)

4. Demidova, E., Fankhauser, P., Zhou, X., Nejdl, W.: Divq: diversification for keyword search over structured databases. In: SIGIR 2010: Proceeding of the 33rd International ACM SIGIR Conference on Research and Development in Information Retrieval, pp. 331–338. ACM, New York (2010)

5. Dou, Z., Hu, S., Chen, K., Song, R., Wen, J.-R.: Multi-dimensional search result diversification. In: Proceedings of the Fourth ACM International Conference on Web Search and Data Mining, WSDM 2011, pp. 475–484. ACM, New York (2011)

6. Drosou, M., Pitoura, E.: Search result diversification. SIGMOD Rec. 39(1), 41–47 (2010)

7. Giunchiglia, F., Kharkevich, U., Zaihrayeu, I.: Concept search: Semantics enabled syntactic search. In: SemSearch, pp. 109–123 (2008)

8. Gollapudi, S., Sharma, A.: An axiomatic approach for result diversification. In: WWW 2009: Proceedings of the 18th International Conference on World Wide Web, pp. 381–390. ACM, New York (2009)

9. Gonzalez, T.F.: Clustering to minimize the maximum intercluster distance. Theoretical Computer Science 38, 293–306 (1985)

10. Liu, Z., Sun, P., Chen, Y.: Structured search result differentiation. Proc. VLDB Endow. 2(1), 313–324 (2009)

11. Martinenghi, D., Tagliasacchi, M.: Proximity rank join. PVLDB 3(1), 352–363 (2010)

12. Rafiei, D., Bharat, K., Shukla, A.: Diversifying web search results. In: WWW 2010: Proceedings of the 19th International Conference on World Wide Web, pp. 781–790. ACM, New York (2010)

13. Skoutas, D., Alrifai, M., Nejdl, W.: Re-ranking web service search results under diverse user preferences. In: PersDB 2010 (September 2010)

14. Soliman, M.A., Ilyas, I.F., Saleeb, M.: Building ranked mashups of unstructured sources with uncertain information. PVLDB 3(1), 826–837 (2010)
15. Vee, E., Srivastava, U., Shanmugasundaram, J., Bhat, P., Yahia, S.A.: Efficient computation of diverse query results. In: ICDE 2008: Proceedings of the 2008 IEEE 24th International Conference on Data Engineering, pp. 228–236. IEEE Computer Society, Washington, DC (2008)
16. Zhai, C.X., Cohen, W.W., Lafferty, J.: Beyond independent relevance: methods and evaluation metrics for subtopic retrieval. In: SIGIR 2003: Proceedings of the 26th Annual International ACM SIGIR Conference on Research and Development in Informaion Retrieval, pp. 10–17. ACM, New York (2003)

Twinder: A Search Engine for Twitter Streams

Ke Tao, Fabian Abel, Claudia Hauff, and Geert-Jan Houben

Web Information Systems, Delft University of Technology
{k.tao,f.abel,c.hauff,g.j.p.m.houben}@tudelft.nl

Abstract. How can one effectively identify relevant messages in the hundreds of millions of Twitter messages that are posted every day? In this paper, we aim to answer this fundamental research question and introduce Twinder, a scalable search engine for Twitter streams. The Twinder search engine exploits various features to estimate the relevance of Twitter messages (tweets) for a given topic. Among these features are both topic-sensitive features such as measures that compute the semantic relatedness between a tweet and a topic as well as topic-insensitive features which characterize a tweet with respect to its syntactical, semantic, sentiment and contextual properties. In our evaluations, we investigate the impact of the different features on retrieval performance. Our results prove the effectiveness of the Twinder search engine - we show that in particular semantic features yield high precision and recall values of more than 35% and 45% respectively.

1 Introduction

Microblogging sites such as Twitter[1] have emerged as large information sources for exploring and discussing news-related topics [1]. Twitter is also used as a major platform for publishing and disseminating information related to various topics such as politics or sport events[2]. For trending topics, thousands of Twitter messages (tweets) are posted per second. Moreover, the number of posts published per day typically exceeds several hundred million[3]. Thus, searching for tweets that are relevant to a given topic is a non-trivial research challenge.

Teevan et al. revealed that users exhibit a different search behaviour on Twitter compared to Web search [2]. For example, keyword queries on Twitter are significantly shorter than those issued for Web search: on Twitter people typically use 1.64 words to search while on the Web they use, on average, 3.08 words. This can be explained by the length limitation of 140 characters per Twitter message: as long keyword queries easily become too restrictive, people tend to use broader and fewer keywords for searching.

Given the drawbacks of keyword search as provided by Twitter, researchers recently started to investigate alternative search interfaces. Bernstein et al. [3] presented Eddi, an interface which categorizes the tweets in the personal timeline

---

[1] http://twitter.com/

[2] http://yearinreview.twitter.com/en/tps.html

[3] http://blog.twitter.com/2011/06/200-million-tweets-per-day.html

M. Brambilla, T. Tokuda, and R. Tolksdorf (Eds.): ICWE 2012, LNCS 7387, pp. 153–168, 2012.
© Springer-Verlag Berlin Heidelberg 2012

of a user into topics and provides access to these tweets by means of tag clouds. In previous work [4], we studied the utility of a faceted search interface for Twitter that allows users to explore topics along different facets such as persons or locations. Moreover, researchers explored various solutions for representing Twitter search results [5], for ranking Web pages that are currently trending on Twitter [6] or for recommending Twitter conversations [7]. However, none of these works focuses on engineering search engines for microblogging data that allow for estimating the relevance of tweets for a given topic.

In this work, we tackle this challenge and introduce *Twinder*, a scalable search engine for Social Web and Twitter streams in particular. Twinder analyzes various features to estimate the relevance of a tweet for a given topic ranging from syntactical characteristics as proposed by [8] (e.g. presence of URLs) to semantic and contextual information (e.g. semantic distance to topic). We explore both *topic-insensitive* features, which can be pre-computed independently from a given topic on a cloud computing infrastructure[4], and *topic-sensitive* features, which are calculated at query time. To analyze the effectiveness of the different features and to investigate how well Twinder can deliver tweets which are *interesting* and *relevant* to a given topic, we evaluated Twinder on a large benchmark dataset of more than 16 million tweets that features relevance judgements for a set of 49 topics. The main contributions of this paper are:

- We present Twinder, a search engine for Twitter streams that analyzes various features in order to identify tweets that are relevant for a given topic. Twinder is designed to run in a cloud computing infrastructure (Section 3).
- We propose methods for extracting novel features from Twitter messages that allow Twinder to predict the relevance of a message for a given topic. In particular, our semantic features go beyond the state of the art (Section 4).
- We evaluate the effectiveness of Twinder for searching Twitter messages and conduct an in-depth analysis to investigate the impact of the different features on retrieval effectiveness (Section 5).

2   Related Work

Since its launch in 2006 Twitter has attracted a lot of attention, both among the general public and among the research community. Researchers started studying microblogging phenomena to find out what kind of topics are discussed on Twitter [1], how trends evolve [9], or how one detects influential users on Twitter [10]. Applications have been researched that utilize microblogging data to enrich traditional news media with information from Twitter [11], to detect and manage emergency situations such as earthquakes [12] or to enhance search and ranking of Web sites which possibly have not been indexed yet by Web search engines.

---

[4] For example, the supporting website contains a MapReduce-based solution to generate topic-insensitive features [15].

So far though, search on Twitter has not been studied extensively. Tevaan et al. [2] compared the search behaviour on Twitter with traditional Web search behaviour as discussed in the introduction.

Bernstein et al. [3] proposed an interface that allows for exploring tweets by means of tag clouds. However, their interface is targeted towards browsing the tweets that have been published by the people whom a user is following and not for searching the entire Twitter corpus. Jadhav et al. [11] developed an engine that enriches the semantics of Twitter messages and allows for issuing SPARQL queries on Twitter streams. In previous work, we also followed such a semantic enrichment strategy to provide faceted search capabilities on Twitter [4]. Duan et al. [8] investigate features such as Okapi BM25 relevance scores or Twitter specific features (length of a tweet, presence of a hashtag, etc.) in combination with RankSVM to learn a ranking model for tweets. In an empirical study, they found that the length of a tweet and information about the presence of a URL in a tweet are important features to rank relevant tweets.

Our research builds on these previous works. In this paper, we introduce the Twinder search engine for Twitter stream. We re-visit a number of features that were proposed by Duan et al. [8]. Additionally, we also developed a number of novel semantic measures to further boost the retrieval effectiveness of Twinder.

3   Twinder Search Engine

Twinder (*Twi*tter F*inder*) is a search engine for Twitter streams that aims to improve search for Twitter messages by going beyond keyword-based matching. Different types of features ranging from syntactical to contextual features are considered by Twinder in order to predict the relevance of tweets for a given search query. Figure 1 shows the core components of the Twinder architecture. Different components are concerned with extracting features from the incoming messages of a Twitter stream. Given the huge amount of Twitter messages that are published every day, the system is designed to be scalable. For this reason, Twinder makes use of cloud computing infrastructures for processing-intensive tasks such as feature extraction and indexing. Below, we introduce the core components of the *Twinder Search Engine* (see blue boxes in Figure 1) and compare the runtime performances of our engine when running on an cloud computing infrastructure vs. a multi-core server environment.

3.1   Core Components

Feature Extraction. The features used for relevance estimation are extracted by the *Feature Extraction* component. It receives Twitter messages from *Social Web Streams* and implements a suite of functions that allow for representing the tweets via (i) topic-sensitive features which are computed whenever a new query is received and (ii) topic-insensitive features which are calculated when new tweets are received. The set of features that are currently exploited by Twinder are introduced in Section 4. The computation of some features requires

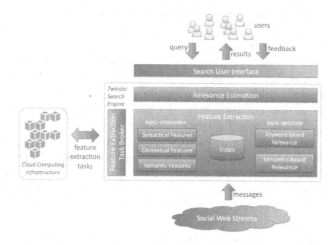

Fig. 1. Architecture of the Twinder Search Engine

further services which offer additional functionalities (e.g. semantic enrichment). Tasks such as obtaining contextual information about the creator of tweets or the actual construction of the multifaceted index of Twinder are repeated periodically. To update its multifaceted index and to compute topic-insensitive features, Twinder provides MapReduce-based implementations and can thus utilize cloud computing infrastructure.

Feature Extraction Task Broker. MapReduce-based implementations are efficient at processing batch tasks with large volume of data and are typically executed on large cloud computing infrastructures. Twinder is designed to take advantage of MapReduce and cloud computing infrastructures to allow for high scalability and to allow for frequent updates of its multifaceted index. For example, the extraction of topic-insensitive features that are not directly available via the Twitter API and the indexing process may be time-consuming tasks for massive amounts of data. Therefore, the *Feature Extraction Task Broker* allows for dispatching feature extraction tasks and indexing tasks to cloud computing infrastructures.

Relevance Estimation. The *Relevance Estimation* component is the most crucial part of Twinder as it determines for a given topic the relevance of tweets which are represented through their calculated features. Technically, the component accepts search queries from a front-end module and passes them to the *Feature Extraction* component in order to compute the features required for the relevance estimation. Tweets that are classified as relevant can be delivered to the front-end for rendering. The relevance estimation is cast into a classification problem where the tweets have to be classified as relevant or non-relevant with respect to a topic. Given a training dataset, Twinder can learn the classification model. At runtime, the learned model is applied to the feature representation of the tweets to identify relevant tweets. In future work, we also

Table 1. Comparison of indexing times: Amazon EMR vs. a single machine

Corpus Size	Mainstream Server	EMR (10 instances)
100k (13MBytes)	0.4 min	5 min
1m (122MBytes)	5 min	8 min
10m (1.3GBytes)	48 min	19 min
32m (3.9GBytes)	283 min	47 min

plan the integration of further user feedback to continuously improve the learned model. For example, we envision the exploitation of re-tweeting activities or favourite markings as additional training data.

3.2 Efficiency of Indexing

As described in Section 3.1, Twinder is capable of leveraging a cloud computing infrastructure to execute data-intensive jobs. In order to demonstrate that it is beneficial to assign tasks with a large amount of data to a cloud computing infrastructure, we compare the performance of creating an inverted index on Amazon ElasticMapReduce (EMR)[5] and a multi-core server[6]. We evaluated the runtime of four different Twitter corpora, ranging in size from 100 thousand to 32 million tweets. On EMR, the indices were built by using ten instances[7], where each instance contains one virtual core, in contrast to the 8 cores in the multi-core server.

As shown in Table 1, if the corpora are small, the index can be efficiently created with a dedicated toolkit on a single machine. However, as the corpus size increases, utilizing cloud infrastructure offers significant speed gains. Therefore we conclude that Twinder can achieve a better runtime performance by employing cloud computing infrastructure.

4 Features of Microposts

In this section, provide an overview of the different features that are analyzed by Twinder.We distinguish two types of features: topic-sensitive features, which are computed at query time and express the relevance of a Twitter message with respect to the query, and topic-insensitive features, which are evaluated before a query is issued and characterize syntactical, semantic or contextual properties of a Twitter message.

4.1 Topic-Sensitive Features

Keyword-Based Relevance Features. A straightforward approach is to interpret Twitter messages as traditional Web documents and apply standard text retrieval measures to estimate the relevance of tweet for a given topic.

---

[5] http://aws.amazon.com/elasticmapreduce/

[6] We wrote our own indexer in Hadoop and relied on the Lemur Toolkit for Information Retrieval to create the index on the single server: http://www.lemurproject.org/.

[7] Specifically, we used ten instances of type m1.small.

Feature F1: keyword-based relevance score. To calculate the retrieval score for pair of (topic, tweet), we employ the language modeling approach to information retrieval [13]. A language model θ_t is derived for each document (tweet). Given a query Q with terms $Q = \{q_1, ..., q_n\}$ the document language models are ranked with respect to the probability $P(\theta_t|Q)$, which according to the Bayes theorem can be expressed as follows.

$$P(\theta_t|Q) = \frac{P(Q|\theta_t)P(\theta_t)}{P(Q)} \propto P(\theta_t) \prod_{q_i \in Q} P(q_i|\theta_t). \tag{1}$$

This is the standard query likelihood based language modeling setup which assumes term independence. Usually, the prior probability of a tweet $P(\theta_t)$ is considered to be uniform, that is, each tweet in the corpus is equally likely. The language models are multinomial probability distributions over the terms occurring in the tweets. Since a maximum likelihood estimate of $P(q_i|\theta_t)$ would result in a zero probability of any tweet that misses one or more of the query terms in Q, the estimate is usually smoothed with a background language model, generated over all tweets in the corpus. We employed Dirichlet smoothing [13].

Hypothesis H1: the greater the keyword-based relevance score (that is, the less negative), the more relevant and interesting the tweet is to the topic.

Semantic-Based Relevance Features. Based on the semantics that are extracted from the Twitter messages, we calculate two further relevance features. *Feature F2: semantic-based relevance score.* This feature is a retrieval score calculated as in Section 4.1 though with a different set of terms. Since the average length of search queries submitted to microblog search engines is lower than in traditional Web search, it is necessary to understand the information need behind the query. The search topics provided as part of the TREC data set contain abbreviations, part of names, and nicknames. For example, the name "Jintao" (query: "Jintao visit US") refers to the president of China. However, in tweets he is also referred to as "President Hu", "Chinese President", etc. If these semantic variants of a person's name are considered when deriving an expanded query then potentially more relevant tweets can be found. We utilize the Named-Entity-Recognition (NER) service DBPedia Spotlight[8] to identify names and their synonyms in the query. We merge the found concepts into an expanded query which is then used as input to the retrieval approach described earlier.

Hypothesis H2: the greater the semantic-based relevance score, the more relevant and interesting the tweet is.

Feature F3: isSemanticallyRelated. It is a boolean value that shows whether there is a semantic overlap between the topic and the tweet. This feature requires us to employ DBpedia Spotlight on the topic as well as the tweets. If there is an overlap in the identified concepts then it is set to *true*.

Hypothesis H3: if a tweet is considered to be semantically related to the query then it is also relevant and interesting for the user.

---

[8] http://spotlight.dbpedia.org/

4.2   Topic-Insensitive Features

Syntactical Features. Syntactical features describe elements that are mentioned in a Twitter message. We analyze the following properties:

Feature F4: hasHashtag. This is a boolean property that indicates whether a given tweet contains a hashtag. Twitter users typically apply hashtags in order to facilitate the retrieval of the tweet. For example, by using a hashtag people can join a discussion on a topic that is represented via that hashtag. Users, who monitor the hashtag, will retrieve all tweets that contain it. Therefore, we investigate whether the occurrence of hashtags (possibly without any obvious relevance to the topic) is an indicator for the interestingness of a tweet.

Hypothesis H4: tweets that contain hashtags are more likely to be relevant than tweets that do not contain hashtags.

Feature F5: hasURL. Dong et al. [6] showed that people often exchange URLs via Twitter so that information about trending URLs can be exploited to improve Web search and particularly the ranking of recently discussed URLs. Hence, the presence of a URL (boolean property) can be an indicator for a relevant tweet.

Hypothesis H5: tweets that contain a URL are more likely to be relevant than tweets that do not contain a URL.

Feature F6: isReply. On Twitter, users can reply to the tweets of other people. This type of communication may be used to comment on a certain message, to answer a question or to chat. For deciding whether a tweet is relevant to a news-related topic, we therefore assume that the boolean *isReply* feature, which indicates whether a tweet is a reply to another tweet, can be a valuable signal.

Hypothesis H6: tweets that are formulated as a reply to another tweet are less likely to be relevant than other tweets.

Feature F7: length. The length of a tweet (the number of characters) may also be an indicator for the relevance. We hypothesize that the length of a Twitter message correlates with the amount of information that is conveyed it.

Hypothesis H7: the longer a tweet, the more likely it is to be relevant.

For the above features, the values of the boolean properties are set to 0 (false) and 1 (true) while the length of a Twitter message is measured by the number of characters divided by 140 which is the maximum length of a Twitter message.

There are further syntactical features that can be explored such as the mentioning of certain character sequences including emoticons, question marks, etc. In line with the *isReply* feature, one could also utilize knowledge about the re-tweet history of a tweet, e.g. a boolean property that indicates whether the tweet is a copy from another tweet or a numeric property that counts the number of users who re-tweeted the message. However, in this paper we are merely interested in original messages that have not been re-tweeted yet and therefore also only in features which do not require knowledge about the history of a tweet. This allows us to estimate the relevance of a message as soon as it is published.

Semantic Features. In addition to the semantic relevance scores described in Section 4.1, we can also analyze the semantics of a Twitter message independently from the topic of interest. We therefore utilize again the NER services provided by DBpedia Spotlight to extract the following features:

Feature F8: #entities. The number of DBpedia entities that are mentioned in a Twitter message may also provide evidence for the potential relevance of a tweet. We assume that the more entities can be extracted from a tweet, the more information it contains and the more valuable it is. For example, in the context of the discussion about birth certificates we find the following two tweets in our dataset:

t_1: *"Despite what her birth certificate says, my lady is actually only 27"*
t_2: *"Hawaii (Democratic) lawmakers want release of Obama's birth certificate"*

When reading the two tweets, without having a particular topic or information need in mind, it seems that t_2 has a higher likelihood to be relevant for some topic for the majority of the Twitter users than t_1 as it conveys more entities that are known to the public and available on DBpedia. In fact, the entity extractor is able to detect one entity, *db:Birth_certificate*, for tweet t_1 while it detects three additional entities for t_2: *db:Hawaii*, *db:Legislator* and *db:Barack_Obama*.

Hypothesis H8: the more entities a tweet mentions, the more likely it is to be relevant and interesting.

Feature F9: diversity. The diversity of semantic concepts mentioned in a Twitter message can be exploited as an indicator for the potential relevance of a tweet. Here, we count the number of distinct types of entities that are mentioned in a Twitter message. For example, for the two tweets t_1 and t_2, the diversity score would be 1 and 4 respectively as for t_1 only one type of entity is detected (*yago:PersonalDocuments*) while for t_2 also instances of *db:Person* (person), *db:Place* (location) and *owl:Thing* (the role *db:Legislator* is not further classified) are detected.

Hypothesis H9: the greater the diversity of concepts mentioned in a tweet, the more likely it is to be interesting and relevant.

Feature F10: sentiment. Naveed et al. [14] showed that tweets which contain negative emoticons are more likely to be re-tweeted than tweets which feature positive emoticons. The sentiment of a tweet may thus impact the perceived relevance of a tweet. Therefore, we classify the semantic polarity of a tweet into positive, negative or neutral using *Twitter Sentiment*[9].

Hypothesis H10: the likelihood of a tweet's relevance is influenced by its sentiment polarity.

Contextual Features. In addition to the aforementioned features, which describe characteristics of the Twitter messages, we also investigate features that

---

[9] http://twittersentiment.appspot.com/

describe the context in which a tweet was published. In our analysis, we focus on the *social context*, which describes the creator of a Twitter message, and investigate the following four contextual features:

Feature F11: #followers. The number of followers can be used to indicate the influence or authority of a user on Twitter. We assume that users who have more followers are more likely to publish relevant and interesting tweets.

Hypothesis H11: the higher the number of followers a creator of a message has, the more likely it is that her tweets are relevant.

Feature F12: #lists. On Twitter, people can use so-called *lists* to group users, e.g. according to the topics about which these users post messages. If a user appears in many Twitter lists then this may indicate that her messages are valuable to a large number of users. Twinder thus analyzes the number of lists in which a user appears in order to infer the value of a user's tweets.

Hypothesis H12: the higher the number of lists in which the creator of a message appears, the more likely it is that her tweets are relevant.

Feature F13: Twitter age. Twitter was launched more than five years ago. Over time, users learn how to take advantage of Twitter and possibly also gain experience in writing interesting tweets. Therefore, we assume that the experienced users are more likely to share interesting tweets with others. Twinder measures the experience of a user by means of the time which passed since the creator of a tweet registered with Twitter.

Hypothesis H13: the older the Twitter account of a user, the more likely it is that her tweets are relevant.

Contextual features may also refer to temporal characteristics such as the creation time of a Twitter message or characteristics of Web pages that are linked from a Twitter message. One could for example categorize the linked Web pages to discover the types of Web sites that usually attract attention on Twitter. We leave the investigation of such additional contextual features for future work.

5   Analysis and Evaluation of Twinder

Having introduced the various features we now turn to analyzing the overall search effectiveness of Twinder. In a second step, we investigate how the different features impact the performance.

5.1   Dataset, Feature Characteristics and Experimental Setup

Dataset. For our evaluations, we use the Twitter corpus which was introduced in the microblog track of TREC 2011[10]. The original corpus consists of approx. 16 million tweets, posted over a period of 2 weeks (Jan. 24 until Feb. 8, inclusive).

---

[10] The dataset is available via http://trec.nist.gov/data/tweets/

Table 2. The dataset characteristics and the relevance prediction across topics. The feature coefficients were determined across all topics. The total number of topics is 49. The five features with the highest absolute coefficients are underlined.

Category	Feature	Relevant	Non-relevant	Coefficient
keyword relevance	keyword-based	-10.699	-14.408	0.1716
semantic relevance	semantic-based	-10.298	-14.206	0.1039
	isSemanticallyRelated	25.3%	4.7%	0.9559
syntactical	hasHashtag	19.1%	19.3%	0.0627
	hasURL	81.9%	53.9%	1.1989
	isReply	3.4%	14.1%	-0.5303
	length (in characters)	90.282	87.819	0.0007
semantics	#entities	2.367	1.882	0.0225
	diversity	1.796	1.597	0.0243
	positive sentiment	2.4%	10.7%	-0.6670
	neutral sentiment	92.7%	82.8%	0.2270
	negative sentiment	4.9%	6.5%	0.4906
contextual	#followers	6501.45	4162.364	0.0000
	#lists	209.119	101.054	0.0001
	Twitter age	2.351	2.207	0.1878

We utilized an existing language detection library[11] to identify English tweets and found that 4,766,901 tweets were classified as English. Employing named entity extraction on the English tweets resulted in a total over 6 million entities among which we found approximately 0.14 million distinct entities. Besides the tweets, 49 search topics were given. TREC assessors judged the relevance of 40,855 topic-tweet pairs which we use as ground truth in our experiments. 2,825 topic-tweet pairs were judged relevant while the majority (37,349) were marked non-relevant.

Feature Characteristics. In Table 2 we list the average values of the numerical features and the percentages of true instances for boolean features that have been extracted by Twinder's feature extraction component. Relevant and non-relevant tweets show, on average, different values for the majority of the features. As expected, the average keyword-based and semantic-based relevance scores of tweets which are judged as relevant to a given topic, are much higher than the ones for non-relevant tweets: −10.7 and −10.3 in comparison to −14.4 and −14.2 respectively (the higher the value the better, see Section 4.1). Similarly, the semantic relatedness is given more often for relevant tweets (25.3%) than for non-relevant tweets (4.7%). For the topic-sensitive features, we thus have first evidence that the hypotheses hold (H1-H3).

With respect to the syntactical features, we observe that 81.9% of the relevant tweets mention a URL in contrast to 53.9% of the non-relevant tweets. Hence, the presence of a URL seems to be a good relevance indicator. Contrary to this, we observe that *hasHashtag* and *length* exhibit, on average, similar values for the relevant and non-relevant tweets. Given an average number of 2.4 entities per tweet, it seems that relevant tweets feature richer semantics than non-relevant

---

[11] Language detection, http://code.google.com/p/language-detection/

Table 3. Performance results of relevance estimations for different sets of features.

Features	Precision	Recall	F-Measure
keyword relevance	0.3036	0.2851	0.2940
semantic relevance	0.3050	0.3294	0.3167
topic-sensitive	0.3135	0.3252	0.3192
topic-insensitive	0.1956	0.0064	0.0123
without semantics	0.3410	0.4618	0.3923
without sentiment	0.3701	0.4466	0.4048
without context	0.3827	0.4714	0.4225
all features	0.3725	0.4572	0.4105

tweets (1.9 entities per tweet). Furthermore, the semantic diversity, i.e. the distinct number of different types of concepts that are mentioned in a tweet, is more than 10% higher for relevant tweets.

As part of the sentiment analysis the majority of the tweets were classified as neutral. Interestingly, Table 2 depicts that for relevant tweets the fraction of negative tweets exceeds the fraction of positive tweets (4.9% versus 2.4%) while for non-relevant tweets it is the opposite (6.5% versus 10.7%). Given the average sentiment scores, we conclude that relevant and interesting tweets seem to be more likely to be neutral or negative than tweets that are considered as non-relevant.

The average scores of the contextual features that merely describe characteristics of the creator of a tweet reveal that the average publisher of a relevant tweet has more followers (*#followers*), is more often contained in Twitter lists (*#lists*) and is slightly older (*Twitter age*, measured in years) than the average publisher of a non-relevant tweet. Given these numbers, we gain further evidence for our hypotheses (H11-H13). Thus, contextual features may indeed be beneficial within the retrieval process.

Experimental Setup. To evaluate the performance of Twinder and to analyze the impact of the different features on the relevance estimation, we relied on logistic regression to classify tweets as relevant or non-relevant to a given topic. Due to the small size of the topic set (49 topics), we use 5-fold cross validation to evaluate the learned classification models. For the final setup of the Twinder engine, all 13 features were used as predictor variables. As the number of relevant tweets is considerably smaller than the number of non-relevant tweets, we employed a cost-sensitive classification setup to prevent the relevance estimation from following a best match strategy where simply all tweets are marked as non-relevant. In our evaluation, we focus on the precision and recall of the relevance classification (the positive class) as we aim to investigate the characteristics that make tweets relevant to a given topic.

5.2   Influence of Features on Relevance Estimation

Table 3 shows the performances of the Twinder's relevance estimation based on different sets of features. Learning the classification model solely based on the keyword-based or semantic-based relevance scoring features leads to an F-measure of 0.29 and 0.32 respectively. Semantics thus yield a better performance than the keyword-based relevance estimation. By combining both types of features (see topic-sensitive in Table 3) the F-measure increases only slightly from 0.3167 to 0.3192. As expected, when solely learning the classification model based on the topic-independent features, i.e. without measuring the relevance to the given topic, the quality of the relevance prediction is extremely poor (F-measure: 0.01). When all features are combined (see *all features* in Table 3), a precision of 0.37 is achieved. That means that more than a third of all tweets, which Twinder classifies as relevant and thus returns as results to the user, are indeed relevant, while the recall level (0.46) implies that our approach discovers nearly half of all relevant tweets. Since microblog messages are very short, a significant number of tweets can be read quickly by a user when presented in response to her search request. In such a setting, we believe such a classification accuracy to be sufficient.

Overall, the semantic features seem to play an important role as they lead to a performance improvement with respect to the F-measure from 0.39 to 0.41. allow for an increase of the F-measure. However, Table 3 also shows that contextual features seem to have a negative impact on the retrieval performance. In fact, the removal of the contextual features leads to a performance improvement in recall, precision and F-measure.

We will now analyze the impact of the different features in more detail.

One of the advantages of the logistic regression model is, that it is easy to determine the most important features of the model by considering the absolute weights assigned to them. For this reason, we have listed the relevant-tweet estimation model coefficients for all involved features in the last column of Table 2. The features influencing the model the most are:

- *hasURL*: Since the feature coefficient is positive, the presence of a URL in a tweet is more indicative of relevance than non-relevance. That means, that hypothesis H5 holds.
- *isSemanticallyRelated*: The overlap between the identified DBpedia concepts in the topics and the identified DBpedia concepts in the tweets is the second most important feature in this model, thus, hypothesis H3 holds.
- *isReply*: This feature, which is *true* ($= 1$) if a tweet is written in reply to a previously published tweet has a negative coefficient which means that tweets which are replies are less likely to be in the relevant class than tweets which are not replies, confirming hypothesis H6.
- *sentiment*: The coefficient of the positive and negative sentiment features are also strong indicators for estimating the relevance of a tweet which is in line with our hypothesis H8. In particular, the coefficients suggest that negative tweets are more likely to be relevant while positive tweets are more likely to be non-relevant.

We note that the keyword-based similarity, while being positively aligned with relevance, does not belong to the most important features in this model. It is superseded by semantic-based as well as syntactic features. Contextual features do not play an important role in the relevance estimation process.

When we consider the topic-insensitive features only, we observe that interestingness is related to the potential amount of additional information (i.e. the presence of a URL), the overall clarity of the tweet (a reply tweet may only be understandable in the context of the contextual tweets) and the different aspects covered in the tweet (as evident in the diversity feature).

5.3   Influence of Topic Characteristics on Relevance Estimation

In all reported experiments so far, we have considered the entire set of topics available to us. We now investigate to what extent certain topic characteristics impact the performance of Twinder's relevance estimation and to what extent those differences lead to a change in the logistic regression models. Our ambition is to explore to what extent it is useful to adapt Twinder's configuration to the particular type of search topic. We categorized the topics with respect to three dimensions:

- Popular/unpopular: The topics were split into popular (interesting to many users) and unpopular (interesting to few users) topics. An example of a popular topic is *2022 FIFA soccer* (MB002[12]) - in total we found 24. In contrast, topic *NIST computer security* (MB005) was classified as unpopular (as one of 25 topics).
- Global/local: In this split, we considered the interest for the topic across the globe. The already mentioned topic MB002 is of global interest, since soccer is a highly popular sport in many countries, whereas topic *Cuomo budget cuts* (MB019) is mostly of local interest to users living in New York where Andrew Cuomo is the current governor. We found 18 topics to be of global and 31 topics to be of local interest.
- Persistent/occasional: This split is concerned with the interestingness of the topic over time. Some topics persist for a long time, such as MB002 (the FIFA world cup will be played in 2022), whereas other topics are only of short-term interest, e.g. *Keith Olbermann new job* (MB030). We assigned 28 topics to the persistent and 21 topics to the occasional topic partition.

Our discussion of the results focuses on two aspects: (i) the performance differences and (ii) the difference between the models derived for each of the two partitions (denoted $M_{splitName}$). The results for the three binary topic splits are shown in Table 4.

Popularity: We observe that the recall is considerably higher for unpopular (0.53) than for popular topics (0.41). To some extent this can be explained when considering the amount of relevant tweets discovered for both topic splits: while on average 67.3 tweets were found to be relevant for popular topics, only 49.9 tweets were found to be relevant for unpopular topics (the average number of relevant tweets across the entire topic set is 58.44). A comparison of the most

---

[12] The identifiers of the topics correspond to the ones used in the official TREC dataset.

Table 4. Influence comparison of different features among different topic partitions. There are three splits: popular vs. unpopular topics, global vs. local topics and persistent vs. occasional topics. While the performance measures are based on 5-fold cross-validation, the derived feature weights for the logistic regression model were determined across all topics of a split. For each topic split, the three features with the highest absolute coefficient are underlined.

Performace	Measure	popular	unpopular	global	local	persistent	occasional
	precision	0.3702	0.3696	0.3660	0.3727	0.3450	0.4308
	recall	0.4097	0.5345	0.4375	0.4748	0.4264	0.5293
	F-measure	0.3890	0.4370	0.3986	0.4176	0.3814	0.4750
Category	Feature	popular	unpopular	global	local	persistent	occasional
keyword-based	keyword-based	0.1035	0.2465	0.1901	0.1671	0.1542	0.1978
semantic-based	semantic-based	0.1029	0.1359	0.1018	0.0990	0.0808	0.1583
	semantic distance	<u>1.1850</u>	<u>0.5809</u>	<u>0.9853</u>	<u>0.9184</u>	<u>0.8294</u>	<u>1.1303</u>
syntactical	hasHashtag	0.0834	0.0476	0.1135	0.0429	0.0431	0.0803
	hasURL	<u>1.2934</u>	<u>1.1214</u>	<u>1.2059</u>	<u>1.2192</u>	<u>1.2435</u>	<u>1.0813</u>
	isReply	-0.5163	<u>-0.5465</u>	-0.6179	-0.4750	-0.3853	-0.7712
	length	0.0016	-0.0001	0.0003	0.0009	0.0024	-0.0023
semantics	#entities	0.0468	-0.0072	0.0499	0.0107	0.0384	-0.0249
	diversity	-0.0540	0.1179	-0.1224	0.0830	0.0254	0.0714
	negative sentiment	0.8264	0.0418	0.6780	0.3798	0.0707	<u>0.8344</u>
	neutral sentiment	0.2971	0.2102	0.1695	0.2653	0.3723	0.0771
	positive sentiment	<u>-1.0180</u>	-0.3410	<u>-0.7119</u>	<u>-0.6476</u>	<u>-0.6169</u>	-0.6578
contextual	#followers	0.0000	0.0000	0.0000	0.0000	0.0000	0.0000
	#lists	0.0002	0.0001	0.0002	0.0001	0.0004	0.0001
	Twitter age	0.1278	0.2743	0.0477	0.2646	0.1588	0.2377

important features of $M_{popular}$ and $M_{unpopular}$ shows few differences with the exception of the sentiment features. While sentiment, and in particular positive and negative sentiment, are among the most important features in $M_{popular}$, these features (in particular the negative sentiment) are ranked much lower in $M_{unpopular}$. We hypothesize that unpopular topics do not evoke strong emotions in the users so that sentiment features play a less important role.

Global vs. local: This split did neither result in major differences in the retrieval performances nor in models that are significantly different from each other, indicating that—at least for our currently investigated features—a distinction between global and local topics is not useful.

Temporal persistence: It is interesting to see that the performance (all metrics) is considerably higher for the occasional (short-term) topics than for the persistent (long-term) topics. For topics that have a short lifespan, recall and precision are notably higher than for the other types of topics. In the learnt models, we observe again a change with respect to sentiment features: while the negative sentiment is an important indicator for occasional topics, it is among the least important features for topics that are more persistently discussed on Twitter.

The observation that certain topic splits lead to models that emphasize certain features also offers a natural way forward: if we are able to determine for each topic in advance to which theme or topic characteristic it belongs to, we can select the model that fits the topic best and therefore further optimize the performance of the Twinder search engine.

6   Conclusions

In this paper, we have introduced the Twinder search engine which analyzes various features to determine the relevance and interestingness of Twitter messages for a given topic. We also demonstrated the scalability of the Twinder search engine. In an extensive analysis, we investigated tweet-based and tweet-creator based features along two dimensions: topic-sensitive features and topic-insensitive features. We gained insights into the importance of the different features on the retrieval effectiveness. Our main discoveries about the factors that lead to relevant tweets are as follows:

- The learned models which take advantage of semantics and topic-sensitive features outperform those which do not take the semantics and topic-sensitive features into account.
- Contextual features that characterize the users who are posting the messages have little impact on the relevance estimation.
- The importance of a feature differs depending on the topic characteristics; for example, the sentiment-based features are more important for popular than for unpopular topics.

In the future, we plan to further investigate whether one can adapt the relevance estimation in Twinder to the given search topics. Moreover, we would like to study to what extent personal interests of the users (possibly aggregated from different Social Web platforms) can be utilized as features for personalized retrieval of Twitter messages.

Acknowledgements. The research has received funding from the European Union Seventh Framework Programme, grant agreement no ICT 257831 (Im-REAL project).

References

1. Kwak, H., Lee, C., Park, H., Moon, S.: What is twitter, a social network or a news media? In: WWW, pp. 591–600. ACM (2010)
2. Teevan, J., Ramage, D., Morris, M.R.: #TwitterSearch: a comparison of microblog search and web search. In: WSDM, pp. 35–44. ACM (2011)
3. Bernstein, M.S., Suh, B., Hong, L., Chen, J., Kairam, S., Chi, E.H.: Eddi: interactive topic-based browsing of social status streams. In: UIST, pp. 303–312. ACM (2010)
4. Abel, F., Celik, I., Houben, G.-J., Siehndel, P.: Leveraging the Semantics of Tweets for Adaptive Faceted Search on Twitter. In: Aroyo, L., Welty, C., Alani, H., Taylor, J., Bernstein, A., Kagal, L., Noy, N., Blomqvist, E. (eds.) ISWC 2011, Part I. LNCS, vol. 7031, pp. 1–17. Springer, Heidelberg (2011)

5. Golovchinsky, G., Efron, M.: Making sense of twitter search. In: CHI Workshop on Microblogging: What and How Can We Learn From It? (2010)

6. Dong, A., Zhang, R., Kolari, P., Bai, J., Diaz, F., Chang, Y., Zheng, Z., Zha, H.: Time is of the essence: improving recency ranking using twitter data. In: WWW, pp. 331–340. ACM (2010)

7. Chen, J., Nairn, R., Chi, E.H.: Speak Little and Well: Recommending Conversations in Online Social Streams. In: CHI. ACM (2011)

8. Duan, Y., Jiang, L., Qin, T., Zhou, M., Shum, H.Y.: An empirical study on learning to rank of tweets. In: COLING, Association for Computational Linguistics, pp. 295–303 (2010)

9. Mathioudakis, M., Koudas, N.: Twittermonitor: trend detection over the twitter stream. In: SIGMOD, pp. 1155–1158. ACM (2010)

10. Weng, J., Lim, E.P., Jiang, J., He, Q.: Twitterrank: finding topic-sensitive influential twitterers. In: WSDM, pp. 261–270. ACM (2010)

11. Jadhav, A., Purohit, H., Kapanipathi, P., Ananthram, P., Ranabahu, A., Nguyen, V., Mendes, P.N., Smith, A.G., Cooney, M., Sheth, A.: Twitris 2.0: Semantically Empowered System for Understanding Perceptions From Social Data. In: Semantic Web Challenge (2010)

12. Sakaki, T., Okazaki, M., Matsuo, Y.: Earthquake shakes Twitter users: real-time event detection by social sensors. In: WWW, pp. 851–860. ACM (2010)

13. Zhai, C., Lafferty, J.: A study of smoothing methods for language models applied to Ad Hoc information retrieval. In: SIGIR, pp. 334–342. ACM (2001)

14. Naveed, N., Gottron, T., Kunegis, J., Alhadi, A.C.: Bad news travel fast: A content-based analysis of interestingness on twitter. In: WebSci. ACM (2011)

15. Tao, K., Abel, F., Hauff, C., Houben, G.J.: Supporting website with additional material (2012), http://www.wis.ewi.tudelft.nl/twinder/

Social Event Detection on Twitter

Elena Ilina[1], Claudia Hauff[1], Ilknur Celik[2], Fabian Abel[1],
and Geert-Jan Houben[1]

[1] Web Information Systems, Delft University of Technology
{e.a.ilina,c.hauff,f.abel,g.j.p.m.houben}@tudelft.nl
[2] Middle East Technical University Northern Cyprus Campus
cilknur@metu.edu.tr

Abstract. Various applications are developed today on top of microblogging services like Twitter. In order to engineer Web applications which operate on microblogging data, there is a need for appropriate filtering techniques to identify messages. In this paper, we focus on detecting Twitter messages (tweets) that report on social events. We introduce a filtering pipeline that exploits textual features and n-grams to classify messages into event related and non-event related tweets. We analyze the impact of preprocessing techniques, achieving accuracies higher than 80%. Further, we present a strategy to automate labeling of training data, since our proposed filtering pipeline requires training data. When testing on our dataset, this semi-automated method achieves an accuracy of 79% and results comparable to the manual labeling approach.

Keywords: microblogging, Twitter, event detection, classification, semi-automatic training.

1 Introduction

Twitter is a popular micro-blogging web application serving millions of users. Twitter users chat and share information on news, work-related issues and community matters [1]. Despite the noise in Twitter blogs [2], Web applications can exploit the blogs' content as a source of information to identify natural disasters [3], news [2], or social events [4]. Since the existing Twitter search is cumbersome in finding event-related information [5], a targeted search aiming at finding tweets specifically related to real-life events might be useful. The capability of searching real-life events would be of great benefit for personalization purpose in search.

Accordingly, our motivation is to separate event-related content from the rest of micro-posts. For this, the large volume of non-event-related messages is one of the paramount challenges to be solved. Our approach could be used as a first filtering step before applying other techniques for finding event-related content. The goal is to identify tweets related to real-life events, social events such as music concerts and festivals. Based on Twitter content published by event broadcasters, we train our classification model to distinguish social events from other tweets. The proposed approach is based on a text classification technique, which enables to classify content into two mutually exclusive groups.

M. Brambilla, T. Tokuda, and R. Tolksdorf (Eds.): ICWE 2012, LNCS 7387, pp. 169–176, 2012.

We employ the Naive Bayes classification algorithm utilizing features extracted from the Twitter messages. For training our classifier, we assume, that the selected event broadcasters publish only event-related tweets. Tweets published by other users are initially assigned to the *Other* class. We apply heuristic rules defining the presence of event-related aspects such as time, persons involved and locations. In the presence of these three aspects, the *Events* class is assigned, otherwise the class *Other*. This semi-automatic training approach enables automatic identification of event-related Twitter content and helps to achieve comparable results with supervised learning approach, while reducing efforts of manually labeling training datasets.

Our main contributions include: a semi-automatic training approach for training a classification model which assists in determining event-related tweets, the application of a Naive Bayes classification to identify tweets related to social events based on the proposed semi-automated approach, text preprocessing strategies to improve tweet classification outcomes, an evaluation of the semi-automated learning approach and classifier.

2   Related Work

Twitter received much attention in recent years. Twitter data is openly available, motivating research in social interactions on the Web, micro-blogging and data mining. At the same time, Twitter differs from other blogging software due to its shorter messages, facilitating up-to-date publishing [1]. Researchers have been motivated to analyze Twitter as a source of sensory information provided by Twitter users, reacting on real-life events such as social events [6,7] or natural occurrences as earthquakes [3].

The most prominent works investigating event detection on Twitter are based on statistical [3] and machine learning techniques [8,7]. Sakaki et al. [3] applied classification and particle filtering methods to event detection from Twitter messages, reporting a significant accuracy in detecting earthquakes. Chakrabarti and Punera [9] proposed an approach to group event-related tweets in real-time applying Hidden Markov Models. Their approach can be used for well-structured events, but requires prior knowledge on events, participating athletes and defined event-related hashtags. [8] applied an online clustering approach, grouping tweets with similar content together. After manually labeling clusters as event-related and not event-related, they trained a Naive Bayes text classifier for identifying event-related tweets. This approach, however, requires calculating pairwise similarities before actually identifying tweets as related to events. Popescu et al. [7] used named entity recognition and decision trees, calculating the quantity of found named entities in time.

Other works identify event content using other information sources besides Twitter. Benson et al. [4] align tweets with particular events mentioned in a city guide, employing a distant-supervision approach for training their event classification model. Social blogging content as a source of information for user opinions on events was investigated by [6], which created software that retrieves tweets related to events published on the *Upcoming* web site.

Due to the inherent lack of structure in micro-posts, Twitter is a challenging media platform to work particularly when it comes to identifying relevant tweets [5]. Sankaranarayanan et al. [2] stated that the noise of Twitter messages leads to large volumes of unrelated tweets, introducing an increased complexity of events identification. None of the aforementioned works, however, investigate in-depth the problem of identifying tweets related to social events based solely on the tweets' content. We close this gap by focusing on social event detection, applying a semi-automated learning classification technique similar to [8]. In contrast, our semi-automated classification approach is based on tweets content and does not require additional data sources, clustering or named entity recognition steps. Our approach can be used for filtering event-related content on microblogs.

3   Social Events on Twitter

Twitter microblog posts may include any free-text, special tags or links to other Web resources and are limited to 140 characters. This is why tweets' content often include abbreviations, shortened words or phrases, as well as shortened Uniform Resource Locators (URLs). Forwarding services such as *bit.ly* or *oil.ly* are used to decode the shortened links. Given these limitations, Twitter users try to convey their ideas in a very concise form and make use of special labels, so-called *hashtags*, for tagging the topics of their tweets. For referring to other Twitter users or replying to them, the "@"-symbol is used.

Twitter user profiles are usually linked with profiles of other users, called followers and friends. Twitter can be used for communicating with networking partners, organizations, music bands and even famous people. Twitter assists in marketing and promotion and is therefore widely used by advertising agencies and social media broadcasters to inform on social happenings such as touring artists or upcoming concerts.

In previous works such as [3], events are typically defined using the time and location dimensions. Since social occasions such as music concerts involve musicians and music bands, social events can also be defined by the personalities and/or organizations involved. Therefore, we choose to describe a social event such as a music festival by three main dimensions: "agents involved", "time" and "location". When a particular tweet does not mention all three dimensions, missing dimensions have to be inferred from its content. For instance, we have observed that time references were included in less than 30% of 333 tweets randomly selected from our initial dataset. Only 10% of the 333 tweets mentioned all the three event dimensions, of which 9% were event-related tweets and 1% of tweets were not related to events. This implies that the majority of event-related tweets contain references to these three dimensions, while most of the tweets referring only to one dimension are likely not to be related to social events. Overall, the largest discrepancy was detected for the combinations of event dimensions "Location+Artist+Time" and "Location+Time", which were identified 9 and 6 more times respectively for event related tweets compared to non-event related tweets. This means that time and location dimensions are paramount for finding event-related tweets, whilst adding the artist dimension increases the identification of event-related tweets.

4   Classification Approach

For the implementation, we adapt the standard Naive Bayes classification [10] approach and employ n-gram features. Kanaris et al. [11] argue that character sequence n-gram classification models are relatively resilient towards spelling errors, do not require stemming procedures and can help in decreasing a feature set when compared with word level n-grams. The reason for this is, that there are more n-gram word combinations compared to the number of character n-gram combinations defined by the number of characters used in a particular vocabulary. The lexical benefits of the character n-grams was a motivation for us to create the character n-gram classifier for working with Twitter data. Based on our goal of determining if a particular tweet is related to an event or not, we formulate the following binary classification problem:

Tweet Classification Problem: *Given a tweet $t \in T$, the classification algorithm is used to label the tweet as event related or non-event related by approximating the function $F : T \longrightarrow C$ mapping tweets to their respective classes $C = \{Events, Other\}$*

Based on the Bayes theorem [10], we can calculate the probability $P(C|t)$ of a tweet t belonging to the class C using:

$$P(C|t) = P(t|C) * P(C)/P(t) \ , \tag{1}$$

with $P(t|C)$ the conditional probability of observing tweet t in class C, $P(C)$ the unconditional probability of observing class C, and $P(t)$ the probability of observing tweet t. Next, each tweet we break into a set of n-grams, called $g_1, \ldots, g_m$. For calculating the likelihood that an n-gram appears in the class C, we calculate the product of probabilities of all n-grams based on the Naive Bayes assumption that n-grams appear independently from each other:

$$P(t|C) \simeq P(g_1|C) * P(g_2|C) * \ldots * P(g_m|C) \ . \tag{2}$$

For calculating the probability of a particular n-gram g belonging to the class C, we divide the number of times n-gram g appears in the class C by the total number of n-grams in the class C. The likelihood of class C is computed by dividing the total number of n-grams of the class C by the total number of n-grams in both categories, *Events* and *Other*. Finally, we identify the largest $P(C|t)$, which will be the classification class (*Events* or *Other*) assigned to the tweet t, while ignoring $P(t)$, which is the same for both classes.

For training our classification models we consider manual and semi-automatic labeling. In both cases, we apply several heuristic rules rather than selecting training instances randomly. The reasoning behind this choice is that in our dataset, the ratio between "event" and "not event" tweets from the tweets sample of 333 tweets mentioned above was 0.25. Our aim was to increase the number of training instances while ensuring a satisfactory classification performance. For manual labeling, we follow shortened URLs as generated by shortening services such as *bit.ly* or *oil.ly* and considered only tweets including the sub-strings: "/event/", "/artists/" or "/venue/". Interestingly, only roughly two out of three tweets having such URLs are event-related.

For semi-automated labeling, we include the tweets of the selected event broadcasters into our training dataset of positive instances (*Events* class), when they include the mention of time concepts, references to other users, and words starting with capital letters. For identifying time dimensions, we consider date and time mentions, or words and phrases such as "today", "this evening" or "this summer". In order to relate tweet content elements to the "involved agents" dimension, we consider not only accurately spelled artist names, but also their twitter names. This way we avoid a named entity recognition step for detecting artist and location names. Tweets that do not satisfy heuristic rules of the positive class are assigned to the negative training set (*Other* class).

Hovold [12] demonstrated that the removal of stopwords improves classification accuracy in the context of spam detection and that punctuation marks can have a negative effect on classification. We experiment with removing stopwords, punctuation marks, shortened URLs, hashtags and user mentions for selecting our text-preprocessing strategy applied to Twitter content.

5 Evaluation

In this section we evaluate our Twitter content classification approach. We identify which of the proposed text preprocessing strategies and n-gram sizes are best suited for manual evaluation. The selected n-gram size and text preprocessing strategy are further applied to compare supervised and semi-automated learning approaches.

For running our classification experiments, we created six datasets[1]. The datasets have quite different proportions of "event-related" and "not event-related" tweets (which we denote as R_e ratio), due to their different origin. Datasets $TEST_{MIT}$ (total number of instances N=334, R_e=1) and $TRAIN_{MIT}$ (N=2400, R_e=1) were created by selecting tweets which content overlaps with strings from the New York city guide and provided by [4]. The rest of datasets were published by event broadcasters having more than 1000 of followers and being included in at least ten public lists. For each of the selected 30 broadcasters we followed their 1000 random followers, which posted at least 200 tweets each. Datasets $TRAIN_{auto_1}$ (N=13615, R_e=0.36) and $TRAIN_{auto_2}$ (N=267938, R_e=0.12) were automatically labeled as described in the previous section. Datasets $TRAIN_{TUD}$ (N=2400, R_e=1) and $TEST_{TUD}$ (N=333, R_e=0.33) were labeled manually.

First, based on the manually labeled datasets, $TEST_{TUD}$ and $TRAIN_{TUD}$, we have found that removal of URLs, hashtags, user mentions and punctuation marks

---

[1] See: http://www.wis.ewi.tudelft.nl/people/elena/elenaprojects/events/

has a positive influence on classification performance, increasing F_1-measure in 17% and accuracy from 81% to 84%. Removal of stopwords had a negative impact on all performance metrics. Second, after removing hashtags, URLs, user mentions and punctuation marks from tweets, we identify the best performing n-gram size of 4, resulting in a precision of 96% of events detection for the manually labeled dataset. Therefore, in the next experiments we employed 4-grams, we left stopwords and removed other syntactic elements mentioned above.

Table 1 summarizes the tests we performed with cross-validation of testing and training datasets. The first two tests were performed on manually labeled training sets and achieved an above baseline accuracy of 50%. However, in the second test using the $TEST_{MIT}$ and the $TRAIN_{TUD}$ datasets, we achieved a lower performance for all metrics. Test 4 using $TEST_{TUD}$ testing set and $TRAIN_{MIT}$ training set did not achieve an accuracy of baseline accuracy value. We explain this by the different features used for creating the classification models. Both training sets have different historic data, while our tweets selection strategy differs considerably.

Table 1. Performance on Different Testing Datasets (percentages), where $A_{baseline}$ and $A_{achieved}$ are respective accuracies

Test	Testing	Training	$A_{baseline}$	$A_{achieved}$	Precision	Recall	F_1
1	$TEST_{MIT}$	$TRAIN_{MIT}$	50	71	66	83	74
2	$TEST_{MIT}$	$TRAIN_{TUD}$	50	58	88	18	30
3	$TEST_{TUD}$	$TRAIN_{TUD}$	75	83	96	32	48
4	$TEST_{TUD}$	$TRAIN_{MIT}$	75	43	25	67	36
5	$TEST_{TUD}$	$TRAIN_{auto_1}$	75	79	63	41	50
6	$TEST_{MIT}$	$TRAIN_{auto_2}$	50	60	52	20	29

Figure 1 (a) shows that accuracy of classification using the semi-automatic training improves with a growing number of training instances. After reaching about 5000 training instances, the classification accuracy is above the baseline classification[2] accuracy of 75% when tested on the $TEST_{TUD}$ dataset. The F_1-measure stays above the F_1-measure of the manually-trained classifier. In test 5, we employ $TEST_{TUD}$ and achieve comparable results with the test 3 performed on manually labeled dataset. We observe a drop in precision from 96% to 63%, while, for recall and F_1-measure, we have a slight improvement for the semi-automatic training approach.

In test 6 performed on the $TEST_{MIT}$ dataset, we increase the number of training instances up to 267938. As shown in the Figure 1 (b), we achieve an accuracy of 60%, which is comparable with the accuracy achieved when using the manual labeling approach in test 2. We achieve very similar performance values for tests 2 and 6; however, in test 6 we observe decreased precision.

---

[2] In our case the baseline classifier is a default classifier predicting a majority class of non-events.

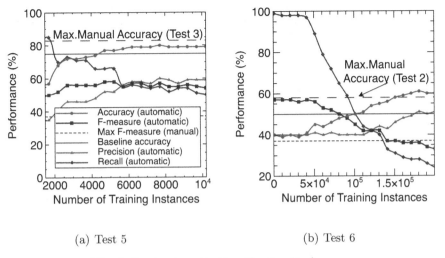

(a) Test 5   (b) Test 6

Fig. 1. Semi-automatic Classification Performance

6   Conclusion and Future Work

In the foregoing, we propose a semi-automatic approach for detecting event-related tweets. This will allow to exploit large volumes of micro-blogging content for providing information on social events. The aim is eventually to use for instance Twitter content in web applications listing concerts, taking into account factors like a specific time or date, location or performers. For this, we use a classification approach based on Naive Bayes and n-gram features extracted from Twitter content of event broadcasters and their followers. The training and testing datasets are built up on a classifier of manually labeled tweets, with which we achieve high precision and accuracy. Training the classifier in a semi-automatic way using content of pre-selected broadcasters would allow to reduce manual labeling efforts. With a growing number of training instances, the prediction accuracy of the classifier using the proposed semi-automatic training approach is comparable to the classifier created on a manually labeled training set. Future work will include using the classifier with different and larger scale datasets derived from Twitter content, developing a classifier that could outperform one requiring manual labeling.

Acknowledgments. This work is partially sponsored by the ImREAL project (http://imreal-project.eu).

References

1. Java, A., Song, X., Finin, T., Tseng, B.: Why we twitter: understanding microblogging usage and communities. In: Proceedings of the 9th Workshop on Web Mining and Social Network Analysis (WebKDD), pp. 56–65. ACM (2007)

2. Sankaranarayanan, J., Samet, H., Teitler, B., Lieberman, M., Sperling, J.: Twitterstand: news in tweets. In: Proceedings of the 17th International Conference on Advances in Geographic Information Systems (SIGSPATIAL), pp. 42–51. ACM (2009)

3. Sakaki, T., Okazaki, M., Matsuo, Y.: Earthquake shakes Twitter users: real-time event detection by social sensors. In: Proceedings of the 19th International Conference on World Wide Web (WWW), pp. 851–860. ACM (2010)

4. Benson, E., Haghighi, A., Barzilay, R.: Event discovery in social media feeds. In: Proceedings of the 49th Annual Meeting of the Association for Computational Linguistics (ACL-HLT 2011), pp. 389–398. Association for Computational Linguistics (2011)

5. Abel, F., Celik, I., Houben, G.-J., Siehndel, P.: Leveraging the Semantics of Tweets for Adaptive Faceted Search on Twitter. In: Aroyo, L., Welty, C., Alani, H., Taylor, J., Bernstein, A., Kagal, L., Noy, N., Blomqvist, E. (eds.) ISWC 2011, Part I. LNCS, vol. 7031, pp. 1–17. Springer, Heidelberg (2011)

6. Becker, H., Chen, F., Iter, D., Naaman, M., Gravano, L.: Automatic identification and presentation of twitter content for planned events. In: Proceedings of the 5th International AAAI Conference on Weblogs and Social Media (ICWSM 2011), pp. 655–656. AAAI Press (2011)

7. Popescu, A., Pennacchiotti, M., Paranjpe, D.: Extracting events and event descriptions from Twitter. In: Proceedings of the 20th International Conference on World Wide Web (WWW), pp. 105–106. ACM (2011)

8. Becker, H., Naaman, M., Gravano, L.: Beyond trending topics: Real-world event identification on twitter. In: Proceedings of the 5th International AAAI Conference on Weblogs and Social Media (ICWSM), North America, pp. 438–441. AAAI Press (July 2011)

9. Chakrabarti, D., Punera, K.: Event summarization using tweets. In: Proceedings of the 5th International Conference on Weblogs and Social Media (ICWSM), pp. 66–73. AAAI Press (2011)

10. Lewis, D.: Naive (Bayes) at Forty: The Independence Assumption in Information Retrieval. In: Nédellec, C., Rouveirol, C. (eds.) ECML 1998. LNCS, vol. 1398, pp. 4–15. Springer, Heidelberg (1998)

11. Kanaris, I., Kanaris, K., Houvardas, I., Stamatatos, E.: Words vs. character n-grams for anti-spam filtering. International Journal on Artificial Intelligence Tools 16(6), 1047–1067 (2007)

12. Hovold, J.: Naive bayes spam filtering using word-position-based attributes. In: Proceedings of the Second Conference on Email and Anti-Spam (CEAS 2005), Stanford University, California, USA, pp. 1–8 (2005)

Temporal Semantic Centrality for the Analysis of Communication Networks

Damien Leprovost[1], Lylia Abrouk[1],
Nadine Cullot[1], and David Gross-Amblard[2]

[1] Le2i CNRS Lab, University of Bourgogne, Dijon, France
`firstname.lastname@u-bourgogne.fr`
[2] IRISA, University of Rennes 1, France
`firstname.lastname@irisa.fr`

Abstract. Understanding communication structures in huge and versatile online communities becomes a major issue. In this paper we propose a new metric, the *Semantic Propagation Probability*, that characterizes the user's ability to propagate a concept to other users, in a rapid and focused way. The message semantics is analyzed according to a given ontology. We use this metric to obtain the *Temporal Semantic Centrality* of a user in the community. We propose and evaluate an efficient implementation of this metric, using real-life ontologies and data sets.

Keywords: semantic analysis, centrality, community, communication network, ontology.

1 Introduction

With the advent of the collaborative Web, each website can become a place for expression, where users' opinions are exchanged. User messages are valuable for the site owner: in addition to a proof of interest for the website, they allow the owner to understand users'judgments and expectations. However, if this reasoning is humanly manageable on a small number of messages, it is reckless for larger systems, handling thousands of users posting thousands of messages per month.

Nowadays, users and community profiling is a growing challenge [1]. Many approaches have been developed, initialy relied on a basic relationship between users like friendship in social networks or answers / citations in social communication networks (like forums or emails).

In this paper we consider as a communication network any system where users are able to exchange messages, such as forums, tweets, mailboxes, etc. In this context, we first use a method for the identification of hot topics and thematic communities. These topics are identified within user messages using a target *ontology*, which can be generic or specialized for a given domain.

We then present a method for the discovery of central users who play an important role in the communication flow of each community. For this purpose we introduce new semantic measures called the *Semantic Propagation Probability*

M. Brambilla, T. Tokuda, and R. Tolksdorf (Eds.): ICWE 2012, LNCS 7387, pp. 177–184, 2012.
© Springer-Verlag Berlin Heidelberg 2012

(SPP) and *Temporal Semantic Centrality* (TSC) that take into account both semantics and communication timestamps *at once*.

A potential limitation of using an ontology is to limit a priori the set of topics of interest, what may prevent the discovery on new topics. But the main advantages is to focus the analysis on a known domain that can be extended at will, but in a controlled way. A basic example is to understand the behavior of a forum according to brand product ontologies. Another advantage is to rely on the permanently increasing set of generic or specialized ontologies that are linked to other resources or services.

The paper is organized as follows. We present hot topics and community identification in Section 2 and our metric in Section 3. We show our experiments in Section 4. Section 5 discusses the obtained results and Section 6 covers related approaches. Finally, Section 7 concludes[1].

2   Communication Networks and Thematic Communities

Overview. We reason according to an ontology $O = (C, is - a)$, where C is a set of concepts and $is - a$ is the subsumption relation. We equip C with a semantic similarity measure $d_C(c, c')$ with c and c' in C. Let δ be a similarity threshold. We say that two concepts are similar if their distance d_C is smaller than δ.

We consider a communication network $G = (U, S)$, where U is a set of users and $S \subseteq U \times U \times \mathbb{N}$ is the timed directed *send* relation of a message $m = (u, v, t)$ from user u to user v at time t. We take $\mathbb{N}$ as a clock for the sake of simplicity. Perfectly simultaneous messages are possible in this model, and their occurrence is taken into account . This simple model assumes that the originator and receptor of a given message are known. The *content* function maps a message $m = (u, v, t)$ to its plain textual content $content(m)$. In order to focus on concepts in C, the $content_C$ function maps m to the set of concepts of C which appear in $content(m)$. This function encompasses details like stemming.

Identifying Hot Concepts. The first step of our method is to determine the hot topics of the communication network, as a subset of concepts of O. We associate with each user a *semantic profile*. At the communication network level, we aggregate all the user profiles to build a system profile. Hot concepts are the top-n concepts which are most present in users' profiles. Due to a lack of space, we do not provide here a full description of the profile construction of the system, which is available in our previous work [8].

Building Thematic Communities. Once hot concepts are well identified, our goal is to divide the communication network G into k thematic communities $G_1 \ldots, G_k$, each G_i being labeled with one set of concepts $L_i \subseteq C$. We will filter users according to their semantic profiles. In order to control the number of

---

[1] A detailed version of the method is available as a technical report:
http://hal.archives-ouvertes.fr/hal-00692289

thematic communities, we allow users to be gathered according to their common and similar concepts. The similarity of two concepts of the target ontology O is measured using a semantic distance. We rely here on the Wu-Palmer distance [13] restricted to concepts *hierarchies* (trees), which has already been applied to similar cases [3]. The similarity is defined with respect to the distance between two concepts in the hierarchy, and also by their position relative to the root. The semantic similarity between concepts c_1 and c_2 is

$$sim_{Wu\&Palmer}(c_1, c_2) = \frac{2 * depth(c)}{depth(c_1) + depth(c_2)} \ ,$$

where c is the nearest top edge of c_1 and c_2 and $depth(x)$ the number of edges between x and the root. As stated in the beginning of this section, two concepts c_1 and c_2 will be considered as similar if $d_C(c_1, c_2) \leq \delta$, where δ is the similarity threshold:

$$d_C(c_1, c_2) = 1 - sim_{Wu\&Palmer}(c_1, c_2).$$

We then turn to thematic communities. Let $N_i^+(G_i)$ be the in-degree of community G_i, that the number of posts from members of G_i to members of G_i which contain concepts (similar to) a concept in L_i. Conversely, let $N_i^-(G_i)$ be its out-degree, that is the number of posts from members of G_i to members outside G_i which contain concepts (similar to) a concept in L_i. We can now define a thematic community:

Definition 1. *A set $G_i \subseteq G$ is a thematic community on concepts $L_i \subseteq C$, if, when restricting G_i to posts that contain a concept (similar to) a concept in L_i, the in-degree of G_i is greater than its out-degree (thus, $N_i^+(G_i) > N_i^-(G_i)$).*

Traditional approaches by Flake et al. [5] and various optimizations [7,4] allow us to effectively group users linked by a binary relation in communities. We take a leaf out of them to define a cutting method, given the resulting simplification of the Definition 1. For each community G_i, we maintain for each user u , two sets of messages $N_i^+(u)$ and $N_i^-(u)$, representing respectively communications inside G_i and communications outside G_i, with concepts similar to L_i. A message m_k is considered by default in $N_i^-(u)$. Each message m_k to user u is considered initially as unhandled. So, we add the message to $N_i^-(u)$. After that, if one or more message m_l is emitted from u, with $d(m_l, m_k) \leq \delta$. At any time, communities are $G_i = (U_i, S_i)$, where $U_i = \{u \in U : N_i^+(u) \leq N_i^-(u)\}$ and $S_i \subseteq U_i \times U \times \mathbb{N}$. Algorithm 1 and 2 presents this community clustering.

3   Temporal Semantic Centrality

Dispersion and Lag. Inside a thematic community labeled by concepts L_i, all users are known to discuss frequently about topics of L_i or similar topics. We would like to rank these users according to their centrality, i.e. to identify the most important information participants inside the community. In this proposal, we base our ranking on *both semantics and time*. We define a *temporal semantic*

Algorithm 1. Message	**Algorithm 2.** Communities
Require: message m, concepts $L_1, \ldots, L_i, \ldots, L_k, \delta$	**Require:** $G = (U, S)$, $L_1, \ldots, L_i, \ldots, L_k$

Algorithm 1. Message

Require: message m,
    concepts $L_1, \ldots, L_i, \ldots, L_k, \delta$
1: **for all** $c \in L_i, c \in context(m)$ **do**
2:    **if** m is incoming **then**
3:       $N_i^-(u) = N_i^-(u) \cup m$
4:    **else**
5:       **for all** m_λ to u with $d(m, m_\lambda) \leq \delta$ **do**
6:          $N_i^+(u) = N_i^+(u) \cup m \cup m_\lambda$
7:          $N_i^-(u) = N_i^-(u) - m$
8:       **end for**
9:    **end if**
10: **end for**

Algorithm 2. Communities

Require: $G = (U, S)$, $L_1, \ldots, L_i, \ldots, L_k$
1: **for all** G_i **do**
2:    **for all** $u \in U$ **do**
3:       **if** $N_i^+(u) \leq N_i^-(u)$ **then**
4:          $U_i = U_i \cup u$
5:       **end if**
6:    **end for**
7: **end for**

centrality, using a concept-driven measure, the *semantic propagation probability*, denoted as SPP in the sequel. Globally speaking, this measure aims at capturing:

- how focused are the answers of a user according to an input post,
- how fast are these answers, relatively to the general pace of the community.

Users with a high SPP are more likely to answer or relay messages, semantically relevant to the community.

Let us consider an oriented communication: $u \to_t u' \to_{t'} u''$, which means that there exists in the communication graph G a message $m = (u, u', t)$ from u to u' at time t, and a messages $m' = (u', u'', t')$ from u' to u'' at time t'. For $t' > t$, m' can be seen as a relay of m in a very broad sense. Globally speaking, user u' is impacted (in various ways) by the reception of m before sending m'. Also, the content of m' can be related to m or completely independent from it. We will measure this relation so that it depends on the *semantic dispersion* of the sent message, and its *lag*.

The *dispersion* of a message m according to concept c, noted $dispersion_c(m)$, is the ratio between the minimum semantic distance between c and concepts in m, and the maximum semantic distance between c and the concepts of the target ontology:

$$dispersion_c(m) = \frac{\min_{c' \in content(m)} d_C(c, c')}{\max_{c' \in C} d_C(c, c')}.$$

If the message uses concept $c \in content(m)$, then $dispersion_c(m) = 0$. Observe also that the dispersion is at most 1. For the special case where the message has no relevant concept ($content(m)$ is empty), we consider that $dispersion_c(m) = 1$.

Similarly, we define the *lag* between a message received by u_i at time t_{i-1} and a message sent by u_i at time t_i as the duration between them, *relatively to the natural pace of the community*. Indeed, some news-focused or work-oriented communities suppose a rapid pace from its users (say hours, minutes, at most 2 days), while some technical communities may consider a month a natural duration for a specific topic.

The *meanpace*$_{L_i}$ of a community labeled by L_i is the average of the duration of message transmission between users of the community labeled by L_i:

$$meanpace_{L_i} = avg_{m=(u,u',t),m'=(u',u'',t') \text{ with } u,u',u''\in G_i,t'>t}(t'-t).$$

The *lag* between two message $m = (v, u, t)$ and $m' = (u, v', t')$, relative to the mean pace *meanpace*$_{L_j}$ of community G_j labeled by concepts L_j is defined by:

$$lag(m,m') = \begin{cases} \infty \text{ if } t' \leq t, \\ \frac{t'-t}{meanpace_{L_j}} \text{ otherwise.} \end{cases}$$

Note that the infinite lag is used to enforce communication chains with an increasing timestamp and to discard simultaneous messages $(t = t')$.

Semantic Propagation Probability and Temporal Semantic Centrality. We can now turn to the definition of the *Semantic Propagation Probability (SPP)*. The *SPP* of user u according to messages m and m' is defined by:

$$SPP_c(u,m,m') = \frac{(1 - dispersion_c(m) \times dispersion_c(m'))}{1 + lag(t,t')}.$$

For example, a user receiving a message talking about c and sending a message about c immediately after (that is $t' \approx t$ in our discretized model), has a SPP_c arbitrary close to 1.

Finally, the temporal semantic centrality $TSC_{L_i}(u)$ of user u within the community labeled by L_i is computed on all incoming and sent messages of u:

$$TSC_{L_i}(u) = avg_{c\in L_i}\Big(\sum_{m=(u,u',t)\in G} \sum_{m'=(u',u'',t')\in G,t'>t} SPP_c(u,m,m')\Big).$$

Approximation for Efficiency. In our implementation of SPP_c, the semantic distance is computed in two phases. An initial phase, done once per ontology, builds an index matching each concept to its ancestor and depth in the ontology. In the second phase, for a new message with at most k distinct concepts, the computation of its dispersion according to concept c requires k queries to the index. The overall computation time is then $O(kM)$, where M is the total number of hot concepts.

Computing the TSC naively is a time consuming operation, as (1) the ontology may be extremely large and (2) all incoming messages have to be matched with all potential outcoming messages. For the first difficulty, we focus on the identified hot concepts, and compute the set of concepts in the relevant neighborhood of at least one of them (that is, with a semantic distance smaller than the prescribed relevance threshold).

For the second difficulty, it should be observed that a message can impact the TSC only during a short time window, due to the lag function. Outside this window, the TSC contribution is close to zero. This suggests a sliding-window algorithm, where only a finite set $INBOX(u)$ of messages recently received by u is kept in main memory. Outcoming messages are then compared to messages in this window.

4   Experiments

Data Sets. We have taken as a data source the Enron Email data set[2] for its complete communication network with a send relation and precise timestamps. This data set consists in emails collected from about 150 users, mostly senior management of Enron, made public by US federal authorities during its investigation on Enron scandal. The set contains a total of about 500'000 messages.

Ontology. We use WordNet as an ontology, with the *hypernym* relation playing the role of the $is - a$ relation, and the *entity* synset as root. We perform a relational mapping of the resulting ontology.

Communities. As explained in the model, we parse every mail, and extract their main topics. We generalize and summarize them, to obtain the top concepts. We extract and cluster the main community topics, as shown in Table 1.

Table 1. Concept clusters of communities

rank	concepts	rank	concepts
#1	{market,services,providence,questioning,management}	#6	{time,change}
#2	{forward,informant,attache,reporter}	#7	{company,business}
#3	{pleasing,contraction}	#8	{newness}
#4	{subjectivity}	#9	{thanks}
#5	{energy,gas}	#10	{power}

Temporal Semantic Centrality. Based on this clusters, we compute SPP and centralities for each community. Table 2 shows results for one of them. It is interesting to note that the centrality does not appear to be directly related to activity (set of posts) within the community. The best example is the announcement address. Despite a strong activity in each of the identified communities, it does not have any centrality. This reflects the fact that if it writes to all, no one communicate with it. It is therefore absent of any communication path identified.

Table 2. Centralities of #1{market,services,...} community

login	$N^+ - N^-$	centrality	position
kate.symes	4310	5438	Employee
kay.mann	14332	3208	Assistant General Counsel
vince.kaminski	8432	1170	Managing Director for Research
	...		
steven.kean	4571	348	Vice President & Chief of Staff
	...		
enron.announcements	7284	0	Mailing list

---

[2] Available at http://www.cs.cmu.edu/~enron/

5 Discussion

Community Analysis. The implementation on the Enron data set allows us to compare our results with the reality of this company and its communication network. An interesting point about this is that although the data set contains a high proportion of spam, no content of this type has emerged from the analysis. This is a great advantage of taking into account the semantic centrality compared to simple raw frequencies. It is also interesting to note the role of senior managers. Although their communication is important, and their centrality honorable, they are rarely well positioned in our ranking. This can be explained by their position in the company. As leaders, they are often the start or the end of the communication chain. That is why the best centrality is often held by an employee. We speculate that central employees seem to be those responsible for secretarial outsourced tasks: requiring strong two-ways communications, such tasks become the centers. But the lack of data on staff assignments in the data set does not allow us to validate this conclusion further.

Properties of *TSC*. It should be observed that a user forwarding received emails systematically will be granted a high TSC. Indeed, this centrality does not measure information addition to a message, but the probability to transmit information efficiently. We identified in this respect the forwarding robot of Enron emails as a central "user". This robot is central as it represents a efficient way of propagating messages. Second, we do not favor explicitly co-occurrences of concepts in emails. For example, it seems natural to weight higher a user who conveys concepts $\{a, b\} \in L_i$ in a unique message m_1 rather than a user conveying a then b in two distinct messages m_2 and m_3. But the definition of SPP takes this co-occurrence into account, as m_1 will contribute twice with the same lag, and m_2 (resp. m_3) will contribute once, with a longer lag (unless m_2 and m_3 are simultaneous).

6 Related Work

Models have been proposed to modelize users' influence applying data mining techniques [11], or centrality metrics [6]. We differ from their approaches by the incorporation of a structured semantics, the role of each user in the communication, and the incremental possibilities of our computations. Several studies have focused on the importance of comment activity on blogs or news sites [9] and highlight the social role of comments. It allows to determine popular topics, conflicts of opinion [10], or relational implications between users [2]. Different approaches focus on mapping the user interests to an ontology [12], based on the user's Web browsing experience. Our method relies on richer users contributions (posts), with a common ontology for all users.

7 Conclusion

We presented in this paper an approach to detect central users in a communication network by building semantic-driven communities and evaluating message quality. For this purpose, we have introduced a new measure, the *Semantic Propagation Probability* to take into account semantic accuracy and time delay. As a future direction, we will consider the transformations that a message undergoes in a communication path, in order to find the user's position (adviser, accountant, etc.), or determine the user's capabilities like computation, correction, etc.

References

1. Bilenko, M., Richardson, M.: Predictive client-side profiles for personalized advertising. In: ACM International Conference on Knowledge Discovery and Data Mining (SIGKDD), pp. 413–421. ACM, New York (2011)
2. De Choudhury, M., Mason, W.A., Hofman, J.M., Watts, D.J.: Inferring relevant social networks from interpersonal communication. In: International Conference on World Wide Web (WWW), pp. 301–310. ACM, New York (2010)
3. Desmontils, E., Jacquin, C.: Indexing a web site with a terminology oriented ontology. In: International Semantic Web Working Symposium, pp. 181–198. IOS Press (2002)
4. Dourisboure, Y., Geraci, F., Pellegrini, M.: Extraction and classification of dense communities in the web. In: International Conference on World Wide Web (WWW), pp. 461–470. ACM, New York (2007)
5. Flake, G.W., Lawrence, S., Giles, C.L.: Efficient identification of web communities. In: ACM International Conference on Knowledge Discovery and Data Mining (SIGKDD), pp. 150–160. ACM, New York (2000)
6. Fuehres, H., Fischbach, K., Gloor, P.A., Krauss, J., Nann, S.: Adding Taxonomies Obtained by Content Clustering to Semantic Social Network Analysis. In: Bastiaens, T.J., Baumöl, U., Krämer, B.J. (eds.) On Collective Intelligence. AISC, vol. 76, pp. 135–146. Springer, Heidelberg (2010)
7. Ino, H., Kudo, M., Nakamura, A.: Partitioning of web graphs by community topology. In: International Conference on World Wide Web (WWW), pp. 661–669. ACM, New York (2005)
8. Leprovost, D., Abrouk, L., Gross-Amblard, D.: Discovering implicit communities in web forums through ontologies. Web Intelligence and Agent Systems: An International Journal 10, 93–103 (2011)
9. Menchen-Trevino, E.: Blogger motivations: Power, pull, and positive feedback. Internet Research 6.0 (2005)
10. Mishne, G., Glance, N.: Leave a reply: An analysis of weblog comments. In: WWW 2006 Workshop on the Weblogging Ecosystem (2006)
11. Richardson, M., Domingos, P.: Mining knowledge-sharing sites for viral marketing. In: ACM International Conference on Knowledge Discovery and Data Mining (SIGKDD), pp. 61–70. ACM, New York (2002)
12. Sieg, A., Mobasher, B., Burke, R.: Web search personalization with ontological user profiles. In: ACM Conference on Information and Knowledge Management, CIKM 2007, pp. 525–534. ACM, New York (2007)
13. Wu, Z., Palmer, M.: Verbs semantics and lexical selection. In: Association for Computational Linguistics (ACL), pp. 133–138. Association for Computational Linguistics, Stroudsburg (1994)

Systematic Evolution of WebML Models by Coupled Transformations

Manuel Wimmer, Nathalie Moreno, and Antonio Vallecillo

Universidad de Málaga, Spain
{mw,moreno,av}@lcc.uma.es

Abstract. Model-driven Web Engineering is an effective approach for improving the development of Web applications by providing appropriate abstraction mechanisms and different viewpoints. However, maintaining existing Web models still presents some significant research challenges. In particular, maintenance and evolution tasks are based on fine-grained atomic changes, and there is no automated reconciliation support for change propagation among viewpoints. In this paper we present an approach based on coupled transformations to ease the evolution of content models and the corresponding reconciliation of dependent hypertext models. The approach is illustrated by using the well-known *Extract-Class* refactoring for WebML models.

1 Introduction

Model-driven Web Engineering (MDWE) [13] is an effective approach to Web application development that uses models, metamodels, and model transformation as key elements of the development process. It incorporates a higher level of abstraction in the specification of systems guided by the *separation of concerns principle* using *viewpoints* that allows the (semi)-automated derivation of the final implementation code from platform-independent multi-viewpoint specifications. In this sense, existing Web engineering approaches such as WebML [1] and UWE [11] to name just a few (for a survey, cf., [15]) match the MDWE principles.

Most MDWE approaches identify three key viewpoints for the design of Web applications: *content*, *hypertext*, and *presentation*. Although these viewpoints are separately specified and developed, they are not completely independent. For instance, the hypertext models reference elements defined in content models, because they describe how to navigate through the content model. Maintaining manually these references and the consistency between the different viewpoints is a cumbersome task, for which there is little automated support. Furthermore, the integration and synchronization of multi-viewpoint systems is an open issue, not only in MDWE but also in other application fields of model-driven engineering in general [7].

The maintenance and evolution of Web models in the majority of MDWE approaches is currently hampered by two main shortcomings: (i) *missing evolution support*, since changes are applied and identified at very low level of abstraction (basically as atomic changes to the model elements such us additions, deletions, and updates); (ii) *missing reconciliation support*, since the propagation of changes among viewpoints is currently

M. Brambilla, T. Tokuda, and R. Tolksdorf (Eds.): ICWE 2012, LNCS 7387, pp. 185–199, 2012.

difficult and cumbersome because the reconciliation is also achieved by manually applying atomic changes.

To tackle these shortcomings, we propose to manage the evolution of content models by using *coarse-grained changes*, which are specified as *model transformations*.
To reason about the impact of the coarse-grained content model changes, we specify
the changes by stating not only the structural transformation of content models, but
also the implications for their instances, i.e., the data of the Web application, by applying *coupled model transformations* [12] for the instance models. This approach allows
describing in a precise way the semantics of the coarse-grained changes—which is a
prerequisite for reasoning about the reconciliation of dependent hypertext models.

Based on the coarse-grained content model changes, we present a catalogue of reconciliation patterns for hypertext models specified as coupled model transformations.
As an example, we present how hypertext models have to co-evolve when a content
model evolve by an *ExtractClass* refactoring. This catalogue of reconciliation patterns
is based on the core modeling elements of Web modeling languages, which have been
jointly developed in the MDWEnet initiative [14,18]. For demonstrating the proposed
approach, we use WebML as selected MDWE protagonist. Although the presented (coupled) transformations are specific to WebML, the used modeling concepts are shared by
the majority of MDWE approaches. Thus, they results are not limited to WebML but
may be also transferred to other MDWE approaches. As a spin-off, during our investigations we explored some limitations of WebML for which we propose two extensions.

This paper is structured as follows. Section 2 briefly outlines WebML and introduces
the running example used throughout the paper. Then, Section 3 presents our approach
and Section 4 describes the catalogue of reconciliation patterns for hypertext models
when *ExtractClass* refactorings have been applied on content model. Finally, Section 5
relates our work to similar approaches and Section 6 concludes.

2   Background: WebML By-Example

WebML describes Web applications with three viewpoints: *content* (data), *hypertext*
(navigation between pages), and *presentation* (look&feel). The *content model* is specified using an Entity-Relationship model (or, equivalently, a simplified UML class diagram), comprising *classes*, *attributes*, *single inheritance*, and *binary relationships* as
shown in the WebML metamodel (cf. Fig. 1). The front-end is specified using the *hypertext model*, which is structured into *pages*.

Pages are the basic interface containers: they can be structured in sub-pages and
comprise content units. A *content unit* is defined as a component that publishes some
content in a page; the published content can be extracted dynamically from the objects
specified in the content model or specified statically in the hypertext model (e.g., an
entry form consisting of multiple input fields). In addition to content units, WebML
provides *operation units*, defined as components for executing commands (mostly on
the database). Operation units, unlike content units, do not publish content and thus
are positioned outside pages. Components (content and operation units) may have *input
and output parameters* (e.g., the OID of the object to display or modify, etc.). Parameter
passing is expressed as a side effect of navigation (values are transported from source

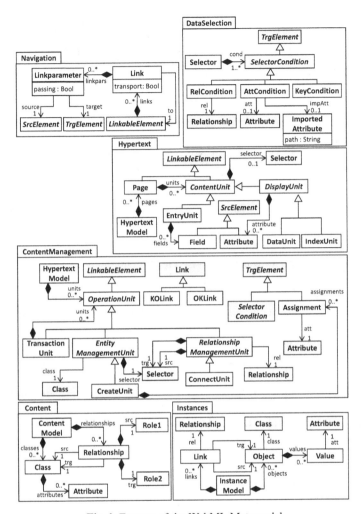

Fig. 1. Excerpt of the WebML Metamodel

elements of link parameters to their targets): components are connected by *links*, which have a threefold purpose: enabling the user's navigation, supporting the passage of parameters, and triggering the execution of components. In particular, *OK links* and *KO links* are output links of operations, respectively followed after execution success or failure. How all these concepts are related to each other is illustrated in an excerpt of the metamodel shown in Fig. 1.

Running example: The Agenda system. At the beginning, this Web application was designed with the only goal of allowing users to maintain a simple list of contacts. Following the WebML methodology, the content and hypertext models were designed as shown in Fig. 2. Given the simplicity of our requirements, one class was enough to store the contacts' information and, based on it, the hypertext model was established, comprising a *DataUnit* and an *IndexUnit* for retrieving information from the content

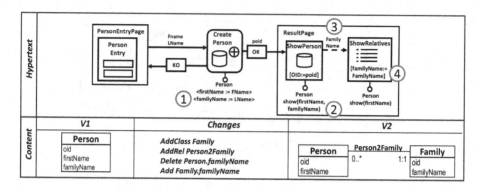

Fig. 2. Running Example: Content Model Evolution and Impact on Hypertext Model

model as well a *CreateUnit* and an *EntryUnit* for inserting and storing information. However, the content model was later revised to add, among other changes, the *Family* class for grouping contacts based on their family ties. This meant to *extract* a class from the *Person* class, and to *move* the attribute *familyName* from *Person* to the new class.

When describing the changes as refactorings, this high-level of abstraction is the natural way in which modelers usually thinks and discuss about a system evolution. However, when these changes are detected by any of the existing model difference tools, what we obtain is a very large number of atomic changes that need to be applied to the individual model elements (*AddClass Family, AddRel Person2Family, Delete Person.familyName, Add Family.familyName*, etc.). Understanding and manipulating atomic changes to propagate them from one view to the rest can become a complex and brittle task. Just thinking about, e.g., the *ExtractClass* refactoring that we have previously mentioned. In order to guarantee that the hypertext model still works as before, the modeler has to adjust several elements in the hypertext model (around 22 atomic changes as we shall see later) for this small example because of four issues:

1. The *CreateUnit* has an assignment to the attribute *familyName* (cf. ① in Fig. 2) which is now no longer contained the class *Person*. In WebML, only attributes contained by the class which is referenced by the *CreateUnit* can be used in assignments. Furthermore, the *CreateUnit* is only able to produce a *Person* instance, but actually, also a *Family* instance is needed that is linked to the *Person* instance to populate the same information in the database for the given inputs of the *EntryUnit*.
2. The *DataUnit* shows two attributes, namely *firstname* and *familyname* (cf. ② in Fig. 2). However, as mentioned before, the attribute *familyName* is no longer available in the class *Person*. As for *CreateUnits*, also *DataUnits* can only use attributes which are directly contained by their referenced class.
3. The automatic transport link between the *DataUnit* and the *IndexUnit* comprises a *LinkParameter* transferring the *familyName* value (cf. ③ in Fig. 2) from the source unit to the target unit. However, this value is not accessible in the source unit.
4. A similar issue arises for the *SelectorCondition* of the *IndexUnit* which also accesses the moved attribute *familyName*.

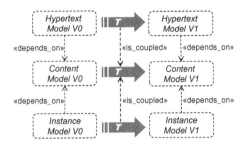

Fig. 3. Coupled Transformations for Web Model Evolution at a Glance

3   Transformations for Web Model Evolution: An Overview

In WebML, the content model is the cornerstone around which all other views are articulated. This fact is not a particular feature of WebML, but shared by most modeling approaches for data-intensive Web applications. So, given its importance, we have focused our research on the evolution of Web application models when evolution is triggered by the content model.

Fig. 3 illustrates our proposed approach for the systematic evolution of Web models when coarse-grained content model changes are applied. While the upper area of this figure is concerned with the reconciliation of the changed content model and the initial hypertext model, the lower area is dealing with the co-evolution of the content model and its instances. So to speak, we have *initiator changes* on the content models expressed as *model transformations*, and *reconciliation changes* for the instance models and hypertext models expressed as *coupled model transformations* [12], which are transformations that involve multiple software artefacts, such that changes in one artefact trigger co-changes in other artefacts.

3.1   Coarse-Grained Content Model Changes as Transformations

A transformation describing a coarse-grained change is much more than a *set of atomic changes*. In fact, its definition includes *pre-* and *post-conditions* which have to be fulfilled for an appropriate application. A natural way of implementing coarse-grained changes is by means of *in-place* transformations. As a matter of fact, the term *in-place transformations* stands for transformations rewriting a model, as opposed to producing a model from scratch which is done by *out-place* transformations.

In-place transformations can be described in many ways. Rule-based descriptions are elegant and easy to understand. Such descriptions have declarative model rewriting rules as their primitive building blocks. A rule consists of a *Left Hand Side* (LHS) pattern that is matched against a model. If a match is found, this pattern is updated, in the model, based on what is specified in the *Right Hand Side* (RHS) of the rule. Additionally, *Negative Application Condition* (NAC) patterns may be used, specifying which patterns should not be found in the model (match for non-existence) for applying the rule.

Coarse-grained changes such as refactorings are implemented by specifying its pre- and post-conditions as well as the actions that have to be executed for applying the

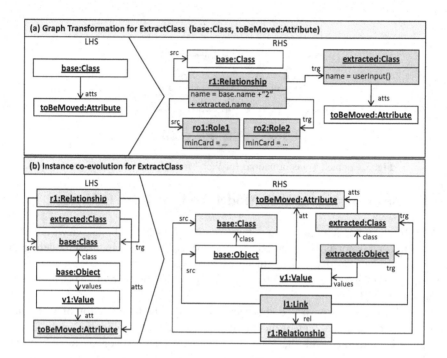

Fig. 4. Formalization of ExtractClass Refactoring

change. Most of them need also some input parameters that should be properly instantiated by the user. Let us go back to our example. The corresponding graph transformation rule for the refactoring *ExtractClass* is depicted in Fig. 4(a). Thereby, the LHS of the rule represents the pre-condition of the operation and the post-condition is specified in the RHS whereas actions that are going to carry out are implicitly defined in both sides. More precisely, the execution of a transformation rule produces the following effects: (i) all elements that only reside in the LHS are deleted; (ii) all elements that only exist in the RHS are added, and (iii) all elements that reside in both sides are preserved. To mark that an element in the RHS is equivalent to an element in the LHS, both elements must have the same identifier. Note that the *ExtractClass* refactoring requires that a class and an attribute are given as input by the user.

The graph transformation rules that describe the content model changes may be coupled with other rules which take care of the reconciliation of the existing instances for the content model (cf. Fig. 3). This coupling is a crucial aspect, because the semantics of the content model changes are described by the corresponding changes on the instances. For example, moving an attribute from one class to the other can have several meanings, depending on the intended behaviour on the instances: either the attribute is supposed to be deleted and then created (and therefore the values for the old attribute are lost, and the newly created attribute gets fresh values), or the attribute is supposed to be *moved* (and hence the values of the attribute should not be deleted but reused for the newly introduced attribute).

3.2   Instance Reconciliation as Coupled Transformations

If instances of content models are again considered as models, transformations can be applied for their reconciliations. To represent instance models on a conceptual level, we reuse UML object diagrams for modeling *objects* (instances of classes), *values* (instances of attributes), and *links* (instances of relationships). Thus, we have included in the WebML metamodel a package for modeling instance models (Fig. 1).

Considering again the *ExtractClass* refactoring, expressing the effect at the instance level, a coupled transformation is needed. Fig. 4(b) shows the effect on the instance model as a transformation rule. For each object of the *base* class (which stands for an arbitrary class on which an *ExtractClass* refactoring has been applied), an additional object of the *extracted* class is created and linked to the *base* object. Finally, the value of the moved attribute is shifted from the *base* object to the *extracted* object.

The benefits of having a conceptual representation of the instance level evolution is twofold. First, the intend of the refactoring is concisely represented by stating the effects on the instances, thus we have the basis for reasoning on the impact of the change on the hypertext level. Second, the conceptual representation may be used to derive platform specific reconciliation rules, e.g., SQL-based migration rules for relational data, automatically.

3.3   Hypertext Reconciliation as Coupled Transformations

It is likely that reconciliations in the hypertext models are necessary when the underlaying content model has been changed. In this sense, the hypertext model has to be reconciled to guarantee interaction requirements supported by the system before evolution.

Some effects that content model evolution implies on the hypertext model may be easily inferred by looking at broken correspondence links between hypertext and content model. Let us consider the *ExtractClass* refactoring. In the hypertext, all *Units* that reference the moved attribute (for applying any CRUD operation on it) need to be split into two in order to consider the new container of the attribute, i.e., the *Family* class. To preserve the system's initial navigation structure and behavior, added elements on the hypertext model must be properly linked by using suitable navigation links. In next section, we will explain in detail how coupled transformations are used to reconcile hypertext models with evolved content models.

4   Co-evolution Patterns for WebML Hypertext Models

When propagating changes from content models to hypertext models, equivalence properties have to be preserved for the initial hypertext model (H) and the revised version (H') such that the observable behavior of the Web application is equivalent between H and H' from a user point of view. In particular, we have derived three equivalence properties which are directly related to the three core behavioral element types of hypertext model, namely *ContentUnit*, *OperationUnit*, and *Link* shown in Figure 1:

- **Amount of information per page**. The *content units* located in a *page* should display in total the same amount of information in H and H', i.e., the same attribute values have to be shown on the page before and after evolution for given input values.
- **Effects on the database**. Having a set of input values for a *operation unit* in H should have the same effect as having these input values for the corresponding sequence of *operation units* in H'. This means, when a *operation unit* in H is executed on the initial content model and the data is subsequently migrated to the new content model, it should lead to the same result as executing the corresponding sequence of *operation units* in H on the new content model.
- **Navigation paths**. If a node b is reachable from node a in H then node b has to be reachable from node a in H' with the same parameter values transported.

In the following, we present co-evolution patterns for reconciling hypertext models after a *ExtractClass* refactoring has been executed in the associated content model. The co-evolution patterns are described by recapturing the issue that has to be resolved in the hypertext model, the reconciliation strategy, and the corresponding graph transformation rule.

4.1   Rule 1: CreateUnit Reconciliation

Issue: A *CreateUnit* refers to a *Class* in the content model on which the *ExtractClass* refactoring has been executed. As a result, the moved attribute may be used in an assignment of the *CreateUnit*; a situation which does not represent a valid model structure in WebML. Furthermore, to preserve the operational semantics of the hypertext model, not only an instance of the base class has to be created, but also an instance of the extracted class linked to the instance of the base class is needed.

Reconciliation Strategy: In addition to the already existing *CreateUnit* for instantiating the base class, an additional *CreateUnit* for instantiating the extracted class and a *ConnectUnit* for linking instances of the base class and of the extracted class have to be introduced. Furthermore, to guarantee the same behavior as before the evolution, a *TransactionUnit* has to be introduced which contains all three operation units. This ensures that only when all three units are successfully executed, the complete information is populated in the database —which corresponds to behavior of the initial hypertext model where one *CreateUnit* is responsible for populating the complete information at once. Furthermore, the assignment of the attribute that has been moved to the extracted class has to be moved to the new *CreateUnit*.

Transformation Rule: The transformation rule[1] for co-evolving the hypertext models based on the mentioned adaptation strategy is illustrated in Fig. 5. The newly introduced elements in the hypertext model are shown in green background color. The content model elements are shown in gray background color. As is illustrated, additional *OperationUnits* connected by *OKLinks* are introduced to simulate the behavior of the single *CreateUnit* in the initial version. The *KOLink* is moved from the *CreateUnit* to the *TransactionUnit* which ensures if one single unit fails, the target of the *KOLink* is shown to the user. Finally, also the source of the initial *OKLink* is relinked to the last unit of the transaction.

---

[1] *LinkParameters* and *SelectorConditions* are not shown due to space limitations.

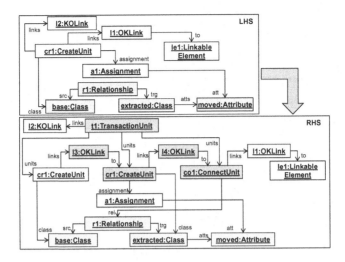

Fig. 5. Co-evolution pattern for *CreateUnits* affected by *ExtractClass* refactorings

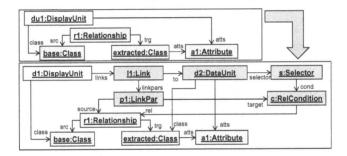

Fig. 6. Co-evolution pattern for *DisplayUnits* effected by *ExtractClass* refactorings

4.2 Rule 2: DisplayUnit Reconciliation

Issue: A *DisplayUnit* refers to a *Class* in the content model which has been effected by the *ExtractClass* refactoring and displays the attribute which has been moved to the extracted class. As for *CreateUnits*, a *DisplayUnit* can only refer to attributes which are directly contained by the referenced class.

Reconciliation Strategy: In order to display the value of the moved attribute, a *DataUnit* has to be introduced which is able to display the attribute, i.e., which refers to the extracted class. This means, also an additional *TransportLink* has to be created to navigate the relationship from the base class to the extracted class to find the appropriate instance which contains the value to display. The *DataUnit* shows the moved attribute and is included in the page containing the initial *DisplayUnit*.

Transformation Rule: The transformation rule for this strategy is shown in Fig. 6.

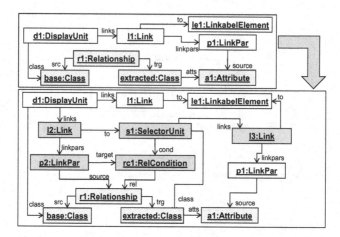

Fig. 7. Co-evolution pattern for *Source Elements* of *LinkParameters* effected by *ExtractClass* refactorings

4.3 Rule 3: LinkParameter.source Reconciliation

Issue: A *Link* may use an *Attribute* as a source element for a *LinkParameter* which is no longer accessible for the source of the *Link*, because it has been moved to the extracted class. Again, the same constraint applies that units cannot access elements outside their referenced classes.

Reconciliation Strategy: In order to transfer the necessary input for the target of the *Link*, a work-around using a so-called *SelectorUnit* is required. A *SelectorUnit* is used to access the attribute and transports the value of the attribute to the target of the *Link*, however, the processing of a *SelectorUnit* does not effect the user interface of the Web application. This additional unit is needed, because the initial source unit of the link is not able to access the moved attribute. But it is possible to access the extracted class by using the relationship between the base class and the extracted class, but it is not possible to access its features directly. Thus, the access of the moved attribute is delegated to the *SelectorUnit* which receives the extracted class instance from which it retrieves the requested attribute value.

Transformation Rule: The transformation rule for reconciling source elements of link parameter which are no longer accessible is shown in Fig. 7.

4.4 Rule 4: LinkParameter.target Reconciliation

Issue: A moved *Attribute* is used as a target element of a *LinkParameter* which is no longer accessible for the target of the *Link*, because it has been moved to the extracted class (inverse case to Rule 3). This case is typically concerned with *AttConditions* of *Selectors*, which act as target elements for *LinkParameters*.

Reconciliation Strategy: In order to the use again the target element for the *LinkParameter*, the *AttCondition* has to point to a so-called *ImportedAttribute* instead of normal *Attribute*. By using *ImportedAttributes* it is possible to access information

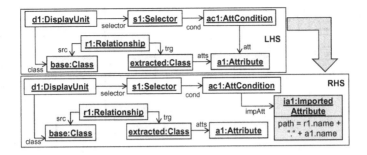

Fig. 8. Co-evolution pattern for *Target Elements* of *LinkParameters* effected by *ExtractClass* refactorings

outside the referred class. Thus, we employ this concept to access the moved *Attribute* by following the relationship from the base class to the extracted class.

Transformation Rule: As can be seen in Fig. 8, the link from the *AttCondition* to the moved *Attribute* is substituted by a link to an *ImportedAttribute*. In particular, the *path* to the moved attribute is calculated by concatenating the relationship name (*r1.name*) followed by the point operator (used to access the features of the target class) and the name of the moved attribute (*a1.name*).

4.5   Application to the Running Example

When applying the presented coupled transformation rules exhaustively (i.e., the model is rewritten until no further match can be found) on the running example, we end up with a hypertext model illustrated in Fig. 9. In particular, when the rules are applied in the order they are presented, the initial hypertext model is rewritten from left to right. First, the *CreateUnit* is rewritten by Rule 1 into a *TransactionUnit* covering the three *OperationUnits*. Second, the ShowPerson *DataUnit* is split by Rule 2 into two *DataUnits*, one visualizing the *firstName* attribute value and the other the *familyName* attribute value of the created person. Third, Rule 3 substitutes the *Link* between the ShowPerson *DataUnit* and the *IndexUnit* by one *Link* activating a *SelectorUnit* for retrieving the family instance for the transferred person instance, followed by another *Link* which is transferring the familyName attribute value from the *SelectorUnit* to the *IndexUnit*. Finally, the *AttCondition* of the *IndexUnit* is rewritten from a "standard" attribute to an *ImportedAttribute* (cf. *Person2Family.familyName*) by Rule 4.

4.6   Critical Discussion

The reconciled hypertext model allows to work with the new content model version in an equivalent way as the initial hypertext model worked with the initial content model w.r.t. the three stated properties in the beginning of this section. However, there are also some minor differences concerning the structure of the Web pages. Because it is not possible to use the notion of *ImportedAttributes* for showing attributes residing outside the classes referenced by *DisplayUnits*, some additional *DisplayUnits* have to be introduced in the hypertext model. This has an effect on the presentation models

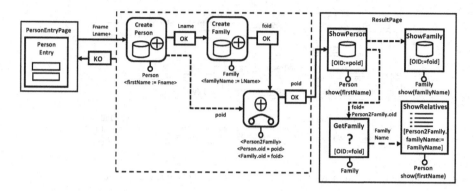

Fig. 9. Reconciled Hypertext Model of the Running Example

of the Web applications, and thus, on the user interfaces. For example, automated test may fail to access some information which is now visualized in a different place on the corresponding Web site.

As a consequence, the *ResultPage* in the reconciled hypertext model (cf. Fig. 9) is more verbose than the initial version because *ImportedAttributes* are not possible either for source elements of *LinkParameters* or for the shown attributes of *DisplayUnits*. Other Web modeling languages such as UWE [11] allow for *ImportedAttributes* for *DisplayUnits* by using some kind of expression language, similar to the one in WebML for defining *ImportedAttributes* for *SelectorConditions*.

When we assume that we have an enhanced modeling support in WebML, i.e., *ImportedAttributes* are also possible for *DisplayUnits* as well as for source elements of *LinkParameters*, the *ResultPage* would be expressible in a more concise manner following the initial page structure as shown in Fig. 10. Instead of using four units in the reconciled hypertext model, only two units—as in the initial hypertext model—are sufficient to work with the new content model version. Thus, the same structure of the Web page is guaranteed which also allows to reuse the presentation model of the initial hypertext version also for the reconciled version.

In addition, having this enhanced modeling support also leads to less complex co-evolution patterns. In particular, *Rule 2* and *Rule 3* only have to substitute the links from the hypertext model elements to the moved attribute with an *ImportedAttribute*. Therefore, we propose the WebML metamodel to have also the possibility to use *ImportedAttributes* for *DisplayUnits* and for source elements of *LinkParameters*. By this not only the reconciliation rules and the resulting reconciled hypertext models are simpler, but also modeling Web applications in WebML from scratch may be enhanced by having such modeling support.

4.7   Implementation

We have implemented the presented approach by defining WebML models in the Eclipse Modeling Framework (EMF). For representing WebML models in EMF, we have developed an Ecore-based WebML metamodel. This opens the door for using transformation approaches available for EMF-based models. We selected the Eclipse Modeling

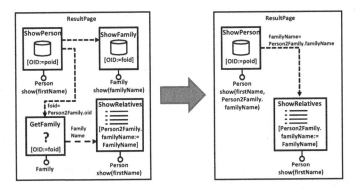

Fig. 10. Possible improvements of the *ResultPage* using *ImportedAttributes* for *DisplayUnits* and *Source Elements* of *LinkParameters*

Operation (EMO) project (*http://www.modelversioning.org/emf-modeling-operations*) which is a dedicated transformation framework for implementing and executing model refactorings. Based on EMO, we have implemented the transformations for the content models as well as the coupled transformations for the instance models and the hypertext models. EMO allows also the interactive execution of the transformations by preselecting model elements in the modeling editor. The execution engine of EMO completes the bindings of the model elements in case only a partial pre-binding for the transformation rule has been provided by the user. Finally, EMO also allows for user input during transformation execution, e.g., to give the name for the extracted class.

5 Related Work

With respect to the contribution of this paper, namely evolution and reconciliation support for Web models, we identify two main lines of related work: (i) model refactoring and (ii) multi-viewpoint model synchronization.

Model Refactorings. Compared to refactorings established in the field of object-orientation modeling [16,20], only some initial proposals for Web models exist. Most notable is the work of Cabot and Gómez [2] in which a catalogue of refactorings for improving the navigation between pages has been documented. The presented refactorings are defined on a high-level of abstraction considering links, pages, and navigation paths so they can be translated to any Web modeling methodology as we do. However, their approach only covers one single viewpoint and does not consider the change impact on dependent viewpoints. Mitigating this shortcoming, the work in [8] focuses on the navigation and presentation viewpoints and how they must co-evolve for propagating changes in a consistent way. In particular, they make an OOHDM dependent, fine-grained characterization of different kinds of refactorings. They combine also atomic changes to achieve more complex transformations. In contrast, our approach considers the co-evolution problem between content models and hypertext models.

Model Synchronization. A large number of approaches in other disciplines address the problem of multi-viewpoint synchronization [3,5,6,7,9,10,19]. All these approaches have in common that they consider only atomic changes when reconciling models to satisfy again given modeling language constraints. However, when structuring changes to composite ones, more appropriate reconciled models may be found. For Web applications, instance migration support for evolving databases is presented in [17], but the impact on the hypertext level is not discussed. Cicchetti et al. [4] propose evolution support for Web models going beyond instance migration. The approach uses state-based model comparison to compute the differences between two content model versions based on fine-grained atomic changes, such as adding and removing elements or modifying some of their values. Two coarse-grained change operators are considered in their work: merge/split of classes. The approach is described in detail for the beContent Web modeling language which does not employ an explicit hypertext layer, and briefly discussed for WebML, for which only the reconciliation of hypertext models in case of deletions of content model elements is discussed. Our work is orthogonal in the sense that coarse-grained changes are considered for reconciling WebML hypertext models.

6   Conclusions and Future Work

In this paper we have presented coarse-grained content model changes formalized as model transformations, which are propagated to dependent viewpoints using coupled transformations. The approach has been demonstrated by the *ExtractClass* refactoring example in the particular context of WebML.

Since the reconciliation strategies are defined for the core of WebML, which is also shared by other Web modeling languages, the results should be transferable to other Web modeling languages. In particular, we have abstracted the patterns as much as possible, e.g., by using generalized classes of the metamodel such as *LinkableElement* or *DisplayUnit* which usually have equivalent concepts in other Web modeling languages. By this, the transformations are not specific to the presented example, but are reusable for others. However, there are language concepts which may require their own reconciliation patterns which are not presented in the paper. For instance, if a *DeletionUnit* refers to a class which has been subject to the *ExtractClass* refactoring, an analogous reconciliation pattern is necessary as for the *CreateUnit* to ensure that the instances of the base class and the extracted class are deleted.

As future work we plan to extend the presented catalogue of reconciliation patterns, and identify/resolve possible conflicts between them based on graph transformation theory, in particular, using critical pairs analysis. Furthermore, our patterns aim to preserve the consistency and observable behavior of the system by fulfilling a set of equivalence properties before and after co-evolution models happen. However, coarse-grained changes can be translated to the hypertext viewpoint in different ways, i.e., producing different models where some of them are more efficient than others. In this sense, we want to improve our proposal to determine the most optimal pattern in each case by exploring quality properties such as usability and accessibility of hypertext models. Finally, we want to investigate a hybrid reconciliation approach by using in the first phase the presented approach for coarse-grained changes and in the second phase a constraint-based approach for atomic changes which could not be composed into coarse-grained changes.

Acknowledgements. This work has been partially funded by the Austrian Science Fund (FWF) under grant J 3159-N23, and by Spanish Research Project TIN2011-23795.

References

1. Acerbis, R., Bongio, A., Brambilla, M., Butti, S., Ceri, S., Fraternali, P.: Web Applications Design and Development with WebML and WebRatio 5.0. In: Paige, R.F., Meyer, B. (eds.) TOOLS EUROPE 2008. LNBIP, vol. 11, pp. 392–411. Springer, Heidelberg (2008)
2. Cabot, J., Ceballos, J., Gómez, C.: On the Quality of Navigation Models with Content-Modification Operations. In: Baresi, L., Fraternali, P., Houben, G.-J. (eds.) ICWE 2007. LNCS, vol. 4607, pp. 59–73. Springer, Heidelberg (2007)
3. Cicchetti, A., Ruscio, D.D.: Decoupling Web Application Concerns through Weaving Operations. Science of Computer Programming 70(1), 62–86 (2008)
4. Cicchetti, A., Ruscio, D.D., Iovino, L., Pierantonio, A.: Managing the Evolution of Data-Intensive Web Applications by Model-Driven Techniques. In: SoSym, pp. 1–31 (2012)
5. Diskin, Z., Xiong, Y., Czarnecki, K.: Specifying Overlaps of Heterogeneous Models for Global Consistency Checking. In: Dingel, J., Solberg, A. (eds.) MODELS 2010. LNCS, vol. 6627, pp. 165–179. Springer, Heidelberg (2011)
6. Eramo, R., Pierantonio, A., Romero, J.R., Vallecillo, A.: Change Management in Multi-Viewpoint Systems using ASP. In: WODPEC 2008. IEEE (2008)
7. Finkelstein, A., Gabbay, D.M., Hunter, A., Kramer, J., Nuseibeh, B.: Inconsistency Handling in Multi-perspective Specifications. In: Sommerville, I., Paul, M. (eds.) ESEC 1993. LNCS, vol. 717, pp. 84–99. Springer, Heidelberg (1993)
8. Garrido, A., Rossi, G., Distante, D.: Model Refactoring in Web Applications. In: 9th International Workshop on Web Site Evolution, pp. 89–96. IEEE (2007)
9. Grundy, J., Hosking, J., Mugridge, W.B.: Inconsistency Management for Multiple-view Software Development Environments. IEEE Trans. Softw. Eng. 24(11), 960–981 (1998)
10. Hofmann, M., Pierce, B.C., Wagner, D.: Symmetric lenses. In: POPL 2011, pp. 371–384. ACM (2011)
11. Koch, N., Knapp, A., Zhang, G., Baumeister, H.: UML-Based Web Engineering: An Approach Based on Standards. In: Web Engineering: Modelling and Implementing Web Applications. Human-Computer Interaction Series, vol. 12, ch. 7, pp. 157–191. Springer (2008)
12. Lämmel, R.: Coupled Software Transformations (Extended Abstract). In: First International Workshop on Software Evolution Transformations (2004)
13. Moreno, N., Romero, J.R., Vallecillo, A.: An Overview Of Model-Driven Web Engineering and the MDA. In: Web Engineering: Modelling and Implementing Web Applications, ch.12, pp. 353–382. Springer (2008)
14. Moreno, N., Vallecillo, A.: Towards Interoperable Web Engineering Methods. JASIST 59(7), 1073–1092 (2008)
15. Schwinger, W., et al.: A Survey on Web Modeling Approaches for Ubiquitous Web Applications. IJWIS 4(3), 234–305 (2008)
16. Sunyé, G., Pollet, D., Le Traon, Y., Jézéquel, J.-M.: Refactoring UML Models. In: Gogolla, M., Kobryn, C. (eds.) UML 2001. LNCS, vol. 2185, pp. 134–148. Springer, Heidelberg (2001)
17. Vermolen, S.D., Wachsmuth, G., Visser, E.: Generating Database Migrations for Evolving Web Applications. In: GPCE 2011, pp. 83–92. ACM (2011)
18. Wimmer, M., Schauerhuber, A., Schwinger, W., Kargl, H.: On the Integration of Web Modeling Languages. In: MDWE 2007. CEUR Workshop Proceedings, vol. 261 (2007)
19. Xiong, Y., Liu, D., Hu, Z., Zhao, H., Takeichi, M., Mei, H.: Towards Automatic Model Synchronization from Model Transformations. In: Proc. of ASE 2007, pp. 164–173. ACM (2007)
20. Zhang, J., Lin, Y., Gray, J.: Generic and Domain-Specific Model Refactoring using a Model Transformation Engine. In: Model-driven Software Development—Research and Practice in Software Engineering, pp. 199–217. Springer (2005)

From Requirements to Web Applications
in an Agile Model-Driven Approach

Julián Grigera[1], José Matías Rivero[1,2], Esteban Robles Luna[1],
Franco Giacosa[1], and Gustavo Rossi[1,2]

[1] LIFIA, Facultad de Informática, UNLP, La Plata, Argentina
{julian.grigera,mrivero,franco.giacosa,
esteban.robles,gustavo}@lifia.info.unlp.edu.ar
[2] Also at Conicet

Abstract. Web applications are hard to build not only because of technical reasons but also because they involve many different kinds of stakeholders. Involving customers in the development process is a must, not only while eliciting requirements but also considering that requirements change fast and they must be validated continuously. However, while model-driven approaches represent a step forward to reduce development time and work at a higher level of abstraction, most of them practically ignore stakeholders' involvement. Agile approaches tend to solve this problem, though they generally focus on programming rather than modeling. In this paper we present an extension to an approach that combines the best of both worlds, allowing a formal and high-level design style with constant involvement of customers, mainly in the definition of navigation, interaction and interface features. We extended it by adding transformation features that allow mapping requirement models into content and navigation ones. We provide a proof of concept in the context of the WebML design method and an empiric validation of the approach's advantages.

1   Introduction

Developing Web applications is a complex task, involving different specialists through different stages. At the end of the process, it is usual to find out that the final result does not reflect the customers' wishes with accuracy, since while going through the different stages the team may slowly steer away from the original requirements. The difference between requirements and the final result grows broader as new changes are introduced. These problems are in part caused by communication issues, but they also arise as a consequence of the development approach.

In a previous work [17] we argued that most model-driven Web engineering approaches (MDWE) [1, 8, 12, 19] tend to focus on the design artifacts and their automatic transformation onto running applications, therefore leaving the customer aside (at least in part) throughout the process. Interaction and interface issues are usually left as final concerns, while being, in many applications, the most important aspects for customers. At the same time agile approaches[1] focus on customers' involvement,

---

[1] Principles behind the Agile Manifesto –
http://agilemanifesto.org/principles.html

M. Brambilla, T. Tokuda, and R. Tolksdorf (Eds.): ICWE 2012, LNCS 7387, pp. 200–214, 2012.
© Springer-Verlag Berlin Heidelberg 2012

while being less *formal* from the technical point of view. We then proposed to bridge both approaches by using Test-Driven Development (TDD) in a model-driven setting. With short development cycles, the mismatch between requirements and implementation is usually kept under control. We already proposed a requirement engineering language, named WebSpec [18] to capture navigation and interaction requirement. Associated with customer-generated mockups, WebSpec diagrams provide simulations to share an early view of the application with stakeholders and automatically derive acceptance tests (using test frameworks like Selenium[2]).

In this paper we go one step further from these two previous contributions by showing how to semi-automatically derive navigation and domain models from requirements captured with mockups and WebSpec diagrams. Interface mockups are not thrown away as usual (even in agile approaches) but evolve into the final applications' interface. The approach, which incorporates requirements into the model-driven cycle, is still agile in that it is based in short cycles with heavy customers intervention, since the used requirements artifacts (Webspec diagrams and mockups) can be manipulated by them; however it can also be used in a conventional "unified" model-driven style.

Though the approach is agnostic to the underlying design method, we illustrate it with the WebML [1] notation and its associated tool WebRatio[3] with which we have made extensive experiments. We also show that the approach does not necessarily depend on interaction tests as driving artifacts for the development (like most TDD approaches do); therefore it can be used either with organized agile styles like Scrum, or even with more "extreme" approaches [6].

The main contributions of the paper are: first, from a process point of view, a way of bridging agile and MDWE from requirements to implementation, easing customer participation from early stages of development using interface mockups and fast prototype generation as a common language to discus requirements; second, we provide a shorter path from requirements to models through a set of heuristics to transform requirement models (expressed as WebSpec diagrams plus interface mockups) onto navigation, presentation and content models. We illustrate these contributions with a set of running examples and describe an experiment that validates our claims.

The rest of the paper is structured as follows: in Section 2 we present a brief background of our work emphasizing on WebSpec diagrams and interface mockup annotations. Next, in Section 3 we explain our approach in detail. In section 4 we show a simple but meaningful example. Section 5 shows an experiment that validates the approach and Section 6 presents some related work on this subject. Section 7 concludes the paper and discusses some further work we are pursuing.

2   Background

The first stage of our process involves two main artifacts that help to state clearly what customers need, and how they want it to look and behave. Graphical user interface (GUI) mockups combined with WebSpec diagrams will not only help through this stage, but also in the following, as we will explain later on section 4. Besides these artifacts, we will organize the requirements gathering with User Stories [6] as functional units, though Use Cases [5] can also be used for the same purpose.

---

[2] Selenium web application testing system - http://seleniumhq.org/
[3] WebRatio – http://www.webratio.com

2.1   GUI Mockups

GUI mockups serve well as first requirement artifacts, since they are really close to customers in terms of interfaces and interaction, resulting much clearer than textual specifications. Mockups act as tools to communicate software requirements in a *common language* shared between customers and the development team [10]. It has been shown that screen mockups effectively increase general software comprehension without involving a high cost in the development process [15]. Besides, we have shown that they also work as specifications for building user interface models [16]. When built using digital tools, mockups represent an incomplete, yet non-ambiguous, description of the UI. However, in most cases mockups are used only during the requirements specification and thrown away shortly after. We have also shown that, because of the common fidelity (i.e., the shared abstraction level and metamodel elements) between MDWE presentation models and modern mockup building tools, we can easily translate mockups to UI models using a transformation process [16].

In this work we employ user interface mockups as the initial artifacts to interact with customers. Once agreed upon them, mockups are derived into the presentation model of the application (that we can generate automatically) and a foundation to specify further features, like navigation and content aspects.

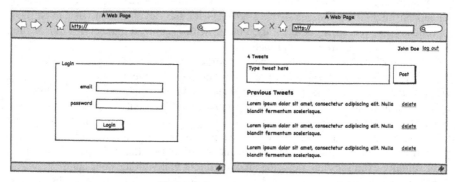

Fig. 1. Sample GUI mockups

Figure 1 shows two simple low-fi mockups of a login and home screen to a Twitter-like application. Later in the paper we show how they can be combined with a WebSpec diagram to describe the navigation features these artifacts lack.

2.2   WebSpec

WebSpec [18] is a DSL designed to capture navigation and interaction aspects at the requirements stage of a Web applications development process. A WebSpec diagram contains *Interactions* and *Navigations*. An Interaction represents a point where the user consumes information (expressed as a set of interface widgets) and interacts with the application by using its widgets. Some actions like clicking a button, or typing some text in a text field might produce navigation from one Interaction to another, and as a consequence, the user moves through the application's navigation space. These actions are written in an intuitive domain specific language. Figure 2 shows a diagram that will let the user tweet, see how many tweets she has, and allow her to logout from the application. From the Login interaction, the user types username and password and clicks on the login button (navigation from Login to Home interaction). Then, she can add messages by typing in the message text field (messageTF attribute) and clicking on the post button (navigation from Home to Home interaction).

Fig. 2. WebSpec of Tweet's interaction

From a WebSpec diagram we automatically generate a set of interaction tests that cover all the interaction paths specified in it [18], avoiding the translation problem of TDD between tests and requirements. Unlike traditional Unit Tests, interaction tests simulate user input into HTML pages, and allow asserting conditions on the results of such interactions. Since each WebSpec Interaction is related to a mockup, each test runs against it and the predicates are transformed into tests assertions. These failing series of tests set a good starting point for a TDD-like approach and (even when using another agile approach) they can be used later as the application's acceptance tests.

3   The Approach in a Nutshell

To bridge the gap between requirements specifications and implementation, we have devised model transformation rules for turning requirements artifacts into content and navigation models. We depict the approach in Figure 3 assuming a TDD cycle.

The process begins with a small group of initial requirements, related to a single User Story. We gather presentation and interaction requirements by building interface mockups, which help to agree upon the look and feel of the new application, and will also provide the basis for WebSpec diagrams.

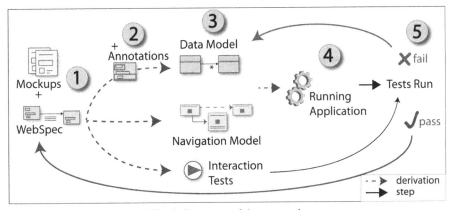

Fig. 3. Summary of the approach

After building the mockups, we specify navigation features through WebSpec diagrams. Since WebSpec can express interaction requirements (including navigation), general hypertext specifications can be derived directly from it, but backend features are missed, being the most important the underlying content model. To fulfill this gap, we annotate WebSpec widgets to represent content model features, in terms of classes (or entities) and attributes. These annotations are extremely simple and easy to apply and will help to build the content model incrementally and in an *on-demand* fashion.

Once we have both mockups and the annotated WebSpec diagrams, we derive a first set of content and navigation models. We generate the navigation model from the WebSpec diagrams directly, and we make use of the annotations made on them to derive the content model. Both models are linked together automatically since they stem from the same diagrams. Additionally, WebSpec diagrams are used to generate the interaction tests [18] that will guide the rest of the development in an agile style.

Having created the models with their corresponding interaction tests, the developers apply the presentation according the mockups devised in the first stage and derive a running application, which must be validated with such interaction tests. When using a TDD style, if tests fail, the models must be tweaked until they pass, and then move forward to another User Story for the following iteration towards the final application. The reason why interaction tests might fail is because the transformation rules can sometimes be inaccurate, and while these misinterpretations are mostly due to insufficient information in the WebSpec diagrams or their annotations, some can also be due to ambiguous customer's specifications. In such cases, the type of corrections required to adjust the models to their correct semantics have proven to be recurrent, so we devised a list of frequent model adjustments in a pattern-like style.

In the following subsections we detail how we specify WebSpec diagrams, then turn them into navigation and content models through a set of transformation rules, and the main required refactorings we detected for correcting the derived models.

3.1   Gathering Navigation Requirements with WebSpec Diagrams

We use the existing tooling support for WebSpec to import and group existing mockups as defined in the initial User Stories. For every mockup in each User Story, a WebSpec Interaction is created to specify the behavior mockups cannot express. With assistance of the tool, mockup widgets can be *projected* to WebSpec diagrams in order to be included in interaction specifications.

It is important to note that a single mockup can be referenced by two or more WebSpec Interactions in different diagrams, since many User Stories can be partially

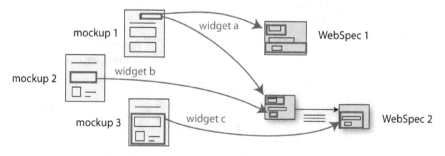

Fig. 4. Overlapping mockups and WebSpec diagrams

related to the same user interface in the Web application. Conversely, two or more mockups can be referenced in a single WebSpec diagram, given it specifies navigation from one to another. This is shown schematically in Figure 4.

3.2 Obtaining Data Model through Annotations

After creating the WebSpec diagrams, we apply lightweight content annotations on their widgets (for a complete reference on widgets see our previous work on WebSpec [18]); this will allow us to generate content models *on the fly* together with interaction specs. Generating content models from structured UIs have been already proposed and implemented [14], here we define an extremely simple annotation schema that can be applicable directly with the annotation facilities provided with mockup tools:

- Composite widgets (Panels and ListPanels) are annotated with a single string that denotes the class (or entity) it handles (e.g., @Employee in Figure 5.a).
- Simple input widgets (like TextFields or Checkboxes) are annotated with the syntax `<class>.<attributeName>` (@Employee.Role in Figure 5.b), also applied to simple widgets referring other classes' instances (like ComboBoxes or Lists).

a   b

Fig. 5. Annotated WebSpec diagrams

3.3 Deriving Models

In this section we show how we obtain navigation and data models from WebSpec diagrams. We begin with some basic transformations that intuitively map simple WebSpec constructions into WebML elements, shown in table 1.

Table 1. Basic WebSpec to WebML transformations

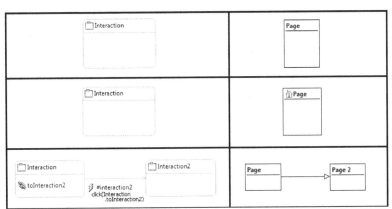

The first transformation rule maps a Webspec Interaction to a WebML Page. Every WebSpec diagram is initialized with a Starting Interaction component that will be represented using a WebML Home Page. A link between Interactions will be turned into a Normal Link in WebML.

The annotation schema (explained in section 3.2) combined with the WebSpec model allows us to derive a WebML Data Model as well. In table 2 we depict some transformation rules including content model annotations.

Table 2. From annotated WebSpec to Data Models

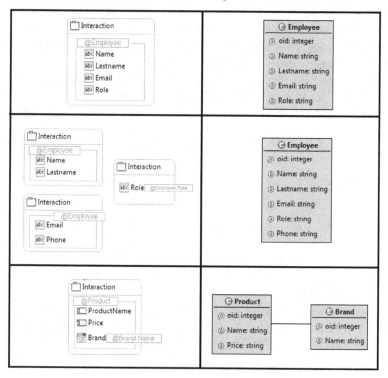

The @Class annotation (e.g. @Employee) allows specifying that the underlying composite widget will manage instances of the Class entity. As a consequence, a corresponding WebML Entity will be created in the WebML Data Model and every simple widget in it will be transformed as an attribute (the OID attribute will be added by default to each new entity). If an entity is spread in several diagrams, a union operation will be applied to create the entity. Each simple widget found either by been inside a Composite Widget annotated with @Class or by being annotated with the @Class.attribute label, will be gathered an put inside a single Entity as long as they share the same Class. If a Simple Widget inside a Composite Widget has a different class annotation than its parent, a relationship between the class of the Composite Widget and the one of the Simple Widget will be created. After deriving a Data Model, now we can start mapping the above WebML Web Model, as we show in the transformations portrayed in Table 3.

Table 3. Obtaining full WebML models

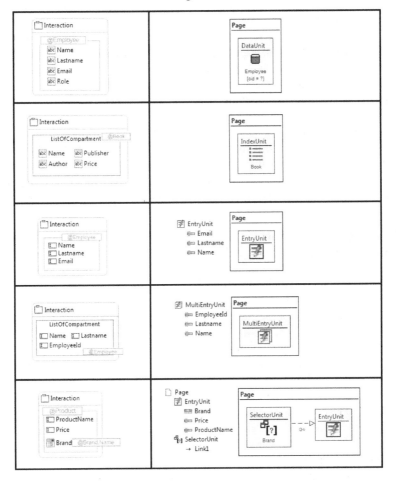

The transformations introduced in Table 3 are the following: (1) A Panel used to show data (e.g a panel of labels) with a `@Class` annotation is transformed to a Data Unit pointing at the specified class, (2) A List used to show data (e.g. a list of labels) with a `@Class` annotation is transformed to an Index Unit pointing at the specified class, (3) A Panel used to input data (e.g. a panel composed by input widgets) with a `@Class` annotation is transformed to an Entry Unit and each input widget in the panel will be mapped to a WebML input field, (4) A List used to input data (e.g. a list composed by input widgets) with a `@Class` annotation is transformed to an Multi Entry Unit and each input widget in the List will be mapped to a WebML input field and (5) if inside an Input Panel there is a Combo Box annotated with a different class (e.g.: `@Brand.name`), a selection field will be created in the Entry Unit, and it will be filled with a Selector Unit pointing at the specified entity annotated in the Combo Box.

Before the derived models are ready to generate a running application, some fixes might need to be made. We will discuss these in the next section.

3.4   Adjusting the Models

Applying the described transformations to the initial requirement artifacts, both navigation and data models are generated in conjunction with a set of interaction tests, as depicted in Figure 3. Using the code generation capabilities of the chosen MDWE approach, a running application is generated in order to run the interaction tests over it to check the functionality. In some cases, tests may fail on their first run, due to missing or unexpected presentation details or layout specifications in the final user interface. However, in some cases they can also fail because of ambiguous or insufficient behavior inferred from the models derived with the described rules. Regarding data and business logic, we found a list of *fail patterns* and devised some heuristics to detect them and suggest potential corrections. Depending of its importance and obviousness, fail patterns are presented to the designer as a refactoring [4] suggestion in the tool or they are applied automatically as a final part of the generation process. We detail two notorious examples below:

- **Non-normalized Attribute**
  - Explanation: a simple widget is bound to an individual attribute of a mapped class, but in fact it must be bound to an attribute of a different class related to the former through an association.
  - Example: a product panel tagged as @Product has a label called brandName. This label must not be data-bound as an attribute of Product, but to an attribute of Brand, a class associated to Product. Then, a proper @Brand.name annotation must be placed in it (see Figure 6).
  - Fail reason: data is not normalized and fails occur when updating information within the execution of a WebSpec test (e.g., the brand name of a product is changed, and when the test checks the name in a second product of the same brand, it has the old one and an equality assertion fails).
  - Detection Heuristic: analyze widget name and search for the name of a previously mapped class within it. Suggest an association to this class.
- **Missing Filter in Index**
  - Explanation: an input panel and a list exist in an interaction. The panel contains widgets that specify filtering conditions to the elements that are shown on the list. Both widgets are annotated with the same class and a transition from the interaction to itself exist. According to the translation rules, a WebML Index Unit will be generated in the model for the list and an Entry Unit must be created for the input panel. However, no filtering is generated by default.
  - Example: an interaction contains a panel with a textbox that allows searching products by its name. Below, a list of products found with the matching name is shown (see Figure 7).
  - Fail reason: items in the index are the same after changing the *filter widgets* values in the panel and updating the page. Thus, an equality assertion fails.
  - Detection Heuristic: analyze the interaction to find a panel and a list annotated with the same class and a recursive transition.

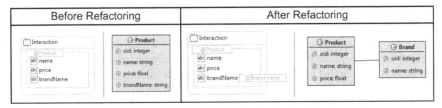

Fig. 6. Non-Normalized fail pattern and refactored diagram

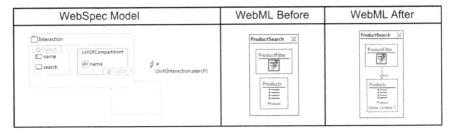

Fig. 7. Missing *Filter in Index* fail pattern and refactored diagram

4   Proof of Concept

For a better understanding of the approach, we will show a full cycle of our process in the ongoing development of a sample application: a Customer Satisfaction system, where different users manage customers' complaints through different departments.

We will take the development from an advanced status, and show how a new User Story is implemented. We will start from a point where the system allows creating new complaints, viewing their details and delegating them between departments. The next functionality to implement is the ability to make comment on the complaints.

As a first step, the previous mockup for the detailed view of a complaint is extended to show comments and a new form is added for the user to leave comments.

Fig. 8. Mockups for new functionality

Figure 8 shows the previous mockup for the details page of a complaint, and the new mockup that contemplates the comments.

Once we have agreed on the new functionality's look and feel, we move on to the WebSpec diagrams. Since the interaction for viewing a complaint was already present, we just extend it with the list of comments and the form for adding comments, with the corresponding navigation functionality. Figure 9 shows both previous and modified diagrams.

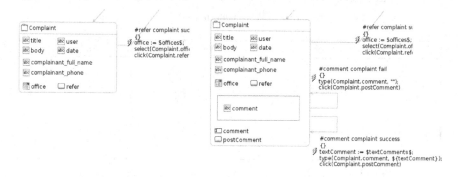

Fig. 9. Extended WebSpec model for comments feature

We next tag the new components of the diagram with annotations for deriving the missing content model. Then, the only step left is derivation. The extended WebSpec diagram generates new features for the existing navigation model, while the annotations generate a simple model for the comments, and their relationships with the complaints on the current data model. New interaction tests are also generated to check for the creation of new comments.

As a last step we regenerate the application from the derived models, and run the automatically generated interaction tests to validate the new functionality. If the tests pass, we move on to another User Story; if they don't, we must check for possible inaccurate derivations. For example, in this case we could have specified the author's name for the comments as a plain attribute for the Comment entity, instead of being a foreign attribute from the User entity, which should be related to the first (*Non-normalized Attribute* fail pattern). Fixing the data model will require also fixing the navigation model, and re-running the tests to check for the functionality.

5   Assessing the Approach

To make a first assessment of our approach we ran an experiment with 10 developers, each going through a complete development cycle for a simple application: the Complaint Management System presented as example in section 3.

We split the subjects in 2 groups of 5 developers, each group using different approaches in the requirements elicitation and WebRatio as development tool. A first group (group A) used only User Stories and UI Mockups, while the second one (group B) added also WebSpec and tagging, completing the full approach proposed in this paper, relying on the models derivation features.

We had a first meeting with each subject playing the role of customers. Depending on the group they belonged, they gathered requirements using different artifacts. They were also provided with ready-made User Stories. Before the second stage, the developers from group B automatically derived content and navigation models from the WebSpec diagrams they had created and tagged. Then, all subjects developed the complete application measuring the time taken to implement each User Story individually. Additionally, developers from group B measured the time taken to alter the derived models to make up for eventual derivation mistakes. The third stage involved acceptance tests to check all functionality in both groups' resulting applications.

In this experiment we measured two key aspects: time and satisfaction. The latter measures the functionality's accuracy to what users expected, in a scale ranging from 1 to 5. We found an improvement in both aspects. In figure 10 we depict the average time in minutes it took for each group for completing each User Story.

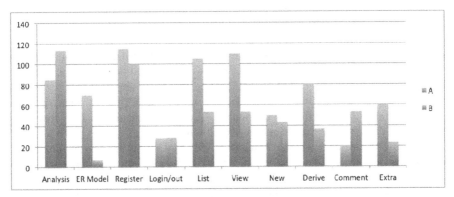

Fig. 10. Time measured for development

As the graphic shows, the time taken by the group A was considerably higher than group B's, mostly owed to the fact that group B only adjusted models, while group A had to create them from scratch, including the data model (marked as ER in the chart). Also, group A took more time to develop extra features that were not asked for in the requirements documents. However, Group B took longer to capture requirements, since they had more artifacts to put together.

As for the satisfaction aspect, the results were not as much conclusive as the previous ones, although they did show an improvement in most User Stories. After

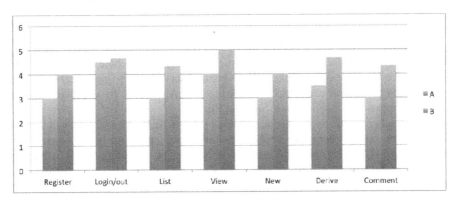

Fig. 11. Satisfaction measured for development

revising the applications we concluded that using WebSpec did improve the fidelity of the final application with respect to the requirements elicitation. Figure 11 shows the average satisfaction ratings for all functionalities developed by both groups.

It should be mentioned that the validity of these first results was somewhat threatened by a number of biases, mainly due to time and resources limitations. Some of them were: the application's scale (which is by no means a real scale development), the small number of subjects and the difference in their skills. The novelty in the use of WebSpec was also a factor, manifested in the higher analysis times on Group B. We plan to make further experiments with more experienced subjects on the use of WebSpec and it's tools, to confirm the presumption that analysis times will drop, at least to the levels of a traditional approach.

6   Related Work

Derivation of requirement models has been already considered with the aim of automatically generating UWE models [7]. In this work, the authors present a modeling language for requirements called WebRE, using the NDT approach [2] for the requirements capture and definition, and specify a set of transformation rules, specified at the meta-model level in the QVT language. The transformation process covers the derivation of content, navigation and presentation models.

Following the same lead, the Ariadne CASE tool [9] generates design models from requirement models, in the context of the ADM model-driven approach, used in turn to generate light prototypes of the final application. The tool leans on domain-specific patterns for generating conceptual models.

Also in this field, Valderas et al [21] propose an improvement on their automatic code generation from OOWS, in which they include graphic designers into the development. To do this, they automatically extract information and functionality from the requirements models. This allows the designers to make changes on a living application for a better experience in the requirements gathering stage, but the presentations are not part of the requirements models from which the information and functionality is extracted.

Our process differs from the aforementioned approaches in that it is focused on short agile development cycles. Being based on GUI Mockups and WebSpec, which is in turn based on User Stories, we not only favor an agile style, but also are able to generate interaction tests to check the resulting applications, in a way that lets us take advantage of the features of TDD approaches as well.

With respect to the artifacts used in our approach, GUI Mockups as requirements gathering tools have been evaluated in several studies. In the context of agile development processes, interface mockups have been observed as an irreplaceable artifact to effectively introduce early usability testing [3]. Also, they have proven to help refining concepts expressed in User Stories [20].

On the other hand, user interface mockups have been included in well known Model-Driven methodologies to improve requirements gathering. In the work of Panach et al. [11], the drawing of user interface sketches is proposed as a way of capturing underlying task patterns using the ConcurTaskTree [13] formalism. Other authors propose directly to include mockups as a metamodel itself to describe interaction from them [10].

7   Concluding Remarks and Further Work

Through this paper we have shown how we improved an agile model-driven Web development process by including digital requirement artifacts to keep the whole process model-driven; in this way we bridge the gap between requirements and implementation by introducing model transformations that automatically map requirement models into content and navigation models; this models are ready to be used to generate a running application, which can be in turn validated using the automatically generated interaction tests.

By driving an experiment with developers, we have shown the strengths of the approach, concerning not only requirements gathering stage but also the rest of the development process. The experiment has also exposed some weaknesses in the derivation process as well as in the process itself, on which we are already working to improve, before running a new, more comprehensive, experiment. In the same way we discovered the current transformation rules, we noticed that the combination of data annotations and navigation features of WebSpec models has still potential for new transformation rules that require further experimentation in order to be correctly stated. We are also finishing derivation rules for object-oriented approaches like UWE [8], which are resulting straightforward since we are working at the meta-model levels of WebSpec and UWE. At the same time we are also extending the WebSpec meta-model to introduce new requirement features.

Regarding the model adjustments, we are working on a suggestion mechanism that will be integrated into our tool, in order to detect possible miscarried derivations and correct them automatically, prompting a set of applicable corrections to the user for him to pick the most suitable one.

Another concern we are working on is the relationship between requirements and implementation models after the transformations. In order to keep track of such relationship and being able to generate changes incrementally, at this point we do not allow for mayor modifications on the application's models. The only modifications allowed should be those that do not introduce changes in the requirements – i.e. what WebSpec diagrams express. Nevertheless, we intend to handle these cases in such a way that allows us to suggest changes on the WebSpec diagrams, so the link between them and the generated models is never broken.

References

1. Ceri, S., Fraternali, P., Bongio, A.: Web Modeling Language (WebML): A Modeling Language for Designing Web Sites. Computer Networks and ISDN Systems 33(1-6), 137–157 (2000)
2. Escalona, M.J., Aragón, G.: NDT. A Model-Driven Approach for Web Requirements. IEEE Trans. Softw. Eng. 34(3), 377–390 (2008)
3. Ferreira, J., Noble, J., Biddle, R.: Agile Development Iterations and UI Design. In: AGILE 2007 Conference (2007)
4. Fowler, M., Beck, K., Brant, J., Opdyke, W., Roberts, D.: Refactoring: Improving the Design of Existing Code. Addison-Wesley Professional (1999)
5. Jacobson, I.: Object-Oriented Software Engineering: A Use Case Driven Approach. ACM Press/Addison-Wesley (1992)

6. Jeffries, R.E., Anderson, A., Hendrickson, C.: Extreme Programming Installed. Addison-Wesley Longman Publishing Co., Inc. (2000)

7. Koch, N., Zhang, G., Escalona, M.J.: Model transformations from requirements to web system design. In: Proceedings of the 6th International Conference on Web Engineering (ICWE 2006), pp. 281–288. ACM, New York (2006)

8. Koch, N., Knapp, A., Zhang, G., Baumeister, H.: UML-Based Web Engineering, An Approach Based On Standards. In: Web Engineering, Modelling and Implementing Web Applications, pp. 157–191. Springer, Heidelberg (2008)

9. Montero, S., Díaz, P., Aedo, I.: From requirements to implementations: a model-driven approach for web development. European Journal of Information Systems 16(4), 407–419 (2007)

10. Mukasa, K.S., Kaindl, H.: An Integration of Requirements and User Interface Specifications. In: 6th IEEE International Requirements Engineering Conference (2008)

11. Panach, J.I., España, S., Pederiva, I., Pastor, O.: Capturing Interaction Requirements in a Model Transformation Technology Based on MDA. Journal of Universal Computer Science 14(9), 1480–1495

12. Pastor, Ó., Abrahão, S., Fons, J.J.: An Object-Oriented Approach to Automate Web Applications Development. In: Bauknecht, K., Madria, S.K., Pernul, G. (eds.) EC-Web 2001. LNCS, vol. 2115, pp. 16–28. Springer, Heidelberg (2001)

13. Paternò, F.: ConcurTaskTrees: An Engineered Notation for Task Models. In: Diaper, D., Stanton, N. (eds.) The Handbook of Task Analysis for Human-Computer Interaction, pp. 483–503. Lawrence Erlbaum Associates (2003)

14. Ramdoyal, R., Cleve, A., Hainaut, J.-L.: Reverse Engineering User Interfaces for Interactive Database Conceptual Analysis. In: Pernici, B. (ed.) CAiSE 2010. LNCS, vol. 6051, pp. 332–347. Springer, Heidelberg (2010)

15. Ricca, F., Scanniello, G., Torchiano, M., Reggio, G., Astesiano, E.: On the effectiveness of screen mockups in requirements engineering. In: 2010 ACM-IEEE International Symposium on Empirical Software Engineering and Measurement (2010)

16. Rivero, J.M., Grigera, J., Rossi, G., Robles Luna, E., Koch, N.: Towards agile model-driven web engineering. In: Nurcan, S. (ed.) CAiSE Forum 2011. LNBIP, vol. 107, pp. 142–155. Springer, Heidelberg (2012)

17. Robles Luna, E., Grigera, J., Rossi, G.: Bridging Test and Model-Driven Approaches in Web Engineering. In: Gaedke, M., Grossniklaus, M., Díaz, O. (eds.) ICWE 2009. LNCS, vol. 5648, pp. 136–150. Springer, Heidelberg (2009)

18. Robles Luna, E., Rossi, G., Garrigós, I.: WebSpec: a visual language for specifying interaction and navigation requirements in web applications. Requir. Eng. 16(4), 297–321 (2011)

19. Rossi, G., Schwabe, D.: Modeling and Implementing Web Applications using OOHDM. In: Web Engineering, Modelling and Implementing Web Applications, pp. 109–155. Springer, Heidelberg (2008)

20. Ton, H.: A Strategy for Balancing Business Value and Story Size. In: AGILE 2007 Conference (2007)

21. Valderas, P., Pelechano, V., Pastor, Ó.: Introducing Graphic Designers in a Web Development Process. In: Krogstie, J., Opdahl, A.L., Sindre, G. (eds.) CAiSE 2007. LNCS, vol. 4495, pp. 395–408. Springer, Heidelberg (2007)

Assessment of Effort Reduction due to Model-to-Model Transformations in the Web Domain[*]

Nora Koch[1,2], Alexander Knapp[3], and Sergej Kozuruba[1]

[1] Ludwig-Maximilians-Universität München, Germany
[2] NTT DATA, Germany
[3] Universität Augsburg, Germany

Abstract. Model-driven engineering (MDE) approaches provide the well-known advantage of software development at a higher level of abstraction. However, in the web engineering domain such approaches still encounter difficulties mainly due to applications that are continuously evolving and the heterogeneity of web technologies. Instead of fully automated generation, we look at MDE as assisting the web engineer in different phases of the software development life cycle. In particular, we use model-to-model transformations to support the generation of model sketches of the different concerns from a requirements specification. In this work, we present a metric to measure the effort reduction that results from applying this kind of model-driven approach. We use the metric to evaluate models of six web applications in the context of UML-based Web Engineering (UWE).

1 Introduction

Requirements models should be the result of an intensive communication with the customer and provide the representation of the business decisions related to the application to be developed. The more accurate the models produced in this early development phase, the less error-prone are the models and the code generated later. This relationship between the quality of the requirements specification and the implemented system has been analyzed and confirmed several times [4]. However, in practice, many projects start too soon with the technical design and the implementation. Even if requirements are specified, they are often partially ignored. The time invested in the requirements specification is very often seen as partially wasted. Therefore it is important to improve the use of the requirements specification in further development steps and to obtain as much information as possible for the so-called design models. In this work, we assess the utility of modeling the requirements and use these models in a model-driven development process (MDD) instead of manual modeling in all stages. We define a metric for measuring the effort reduction due to automatic generation of models against manual creation. Such an effort reduction would represent a measurable benefit for web productivity [4, Ch. 3]. We propose an assessment strategy that consists of the creation and generation of models, their comparison and calculation of the effort reduction indicator.

We have built the models of six web applications using UWE (UML-based Web Engineering [3]); these applications are a simple address book, a movie database, a music

---

[*] This work has been partially sponsored by the EU project ASCENS, FP7 257414, the EU-NoE project NESSoS, GA 256980, and the DFG project MAEWA II, WI 841/7-2.

portal, a social network, a publication management system and the UWE website. Our assessment approach analyzes the model elements and aggregates them for the different concern models. Although the requirements models were rather sketchy (estimated degree of details of 53%), the benefit, i.e. the effort reduction reached by having drawn and used them in the MDD process is calculated to be between 26% and 77%. We have tested as well the robustness of our metric and reasoned about the scalability. An empirical evaluation performed by a set of web engineers is planned for the corroboration of our metric. However, in this work, our focus is on the definition of the assessment strategy and to show the plausibility of the approach.

Related Work. Several model-driven web engineering methods were presented during the last decade [5]. Valderas and Pelechano [7] present a detailed analysis of the MDD characteristics of the most relevant methods. Only some of them include explicitly a requirements phase. OOHDM, UWE and WebML defined proprietary notations for the requirements offering only partial MDD tool support. The most complete though rather complex approach is presented by Object-Oriented Web Solutions (OOWS [7]). The requirements analysis phase is also the focus of the Navigational Development Technique (NDT [2]); the approach of textual templates, however, is less appropriate for the specification of navigational aspects of web applications. More recently, the Mockup-driven development process (MockupDD [6]) was defined which enables smooth transformations into e.g. UWE navigation and presentation models.

Software effort models help project managers to take decisions on methods, techniques, and tools. Mendes et al. [4, Ch. 2] present techniques for effort estimates in web software development, but do not particularly analyze the effort reduction implied by an MDD process. Another approach consists in calculating productivity based on size and effort aggregating different size measures that characterize web applications [4, Ch. 3].

2 Assessment Strategy

Our assessment is defined in terms of reduction of modeling efforts, i.e., measuring to which extent models of web software can be generated by transformations. We focus on comparing the results of the automatic generation of design models of rich web applications — just per mouse click — to the work the designer invests in modeling the application from scratch. Both, the manual modeling and the model-driven development processes use requirements models as source for building the design models.

Research Scope and Questions. The requirements models in our assessment are very simple, i.e. without many details. They contain enough information to discuss the web application with the customer, but abstract from details mainly required for the implementation. Hence, these requirements models are insufficient for the generation of complete design models and code. In fact, our goal is to analyze to which extent these simple requirements models can provide substantial help in building design models.

Our empirical method was designed to answer the following questions: (Q1) How much of the modeling effort can be reduced through automatic generation of design models of web applications? (Q2) Is it worth for the designer to focus on the modeling of the requirements in terms of effort reduction for design models? (Q3) How could web specific modeling tools provide more assistance through partial model-driven support?

Table 1. Similarity scale with associated benefit

Kind (k)	Description	Benefit ($b(k)$)
identical	both model elements have exactly the same features	1
similar	some features are identical; others are missing or erroneous	0.5
erroneous	contains features not included in the original one	−0.25
missing	is not included in the model while the original is included	0

Table 2. Weights for UML model element types

UML model element type (t)	Weight ($w(t)$)	UML model element type (t)	Weight ($w(t)$)
Class	1	Action	1
Attribute	0.5	Object Node	0.75
Association/Dependency	0.5	Pin	0.5
Tag	0.25	Control/Object Flow	0.25
Property	0.75	Use Case	1

Table 3. Effort reduction indicators and scope factor

(1) $E(t) = (\sum_{k=1}^{m} G(k,t) \cdot b(k))/M(t)$ effort reduction per model element type

(2) $E(c) = (\sum_{t=1}^{n} E(t) \cdot w(t))/\sum_{t=1}^{n} w(t)$ effort reduction per concern

(3) $E = (\sum_{c=1}^{v} E(c))/v$ effort reduction for the application

(4) $s = (\sum_{t=1}^{n} R(t) \cdot w(t))/(\sum_{t=1}^{n} M(t) \cdot w(t))$ scope factor

Assessment Process. The methodology for the assessment has as input the requirements models of the application and consists of the following steps: (1a) manual creation of the design models following the principle of separation of concerns, (1b) generation of the basic design models using transformations; (2) comparison and classification of the model elements of the manually created and automatically generated models; and (3) calculation of the *effort reduction* indicator and interpretation of results.

The notation used for our case studies is the UML profile UWE, the tool is Magic-Draw and the MagicUWE plugin with its model-to-model transformations. The requirements of the web applications are modeled with use case diagrams for the functional system properties and activity diagrams for the navigational paths and processes. The design models express the different aspects of content, navigation, presentation, and processes of web applications. These design models are produced twice for our evaluation: in step (1a) manually by the designer, in (1b) automatically by model-to-model transformations from the requirement models (see Sect. 3).

In step (2) the generated model elements, such as classes, attributes, and actions are compared to the manually designed model elements. We distinguish $m = 4$ *kinds of similarity* k for generated model elements: *identical, similar, erroneous,* and *missing* (see Tab. 1). The *benefit factor* $b(k)$ of kind k tells how much the generation contributes to the work of the web engineer. This ranges from $b(identical) = 1$, when nothing has to be changed, to $b(erroneous) = -0.25$, when elements need to be removed.

Finally, in step (3) the *effort reduction* indicator is calculated for model types and aggregated for each concern and for the application; see Tab. 3. The indicator $E(t)$ for a model element type t, like class, attribute, etc., is the sum of the number of the generated elements $G(k, t)$ of a similarity kind k and of the type t weighted with the benefit factor $b(k)$ and divided by the corresponding number of manually generated model elements $M(t)$ (Tab. 3(1)). The effort reduction indicator $E(c)$ for a concern c, such as content, navigation, process, and presentation, is calculated as a linear additive weighted formula of the effort reduction indicator $E(t)$ of the n individual model element types (Tab. 3(2)). The *weight* $w(t)$ in Tab. 2 expresses the relevance a model element type t has for the designer. For example, classes are first-class citizens and attributes are not, as they belong to classes. The effort reduction indicator E for the entire web application is given by the average over all v concerns that are modeled for the web application (Tab. 3(3)). We assume that for the designer all concerns have the same relevance.

With E we provide an estimation of the amount of spared effort when we focus on modeling requirements of a web application and partially generate the design models. We need, however, to complete these draft models with some *additional effort* in order to achieve the same objective as when modeling the different concerns manually. In terms of project productivity each activity in the development process has a measurable, positive cost, with exception of the automated model transformations (we neglect the implementation costs of the transformations as they are reusable for many projects).

Until now, we only assumed that the same requirements model were used for both the manual and the automatically generated design models, but disregarded the quality of the requirements model. We introduce a *scope* factor that gives a very rough estimation of the degree of detail to which the requirements are modeled. This scope factor is calculated as the ratio between the linear additive weighted expression of the number of requirements elements $R(t)$ of a model element type t and the number of design elements $M(t)$ (Tab. 3(4)). We use it to normalize the values obtained for the effort reduction of a web application making different web applications comparable.

3   Model-Based Development of Web Applications in UWE

The assessment strategy for effort reduction in MDD is independent of the approach for developing web applications; only support for modeling the requirements and the different design concerns is required. In this work, we use the UML-based Web Engineering (UWE [3]) notation, method, and tool support for evaluating the strategy. The UWE notation is defined as a UML profile. The cornerstones of the UWE method are the principle of separation of concerns and the model-driven approach. As UWE tool we use the MagicUWE plugin implemented for MagicDraw [1].

We illustrate the modeling process and the results of the model transformations in UWE by a web-based social network application for sharing favorite web links with friends: *Linkbook* is accessible to guests and registered users, providing logging in/out and (un)registering functionality. The homepage shows a list of favorite links grouped by categories and offers search facilities for links and user comments. Registered users can comment links and switch to their personal view for managing their links. Network functionality is offered by a list of friends, giving access to the friends' favorites.

Requirements Modeling. In UWE, a web application's functional requirements are captured by use cases and activities. Figure 1(a) depicts a subset of the *Linkbook* use cases.

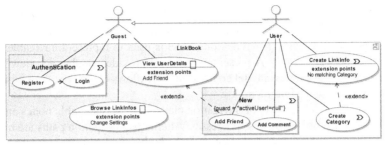

(a) Functional requirements modeled with use cases (excerpt)

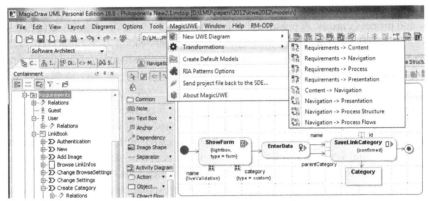

(b) MagicUWE tool with requirements workflow for CreateCategory

(c) Presentation elements: manually modeled (M, left) and automatically generated (G, right)

Fig. 1. *Linkbook* example in MagicUWE

The UWE profile supports web-specific annotations by stereotypes for use cases, like «browsing» (· , pure navigation) and «processing» (· , workflow functionality). Use cases in packages inherit the stereotype of the package.

Each «processing» use case is refined by a workflow using UML activity diagrams, for CreateCategory see Fig. 1(b) (lower right). The workflow specifies the process actions, input/output information with pins or objects, decisions, and rich user interface features. Web-specific annotations can be added to actions, like «displayAction» ( ) for the explicit presentation of elements, «userAction» (·) for asking the user for input, or «systemAction» (·) indicating the processing of data.

Creating Design Models. The UWE method for the design phase follows the principle of "separation of concerns": A content model represents the domain concepts and the relationships between them. A navigation model is used to represent navigable nodes and the links between nodes. A presentation model provides an abstract view on the user interface (UI). A process model contains the workflows of the processes which are invoked from certain navigation nodes.

A navigation model consists of navigation classes for the navigable nodes and process classes for accessing business processes. Alternative navigation paths are handled by menus, multiple instances of navigation paths by indexes, menus, and queries. The basic presentation modeling elements are the «presentationGroup» which are directly based on nodes from the navigation model, i.e. navigation classes, menus, access primitives, and process classes. A presentation group (·) or a «form» (·) are used to include a set of other UI elements, like «textInput» (·) or «selection» (·). Figure 1(c) (left) shows the presentation model for the process AddComment which is related to the «processing» use case with the same name.

Generating Design Models. On the right side of Fig. 1(c) the presentation model of the same AddComment form is shown, but this one was automatically generated by model-to-model transformations. A set of model transformations is defined in MagicUWE with the goal to benefit from the efforts invested in the requirements models and produce initial versions of all design models, i.e., content, navigation, process, and presentation (see Fig. 1(b)). To describe in detail each of these transformations is out of the scope of this work. For the requirements-to-presentation transformation mainly information from the requirements workflow with its action stereotypes is used, like «userAction» asking the user for input.

4   Evaluation Results

Once the modeling part of the process described in Sect. 2 is completed, the evaluation of the MDD approach can be started (steps 2 and 3). We first provide details on how the effort reduction calculations are applied to the *Linkbook*, then we present the assessment results for a set of six web applications and discuss the robustness of our findings.[1]

Assessing Effort Reduction for Linkbook. A counting of model elements of both design models resulting from the requirements, the manually crafted and the generated model, is performed for each concern. The generated elements are classified into the kinds of of Tab. 1. For example, the excerpt of the manually crafted presentation models of *Linkbook* shown in Fig. 1(c) contains 10 model elements (1 class, 4 properties and 5 tags); the generated counterpart contains 7 model elements (1 class, 6 properties and 1 tag); there is no *identical* element, 4 *similar* and 3 *erroneous*. Table 4 presents the results of the counting and categorization of all model elements of the presentation concern. These modeling elements are the presentation group (including those that inherit from it, like input form), the interactive elements (like button, input text, selection), and the output properties (such as text, images).

---

[1] Further details on the example applications (*Address Book, Music Portal, Movie Database, Publication Management System* and the *UWE website*) as well as download links of their models can be found at the UWE website: http://uwe.pst.ifi.lmu.de.

Table 4. Linkbook application: Effort reduction indicators for the presentation concern

Linkbook	Manually modeled	Generated Identical	Similar	Erroneous	Effort reduction indicator (E)
Presentation Groups (Class)	38	13	15	12	0.46
Interactive Elements (Property)	54	32	18	26	0.64
Output Elements (Property)	25	17	8	11	0.73
Presentation Model					0.59

Table 5. Overview on Assessment Results

Web application	Content	Navigation	Presentation	Process	E	Scope	E normalized
Address Book	0.56	0.45	0.51	0.66	0.54	0.75	0.39
Linkbook	0.45	0.57	0.59	0.63	0.56	0.84	0.35
Movie DB	0.25	0.30	0.10	0.33	0.25	0.51	0.26
Music Portal	0.59	0.52	0.46	0.78	0.59	0.41	0.77
Publications MS	0.13	0.33	0.25	0.17	0.22	0.36	0.33
UWE Website	0.40	0.01	0.53	0.78	0.43	0.32	0.72
Average						0.53	0.47

Table 6. Statistics on Linkbook models

Model	Class	Use Case	Action	Attribute	Assoc./ Depend.	Pin	Property	Contr./Obj. Flow	Object Node	Tag	Weighted Average
Req.	0	22	93	0	15	131	0	179	16	93	63.06
Design	80	0	46	33	70	57	135	120	19	114	75.11

The last column of Tab. 4 shows the values of the effort reduction indicators calculated using the equations in Tab. 3: $E(t)$ for each model element type t and the effort reduction indicator $E(c)$ for the entire presentation concern, which is 59%. The effort reduction indicators for the content, navigation and process concerns are computed similarly (see second row of Tab. 5). The effort reduction indicator E for the entire web application *Linkbook* is 56%. As additional modeling effort required after the execution of the model transformation 48 model elements have to be built.

Comparing Effort Reductions of Multiple Applications. Table 5 gives an overview of the effort reduction indicators for all six web applications of the assessment study. The evaluation results show that the execution of the transformations and the resulting first drafts of the different models for the content, navigation, presentation, and process concerns imply an effort reduction between 22% and 59%, but irrespective of the amount of effort that has been invested in the requirements modeling. To correct this bias, we use the scope factor s of Tab. 3(4) based on a relationship between amount and type of model elements used at requirements and design level; see next-to-last column of Tab. 5. The scope factor is then applied to normalize the effort reduction indicator of each application. The normalized values of E (last column) are comparable and are situated in the range between 26% and 77% with an average effort reduction of 47%.

These results allow the following answers to the questions in Sect. 2: (Q1) The modeling effort can be reduced in average by 47% if the degree of detail of the requirements models is estimated in 53%; assuming linearity this would imply that complete require-ments models (100%) would lead to an automatic generation of 88% of the design mod-els. (Q2) The effort reduction values confirm that it is worth to invest in the requirements modeling. (Q3) Tools should allow for separate execution of model transformations for each concern enabling the modeler to select appropriate transformations.

Robustness of the Assessment. We recalculated the effort reduction indicator changing the weights of model elements in Tab. 2. A modification of 0.25 for a navigation element type changes the effort reduction indicator of the concern by max. 3%, in average only 2%. Similarly, in the presentation model changes of 0.25 in average only affect the value of the indicator by 1%, max. 4%. Although these results sound encouraging, there are still some difficulties to be solved. The most important methodological issue is the regeneration of models after changes in the target models have been performed, i.e. how to merge models and identify conflicts. A more technical and tool related problem is the graphical representation of the diagrams corresponding to generated models.

5   Conclusions

We have presented an assessment process and a metric for measuring the effort reduc-tion resulting from using model-transformations instead of manual creation of design models based on the requirements models of web applications. The proposed assess-ment strategy has been applied to six web applications, whose requirements have been specified using the UWE approach. Our evaluation shows that the MDD approach re-duced the effort in more than 45%, which could even be improved if the degree of detail of the source models is increased. We plan to corroborate the results of our evaluation with empirical data obtained by groups of students that will create the models and use the same tool for generating these web applications.

References

1. Busch, M., Koch, N.: MagicUWE – A CASE Tool Plugin for Modeling Web Applications. In: Gaedke, M., Grossniklaus, M., Díaz, O. (eds.) ICWE 2009. LNCS, vol. 5648, pp. 505–508. Springer, Heidelberg (2009)
2. Escalona, M.J., Aragón, G.: NDT. A Model-Driven Approach for Web Requirements. IEEE Trans. Softw. Eng. 34(3), 377–390 (2008)
3. Koch, N., Knapp, A., Zhang, G., Baumeister, H.: UML-Based Web Engineering: An Approach Based on Standards. In: Olsina et al. [5], ch. 7, pp. 157–191
4. Mendes, E., Mosley, N. (eds.): Web Engineering. Springer, Berlin (2006)
5. Olsina, L., Pastor, O., Rossi, G., Schwabe, D. (eds.): Web Engineering: Modelling and Imple-menting Web Applications. Springer (2008)
6. Rivero, J.M., Grigera, J., Rossi, G., Robles Luna, E., Koch, N.: Towards Agile Model-Driven Web Engineering. In: Nurcan, S. (ed.) CAiSE Forum 2011. LNBIP, vol. 107, pp. 142–155. Springer, Heidelberg (2012)
7. Valderas, P., Pelechano, V.: A Survey of Requirements Specification in Model-Driven Devel-opment of Web Applications. ACM Trans. Web 5(2), 10 (2011)

Evaluating the Impact of a Model-Driven Web Engineering Approach on the Productivity and the Satisfaction of Software Development Teams

Yulkeidi Martínez[1], Cristina Cachero[2], and Santiago Meliá[2]

[1] Universidad Máximo Gómez Báez de Ciego de Ávila, Cuba
[2] DLSI. Universidad de Alicante, Spain

Abstract. BACKGROUND: Model-Driven Engineering claims a positive impact on software productivity and satisfaction. However, few efforts have been made to collect evidences that assess its true benefits and limitations.

OBJECTIVE: To compare the productivity and satisfaction of junior Web developers during the development of the business layer of a Web 2.0 Application when using either a code-centric, a model-based (UML) or a Model-Driven Engineering approach (OOH4RIA).

RESEARCH METHOD: We designed a full factorial, intra-subject experiment in which 26 subjects, divided into five groups, were asked to develop the same three modules of a Web application, each one using a different method. We measured their productivity and satisfaction with each approach.

RESULTS: The use of Model-Driven Engineering practices seems to significantly increase both productivity and satisfaction of junior Web developers, regardless of the particular application. However, modeling activities that are not accompanied by a strong generation environment make productivity and satisfaction decrease below code-centric practices. Further experimentation is needed to be able to generalize the results to a different population, different languages and tools, different domains and different application sizes.

1 Introduction

It is a well known fact that the Web Engineering community advocates the use of models in order to improve software development processes for Web applications. However, there are many issues around modeling that are, as of today, cause of controversy and heated debates: to which extent should practitioners model? Which should be the level of detail of these models? Should practitioners strive to maintain the models current, or should these models be disposable? These and others are open questions whose answer currently partly depends on the development culture of the person asked, and partly on the context in which such practices are being adopted. In this respect we claim that, instead, the decision about which is the adequate application of software modeling practices should be answerable based on objective data regarding its impact on well-known process

M. Brambilla, T. Tokuda, and R. Tolksdorf (Eds.): ICWE 2012, LNCS 7387, pp. 223–237, 2012.

and product quality dimensions. From these dimensions, productivity, defined as a ratio of what is produced to what is required to produce it, outstands, due to its impact during the selection of a development process in industry [1]. Also, satisfaction is an important aspect of quality, since, being software development a human process, the developer's satisfaction is a key factor for the successful adoption of such practices [2].

One quite well-known way of classifying modeling practices in industry is according to the extent to which modeling is used to support the development process. Fowler [3] describes three different modes in which modeling languages (and the UML in particular) can be used: sketch, blueprint and programming language.

- Sketches are informal diagrams used to communicate ideas. They usually focus on a particular aspect of the system and are not intended to show every detail of it. It is the most common use of the UML, and the recommended practice in agile, code-centric frameworks like Scrum. When models are used as sketches, tools are rarely used, the modeling activity being mostly performed in front of blackboards where designers join to discuss complex or unclear aspects of the system. They are most useful in code-centric approaches, where the objective is to develop self-explaining code.
- Blueprints are diagrams that show most of the details of a system in order to foster its understanding or to provide views of the code in a graphical form. Blueprints are widely used in Model-Based Development (MBD) practices, such as the ones promoted by frameworks such as the Rational Unified Process (RUP).
- Last but not least, models can be used to fully characterize the application. If such is the case, the diagrams replace the code, and they are compiled directly into executable binaries. This is the modeling use that lies at the core of Web Engineering Model-Driven Development (MDD) approaches.

This classification has led some authors to characterize the modeling maturity level of organizations based on the role of modeling in their software development process, from manual, code-centric, to full, Model-Driven [4]. While code-centric development methods require - at most - an informal use of modeling techniques and languages, both MBD and MDD require a formal use of models, which mainly relies on the use of Computer Aided Software Engineering (CASE) tools. These tools may offer not only modeling environments - including model checkers that may assure syntactical correctness, semantic accurateness, consistency or completion of models, to name a few desirable model characteristics - but also partial or even complete software generation environments that, in the case of MDD CASE tools, are based on model transformations.

Both MBD and MDD tools work under the assumption that designing models that can generate partial or complete code is much simpler and quicker than actually writing such code. This same view is sustained in MBD and MDD related scientific literature. Such literature claims that the two most outstanding advantages of MDD over code-centric or even MBD approaches are (a) short and long term process productivity gains [5] and (b) a significant external software product quality improvement [6,7]. These advantages are justified in literature by the higher level of compatibility between systems, the simplified design process, and the better communication between individuals and teams working on the system that the MDD paradigm fosters [8].However, neither the MBD nor the MDD research community have yet been able to provide practitioners with a sufficient body of practical evidence that soundly backs the purported gains of their recommended modeling practices with respect to code-centric approaches [9,10]. Many authors have written about the importance of providing empirical evidence in software engineering [11] but, unfortunately, the percentage of empirical studies - be them surveys, experiments, case studies or postmortem analyses [12]- that provide data to illustrate the impact of MBD and MDD approaches over different quality characteristics (such as productivity or satisfaction) is still very low, which hampers the generalizability of the results. In order to guarantee such generalizability, we also need to take into explicit consideration many factors that may affect these characteristics, such as tool usage, adaptation of the development methodology to the idiosyncrasy of the particular development team, type, complexity and size of the project, and so on. This situation contrasts with other disciplines and even other areas of Software Engineering [13], and it is often mentioned as one of the causes that explain the low adoption level of modeling practices by the practitioner's mainstream [14].

Given this situation, the aim of this paper is to augment the repository of empirical data that contributes to giving a scientific answer to the following research question: *What is the impact of the development method (be it rooted in a code-centric, an MBD, or an MDD paradigm) on the productivity and satisfaction of junior developers while developing Web 2.0 applications?*

In order to answer this question, Section 2 describes some previous studies that center on the impact of MBD and MDD practices on process productivity and satisfaction with respect to traditional code-centric practices. Section 3 outlines our experiment design, and analyzes its results and threats to validity. Finally, Section 4 presents the conclusions and further lines of research.

2   Background

Although still scarce in number and not always systematically performed [15], in the last years we have witnessed an increase in the number of empirical studies that provide empirical data regarding the impact of MBD and MDD practices on the productivity and satisfaction of software development teams.

Regarding MBD, in [5] initial evidence is provided about the use of models and tools as an effective way to reduce the time of development and to improve software development variables such as productivity and product quality.

Regarding MDD, there is a number of experiments where productivity of developers using different methods - some model-driven, others code-centered - was measured [9,16,17,18,19,20]. The conclusion in all these studies is that, as projects grow larger, the use of MDD development practices significantly increases productivity (results ranging from two up to nine or even twenty times, depending on the study). The only evidence contradicting these findings is an industrial experience presented in [14]. In this paper, the authors reported a set of studies that showed contradictory results, with both software productivity gains and losses, depending on the particular study. They explained the found productivity losses by pointing at the use of immature tools and high start-up costs. Also, these studies showed that modeling was considered to be an activity at least as complex as programming with a traditional third generation language.

Last but not least, although most of the aforementioned studies include some kind of global satisfaction score, there are few studies that center on the developers' subjective perceptions while applying different methods. In [21], the author empirically assessed the satisfaction of an MDD method (called MIMAT) that includes Functional Usability Features (FUFs) in an MDD software development process. The study concluded that the users' satisfaction improves after including FUFs in the software development process. Our experiment does not center on the impact of a method enrichment, but compares different methods with respect to the developer's satisfaction and productivity.

Next, we present the quasi-experiment that we have performed to test the impact of three methods, each one an example of a code-centric, an MBD and an MDD approach respectively, on the productivity and satisfaction of junior software developers.

3   Description of the Experiment

During the months of January and February 2011, a quasi-experiment was conducted at the University of Alicante. A quasi-experiment differs from a true experiment in that subjects are not randomly chosen. Quasi-experiments, although suffering from a lower internal validity, are widely used and deemed useful in the Empirical SE field, since they allow investigations of cause-effect relations in settings such as ours, in which randomization is too costly [22].

3.1   Goals and Context Definition

Following the GQM template [23], our empirical study is aimed at *analyzing* three methods, one representative of the code-centric paradigm, one representative of the MBD paradigm and one representative of the MDD paradigm, *for the purpose of* comparison *with respect to* their productivity and satisfaction *from the point of view of* junior software developers. The context of the study was a set of M.Sc. students developing the business layer of a Web 2.0 application.

The design of the experiment was based on the framework for experimentation in SE suggested by [12]. The whole data set is included in the replication package available at http://www.dlsi.ua.es/ ccachero/labPackages/ Productivity.v1.rar.

The research questions addressed in this study were formulated as follows:

– **RQ1**: Is the team's productivity significantly different among methods, regardless of the particular module being developed?

- **RQ2**: Is the developer's satisfaction significantly different among methods, regardless of the particular module being developed?

These research questions were devised to be answerable by quantitative means.

Subjects and Application. The initial group of subjects were 30 students of the Web Applications Developer Master at the University of Alicante. These students were divided into six teams of 4 to 6 people. From them, the data corresponding to Team 6 had to be dropped due to some of their components abandoning the Master for work reasons soon after the experiment had started. Therefore, the final set of observations corresponds to the observations of the remaining five groups (26 subjects). Since the abandonment of the group had nothing to do with the application being developed, the treatments that the group were applying to his project nor the particular order in which they were applying them, we can assume that the results of the experiments have not been compromised. The final sample comprised 25 men and 1 women, of whom 75% had more than 2 years of professional experience as developers of web applications. The mean age of the participants was 25,6 years old and all of them were Computer Engineering graduates of the University of Alicante. Regarding the subjects' level of knowledge with respect to the different technologies and methods used during the experiment, a questionnaire showed that 81% knew UML, and that another 12% considered that they had a high-level of knowledge of UML. It should also be noted that 76% of the subjects had previously programmed with VS and .NET during their degree courses, although only 12% had applied them in industry. Finally, the subjects acknowledged no previous practical knowledge of MDD, although 56% of them were aware of the existence of the paradigm. By the time the experiment took place, the subjects had received additional training in all three methods. Such training consisted in 30 hours of training in programming in C# using Visual Studio 2010, 20 hours of training in UML modelling with RSM and 10 hours of training in modelling with the OOH4RIA tool.

Each of the five groups developed a social media application for a different domain:

- Trips: the social network for this domain is focused on establishing relationships between people who want to reduce travel costs by sharing their own cars.
- Events: the social network for this domain is centred on organized social events.
- Hospitals: the social network for this domain aims at improving the communication between physicians and patients.
- Academics: the social network for this domain focuses on connecting and sharing teaching contents among teachers and students.
- Facework: the social network for this domain helps workers to share information about different tasks, resources and goals of the company.

All the applications shared the same complexity, which was controlled by defining a set of functional features that all the applications had to support, regardless of the domain. From them, the three functional features that were included in our experiment were:

- Support for the establishment of a community of users (from now on Group) to create contents and relationships among people of different environments (professional, personal, etc., depending on the particular application being developed).
- Support for the organization of events (from now on Events) where people can invite their friends or colleagues to attend to a place where the event is realized (the particular event being a celebration, a work meeting, etc. depending on the particular application being developed)
- Support for an organizational community (from now on Organization) where subjects (be them companies, celebrities, etc., depending on the particular application) can publish content, photos, etc. in a unidirectional way to the social network.

Each one of these functional features was designed as a module. In order to further control the complexity of each module, we strictly defined their architecture, which was based on four main layers: the Business Objects layer (BO), the Data Access Objects layer (DAO), the Data Transfer Objects layer (DTO) and the Database layer (DB). In this way, it was possible to standardize to a certain point the code that had to be developed and facilitate its measurement. Although we are conscious that such strict architecture may hamper the external validity of the experiment, this factor was kept constant across the three treatments, in order to preserve the comparability of the results. The subjects were asked to implement each module following a different method. The time assigned for the implementation of each module was two weeks.

In order to develop the different projects, the students had to follow the Agile Unified Process (Agile UP) methodology [24], a streamlined approach to software development that is based on the IBM's Rational Unified Process (RUP) [25]. The Agile UP lifecycle is serial in the large, iterative in the small, and delivers incremental releases over time. Specifically, our experiment was situated in the construction phase of Agile UP, which is focused on developing the system to the point where it is ready for pre-production testing. The construction phase is made up of a set of disciplines or workflows that groups different tasks of this process. These disciplines, together with the impact of modelling practices on each of them depending on the paradigm, are presented in Table 1. All the students had previously developed at least one application with Agile UP, and they had an additional 10-hour training period to refresh the main concepts.

Table 1. Degree of automation of Agile UP disciplines by development paradigm

Discipline	Code-Centric(.NET)	Model-Based(RSM)	Model-Driven(OOH4RIA)
Model	Sketch or absent	Blueprint	Fully-fledged (DSL)
Implementation	Manual	Semi-automatic	Automatic
Test	Manual	Manual	Semiautomatic

Implementation Language and Case Tools. The development environment for the experiment was set up as follows:

- Code Development Environment: NET framework and NHibernate (Object-Relational Mapping).
- IDE (Integrated Development Environment) Development Tool: Visual Studio 2010.
- Languages: C# and the Extensible Application Markup Language (XAML).
- MBD Modeling Environment: Rational Software Modeler (RSM)
- MDD Modeling Environment: OOH4RIA IDE
- Other tools: Subversion 1.6 (SVN), Jira (Issue Tracking) and Survey Monkey (for questionnaires).

The code-centric treatment relied solely on the development enviroment provided by the Visual Studio 2010 and the use of external tools that permit to manage the collaborative work (Subversion). On the other hand, the MBD treatment required the students to work with the UML class diagram of the RSM tool. Last but not least, for the MDD treatment the students worked with the OOH4RIA approach [26].

Students were scheduled to work on these three modules during six weeks along the months of January and February 2011. By this time of the year, the students had already gone through most of the topics of the master, and had gathered a substantial amount of experience with the different tools and the development environments. The experiment defined a tight timetable of deliverables, one every two weeks. Each deliverable consisted of a set of source files and a domain model. The source code had to contain four specific file types: the Business Object files (BO), the Data Access Object files (DAO), the Data Transfer Object files (DTO) and the Database files (DB). The teams were continuously monitored by a Master instructor whose role in the experiment was to look after the quality of the data gathered, both in class and off-line through the Jira and the SVN report systems.

3.2 Experiment Planning

Given the low number of development teams available, and in order to facilitate the detection of method impact by controlling the variability among subjects, the experiment was conceived as an intra-subject design. The combination team-module-approach was defined using a Factorial Design [27,28] (see Table 2). This kind of design avoids order effects and can provide some unique and relevant information about how variables interact or combine in the effect they have on the dependent variables. Also, this design eliminates any possible order effect. Teams were randomly assigned to each treatment order.

In order to answer the research questions presented in Section 3.1, we have defined the following independent (experimentally manipulated) variables (IV) or factors:

Table 2. Experiment design: a factorial, intra-subject design. Group marked with(*) did not finish the experiment.

Team/Module	Application	Group	Events	Organization
1	Travel	code-centric	MBD	MDD
2	Events	code-centric	MDD	MBD
3	Hospital	MBD	MDD	code-centric
4	Academics	MDD	MBD	code-centric
5	Facework	MBD	code-centric	MDD
6*	Automobile	MDD	code-centric	MBD

- Meth: Method, a categorical variable with three levels: code-centric, MBD, MDD. It is important to note that, in this experiment, when we refer to method we are in fact talking about a compound variable (method*tool), due to the coupling of these two variables in our experimental settings.
- Mod: Module, a categorical variable with three possible values: Groups, Events, Organization.

The Dependent (measurable) variables (DV) are:

- P(Meth, Mod), a ratio variable that measures the productivity of the team with each method and module
- S(Meth,Mod), an interval variable, based on a 7-point Likert scale, that measures the satisfaction of the developers with each method and module

The DV have been measured through the following collection procedures:

1. To measure Productivity we measured both the development time and the size of the modules developed by each team.
   - Development time: The student had to document the time of each development activity through the JIRA tool.
   - Module size: We measure the size of the code produced by students in source lines of code (SLOC). SLOCs come in handly to express the size of software among programmers with low levels of experience [29]. We automated the obtention of this measure through the Line Counter [30] tool.
2. To measure Satisfaction we defined a satisfaction scale (SS) made up of eleven items, where each one was based on a 7-point Likert rating scale.

These measures have been used to test the following testable hypotheses, which are based on the research questions and the existing empirical evidence presented in Section 2:

- Productivity Hypothesis (PH): Prod(MDD)>Prod(MBD)>Prod(code-centric). Developer teams are significantly more productive with the MDD method, followed by the MBD method, followed by the code-centric method.
- Productivity-Module Interaction Hypothesis (PMIH): P(Module*Meth)< 0.05. The effect on P of the particular module to which the method is applied is insignificant compared to the effect of the method.

- Satisfaction Hypothesis (SH): Satisf(MDD)>S(MBD)>S(code-centric). De-velopers are significantly more satisfied with the MDD method, followed by the MBD method, followed by the code-centric method.
- Satisfaction-Module Interaction Hypothesis (SMIH): S(Module*Meth)<0.05. The effect on S of the particular module to which the method is applied is insignificant compared to the effect of the method.

3.3   Instrumentation

Besides the instructional materials, all the students received three booklets:

- Modules Description Booklet: a requirements document describing the func-tional and non functional requirements of the three modules included in the experiment. This booklet was divided in three parts, and it was the same regardless of the order in which the treatments were to be applied.
- Jira Time Reporting Booklet: a document explaining the time reporting conventions that were to be used during the experiment
- Subject Instruction sheet: a set of instructions to the students to correctly perform the experiment.

These instruments are included in the replication package available at http://www.dlsi.ua.es/~ccachero/labPackages/Productivity.v1.rar.
The experiment had the following structure:

1. Subject instruction sheet.
2. Pre-experiment questionnaire: it included demographic questions as well as questions about subjects' previous experience with Web application devel-opment, Web programming and application modeling, etc.
3. Project work: For each treatment, the students spent two weeks working on the corresponding module with the assigned methodology.
4. Post-experiment questionnaire: it included a semantic-differential scale that required developers to judge each method on 11 pairs of adjectives describing the developer's overall satisfaction with such method.

At the end of each module, the students delivered both the Domain Models and the Source Code (BO, DAO, DTO and DB files).

3.4   Data Analysis and Interpretation of Results

The statistical analysis was carried out with PASW (Predictive Analytics Soft-Ware) Statistics [31].
Prior to the assessment of the hypotheses, we checked the reliability of the Satisfaction scale in the context of our experimental settings. For the satisfac-tion scale, all the items showed a correlation higher than 0.3, while the global Cronbach alpha was 0.892, giving proof of a high internal consistency among the scale items. This high correlation has led us to calculate the scale mean for each method, and consider this mean as a global rating of satisfaction with each one of the three treatments (code-centric, MBD, MDD).

RQ1: Impact of Method on Team Productivity. The data gathered to accept/reject the PH and PMIH hypotheses (see section 3.2) are graphically presented in Fig. 1.

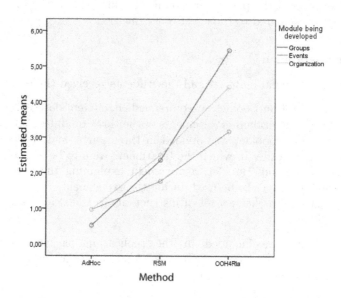

Fig. 1. Productivity: SLOC/Hours

To test the PH and PMIH hypotheses, we applied a 3*5 Mixed Design ANOVA , in which the module (Groups, Events, Organization) was the between-subjects variable, and the calculated P ratings for each method were the within-subjects variables. In order to assure that applying this statistical method made sense, we verified that the principle of sphericity was not violated by applying the W Mauchly's test (W=0,005, p>0,05) [32]. The results showed that MDD produced the highest P (M = 4,60, SD=1,17), followed by MBD (M=2,30, SD=1,10) and then Code-centric (M=0,80, SD=0,29), and that these differences were significant (F=25,395, p=0,001).

The results also showed that the interaction Mod*Meth was not significant (F= 3,009, p>0.05). We can then safely examine the main effects of the two independent variables (Mod and Meth) on these means without needing to qualify the results by the existence of a significant interaction. The main effect of module did not attain significance (F=0,538, p>0.05), while the main effect of method did reach significance, (F=25,39, p<0,01), that is, the differences in P are significantly affected by the method used, regardless of the particular module being developed. The last step of the analysis consisted on studying the pairwise differences among methods through a one-way RM Anova with pairwise comparisons. In order not to augment the risk of a type-1 error, a Bonferroni adjustment was applied. This means reducing the significance threshold to 0.0167 (p = 0.05 / 3 = 0,0167).

With this adjustment, the differences in productivity between the Code-centric and the MBD method did not attain significance (t=-2,69, p=0,054) but the differences between Code-centric and MDD (t=-6,029, p=0,004) and MBD and MDD (t=-6,031, p=0,004) did.

RQ2: Impact of Method on Developer's Satisfaction. The data gathered to accept/reject the SH and SMIH hypotheses (see section 3.2) are graphically presented in Fig. 2.

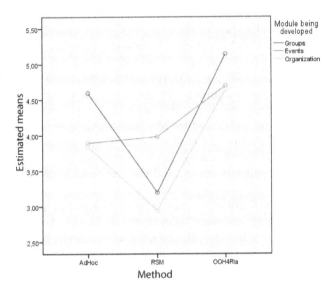

Fig. 2. Satisfaction: Likert Scale

To test the SH and SMIH hypotheses we applied a 3*5 Mixed Design ANOVA , in which the module (Groups, Events, Organization) was the between-subjects variable, and the S ratings for each method were the within-subjects variables. In order to assure that applying this statistical method made sense, we first checked that the principle of spherity was not violated by applying the W Mauchly's test (W=0,838, p=0,142) [32]. The results showed that MDD produced the highest S (M = 4,76, SD=0,73), followed by code-centric (M=4,17, SD=0,72) and then MBD (M=3,48, SD=0,96). The results also showed that the interaction Mod*Meth is not significant (F = 1,768, p>0.05). If we examine the effects of the two independent variables (module and method) we can observe how the Mod inter-subject influence did not attain significance (F=0,167, p>0,05), while the main effect of method did reach significance, (F=18,04, p<0,01), that is, the differences in S are significantly affected by the method used, regardless of the particular module being developed. The last step of the analysis consisted on studying the pairwise differences among methodologies through a one-way

Anova with pairwise comparisons. In order not to augment the risk of a type-1 error, a Bonferroni adjustment was applied. This means reducing the significance threshold to 0.0167 (p = 0.05 / 3 = 0,0167). Even with this conservative adjustment, all the pairwise S differences were significant (p<0,05), which means that, in our experiment, subjects rated significantly differently the three approaches, being MDD the best method rated and MBD the worst.

3.5   Threats to Validity

The analysis of the threats to validity evaluates under which conditions our experiment is applicable and offers benefits, and under which circumstances it might fail. For the classification of these threats, we have followed the classification proposed by Cook and Cambell [33]: internal, external, construction and conclusion.

Threats to conclusion validity refer to the relationship between the treatment and the outcome. In order to minimize the threats, we have strived to automatically capture as many measures as possible, with the help of well-known tracking systems such as JIRA or SVN. Additionally, statistical tests have been chosen conservatively, without making any kind of assumption on variable distributions. However, the fact that the students self-reported the measures, together with the duration of the experiment (six weeks) and the low number of subjects hamper the conclusion validity.

Threats to internal validity are concerned with the possibility of hidden factors that may compromise the conclusion that it is indeed the treatment what causes the differences in outcome. All groups applied all the treatments to different modules at different times, what minimizes many internal threats such as selection, history, maturation or social threads such as compensatory rivalry or resentful demoralization. However, being an intra-subject design, carry-over effects may have occurred.

Threats to construct validity refer to the relationship between theory and observation. In this sense, both the treatments and the measures used to assess productivity and satisfaction have been previously widely used in literature. This notwithstanding, there remains the possibility of an interaction of testing and treatments: the need to self-report certain measures may have changed the behavior of the students. We believe that the fact that the experiment took over six weeks minimizes this risk, since it is very difficult to maintain a 'potentially abnormal' behavior over such a long period of time without it being detected. Also, the hypothesis of the experiment (that is, a higher productivity of MDD environments) was quite easy to guess, so students may have felt bound to report less time when using MBD or MDD. Anyway, the experiment observers took special care not to disclose this hypothesis to the students. Additionally, the experiment suffers from a restricted generalizability across constructs: we have checked a positive outcome between productivity and MDD, but we cannot assure that this does not come at the expense of other characteristic of the developed software, such as modularity, reusability, or any other quality attribute.

Last but not least, external validity is concerned with generalization of the results. In this group of threats we have identified a lack of sample representativeness (M.Sc. students), academic environment, a strict architecture and a restricted domain and complexity. Also, we are conscious of the existing coupling between method and tool: all the methods were accompanied by tools. Although we tried to choose well-known development environment and -when possible- use standards (e.g. UML for the modeling activity in MBD and MDD), we are conscious that the different tools add a different 'flavor' to the methods. Therefore, this experiment needs to be replicated in order to make sure that it is the method used and not the tool what causes the observed differences.

4 Conclusions

During the last years the Web Engineering community has claimed how the use of modeling practices in MDD and MDB approaches significantly improves the productivity and satisfaction of Web applications with respect to code-centric development approaches. However, up to now, the quality and quantity of the empirical analyses that demonstrate the true impact of these modeling techniques over the final developer's productivity or satisfaction are still very low. In this paper, we have presented a rigorous analysis of a quasi-experiment carried out in a controlled environment. The data gathered shows that the productivity and the satisfaction of junior Web developers are significantly affected by the development method but they are independent from the particular module being developed. The main conclusions of our study (that still need to be corroborated with further replications) are:

- The MDD approach seems to significantly increase the productivity of developers with respect to both the MDB and the code-centric approach.
- The MDD approach satisfies the most the expectations of juniors developers, followed by code-centric and, in third position, the MDB approach.

These results are well aligned with with the assumption that model-driven techniques improve the productivity and also the satisfaction among developers when they are accompanied by a generation environment. However, the productivity and the satisfaction can decrease even below code-centric practices when the modeling activities are used exclusively as blueprints to improve the understanding, and the developers must implement manually almost all the final code.

Our study of the impact of MDD on the productivity and satisfaction is just the beginning of a family of experiments in which we want to replicate the same analysis with practitioners in industry and also with more complex Web application client-side models. Moreover, further experimentation is needed to separate the effect of methods from the effect of their accompanying development environments (Visual Studio 2010, RSM or the OOH4RIA tool) and to be able to generalize the results to a different population, different methods and languages, different application types or different application sizes.

Acknowledgements. This paper has been co-supported by the DLSI, the Spanish Ministry of Education, and the University of Alicante under contracts TIN2010-15789 (SONRIA) and GRE10-23 (DISEMRIA). The authors also wish to thank their students to take the time to participate in this empirical study. Besides we would like to thank to Jose Javier Martinez and Juan Antonio Osuna, who contributed to the development of the OOH4RIA Tool.

References

1. CMU/SEI: CMMI Product Development Team, CMMI for Development verion 1.2 (2006)
2. Moore, G.C., Benbasat, I.: Development of an instrument to measure the perceptions of adopting an information technology innovation. Information Systems Research 2(3), 192–222 (1991)
3. Fowler, M.: UML distilled: a brief guide to the standard object modeling language, 3rd edn. Addison-Wesley Longman Publishing Co., Inc., Boston (2004)
4. Kleppe, A.G., Warmer, J., Bast, W.: MDA explained: the model driven architecture: practice and promise. Addison-Wesley Longman Publishing Co., Inc., Boston (2003)
5. Bruckhaus, T., Madhavii, N.H., Janssen, I., Henshaw, J.: The impact of tools on software productivity. IEEE Software 13(5), 29–38 (2002)
6. Genero, M., Manso, M.E., Visaggio, A., Canfora, G., Piattini, M.: Building measure-based prediction models for UML class diagram maintainability. Empirical Software Engineering 12(5), 517–549 (2007)
7. Abrahão, S., Iborra, E., Vanderdonckt, J.: Usability evaluation of user interfaces generated with a model-driven architecture tool. Maturing Usability, 3–32 (2008)
8. Mellor, S.J., Clark, T., Futagami, T.: Model-driven development: guest editors' introduction. IEEE Software 20(5), 14–18 (2003)
9. Heijstek, W., Chaudron, M.R.V.: Empirical investigations of model size, complexity and effort in a large scale, distributed model driven development process. In: 35th Euromicro Conference on Software Engineering and Advanced Applications, SEAA 2009, pp. 113–120. IEEE (2009)
10. Mohagheghi, P.: An Approach for Empirical Evaluation of Model-Driven Engineering in Multiple Dimensions. In: C2M:EEMDD 2010 Workshop- from Code Centric to Model Centric: Evaluating the Effectiveness of MDD, pp. 6–17. CEA LIST Publication (2010)
11. Kitchenham, B., Budgen, D., Brereton, P., Turner, M., Charters, S., Linkman, S.: Large-scale software engineering questions-expert opinion or empirical evidence? IET Software 1(5), 161–171 (2007)
12. Wohlin, C., Runeson, P., Höst, M.: Experimentation in software engineering: an introduction. Springer, Netherlands (2000)
13. Zelkowitz, M.V.: An update to experimental models for validating computer technology. Journal of Systems and Software 82(3), 373–376 (2009)
14. Mohagheghi, P., Dehlen, V.: Where Is the Proof? - A Review of Experiences from Applying MDE in Industry. In: Schieferdecker, I., Hartman, A. (eds.) ECMDA-FA 2008. LNCS, vol. 5095, pp. 432–443. Springer, Heidelberg (2008)
15. Abrahão, S., Poels, G.: A family of experiments to evaluate a functional size measurement procedure for Web applications. Journal of Systems and Software 82(2), 253–269 (2009)

16. Afonso, M., Vogel, R., Teixeira, J.: From code centric to model centric software engineering: practical case study of MDD infusion in a systems integration company (2006)
17. Krogmann, K., Becker, S.: A Case Study on Model-Driven and Conventional Software Development: The Palladio Editor. Software Engineering, 169–176 (2007)
18. Staron, M.: Transitioning from code-centric to model-driven industrial projects–empirical studies in industry and academia. Model Driven Software Development: Integrating Quality Assurance (2008)
19. Kapteijns, T., Jansen, S., Brinkkemper, S., Houët, H., Barendse, R.: A Comparative Case Study of Model Driven Development vs Traditional Development: The Tortoise or the Hare. From code centric to model centric software engineering: Practices, Implications and ROI, 22 (2009)
20. Mellegård, N., Staron, M.: Distribution of Effort among Software Development Artefacts: An Initial Case Study. In: Bider, I., Halpin, T., Krogstie, J., Nurcan, S., Proper, E., Schmidt, R., Ukor, R. (eds.) BPMDS 2010 and EMMSAD 2010. LNBIP, vol. 50, pp. 234–246. Springer, Heidelberg (2010)
21. Panach, J.: Incorporación de mecanismos de usabilidad en un entorno de producción de software dirigido por modelos. Tesis doctotal, Universidad Politécnica de Valencia (2010)
22. Kampenes, V., Dyba, T., Hannay, J., Ksjoberg, D.: A systematic review of quasi-experiments in software engineering. Information and Software Technology 51(1), 71–82 (2009)
23. Perry, D.E., Porter, A.A., Votta, L.G.: Empirical studies of software engineering: a roadmap. In: Proceedings of the Conference on the Future of Software Engineering, pp. 345–355. ACM (2000)
24. Ambler, S.: Agile Modeling: Effective Practices for eXtreme Programming and the Unified Process. Wiley (2002)
25. Kruchten, P.: The rational unified process: an introduction. Addison-Wesley Professional (2004)
26. Meliá, S., Gómez, J., Pérez, S., Díaz, O.: Architectural and technological variability in rich internet applications. IEEE Internet Computing 14(3), 24–32 (2010)
27. Montgomery, D.C.: Design and analysis of experiments. John Wiley & Sons Inc. (2008)
28. Plonsky, M.: Psychological Statistics (2009)
29. Gollapudi, K.: Function points or lines of code?–an insight. Global Microsoft Business Unit, Wipro Technologies (2004)
30. Seato: Counting Lines of Code in C# (2004)
31. SPSS Inc. an IBM CompanyHeadquarters: PASW Statistics 18 - Content Guide (2009)
32. Mauchly, J.W.: Significance test for sphericity of a normal n-variate distribution. The Annals of Mathematical Statistics 11(2), 204–209 (1940)
33. Cook, T.D., Campbell, D.T., Day, A.: Quasi-experimentation: Design & analysis issues for field settings. Houghton Mifflin, Boston (1979)

JSART: JavaScript Assertion-Based Regression Testing

Shabnam Mirshokraie and Ali Mesbah

University of British Columbia
Vancouver, BC, Canada
{shabnamm,amesbah}@ece.ubc.ca

Abstract. Web 2.0 applications rely heavily on JAVASCRIPT and client-side run-time manipulation of the DOM tree. One way to provide assurance about the correctness of such highly evolving and dynamic applications is through regression testing. However, JAVASCRIPT is loosely typed, dynamic, and notoriously challenging to analyze and test. We propose an automated technique for JAVASCRIPT regression testing, which is based on on-the-fly JAVASCRIPT source code instrumentation and dynamic analysis to infer invariant assertions. These obtained assertions are injected back into the JAVASCRIPT code to uncover regression faults in subsequent revisions of the web application under test. Our approach is implemented in a tool called JSART. We present our case study conducted on nine open source web applications to evaluate the proposed approach. The results show that our approach is able to effectively generate stable assertions and detect JAVASCRIPT regression faults with a high degree of accuracy and minimal performance overhead.

Keywords: JavaScript, web, regression testing, assertions, dynamic analysis.

1 Introduction

JAVASCRIPT is increasingly being used to create modern interactive web applications that offload a considerable amount of their execution to the client-side. JAVASCRIPT is a notoriously challenging language for web developers to use, maintain, analyze and test. It is dynamic, loosely typed, and asynchronous. In addition, it is extensively used to interact with the DOM tree at runtime for user interface state updates.

Web applications usually evolve fast by going through rapid development cycles and are, therefore, susceptible to regressions, i.e., new faults in existing functionality after changes have been made to the system. One way of ensuring that such modifications (e.g., bug fixes, patches) have not introduced new faults in the modified system is through systematic regression testing. While regression testing of classical web applications has been difficult [25], dynamism and non-determinism pose an even greater challenge [22] for Web 2.0 applications.

In this paper, we propose an automated technique for JAVASCRIPT regression testing, which is based on dynamic analysis to infer invariant assertions. These obtained assertions are injected back into the JAVASCRIPT code to uncover regression faults in subsequent revisions of the web application under test. Our technique automatically (1) intercepts and instruments JAVASCRIPT on-the-fly to add tracing code (2) navigates the web application to produce execution traces, (3) generates dynamic invariants from the

M. Brambilla, T. Tokuda, and R. Tolksdorf (Eds.): ICWE 2012, LNCS 7387, pp. 238–252, 2012.

```
1    function setDim(height, width) {
2        var h = 4*height, w = 2*width;
3        ...
4        return{h:h, w:w};
5    }

7    function play(){
8        $(#end).css("height", setDim($('body').width(), $('body').height()).↩
             h + 'px');
9        ...
10   }
```

Fig. 1. Motivating JAVASCRIPT example

trace data, (4) transforms the invariants into stable assertions and injects them back into the web application for regression testing.

Our approach is orthogonal to server-side technology, and it requires no manual modification of the source code. It is implemented in an open source tool called JSART (JAVASCRIPT Assertion-based Regression Testing). We have empirically evaluated the technique on nine open-source web applications. The results of our evaluation show that the approach generates stable invariant assertions, which are capable of spotting injected faults with a high rate of accuracy.

2   Motivation and Challenges

Figure 1 shows a simple JAVASCRIPT code snippet. Our motivating example consists of two functions, called setDim and play. The setDim function has two parameters, namely height and width, with a simple mathematical operation (Line 2). The function returns local variables, h and w (Line 4). setDim is called in the play function (Line 8) to set the height value of the CSS property of the DOM element with ID end. Any modification to the values of height or width would influence the returned values of setDim as well as the property of the DOM element. Typical programmatic errors include swapping the order of height and width when they are respectively assigned to local variables h and w or calling setDim with wrong arguments, i.e., changing the order of function arguments.

Detecting such regression errors is a daunting task for web developers, especially in programming languages such as JAVASCRIPT, which are known to be challenging to test. One way to check for these regressions is to define invariant expressions of expected behaviour [17] over program variables and assert their correctness at runtime. This way any modification to height, width, h, or w that violates the invariant expression will be detected. However, manually expressing such assertions for web applications with thousands of lines of JAVASCRIPT code and several DOM states, is a challenging and time-consuming task. Our aim in this work is to provide a technique that automatically captures regression faults through generated JAVASCRIPT assertions.

3   Our Approach

Our regression testing approach is based on *dynamic analysis* of JAVASCRIPT code to infer invariants from a given web application. We use the thus obtained invariants as

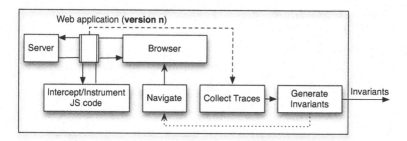

Fig. 2. Overview of the JAVASCRIPT tracing and invariant generation steps (web application version *n*)

runtime assertions in the JAVASCRIPT code to automatically uncover regression errors that can be introduced after changes have been made to the web application in a subsequent reversion. Our approach is largely based on two assumptions (1) the current version of the web application, from which invariants are being generated, is bug-free (2) the inferred invariants capture program specifications that are unlikely to change frequently in the following revisions (we revisit these two assumptions in Section 6). Our regression testing technique is composed of the following four main steps: (1) JavaScript tracing, (2) Invariant generation, (3) Filtering unstable assertions, and (4) Regression testing through assertions. In the following subsections, we will describe each step in details.

3.1   JAVASCRIPT Tracing

In order to infer useful program invariants, we need to collect execution traces of the JAVASCRIPT code. The idea is to log as much program variable value changes at runtime as possible. Figure 2 depicts a block diagram of the tracing step. Our approach automatically generates trace data in three subsequent steps: (i) JAVASCRIPT interception and instrumentation, (ii) navigation, and (iii) trace collection. In the following, we explain each step in details.

JAVASCRIPT Interception and Instrumentation.   The approach we have chosen for logging variables is on-the-fly JAVASCRIPT source code transformation to add instrumentation code. We intercept all the JAVASCRIPT code of a given web application, both in JAVASCRIPT files and HTML pages, by setting up a proxy [3] between the server and the browser. We first parse the intercepted source code into an Abstract Syntax Tree (AST). We then traverse the AST in search of *program variables* as well as *DOM modifications* as described below.

Tracing Program Variables. Our first interest is the range of values of JAVASCRIPT program variables. We probe function entry and function exit points, by identifying function definitions in the AST and injecting statements at the start, end, and before every `return` statement. We instrument the code to monitor value changes of *global variables, function arguments*, and *local variables*. Per program point, we yield information on *script name, function name*, and *line number*, used for debugging purposes. Going back to our running example (Figure 1), our technique adds instrumentation code to trace width, height, h, and w. For each variable, we collect information on *name*, *runtime type*, and *actual values*. The runtime type is stored because JAVASCRIPT is a loosely typed language, i.e., the types of variables cannot be determined syntactically, thus we log the variable types at runtime.

Tracing DOM Modifications. In modern web applications, JAVASCRIPT code frequently interacts with the DOM to update the client-side user interface state. Our recent study [18] of four bug-tracking systems indicated that DOM-related errors form 80% of all reported JAVASCRIPT errors. Therefore, we include in our execution trace how DOM elements and their attributes are modified by JAVASCRIPT at runtime. For instance, by tracing how the CSS property of the 'end' DOM element in Figure 1 is changed during various execution runs, we can infer the range of values for the height attribute.

Based on our observations, JAVASCRIPT DOM modifications usually follow a certain pattern. Once the pattern is reverse engineered, we can add proper instrumentation code around the pattern to trace the changes. In the patterns that we observed, first a JAVASCRIPT API is used to find the desired DOM element. Next, a function is called on the returned object responsible for the actual modification of the DOM-tree. After recognizing a pattern in the parsed AST, we add instrumentation code that records the value of the DOM attribute before and after the actual modification. Hence, we are able to trace DOM modifications that happen programmatically through JAVASCRIPT.

Navigation.   Once the AST is instrumented, we serialize it back to the corresponding JAVASCRIPT source code file and pass it to the browser. Next, we navigate the application in the browser to produce an execution trace. The application can be navigated in different ways including (1) manual clicking (2) test case execution (3) or using a web crawler. To automate the approach, our technique is based on automated dynamic crawling [15]. The execution needs to run as much of the JAVASCRIPT code as possible and execute it in various ways. This can be achieved through visiting as many DOM state changes as possible as well as providing different values for function arguments.

Trace Collection.   As the web application is navigated, the instrumented JAVASCRIPT code produces trace data, which needs to be collected for further analysis. Keeping the trace data in the browser's memory during the program execution can make the browser slow when a large amount of trace data is being produced. On the other hand, sending data items to the proxy as soon as the item is generated, can put a heavy load on the proxy, due to the frequency of HTTP requests. In order to tackle the aforementioned challenges, we buffer a certain amount of trace data in the memory in an array, post the data as an HTTP request to a proxy server when the buffer's size reaches a predefined threshold, and immediately clear the buffer in the browser's memory afterwards. Since the data arrives at the server in a synchronized manner, we concatenate the tracing data into a single trace file on the server side, which is then seeded into the next step (See Figure 2).

3.2   Invariant Generation

The assertion generation phase is involved with analyzing the collected execution traces to extract invariants. Substantial amount of research has been carried out on detecting dynamic program invariants [5,7,9,13]. Our approach is based on Daikon [9] to infer

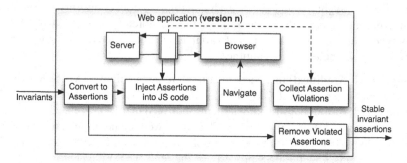

Fig. 3. Overview of the filtering step to remove unstable invariant assertions, for web application version *n*

likely invariants. As indicated with the dotted line in Figure 2, we cycle through the navigation and invariant generation phases until the size of generated invariant file remains unchanged, which is an indication that all possible invariants have been detected.

3.3 Filtering Unstable Invariant Assertions

The next step is to make sure that the generated invariants are truly invariants. An invariant assertion is called unstable when it is falsely reported as a violated assertion. Such assertions result in producing a number of false positive errors during the testing phase. To check the stability of the inferred invariants, we use them in the same version of the web application as assertions. Theoretically, no assertion violations should be reported because the web application has not changed. Hence, any assertion violation reported as such is a false positive and should be eliminated. Our filtering process, shown in Figure 3, consists of the following four processes:

- Converting the inferred invariants into checkable assertions;
- Injecting the invariant assertions into the same version of the web application;
- Navigating the web application;
- Collecting assertion violations and removing them;

From each of the inferred invariants, we generate an assertion in JAVASCRIPT format. We use on-the-fly transformation to inject the assertions directly into the source code of the same version of the web application. Since we have all the information about the program points and the location of the assertions, we can inject the assertions at the correct location in the JAVASCRIPT source code through the proxy, while the code is being sent to the client by the server. This way the assertions can run as part of the client-side code and gain access to the values of all program variables needed at runtime. Once the assertions are injected, we execute the web application in the browser and log the output. Next we collect and remove any violated assertions. The output of this step is a set of *stable* invariant assertions, used for automated regression testing in the next step.

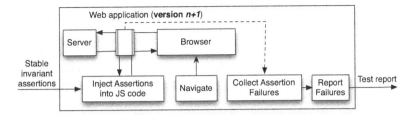

Fig. 4. Overview of the JAVASCRIPT regression testing step through invariant assertions, for web application version *n+1*

3.4 Regression Testing through Assertions

Once a set of stable invariant assertions are derived from version n of a web application, they can be used for automatic regression testing a subsequent version (n+1) of the web application. The regression testing phase is depicted in Figure 4.

We inject the inferred stable assertions to the JAVASCRIPT source code of the modified web application, in a similar fashion to the filtering step in Section 3.3. Once the assertions are injected, the new version of the web application is ready for regression testing. Any failed assertion during the testing phase generates an entry in the test report, which is presented to the tester at the end of the testing step. The generated test report provides precise information on the failed assertion, the file name, the line number, and the function name of the assertion.

```
1   function setDim(height, width) {
2       assert((width < height), 'example.js:setDim:ENTER:POINT1');
3       var h = 4*height, w = 2*width;
4       ...
5       assert((width < height), 'example.js:setDim:EXIT:POINT1');
6       assert((w < h), 'example.js:setDim:EXIT:POINT1');
7       return{h:h, w:w};
8   }

10  function play(){
11      $(#end).css("height", setDim($('body').width(), $('body').height()).h + ←
            'px');
12      assert(isIn($('#end').css('height'), {100, 200,
            300}),'example.js:play:POINT3');
13      ...
14  }
```

Fig. 5. Invariant assertion code for JAVASCRIPT function parameters, local variables and DOM modifications. Injected assertions are shown in bold.

Figure 5 shows the automatically injected invariant assertions for our running example of Figure 1. Note that we do not show all the assertions as they clutter the figure. Each `assert` call has the invariant as the first parameter and the corresponding debugging information in the second parameter, which includes information about script name, function name, and line number. In this example, the inferred invariants yield information about the inequality relation between function arguments, width and height, as well as local variables, w and h. The assertions in lines 2 and 5-6 check the corresponding inequalities, at entry and exit points of the setDim function at runtime. The example also shows the assertion that checks the height attribute of the DOM element, after the JAVASCRIPT DOM modification in the play function. The assertion that comes after the DOM manipulation (Line 12) checks the height value by calling the auxiliary isIn function. isIn checks the value of height to be in the given range, i.e., either 100, 200, or 300. Any values out of the specified range would violate the assertion.

4 Tool Implementation

We have implemented our JAVASCRIPT regression testing approach in a tool called JSART. JSART is written in Java and is available for download.[1]

JSART extends and builds on top of our InvarScope [10] tool. For JAVASCRIPT code interception, we use an enhanced version of Web-Scarab's proxy [3]. This enables us to automatically analyze and modify the content of HTTP responses before they reach the browser. To instrument the intercepted code, Mozilla Rhino[2] is used to parse JAVASCRIPT code to an AST, and back to the source code after instrumentation. The AST generated by Rhino's parser has traversal API's, which we use to search for program points where instrumentation code needs to be added. For the invariant generation step, we have extended Daikon [9] with support for accepting input and generating output in JAVASCRIPT syntax. The input files are created from the trace data and fed through the enhanced version of Daikon to derive dynamic invariants. The navigation step is automated by making JSART operate as a plugin on top of our dynamic AJAX crawler, CRAWLJAX [15].[3]

5 Empirical Evaluation

To quantitatively assess the accuracy and efficiency of our approach, we have conducted a case study following guidelines from Runeson and Höst [23]. In our evaluation, we address the following research questions:

RQ1 How successful is JSART in generating stable invariant assertions?
RQ2 How effective is our overall regression testing approach in terms of correctly detecting faults?
RQ3 What is the performance overhead of JSART?

The experimental data produced by JSART is available for download.[1]

5.1 Experimental Objects

Our study includes nine web-based systems in total. Six are game applications, namely, SameGame, Tunnel, TicTacToe, Symbol, ResizeMe, and GhostBusters. Two of the web

---

[1] http://salt.ece.ubc.ca/content/jsart/
[2] http://www.mozilla.org/rhino/
[3] http://www.crawljax.com

Table 1. Characteristics of the experimental objects

App ID	Name	JS LOC	# Functions	# Local Vars	# Global Vars	CC	Resource
1	SameGame	206	9	32	5	37	http://crawljax.com/same-game
2	Tunnel	334	32	18	13	39	http://arcade.christianmontoya.com/tunnel
3	TicTacToe	239	11	22	23	83	http://www.dynamicdrive.com/dynamicindex12/tictactoe.htm
4	Symbol	204	20	28	16	32	http://10k.aneventapart.com/2/Uploads/652
5	ResizeMe	45	5	4	7	2	http://10k.aneventapart.com/2/Uploads/594
6	GhostBusters	277	27	75	4	52	http://10k.aneventapart.com/2/Uploads/657
7	Jason	107	8	4	8	6	http://jasonjulien.com
8	Sofa	102	22	2	1	5	http://www.madebysofa.com/archive
9	TuduList	2767	229	199	31	28	http://tudu.ess.ch/tudu

applications are Jason and Sofa, which are a personal and a company homepage, respectively. We further include TuduList, which is a web-based task management application. All these applications are open source and use JAVASCRIPT on the client-side.

Table 1 presents each application's ID, name, and resource, as well as the characteristics of the custom JAVASCRIPT code, such as JAVASCRIPT lines of code (LOC), number of functions, number of local and global variables, as well as the cyclomatic complexity (CC). We use Eclipse IDE to count the JAVASCRIPT lines of code, number of functions, number of local as well as global variables. JSmeter [4] is used to compute the cyclomatic complexity. We compute the cyclomatic complexity across all JAVASCRIPT functions in the application.

5.2   Experimental Setup

To run the experiment, we provide the URL of each experimental object to JSART. In order to produce representative execution traces, we navigate each application several times with different crawling settings. Crawling settings differ in the number of visited states, depth of crawling, crawling time, and clickable element types. To obtain representative data traces, each of our experimental objects is navigated three times on average. Although JSART can easily instrument the source code of imported JAVASCRIPT libraries (e.g., jQuery, Prototype, etc), in our experiments we are merely interested in custom code written by developers, since we believe that is where most programming errors occur.

To evaluate our approach in terms of inferring stable invariant assertions (RQ1), we count the number of stable invariant assertions generated by JSART before and after performing the filtering step. As a last check, we execute the initial version of the application using the stable assertions to see whether our filtered invariant assertions are reporting any false positives.

Once the stable invariant assertions are obtained for each web application, we perform regression testing on modified versions of each application (RQ2). To that end, in order to mimic regression faults, we produce twenty different versions for each web

---

[4] http://jsmeter.info

Table 2. Properties of the invariant assertions generated by JSART

App ID	Trace Data (MB)	# Total Assertions	# Entry Assertions	# Exit Assertions	# DOM Assertions	# Total Unstable Assertions	# Unstable Entry Assertions	# Unstable Exit Assertions	# Unstable DOM Assertions	# Total Stable Assertions	# Stable Entry Assertions	# Stable Exit Assertions	# Stable DOM Assertions
1	8.6	303	120	171	12	0	0	0	0	303	120	171	12
2	124	2147	1048	1085	14	14	9	5	0	2133	1039	1080	14
3	1.2	766	387	379	0	16	8	8	0	750	379	371	0
4	31.7	311	138	171	2	14	7	7	0	297	131	164	2
5	0.4	55	20	27	8	0	0	0	0	55	20	27	8
6	2.3	464	160	266	38	3	1	2	0	461	159	264	38
7	1.2	29	4	6	19	0	0	0	0	29	4	6	19
8	0.1	20	2	2	16	0	0	0	0	20	2	2	16
9	2.6	163	58	104	1	0	0	0	0	163	58	104	1

application by injecting twenty faults into the original version, one at a time. We categorize our faults according to the following fault model:

1. **Modifying Conditional Statements:** This category is concerned with swapping consecutive conditional statements, changing the upper/lower bounds of loop statements, as well as modifying the condition itself;
2. **Modifying Global/Local Variables:** In this category, global/local variables are changed by modifying their values at any point of the program, as well as removing or changing their names;
3. **Changing Function Parameters/Arguments:** This category is concerned with changing function parameters or function call arguments by swapping, removing, and renaming parameters/arguments. Changing the sequence of consecutive function calls is also included in this category;
4. **DOM modifications:** Another type of fault, which is introduced in our fault model is modifying DOM properties at both JAVASCRIPT code level and HTML code level.

For each fault injection step, we randomly pick a JAVASCRIPT function in the application code and seed a fault according to our fault model. We seed five faults from each category.

To evaluate the effectiveness of JSART (RQ2), we measure the precision and recall as follows:

Precision is the rate of injected faults found by the tool that are correct: $\frac{TP}{TP+FP}$

Recall is the rate of correct injected faults that the tool finds: $\frac{TP}{TP+FN}$

where TP (true positives), FP (false positives), and FN (false negatives) respectively represent the number of faults that are correctly detected, falsely reported, and missed.

To evaluate the performance of JSART (RQ3), we measure the extra time needed to execute the application while assertion checks are in place.

Table 3. Precision and Recall for JSART fault detection

App ID	# FN	# FP	# TP	Precision (%)	Recall (%)
1	2	0	18	100	90
2	4	0	16	100	80
3	1	0	19	100	95
4	2	0	18	100	90
5	0	0	20	100	100
6	1	0	19	100	95
7	0	0	20	100	100
8	0	0	20	100	100
9	1	0	19	100	95

5.3 Results

In this section, we discuss the results of the case study with regard to our three research questions.

Generated Invariant Assertions. Table 2 presents the data generated by our tool. For each web application, the table shows the total size of collected execution traces (MB), the total number of generated JAVASCRIPT assertions, the number of assertions at entry point of the functions, the number of assertions at exit point of the functions, and the number of DOM assertions. The unstable assertions before the filtering as well as the stable assertions after the filtering step are also presented. As shown in the table, for applications 1, 5, 7, 8, and 9, all the generated invariant assertions are stable and the filtering step does not remove any assertions. For the remaining four applications (2, 3, 4, 6), less than 5% of the total invariant assertions are seen as unstable and removed in the filtering process. Thus, for all the experimental objects, the resulting stable assertions found by the tool is more than 95% of the total assertions. Moreover, we do not observe any unstable DOM assertions. In order to assure the stability of the resulting assertions, we examine the obtained assertions from the filtering step across multiple executions of the original application. The results show that all the resulting invariant assertions are truly stable since we do not observe any false positives.

As far as RQ1 is concerned, our findings indicate that (1) our tool is capable of automatically generating a high rate of JAVASCRIPT invariant assertions, (2) the unstable assertions are less than 5% of the total generated assertions, (3) the filtering technique is able to remove the few unstable assertions, and (4) all the remaining invariant assertions that JSART outputs are stable, i.e., they do not produce any false positives on the same version of the web application.

Effectiveness. Since applications 3, 4, and 9 do not contain many DOM assertions, we were not able to inject 5 faults from the DOM modification category. Therefore, we randomly chose faults from the other fault model categories.

In Table 3, we present the accuracy of JSART in terms of its fault finding capability. The table shows the number of false negatives, false positives, true positives, as well as the percentages for precision and recall. As far as RQ2 is concerned, our results show that JSART is very accurate in detecting faults. The precision is 100%, meaning that all the injected faults, which are reported by the tool, are correct. This also implies that our filtering mechanism successfully eliminates unstable assertions as we do not observe any false positives. The recall oscillates between 80-100%, which is caused by a low

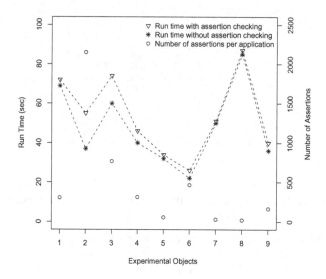

Fig. 6. Performance plot of JSART

rate of missed faults (discussed in Section 6 under Limitations). Therefore, as far as RQ2 is concerned, JSART is able to successfully spot the injected faults with a high accuracy rate.

Performance. Figure 6 depicts the total running time needed for executing each web application with and without the assertion code. Checking a fairly large number of assertions at runtime can be time consuming. Thus, to capture the effect of the added assertions on the execution time, we exploit a 2-scale diagram. As shown in Figure 6, each experimental object is associated with two types of data. The left-hand Y-axis represents the running time (seconds), whereas the right-hand Y-axis shows the number of assertions. This way we can observe how the number of assertions relates to the running time. As expected, the figure shows that by increasing the number of assertions, the running time increases to some degree. While the time overhead of around 20 seconds is more evident for the experimental object 2 (i.e., Tunnel with 2147 number of assertions), it is negligible for the rest of the experimental objects. Considering that Tunnel has 260 statements in total, the number of assertions instrumented in the code is eight times more than the number of statements in the original version. Therefore, it is reasonable to observe a small amount of overhead. Though assertions introduce some amount of overhead, it is worth mentioning that we have not experienced a noticeable change (i.e., freezing or slowed down execution) while running the application in the browser.

Thus, as far as RQ3 is concerned, the amount of overhead introduced by our approach is 6 seconds on average for our experimental objects, which is negligible during testing. Furthermore, based on our observations, the assertions do not negatively affect the observable behaviour of the web applications in the browser.

Table 4. Manual effort imposed by our approach for deriving stable invariant assertions.

App ID	Total Time (min)	Manual Effort (min)
1	13	4
2	11.5	3
3	15.5	5
4	11	3
5	6.5	2.5
6	9	4.5
7	7.5	3.5
8	6.5	2
9	18	13

6   Discussion

Unstable Assertions.   As mentioned in Section 3.3, we observe a few number of unstable invariant assertions initially, which are removed by our filtering mechanism. By analyzing our trace data, we observe that such unstable assertions arise mainly because of the multiple runtime types of JAVASCRIPT variables. This is based on the fact that in JAVASCRIPT it is possible to change the type of a variable at runtime. However, Daikon treats variables as single type, selects the first observed type, and ignores the subsequent types in the trace data. This results in producing a few number of unstable invariant assertions for JAVASCRIPT. We remove such unstable assertions in our filtering step. A drawback of removing these assertions, is that our tool might miss a fault during the regression testing phase. However, according to our observations, such unstable assertions form only around 5% of the total generated assertions. Thus, we are still able to achieve high accuracy as presented in the previous section.

Limitations.   Our approach is not able to detect syntax errors that are present in the JAVASCRIPT code. Furthermore, tracing DOM manipulations using APIs other than the standard DOM API or jQuery is currently not supported by JSART. Further, a regression fault either directly violates an invariant assertion, or it can violate closely related assertions, which have been affected by the fault. However, if the tool is not able to infer any invariants in the affected scope of the error, it fails to detect the fault. This results in observing a low rate of false negatives as illustrated in Section 5.

Revisiting the Assumptions.   As we mentioned in Section 3, we assume that the current version of the web application is bug-free. This is based on the fact that in regression testing a gold standard is always needed as a trusted version for comparing the test results against [4] to detect regression faults. However, if the original version of the application does contain an error, the generated assertions might reflect the error as well, and as such they are not able to detect the fault. Our second assumption states that the program specifications are unlikely to change frequently in revisions. Here we assume that software programs evolve gradually and regression faults are mostly due to small changes. However, if major upgrades occur in subsequent revisions such that the core specification of the application is affected, the inferred invariants from the original version may not be valid any longer and new invariant assertions need to be generated.

Automation Level.   While the testing phase of JSART is fully automated, the navigation part requires some manual effort. Although the crawling is performed automatically, we do need to manually setup the tool with different crawling configurations per application execution. Moreover, for each application run, we manually look at the size of the invariant output to decide whether more execution traces (and thus more crawling sessions) are needed. We present the manual effort involved with detecting stable invariant assertions in Table 4. The table shows the total time, which is the duration time of deriving stable assertions including both automatic and manual parts. The reported manual effort contains the amount of time required for setting up the tool as well as the manual tasks involved with the navigation part. The results show the average manual effort is less than 5 minutes.

7 Related Work

Automated testing of modern web applications is becoming an active area of research [2,14,16,19]. Most of the existing work on JAVASCRIPT analysis is, however, focused on spotting errors and security vulnerabilities through static analysis [11,12,27]. We classify related work into two broad categories: web application regression testing and program invariants.

Web Application Regression Testing.   Regression testing of web applications has received relatively limited attention from the research community [26,25]. Alshahwan and Harman [1] discuss an algorithm for regression testing of web applications that is based on session data [24,8] repair. Roest et al. [22] propose a technique to cope with the dynamism in Ajax web interfaces while conducting automated regression testing. None of these works, however, target regression testing of JAVASCRIPT in particular.

Program Invariants.   The concept of using invariants to assert program behaviour at runtime is as old as programming itself [6]. A more recent development is the automatic detection of program invariants through dynamic analysis. Ernst et al. have developed Daikon [9], a tool capable of inferring likely invariants from program execution traces. Other related tools for detecting invariants include Agitator [5], DIDUCE [13], and DySy [7]. Recently, Ratcliff et al. [20] have proposed a technique to reuse the trace generation of Daikon and integrate it with genetic programming to produce useful invariants. Conceptually related to our work, Rodríguez-Carbonell and Kapur [21] use inferred invariant assertions for program verification.

Mesbah et al. [16] proposed a framework called ATUSA for manually specifying generic and application-specific invariants on the DOM-tree and JAVASCRIPT code. These invariants were subsequently used as test oracles to detect erroneous behaviours in modern web applications. Pattabiraman and Zorn proposed DoDOM [19], a tool for inferring invariants from the DOM tree of web applications for reliability testing.

To the best of our knowledge, our work in this paper is the first to propose an automated regression testing approach for JAVASCRIPT, which is based on JAVASCRIPT invariant assertion generation and runtime checking.

8 Conclusions and Future Work

JAVASCRIPT is playing a prominent role in modern Web 2.0 applications. Due to its loosely typed and dynamic nature, the language is known to be error-prone and difficult to test. In this paper, we present an automated technique for JAVASCRIPT regression testing based on generated invariant assertions. The contributions of this work can be summarized as follows:

- A method for detecting JAVASCRIPT invariants across multiple application executions through on-the-fly JAVASCRIPT instrumentation and tracing of program variables and DOM manipulations;
- A technique for automatically converting the inferred invariants into stable assertions, and injecting them back into the web application for regression testing;
- The implementation of our proposed technique in an open source tool called JSART;
- An empirical study on nine open source JAVASCRIPT applications. The results of our study show that our tool is able to effectively infer stable assertions and detect regression faults with minimal performance overhead;

Our future work encompasses conducting more case studies to generalize the findings as well as extending the current JAVASCRIPT DOM modifications detector so that it is capable of coping with more patterns in other JAVASCRIPT libraries. In addition, we will explore ways of fully automating the navigation part by generating crawling specifications.

References

1. Alshahwan, N., Harman, M.: Automated session data repair for web application regression testing. In: Proceedings of the Int. Conf. on Software Testing, Verification, and Validation (ICST 2008), pp. 298–307. IEEE Computer Society (2008)
2. Artzi, S., Dolby, J., Jensen, S., Møller, A., Tip, F.: A framework for automated testing of JavaScript web applications. In: Proceedings of the Intl. Conference on Software Engineering (ICSE), pp. 571–580. ACM (2011)
3. Bezemer, C.-P., Mesbah, A., van Deursen, A.: Automated security testing of web widget interactions. In: Proceedings of the 7th Joint Meeting of the European Software Engineering Conference and the ACM SIGSOFT Symposium on the Foundations of Software Engineering (ESEC-FSE 2009), pp. 81–91. ACM (2009)
4. Binder, R.: Testing Object-Oriented Systems: Models, Patterns, and Tools. Addison-Wesley (2000)
5. Boshernitsan, M., Doong, R., Savoia, A.: From Daikon to Agitator: lessons and challenges in building a commercial tool for developer testing. In: Proc. Int. Sym. on Software Testing and Analysis (ISSTA 2006), pp. 169–180. ACM (2006)
6. Clarke, L.A., Rosenblum, D.S.: A historical perspective on runtime assertion checking in software development. ACM SIGSOFT Software Engineering Notes 31(3), 25–37 (2006)
7. Csallner, C., Tillmann, N., Smaragdakis, Y.: DySy: Dynamic symbolic execution for invariant inference. In: Proceedings of the 30th International Conference on Software Engineering (ICSE 2008), pp. 281–290. ACM (2008)
8. Elbaum, S., Rothermel, G., Karre, S., Fisher, M.: Leveraging user-session data to support web application testing. IEEE Trans. Softw. Eng. 31, 187–202 (2005)
9. Ernst, M., Perkins, J., Guo, P., McCamant, S., Pacheco, C., Tschantz, M., Xiao, C.: The Daikon system for dynamic detection of likely invariants. Science of Computer Programming 69(1-3), 35–45 (2007)
10. Groeneveld, F., Mesbah, A., van Deursen, A.: Automatic invariant detection in dynamic web applications. Technical Report TUD-SERG-2010-037, TUDelft (2010)

11. Guarnieri, S., Livshits, B.: Gatekeeper: mostly static enforcement of security and reliability policies for JavaScript code. In: Conference on USENIX Security Symposium, SSYM 2009, pp. 151–168 (2009)

12. Guha, A., Krishnamurthi, S., Jim, T.: Using static analysis for Ajax intrusion detection. In: Intl. Conference on World Wide Web (WWW), pp. 561–570 (2009)

13. Hangal, S., Lam, M.S.: Tracking down software bugs using automatic anomaly detection. In: Proceedings of the 24th International Conference on Software Engineering (ICSE 2002), pp. 291–301. ACM Press (2002)

14. Marchetto, A., Tonella, P., Ricca, F.: State-based testing of Ajax web applications. In: Proc. 1st Int. Conference on Sw. Testing Verification and Validation (ICST 2008), pp. 121–130. IEEE Computer Society (2008)

15. Mesbah, A., van Deursen, A., Lenselink, S.: Crawling Ajax-based web applications through dynamic analysis of user interface state changes. ACM Transactions on the Web (TWEB) 6(1), 3:1–3:30 (2012)

16. Mesbah, A., van Deursen, A., Roest, D.: Invariant-based automatic testing of modern web applications. IEEE Transactions on Software Engineering (TSE) 38(1), 35–53 (2012)

17. Meyer, B.: Applying design by contract. Computer 25(10), 40–51 (1992)

18. Ocariza, F.J., Pattabiraman, K., Mesbah, A.: AutoFLox: An automatic fault localizer for client-side JavaScript. In: Proceedings of the 5th IEEE International Conference on Software Testing, Verification and Validation (ICST 2012), pp. 31–40. IEEE Computer Society (2012)

19. Pattabiraman, K., Zorn, B.: DoDOM: Leveraging DOM invariants for Web 2.0 application robustness testing. In: Proc. Int. Conf. Sw. Reliability Engineering (ISSRE 2010), pp. 191–200. IEEE Computer Society (2010)

20. Ratcliff, S., White, D., Clark, J.: Searching for invariants using genetic programming and mutation testing. In: Proceedings of the 13th Annual Conference on Genetic and Evolutionary Computation (GECCO). ACM (2011)

21. Rodríguez-Carbonell, E., Kapur, D.: Program Verification Using Automatic Generation of Invariants. In: Liu, Z., Araki, K. (eds.) ICTAC 2004. LNCS, vol. 3407, pp. 325–340. Springer, Heidelberg (2005)

22. Roest, D., Mesbah, A., van Deursen, A.: Regression testing Ajax applications: Coping with dynamism. In: Proc. 3rd Int. Conf. on Sw. Testing, Verification and Validation (ICST 2010), pp. 128–136. IEEE Computer Society (2010)

23. Runeson, P., Höst, M.: Guidelines for conducting and reporting case study research in software engineering. Empirical Software Engineering 14(2), 131–164 (2009)

24. Sprenkle, S., Gibson, E., Sampath, S., Pollock, L.: Automated replay and failure detection for web applications. In: ASE 2005: Proc. 20th IEEE/ACM Int. Conf. on Automated Sw. Eng., pp. 253–262. ACM (2005)

25. Tarhini, A., Ismail, Z., Mansour, N.: Regression testing web applications. In: Int. Conf. on Advanced Comp. Theory and Eng., pp. 902–906. IEEE Computer Society (2008)

26. Xu, L., Xu, B., Chen, Z., Jiang, J., Chen, H.: Regression testing for web applications based on slicing. In: Proc. of Int. Conf. on Computer Software and Applications (COMPSAC), pp. 652–656. IEEE Computer Society (2003)

27. Zheng, Y., Bao, T., Zhang, X.: Statically locating web application bugs caused by asynchronous calls. In: Proceedings of the Intl. Conference on the World-Wide Web (WWW), pp. 805–814. ACM (2011)

A Framework for the Development
of Haptic-Enhanced Web Applications

Sara Comai, Davide Mazza, and Andrea Guarinoni

Politecnico di Milano
Department of Electronics and Information (DEI)
Piazza L. Da Vinci 32,
I-20133 Milan, Italy
{sara.comai,davide.mazza}@polimi.it

Abstract. In the last years we have witnessed an increasing adoption
of haptic devices (allowing the user to feel forces or vibrations) in several
fields of applications, from gaming, to mobile, automotive, etc. Some
efforts have been done to enhance also Web applications interfaces with
haptics, either to improve accessibility or, more in general, to improve
usability. Despite the spreading of haptic applications, their development
is still a time consuming task that requires significant programming skills.
In particular, in the Web context no plug-ins or style extensions are
currently available and applications must be developed from scratch. In
this paper we describe a framework to easily include haptic interaction
in Web applications, focusing both on haptic interaction modeling and
on its implementation.

1 Introduction

Haptics, the technology that exploits the human sense of touch by applying
forces, vibrations, or motions to user's hands or body, has received an enormous
attention in the last decades, but only in recent years has reached an important
level of visibility in several fields of applications. The most spread form of haptics is represented by the tactile effects on mobile devices, where the user can
feel vibrations through the skin; similar effects can be found also in the automotive field, where touch surfaces are replacing mechanical buttons, as well as
on cameras and media players' touchscreens. Haptics has been largely exploited
also in the gaming field, where controllers like the DualShock^{TM} by Sony or the
Falcon^{TM} by Novint provide stronger vibrations with different levels of intensi-
ties according to the action of the game.

But vibrations are not the only feedback that can be provided by haptic devices. More sophisticated input/output devices like, e.g., the PHANTOM^{TM}
stylus by Sensable, can provide richer effects, by supporting a bidirectional communication of the forces: the user can *feed* the system with data about his/her
movements (in terms of position, velocity of a movement, or even direct force
supplied through the device) and can *receive* information from the system in
the form of sensations simulating weight, resistance, etc. Such devices have been

M. Brambilla, T. Tokuda, and R. Tolksdorf (Eds.): ICWE 2012, LNCS 7387, pp. 253–267, 2012.
© Springer-Verlag Berlin Heidelberg 2012

traditionally employed to improve virtual reality systems and simulators, but different works show how to use them also in the context of Web applications [7, 12–14].

Haptic-enhanced Web applications offer new modalities of interactions and new possible scenarios. Beside navigating the Web by associating events with vibrations in a way similar to what mobile devices provide (e.g., to confirm user's inputs or as non-intrusive alerts when calls/messages arrive), force feedback devices such as mice, joysticks, pens, etc. can supply richer kinesthetic forces producing moderate attractive/repulsive effects, so that the following use scenarios can be devised [7, 13, 15]:

- when the user presses a button, the visual aspect of the button may change and the user may "feel" the simulation of "mechanical" pressure, thus providing an immediate and more realistic confirmation of user's action;
- while the user reads the main content of the page, he can "feel" the scrollbar without the need of looking at it, thus reducing his/her workload and avoiding distractions from his/her main task;
- when the cursor is over a button or a form field, the user feels a "snap-to" effect that avoids slip-offs, thus reducing possibilities of errors and guaranteeing a more precise execution of the task;
- when the user accesses a complex page, with rich content, haptic cues can highlight or indicate the importance of user actions or of the displayed information (e.g., recency of news), without overloading the visual channel; or when ads or auxiliary content can lead to visual distractions, a gentle guided movement of the cursor towards core contents can be provided.

Experimental works show that the integration of haptics in Web applications is helpful, in particular, in terms of reduced workload and reduced number of errors [15]; moreover, in case of applications targeted to visually impaired users, also accessibility can be improved [12, 14].

However, in the current practice, the development of haptic applications is still a time consuming task and requires significant programming skills. The solutions proposed in literature for adding haptic interactions into Web pages are mainly hand-crafted and specifically tailored to the needs of each work: the field would surely benefit of a more structured approach to be integrated into existing methodologies and tools, according to the usual Web engineering principles.

At this aim, we propose a framework to include haptic interaction in HTML-based Web applications, supporting a flexible design of haptic effects and separating device-independent features to be easily extendable to different haptic devices. After an initial overview in Section 2 of the related works proposed in literature, both on the introduction of haptic interactions in the Web and on the current practice for the development of haptic applications, Section 3 introduces the basic concepts underlying haptic interactions. Section 4 presents the design of our framework, while Section 5 describes an associated tool to ease the development of haptic-enhanced applications. Section 6 analyzes the impact of adding haptic interaction in the usual Web browsing activity and, finally, in Section 7 conclusions are drawn.

2   Related Work

The research in the last decade has shown an increasing trend of interest in the adoption of haptics in common applications. However, in order to be applied in the Web context, several issues need still to be investigated.

The problem of how to interact with the Web through a haptic device has been first treated in [6, 11, 19]. [11] tries to introduce haptic modalities for the *exploration* of Web pages, by assigning forces or vibrating effects to the different widgets of a page (e.g., textfields, buttons, images). The proposed approach is targeted to people with visual disabilities and the original Web page is mapped into a 3D virtual environment, where each widget of the original Web page is represented by a typed 3D object providing both haptic and audio feedbacks (e.g., texts are mapped into "T" objects having a particular shape and friction, hyperlinks into "arrow" objects having a different shape and surface characteristics, and so on). Also [19] aims at improving accessibility on the Web by means of a "content-aware" Web browser plug-in, where audio and haptic modalities are supported: the user can be informed when (s)he is in the vicinity of an image or an hyperlink, to increase the level of spatial awareness, and can "feel" the different types of objects by means of effects associated with users' actions like hovering a link, an image and so on. In a similar way, [6] utilizes haptic feedback and speech recognition to aid browsing, but with a limited set of haptic effects. Also maps, images, and other graphical contents can be haptically rendered with groove, texture, or vibration effects so that the user can "feel" the pictures: for example, city maps can be explored by following groove lines representing the streets [12]; charts can be associated with haptic effects proportional to the quantitative information they represent [16]. Effects have been applied effectively also to better locate objects in the space of interaction [15] or to be directed to a specific target (e.g., after filling a search box the user is guided to the submit button) [13], according to the user's task.

While the design of haptic interactions and their inclusion in Web applications have been studied by different researchers, the development methodology used for haptic applications is still a critical aspect in this field. In general, the current practice in the development of software with haptic interfaces consists mainly in writing the corresponding code manually by including API libraries or SDK provided by the device manufacturer.

Commercial libraries depend on the device itself: for example, for the Sensable PHANTOM [5] the HDAPI / HLAPI [10] are available. The different APIs are incompatible, but some efforts have been done to realize *device-independent* libraries that try to integrate the features supported by different haptic devices. The most known examples are represented by the Haptik library [17] and by the library provided by Novint [4], which offer *Hardware Abstraction Layers* for accessing the device features.

Among the academic proposals, CHAI3D [1] is a set of open-source libraries to be used for the development of applications with the C++ language. The APIs focus primarily on the management of scene graphs (through OpenGL) and on integrating haptic effects into a 3D scene. JTouchToolkit [3] is another open source library that can be used to introduce haptic interactions in a Java environment.

At a higher level of abstraction, [9] proposes HAML, an XML-based specification language that couples applications with haptic devices, defining the hardware properties of the haptic tool and modeling the haptic response of objects' surfaces in terms of stiffness, resistance, and so on. The HAML formalism is completely textual and is supported by the authoring tool HAMLAT [8], which allows users to render the haptical properties of a virtual environment with no programming skills. However, all the proposed libraries and specification languages are very general and address mainly hardware aspects, and/or are typically conceived for 3D graphics.

3   A Model for Haptic Interaction in Web Applications

The elements of the graphical interface of a Web application are usually interpreted as passive components: the user decides to interact with them according to his/her own will or the task (s)he would like to perform. However, each element can become *active*, by adding proper haptic effects that may guide the user during the navigation.

Systems involving haptic interactions are typically based on the architecture shown in Figure 1 [18], which includes:

- The *haptic device*, providing in input to the system the position of its proxy, and rendering in output a force;
- The *video* rendering the visual aspects of the application;
- A module devoted to the *haptic rendering*;
- A module devoted to the *visual rendering*;
- A module containing the *objects of the environment* to be rendered visually and associated with haptic effects.

The haptic rendering pipeline is composed of three main blocks:

- *Collision detection*: given the current position of the haptic proxy, it determines which virtual objects collide with the proxy;
- *Force response*: the interaction force between the proxy and the virtual objects is computed. Force computation is based on the *mathematical* representation (model) of the force, that is a function of the input provided to the device (typically, the position of the haptic proxy, but also its velocity and acceleration) and, possibly, of the features of the object associated with the haptic behavior. The mathematical model is used to compute the intensity and the direction of the force to render: the output may be perceived by the user as a change of the position of the proxy, possibly with a given velocity and acceleration.

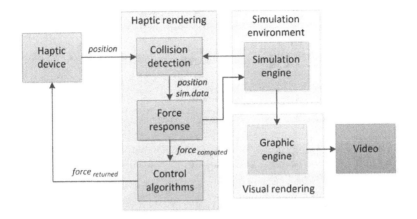

Fig. 1. Basic architecture for haptic rendering

- *Control algorithm*: the computed force is approximated according to the device's capabilities (e.g., maximum output force) and rendered to the user.

Considering Web applications, any element of the page may be associated with an effect that the user will perceive during navigation. From a conceptual point of view we need to identify such elements and to understand when and how forces need to be computed and rendered. At this aim, haptic interaction can be modeled through the specification of a set of tuples of the type $\langle obj, event, effect, action \rangle$ where:

- *obj* is the *target object*/widget of the application associated with a haptic effect; in a HTML page it may be any object registered inside the Document Object Model (DOM) of the page (from a *HTMLDivElement* to a *HTMLInputElement* or *HTMLDocumentElement* etc.);
- *event* is the *event* associated to *obj*: it may be a native event of the browser (like click, load, mouseover, etc.) or an application-dependent event defined by the developer[1];
- *effect* is the *effect* generated by the haptic device and felt by the user. Examples of effects include: vibration effects or attraction/repulsion forces. They are specified by means of mathematical models, as exemplified next. Effects may be:
  - *Single*: they are defined by means of a single (possibly complex) expression. Single effects are associated with a *timeout* specifying a time duration (e.g., 1000 ms);
  - A *Concatenation* of effects (Eff_1, Eff_2, ..., Eff_n), where each effect may be in turn either a single effect or a concatenation of effects: in this case, one effect a time is rendered, and the whole sequence may be associated with a number of *iterations*, to be possibly repeated several times.

---

[1] Application-dependent events may be defined by means of the *Object.createEvent()* function, according to the ECMAScript 5 specifications.

Force model	Description	Parameters	Input	Expression
Spring	Elastic force depending on the position of the proxy	Elastic constant $(\overrightarrow{k_e})$ Point Of Interest $(\overline{POI})$	Position $(\vec{x})$	$\vec{F} = \overrightarrow{k_e} * (\vec{x} - \overline{POI})$
Magnet	Magnetic force depending on the position of the proxy	Max attraction $(\vec{k})$ Point Of Interest $(\overline{POI})$ Gradient $(\vec{\partial})$	Position $(\vec{x})$	$\vec{F} = \vec{k}/(\vec{x} - \overline{POI})^{\partial}$
Damper	Damping force depending on the velocity of the proxy	Viscous constant $(\overrightarrow{k_v})$	Velocity $(\vec{v})$	$\vec{F} = \overrightarrow{k_v} * \vec{v}$
Mass	Force depending on the acceleration of the proxy	Virtual mass (m)	Acceleration $(\vec{a})$	$\vec{F} = m * \vec{a}$
Vibration	Vibration force generated by a sinusoidal oscillation	Amplitude $(\vec{A})$ Angular frequency $(\vec{\omega})$	Time elapsed (t)	$\vec{F} = \vec{A} * \sin(\vec{\omega} * t)$
NullModel	Idle force returning a null value	---	---	$\vec{F} = 0$

Fig. 2. Examples of force models

– *action* specifies if, upon the event, the associated haptic effect must be *started*, *stopped*, or definitely *removed* from the page. Stopped effects can be restarted when the event associated to the object occurs again; instead, removed effects can occur only once for the loaded page. Given an effect, stop/remove actions may be not specified, since timeouts and iterations are enough to stop the rendering of the effect; when both are specified, the effect will cease upon the occurrence of the first blocking event (timeout or stop/remove).

This model extends our previous proposal done in [7] by taking into account the specific field of application. In our work we have implemented some predefined effects. Examples of such effects are reported in Figure 2: each effect is specified by means of a mathematical expression that depends on inputs received from the device (e.g., the position of the proxy) and possibly on other parameters.

Figure 3 shows an example of Web page enhanced with haptic effects applied to the HTML elements of the Google homepage. Due to the lack of guidelines for introducing haptic effects to enhance user interaction, we enriched the visual information with haptic feedbacks conveying messages not already communicated

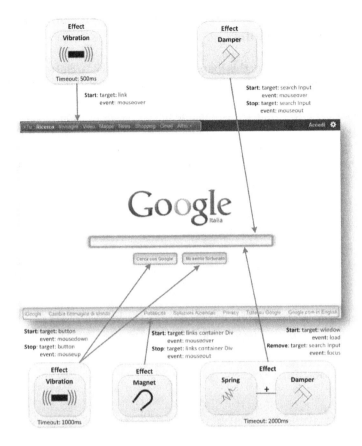

Fig. 3. An example of page enriched with haptic effects

to the user. For example, we assigned a time-dependent vibration perceivable by the user as soon as (s)he moves the mouse over the individual links listed in the upper part of the page, or over the buttons near the search bar, to confirm user's action (typically not emphasized in a visual way). Moreover, in order to assist the user during the navigation, the menu items at the bottom of the page are associated with a slight magnetic attraction to improve the cursor control and avoid mouse slippery on click. In the same way, a gentle guided movement over the input field has been obtained as a composition of the spring and the damper force models; this effect is rendered as soon as the loading process of the page is completed, while a viscous (damper) effect is perceived whenever the cursor moves over the input field. The playback of each single haptic effect is regulated by means of the associated events/actions, which specify the execution criteria of the handlers that activate and deactivate the effect. For example, on the two buttons in the middle of the page, the haptic effect will start whenever the *mousedown* event occurs and will stop either after 1000 ms or before, if a *mouseup* event is fired.

4 A Framework for the Addition of Haptic Effects in Web Applications

The framework proposed in this paper is based on the architecture depicted in Figure 4, which contextualizes the classical schema of Figure 1 for the Web realm. The Web page is extended with Javascript code exploiting a Javascript library (called *JHaptic*) that is responsible for the computation of the force and its scaling (i.e., of the Force Response and Control Algorithm steps of the haptic rendering pipeline). A browser plug-in has been developed to enable the interaction with the physical device through the APIs exposed by it (see Section 4.2).

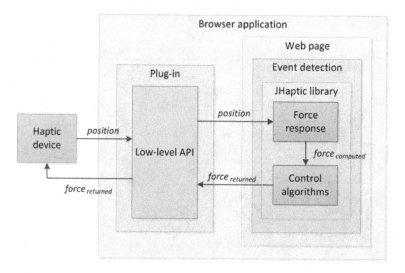

Fig. 4. The working architecture of the proposed library

Compared to the classical haptic rendering pipeline, the collision detection step can be obtained by exploiting the event model of the browser rendering engine itself. Indeed, it is possible to monitor events like *mouseover* or *mouseout*, over any element (visible or not) stored in the Document Object Model (DOM).

The communication among the different modules depicted in the figure is carried out as follows:

1. The current position of the haptic interface is taken in input; this is processed by the low-level libraries provided with the selected device and interfaced through a plug-in with the Web page loaded in the browser;
2. A Javascript library is integrated within the HTML document; it receives the position of the device proxy, maps it to the corresponding point both in the desktop and in the Web page and computes the forces to be reproduced in output; effects are included in the Web application code by invoking the corresponding library functions;

3. The value of the computed force is scaled so that the hardware limits of the adopted device are not beyond its force magnitude rendering capabilities;
4. By exploiting the low-level APIs through the plug-in, the computed force impulse is sent to the device, so that it is perceived by the user.

The library therefore manages the whole rendering process and exploits an external plug-in (a Dynamic-link library) to access the APIs needed to interact with the physical device.

In order to allow Web contents browsing, the mouse cursor has been firmly associated to the end-effector of the haptic device so that a movement of it produces a proportional shift in the position of the mouse arrow on the screen. This way, the user can do actions and fire events as with the usual mice, and haptic effects ca be rendered (started, stopped, etc.) upon a particular occurring condition (e.g., click on a button, hovering a link, missing data in an input field, etc.) of a given element (or node) of the page.

The framework can supports any kind of device, from (2D) mice to haptic devices moving in a 3D working space: in the latter case, the position of the haptic proxy must be mapped into the bi-dimensional position of the pointer on the screen; in our model, the user screen space has been vertically centered onto the workspace of the physical device, represented as a parallelepiped. The currently displayed area of the Web page (*viewport*) is conceived as a vertical flat surface, so that the three-dimensional position of the end-effector is projected on the vertical plane in which the Web page resides, thus providing the bi-dimensional coordinates of the mouse on the screen (see the Virtual I/O panel in Figure 6).

4.1   JHaptic Library

The conceptual elements introduced in Section 3 to model haptic interaction inside a Web page have been integrated into the JHaptic library according to the UML diagram in Figure 5. It represents only the most significative objects composing the project and their fundamental properties.

The library presents some first-class objects to model the haptic interaction. The *Device* class models the features offered by a generic haptic device like its inputs (*position, speed,* and *acceleration*) and ouptut (*output force*). The size of the physical workspace and the intensity of the maximum playable force are obtained directly from the parameters exposed by the plug-in, allowing the library to abstract from the device type.

A *Virtual Device* is also defined emulating the functionalities of a basic haptic device, so that the testing of the application is possible also without the need of a connected physical device (see Section 5).

The *ForceModel* class, and in particular its *func* property, represents the mathematical model of the effect to render. To consider the most general working space of haptic devices, all input and output data are represented by 3D vectors (class *Vector*). Some widely-used models have been predefined and represented by utility classes such as the *Spring, Damper,* or *Vibration* force models, etc.,

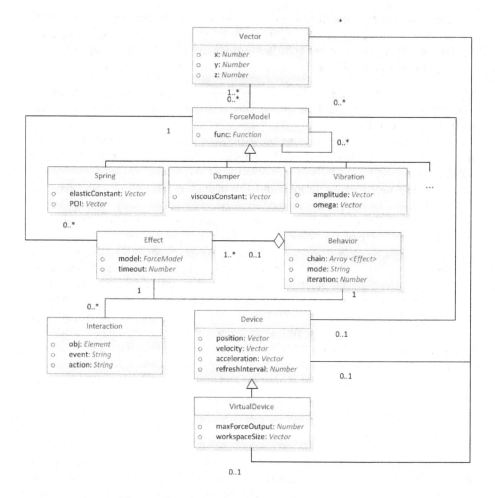

Fig. 5. The UML model of the developed library

just to mention the ones depicted in Figure 5. Anyway, the developer can customize the effects to render to face user's needs: the class *Effect* allows to specify a duration in time of the force feedback generated by the defined model; moreover, effects can also be composed, in order to obtain a time-sequenced effects or specifically designed patterns: this effects composition is possible with the *Behavior* class which supports the concatenation of effects, to reproduce them for a specified number of times.

4.2   The Plug-in for the Browser

The developed plug-in has been designed to be used with NPAPI-compliant browsers, e.g., Mozilla Firefox, Google Chrome, Gecko, Safari, etc. Among all the browsers, we have considered Google Chrome and for the development of the plug-in we have used Firebreath [2], a framework that allows the creation and development of simple plug-ins for most of the popular browsers integrating the NPAPI functionalities.

The plug-in has been implemented taking into account two main requirements:

- *Low complexity*: the minimal functions needed to manage the communication with the device are included. In this way, the creation of new plug-ins to extend the library support to more devices becomes simpler and faster, since no algorithms for the computation and management of the haptic rendering need to be redefined.
- *High compatibility*: the APIs exhibited by the plug-in should represent the basic set of functions needed to interface with a haptic device. The plug-in is the main interface for the JHaptic library: if the plug-in exhibits a fixed set of APIs, compatible with all the devices, this will simplify a possible change of the employed haptic device.

To maximize the compatibility with more devices, 3 DOFs (degrees of freedom) have been considered. At this aim a basic set of methods and variables that the plug-in should exhibit to the JHaptic library has been identified, including:

- a set of methods to control the device, i.e., to start and stop the communication with the device;
- a method to send the force value to be instantaneously rendered;
- a method to obtain the force applied to the device;
- a method to obtain the current coordinates of the proxy;
- a method to set the working space (2D or 3D) and a variable to set its maximum dimensions;
- a variable to set the maximum force value that can be rendered by the device.

For further details the reader can refer to the official Web site of the JHaptic library project[2], where the complete framework (library and plug-in) can be downloaded, more specific documentation can be found, and examples of Web pages enriched with haptic effects are available.

In our tests we have used the Sensable PHANTOM^{TM}, which is a 6-DOF device: the additional 3 DOFs exhibited by the end-effector of this specific device have not been considered.

In order to decouple the implementation from a specific device, we have not used any proprietary library associated with a particular haptic interface, but we have written the plug-in code with the help of the multi-device CHAI3D open-source library [1], which allows the automatic detection and adaptation of the plug-in functionalities to other haptic device.

The plug-in takes care also of the movements of the mouse pointer on the screen according to the movements of the haptic end-effector, by mapping the corresponding coordinates as explained in Section 4. To handle the positioning of the mouse cursor at the computed screen coordinates, appropriate operating system APIs are called from the plug-in, since this is not possible using Javascript code.

---

[2] `http://home.dei.polimi.it/mazza/jhaptic`

Device-Independency. A note on the device-independency of the overall design is here worth saying. The whole framework has been designed to be device-independent: the Javascript library is based on a conceptual model specifying the haptic interaction, and also the plug-in has been implemented using a device-independent library such as CHAI3D and has been designed considering 3-DOF devices, so that it can be easily adapted to be used with different physical interface: in case of 2-DOF devices the z-coordinate of the Vector is simply ignored; for devices with more than 3 DOFs, only the main 3 DOFs are considered.

5   Console for Debugging and Testing

In order to support the developer in the usage of the proposed library we realized a browser-integrated tool to simplify the debugging and testing process of a Web page extended with haptic feedback. The solution provided is made up of a console and a simulator. Both components are implemented in Javascript so that they can be exploited directly within the browser, thus overcoming the problems related to the architecture or the operative system of the developer's machine. The structure of the debugging tool is shown in Figure 6.

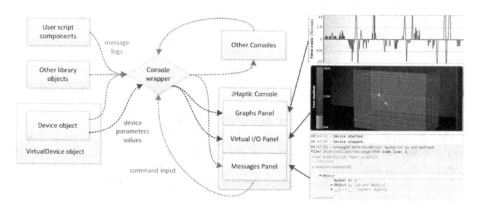

Fig. 6. The structure of the debugging tool

By means of the console, injectable on request within the HTML document, the developer is able to visually monitor the behavior of the haptic device by exploiting three panels:

1. The *Graphs* panel, displaying a chronological visualization of the changes occurring during haptic interaction in terms of wave forms representing the force pulses reproduced by the device; it is also possible to visualize the variations of the other measures computed during the haptic rendering process (like position, velocity, refresh rate, etc.) by means of multiples real-time quoted plots;

2. The *Virtual I/O* panel, graphically rendering in the 3D workspace the representation of the current position of the proxy and the magnitude and direction of the output force, along with other auxiliary information such as the arrangement of the desktop area or the virtual placement of the page viewport plane;
3. The *Messages* panel, used to monitor the log, warning and error messages related to the functioning of the Web page and of the library components.

Through the console it is also possible to directly edit at runtime the haptic effects set in the Web page, taking advantage of the code injecting feature that has been developed.

All the information and functionalities provided by the console are accessible either using a real device, controlled by means of a browser plug-in, or using a simulated one, to allow the test of an application without the need of a physical device connected to the system. At this aim, the simulator emulates the three-dimensional input received from a real device by conveying the correct position calculated by parsing the events related to the mouse positions and buttons, according to the workspace size defined by the developer; the output is shown in the console.

6   Evaluation and Experience

In order to understand the impact of the introduction of haptic interaction on Web navigation, we have done some performance tests on different hardware configurations by extending different pages with multiple haptic feedbacks. We evaluated more usage conditions for the library, exploiting both the simulator and the real device used through the developed plug-in. The tests were performed on mid-range systems: 1) CPU Intel Core 2 Duo T6500 2.1GHz, RAM 4GB DDR2 800MHz, GPU Ati Mobility Radeon 4650; 2) CPU Intel Core 2 Duo E8400 3GHz, RAM 4GB DDR2 800MHz, GPU nVidia Geforce 9600GT; the Google Chrome (v.17) browser on the Microsoft Windows 7 32-bit operative system has been employed. The following parameters have been monitored: 1) the *haptic refresh rate*, i.e., the real frequency with which the force pulses are computed and sent to the device 2) the *CPU workload*, i.e., the processing power required to perform the calculation of the forces set, keeping the ideal refresh rate to 1 kHz. Results show that the rendering of a low number of haptic effects within the HTML document does not lead to a significant increase of the resources usage. In particular, the playback of a single force model among those already provided in the library does not cause a tangible variation of the CPU workload, while the real refresh rate remains close to 1 kHz. By increasing the amount of the haptic effects simultaneously rendered, we observed a slight linear rise of the CPU power demand, whereas the average haptic refresh on the low-end system showed more frequent peaks of delay. Anyway, several force models to be reproduced simultaneously within a Web page is a situation that will hardly occur in practice: user studies presented in literature demonstrated that the design of the Web page should enable one - possibly complex - effect at a time, to avoid a chaotic sensations to the user receiving too many information from different channels [13]. Moreover, the CPU usage is never overloaded, allowing the execution of other applications in parallel to the Web browsing activity. Finally, no performance difference has been identified in the use of the real and the simulated device.

On the development experience side, the framework presents mainly two benefits: 1) compared to manual coding, the JHaptic library, together with the plug-in interfacing the physical device, simplifies the addition of the haptic effects to a Web application; 2) moreover, the framework can be extended with any new effect, by means of additional Javascript function(s) that model the effects to render by exploiting the already existing JHaptic library APIs; extensibility is an important aspect, especially when common standards are lacking, like in the case of haptics.

7   Conclusions and Future Works

In this work we have designed and realized a framework for the introduction of haptic interactions into Web applications. To our knowledge, this is the first framework supporting a flexible design of effects, providing a set of browser-integrated tools to help the Web developer in the definition and testing of haptic effects, and designed to be device-independent.

As future work we plan to extend the capabilities of the developed library with the integration of a graphical engine, for the specification of haptic effects within a three-dimensional environments rendered in the browser. Another aspect worth studying concerns the usability of haptic-enhanced Web applications, considering the type of device, the context of use, and the type of target users, in order to identify guidelines and design patterns.

More room there will be in the future for haptic technologies: the research trend emerged in recent years pays particular attention to the design and development of devices exploiting the sense of touch, also the W3C, has set up two relevant initiatives[3] to face the emerging new ways of interactions and the supporting devices. Haptics is going to strongly influence consumers' habits and research domains for the next years.

References

1. Chai 3d, http://www.chai3d.org
2. Firebreath, http://www.firebreath.org
3. Jtouchtoolkit, https://jtouchtoolkit.dev.java.net/
4. Novint, http://home.novint.com/
5. Sensable phantom omni, http://www.sensable.com/haptic-phantom-omni.htm
6. Caffrey, A., Mccrindle, R.: Mccrindle r. developing a multi-modal web application. In: Proceedings of ICDVRAT 2004, pp. 165–172 (2004)

---

[3] The Device APIs Working Group: http://www.w3.org/2009/dap/
The Vibration API: http://www.w3.org/TR/2012/WD-vibration-20120202/

7. Comai, S., Mazza, D.: Introducing haptic interactions in web application modeling. In: WSE, pp. 43–52 (2010)
8. Eid, M., Andrews, S., Alamri, A., El Saddik, A.: HAMLAT: A HAML-Based Authoring Tool for Haptic Application Development. In: Ferre, M. (ed.) EuroHaptics 2008. LNCS, vol. 5024, pp. 857–866. Springer, Heidelberg (2008)
9. Eid, M., Mansour, M., Iglesias, R., Saddik, A.E.: A device independent haptic player. In: Proceedings of the 2007 IEEE International Conference on Virtual Environments, Human-Computer Interfaces, and Measurement Systems. IEEE (2007)
10. Itkowitz, B., Handley, J., Zhu, W.: The openhaptics toolkit: A library for adding 3d touch navigation and haptics to graphics applications. In: Proceedings of First Joint Eurohaptics Conference and Symposium on Haptic Interfaces for Virtual Environment and Teleoperator Systems (WHC 2005). IEEE (March 2005)
11. Kaklanis, N., Calleros, J.G., Vanderdonckt, J., Tzovaras, D.: A haptic rendering engine of web pages for blind users. In: Proceedings of the Working Conference on Advanced Visual Interfaces, AVI 2008, pp. 437–440 (2008)
12. Kaklanis, N., Votis, K., Moschonas, P., Tzovaras, D.: Hapticriamaps: towards interactive exploration of web world maps for the visually impaired. In: W4A, p. 20 (2011)
13. Kuber, R., Yu, W., McAllister, G.: Towards developing assistive haptic feedback for visually impaired internet users. In: CHI, pp. 1525–1534 (2007)
14. Kuber, R., Yu, W., O'Modhrain, M.S.: Evaluation of haptic html mappings derived from a novel methodology. TACCESS 3(4), 12 (2011)
15. Oakley, I., McGee, M.R., Brewster, S.A., Gray, P.D.: Putting the feel in look and feel. In: CHI, pp. 415–422 (2000)
16. Panëels, S.A., Roberts, J.C.: Review of designs for haptic data visualization. IEEE T. Haptics 3(2), 119–137 (2010)
17. Pascale, M.D., Prattichizzo, D.: The haptik library. IEEE Robotics & Automation Magazine 14(4), 64–75 (2007)
18. Salisbury, K., Conti, F., Barbagli, F.: Haptic rendering: Introductory concepts. IEEE Comput. Graph. Appl. 24(2), 24–32 (2004)
19. Yu, W., Kuber, R., Murphy, E., Strain, P., McAllister, G.: A novel multimodal interface for improving visually impaired people's web accessibility. Virtual Reality 9(2-3), 133–148 (2006)

Supporting Users Tasks with Personal Information Management and Web Forms Augmentation

Sergio Firmenich[1,2], Vincent Gaits[2], Silvia Gordillo[1,3],
Gustavo Rossi[1,2], and Marco Winckler[4]

[1] LIFIA, Facultad de Informática
[2] Universidad Nacional de La Plata and Conicet Argentina
[3] CiCPBA
[4] IRIT, Université Paul Sabatier, France
{sergio.firmenich,vgaits,gordillo,gustavo}@lifia.info.unlp.edu.ar,
winckler@irit.fr

Abstract. Currently, many tasks performed on the Web prompt users to provide personal information through forms. Despite the fact that most users are familiarized with this kind of interaction technique, the use of Web forms is not always straightforward. Indeed, some users might need assistance to understand labels and complex data format required to fill in form fields that, quite often, vary from a Web site to another even when requesting similar data. Filling in forms can be tedious and repetitive as many Web sites request similar information. In this work we analyze user's interactions with Web forms and propose an approach for enhancing Web forms using client-side adaptation techniques in order to assist users to fill in Web forms. As the use of Web forms is closely related to the management of personal information our approach includes the support for data exchange between user's personal information management systems (PIMs) and third-party Web forms. The approach is illustrated by a set of client-side adaptation tools and a pervasive Personal Information Management Systems called PIMI.

1 Introduction

For many Web applications, forms are essential components that allow users to provide data and interact with the system. Despite the fact that forms can be very effective for gathering information, the tasks users engage when filling in forms can be complex: at first, users must to *understand how to fill in the forms*; users should also be able to *recall information* that should be entered into form fields; only then users can start typing to *fill in the forms;* it is worth noting that quite often users need to *record data used in forms* in their personal information management systems (PIMs) for later use. If these users' tasks are not supported properly they might raise several usability problems. For example, users can make mistakes if they don't understand labels or if they do not know how to enter data in the expected data format [3]. Users can also left form fields blank if mandatory fields are not clearly indicated. Recalling information is cognitively demanding [14] and particularly painful if users should recall the information provided to every Web form. Whilst typing in form fields, users can introduce typos. Filling in Web forms can also be tedious and repetitive [5]; this is particularly true because, quite often, different Web forms will request similar personal information from users [25].

M. Brambilla, T. Tokuda, and R. Tolksdorf (Eds.): ICWE 2012, LNCS 7387, pp. 268–282, 2012.

In the last years, several strategies have been developed to assist users to fill in forms. On one hand there are techniques focused on the system design for example, guidelines aimed to provide advices for building usable Web forms [14]. Another example is third-party applications that include a user personal space on the server-side for providing pre-filled forms on the client-side.

On the other hand, some enhanced Web browsers and plug-ins implement techniques for assisting users to fill in forms such as auto-filling techniques [10] and auto-completion [22]. The auto-filling techniques [10] can "remember" which values were entered by the users in a given form in a previous visit to the Web site. Some Web browsers like Safari[1] implement by default an auto fill form mechanism that reuses previously filled form for automatically filling out different forms with data. However this will ultimately require users to login and record Web forms requesting personal data, which implies that users should remember their login information.

Despite the fact that all these solutions provide undeniable help, they suffer of at least one of the following limitations:

- We depend on the diligence of Web-browsers designers and developers of third-party Web applications;
- These solutions focus on a single problem, quite often limited to automating filling in forms and neglecting overall user tasks with Web forms;
- There is no integration between data available on users' personal information management systems and Web forms. Even if many Web applications can keep updated records of personal information in remote servers, there are legal and technical issues that prevent them from sharing personal data among different applications. Moreover, users must keep multiple accounts which increase the complexity of personal data management [15].

In order to assist users in all the tasks they engage whilst interacting with Web forms this paper proposes an approach based on Web forms augmentation to support a straightforward interaction between third-party Web forms and users' personal information management systems.

The underlying premise for the current work is that users will be more efficient whilst filling in forms if they were allowed to reuse data from their personal information management systems (PIMs). This work also assumes that some of the usability problems occur because users have to interact with different Web forms and it is virtually impossible to create a uniform presentation for all third-part Web forms available on the Web. In the following sections we describe the general approach and the tools that have been developed to solve these problems.

2   Task Analysis of User Interaction with Web Forms

2.1   Motivating Scenario

Some of the inner difficulties for interacting with Web forms only become evident when users have to accomplish the same tasks across different Web forms. To illustrate this, we present below a trip planning scenario which ultimately requires users to provide the same data on different third-party Web forms, as follows:

---

[1] Safari - Auto Fill: Personal Information, http://www.apple.com/safari

> *"John wants to bring his wife Judy to Berlin for her birthday, for that he is booking a flight, a hotel and a car at the following Web sites: expedia.com, booking.com and hertz.com. By doing so, John fills in three Web forms with information about the travel (i.e. dates, city of origin and destination) and the people travelling (i.e. name, personal address, billing address, credit card information, frequent flyer number, driver license, and passport number). Interesting enough, the three Web sites propose different names for form fields requesting similar information. John knows by heart his personal information but it does not go the same for Judy's passport information and frequent flyer number. Whilst filling in the forms, John is puzzled to see that the Web site could recall his credit card number and passport (he does not remember to have asked the web site to record such information in the past…). Moreover, the Web site recalls John's old passport number which John didn't realize immediately but he was very precautious to crosscheck it and change the information in time. After completing the booking, John has a last task to collect information for his travel (e.g. addresses of hotels, car rental…). John also takes note one of his many credit cards he used with the different Web sites."*

Whilst performing the scenario above, it is possible to observe some issues that make the following users tasks difficult. As illustrated at Fig. 1, these tasks have several implications on the user side (concerning user requirements for accomplish the task), on the system side (impact on the design of Web forms), or both (the system implementation has an impact on users tasks).

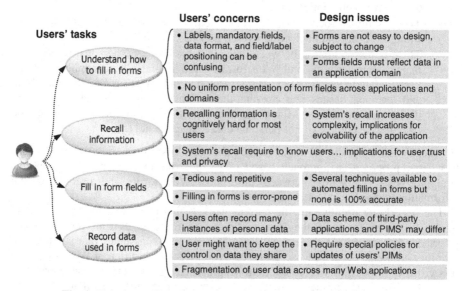

Fig. 1. Main issues for supporting common users' tasks with Web forms

2.2   Rational for Improving User Interaction with Web Forms

An overview in the current literature will point out several recommendations for solving each individual issue described at Fig. 1. Hereafter we present possible solutions for each task:

- Understand how to fill in forms
    - *Provide the same form structure through different Web sites;*
    - *Always describe the information demanded with standardized labels;*
    - *Provide a help page to explain the form;*
    - *Provide contextual help for filling every form field;*

- Recall information
  - ○ *Store information in the browser/server-side to recall users of previously entered data on Web forms;*
  - ○ *Provide users with a pervasive access to their personal space*
- Filling in forms
  - ○ *Support user profiles to complete some data automatically;*
  - ○ *Give to users full control over data used for filling in forms;*
  - ○ *Manage a PIM and establishing semantic correspondence with forms.*
- Record data used in forms
  - ○ *Allow users to record into their personal space the data provide to Web forms;*
  - ○ *Allow users to collect information in Web sites and make it available across the Web at client-side.*

It is interesting to notice that existing solutions will focus on a single issue at a time. Moreover, some solutions such as labels standardization among the Web seem technically possible but unrealistic in practice as application domains might vary and Web developers are usually "creative" in their designs. Indeed, existing solutions will present two main drawbacks: dependency on the diligence of designers of Web applications and/or lack of support for integrating personal information space and Web forms. In order to solve these problems we propose below some alternative solutions:

- *Allow users community to describe the form entries and show these descriptions in the form page.*
- *Provide a pervasive personal information space with seamless integration with Web forms. This solution could help users to recall their personal information that could also be used for filling in forms.*
- *Allow users to collect information in Web sites and make it available across the Web at client-side.*

3   Outline of the Approach

Our approach relies in a distributed architecture encompassing a set of independent Web applications that can be combined as shown by Fig. 2. The architecture is conceived to support user interaction with Web forms provided by third-party applications. The personal information space is a piece of software whose main task is to store users' personal data (e.g. address, bank account...). The personal information space is deployed into a Web server, rather than on the Web browser, to provide users with a pervasive access to their personal data. The third element in this architecture is the personal assistant for filling forms, which is a piece of software implementing client-side adaptation techniques for supporting Web form augmentation and ensuring data interoperability between the personal information space and third-party Web applications. The main principles that underlying the approach are: i) third-party Web form augmentation through the use of client-side adaptation techniques; ii) the availability of a pervasive personal information management system; iii) the development of an annotation service for supporting data interoperability between third-party Web forms and user personal information systems. The rest of this section describes the rationale behind every element of this architecture.

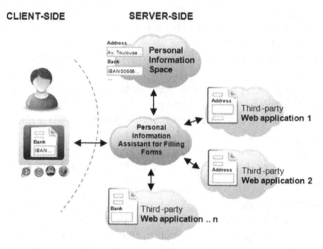

Fig. 2. Overview of architecture of our approach for Web form augmentation

3.1   Web Form Augmentation

Previous works [4][7] have demonstrated that client-side adaptation techniques are an effective way to empower users in order to adapt Web sites according with their concern. For example, client-side adaptation techniques may be used to create small software packages called *augmenters* [7] that can modify, in the Web browser, the content of third-party Web applications. *Augmenters* are built as generic adaptations featuring behaviors such as adding user defined links to Web pages, highlighting text, etc. Technically speaking, an *augmenter* is just a script (written in JavaScript) that is able to modify the DOM. *Augmenters* are developed using the CSN framework [7] and then installed in the browser as a plug-in. Whilst navigating the Web, end-users can use the framework to trigger *augmenters* whenever they are needed to improve the user interaction. In our previous work [7] we have explained how to use the CSN framework to build not only individual *augmenters* for supporting opportunistic user tasks but also how to combine different *augmenters* to supporting complex scenarios.

The present work borrows the basic infrastructure provided by the CSN framework to build client-side adaptations and it extends it by describing a set of useful *augmenters* supporting Web form augmentation (i.e. *augmenters* aimed to help users to interact with Web forms). These augmenters can be triggered either by the users (i.e. manually) or programmed to execute automatically under certain circumstances. In this way, users may perform adaptations under demand, but the same adaptations may be executed automatically by the tool (a Web browser plug-in).

3.2   A Pervasive Personal Information Management System

The second main element in our approach is a pervasive information space for storing user's personal data. Managing large sets of information is strongly related to the domain of Personal Information Management systems (PIMs), which corresponds [15] to the research field addressing the way people manage their physical documents (books, notebooks, sheets, etc.), as well as their electronic documents (files, emails,

Web pages, etc.), with the aim of designing tools that support the management of electronic documents (PIM tools). While the PIMs area usually covers many contexts and activities, in this paper we look at PIMs in a more specific way: the individual information items people keep on various notes, cards, forms, agendas, etc., the ones that user are mostly have to use when interacting with Web forms.

Our approach relies on a Personal Information Management system (PIMs) as a tool allowing users to persist information which may be used when they it is needed. In this way, users may have always relevant information for performing tasks, specifically those which require forms. The pervasive aspect for the PIMs is aimed to reduce information fragmentation and for making information fully accessible to the users.

3.3   Data Interoperability through Web Forms Annotation

The Web forms provided by third-party applications might have different structure and inner organization. For example, form fields can have diverse names such as city, town, locality, etc; an address can include (or not) the state and mailbox; and so on. Therefore, a mapping process is required to ensure that data can be exchanged between applications. In our approach data operability is ensured by complying form fields with an emerging standard such as Microformats [17] and Microdata [12]. Our approach can support diverse data formats, but for the purposes of the illustration, the current implementation is built upon Microformats.

The choice for Microformats is motivated by the fact that they can embedded into other data formats such as (X)HTML, Atom, RSS, and arbitrary XML. Moreover, there are several plug-ins that can detect automatically the presence of data into Web pages encoded accordingly to Microformats. Fig. 3 shows the structure of the *Microformat* hcard. The tag *vcard* indicates the class of the *Microformat*; the *hcard* was originally proposed upon the standard vCard RFC 2426 (Card MIME Directory Profile) to identify individuals. The tag *fn* is used for full name and it is the only mandatory element. The tags *org, adr, street-address, locality, region, postal-code*, and *country-name* are some of other 29 optional tags can be used to identify a person.

```
<div class="vcard">
<span class="fn">Marilyn Monroe</span>
<div class="adr">
<div class="street-address"> Pennsylvania Avenue</div>
<span class="locality"> Brentwood</span>,
<span class="region">CA</span>,
<span class="postal-code"> 90049</span>
<span class="country-name">United States</span>
</div>
```

Fig. 3. Excerpt of the Microformats *hcard*

In our approach, Microformats are used as a kind of *lingua franca* that supports data exchange between the different elements described in Fig. 2. The use of Microformats is spreading fast on the Web, but not all Web pages are built using Microformats. Thus, we have to face two possible scenarios: a) forms fields were built using Microformats structures; b) Forms fields do not embed Microformats. In the first case (a) Web forms already integrate Microformats so that forms can be used as such with the personal assistant for filling forms. In the second case (b) the original Web forms must be annotated with Microformats.

Fig. 4 illustrates how the approach supports the detection of Microformats in Web pages and the corresponding annotation of third-party Web forms with Microformats. It is important to notice that annotations are necessary to make Web forms compatible with the users' data stored into their personal information. Annotations are stored as external files in a dedicated database. If known annotations for a Web form exist, they are added to the original Web form to produce a modified form featuring Microformats. Notice that Web forms are not modified on the third-party Web server making the solution independent of the Web form provider.

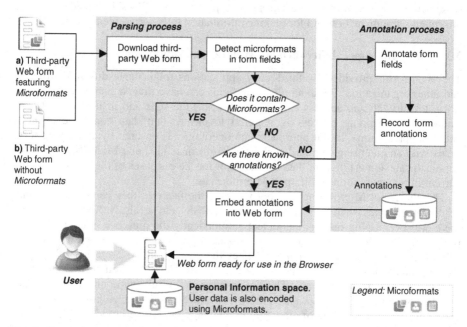

Fig. 4. Annotation process for supporting interoperability between third-party Web forms and user's personal information space using Microformats

Annotations can be done in many ways either manually coding the annotations into a text file or by using several annotation tools such as Greasemonkey scripts[2] and open annotation services [21]. We consider that annotation should be done by web developers, but since the use of annotation tools require little training they can be also mastered by experienced Web users. The efforts of annotating are reduced by the collective effort. Therefore most users will not need to annotate forms before using them. The process for modifying Web pages using external annotations is supported by some tools such as [11][13]. Despite the fact that we assume that annotation of forms could be easily performed by advanced Web users, we do not exclude the possibility that the annotation process could be automated. Indeed, tools such as Carbon [1] and Opal [9] are able to analyze Web forms with respect to their fields and labels. For example, Opal [9] interprets form labels and classifies the fields according to a given domain Ontology. This classification mechanism could be exploited to support automated annotation of Web forms.

---

[2] Greasemonkey, http://www.greasespot.net/

3.4   User Control on Data Transfer

Most of available techniques will fill in forms with data without prompting users. As users do not know beforehand which data will be automatically entered, they must cross-check all form fields. Wrong predictions of data put into form fields might cause frustration and ultimately reduce user performance. Moreover, users' confidence on the system might decrease if they do not fell in control of the data transfer. This aspect of the user interaction has become an essential aspect for the design of new applications [16]. In other to prevent these drawbacks, our approach defines user's control on automatic form fill in as follows:

- Users should be able to create as many records of personal information as needed, (e.g. home address, secondary house, etc);
- Users should be able to control data flowing from/to the personal information space from/to Web forms;
- The personal information space can be update at any time;
- Users must be allowed to modify partially/totally the content of form fields even after the personal assistant has previously filled them in with data chose by users;
- Personal data must be accessible from everywhere so that users can keep control of their personal data regardless the browser and/or the computer they are using.

4   Case Study and Tool Support

In order to demonstrate the feasibility of the approach we have developed a set of tools including a *personal information space*, a *personal assistant for filling forms* that provides support for Web form augmentation and an *annotation service*. Actually these tools have been combined in a single user interface called PIMI, which was built upon the CSN framework [7]. As shown in Fig. 5, PIMI is delivered as a Firefox extension that, when activated, appears at the left-hand side (see Fig. 5.a) of the Web browser whilst users are navigating on the Web at the right-hand side (see Fig. 5.b). Fig. 5.a, Fig. 5.c and Fig. 5.d shows the corresponding screenshots when the user can log into PIMI (a), create a new account (b) and access to the main menu that give access to the tools for supporting users in filling forms while they perform their tasks.

The rest of this section is organized as follow: section 4.1 presents how user can use PIMI to manage their personal information; section 4.2 illustrates how PIMI supports automated filling in forms; section 4.3 describes the annotation service for making new forms interoperable with the user personal information space.

4.1   Personal Information Space

One of the main features of our approach is that users should be able to connect their personal information system with third-party Web forms. In order to ensure a pervasive access to users' personal data, PIMI includes a data server from where users can manage their personal records. Such personal information space can be seen as a standalone application. However, PIMI integrates data from user's personal spaces for allowing them to reuse such data whilst they are also navigating third-party applications as shown by Fig. 6.

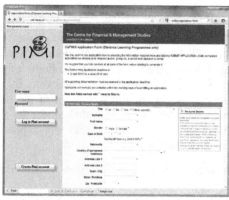

| a) PIMI login |... b) third-party web forms ....| |c) new account| |d) main menu |

Fig. 5. Views PIMI inside the Web browser whilst navigating the Web

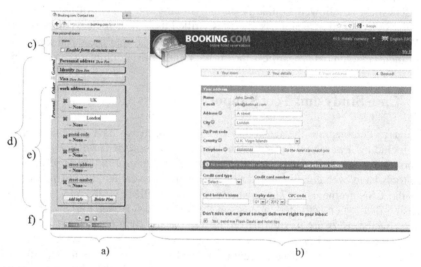

Fig. 6. Overview of the personal information space at PIMI: *a) PIMI; b) third-party application; c) tools menu; d) personal records items; e) expanded items; f) items menu*

Once connected to his account, the user can see his personal information space at the left-hand side of the Web browser (Fig. 6.a) and the third-party web form at the right-hand side (Fig. 6.b). The personal records are organized in the form of cards that can be piled up and managed as electronic posts-it containing a simple label (see Fig. 6.d). Each personal record can be expanded to show all detailed information; for instance, Fig. 6.e shows all the fields associated to the label *work address*. The current structure of these cards is based on existing *Microformats* and only accessible from PIMI. However, it would be possible to extend it to use other data format. Fig. 6.f shows the menu for creating new personal records using existing Microformats elements. On the top (Fig. 6.c) there is a menu for allowing navigation to the other tools delivered with PIMI including the navigation to the main menu (as shown at Fig. 5d), the personal assistant to filling forms (see section 4.4) and the annotation service (see section 4.5).

4.2   Personal Assistant for Filling Forms

The personal assistant for filling forms is a tool that implements a set of client-side adaptation techniques that can modify third-party Web applications and thus making them compatible with the user's personal information space. One of the most interesting features of this tool is the automated fill in of Web forms that is supported by a simple "drag and drop" (D&D) of information items as shown by Fig. 7.a. The tool is able to detect if the Web page embeds Microformats that can be used to support the exact mapping between personal user data and the form fields. Such D&D is possible because both input and property have the same Microformat. Notice that users do not need to move every field (e.g. *street number*), but instead they manipulate the whole block of information (i.e. *personal address*). The entire set of data is copied into form fields whenever there is a correspondence between the data type. If form fields already contain data, the D&D action will replace it with the data from the personal information space. The opposite operation is also possible so that users can also populate their personal information space by performing a D&D from a Web form towards the personal information space. For that, the user just needs to enable the option "*Enabling form elements save*" on the top menu before performing the D&D.

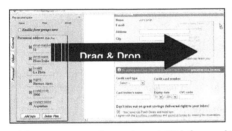 

a) from user personal space towards Web form   b) Web form towards personal information space

Fig. 7. Personal assistant for filling forms using D&D

The personal assistant for filling form implements that *parsing* process already described in Fig. 4. At first it tries to detect if the third-party Web forms have been built with Microformats, or if there are known annotations for the Web form that would make the Web form compatible with Microformats. Otherwise the users should annotate the Web form before being able to perform D&D operations.

4.3   Tool Support for Annotation of Web Forms

In our approach, annotations are a key step for implementing Web forms augmentation. On one hand, annotations are needed for providing users with contextual help to labels and thus help them to fill in forms. On the other hand, annotations can be used to make third-party Web forms interoperable with the user's personal information. Our tools support two kinds of annotations: a) semantic annotation of form fields to make them compliant with Microformats; b) textual annotations that can be used as contextual help.

Fig. 8 illustrates the annotation process of the Web form available at the Web site Expedia.com. By navigating on the top menu it is possible to reach the annotation tab that basically shows a list of existing Microformats. So far the current Microformats are supported: *Hcalendar, Hcard, Hreview, Xoxo, Haddress, Hbank, Hcontct, Hidentity,*

Hlog. To annotate a form field, the only thing the user should do is to select an ***input type*** of a Microformats (for example the property *value* of the field *email* embedded into Microformats *Hcard*; Fig. 8.a) and then perform a D&D to the ***target input*** in the Web form. When doing so, the target form field becomes green to show that it has been annotated (see at Fig. 8.a, ***target input***). Whilst the form field is selected, users can also add a description to it using the field ***input description***. This operation should be repeated in all fields that require annotations. The tool will automatically record these annotations in a dedicated database. Once annotated, the event *mouse over* will trigger the contextual help embedding the user-defined annotations as a virtual post-it as shown in Fig. 8.b. Web forms annotated in this way will became semantically compatible with Microformats and thus enabling integration with data from the user personal space (as described in section 4.2).

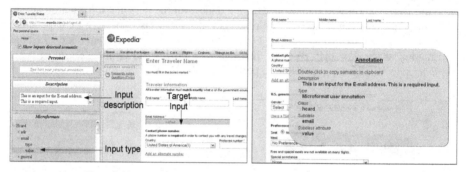

a) Annotation of form fields using Microformats   b) Contextual help provided by annotations

Fig. 8. Overview of form annotations in Expedia.com

In the current implementation, annotations performed by a user will automatically become available to users visiting the same Web forms, provided that other users also have a PIMI account. This feature is aimed to support a crowdsourcing approach for annotations of Web forms so that users create new annotations that are shared with the community and then any other user can profit from the new annotations.

4.4   Evaluation of Tool Support

The tools presented above are full operational and have been used with a large set of third-party Web forms.

In order to highlight the contributions of these tools, we present in this section a quantitative assessment of user tasks with Web forms accordingly to the GOMS-Keystroke (KLM) model [6]. GOMS ("Goals, Operators, Methods, Selection rules") is a cognitive formal model used to rigorously evaluate how efficiently a trained person can interact with a given software system or program. GOMS is a human information processing model that is built upon a detailed sequence of users operations with a system. The GOMS-Keystroke (KLM) is a variant of that model which includes values to known users' actions; so that it is possible to predict the time skilled users will spend in seemingly unpredictable situations. For example, the average time to perform the action *reach for mouse is of 0.40 seconds, click on a field is of 0.20 seconds, etc.* Thus by providing a detailed scenario of user actions with tools including low-level user actions, it is possible to use GOMS-KLM to predict performance of computers (e.g., speed).

Due to the limited space, Table 1 presents a summary of the results obtained by applying the GOMS-KLM over some tasks identified in the scenario "planning a travel to Berlin" described in section 2. The last line in the table provides the estimated time for the full scenario. We compare tasks performed using PIMI and without PIMI. As we shall see, the estimated time for some tasks in the scenario such as *"Search Flights"* and *"Selecting Flights"* are the same. However users will save time when reusing data that is already on the personal information space as the D&D is faster than typing every word in the form field. At Table 1 we can also see that some new tasks will appear when using PIMI as users will be requested to *create an account* and eventually populate the information space with data such as *personal contact* and *credit card*. It also includes the estimated time for annotating third-party form fields using PIMI; ex. annotating fields related to credit cards is estimated to 15 sec. Whilst users spend some time populating the personal information space, they will save time reusing that information in future operations.

Table 1. Estimated performance of some tasks accordingly to GOMS-KLM model

Tasks	Without PIMI	With PIMI
Search Flights in Expedia.com	6.3 sec	6.3 sec
Selecting Flights in Expedia.com	32 sec	32 sec
Filling in form with passenger information in Expedia.com	26 sec	9.9 sec
Filling in form with credit card information in Expedia.com	67 sec	11.9 sec
Create an account in PIMI	-	27.6 sec
Add personal contact into personal information space	-	27.5 sec
Add credit card information into personal information space	-	41 sec
Annotated form fields related to credit card (bank, account number...)	-	15 sec
Total task: travel planning buying flights tickets (expedia.com), booking accommodation (Booking.com)	**240.6 sec**	**116.8 sec**

Note that, besides these quantitative time estimations, the approach and the tool support help to add overcome limitations of existing forms with respect to the lack of contextual help and seamless management of personal information.

5   Discussion and Related Work

The approach presented in this paper opens questions of practical and theoretical significance including: What makes the task of filling forms so difficult for users? Which functions could be implemented to provide better support for helping users to fill in Web forms? How to support a better integration between Web forms and personal information management? Which is the best standard for describing personal user data? How to support data interoperability between different third-party web forms? How to make third-part Web forms interoperable?

The study of interaction techniques for improving the user interaction with Web forms is not a new research theme. Specifically, the lack of standardization in data entry forms is not a new problem [8], however, it is still a standing one. The diversity of structure and organization of Web forms is a major constraint that still prevents the development of a seamless solution for automating filling in Web forms. Most of currently available techniques focus on the automation of the tasks of filling in forms (i.e. for Auto-complete [22] and Auto-filling [2]). Some recent work [1][9][23] try to tackle the problem by using similarity functions to predict which personal information is expected for each form fields. However, prediction techniques fail to provide users with full control of their own data exchange; this issue might have an impact on trust and potential of user adoption of the final solution.

Other authors [5][24] investigate the use of Semantic Web technology for developing data bindings schemas. Data binding patterns are established techniques that help to connect user interface elements and data objects of applications [11]. The main drawback with such techniques is that one must have an Ontology describing third-party applications before performing the data integration. OpenID [20] technology allows users to provide certified identification and share information with trusted Web sites. Personal records can then be used to automatically fill in Web forms of trusted Web sites. One of the inconvenient of such approaches is that it requires the agreement of third-party Web sites to operate. Despite the fact that OpenID has been around for some years, its use is still limited to a few specialized Web sites. Moreover, the reinforced user identification promoted by OpenID is not always a mandatory requirement for user interaction with most Web forms. Instead of focusing on a custom Ontology for particular Web applications, some binding schemas relies on the emergence of open standard data types such as Microformats [17] and Microdata [12]. Microdata is an under development standard of the World Wide Web Consortium whose aim is to integrate complex data as native types in XML-like technologies. The structure and underlying approach of Microformats and Microdata are pretty similar. However, Microformats have the advantage of an open community and already existing tools to support it.

This work is also closely related to the emergence of Personal Information Management Systems (PIMs) [15]. PIMs studies have mostly focused on very large data sets, such has the whole content of a user hard drive, and therefore has mainly concentrated on search/ retrieval issues, with some findings about the great variability in which people search their own information. However, in more recent years some authors started investigating the management of personal information over the Web [18][19]. For example, [19] proposes a complete architecture based on Web 2.0 technology enabling users to manage their personal records on the Web and synchronize them with other Web applications, in particular social networks. Notwithstanding, these efforts are mainly related to textual flat data and do not take into account interactive users tasks such as filling in forms. Our approach is another motivating example for promoting the development of pervasive PIMs [26].

The approach introduced in this paper also made use of client-side adaptation techniques for modifying third-party applications. Indeed, the tool support delivered with the approach is able to add new interactors on third-party Web forms (i.e. highlight, new buttons and D&D interaction techniques) for supporting users' tasks. The adaptation on the client of Web pages is an emerging topic of research. Our tool demonstrates that client-side adaptation is feasible from a technical point of view. As far as the adaptation occurs in the client-side, neither the information system hosted in the server-side or the Web forms it provides needs to be changed, and so our approach has virtually no impact on the server-side. However, client-side adaptation is not yet widely known by users so that more research is required to investigate the effect of such technology on the user experience.

Another challenge is to manage possible inconsistencies in the annotations made by the community. A possible solution for that is to rank the annotations in order to determine which are the more reliable annotations.

6   Conclusions and Future Work

One of the contributions of this paper is to highlight the user tasks while interacting with Web forms. Despite of some progress in terms of new interaction techniques for filling in forms, most existing approaches do not provide a big picture of user tasks with Web forms. In this respect, the task analysis presented in this paper can provide new insights. This paper also envisages a possible solution to these problems. For that we have presented an approach based on Web form augmentation for supporting users' tasks when interacting with Web forms. The approach is driven by the fact that users need a better integration of third-party Web forms and their personal information space. For that purpose we combine several techniques including client-side adaptation for form augmentation, annotation of Web pages, and personal information management systems. One of the originalities of the contributions is to combine all these techniques into a single approach. The approach is fully supported by a set of tools named PIMI that were built upon client-side adaptation techniques. Despite the fact that only a few augmenters have been implemented, they provided undeniable support for several user tasks with Web forms. We are currently extending the set of these augmenters for supporting user interaction with Web forms. Anyway, the web site http://www.vincent.gaits.fr/piaff.php contains a set of videos illustrating the use of PIMI and it provides the link for downloading and installing the tool. One of the next steps in this research will be to deploy these tools for investigating the crowdsourcing potential of the approach. Other aspects include the integration of other personal information space that could become available via the tool PIMI.

References

1. Araujo, S., Gao, Q., Leonardi, E., Houben, G.-J.: Carbon: Domain-Independent Automatic Web Form Filling. In: Benatallah, B., Casati, F., Kappel, G., Rossi, G. (eds.) ICWE 2010. LNCS, vol. 6189, pp. 292–306. Springer, Heidelberg (2010)
2. Autofill Forms - Mozilla Firefox add-on, http://autofillforms.mozdev.org/
3. Bargas-Avila, J.A., Orsini, S., Piosczyk, H., Urwyler, D., Opwis, K.: Enhancing online forms: Use format specifications for fields with format restrictions to help respondents. Interacting with Computers 23(1), 33–39 (2011),
   http://dx.doi.org/10.1016/j.intcom.2010.08.001
4. Bouvin, N.O.: Unifying Strategies for Web Augmentation. In: Proc. of the 10th ACM Conference on Hypertext and Hypermedia (1999)
5. Bownik, L., Gorka, W., Piasecki, A.: Assisted Form Filling. In: Soomro, S. (ed.) Engineering the Computer Science and IT. InTech (October 2009) ISBN 978-953-307-012-4
6. Card, S., Moran, T., Newell, A.: The psychology of human-computer interaction, 448 p. Lawrence Erlbaum Associates, Hillsdale (1983)
7. Firmenich, S., Winckler, M., Rossi, G., Gordillo, S.: A Framework for Concern-Sensitive, Client-Side Adaptation. In: Auer, S., Díaz, O., Papadopoulos, G.A. (eds.) ICWE 2011. LNCS, vol. 6757, pp. 198–213. Springer, Heidelberg (2011)
8. Girgensohn, A., Leeb, A.: Seamless integration of interactive forms into the Web. Computer Networks and ISDN Systems 29(8-13), 1531–1542 (1997)

9. Guo, X., Kranzdorf, J., Furche, T., Grasso, G., Orsi, G., Schallhart, C.: OPAL: A Passe-partout for Web Forms. In: Proc. 21st Int. Conf. World Wide Web (WWW 2012 Companion), pp. 353–356. ACM, New York (2012)

10. Hartmann, M., Muhlhauser, M.: Context-Aware Form Filling for Web Applications. In: Proceedings of the 2009 IEEE International Conference on Semantic Computing (ICSC '09), pp. 221–228. IEEE Computer Society, Washington, DC (2009)

11. Heinrich, M., Gaedke, M.: WebSoDa: A Tailored Data Binding Framework for Web Programmers Leveraging the WebSocket Protocol and HTML5 Microdata. In: Auer, S., Díaz, O., Papadopoulos, G.A. (eds.) ICWE 2011. LNCS, vol. 6757, pp. 387–390. Springer, Heidelberg (2011), doi:10.1007/978-3-642-22233-7_32

12. Hickson, I.: HTML Microdata (2011), http://www.w3.org/TR/microdata/

13. Hori, M., Kondoh, G., Ono, K.: Annotation-based Web content transcoding. In: Proc. of the 9th Int. World Wide Web Conference, pp. 197–211. North-Holland Publishing Co., Amsterdam (2000)

14. Jarrett, C., Gaffney, G.: Forms that Work: Designing Web Forms for Usability, 288 Pages. Morgan Kaufmann (November 2008) ISBN 1-55860-710-2

15. Jones, W., Teevan, J.: Personal Information Management, p. 334. University of Washington Press, Seattle (2007)

16. Olsen, K.A., Malizia, A.: Interfaces for the ordinary user: can we hide too much? Commun. ACM 55(1), 38–40 (2012)

17. Khare, R.: Microformats: The Next (Small) Thing on the Semantic Web? IEEE Internet Computing 10(1), 68–75 (2006)

18. Leone, S., Grossniklaus, M., de Spindler, A., Norrie, M.C.: Synchronising Personal Data with Web 2.0 Data Sources. In: Chen, L., Triantafillou, P., Suel, T. (eds.) WISE 2010. LNCS, vol. 6488, pp. 411–418. Springer, Heidelberg (2010)

19. Norrie, M.C.: PIM Meets Web 2.0. In: Li, Q., Spaccapietra, S., Yu, E., Olivé, A. (eds.) ER 2008. LNCS, vol. 5231, pp. 15–25. Springer, Heidelberg (2008)

20. Recordon, D., Reed, D.: OpenID 2.0: a platform for user-centric identity management. In: Proceedings of the Second ACM Workshop on Digital Identity Management (DIM 2006), pp. 11–16. ACM, New York (2006)

21. Signer, B., Norrie, M.C.: A Model and Architecture for Open Cross-Media Annotation and Link Services. Information Systems 36(3) (May 2011)

22. Stocky, T., Faaborg, A., Lieberman, H.: A commonsense approach to predictive text entry. In: CHI 2004 Extended Abstracts of CHI 2004, Vienna, Austria, April 24 -29, pp. 1163–1166. ACM, New York (2004)

23. Toda, G.A., Cortez, E., da Silva, A.S., de Moura, E.: A probabilistic approach for automatically filling form-based Web interfaces. Proc. VLDB Endow. 4(3), 151–160 (2010)

24. Wang, Y., Peng, T., Zuo, W., Li, R.: Automatic Filling Forms of Deep Web Entries Based on Ontology. In: Proceedings of the, International Conference on Web Information Systems and Mining (WISM 2009), pp. 376–380. IEEE Computer Society, Washington, DC (2009)

25. Winckler, M., Gaits, V., Vo, D.-B., Firmenich, S., Rossi, G.: An Approach and Tool Support for Assisting Users to Fill-in Web Forms with Personal Information. In: Proc. of the ACM SIGDOC 2011, Pisa, Italy, October 3-5 (2011)

26. Zhou, D., Chander, A., Inamura, H.: Optimizing user interaction for Web-based mobile tasks. In: Proceedings of the 19th International Conference on World wide Web (WWW 2010), pp. 1333–1336. ACM, New York (2010)

Model-Based Service Discovery and Orchestration for OSLC Services in Tool Chains

Matthias Biehl[1], Wenqing Gu[1,2], and Frédéric Loiret[1]

[1] Royal Institute of Technology, Stockholm, Sweden
{biehl,floiret}@md.kth.se
[2] Ericsson AB, Kista, Sweden
wenqing.gu@ericsson.com

Abstract. Globally distributed development of complex systems relies on the use of sophisticated development tools but today the tools provide only limited possibilities for integration into seamless tool chains. If development tools could be integrated, development data could be exchanged and tracing across remotely located tools would be possible and would increase the efficiency of globally distributed development. We use a domain specific modeling language to describe tool chains as models on a high level of abstraction. We use model-driven technology to synthesize the implementation of a service-oriented wrapper for each development tool based on OSLC (Open Services for Lifecyle Collaboration) and the orchestration of the services exposed by development tools. The wrapper exposes both tool data and functionality as web services, enabling platform independent tool integration. The orchestration allows us to discover remote tools via their service wrapper, integrate them and check the correctness of the orchestration.

Keywords: Service Discovery, Service Orchestration, Model-driven Development, Tool Integration.

1 Introduction

Globally distributed software development teams need tool chains that are flexible, distributed and tailored to their development processes [12]. To deal with these new requirements, modern tool chains apply the principles of service-oriented computing [8,11], which deals with the generic integration of distributed services [9]. When applying the service-oriented principles to tool integration, tools expose both their data and functionality as services; these services are orchestrated to form a tool chain. The industry initiative Open Services for Lifecycle Integration (OSLC) [15], advocates a service-oriented, RESTful [7] architecture for managing tool data.

The challenge in adopting the OSLC approach for tool integration lies in finding appropriate mechanisms for discovering the RESTful services of remotely deployed development tools and to orchestrate the RESTful services of remote

M. Brambilla, T. Tokuda, and R. Tolksdorf (Eds.): ICWE 2012, LNCS 7387, pp. 283–290, 2012.

development tools. However, there is currently no standard and no practical support for discovering and orchestrating RESTful web services [17]. Due to the lack of a high-level design language for orchestration of RESTful web services, solutions are typically directly implemented in code; an overview of the details of this challenge is provided in [16]. As a result, the orchestration of tools requires a lot of manual work. In addition, inconsistencies can only be found on code-level, which is difficult, time-consuming and expensive.

In this paper, we propose a model-based approach to address both discovery and orchestration for RESTful services in the domain of tool integration. We introduce a domain-specific modeling language for tool integration that allows us to describe both the tool chain as an orchestration of tools and the specification of the services of each tool. This specification is the basis for both the discovery of tool services and the generation of an implementation. The domain specific model allows us to perform early correctness checks between the service usage and the service definition in the service specification.

2   Approach

To close the gap between discovery and orchestration of RESTful services for OSLC tool integration, our approach interleaves service discovery and service orchestration for tool integration, as illustrated in figure 1. We propose a model-based approach, which seamlessly integrates the results of service discovery with orchestration facilities. The pivot point of this approach is the discovered ToolAdapter metamodel; it is the central connection point between the service discovery and the service orchestration.

The automated process of service discovery is displayed on the vertical axis in figure 1 and explained in section 4. Discovery automatically deduces details

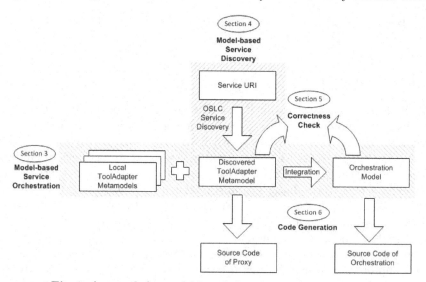

Fig. 1. Approach for model-based discovery and orchestration

of an already deployed tool adapter service, from which only a URL is known as an entry point. Discovery starts with the service URL, extracts the ToolAdapter metamodel using the OSLC *ServiceCatalogs* and *ServiceProviders* and finally generates code for the service proxies.

The process of service orchestration is displayed on the horizontal axis in figure 1 and explained in section 3. It starts with several ToolAdapter metamodels, which might be discovered or newly created and integrates the ToolAdapters into an orchestration model. The formalized ToolAdapter metamodel can even be used for verifying the discovered service definition against its usage in the orchestration model by a number of correctness checks, as described in section 5. Finally we generate code for the orchestration, as detailed in section 6.

3   Service Orchestration for Tool Integration with TIL

Tool chains are often put together in an ad-hoc manner. We promote a systematic development process, where a high-level design of the tool chain is created first. We would like to describe the design of a tool chain in such a way that all important design decisions of a tool chain can be reflected in it. This is why we apply the Tool Integration Language (TIL) [3], a domain specific modeling language for describing tool chains. TIL allows us not only to model a tool chain, but also to analyze it and generate code from it. Here we can only give a short overview of this language and for a detailed explanation of the semantics of TIL, we refer to [3].

In TIL, a tool chain is described in terms of *ToolAdapters* and the relation between them. For each tool, a *ToolAdapter* defines the set of data and functionality that is exposed by that tool in form of a ToolAdapter metamodel. The ToolAdapter metamodel is realized using EMF (Eclipse Modeling Framework)[1]. The relation between the ToolAdapters is realized by any of the following Channels: a *ControlChannel* describes a service call, a *DataChannel* describes data exchange or a *TraceChannel* describes the possibility to create traces. A trace is a link between two elements of tool data, which may reside in different tools. TIL offers three kinds of *ToolAdapters*. A *GeneratedToolAdapter* is newly created, locally deployed and the ToolAdapter metamodel is used as specification. A *BinaryToolAdapter* is included into the tool chain by locally deploying existing binaries and then binding to them. A *DiscoveredToolAdapter* is included into the tool chain by binding to an already deployed *ToolAdapter* on a remote server, it is merely specified by a URL. Realizing the binding in TIL requires a discovery process, which is described in section 4.

4   Service Discovery for Tool Integration

OSLC provides a catalog of linked metadata descriptions. The general idea is to use the catalog for remote discovery of tool adapters by following the links

---

[1] http://www.eclipse.org/modeling/emf

and parsing the metadata. We can discover the details of remotely deployed ToolAdapters that follow the OSLC specification. The key task of the discovery process is to interact with the OSLC directory services to extract a ToolAdapter metamodel. This ToolAdapter metamodel describes the data and functionality provided by the tool adapter and acts as an intermediate model in the discovery algorithm.

When parsing the OSLC metadata, we need to make some assumptions, because the OSLC catalog is not originally intended for the purpose of service discovery, but it contains useful information. The starting point for discovering services is the URI of the *ServiceProviderCatalog*. From the content of the *ServiceProviderCatalog* the algorithm follows to *ServiceProviders* and *ResourceShapes*. All these resources are described in RDF [13] and we parse them with the Jena framework[2].

- **Step 1 - Parse ServiceProviderCatalog:** By parsing the response of an HTTP-GET on the URI of the *ServiceProviderCatalog*, we can identify a set of *ServiceProvider* resources. OSLC related information concerning the *ServiceProviderCatalog* is extracted and saved. For each *ServiceProvider* resource we continue with step 2.
- **Step 2 - Data or Control Service:** We perform a GET on the URIs of all *ServiceProviders*. We make the following assumptions for OSLC directory services: data and control services are encapsulated in separate *ServiceProvider* resources. For a control *ServiceProvider* only inlined *CreationFactory* resources exist, for a data *ServiceProvider* both *CreationFactory* and *QueryCapability* resources exist. With these assumptions we can identify the correct type of *ServiceProvider* by checking if the current *ServiceProvider* contains any *QueryCapability* resources. For a data *ServiceProvider* we proceed with step 3, for a control *ServiceProvider* we proceed with step 6.
- **Step 3 - Find Data Resources:** Each inlined *CreationFactory* or *QueryCapability* property represents one data resource, however, for the name of this data resource we have to assume it is contained in the URI of the inner property *resourceShape*, *resourceType*, *creation* or *queryBase*. With the listed sequence, we anticipate the resource name by extracting the last word of the URI. We use the simplest way to anticipate the correct name, which is to select the first URI in the listed sequence. For each data resource, we check if the URI of *ResourceShape* resource is given in the response. If it is provided, details of this data resource can be constructed by parsing the *ResourceShape* given, otherwise we query one or more specific objects of this data type to anticipate the structure of the resource. We follow step 4 if the URI of *ResourceShape* is given and step 5 otherwise.
- **Step 4 - Construct Data Resource Structures by Parsing the *ResourceShape*:** Properties of the current data resource are analyzed and added to the corresponding *class* in the ToolAdapter metamodel as *attributes* or *references*. More specifically, for properties of primitive data types like *string*, *int*, etc. an *attribute* is added to the *class*. For other types we determine the referenced data type by analyzing the URI of the given *valueShape*

---

[2] http://incubator.apache.org/jena/

or *valueType* property as described in step 3 and add a corresponding *reference* to the current *class*. In OSLC, the multiplicity is described by the *occurs* property. Possible values are *Zero-or-one*, *Exactly-one*, *One-or-many* and *Zero-or-many*. After the structure of the data has been discovered, the ToolAdapter metamodel is updated.

- **Step 5 - Construct Data Resource Structures by Querying Object Details:** If there is no annotated *ResourceShape* given for a specific resource, we have to discover the structure of this resource by querying a specific instance of this data type. We obtain the list of objects by following the URI of *QueryCapability*. By analyzing the content of the response, we can obtain the attributes or references of the current data type. Since attributes are optional in RDF, we may need to query several objects, to increase the probability of acquiring a complete set of all the properties. We assume that the name of the attributes or references can be deduced from the local name in the properties of the response, and the referenced data type is directly from the local name of the resource type following the resource URI.

- **Step 6 - Find Control Resources:** By analyzing the URIs of the *creationFactory*, we can obtain a list of provided control resources. The resource name is obtained from the URI of *creation*.

- **Step 7 - Persist Discovered Tool Adapter Metamodel:** The discovery is finished and we save the discovered ToolAdapter metamodel.

5   Correctness Check

A correct and consistent TIL model is a prerequisite for the generation of correct source code that realizes the tool chain. We check the TIL model for correctness by analyzing if all service usages comply with their definitions. The definitions of the ToolAdapter services are located in the ToolAdapter metamodels. The usage of ToolAdapter services is specified in the TIL model, more specifically in the different types of Channels. The correctness check ensures that the usages of language concepts are conform to their definitions. The checks are performed early in the development process of a tool chain, on a model-level, before code is involved. Thus errors are relatively easy to detect and correct.

6   Code Generation

We describe the code generation in this section by describing (1) the chosen implementation framework, (2) the mapping of high-level concepts of TIL to the implementation and (3) the creation of proxies for DiscoveredToolAdapters.

Our approach is implemented using the Service Component Architecture (SCA) [2], a set of specifications for developing distributed Service-Oriented Architectures (SOA). SCA combines SOA principles [6] with principles of Component-Based Software Engineering (CBSE). While SOA provides the notion of loosely-coupled services, CBSE provides composability of software components.

SCA is a component model for implementing and composing heterogeneous services. We use the SCA implementation FraSCAti [19], which manages the web server infrastructure, produces the necessary glue code and also provides remote deployment, introspection and reconfiguration at runtime. SCA allows us to define RESTful services and bindings, which makes it possible to implement a tool chain according to OSLC. We found that SCA is an appropriate technology for realizing service-oriented tool chains based on OSLC.

The tool chain is an orchestration of services provided by both locally deployed *GeneratedToolAdapters* and remotely deployed *DiscoveredToolAdapters*. The latter are represented by local proxies bound to the remotely deployed tool adapter implementation. For implementing the interface we use the Service Component Architecture (SCA). By specifying the binding address of the remotely deployed ToolAdapter, SCA tool support can generate the proxy implementation that forwards calls to it. For each *DiscoveredToolAdapter* an SCA component is generated, acting as a local proxy of the discovered adapter. As a proxy, it provides the services of the ToolAdapter metamodel that were retrieved by the discovery process. The services of the local proxy are bound to the remote services provided by the remotely deployed ToolAdapters. SCA allows the specification of remote bindings that are managed transparently by the SCA runtime platform. The orchestration components are SCA components generated from the *ControlChannels* and the *DataChannels*, and bound to the proxy components according to the control and data flows they specify in the orchestration model.

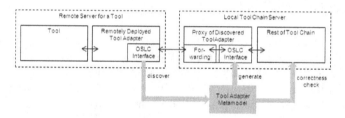

Fig. 2. Architecture of the Discovered ToolAdapter

We use the discovered ToolAdapter metamodel for generating code proxies for the ToolAdapter, which can be used to bind to the remotely deployed ToolAdapter instance. The complete ToolAdapter architecture is represented in figure 2. We distinguish between the remotely deployed ToolAdapter and the DiscoveredToolAdapter. The remotely deployed ToolAdapter already exists and is usually deployed on the same machine as the tool. In the implementation of the remotely deployed ToolAdapter, we separate the code that deals with the integration technology from the code that interacts with the tool. The external part of the remotely deployed ToolAdapter deals with the integration technology, the internal part interacts with the tool, e.g. via local APIs. The Discovered-ToolAdapter is a proxy to the remotely deployed ToolAdapter. It has the same interface as the external part of the remotely deployed ToolAdapter and its implementation merely forwards the service calls. Note that our approach is built for the case in which we do not have access to the source code of the remotely deployed ToolAdapter. The benefits of automated generation are time, effort and cost saving. They can be achieved since the developers of the ToolAdapter do not need to learn the integration technology, nor do they need to implement any code that deals with the integration technology. A model-to-text transformation automatically generates the source code of the DiscoveredToolAdapter.

7   Related Work

Related work can be found in the areas of tool integration, service discovery and orchestration. We list the approaches by fields and point out approaches that are in the intersection of both fields.

Tool Integration: Model-based integration frameworks [1] use metamodeling for describing the tool data. However, these approaches provide neither concepts to model a complete tool chain nor concepts to describe the orchestration architecture of the tool chain. Model-based tool chains are usually realized locally. Tool chains based on the integration framework ModelBus [11] may be distributed. ModelBus uses the SOAP protocol, so discovery, orchestration and correctness checks can be performed.

Service Discovery and Orchestration: Web services based on SOAP [20] are usually described using WSDL (Web Service Description Language) [5]. WSDL is a W3C standard and is widely supported. In order to orchestrate WSDL-based web services, typically BPEL (Business Process Execution Language) [14] is used. The discovery and orchestration of RESTful web services is not equally well supported. The current BPEL 2.0 only supports WSDL 1.1, which is incompatible with RESTful services. RESTful web services can be described in WADL [10] and WSDL 2.0 [4], which is currently not supported by BPEL. Even if the next version of BPEL will support WSDL 2.0, a lot of manual work is required to consume the RESTful services provided, since the burden of creating the WSDL file has shifted from the service supplier to the BPEL designer. The reason is that no WSDL descriptions are provided by the RESTful service supplier. The main alternative is manual coding of the orchestration. A number of approaches for the orchestration of RESTful services have recently been proposed. The extension BPEL for REST [17] and the language Bite [18] have been developed for integration of RESTful services. In SCA, the binding of RESTful web services is possible, however a common Java interface must be used to invoke the web services. The added value of our approach is the domain specific support for OSLC, the correctness check of the orchestration and the code generation facilities.

8   Future Work and Conclusion

In the future we would like to improve the precision of the discovery algorithm and perform additional case studies of tool chains for different development processes. The cornerstone of this approach is the language TIL that describes both the orchestration of ToolAdapters and the ToolAdapter as models. The discovery algorithm finds the details of an initially unknown ToolAdapter and represents them as a model. Both the orchestration and the results of the discovery are models, which allows us to verify their compatibility and correctness. As a consequence of this automated support for discovery, orchestration and correctness checks, distributed tool chains can be built faster and with less errors.

References

1. Amelunxen, C., Klar, F., Königs, A., Rötschke, T., Schürr, A.: Metamodel-based tool integration with MOFLON. In: ICSE 2008, pp. 807–810 (2008)
2. Beisiegel, M.: Service Component Architecture, Tech. Rep (November 2007)
3. Biehl, M., El-Khoury, J., Loiret, F., Törngren, M.: A domain specific language for generating tool integration solutions. In: MDTPI 2011 (June 2011)
4. Chinnici, R., Moreau, J.J., Ryman, A., Weerawarana, S.: Web services description language (WSDL) version 2.0 W3C, 26 (2007)
5. Christensen, E., Curbera, F., Meredith, G., Weerawarana, S.: Web service definition language (WSDL). Technical report, W3C (March 2001)
6. Erl, T.: SOA Principles of Service Design. Prentice Hall (July 2007)
7. Fielding, R.T.: Architectural Styles and the Design of Network-based Software Architectures. PhD thesis, University of California, Irvine (2000)
8. Frost, R.: Jazz and the Eclipse way of collaboration. IEEE Software (2007)
9. Gilmore, S., Gönczy, L., Koch, N., Mayer, P., Tribastone, M., Varró, D.: Non-functional properties in the MDD of SOS. In: SoSyM (2011)
10. Hadley, M.J.: Web application description language (WADL). W3C (2006)
11. Hein, C., Ritter, T., Wagner, M.: Model-Driven tool integration with ModelBus. In: Workshop Future Trends of Model-Driven Development (2009)
12. Herbsleb, J.D.: Global software engineering: The future of socio-technical coordination. In: FOSE 2007 (2007)
13. Klyne, G., Carroll, J.: RDF: Concepts and abstract syntax (2004)
14. OASIS. Web Services Business Process Execution Language, WSBPEL (2007)
15. OSLC Workgroup. OSLC Core Specification, version 2.0 (2010)
16. Pautasso, C.: On Composing RESTful Services. In: Software Service Engineering (2009)
17. Pautasso, C.: RESTful web service composition with BPEL for REST. Data Knowledge Engineering (2009)
18. Rosenberg, F., Curbera, F., Duftler, M.J., Khalaf, R.: Composing RESTful Services and Collaborative Workflows: A Lightweight Approach. IEEE Internet Computing (2008)
19. Seinturier, L., Merle, P., Rouvoy, R., Romero, D., Schiavoni, V., Stefani, J.: A Component-Based Middleware Platform for Reconfigurable Service-Oriented Architectures. In: Software: Practice and Experience (2011)
20. W3C. Simple Object Access Protocol (SOAP) 1.2. W3C (2007)

On the Systematic Development
of Domain-Specific Mashup Tools for End Users

Muhammad Imran, Stefano Soi, Felix Kling, Florian Daniel, Fabio Casati,
and Maurizio Marchese

Department of Information Engineering and Computer Science
University of Trento, Via Sommarive 5, 38123, Trento, Italy
lastname@disi.unitn.it

Abstract. The recent emergence of mashup tools has refueled research
on *end user development*, i.e., on enabling end-users without programming skills to compose their own applications. Yet, similar to what hap-
pened with analogous promises in web service composition and business
process management, research has mostly focused on technology and, as a
consequence, has failed its objective. In this paper, we propose a *domain-
specific* approach to mashups that is aware of the terminology, concepts,
rules, and conventions (the domain) the user is comfortable with. We
show what developing a domain-specific mashup tool means, which role
the mashup meta-model and the domain model play and how these can
be merged into a domain-specific mashup meta-model. We exemplify the
approach by implementing a mashup tool for a specific domain (research
evaluation) and describe the respective user study. The results of the
user study confirm that domain-specific mashup tools indeed lower the
entry barrier to mashup development.

1 Introduction

Mashups are typically simple web applications that, rather than being coded
from scratch, are developed by integrating and reusing available data, functionalities, or pieces of user interfaces accessible over the Web. **Mashup tools**, i.e.,
online development and runtime environments for mashups, ambitiously aim
at enabling non-programmers to develop their own applications. The mashup
platforms developed so far either expose too much functionality and too many
technicalities, so that they are powerful and flexible but suitable only for programmers, or only allow compositions that are so simple to be of little use
for most practical applications. Yet, being amenable to non-programmers is increasingly important, as the opportunity given by the wide range of applications
available online and the increased flexibility that is required in both businesses
and personal life management raise the need for situational applications.

We believe that **the heart of the problem** is that it is impractical to design
tools that are *generic enough* to cover a wide range of application domains, *powerful enough* to enable the specification of non-trivial logic, and *simple enough*
to be actually accessible to non-programmers. At some point, we need to give

M. Brambilla, T. Tokuda, and R. Tolksdorf (Eds.): ICWE 2012, LNCS 7387, pp. 291–298, 2012.
© Springer-Verlag Berlin Heidelberg 2012

up something. In our view, this something is generality. Giving up generality in practice means narrowing the focus of a design tool to a well-defined *domain* and tailoring the tool's development paradigm, models, language, and components to the specific needs of that domain only.

As an example, in this paper we report on a mashup platform we specifically developed for the domain of research evaluation, that is, for the assessment of the performance of researchers, groups of researchers, departments, universities, and similar. There are no commonly accepted criteria for performing such analysis in general, and evaluation is highly subjective. Computing evaluation metrics that go beyond the commonly adopted h-index is still a complex, manual task that is not adequately supported by software instruments. In fact, computing an own metric may require extracting, combining, and processing data from multiple sources, implementing new algorithms, visually representing the results, and similar. In addition, the people involved in research evaluation are not necessarily IT experts and, hence, they may not be able to perform such IT-intensive tasks without help. In fact, we may need to extract, combine, and process data from multiple sources and render the information via visual components, a task that has all the characteristics of a data mashup.

In this paper, we champion the notion of **domain-specific mashup tools** and describe what they are composed of, how they can be developed, how they can be extended for the specificity of any particular application context, and how they can be used by non-programmers to develop complex mashup logics within the boundaries of one domain. Specifically, (1) we provide a *methodology* for the development of domain-specific mashup tools, defining the necessary concepts and design artifacts; (2) we detail and exemplify all *design artifacts* that are necessary to implement a domain-specific mashup tool; (3) we apply the methodology in the context of an *example mashup platform* that aims to support research evaluation, (4) we perform a *user study* in order to assess the viability of the developed platform.

Next we outline the methodology we follow to implement the domain-specific mashup tool. In Section 3 we briefly describe the actual implementation of our prototype tool, and in Section 4 we report on our preliminary user study. In Section 5, we review related works. We conclude the paper in Section 6.

2   Methodology

Our development of a specific mashup platform for research evaluation has allowed us to conceptualize the necessary tasks and to structure them into the following **methodology** steps:

1. Definition of a *domain concept model* (CM) to express domain data and relationships. The domain concepts tell the mashup platform what kind of *data objects* it must support. This is different from generic mashup platforms, which provide support for generic data formats, not specific data objects.
2. Identification of a generic *mashup meta-model* (MM) that suits the composition needs of the domain. A variety of different mashup approaches, i.e.,

meta-models, have emerged over the last years and before focusing about domain-specific features, it is important to identify a meta-model that accommodates the domain processes to be mashed up.

3. Definition of a *domain-specific mashup meta-model*. Given a generic MM, the next step is understanding how to inject the domain into it. We approach this by specifying and developing:

   (a) A *domain process model* (PM) that expresses classes of domain activities and, possibly, ready processes. Domain activities and processes represent the dynamic aspect of the domain.

   (b) A *domain syntax* that provides each concept in the domain-specific mashup meta-model (the union of MM and PM) with its own symbol. Domain concepts and activities must be represented by visual metaphors conveying their meaning to domain experts.

   (c) A set of *instances of domain-specific components*. This is the step in which the reusable domain-knowledge is encoded, in order to enable domain experts to mash it up into new applications.

4. *Implementation* of the domain-specific mashup tool (DMT) as a tool whose expressive power is that of the domain-specific mashup meta-model and that is able to host and integrate the domain-specific activities and processes.

In the next subsections, we expand each of these steps.

2.1   The Domain Concept Model

The **domain concept model (CM)** is obtained via interactions between an IT expert and a domain expert. We represent it as ER diagram or XSD schema. It describes the *conceptual entities* and the *relationships* among them, which, together, constitute the domain knowledge. For example in the chosen domain we have *researchers, publications, conferences, metrics, etc.* The core element in the evaluation of scientific production and quality is the *publication*, which is typically published in the context of a specific *venue*, e.g., a conference or journal, and printed by a *publisher*. It is written by one or more *researchers* belonging to an *institution*.

2.2   The Generic Mashup Meta-model

We first define a generic mashup meta-model, which may fit a variety of different domains, then we show how to define the domain-specific mashup meta-model, which will allow us to draw domain-specific mashup models. Specifically, the generic **mashup meta-model (MM)** specifies a *class* of mashups and, thereby, the *expressive power*, i.e., the concepts and composition paradigms, a mashup platform must know in order to support the development of that class of mashups. Thus the MM implicitly specifies the expressive power of the mashup platform class. Identifying the right features of the mashups that fit a given domain is therefore crucial. For our domain, we start from a very simple MM, both in terms of notation and execution semantics, which enables end-users to model their own mashups. Indeed, it can be fully specified in one page:

- A **mashup** $m = \langle C, P, VP, L \rangle$, consists of a set of *components* C, a set of data *pipes* P, a set of view ports VP that can host and render components with own UI, and a *layout* L that specifies the graphical arrangement of components.
- A **component** $c = \langle IPT, OPT, CPT, type, desc \rangle$, where $c \in C$, is like a task that performs some data, application, or UI action. Components have *ports* through which pipes are connected. Ports can be divided in *input* (IPT) and *output* ports (OPT), where input ports carry data into the component, while output ports carry data generated by the component. Each component must have at least either an input or an output port. Components with no input ports are called *information sources*. Components with no output ports are called *information sinks*. Components with both input and output ports are called *information processors.Configuration* ports (CPT) are used to configure the components. They are typically used to configure filters or to define the nature of a query on a data source. The configuration data can be a constant (e.g., a parameter defined by the end user) or can arrive in a pipe from another component. Conceptually, constant configurations are as if they come from a component feeding a constant value. The type $(type)$ of the components denotes whether they are *UI components*, which display data and can be rendered in the mashup, or *application components*, which either fetch or process information. Components can also have a description *desc* at an arbitrary level of formalization, whose purpose is to inform the user about the data the components handle and produce.
- A **pipe** $p \in P$ carries data (e.g., XML documents) between the ports of two components, implementing a data flow logic. So, $p \in IPT \times (OPT \cup CPT)$.
- A **view port** $vp \in VP$ identifies a place holder, e.g., a DIV element or an IFRAME, inside the HTML template that gives the mashup its graphical identity. Typically, a template has multiple place holders.
- Finally, the **layout** L defines which component with own UI is to be rendered in which view port of the template. Therefore $l \in C \times VP$.

In the model above there are *no variables* and *no data mappings*. This is at the heart of enabling end-user development as this is where much of the complexity resides. It is unrealistic to ask end-users to perform data mapping operations. Because there is a CM, each component is required to be able to process any document that conforms to the model.

The **operational semantics** of the MM is as follows: execution of the mashup is *initiated* by the user. All the components that are *ready* for execution are identified. A component is ready when all the input and configuration ports are filled with data, that is, they have all necessary data to start processing. All ready components are *executed*. They process the data in input ports, consuming the respective data items form the input feed, and generate output on their output ports. The execution proceeds by identifying ready components and executing them, until there are no components to be executed left.

Developing mashups based on this meta-model, i.e., graphically composing a mashup in a mashup tool, requires defining a **syntax** for the concepts in the

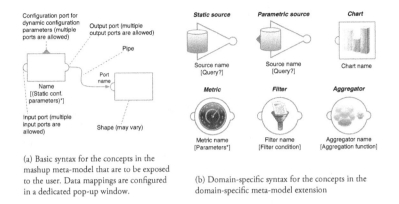

(a) Basic syntax for the concepts in the mashup meta-model that are to be exposed to the user. Data mappings are configured in a dedicated pop-up window.

(b) Domain-specific syntax for the concepts in the domain-specific meta-model extension

Fig. 1. Generic and domain-specific syntax for research evaluation

MM. In Figure 1(a) we map the above MM to a basic set of generic graphical symbols and composition rules. In the next section, we show how to configure domain-specific symbols.

2.3   The Domain-Specific Mashup Meta-model

The mashup meta-model (MM) described in the previous section allows the definition of a class of mashups that can fit into different domains. Thus, it is not yet tailored to a specific domain. Now we want to push the domain into the mashup meta-model. The next step is therefore understanding the dynamics of the concepts in the model, that is, the typical classes of processes and activities that are performed by domain experts. What we obtain from this is a *domain-specific mashup meta-model*. Each domain-specific meta-model is a specialization of the mashup meta-model along three dimensions: (i) domain-specific activities and processes, (ii) domain-specific syntax, and (iii) domain instances.

The ***domain process model (PM)*** describes the classes of *processes* or *activities* that the domain expert may want to mash up to implement composite, domain-specific processes. Operatively, the PM is again derived by specializing the generic meta-model based on interactions with domain experts. This time the topic of the interaction is aimed at defining classes of components, their interactions and notations. In the case of research evaluation, this led to the identification of the following classes of activities, i.e., classes of components: *source extraction*, *metric computation*, *filtering*, and *aggregation* activities.

A possible ***domain-specific syntax*** for the classes in the PM is shown in Figure 1(b). Its semantic is the one described by the MM in Section 2.2.

A set of ***instances*** of domain activities must be implemented, providing concrete mashup components. For example, the *Microsoft Academic Publications* component is an instance of *source extraction* activity with a configuration port (*SetResearchers*) that allows the setup of the researchers for which publications are to be loaded from Microsoft Academic.

3   The ResEval Mash Tool

The ResEval Mash platform is composed of two parts, i.e., client side and server side. The heart of the platform is the *mashup execution engine* on the client side, which support client-side processing, that is, it controls data processing on the server from the client. The engine is responsible for running a mashup composition, triggering the component's actions and managing the communication between client and server. The client side *composition editor* (shown in Figure 2) provides the mashup canvas and a list of components from which users can drag and drop components onto the canvas and connect them. The composition editor implements the *domain-specific mashup meta-model* and exposes it through the *domain syntax*. The platform also comes with a *component registration interface* for developers to set up and configure new components for the platform. On the server side, we have a set of RESTful web services, i.e., the *components services, authentication services, components and composition repository services*, and *shared memory services*. Components services allow the invocation of those components whose business logic is implemented as a server-side web service. These web services, together with the client-side components, implement the *domain process model*. Authentication services are used for user authentication and authorization. Components and composition repository services enable CRUD operations for components and compositions. Shared memory services provide an interface for external web services (i.e., services which are not deployed on our platform) to use the shared memory. The *shared memory manager* provides and manages a space for each mashup execution instance on the server side. The *common data model (CDM) module* implements the *domain concept model* (CM) and supports the checking of data types in the system. CDM configures itself using an XSD (i.e., an XML schema representing domain concept model). All services are managed by a *server side engine*, which fulfills all requests coming from the client side. A demo of ResEval Mash is described in [3] and a prototype is available online at `http://open.reseval.org/`.

4   User Study and Evaluation

In order to evaluate our domain-specific mashup approach, we conducted a user study with 10 users. Participants covering a broad range of domain and technical expertise were invited to use ResEval Mash. At the beginning participants were asked to fill in a questionnaire reporting their computing skills and to watch a video tutorial followed by a set of tasks to complete.

Overall, the tool was deemed to be usable and the participants were comfortable using it. Independently of their level of computing knowledge, all participants were able to accomplish the tasks with minimal or no help at all. The only visible difference was a different level of confidence in task execution. IT experts appeared to be more confident during the test. The results of our study indicate real potential for the domain-specific mashup approach to allow people with no computing skills to create their own applications. The definition of the

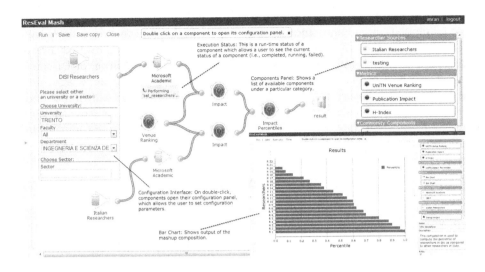

Fig. 2. Composition editor and example mashup output

mappings among the components, which is a well-acknowledged problem known form several user studies of EUD tools [6], did not occur at all in the our study. This preliminary study suggests that ResEval Mash is a successful tool appealing to both expert programmers and end-users with no computing skills.

5   Related Work

The idea of focusing on a particular domain and exploiting its specificities to create more effective and simpler development environments is supported by a large number of research works [5,1]. Mainly these areas are related to Domain Specific Modeling (DSM) and Domain Specific Language (DSL). In DSM, domain concepts, rules, and semantics are represented by one or more models, which are then translated into executable code. Managing these models can be a complex task that is typically suited only to programmers but that, however, increases his/her productivity. In the DSL context, although we can find solutions targeting end users (e.g., Excel macros) and medium skilled users (e.g., MatLab), most of the current DSLs target expert developers (e.g., Swashup [4]). Also here the introduction of the "domain" raises the abstraction level, but the typical textual nature of these languages makes them less intuitive and harder to manage and less suitable for end users compared to visual approaches. Benefits and limits of the DSM and DSL approaches are summarized in [1] and [5].

Web mashups [8] have emerged as an approach to provide easier ways to connect together services and data sources available on the Web [2], together with the claim to target non-programmers. Yahoo! Pipes (`http://pipes.yahoo.com`), for instance, provides an intuitive visual editor that allows the design of data processing logics. Support for UI integration is missing, and support for service integration is still poor while it provides only generic programming features (e.g., feed manipulation, looping) and typically require basic programming knowledge. The CRUISe project [7] specifically focuses on composability and context-aware presentation of UIs, but does not support the seamless integration of UI components with web services. The ServFace project (http://www.servface.eu), instead, aims to support normal web users in composing semantically annotated web services. The result is a simple, user-driven web service orchestration tool, but UI integration and process logic definitions are rather limited and again basic programming knowledge is still required.

6   Status and Lessons Learned

The work described in this paper resulted from actual needs within our university and within the context of an EU project, which were not yet met by current technology. It also resulted from the observation that in general composition technologies failed to a large extent to strike the right balance between ease of use and expressive power. They define seemingly useful abstractions and tools, but in the end developers still prefer to use (textual) programming languages, and, at the same time, domain experts are not able to understand and use them. What we have pursued in our work is, in essence, to constrain the language to the domain (but not in general in terms of expressive power) and to provide a domain-specific notation so that it becomes easier to use and in particular does not require users to deal with one of the most complex aspect of process modeling (at least for end-users), that of data mappings.

References

1. France, R., Rumpe, B.: Domain specific modeling. Software and Systems Modeling 4, 1–3 (2005)
2. Hartmann, B., Doorley, S., Klemmer, S.: Hacking, Mashing, Gluing: A Study of Opportunistic Design and Development. Pervasive Computing 7(3), 46–54 (2006)
3. Imran, M., Kling, F., Soi, S., Daniel, F., Casati, F., Marchese, M.: ResEval Mash: A Mashup Tool for Advanced Research Evaluation. In: Proceedings of WWW 2012, pp. 361–364 (2012)
4. Maximilien, E.M., Wilkinson, H., Desai, N., Tai, S.: A Domain-Specific Language for Web APIs and Services Mashups. In: Krämer, B.J., Lin, K.-J., Narasimhan, P. (eds.) ICSOC 2007. LNCS, vol. 4749, pp. 13–26. Springer, Heidelberg (2007)
5. Mernik, M., Heering, J., Sloane, A.M.: When and how to develop domain-specific languages. ACM Comput. Surv. 37(4), 316–344 (2005)
6. Namoun, A., Nestler, T., De Angeli, A.: Service Composition for Non Programmers: Prospects, Problems, and Design Recommendations. In: Proceedings of ECOWS, pp. 123–130. IEEE (2010)
7. Pietschmann, S., Voigt, M., Rümpel, A., Meißner, K.: CRUISe: Composition of Rich User Interface Services. In: Gaedke, M., Grossniklaus, M., Díaz, O. (eds.) ICWE 2009. LNCS, vol. 5648, pp. 473–476. Springer, Heidelberg (2009)
8. Yu, J., Benatallah, B., Casati, F., Daniel, F.: Understanding Mashup Development. IEEE Internet Computing 12, 44–52 (2008)

Adding Non-functional Preferences to Service Discovery

Fernando Lemos[1], Daniela Grigori[2], and Mokrane Bouzeghoub[1]

[1] Versailles University, 45 Av. des États Unis 78000 Versailles, France
{fernando.lemos,mokrane.bouzeghoub}@prism.uvsq.fr
[2] Paris-Dauphine Univ., Pl. Maréchal de Lattre de Tassigny 75775 Paris, France
daniela.grigori@dauphine.fr

Abstract. The growth of the number of published services rendered searching for a specific service within repositories a critical issue. In this paper, we present an approach to extend structure-based service discovery by making it sensitive to user preferences over service quality defined at different granularity levels of the service structure.

Keywords: Web services, QoS, preferences, process model matching.

1 Introduction

In the last years, the number of published services has been increasingly growing since more and more organizations invested on service management practices. However, this growth rendered searching for a specific service within repositories a critical issue for the success of service computing in general. For the functional aspect of the search, some approaches allow users to detail the process model (PM) describing the structure of the requested service, and thus PM matching techniques have been proposed to find the services best matching the query. However, current PM matching approaches [1,2] still return a large number of services offering similar functionalities [2]. On the non-functional aspect of the search, non-functional requirements such as quality preferences (e.g., response time) are one way to discriminate between structurally similar services. Nevertheless, current works consider Web services as black boxes, limiting the approaches to the profile level [3,4,5], which is not sufficient and do not fulfill user needs as non-functional aspects can be *hidden within the specification of the service structure*.

In our vision, service discovery should be based on both structural specification and non-functional aspects of services. Targeting this goal poses challenges at two levels. (i) At the description level, provide a formal model that allows one to specify, at different granularity levels, non-functional attributes as annotations of the functional specification; and allow the user to enrich his query with (required and preferred) non-functional requirements. (ii) At the discovery level, define a similarity measure aggregating both functional and non-functional similarities and provide algorithms combining the structural matching and the non-functional matching.

M. Brambilla, T. Tokuda, and R. Tolksdorf (Eds.): ICWE 2012, LNCS 7387, pp. 299–306, 2012.

In this work, we extend service matching algorithms based on the PM specification by making them sensitive to user preferences concerning service quality. Our contributions to the above challenges are: (i) we extend the PM representing service structure with adornments for non-functional factors. Each annotation is defined either at the activity level or at level of the service itself. The user query is also a PM complemented with a set of selection clauses, which are defined either as required or preferred criteria in order to avoid empty or overloading answers. (ii) The service discovery is seen as a matching process between the user query PM and a target PM, in which, at the different stages, quality preferences are taken into account. To the best of our knowledge, there is no other approach addressing user preferences on quality factors in the service matching process.

Section 2 presents our model. Section 3 details our approach and experimental results. Section 4 discusses related works. Section 5 concludes the paper.

2   Abstract Representation of Service Process Model

Process models consists of a set of atomic activities, combined using control flow structures to construct complex processes. To abstract from a specific PM description language (e.g., WS-BPEL and OWL-S) and provide a broader general approach, we introduce a graph-based model, as follows. A **process model** is a directed labeled graph $G = (V, E)$, where V is a set of activities and connector nodes and E is a set of edges. An **activity node** is described by its name, inputs and outputs. **Connector nodes** are: *(i) start* or *end*, representing the beginning or the termination of the process execution, respectively; (ii) *AND-split*, triggering all of its outgoing concurrent branches that are synchronized by a corresponding (iii) *AND-join*; (iv) *XOR-split*, representing a choice between one of several alternative branches that are merged by a corresponding (v) *XOR-join*.

For example, the service PM graph depicted in Figure 1(a) converts common types of documents to PDF. It receives as input a file and its extension and executes a pre-flight activity to check whether the file can be converted. If so, *createPDF* activity converts the file to PDF and activity *createLink* returns a link so user can download the converted file. Otherwise, an error message is sent.

QoS information is added by service providers as graph **annotations** of the form (m, r), where r is a value for a QoS attribute m. They can characterize the service as a whole (**profile annotations**) or specific activities (**activity annotations**). Figure 1(a) shows the previous service PM graph adorned with the profile annotations a_1 and a_2 indicating the cost and response time and several activity annotations a_3 to a_9 indicating the response time, reliability and security. We precise that service PMs are considered to be already annotated with QoS attributes by their providers using techniques like in [6].

Providers can also define aggregation functions to automatically calculate global QoS information from activity annotations. An **aggregation function** is a function of the form $f_{[m]} : G \rightarrow R$, where m is a QoS attribute, G is a PM graph and R is a set of atomic values. We denote by F the **set of aggregation functions**. Specifications of such functions can be found in [6].

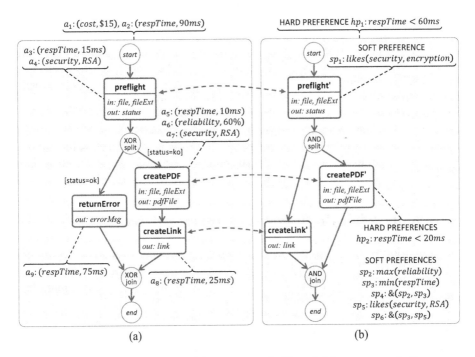

Fig. 1. Mapping between (a) target graph T_1 and (b) query graph Q_1

A user query is specified by (i) a PM graph describing structural requirements and (ii) a set of preferences describing QoS requirements, which are defined for the service as a whole (**profile preferences**) or for specific activities (**activity preferences**). Preferences can also be: (i) **hard**, when they must be satisfied and they are specified as relational expressions of the form (m, o, r), where o is a relational operator and r is a value for QoS attribute m[1]; or (ii) **soft**, when their satisfaction is optional, but desirable.

A soft preference is specified using a subset of the preference constructors proposed by *Preference SQL* [7], one of the first ones to provide a declarative and semantically intuitive model of preferences. The constructors are: (i) *around* $(m, r_{desired})$: it favors the value $r_{desired}$ for attribute m; otherwise, it favors those close to $r_{desired}$; (ii) *between* (m, r_{low}, r_{up}): it favors the values inside the interval $[r_{low}, r_{up}]$; otherwise, it favors those close to the limits; (iii) *max* (m): it favors the highest value; otherwise, the closest value to the maximum is favored; (iv) *min* (m): it favors the lowest value; otherwise, the closest value to the minimum is favored; (v) *likes* $(m, r_{desired})$: it favors the value $r_{desired}$; otherwise, any other value is accepted; (vi) *dislikes* $(m, r_{undesired})$: it favors the values different from $r_{undesired}$; otherwise, $r_{undesired}$ is accepted; (vii) $\otimes (p_i, p_j)$: it states that the soft preferences p_i and p_j are equally important; (viii) $\& (p_i, p_j)$: it states that the soft preference p_i is more important than the soft preference p_j.

---

[1] *We abstract from the different units in which a value can be described.*

Preference SQL distinguishes two types of preferences: *atomic* (*around*, *between*, *max*, *min*, *likes* and *dislikes*) and *complex* ($\otimes$ and &). It also distinguishes two types of atomic preferences: *numerical* (*around*, *between*, *max* and *min*) and *non-numerical* (*likes* and *dislikes*). In this work, the values in non-numerical preferences are taken from a global ontology O given by the user. As specified, complex preferences can be defined over existent complex preferences.

Figure 1(b) shows a sample user query annotated with hard and soft preferences: (i) the profile preference hp_1 indicates the response time must be less than 60 ms; (ii) the soft preference sp_2 indicates that user prefers services having activity B with maximal reliability; (iii) the complex preference sp_4 indicates that to satisfy preference sp_2 is more important than the satisfaction of sp_3.

3   Dealing with Preferences in Service Discovery

The evaluation of query preferences is strongly dependent of a structural mapping between the PMs of query and target services, as described in Subsections 3.1 and 3.2. An important class of solutions to the problem of finding a mapping between PMs is that of *approximate matching* algorithms [1,2], that allow to find target PMs similar to user query. Early approaches of this class reduce the problem to the discovery of a (sub) graph isomorphism between two PMs [2].

Our recent work [2] proposes an algorithm based on state-space searching to discover the best mapping between two PM graphs. To reduce the space search, a *pruning function* is proposed. The returned mapping has a *structural similarity* SS that defines a total order between targets [2], but cannot distinguish between graphs having similar structure and different quality. Moreover, targets very similar to the query and better satisfying the preferences should top the ranking. For these reasons, we extend the PM matching by: (i) evaluating hard preferences during the matching task to reduce the space-search; and (ii) evaluating the soft preferences to rank potential graphs considering structural and quality aspects.

3.1   Evaluating Hard Preferences in Service Matching

The evaluation of query profile preferences against target profile annotations may reduce the number of target service PMs to be matched. However, the structural mapping between query and target may "change" some profile attributes. For example, by considering the matching between Q_1 and T_1 in Figure 1, found by a matching algorithm like in [2], the trace containing activity *returnError* will never be consumed (executed). Thus, recalculating the response time of T_1 ignoring activity *returnError* gives 50 ms. According to the profile preference hp_1, if the recalculation had not been done, T_1 would be discarded.

The recalculation of profile annotations is done over the target's *consumable graph*, which is a graph containing only the consumable paths of the target according to its structural mapping with the query. More formally, a **consumable graph** of a graph G w.r.t. to a mapping M is the graph obtained by eliminating from each block b of G the branches containing no activity mapped by M.

A **block** is any subgraph limited to a split node, its respective join node and the branches between them. Therefore, our algorithm is composed of two steps:

Step 1: Evaluation of Hard Activity Preferences. The first step in evaluating the hard preferences of a query activity is to discover the target activity that semantically corresponds to it. For this, we propose to extend the pruning technique of the PM matching algorithm described in [2] to also discard non-promising mappings according to hard preferences. Thus, a target activity semantically equivalent to a query activity must also satisfy all the hard preferences of the query activity. Given an activity hard preference $hp = (m, o, r)$ and a target annotation $a = (m, v)$, a satisfies hp iff the expression (v, o, r) is true.

Step 2: Evaluation of Hard Profile Preferences. Once a target satisfying all activity preferences is discovered, its hard profile preferences are evaluated. The evaluation algorithm (i) recalculates the profile annotations using the consumable graph and the aggregation functions, and then (ii) checks if all hard profile preferences are satisfied by the target profile annotations. In Figure 1, the consumable graph of T_1 satisfies all the hard preferences of Q_1.

3.2   Dealing with Soft Preferences in Service Selection

The *satisfaction degree* (δ) is our metric to define how well the annotations of a target satisfy the soft preferences of a user query. First, we calculate the satisfaction degree between each soft atomic preference and its corresponding annotation. Then, we aggregate the satisfaction degrees of atomic preferences according to the order of importance defined by the complex preferences.

The **Evaluation of Soft Atomic Preferences** depends on their type. For a numerical preference p, given its corresponding annotation $a = (m, r)$, the satisfaction degree $\delta(p, a)$ between them is given by the equation $\delta(p, a) = 1/(1+d(p,a))$. This equation normalizes the *Satisfaction Distance* $d(p, a)$, which measures how far is the value r in annotation a from those favored by preference p. The satisfaction distance depends on the type of p as described in Table 1.

For non-numerical preferences, the satisfaction degree is based on the semantic similarity between concepts given by $wp(O_G, c_1, c_2)$, where c_1 and c_2 are the concepts to be compared according to an ontology O_G. Among the similarity metrics defined in the literature [8], we applied the classic edge counting technique proposed in [9]. Given a non-numerical preference p and an annotation a, the satisfaction degree $\delta(p, a)$ between them is presented in Table 2.

Based on the mapping of Figure 1 and on the ontology in Figure 2, the satisfaction degrees of soft preferences of query Q_1 are $\delta(sp_1, a_4) = 1$, $\delta(sp_2, a_6) = 0.03$, $\delta(sp_3, a_5) = 0.09$ and $\delta(sp_5, a_7) = 1$, where $d(sp_2, a_6) = 40$ and $d(sp_3, a_5) = 10$.

The **Evaluation of Soft Complex Preferences** aims, at first, to assign weights to the satisfaction degrees of atomic preferences to capture the order of importance defined by complex preferences. Then, these weighted degrees are aggregated to provide the satisfaction degree between the query and the target. The evaluation the complex preferences is composed of the following steps:

Table 1. Satisfaction distance of numerical preference p w.r.t. annotation $a = (m, r)$

Numerical Preference p	Satisfaction Distance $d(p, a)$
$around\,(m, r_{desired})$	$d(p, a) = |r - r_{desired}|$
$between\,(m, r_{low}, r_{up})$	$d(p, a) = \begin{cases} 0, & r \in [low, up] \\ low - r, & r < low \\ r - up, & r > up \end{cases}$
$max\,(m)$	$d(p, a) = r_{max} - r$, where r_{max} is the highest value
$min\,(m)$	$d(p, a) = r - r_{min}$, where r_{min} is the lowest value

Table 2. Satisfaction degree of non-numerical preference p w.r.t. annotation $a = (m, r)$

Non-numerical Preference p	Satisfaction Degree $\delta(p, a)$
$likes\,(m, r_{desired})$	$\delta(p, a) = \begin{cases} 1, & r_{desired} = r \\ 1, & r_{desired} \text{ subsumes } r \\ wp(O_G, r_{desired}, r), & otherwise \end{cases}$
$dislikes\,(m, r_{undesired})$	$\delta(p, a) = 1 - likes\,(m, r_{undesired})$

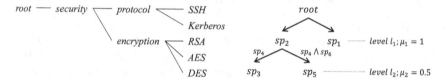

Fig. 2. Sample Security ontology   **Fig. 3.** Preference tree of query Q_1

Step 1. We construct a *preference tree* t_{sp} whose nodes represent atomic preferences, edges represent a *prioritized* ($\&$) preference, from parent to child, and each level l_i of the tree has weight $\mu_i = 1/i$. We denote by $p.l$ the level assigned to preference p. We consider that user has not defined any contradictory preference.

The construction of the tree first addresses each preference $\&\,(p_i, p_j)$ by (i) if $p_i.l = null$, then $p_i.l \leftarrow l_1$ and $p_j.l \leftarrow l_2$, and (ii) if $p_i.l \neq null$, then $p_j \leftarrow p_i.l+1$. Next, it evaluates each preference $\otimes\,(p_i, p_j)$ by applying the following rules:

Rule 1: $p_i.l \neq null \wedge p_j.l = null$ then $p_j.l \leftarrow p_i.l$; *Rule 2:* $p_i.l = null \wedge p_j.l \neq null$ then $p_i.l \leftarrow p_j.l$; *Rule 3:* $p_i.l = null \wedge p_j.l = null$ then $p_i.l \leftarrow l_1$ and $p_j.l \leftarrow l_1$; *Rule 4:* $p_i.l \neq null \wedge p_j.l \neq null$ then: (a) $p_i.l < p_j.l$ then $p_j.l \leftarrow p_i.l$ and the levels of p_j descendants are updated accordingly; (b) $p_j.l < p_i.l$ then $p_i.l \leftarrow p_j.l$ and the levels of p_j descendants are updated accordingly; *Rule 5:* level l_1 is assigned to remaining preferences. Figure 3 shows the tree of Q_1.

Step 2. The satisfaction degree between a query Q and a target T w.r.t. a mapping M is given by $\delta(Q, T, M) = \sum_{p \in S_{sp}} \delta(p, a) \times \mu_{p.l} / \sum_{p \in S_{sp}} \mu_{p.l}$, where a is the annotation corresponding to the QoS attribute of preference p. This equation is a sum of the satisfaction degrees of atomic preferences affected by the weights of their levels in the tree. In our example, $\delta(Q_1, T_1, M_1) = 0.53$.

3.3   Service Ranking Based on Structural and Quality Aspects

Two classic methods are used to order the potential targets of a given query according to structural and quality aspects. The first is the *lexicographic order*: targets are ordered according to the structural similarity degree SS and the preference satisfaction degree is used to break ties. The second is the *weighted average* $wa\,(TQ, M) = \mu_{SS} \times SS\,(M) + (1 - \mu_{SS}) \times \delta\,(Q, T, M)$, where $0 < \mu_{SS} < 1$ is the weight assigned to the semantic similarity degree. The user can specify the contribution of each degree to the calculation of the overall similarity.

3.4   Preliminary Experimental Results

To evaluate our approach, we implemented a prototype on top of the service matching platform proposed by [2]. Our experiments considered 64 services of average size of 15 activities and providing 12 quality properties. The first experiments measured the evaluation time of (i) hard preferences in the matching algorithm and (ii) soft preferences after the matching step. In both cases, the extra time represents less than 1% of the matching time.

The last experiments measured the ranking effectiveness. Clearly, a discovery process that takes into account the quality aspect beyond the structural one provides better responses than a structure-based method. Thus, we were interested in measuring how close is the ranking of our solution compared to the ranking of an expert. For this, an expert manually compared each query to each target and noted it in a *Likert* scale. Then, the results were sorted according to their similarities and compared with our ranking using the NDCG formula. The results obtained for weighted average and lexicographic order rankings were 0.996967 and 0.998752, respectively, which shows that our solution provides a ranking that is strongly close to that defined by the experts in all of our experiments.

4   Related Work

Many approaches for service retrieval based on non-functional characteristics have been proposed in the literature [3,10,11,4]. In these works, quality preferences are specified by (i) relational expressions [3], evaluated to a distance between the preference and the QoS information provided by the service; (ii) fuzzy sets [10], described by membership functions mapping each value of quality attributes to the degree at which the user is satisfied with it; (iii) linguistic variables [4], whose values are terms (e.g., *fast*, *slow*) and whose evaluation returns a match degree in a qualitative scale; or (iv) utility functions [11], similar to fuzzy sets, but can be specified over a discontinuous domain.

The order of importance between preferences is not addressed by these approaches. Instead weights are attributed to QoS properties to be multiplied with the satisfaction degrees of the preferences. These weights are specified by the user at query definition time [11], by an expert at design time [10], or they are fixed in the evaluation process [3]. The aggregation of satisfaction degrees is done via aggregation functions like the sum [3,11], via solutions to the *constraint satisfaction problem* [10], or using match degrees in a qualitative scale [4].

These approaches do not propose preference constructors to help user better define his preferences and they are not abstract enough to be adapted to different non-functional contexts. More important, these approaches consider services as black boxes, so quality requirements for internal activities are not addressed.

5   Conclusions

We presented an approach for service discovery considering structure and quality requirements. First, we proposed a formal model to annotate service PMs with quality properties and user queries with quality preferences. Then, we showed how preferences are addressed in the service discovery process. Our approach can be easily applied to other non-functional requirements. As future work, we intend to study preferences considering user's viewpoint and semantic compositions of structural similarity and preference satisfaction.

Acknowledgment. This work has received support from the French National Agency for Research (ANR) on the reference ANR-08-CORD-009.

References

1. Dijkman, R., Dumas, M., García-Bañuelos, L.: Graph Matching Algorithms for Business Process Model Similarity Search. In: Dayal, U., Eder, J., Koehler, J., Reijers, H.A. (eds.) BPM 2009. LNCS, vol. 5701, pp. 48–63. Springer, Heidelberg (2009)
2. Grigori, D., Corrales, J.C., Bouzeghoub, M., Gater, A.: Ranking bpel processes for service discovery. IEEE TSC 3, 178–192 (2010)
3. Mokhtar, S.B., Preuveneers, D., Georgantas, N., Issarny, V., Berbers, Y.: Easy: Efficient semantic service discovery in pervasive computing environments with QoS and context support. Journal of Systems and Software 81(5), 785–808 (2008)
4. Şora, I., Lazăr, G., Lung, S.: Mapping a fuzzy logic approach for QoS-aware service selection on current web service standards. In: ICCC-CONTI, pp. 553–558 (2010)
5. Zhang, Y., Huang, H., Yang, D., Zhang, H., Chao, H.C., Huang, Y.M.: Bring QoS to P2P-based semantic service discovery for the universal network. Personal Ubiquitous Computing 13(7), 471–477 (2009)
6. Dumas, M., García-Bañuelos, L., Polyvyanyy, A., Yang, Y., Zhang, L.: Aggregate Quality of Service Computation for Composite Services. In: Maglio, P.P., Weske, M., Yang, J., Fantinato, M. (eds.) ICSOC 2010. LNCS, vol. 6470, pp. 213–227. Springer, Heidelberg (2010)
7. Kießling, W.: Foundations of preferences in database systems. In: VLDB, pp. 311–322 (2002)
8. Cross, V.: Fuzzy semantic distance measures between ontological concepts. In: NAFIPS, vol. 2, pp. 635–640 (2004)
9. Wu, Z., Palmer, M.S.: Verb semantics and lexical selection. In: ACL, pp. 133–138 (1994)
10. Xiong, P., Fan, Y.: QoS-aware web service selection by a synthetic weight. In: FSKD, pp. 632–637 (2007)
11. Agarwal, S., Lamparter, S., Studer, R.: Making web services tradable: A policy-based approach for specifying preferences on web service properties. JWS 7(1), 11–20 (2009)

A Semantic Scoring Approach for Service Offers

Ikbel Guidara, Kaouthar Fakhfakh, and Tarak Chaari

ReDCAD Laboratory, University of Sfax
B.P. 1173, 3038 Sfax, Tunisia
{ikbel.guidara,kouthar.fakhfakh}@gmail.com,
tarak.chaari@redcad.org

Abstract. Automating service selection using semantic approaches have been extensively studied in recent years. In fact, given the big number of provider offers, sourcing of the most relevant service to the client intentions is a complex task especially when providers and customers don't share the same knowledge degree. In particular, differentiating between very similar offers satisfying the same number of client constraints is still a challenging task. In this paper, we present a novel semantic scoring approach that helps clients to select the most appropriate service offer according to their intentions. Our approach detects direct and indirect semantic correspondences between these intentions and the available offers using ontological models. It fairly evaluates these offers and ranks them according to their semantic closeness to the client intentions taking into account both functional and QoS properties. Our ranking is based on a deep examination of provider offers and can distinguish between services that look the same for non expert clients.

Keywords: Ontologies, Quality of Service (QoS), Semantic Web, Service Sourcing.

1   Introduction

With the continued growth of Service Oriented Architectures, the sourcing of the most relevant service becomes a challenge. In fact, generally, providers define their services using fixed and predefined choices and technical terms [5]. Because of their limited knowledge, clients may not understand these complex terms. As a result, they may not choose the best offer and may select a service that does not adequately satisfy their needs. In addition, there is often the case when several services fulfill client's requirements and satisfy the same number of client's constraints. Among these services, which one will be selected is a very difficult task. This issue is still insufficiently tackled in the literature since many service sourcing approaches cannot differentiate between similar offers [3, 4]. To address these problems, a tool that helps customers to freely express their requirements and to easily select the best service, has become highly recommended. The challenge of our work is to propose a fair service sourcing approach that helps clients to select the most appropriate service offer according to their intentions while giving them the ability to freely express their

M. Brambilla, T. Tokuda, and R. Tolksdorf (Eds.): ICWE 2012, LNCS 7387, pp. 307–314, 2012.
© Springer-Verlag Berlin Heidelberg 2012

functional and QoS-based requirements using their own knowledge and language. Our approach is based on computing a score for each service offer according to its semantic closeness to the client requirements.

In this paper, we propose a new service sourcing approach which is based on semantic enabled models for client intentions and provider offers using ontologies. Based on these models, the first step of our approach consists in finding correspondences between the description of the services offered by providers and the required ones by the client. The matching step allows detecting direct and indirect correspondences between client and providers terms. The direct correspondences consist in finding semantic equivalence between these terms using a similarity measure. The indirect correspondences are automatically generated using a QoS ontology that bridges the gap between the client and the provider terms. For example, the customer can define his requirements using the expression "*download time*" while the provider defines his offer according to the "*film size*" and the "*throughput*" offered to the client. Correspondences generated in the matching phase are then stored in a matching ontology to be used in the selection process. The second step of our approach is to define a fair classification method of service offers according to their semantic closeness to the client intentions. This method computes the score of each offer based on the number of the satisfied requirements and the distance between the values proposed by the provider and those wanted by the customer for each requirement. The models used in our approach and the semantic matching process are detailed in our ontology driven approach for automatic establishment of service level agreements (ODACE SLA) [1]. In the remaining parts of this paper we detail our service sourcing process and we present how it produces more accurate results than the existing approaches.

This paper is structured as follows: section 2 provides related works about service selection. Section 3 details our semantic approach for service sourcing. Before concluding, we present a case study to illustrate that our approach produces more fair and accurate results than the existing service selection methods.

2   Related Work

There are several approaches in the literature that tackled the problem of service selection. Several criteria can be considered when selecting the best service. The selection of services can be entirely based on price [2] or on some predefined criteria for the comparison of the values of services such as security and response time [3], [4] and [5]. These criteria may not be sufficient to correctly classify the service providers and don't allow clients to freely express their own requirements based on different and high level terms. In addition, these approaches don't control the values given by providers who can give incorrect values to increase their chances to be selected. In their work [6], Comuzzi et al have defined a set of admissible values for each QoS parameter. The values given by customers and providers must belong to the admissible values. However, the authors propose to translate the values of QoS parameters into levels. This may not give a fair classification especially in the case of a large spectrum of values. In addition, this work does not allow the comparison of linguistic terms and only the numeric values are considered. In [7], authors present a semantic web service discovery approach using the SPARQL language to evaluate preconditions and postconditions of services and check if they satisfy the required goals. Nevertheless, this approach doesn't take into account non functional properties in the selection process. In addition, authors do not provide matching capabilities especially when the client is not an IT expert.

According to this study, we conclude that the major part of the existing work doesn't provide an effective mechanism to differentiate between similar offers especially those satisfying the same number of client's constraints. In addition, these works generally omitted scoring literal terms and they are focused only on the scoring of numeric values. In our approach, we aim to use a better expression and analysis of semantics to help the clients finding the best adequate service they need. In the next section, we detail the different steps of our service sourcing approach.

3   Semantic Service Selection Approach

In this section, we detail our approach to select the most appropriate service according to the client preferences. We start by presenting our scoring method to compute the score of each provider value. Then, we detail our selection algorithm based on the defined scores. Finally, we explain the functions that compute these scores.

3.1   Service Offers Scoring Methodology

To compute the final score (FS) of each provider value, we define two types of scores:

The Satisfaction Score (SS): This score tests if the offered value of the provider satisfies the client's constraint. It allows computing the number of constraints satisfied by each provider, but it does not distinguish similar candidates and offers that satisfy the same number of the client constraints.

The Satisfaction Degree (SD): This score gives more precision to the satisfaction score according to the closeness of the values offered by the provider to the client constraints. The closer the provider value to the required one by the client is, the higher the SD will be. In our approach, we propose to grant more importance to the client constraint satisfaction than its closeness to the value of the client. For this reason, we consider that the SD shouldn't be higher than the SS. Consequently, we propose that the sum of all the SDs of each combination of provider values must not exceed 1 (which presents the maximum SS that can be assigned to a constraint value). Then, we choose a threshold that is equal to $\alpha(n_c)$ for each SD with n_c is the number of constraints required by the client. As a result, each value of SD must be between 0 and $\alpha(n_c)$ with:

$$\alpha(n_c) = \frac{1 - \varepsilon}{n_c} \qquad \text{Where} \qquad 0 < \varepsilon < 1 \qquad (1)$$

The final score of each provider value is the sum of these two scores. Thus, a provider value that satisfies the client constraint will have a FS between 1 and $1 + \alpha(n_c)$ and the one that doesn't satisfy the client constraint will have a FS between 0 and $\alpha(n_c)$. Consequently, if a provider doesn't satisfy any constraint, his final score will not exceed $n_c * \alpha(n_c)$ which is equal to $(1-\varepsilon)$. In this case, it will never have a higher score than a provider who satisfies at least one constraint and who will have a minimum score equals to 1.

3.2   Best Service Offer Selection Algorithm

The selection phase is mainly based on checking the satisfaction of the client constraints by each provider offer. It allows evaluating and selecting service providers according to their closeness to satisfy client preferences. In this section, we present our selection algorithm which allows ranking service providers on the basis of their ability to satisfy the client requirements. The first step of our algorithm is to gather all the client constraints from the intention instance. For each constraint, we consider its property, its operator and its threshold from the client ontology. Then, if the threshold value is numeric, we consider its admissible values from the QoS ontology using the correspondences generated in the matching phase. In this step, we select QoS values that have valid correspondences with the client property (we refer to $VQ_{k,min}$ and $VQ_{k,max}$ respectively, the minimum and maximum admissible values identified by the expert for the parameter associated to the kth constraint of the client). A correspondence is considered valid if its certainty is above a minimum acceptance threshold. This threshold is identified using information science measures as precision, recall and F-measure [8]. After that, we retrieve all the corresponding values for each client constraint from the provider ontology.

- For the direct correspondences, we select the provider values that have valid correspondences with the client property and we try to get the value $VP_{ij,k}$ of each selected instance. $VP_{ij,k}$ denotes the value of the offer j of the provider number i which corresponds to the client constraint number k.

- For the indirect correspondence, we retrieve the QoS instances that have valid correspondences with the client property. For each selected instance found, we collect its function and its operands. The next step is to find the set of values from the provider ontology which have valid correspondences with these operands. Then, we compute the function result that presents the provider value $VP_{ij,k}$.

After retrieving all the possible values of each provider corresponding to the client constraints, we compute the final score $FS_{ij,k}$ of each value $VP_{ij,k}$ according to its closeness to the value given by the client. This final score uses the admissible values retrieved from the QoS ontology. If a constraint given by the client has no semantic (direct or indirect) correspondence with a valid term of the provider ontology, this it will be considered as an unsatisfied constraint and its final score will be equal to 0. After computing the score of each provider's value, the last step is identifying the best combination of values that gives the best score OS_{ij} of each offer O_{ij} for the provider P_i using the formula (2).

$$OS_{ij} = \frac{\sum_{k=1}^{n_c} FS_{ij,k}}{n_c * (1 + \alpha(n_c))} \qquad (2)$$

These steps will be repeated for each provider to rank all the available offers according to their scores. Finally, the offer that has the best score will be selected.

3.3   Scoring Functions

In this section, we define the functions that we propose to compute the scores of provider values. We distinguish two categories: linguistic terms and numeric values. To give a fair classification method, it is necessary that both scores of linguistic terms and those of numeric values belong to the values ranges specified in section 3.1.

Computing Scores of Linguistic Terms

In our approach, we aim to identify and use the several semantic relations that can exist between terms. For this reason, we present in the following our method to compute scores of linguistic terms using similarity measures.

-To compute the SS we distinguish two possible cases:

Case 1: If the client gives a single possible term VC_k for the constraint number k (i.e. the operator is *"equal"*), we assume that the client constraint is satisfied if the degree of similarity between the client term and its corresponding provider term is greater than or equal the acceptance threshold.

Case 2: If the client gives more than one term (i.e. the operator is *"in"*), we assume that the constraint of the client is satisfied if there is at least one of the terms proposed by the client that has a similarity degree greater than or equal to the acceptance threshold with the corresponding provider term.

- The SD of linguistic terms is equal to the semantic similarity degree between the client term and the provider term multiplied by $\alpha(n_c)$ in the case where the operator is *"equal"*. It will be equal to the maximum similarity degree computed between the provider term and the set of all client terms multiplied by $\alpha(n_c)$ in the case where the operator is *"in"*. Note that the similarity degree must be a value between 0 and 1, so that the SD will be not above the threshold defined at section 3.1 which is equal to $\alpha(n_c)$.

Computing Scores of Numeric Values

To compute the final score of the numeric values, we suppose that:

- The SS is equal to 1 if the value of the provider satisfies the client constraint and 0 otherwise according to the required operator.

-The SD is computed according to two possible cases:

Case 1: Numeric values that have a better value direction (BVD) which can be "down" or "up". These values can be used to determine if the client prefers the minimum or the maximum value among the values offered by providers. The value "down" indicates that the SD is inversely proportional to the value of the provider. The value "up" indicates that the SD is proportional to the value of the provider. For example, "response time" has a "down" better value direction. Taking inspiration from functions defined in [4], we propose to use the formula (3).

$$SD_{ij,k} = \begin{cases} \alpha(n_c) * \dfrac{VQ_{k,max} - VP_{ij,k}}{VQ_{k,max} - VQ_{k,min}} & if \quad BVD = "down" \\ \alpha(n_c) * \dfrac{VP_{ij,k} - VQ_{k,min}}{VQ_{k,max} - VQ_{k,min}} & if \quad BVD = "up" \end{cases} \qquad (3)$$

Case 2: Numeric values that don't have a better value direction. In this case, we adopt that the more the value of the provider is closer to the value of the client, the more its SD is bigger. We distinguish three cases according to the operator used by the client.

- If the client gives one value (i.e. the operator is *"equal"*, *"greaterThan"* or *"lessThan"*). We propose to compute the SD by the formula (4):

$$SD_{ij,k} = \alpha(n_c) * (1 - \frac{|VP_{ij,k} - VC_k|}{n_1})$$
(4)

With $n_1 = \max\{(VQ_{k,max}-VC_k);(VC_k - VQ_{k,min})\}$

- If the client gives a range of values, we propose the formula (5):

$$SD_{ij,k} = \begin{cases} \alpha(n_c) * (1 - \dfrac{VC_{k,min} - VP_{ij,k}}{n_2}) & if \quad VP_{ij,k} \in [VQ_{k,min};VC_{k,min}[\\ \alpha(n_c) & if \quad VP_{ij,k} \in [VC_{k,min};VC_{k,max}] \\ \alpha(n_c) * (1 - \dfrac{VP_{ij,k} - VC_{k,max}}{n_2}) & if \quad VP_{ij,k} \in]VC_{k,max};VQ_{k,max}] \end{cases}$$
(5)

With $n_2 = \max\{(VQ_{k,max}-VC_{k,max});(VC_{k,min}- VQ_{k,min})\}$

- If the client gives two or more values (i.e. the operator is *"in"*), we propose to compute the SD using the formula (6):

$$SD_{ij,k} = \max\left\{\alpha(n_c) * (1 - \frac{|VP_{ij,k} - VC_{k,m}|}{n_3}), 0 < m \le NV_k\right\}$$
(6)

With $n_3 = \max\{(VQ_{k,max}-VC_{k,m});(VC_{k,m}- VQ_{k,min}), 0 < m \le NV_k$, NV_k is the number of the possible client values for the kth constraint}

4   Case Study

To better illustrate our approach, we consider an example in which the client specifies four constraints in his intention. He wants to download "Comedy" or "Adventure" films (C_1) from a service with a greater availability than 97% (C_2), a download time less than 10 minutes (C_3) and a price less than or equal 3 Euros per film (C_4).

Table 1. An example of provider offers scores

	O_{ij}	SS	SD	FS	OS_{ij}
Provider 1	$VP_{11,1}$=Comedy	1	0,2475	1,2475	
	$VP_{11,2}$=99%	1	0,245	1,245	0,771
	$VP_{11,3}$=9 mn	1	0,214	1,214	
	$VP_{11,4}$=3.1	0	0,143	0,143	
Provider 2	$VP_{12,1}$=Action	0	0,077	0,077	
	$VP_{12,2}$=97%	1	0,24	1,24	0,73
	$VP_{12,3}$=8.5 mn	1	0,216	1,216	
	$VP_{12,4}$=3	1	0,148	1,148	
Provider 3	$VP_{13,1}$=Documentary	0	0,037	0,037	
	$VP_{13,2}$=93%	0	0,23	0,23	0,52
	$VP_{13,3}$=8 mn	1	0,218	1,218	
	$VP_{13,4}$=2.9	1	0,153	1,153	

On the other side, we consider the offers of three providers presented in Table 1. Download time values of provider offers are computed using indirect correspondences. Table 1 shows the scores of the provider offers according to the formulas presented in section 3 of this paper. In this case study, we respectively considered these admissible values for the client constraints on "availability", "download time" and "price": $VQ_{2,min}=0$, $VQ_{2,max}=100$, $VQ_{3,min}=1$, $VQ_{3,max}=60$, $VQ_{4,min}=1$ and $VQ_{4,max}=6$ and ε is equal to 0,01. To compute the linguistic terms scores, we used WordNet::Similarity measures [9].

To better illustrate the advantages of our service sourcing approach, we have compared its results with some existing works [3] and [4]. These two works give the same results. In the existing approaches, the scores of the linguistic terms cannot be computed and indirect correspondences are not taken into account. Consequently, we considered the score of linguistic terms equal to 1 if the terms are syntactically equivalent and 0 otherwise for these approaches. Figure 1 shows that the first provider will have the highest score using our approach whereas the second provider will be selected in the other approaches. In addition, these approaches give the same score to the first and the third provider despite that the first provider gives better offers than the other providers. Consequently, we conclude that our approach gives better results than the existing service sourcing methods. In fact, it allows selecting offers according to both high level functional and non functional constraints given by the client. These constraints can be based on literal values (such as C1 in this case study) or numeric values (such as C2 and C3) using several mathematical operators. Moreover, our approach can detect indirect correspondences between intentions and offers (like C3) which are not detectable by other service sourcing works. The use of two types of scores offers a fair and accurate classification method of service providers. This classification ranks provider offers according to the number of the satisfied constraints presented by the score SS and then enhances these scores by the score SD. The final score gives better ranking precision especially when some offers satisfy the same number of constraints (the case of the providers 1 and 2 in Table 1).

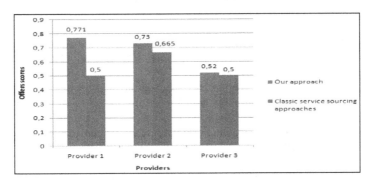

Fig. 1. Case study experimental results

5   Conclusion

Given the continuous growth of multi-service providers, the establishment of an approach that helps clients selecting the appropriate offers to their requirements is highly recommended. In fact, many offers can be distinguished even if they look similar for non-expert clients especially when the providers use complex terms that cannot be easily understood by the clients. To achieve this goal, we defined a novel semantic approach for service sourcing. This approach helps the clients to freely express their intentions using their own language and knowledge that can be different from the provider offers. In our approach, we started by generating direct and indirect correspondences between the client and the provider terms in order to evaluate the available offers. In a second step we defined a fair and accurate scoring algorithm that can distinguish offers satisfying the same number of the client constraints and having close values. In fact, the computed scores depend on admissible ranges defined in a QoS ontology to allow a fair classification of these offers. In addition, these scores depend on the number of the satisfied functional and QoS constraints on one hand and the semantic distance between the linguistic and numeric values proposed by the provider and those required by the client on the other hand. Moreover, our approach can evaluate the provider offers using indirect QoS correspondences which are not detectable using the existing service sourcing algorithms.

As a future work, we aim to evaluate the performance of our algorithms and optimize our approach by reducing its execution time. In fact, dealing with a large number of offers can cause scalability issues. This can be avoided by deploying our algorithms on parallel environments like grids. We also intend to extend our sourcing approach to support the selection of service compositions.

References

1. Kaouthar, F., Tarak, C., Saïd, T., Mohamed, J., Khalil, D.: ODACE SLA: Ontology Driven Approach for Automatic Establishment of Service Level Agreements. IJSSOE 1(3), 1–20 (2010)
2. Lamparter, S., Ankolekar, A., Studer, R., Grimm, S.: Preference based selection of highly configurable web services. In: Proceedings of the 16th International Conference on the World Wide Web WWW 2007, pp. 1013–1022 (2007)
3. Wang, X., Vitvar, T., Kerrigan, M., Toma, I.: A QoS-Aware Selection Model for Semantic Web Services. In: Dan, A., Lamersdorf, W. (eds.) ICSOC 2006. LNCS, vol. 4294, pp. 390–401. Springer, Heidelberg (2006)
4. Zeng, L.Z., Benatallah, B., Ngu, A.H.H.: QoS-aware middleware for Web services composition. IEEE Transaction on Software Engineering 30(5), 311–327 (2004)
5. Andrikopoulos, V., Fugini, M., Papazoglou, M., Parkin, M., Pernici, B., Siadat, S.H.: QoS Contract Formation and Evolution. In: Proceedings of the 11th International Conference on Electronic Commerce and Web Technologies (EC-WEB 2010), pp. 119–130 (2010)
6. Comuzzi, M., Pernici, B.: A framework for QoS-based Web service contracting. ACM Transactions on the Web (TWEB) 3(3) (June 2009)
7. Marco, L.S., David, M., Claude, M.: Discovering Semantic Web services using SPARQL and intelligent agents. Journal of Web Semantics 8, 310–328 (2010)
8. van Rijsbergen, C.J.: Getting into Information Retrieval. In: Agosti, M., Crestani, F., Pasi, G. (eds.) ESSIR 2000. LNCS, vol. 1980, pp. 1–20. Springer, Heidelberg (2001)
9. Siddharth, P.: Incorporating dictionary and corpus information into a context vector measure of semantic relatedness. Master's thesis, University of Minnesota, Duluth (2003)

Rich Communication Patterns for Mashups

Stefan Pietschmann, Martin Voigt, and Klaus Meißner

Technische Universität Dresden
01062 Dresden, Germany
{Stefan.Pietschmann,Martin.Voigt,Klaus.Meissner}@tu-dresden.de

Abstract. Mashups imply the lightweight combination of distributed web resources – a paradigm which can be also applied to the presentation layer to build interactive web applications. However, current solutions are limited to very basic composition patterns and do not reflect the coordination needs of the user interface. To tackle this problem, we propose a novel approach for modeling rich communication patterns as part of a mashup composition model, which supports the synchronization between widgets, asynchronous data requests to backend services, and interaction techniques like drag-and-drop. The concepts were realized and validated with a number of sample applications.

1 Introduction

Mashups have become a prominent approach for building web applications from distributed web resources, which has resulted in a multitude of mashup platforms. Recently, research has addressed both formal, platform-independent models and the integration of user interface (UI) parts as first-class citizens into mashups, e.g. in mashArt [1] or CRUISe [5]. However, the current solutions are very limited when it comes to the "glue", i.e., the means to connect the resources. The latter are typically loosely coupled by "wiring" their outputs and inputs with unidirectional links mapped on a publish/subscribe system, which is supposed to offer the highest flexibility [2]. This results in a "fire-and-forget" communication, which is simple at the first sight, but leads to more complex models when data requests and synchronization between components are needed.

In the light of "universal composition" approaches, which equally integrate backend and frontend components, new communication and coordination requirements arise: The seamless integration of backend services as well as the synchronization within the presentation layer are just two examples, which are hard to realize with prevalent solutions.

To emphasize the **requirements**, we introduce a use case which serves as a **reference scenario** throughout this paper. The application *StockMash* shown in Fig. 1 gives an overview of stock indexes ① ②, allows for comparing stock performance ④ and managing a personal depot ③ ⑤. The most basic coordination need is resembled by the green arrows: *unidirectional* connections, e.g., to notify ② when the stock index in ① changes. Further, the stock selection in ① may serve as input for different components, e.g., for comparison using ④.

M. Brambilla, T. Tokuda, and R. Tolksdorf (Eds.): ICWE 2012, LNCS 7387, pp. 315–322, 2012.

As the "target" depends on the context, the user needs to decide where to direct the data (blue arrows). This can be achieved by platform-specific techniques, like drag-and-drop. As the data is supplied by backend services, UI components must be able to actively *request* it and receive *asynchronous updates* (to prevent extensive polling). Finally, the stock comparison using ④ underlines the need for the *synchronization* of components, e.g., to adjust the time frame in both views (brown arrow).

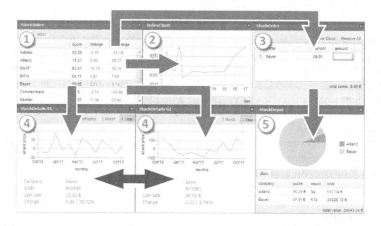

Fig. 1. Coordination relations in the use case *StockMash*

The **contributions** of this paper are twofold. First, we present an advanced communication model comprising different coordination types, which are modeled as extensions of an event-based composition model. Second, we discuss its interpretation and application within an existing composition infrastructure, and show how drag-and-drop interaction can be mapped to this model.

Our paper is structured as follows: In Sect. 2, we introduce the design-time concepts to model rich communication. Then, Sect. 3 presents the runtime concepts and realization, including the communication system and extensions towards drag-and-drop, with the help of our reference scenario. In Sect. 4 we conclude this paper and give an outlook on future work.

2   Modeling Rich Coordination in Mashup Applications

Our solution builds on the universal composition approach of CRUISe, which facilitates the model-driven development and deployment of adaptive, composite web applications. Therefore, we rely on its event-based component and composition models described in [5]. Therein, components of a mashup are described declaratively with the *Semantic Mashup Component Description Language* (SM-CDL) using three abstractions, namely *Property*, *Event*, and *Operation*. Based on these abstractions, developers can compose interactive mashup applications using the *Mashup Composition Model* (MCM).

In the following, we present an extension of these concepts to foster the above-mentioned coordination needs.

2.1 Modeling Static Communication Patterns with Links

Communication and coordination in mashup systems are usually expressed by "wiring" inputs and outputs of components. In our solution, those wires are called *links* which connect n events with m operations in case their parameters are semantically compatible. Thus, when one component issues an event indicating a state change, all operations registered at the same link are invoked with the event data. Since the link acts as a mediator between events and operations, all components remain loosely-coupled.

To support *unidirectional*, *bidirectional* and *synchronization* connections, we introduce different *link types*, which are discussed in the next few paragraphs.

Links represent the basic type of **unidirectional** communication as supported by the majority of composition approaches. They allow for connecting n events with m operations, so the data of an event is published to all registered operations. A response is not expected, thus, a **one-way** communication is established. Every link is implicitly typed by the data, i.e., the parameters it carries. Hence, only events and operations whose parameter signatures are semantically equal can be linked. The MCM does offer means for manipulating and mapping parameter signatures, yet, those concepts are out of the scope of this paper.

BackLinks represent **bidirectional**, i.e., request-response connections between components, as usually required for data requests to backend components. As illustrated by Fig. 2-1, BackLinks indicate an implicit callback (link) created at runtime, which returns requested information to the publisher of the initial link. To avoid ambiguities between the returning messages, BackLinks are established between n requesters (events) and only *one* replier (operation).

As soon as an event is published on a BackLink, the target operation is invoked, just as with a Link. However, upon completion, it issues a *CallbackEvent* with a return message, which is routed to invoke the *CallbackOperation* of the

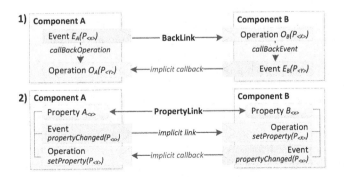

Fig. 2. Communication using Back- or PropertyLinks

initial event. Consequently, to model such a connection, the information about callback events and operations must be available at design time. Therefore, we extended the SMCDL with these two cross references, indicating the implicit connections between incoming and outgoing messages of a component.

By default, the implicit response channel is closed after the callback message has been sent (*single pull*). However, it can be kept open by the replier to facilitate asynchronous updates (*active push*). This needs to be explicitly supported by the replying component as expressed by the operation attribute (*syncable*) within its SMCDL. Using the attribute *syncThreshold* of the BackLink, model authors may set the minimum time interval (in s) between new updates, e. g., to limit the communication and performance overhead.

PropertyLinks allow for the **synchronization** of the stateful components by connecting their properties. This is especially useful for multiple views on shared data, which necessitates their filters to be synchronized. In our reference scenario, this is exemplified by the stock details component showing different stocks, yet in a synchronized time interval.

As illustrated in Fig. 2-2, PropertyLinks can be seen as an abstraction layer on top of the event model. They connect properties – something end-users can more easily understand – but are actually mapped to the corresponding change events and setter operations automatically. The synchronization works mutually, so all participants of this pattern are uniformly modeled as *SyncTargets*.

The introduction of PropertyLinks does not only reduce the complexity and redundancy in the MCM by replacing $n!$ Links with only one PropertyLink with n SyncTargets. Even more importantly, it allows runtime platforms to handle cycles, which would result from using normal Links ($A \Rightarrow B \Rightarrow A$).

2.2 On-Demand Coordination

If the static definition of a mashup's internal data flow is either not desirable or not possible, on-demand coordination becomes necessary. With regard to our reference scenario, this is the case for the stock details components ④. As the stock list ① has only one output – the selected stock – it cannot be connected with both detail views without both of them showing the same data. Thus, the choice, which stock to show in which view, is to be made on-demand at runtime by the user, e. g., by drag-and-drop or other techniques available.

To support this, components need to specify a *dataSource* as part of their interface description. As with any property, it comprises a number of semantically typed parameters representing the data to be shared. Potential targets of an interaction are already specified in the form of operations, as they define which data can be consumed by components, regardless of how it is invoked.

The basic idea of on-demand coordination is: If a dataSource of a component is active, e. g., upon a drag or voice command, any compatible operation within the mashup may act as data sink. The detection of the trigger as well as the coordination between the data source and sink is up to the platform, which hides components from the peculiarity of specific interaction techniques.

2.3   Modeling the Reference Scenario

To prove the feasibility and practicability of our model and composition system, we built several composite applications, one of which represents the use case introduced in Sect. 1. Fig. 3 illustrates the coordination of its stock details components ④ as modeled in the MCM. As soon as a stock has been selected, they request its data via a BackLink and from this point receive updated values every 5 s. Further, a PropertyLink connects the *interval* property of both instances, so that the time span shown in both views is always the same.

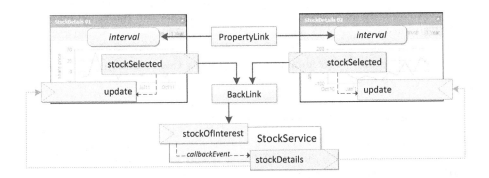

Fig. 3. Coordination links within the sample application

This practical example also illustrates the simplification of the MCM: In comparison with a traditional version, where requests and synchronizations were mapped to normal Links, the novel model allowed for a reduction of connections from 19 to 8, not even considering the additional possibilities of permanent, asynchronous updates and the handling of cycles.

3   Supporting Rich Communication Patterns at Runtime

As mashup components are developed independently and can be composed dynamically, realizing the above-mentioned communication patterns is a challenging task. In the following, we sketch the basic principles of a corresponding communication system, which was implemented as extension of the CRUISe platform.

3.1   Message Format

To realize the data exchange between components developed by different vendors with different technologies a uniform vocabulary is needed. Therefore, all components must adhere to a platform-independent message format. The universal composition implies the communication between components of different application layers and complexity, so the format we have developed is generic, simple, yet extensible. It is divided in control information and the actual payload. The latter forms the *body* of a message and contains the actual data represented by event and operation parameters. The control information in the *header* includes – among others – the following elements:

Status indicates the success or failure of message distribution and data transfer. To this end, we adopt the HTTP status codes.

Name equals the event name which, combined with the component name, results in a unique ID is used to resolve link subscriptions for the message.

CallbackID is an identifier for a certain bidirectional connection. It is automatically added by the MRE, forwarded by replying components and thus used to identify associated messages and subscribers on the BackLink.

SyncThreshold is an optional parameter which defines a threshold for permanent updates (cf. Sect. 2.1). For unidirectional messages, this field is left blank, while any other numeric value defines the minimum time interval between two updates to be enforced by the channel.

3.2   Link Interpretation and Realization

To support the different link types at runtime, we employ the broker pattern [3], which nicely fits with the event-based nature of the model. The **Event Broker** – a module of the mashup platform – is responsible for managing all the channels specified in the MCM. Further, it offers an API to create, configure and send messages. Thereby, components can easily create and send messages, including life-cycle events, change-events for properties, as well as "ordinary" events specified in the SMCDL. Apart from message and type validations, the Event Broker's main responsibility lies in distributing messages according to the links in the MCM, as discussed in the following.

Links can be mapped directly to the existing infrastructure: Components simply create a new message and publish it, using the broker's API. Using the combination of event and component name as unique ID, the message can be assigned to all the Links it is part in. Following optional mediation steps (cf. [4]), it is then used to invoke all the operations registered with the Link. Upon completion, the broker returns a message to the publishing component, which includes a status code to indicate the success of the data transfer. It is up to component developers if and how this information is interpreted.

BackLinks pose additional challenges to the communication architecture. While the initialization and distribution of messages follow the workflow described for Links, the handling of the response requires additional steps. This is, where the CallbackID from Sect. 3.1 comes into play. It is added by the broker to every message published on a BackLink and forwarded by the replier in the Callback-Event. Thereby, returning messages can be distinguished from "ordinary" ones published by a component and can be forwarded to the CallbackOperation of the initial requester (cf. Fig. 2-1). Asynchronous updates published via CallbackEvents are handled likewise; however, the broker additionally enforces the *syncThreshold* defined in the MCM.

Overall, the BackLink is a simple yet effective mechanism to realize data requests between UI and backend components. In our use case scenario, both the automatic update of stock and index information as well as of the depot data can be realized this way. Instead of polling the information, the data is permanently updated from the backend by keeping the channel open.

PropertyLinks offer an abstraction to the event model and are thus harder to interpret. Basically, they are mapped to Links between change events and setter operations of the corresponding properties. However, the following challenges must be handled: (1) The synchronization affects all participants of the PropertyLink, including the trigger component. Thus, in order to prevent the distribution of a state change to the originator, the latter must be filtered out by the broker dynamically. (2) Once the new property value is set for all registered components, they send change events in return. To prevent communication overhead, the broker caches the state of a PropertyLink, i.e., the current property value. If the payload of an update message equals the cached state, the distribution of this message is skipped. 3) Finally, property changes may overlap, which may lead to data loss if change events are issued while the previous synchronization has not been finished. Thus, the Event Broker employs a FIFO queue, which saves incoming updates and delays them, until the current update is finished.

With regard to our reference scenario, PropertyLinks can be used to realize the synchronization of the time interval (property) in the stock detail components ④ to improve the comparability of the stocks charts.

3.3   Supporting On-Demand Coordination

Realizing on-demand coordination using device- or platform-specific interaction techniques poses additional challenges. On the one hand, the trigger interaction is generally recognized by the source component itself. However, as it has no knowledge of the surrounding platform and components, the platform needs to handle the coordination by mapping the interaction to the link model, so that the target component remains independent from any technological peculiarities. This mediation is carried out as follows:

Starting point of an on-demand coordination is a dataSource (Sect. 2.2) which is defined in the SMCDL and, thus, represented in the MCM. If a component detects the trigger interaction, e. g., dragging of data, it publishes a corresponding event. The message contains a reference to the dataSource and its typed parameters. As a result, the MRE creates invisible *data sinks*, e. g. drop zones. Sinks are only enabled for such components that comprise at least one operation compatible with the dataSource. Finally, when the end of the interaction is detected, e. g., a tangible has been placed, the platform usually receives a corresponding system event. If the target component offers more than one appropriate operation, the user may select the action to take. Then, the data sinks are removed and the platform realizes the data flow: Therefore, it requests the data in question from the source component and invokes the selected operation of the target component.

4   Conclusion and Future Work

Recently, mashup development has moved towards the presentation layer, resulting in universal mashups which enable the lightweight combination of distributed backend and frontend resources. However, current solutions are limited to basic communication patterns and do not support the coordination needs implied by the UI, e. g., data requests to backend services, synchronization of widgets, and on-demand coordination using interaction techniques, such as drag-and-drop.

In this paper, we have introduced a novel concept for modeling advanced communication patterns as part of a universal composition model. In contrast to prevalent solutions, it supports active pull and push connections as well as component synchronization. Further, we have shown, how to support on-demand coordination, e. g., using drag-and-drop, and how all these types of coordination can be mapped to common event-based coordination mechanisms.

By realizing the use case scenario, among others, the solutions could be validated and proved to be feasible and practicable. They both simplify the modeling effort and allow unleashing the full potential of universal composition, as they enhance its coordination capabilities with respect to the needs implied by the interactivity of the applications.

Currently, we are working on mechanisms to support end-users in dynamically establishing coordination, i. e., property links, themselves. After that, we plan to conduct extensive user studies, which include the on-demand coordination concepts described here.

Acknowledgments. The work of Martin Voigt is funded by the German Federal Ministry of Education and Research under promotional reference number 01IA09001C. Further, we would like to thank our student Robert Wende for his valuable contributions to this work.

References

1. Daniel, F., Casati, F., Benatallah, B., Shan, M.-C.: Hosted Universal Composition: Models, Languages and Infrastructure in mashArt. In: Laender, A.H.F., Castano, S., Dayal, U., Casati, F., de Oliveira, J.P.M. (eds.) ER 2009. LNCS, vol. 5829, pp. 428–443. Springer, Heidelberg (2009)
2. Eugster, P.T., Felber, P.A., Guerraoui, R., Kermarrec, A.M.: The many faces of publish/subscribe. ACM Comput. Surv. 35, 114–131 (2003)
3. Gamma, E., Helm, R., Johnson, R.E., Vlissides, J.: Design Patterns: Elements of Reusable Object-Oriented Software. Addison-Wesley (March 1995)
4. Pietschmann, S., Radeck, C., Meißner, K.: Semantics-based discovery, selection and mediation for presentation-oriented mashups. In: Proc. of the 5th Intl. WS on Web APIs and Service Mashups. ACM (September 2011)
5. Pietschmann, S., Tietz, V., Reimann, J., Liebing, C., Pohle, M., Meißner, K.: A metamodel for context-aware component-based mashup applications. In: Proc. of the 12th Intl. Conf. on Information Integration and Web-based Applications & Services. ACM (November 2010)

Supporting View Transition Design of Smartphone Applications Using Web Templates

Kazuki Nishiura[1], Yuta Maezawa[1], Fuyuki Ishikawa[2], and Shinichi Honiden[1,2]

[1] The University of Tokyo, 7-3-1 Hongo, Bunkyo-ku, Tokyo, Japan
[2] National Institute of Informatics, 2-1-2 Hitotsubashi, Chiyoda-ku, Tokyo, Japan
{k-nishiura,maezawa,f-ishikawa,honiden}@nii.ac.jp

Abstract. Many developers have implemented native smartphone applications (NSAs) that have the same functionalities as those of existing web applications (WAs). They need to redesign web pages as views of NSAs owing to their constraints, such as compact displays. However, it can produce a NSA with low global navigability. We propose a framework that can support developers in designing view transitions of NSAs on the basis of WAs. We focus on web templates to leverage well-designed web page transitions. Our framework 1) extracts a page transition model from a WA to create candidate view transitions of a NSA, 2) provides an interface where developers design these views to solve the constraints, and 3) suggests design modifications to increase global navigability calculated by proposed criteria of navigation costs for users. After examining case studies, we concluded that our framework could support developers to design easy-to-navigate NSAs.

1 Introduction

The rapid spread of smartphones[1] has enabled users to access the web almost anywhere. However, owing to features of smartphones, such as small screens and touch panels, users cannot comfortably browse web applications (WAs) designed for desktop computers. To meet demands of smartphone users, many WA providers have published native smartphone applications (NSAs).

Many efforts have addressed the problem of web browsing on small devices [1]. Some researches took user input to custom pages [2], and others automatically reorganized structures of pages by using heuristic rules and machine learning techniques [3]. Although they focused on individual pages or single tasks, developers should consider global navigability of applications in order to increase usability. Owing to the importance of transition designs in WA development [4], researchers have attempted to improve navigability of web sites [5].

In this paper, we propose a framework that can support developing NSAs on the basis of existing WAs. Developers will be able to not only inherit well-designed page transitions of WAs but also provide users consistent navigation with WAs,

---

[1] http://www.gartner.com/it/page.jsp?id=1543014

M. Brambilla, T. Tokuda, and R. Tolksdorf (Eds.): ICWE 2012, LNCS 7387, pp. 323–331, 2012.
© Springer-Verlag Berlin Heidelberg 2012

which will increase usability of NSAs [6]. Our framework extracts a transition model of WAs to provide candidate view transitions of NSAs. To handle dynamic web pages, our model focuses on web templates that are de-facto standards in WA development [7]. Using our framework, developers can design views of a NSA from web templates in order to overcome the display size constraints. They can (i) extract elements from web templates and (ii) divide views to create a child view linked from the original view to reduce the number of elements in each view. Although these operations affect global navigability of the NSA, developers cannot perceive whole transitions in the NSA when designing a single view. Therefore, our framework estimates global navigability by defining a formula for navigation costs of users. Our framework suggests modifications of view transition design to increase the estimated navigability. Our suggestions consist of (i) recovering a link removed by developers, (ii) deleting a link, and (iii) shifting a link from or to child views. Developers can design view transitions interactively by accepting or rejecting these suggestions in accordance with their heuristics.

Our contributions are as follows:

- Proposal of leveraging page transitions of WAs when developers design view transitions of NSAs. We focus on web templates to build a transition model.
- Implementation of our framework. Using our framework, developers can design views of NSAs from web templates and receive suggestions for design modifications to increase global navigability of NSAs.
- Evaluation of our framework by means of case studies that showed our tool could support developers in designing easy-to-navigate NSAs.

2   Web Application-Based Native Smartphone Applications

To leverage page transitions of a WA, developers redesign web pages as views of a NSA. This involves two difficulties. First, contents of web pages are changed at runtime. We focus on web template to handle this dynamic nature as described in Sect. 2.1. Second, developers can reduce global navigability of NSAs (Sect. 2.2).

2.1   Web Templates

When developers design views of NSAs using web pages that have dynamic nature, looking at the page in a particular situation is not enough. To handle slight changes of a page, previous work [2] calculated the similarity among elements by using the Document Object Model (DOM). With this approach, however, developers may fail to notice elements hidden when redesigning the page.

Our approach leverages web template files as bases for views of NSAs. Web templates are predesigned web pages that specify fixed aspects of a presentation. They also contain logical specifications (e.g., *if*, *foreach*) that dynamically control the page structure. A library called a template engine combines web templates with dynamic contents to produce a response. Web templates are widely used in WA development [7], because web page designers can separate a presentation from the logic behind the page. Our framework uses web templates that contain all possible structures by their very nature, thus developers can handle all displayable elements regardless of any scenarios. In our prototype tool, we consider PHP-based WAs and the *Smarty* template engine library (www.smarty.net).

2.2 Navigability in Native Smartphone Applications

Developers design views of NSAs on the basis of each single web page. They (i) select elements from a page and (ii) divide elements into multiple views if the page contains too many elements. In other words, they (i) remove unselected links and (ii) place links where they want. These operations decide view transitions, and thus affect global navigability of NSAs.

In Fig. 1, we show examples of page transitions in an online bookstore WA. Boxes represent web pages, and arrows represent links. Look at a link from *Index* to *Audio Books* (b). It helps users reach from *Music* to *Audio Books* in two clicks (a, b), from *Index* to *English* in three clicks (b, c, d), and so on. If developers remove the link, users can follow a detour that goes through a *Books* page (e, f). These examples demonstrate two facts: a link contributes to multiple paths and the impact of deleting a link depends on existences of other links. Therefore, developers cannot estimate an importance of a link by simply looking at its source and destination pages. However, they can barely figure out whole transitions while designing a certain single view or consider all the numerous transitions together.

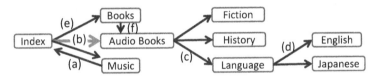

Fig. 1. Simplified page transition graph of an online bookstore web application

3 Proposal Framework

We propose a framework to support developers in designing view transitions of NSAs by using page transitions of existing WAs. Our framework 1) extracts a transition model of a WA to provide candidate view transitions of a NSA, 2) offers an interface where developers redesign web pages of the WA as views of the NSA, 3) calculates global navigability of the NSA, and 4) suggests modifications of transition design to developers in order to increase global navigability.

3.1 Definition of Transition Models

First, our framework generates a Web Application Transition (WAT) model from a WA. To extract the model, we implemented a static path tracer, which pessimistically traces all possible execution paths of a given PHP code and remembers all displayable templates. From given template files, our framework can analyzes transition targets by extracting *a* and *form* tags. The model is then transformed into a Native Smartphone Application Transition (NSAT) model, which reflects the design of developers for the NSA.

Figure 2 shows a meta WAT model given in the Unified Modeling Language (UML). The two main entities in WAs are a *URL* and a *WebPage*. A user sends a request to a URL, and then a WA sends a *response* that contains an appropriate *WebPage* or *redirects* the user to another *URL*. A *WebPage* contains *links* and *forms* by which users send a request to a WA. *WebPages* are *StaticPages* or *DynamicPages* whose contents are fixed or generated at runtime, respectively. Our framework focuses on the WAs using web templates, thus a dynamic page is generated by assigning variables to a web template file.

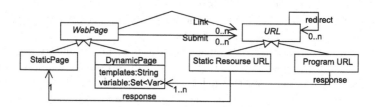

Fig. 2. Meta model of page transitions in general web applications

We model view transitions in NSAs by extending the WAT model (Fig. 3). A *WebPage* is transformed into a *View* of the NSA. In addition, we add *Child-Views* and *internal links*. Note that *ChildView* is a view derived from the source of *internal link*, thus users need not send any additional requests to access it. Additionally, users need not communicate with a server to access *StaticViews*, because NSAs possess layout files on devices. We renamed an association towards *StaticView* as *display*.

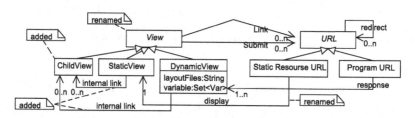

Fig. 3. Meta native smartphone applications transition model. Extension of Fig. 2.

3.2 Estimation of Navigation Costs in Smartphone Applications

In this section, we formulate navigability in NSAs that our framework aims to optimize. Hollink et al. [5] organized previous studies that modeled navigation costs in WAs. They noted that navigation costs for users were determined by the number of pages they visited and the number of choices (i.e., links) on each page. In addition, when they simply assumed these members have a liner relationship to navigation costs, this appeared to fit actual usage logs reasonably.

We extend their formula to model the navigation cost in NSAs generated by our framework. First, we consider *redirections* that consume communication time between clients and servers. Second, among edges in a NSAT graph[2], *display* and *internal link* edges do not require communications with servers, as described in Sect. 3.1. Therefore, we need to consider only the number of *response* in a path. Let α, β, and γ parameters. We can formulate time consumption as follows:

$$Time(Path) = \alpha \mid Responses \mid + \beta \mid Redirections \mid + \gamma \sum choice(View) \quad (1)$$

Here, *Choice* represents the number of links on a view. Using (1), we define *Global Navigability (GN)* as a weighted sum of the minimum navigation time between two arbitrary views in NSAs. Given *ViewPair* (v_1, v_2), we define *ShortestPath* as a path from v_1 to v_2 that minimizes *Time*. In addition, developers specify a *Value* function that returns the importance of a path. They can define the function based on access logs or their own intentions (e.g., leading users to profitable items).

$$GN = \sum (Value(ViewPair) \times Time(ShortestPath(ViewPair))) \quad (2)$$

3.3   Suggestions for Modifications of View Transitions

Our framework suggests three kinds of operations: recovering, deleting, and shifting (Fig. 4). Among candidate operations, the one that improves *GN* the most is suggested. The computation of *GN* requires all-pairs shortest paths, which takes $O(|Views|^3)$ time by simply using Floyd-Warshall algorithm. Here $|Views|$ denotes the number of views in a NSA. Once we calculate *GN*, we can calculate how each operation would change *GN* in $O(|Views|^2)$ time. We can define a *utility* of a link as the difference in *GN* between whether the link exists. Intuitively, our framework aims to leave links with high utility and remove those with low utility.

The recovering (Fig. 4.a) operation recovers a link removed by developers. While developers design each view, they can hardly estimate a link utility that

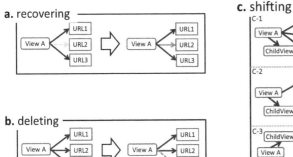

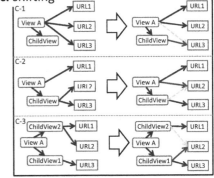

Fig. 4. Transition design of developers (left) and suggestion by our framework (right)

---

[2] The model described in Sect. 3.1 can be re-interpreted as a graph. In the following, we use model and graph terms (e.g., page v.s. node) interchangeably.

is determined by subsequent paths from the link target. Therefore, they might delete useful links. The deleting (Fig. 4.b) operation, in contrast, deletes unnecessary links. The more links on a view, the harder for users to choose the desired link. Therefore, deleting an unimportant link reduces the cost for users to choose links. The shifting (Fig. 4.c) operation shifts a link from a view to its child view (c-1), from child view to its parent view (c-2), or from a child view to another child view (c-3). Creating a child view can distribute costs of choosing links. Our framework assists in shifting less important links to child views and vice versa.

3.4   Tool Implementation

We implemented a prototype tool of our framework (Fig. 5). To design a view of a NSA, developers can select elements from a web template visualized on the left of our tool. Selected elements are displayed on the emulation screen at the center. If a view contains too many elements, developers can create a child view, which is shown on the right. They are required to specify an appropriate text for the link to the child view. After developers finish designing views, our tool suggests modifications to the design in order to improve global navigability of the NSA (Fig. 6). Our tool generates layout files of NSAs for the Android platform (`developer.android.com`). Elements selected by developers are converted into layout files by removing trivial HTML tags (e.g., decoration tags such as b, i) and replacing tags to corresponding GUI elements of NSAs. These transcoding rules are based on our heuristic.

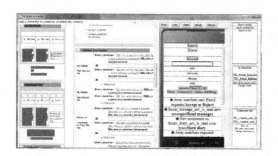

Fig. 5. Designing view (center) ant its child view (right) based on web templates (left)

Fig. 6. Suggestion to improve navigability

4   Evaluation and Discussion

We conducted case studies with *OpenPNE2.14.7* (`www.openpne.jp`)[3], which is an open-sourced social networking service (SNS). The page shown in Fig. 7 contains too many links. Each category has a few item links and a *read more* link that leads to an item list page. Developers delete some links that seem less important, as users can reach these pages via *read more* links anyway. However,

---

[3] We translated pages shown in this section into English.

the destination page of a *post on community board* link contains useful links, such as *send message* and *cancel attending events*. Our framework calculates *GN* and suggests a recovering operation of the link. This case shows that if there are links whose targets have relationships as parent-child or siblings, developers may delete one of them because an alternative path obviously exists. In contrast, developers can hardly estimate tradeoffs between an additional cost incurred by a link deletion and a benefit of decreasing the number of links.

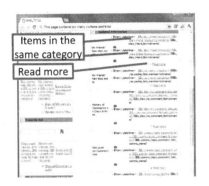   

Fig. 7. Many contents and links on a page   **Fig. 8.** A redundant link on a page

Because this page contains too many elements, developers create child views. They shift some links to leave only useful links in a parent view. Most of the remaining links have a high utility, but a few do not. In addition, the recovering operation recovers a relatively unimportant link, which increases the cost of selecting other important links. Our framework suggests the shifting operation of a *post item review* link that has low utility. A shifting operation can assist the placing of many links among multiple views based on their utility.

Figure 8 shows a community board page. There are links to *topic*, *topic list*, and *post a new topic* pages. Developers decide to use all of them in the NSA. However, users prefer to post a new topic from a *topic list* page after checking existing topics. Our framework suggests a deleting operation of the link to *post a new topic* so that costs of selecting other important links are reduced. Generally, if multiple pages contain links for the same target, developers may use both links. While this choice may increase or decrease navigability, our framework suggests a deleting operation if and only if it works well.

Our framework has some limitations. It cannot deal with links to external WAs nor distinguish different contexts with the same URL and web templates. In addition, our current implementation to extract a WAT model simply traces all execution paths, thus it takes several seconds to trace even a simple code.

5   Related Work

Researchers have attempted to make web pages designed for desktop computers comfortable to browse on narrow screens [1]. Chen et al. [3] utilized both DOM structures and presentations of pages to split them into small pages. Because their successes were based on heuristics and machine learning techniques, their algorithms do not always work optimally. The *Highlight* [2] tool enables users to make task-based mobile WAs from existing WAs. Users can extract elements from each page related to the task to reduce the page size. The tool reapplies the customizations when users visit a page with a similar structure. However, as described in Sect. 2.1, the reapplication may fail owing to dynamics of web pages.

Our method helps WA developers implement NSAs. Titanium SDK (www.appcelerator.com/platform/titanium-sdk) enables NSA development using HTML and JavaScript, which are popular among WA developers. In addition, Prach et al. proposed a mashup framework that could utilize existing web services [8]. However, these approaches did not consider global navigability of NSAs.

Several methods have been proposed to improve web site navigability [5]. Smyth and Cotter [9] reorganized the menu structure to reduce navigation efforts of users modeled by the number of clicks and scrolls. Anderson et al. [10] proposed an algorithm that could suggest shortcut links for mobile web users to reduce the number of communications required. These researchers, however, unrealistically assumed that any two pages could be linked. In fact, modern WAs generate web pages at run time depending on sessions, parameters, and so on.

6   Conclusion and Future Work

We proposed a framework to support developers in designing view transitions of NSAs. We focuses on web templates to extract page transitions in WAs as candidate view transitions in NSAs. Our framework provides an interface to design views of NSAs and suggests design modifications by estimating navigation costs. Using our framework, developers can avoid decreasing global navigability of a NSA while designing each view. By investigating case studies, we conclude that our framework can support designing easy-to-navigate view transitions for NSAs.

Our future work is to implement and publish real world NSAs using our framework. In addition, we aim to extend this work, which leverages page transitions, to handle modern AJAX-based WAs by extracting state transitions on each web page [11]. Moreover, we intend to establish a method for modifying NSAs with keeping consistency in response to frequent updates of WAs.

References

1. Zhang, D., Lai, J.: Can convenience and effectiveness converge in mobile web? a critique of the state-of-the-art adaptation techniques for web navigation on mobile handheld devices. IJHCI 27(12), 1133–1160 (2011)
2. Nichols, J., Hua, Z., Barton, J.: Highlight: a system for creating and deploying mobile web applications. In: UIST, pp. 249–258. ACM (2008)
3. Chen, Y., Xie, X., Ma, W.Y., Zhang, H.J.: Adapting web pages for small-screen devices. IEEE Internet Computing 9(1), 50–56 (2005)
4. Nielsen, J.: User interface directions for the web. CACM 42(1), 65–72 (1999)

5. Hollink, V., Someren, M., Wielinga, B.J.: Navigation behavior models for link structure optimization. UMUAI 17, 339–377 (2007)
6. Gong, J., Tarasewich, P.: Guidelines for handheld mobile device interface design. In: DSI Annual Meeting (2004)
7. Gibson, D., Punera, K., Tomkins, A.: The volume and evolution of web page templates. Special Interest Tracks and Posters of WWW, pp. 830–839. ACM (2005)
8. Chaisatien, P., Prutsachainimmit, K., Tokuda, T.: Mobile Mashup Generator System for Cooperative Applications of Different Mobile Devices. In: Auer, S., Díaz, O., Papadopoulos, G.A. (eds.) ICWE 2011. LNCS, vol. 6757, pp. 182–197. Springer, Heidelberg (2011)
9. Smyth, B., Cotter, P.: The Plight of the Navigator: Solving the Navigation Problem for Wireless Portals. In: De Bra, P., Brusilovsky, P., Conejo, R. (eds.) AH 2002. LNCS, vol. 2347, pp. 328–337. Springer, Heidelberg (2002)
10. Anderson, C.R., Domingos, P., Weld, D.S.: Adaptive web navigation for wireless devices. In: IJCAI, vol. 2, pp. 879–884. Morgan Kaufmann Publishers Inc. (2001)
11. Maezawa, Y., Washizaki, H., Honiden, S.: Extracting interaction-based stateful behavior in rich internet applications. In: CSMR, pp. 423–428. IEEE C.S (2012)

Turn the Page:
Automated Traversal of Paginated Websites*

Tim Furche, Giovanni Grasso, Andrey Kravchenko, and Christian Schallhart

Department of Computer Science, Oxford University,
Wolfson Building, Parks Road, Oxford OX1 3QD
firstname.lastname@cs.ox.ac.uk

Abstract. Content-intensive web sites, such as Google or Amazon, paginate their results to accommodate limited screen sizes. Thus, human users and automatic tools alike have to traverse the pagination links when they crawl the site, extract data, or automate common tasks, where these applications require access to the entire result set. Previous approaches, as well as existing crawlers and automation tools, rely on simple heuristics (e.g., considering only the link text), falling back to an exhaustive exploration of the site where those heuristics fail. In particular, focused crawlers and data extraction systems target only fractions of the individual pages of a given site, rendering a highly accurate identification of pagination links essential to avoid the exhaustive exploration of irrelevant pages.

We identify pagination links in a wide range of domains and sites with near perfect accuracy (99%). We obtain these results with a novel framework for web block classification, BER$_y$L, that combines rule-based reasoning for feature extraction and machine learning for feature selection and classification. Through this combination, BER$_y$L is applicable in a wide settings range, adjusted to maximise either precision, recall, or speed. We illustrate how BER$_y$L minimises the effort for feature extraction and evaluate the impact of a broad range of features (content, structural, and visual).

1 Introduction

Pagination is as old as written information. On the web, no physical limitations force us to paginate articles or result lists. Nevertheless, pagination is just as ubiquitous – for traditional reasons (bookmarking), as well as technical (reducing bandwidth and latency), noble (avoiding information overload), and not quite so noble (maximising page views) ones.

If we are interested in the entire result, e.g., to search through a complete article or to count the number of matching products, pagination quickly becomes a nuisance. This is even more true for automated tools which are interested in extracting all results. Unfortunately, pagination is not a core concept of HTML or the web, but is simulated through links. The ability to distinguish such *pagination links* with *high accuracy* would be a significant advantage for focused crawlers and automated data extraction. Given a reliable

---

* The research leading to these results has received funding from the European Research Council under the European Community's Seventh Framework Programme (FP7/2007–2013) / ERC grant agreement DIADEM, no. 246858.

M. Brambilla, T. Tokuda, and R. Tolksdorf (Eds.): ICWE 2012, LNCS 7387, pp. 332–346, 2012.

method for recognising pagination links, once we reach a page containing relevant, but paginated data, we can crawl, extract, or traverse the entire result set with minimal effort.

Nevertheless, existing crawlers and block classification tools do not incorporate high-accuracy identification of pagination links: (1) Traditional crawlers are unfocused and explore all pages of a site, therefore not requiring link or page classification. Focused crawlers [1–3, 6, 8, 11–13, 15] and data extraction tools [4, 7, 18] considered this a side issue, mostly addressed by manual supervision or simple heuristics combined with an exhaustive fallback strategy. For focused crawlers, this is also influenced by the fact that they already need a mechanism to distinguish relevant pages from irrelevant ones and can apply it also for pagination links. (2) Block classification approaches are more concerned with identifying large page segments, such as navigation menus or advertisements, and are typically tailored for speed over accuracy.

We introduce a novel method for *high accuracy identification of pagination links,* using a novel, flexible framework for block classification called BER_yL, an abbreviation for **B**lock classification with **E**xtraction **R**ules and machine **L**earning. BER_yL combines *logical rules* for *feature extraction* on one hand with *machine learning* for *feature selection and classification* on the other hand. This approach enables different trade-offs between speed, precision, and recall.

Aside of applications in web automation, pagination links are an interesting example for block classification: They appear in a large variety and have themselves a rather simple structure. Together, this makes it hard to identify them accurately with a single class of features. Here, we consider content features, e.g., whether a link text is a number, visual features, e.g., whether a block is in the upper third of a page, or structural ones, such as whether a link is the descendant of a `div`. Figure 1 shows the pagination links on the second page of a paginated result set. There are two *non-numeric* pagination links (‹ and ›) that lead to the next and previous page and 13 *numeric* links leading to the i-th page. For the identification of pagination links we are particularly interested in determining those links that lead to next page in the series, here › and 3 (immediate pagination links). Unfortunately, simple heuristics are not sufficient to achieve high accuracy for the identification of pagination links (as verified in Section 6):

1. *Content features:* Checking the presence of certain keywords or tokens, such as "next" and "›", yields low precision and recall, unable to identify viable links among numeric or image-only pagination links. Since this is a simple baseline heuristic used in some focused crawlers, we investigate it in Section 6, extended with numeric pagination links and some other refinements. We show that it can achieve fairly high precision, but recall remains unacceptable.
2. *Structural features:* It is tempting to assume that such lists of pagination links will be contained in easily identifiable, repeatable HTML structures. But as almost every conceivable abuse of HTML structures indeed occurs in the web, any purely structural approach is limited in its accuracy. Again, we validate in Section 6 that, at least simple, heuristics based on structural features also fail (whether combined with content features or not).
3. *Visual proximity features:* To counter HTML abuse, many data extraction and block classification tools incorporate visual features. We could analyse the visual proximity of links just as well, but although relatively sophisticated, such features fail

‹ 1 2 3 4 5 6 7 8 9 10 11 12 13 14 ›

Fig. 1. Numeric (1, 3 − 14) and non-numeric (‹ and ›)

to contribute significantly towards high accuracy results, either alone or combined with content or structural features, as discussed in Section 6.

4. *Page position features:* Pagination links usually appear on top or below the paginated information. Thus, a link's relative position on a page or whether it occurs in the first screen (at a typical resolution) might seem to constitute a promising feature. Unfortunately, advertisements or navigation headers and footers affect these features significantly (and reliably recognising those blocks is anything but easy). For simple page position features, Section 6 again shows that neither alone nor combined with either content or structural features high accuracy is achieved.

Fortunately, BER$_y$L makes it very easy to extract a large set of features through declarative (Datalog) extraction rules. On the extracted feature model, we employ standard machine learning techniques for automated feature selection and classification. Note that the classifier only needs to be trained *once for all* pages, as demonstrated in Section 6. Our approach is resilient against significant changes in the way HTML is used on the web, as a single re-training of the classifier will suffice for the system to keep functioning properly. With this combination, we achieve near perfect accuracy for identifying pagination links, yet remain comparable in performance to other block classification methods that incorporate visual features, identifying pagination links on most pages within a few seconds. All these approaches are dominated in performance by the underlying page rendering, which is necessary to extract visual features and becomes unavoidable even for content and structural features, as scripted pages reshape the web today. Furthermore, this is easily offset by the fact that a high-accuracy identification of pagination links avoids following many irrelevant links without missing any relevant data, e.g., in focused crawlers or data extraction.

To summarise, we present a novel method for identifying pagination links at a far higher accuracy than previous methods:

1. In BER$_y$L, a **flexible block classification framework**, we combine easy, declarative feature extraction with automatic feature selection and classification (Section 4).
2. Specifically, we define a *comprehensive set of features*, spanning content, structural, and visual features through declarative Datalog rules (Section 5) and BER$_y$L's flexible *feature template rules*.
3. With such a feature set, a *small training set* suffices, yet yields a classifier that uses nearly all these features for effective classification (Section 5.1). The training process is supported by BER$_y$L-Trainer, a visual tool for labeling blocks on web pages.
4. In an *extensive evaluation* (Section 6), we show that this approach achieves **near perfect accuracy** (99%), yet remains highly scalable.
5. We investigate the impact (Section 6) of *removing some features* from the full model and show that neither content, visual, nor structural features alone suffice.

Table 1. Sample pages

Website	n	n_1	n_2	P	R	Screenshot
Real estate FindAProperty	370	1	1	1	1	‹ … | 1 | 2 | 3 | 4 | 5 | 6 | 7 | 8 | 9 | 10 | Next ›
Zoopla	332	1	1	1	1	**Pages:** 1 2 3 4 5 6 7 8 9 10 11 … 58 Next Results per page: 10 | 20 | 50
Savills	234	2	2	1	1	1-10 11-20 21-30 31-40 41-50 Next View all
Cars Autotrader	262	2	2	1	1	Page 1 of 36994 pages. « First ‹ Prev 1 2 3 4 5 6 | Next › Last »
Motors	472	2	2	1	1	1 2 3 4 5 6 7 8 9 10 Next page ▸
Autoweb	103	2	2	1	1	1 2 3 4 5 Next>>
Retail Amazon	448	1	1	1	1	1 2 3 … | Next » ‹ … … … … … ›
Ikea	290	2	0	1	1	1 2 3 4 5 … 11
Lands' End	527	2	2	1	1	Items 1-24 of 37 24 per page ‹ 1 2 »»
Forums TechCrunch	279	0	1	1	1	**PAGE 1** **NEXT PAGE ▶**
TMZ	200	2	2	1	1	(Page 1 of 8) | 1 | 2 | 3 | 4 | 5 | 6 | 7 | Most Recent | Next 15 Comments
Ars Technica	341	2	2	1	1	Comments Page 1 2 3 4 5 Next

2 Pagination Links: A Survey

To motivate the need for pagination link detection and give an impression of some of the issues involved, Table 1 presents a selection of popular websites from the evaluation corpus (on all of which we happen to identify pagination links with 100% precision and recall). n is the number of links on the result page, n_1 (n_2) the number of immediate numeric (non-numeric) pagination links on the page, and P, R are precision and recall for our approach.[1] For each website we also present a screenshot of either its pagination links or a potential false positive. Even in this small sample of webpages, we can observe the diversity of pagination links: Only six of the twelve websites have a typical pagination link layout (non-numeric link containing a NEXT keyword and a list of numeric links with the current page represented as a non-link). Some of the challenges evident from this table are:

1. For FindAProperty and IKEA the index of the current page is a link and thus we need to consider, e.g., its style to distinguish it from the other links.
2. For Zoopla the "50" for the results per page can be easily mistaken for an immediate numeric pagination link.
3. For Savills, numeric links come as intervals. However, our NUMBER annotations also cover numeric ranges (as well as "2k" or "two").
4. For Amazon the result page contains a confusing scrollbar for navigating through related products (right screenshot).
5. For Lands' End the non-numeric pagination link is an image. However, our approach classifies it correctly, based on the context and attribute values.

---

[1] Precision is the percentage of true positives among the nodes identified as pagination links, recall the percentage of identified pagination links among all pagination links (and thus lower recall means more false negatives).

6. TechCrunch contains a single isolated non-numeric pagination link, that we are able to identify due to the keyword present in its text and the proximity to "Page 1".
7. TMZ has a pagination link that carries both a NEXT and a NUMBER annotation. From the context, we nevertheless identify it correctly as non-numeric.

3   Related Work

Our work is mostly related to web-block classification. Although not directly addressing our problem, fields such as focused (or topical) crawling and web data extraction try to recognise relevant links to follow, such as pagination links. *Focused crawlers* [1–3, 8, 13], tailored towards navigating through more restricted collections of pages, mainly aim at efficient exploration of pages relevant to a specific topic. To determine whether a page is relevant, several heuristics are used mostly based on the link context (i.e., the text appearing around the considered link), which is classified using machine learning techniques [1, 3, 6, 11–13, 15]. None of these specifically address pagination links, but rely on the general relevance metrics instead. Unfortunately, these approaches, though requiring significantly more training for the classifiers than our approach, usually reach accuracy below 70%, which is considerable for the general problem, but can be done for pagination links – as shown in this paper – at much higher accuracy.

While focused crawlers are driven by a given topic, *web data extraction* systems often automatise the extraction of data from specific web sites. In this respect, pagination links are fundamental. However, existing unsupervised approaches such as [4, 7, 18] mainly focus on the extraction of records on a page, exploiting repetitive structure, and do not address the task of automatically retrieving pagination links.

Web-block classification approaches typically start with a web-page's corresponding DOM-tree and identify sub-trees or sub-forests of this tree that correspond to particular block types (e.g. advertisements or navigation menus). Most of them employ machine learning techniques. However, to the best of our knowledge, none of these approaches addresses pagination links or even similar block types, but rather focus on larger (multi-node) block types. BERyL is also able to classify such blocks, but in this paper we focus on recognising single-node block types such as pagination links.

Nevertheless, it is worth reviewing briefly how different feature types, content, visual, and structural, are used in these block classification systems. Most of the systems combine content and visual features. For example, [16] focuses on determining two block types (title and body) for one specific domain (news articles) and involves both content and visual features. In a similar way, [14] distinguishes between content and spatial features. In [10] the authors distinguish between stylistic features based on the DOM-tree and visual appearance of nodes and lexical features based on annotation texts of the DOM-nodes, quite similar to the content and visual features in our approach. The authors list site navigation elements among their classification labels, but the F_1 value they achieve for this block (82%) is significantly lower than our result for pagination links (99%) and the definition includes navigation menus and similar blocks. The same is true for [17] and [9]. They also consider navigation blocks, but with a wider definition and significantly lower accuracy (87% and 53%). They are also not able to distinguish pagination links leading to immediate next pages from others.

Block type customization

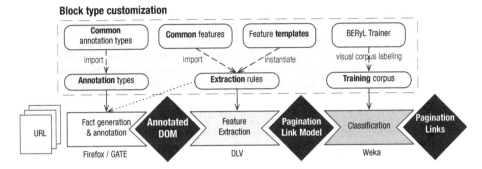

Fig. 2. BER$_y$L: Overview

It may be surprising that we do not incorporate tags or tag paths of pagination links. In [19] the broomstick data-structure is proposed, which employs both the sub-tree rooted at a node (the broom head) and the tag path to it (the broom stick). However, in the case of pagination links, we have observed a high variation among the relevant tags and tag paths.

4   Block Classification with BER$_y$L

Before turning to the specific problem of identifying pagination links, we introduce BER$_y$L, a novel framework for block classification on web pages. BER$_y$L's novelty is the combination of extraction rules formulated in Datalog (with stratified negation and aggregation) and machine learning. Through this combination BER$_y$L allows a user **(1)** to introduce new block types with minimal effort, **(2)** to intermix highly selective, block type specific features alongside more common ones. When we configure BER$_y$L for a specific block type, we decide which of the predefined, *common features* should be considered and define new, block type specific features, mostly through instantiating *feature templates*. Features are specified over the facts on a page's DOM, content, or visual appearance. However, BER$_y$L automatically adjusts the extraction pipeline for a given block type to avoid generating, e.g., visual information if that is not needed by the specific extraction rules. This allows us to tailor BER$_y$L for block types that require fast extraction (possibly through sacrificing in precision or recall).

More specifically, Figure 2 shows an overview of block classification with BER$_y$L. The bottom illustrates the typical stages of classifying the blocks on an individual web page: **(1)** We generate facts about the page's DOM, content, or visual structure depending on the needs of the actual extraction rules. We extract content facts with a set of GATE [5] annotators for entity extraction. These can be customised to the specific block type. Other facts are extracted from a customised Firefox. **(2)** Based on the annotated DOM obtained in the preceding step, we extract a feature model through a set of feature extraction rules (Datalog rules with stratified negation and aggregation). The features for a specific block type are typically a mix of common features, instantiations of *feature templates*, and ad-hoc features. **(3)** Finally, given this feature model, we classify the blocks on the page. The classifier is learned from a training corpus, whose labelling is supported by the BER$_y$L-Trainer, a visual interface for labelling web page blocks.

Table 2. BER$_y$L Annotated DOM

Structural:	
dom::node(N, T, P, Start, End)	DOM node N has tag T, parent P, and start and end label Start and End (position of the start and end tag among the combined list of all start and end tags).
dom::clickable(N)	N is a clickable target (link or has onClick handler).
dom::content(N, v, O, L)	N has (textual) content v, starting at document offset O and having length L.
Visual:	
css::box(N, Left, Top, Right, Bottom)	bounding box of a DOM node N.
css::page(Left, Top, Right, Bottom)	dimensions of the page.
css::resolution(Horizontal,Vertical)	screen resolution.
css::font_family(N, Family)	N is rendered with a font from the given family.
Content:	
gate::annotation(N, A, v)	holds if $\mu(A, N, v)$ holds.

Definition 1. *A* BER$_y$L *feature model is a set of features with values of boolean, integer, string, or tuple types. Each feature is defined through one or more **feature extraction rules**. An instance of a feature model is the result of evaluating those rules on a fact representation of a page. A classifier for a* BER$_y$L *feature model is a ML classifier learned from a set of a training instances for such a model.*

In the following, we briefly describe BER$_y$L, as needed for the identification of pagination links, and in Section 5, we show how to instantiate BER$_y$L for that purpose.

4.1   BER$_y$L Extraction Rules

Fundamentally, BER$_y$L's extraction rules are Datalog$^{\neg,\text{Agg}}$ (i.e., with stratified negation and aggregation) rules on top of an annotated DOM. To ease the definition of new features, we extend this with a template language that allows us to implement many features as simple template instantiations (without affecting the data complexity).

Definition 2. *An **annotated DOM** is a DOM tree P decorated with annotation types from an* annotation schema $\Lambda = (\mathscr{A}, \mu)$ *where* $\mathscr{A}$ *is a set of annotation types and* μ : $\mathscr{A} \times \mathscr{N} \times \mathscr{U}$ *a relation on* $\mathscr{A}$, *the set of DOM nodes* $\mathscr{N}$ *and the union of all attribute domains* $\mathscr{U}$. $\mu(A, n, v)$ *holds if n is a text node containing a representation of a value v of attribute type A.*

For `<b>Oxford,£2k</b>`, we obtain, e.g., $\mu(\text{NUMBER}, t, 2000)$, indicating that there is a number with value 2000 in t, assuming that t is the text node within the `<b>...</b>`.

An annotated DOM is represented in BER$_y$L through three sets of facts, structural, visual, and content (or annotation). Depending on the extraction rules, BER$_y$L automatically detects which of these sets are required and only generates the corresponding facts. In Table 2, we give a sample of the facts from each fact set, as needed for the following discussion. In BER$_y$L, we add namespaces (prefix followed by ::) to separate facts from different fact sets.

```
  std::preceding(X, Y) ⇐ dom::node(X, _, _, _, End),
2   dom::node(Y, _, _, Start, _), End < Start.
  std::proximity(X, Y) ⇐ proximity_dimension(DHor, DVert),
4   css::box(X, LeftX, TopX, _, _), css::box(Y, LeftY, TopY, _, _),
    TopY − DVert ≤ TopX ≤ TopY + DVert, LeftY − DHor ≤ LeftX ≤ LeftY + DHor.
6 std::left_proximity(X, Y) ⇐ std::proximity(X, Y),
    css::box(X, _, _, RightX, _), css::box(Y, LeftY, _, _, _),
8   RightX ≤ LeftY.
  std::first_screen(Left, Top, Right, Bottom) ⇐
10  css::page(Left, Top, _, _), css::resolution(H, V),
    Right = Left + H, Bottom = Top + V.
```

Fig. 3. BER$_y$L standard predicates

Based on these facts, BER$_y$L provides a set of standard predicates and features that a specific block type may import and a set of feature templates for easy instantiation of new features. As for fact sets, BER$_y$L also uses namespaces for different rule sets. Standard predicates are in the std namespace. When instantiating a block type, we use a namespace to separate feature predicates from ordinary ones. Feature predicates are predicates that represent a feature to be used for classification. They come in two varieties, unary for boolean features, and binary for features with a value. Values may be integers, strings, or (flat) tuples of those.

Figure 3 shows some of the standard predicates in BER$_y$L: These range from structural relations between nodes (similar to XPath relations) over visual relations (such as proximity or if a node is to the north-west of another one) to information about the rendering context such as the dimensions of the first and last screen.

BER$_y$L provides a set of standard features such as a nodes's number of characters:

```
<Model>::char_num(X, Num) ⇐ node_of_interest(X), dom::content(X, _, _, Num).
```

node_of_interest is a predicate that specifies which nodes are to be considered for classification (e.g., all nodes, only links, only images). It is provided with the block specific extraction rules, see Section 5.

When we instantiate BER$_y$L for a specific block type, we import only those features that are actually relevant through an import statement such as

```
IMPORT <Model>::char_num INTO <plm>
```

This binds the template variable <Model> to plm and replaces all occurrences of that variable in the rule.

4.2   BER$_y$L Feature Templates

Different block types often have overlapping features, but it is even more common for them to differ only slightly, e.g., with respect to what DOM nodes to consider.

For that reason, we introduce a small template language atop of Datalog. This language allows us to specify a common pattern for features, factoring out constants or predicates in which these features may differ.

Figure 4 shows a sample of feature templates in BER_yL. The first template defines boolean features for any annotation type AType indicating whether a certain node of interest is annotated with AType. We instantiate it for a NUMBER in the plm pagination link model in the following way:

```
INSTANTIATE annotated_by<Model, AType> USING <plm, NUMBER>
```

In a similar way, the second template defines a boolean feature that holds for nodes of interest, if there is another node in their proximity for which Property(Close) is true. To instantiate it to nodes that are annotated with PAGINATION, we write

```
  INSTANTIATE in_proximity<Model,Property(Close)>
2 USING <plm, plm::annotated_by<PAGINATION(Closest)>>
```

Observe, that BER_yL templates thus allow for two forms of template parameters: variables and predicates. More formally,

Definition 3. *A BER_yL template is an expression* **TEMPLATE** $N<D_1,\ldots,D_k>\{p \Leftarrow expr\}$ *such that N is the template name, $D_1,\ldots,D_k$ are template parameters, p is a template atom, expr is a conjunction of template atoms and annotation queries. A template parameter is either a variable or an expression of the shape $p(V_1,\ldots,V_l)$ where p is a predicate variable and $V_1,\ldots,V_n$ are names of required first order variables in bindings of p.*

A template atom $p<C_1,\ldots,C_k>(X_1,\ldots,X_n)$ consists of a first-order predicate name or predicate variable p, template variables $C_1,\ldots,C_k$, and first-order variables $X_1,\ldots,X_n$. If $p(V_1,\ldots,V_l)$ is a parameter for N, then $\{V_1,\ldots V_l\} \subset \{X_1,\ldots,X_n\}$.

An instantiation always has to provide bindings for all template parameters. We extend the usual safety and stratification definitions in the obvious way to a BER_yL template program. Then it is easy to see that the rules derived by instantiating a safe and stratified template program are always a safe, stratified Datalog$^{\neg,\text{Agg}}$ program.

5   Pagination Links with BER_yL

For identifying pagination links with high accuracy, we create a small feature model in BER_yL that consists of content, page position, visual proximity, and structural features. In Section 6, we show that not only BER_yL achieves almost perfect accuracy with this feature model for a wide range of domains and pages, but that these four feature types contribute notably to the overall performance.

Definition 4. *A pagination sequence is a sequence of web pages from the same domain, that is the result of paginating some information such as an article or a result set of a search. Given a DOM P of a page, the (immediate) pagination link identification problem is the problem of identifying those nodes in P that must be clicked to get to the following page in any pagination sequence the page is part of. The pagination links should be distinguished into numerical and non-numerical (such as "Next").*

With BER_yL we reduce this problem to a block classification task over the set of clickable nodes (DOM::clickable). To do so, we need

1. to define appropriate annotation types if necessary,
2. to specify an appropriate feature model, as discussed in Section 4.1, and
3. to train a classifier on a small training set.

```
  TEMPLATE annotated_by<Model,AType> {
2   <Model>::annotated_by<AType>(X) ⇐ node_of_interest(X),
      gate::annotation(X, <AType>, _). }
4 TEMPLATE in_proximity<Model,Property(Close)> {
    <Model>::in_proximity<Property>(X) ⇐ node_of_interest(X),
6   std::proximity(Y,X), <Property(Close)>. }
  TEMPLATE num_in_proximity<Model,Property(Close)> {
8   <Model>::in_proximity<Property>(X,Num) ⇐ node_of_interest(X),
    std::proximity(Close,X), Num = #count(N: <Property(Close)>). }
10 TEMPLATE relative_position<Model,Within(Height,Width)> {
    <Model>::relative_position<Within>(X, (PosH, PosV)) ⇐ node_of_interest(X),
12    css::box(X, LeftX, TopX, _, _), <Within(Height,Width)>,
```

$$PosH = \frac{100 \cdot LeftX}{Width}, \ PosV = \frac{100 \cdot TopX}{Height}. \ \}$$

```
14 TEMPLATE contained_in<Model,Container(Left,Top,Bottom,Right)> {
    <Model>::contained_in<Container>(X) ⇐ node_of_interest(X),
16    css::box(X,LeftX,TopX,RightX,BottomX), <Container(Left,Top,Right,Bottom)>,
      Left < LeftX < RightX < Right, Top < TopX < BottomX < Bottom. }
18 TEMPLATE closest<Model,Relation(Closest,X),Property(Closest),Test(Closest)> {
    <Model>::closest<Relation>_with<Property>_is<Test>(X) ⇐
  node_of_interest(X),
20    <Relation(Closest,X)>, <Property(Closest)>, <Test(Closest)>,
      ¬(<Relation(Y,X)>, <Property(Y)>, <Relation(Y,Closest)>). }
```

Fig. 4. BER$_y$L feature templates

Annotation Types. In addition to the standard annotation type NUMBER, we introduce two annotation types specific to pagination link identification: NEXT and PAGINATION. NEXT collects typical keywords used to indicate immediate non-numerical pagination links, e.g., "next", "»", or "›", PAGINATION includes all those, but also keywords related to previous pagination links, e.g., "previous", and to the number of results, e.g., "page", "results".

Feature Model. Table 3 shows the features used in our approach to pagination link identification. They are split into four types: content, page position, visual proximity, and structural. The corresponding extraction rules are given in Figure 5.

For defining these features, we use a small number of auxiliary predicates as shown below. The first is required in any BER$_y$L feature model and specifies the domain of discourse, here all dom::clickable nodes (links and other click targets). The second is required in feature models that use proximity predicates and specify what we consider to be "in the proximity" of a node.

```
  node_of_interest(X) ⇐ dom::clickable(X).
2 proximity_dimension(Width,10) ⇐ css::page(_, _, Width, _).
  numeric(X, Value) ⇐ gate::annotation(X, NUMBER, Value).
4 numeric(X) ⇐ numeric(X,_).
  different_style(X,Y)⇐css::font_family(X,FX), css::font_family(Y,FY), FX ≠ FY.
```

Table 3. PLM: Pagination Link Model

		Description	Type	Predicate
Content	1	Annotated as NEXT	bool	`plm::annotated_by<NEXT>`
	2	Annotated as PAGINATION	bool	`plm::annotated_by<PAGINATION>`
	3	Annotated as NUMBER	bool	`plm::annotated_by<NUMBER>`
	4	Number of characters	int	`plm::char_num`
Page position	5	Relative position on page	int^2	`plm::relative_position<css::page>`
	6	Relative position in first screen	int^2	`plm::relative_position<std::first_screen>`
	7	In first screen	bool	`plm::contained_in<std::first_screen>`
	8	In last screen	bool	`plm::contained_in<std::last_screen>`
Visual proximity	9	Pagination annotation close to node	bool	`plm::in_proximity<plm::annotated_by<PAGINATION>>`
	10	Number of close numeric nodes	int	`plm::num_in_proximity<numeric>`
	11	Closest numeric node is a link	bool	`plm::closest<std::left_proximity>_with <numeric>_is<non_link>`
	12	Closest numeric node has different style	bool	`<numeric>_is<different_style>`
	13	Closest link annotated with NEXT	bool	`<dom::clickable>_is<plm::annotated_by<NEXT>`
	14	Ascending w. closest numeric left, right	bool	`plm::ascending-numerics`
Structural	15	Preceding numeric node is a link	bool	`plm::closest<std::preceding>_with <numeric>_is<non_link>`
	16	Preceding numeric node has different style	bool	`<numeric>_is<different_style>`
	17	Preceding link annotated with NEXT	bool	`<dom::clickable>_is<plm::annotated_by<NEXT>`

The *content features* 1 − 4 from Table 3 specify whether a node is annotated with one of the three annotation types (NEXT, PAGINATION, and NUMBER) and how many characters it contains. They are defined in Figure 5 by an instantiation and an import of the standard feature char_num. The instantiation creates three instances of the annotated_by template, one for each of the three annotation types.

The *page position features* are the relative position on the first page and on the first screen, as well as whether a node is on the first or last screen. They are defined by two instantiations in Figure 4, one for relative positions (using css::page and std::first_screen, resp.) and one for the presence in the first or last screen.

The *visual proximity features* are the most involved ones. They include a feature on whether there is a node in visual proximity that is annotated with PAGINATION (9), a feature on the number of numeric nodes in the proximity (10), and a feature that specifies whether the node and the closest numeric nodes in the proximity to the left and right form an ascending sequence (14). 11 − 13 ask if the closest node with a certain property passes a given test, e.g., whether the closest numeric node is a link. Accordingly, 11 − 13 are instantiations of closest, 9 and 10 are instantiations of in_proximity and num_in_proximity, and 14 is the only feature in this model that is defined entirely from scratch.

The *structural features* are similar to 11 − 13, but use XPath's preceding instead of visual proximity, E.g., 15 tests if the numeric node, immediately preceding the given node; is a link. Those are omitted from Figure 5 as they are similar to 11 − 13.

```
 1 − 3 : INSTANTIATE annotated_by<Model, AType>
         USING <plm, { NEXT, PAGINATION, NUMBER>
     4 : IMPORT <Model>::char_num INTO <plm>
 5 − 6 : INSTANTIATE relative_position<Model,Within(Height,Weight)>
         USING <plm, {css::page(_,_,Height,Width), std::first_screen(_,_,Height,Width) }>
 7 − 8 : INSTANTIATE contained_in<Model,Container(Left,Top,Bottom,Right)>
         USING <plm, {std::first_screen(Top,Left,Bottom,Right),...}>
     9 : INSTANTIATE in_proximity<Model,Property(Close)>
         USING <plm, plm::annotated_by<PAGINATION(Closest)>
    10 : INSTANTIATE num_in_proximity<Model,Property(Close)>
         USING <plm, numeric(Close)>
11 − 12 : INSTANTIATE closest<Model,Relation(Closest,X),Property(Closest),Test(Closest)>
         USING <plm, std::left_proximity(Closest,X), numeric(Closest),
                     { non-link(Closest), different_style(Closest,X) }>
    13 : INSTANTIATE closest<Model,Relation(Closest,X),Property(Closest),Test(Closest)>
         USING <plm, std::left_proximity(Closest,X), dom::clickable(Closest),
                     plm::annotated_by<NEXT(Closest)>
    14 : plm::ascending-numerics(X) ⇐ node_of_interest(X), numeric(X, ValueX),
         std::left-proximity(Left,X), std::right-proximity(Right,X),
         numeric(Left, ValueLeft), numeric(Right, ValueRight),
         ValueLeft < ValueX < ValueRight,
         ¬(std::left-proximity(Left,LeftN), std::left-proximity(LeftN,X), numeric(LeftN)),
         ¬(std::left-proximity(Left,RightN), std::right-proximity(RightN,X), numeric(RightN)).
```

Fig. 5. Extraction rules for pagination link identification

5.1   Training the Classifier

With this feature model, BER$_y$L derives a classifier based on a small training set. For pagination link classification, a training corpus of only two dozen pages suffices to achieve the high accuracy demonstrated in Section 6. We expect a trade-off between accuracy, corpus size, and complexity of the feature model, but their relation in this triangle remains an open issue.

Figure 6 shows the classification tree derived on a training corpus for real-estate and car websites in the UK and detailed in Section 6. The tree employs almost all features, though the only structural feature considered is 15. For 5, we use both horizontal and vertical position, but at different points in the tree (5.h and 5.v). Visual proximity (9 − −14) and 15 are clearly very distinctive features of pagination links. Feature 1 has a key role in distinguishing numeric and non-numeric pagination links, but 11, 12, and 14 are also required to give an almost perfect distinction, as evident in Section 6.

Our classifier employs almost all of the features we have pre-selected. It places a strong emphasis on the visual features, such as relative vertical and horizontal positions and whether the link to be classified is in the first or last screens. Manually finding rules that correspond to this classifier would be a very error-prone and time consuming task, in particular where thresholds and complex features are involved. This justifies the use of machine learning to obtain the precise classifiers. We further simplify this process by offering a visual tool, BER$_y$L-Trainer . With BER$_y$L-Trainer one can visually label elements on a page very quickly with the correct classification (only numeric and non-numeric are necessary, of course). It is configured with the annotation types and thus can support the user by offering the relevant types and performing a basic validation.

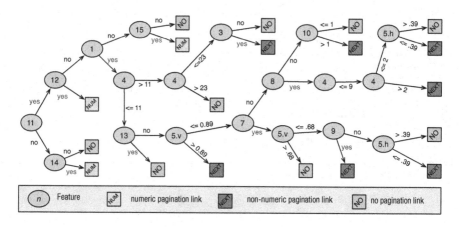

Fig. 6. Classification tree

Given this specific classifier, BER$_y$L is able to quickly identify pagination links. To that end, we first compute the basic content, visual, and DOM facts, then apply the extraction rules and finally classify the feature model instance. Through this approach BER$_y$L achieves almost perfect accuracy, as shown in Section 6.

6   Evaluation

We evaluate our BER$_y$L pagination link classifier on a corpus of 145 websites from four domains (real-estate, used cars, on-line retail, and forums). For each domain, we selected the pages randomly from a listings page (such as yell.com) or a Google search. The latter favours popular sites, but that should not affect the results presented here. For example pages from the evaluation corpus, consider again Table 1 from Section 2.

In Figure 7, we show the results of evaluating quality, feature impact, speed, and per-page speed. Figure 7a illustrates that for all four domains our approach achieves 100% precision with recall never below 96%. This high accuracy means that our approach can be used for crawling or otherwise navigating paginated pages with a very low risk of missing information or retrieving unrelated pages. *Numeric pagination links* are generally harder to classify than non-numeric ones due to their greater variety and the larger set of candidates. Though precision is 100% for both cases, recall is on average slightly lower for numeric pagination links (98% vs. 99%) and in some domains quite notable (e.g., real estate with 96% vs. 99%). Figure 7b shows the overall precision, recall, and F_1 score compared with those for each of the basic feature sets. For space reasons, we do not show the individual impact of all features, but note that all features included in the classification tree contribute at least several percentages to the overall precision and recall. Figure 7b also shows that content and visual proximity features are significantly more important for recall than page position and structural features.

Speed. The speed of feature extraction is crucial for the scalability of our approach. As discussed above, the use of visual features by itself imposes a certain penalty, as a

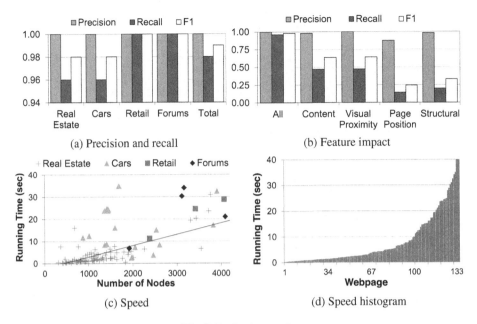

Fig. 7. Evaluation results

page needs to be rendered for those features to be computed. Figure 7c shows that the performance is highly correlated to page size with most reasonably sized pages being processed in well below 10 seconds (including page fetch and rendering). Our experiment was performed on a 3.4 Gz Intel Core i7 machine with 16 GB of RAM, running a 64-bit version of Linux Ubuntu. It is interesting to observe, that those domains where we used Google for generating the corpus and where the corpus is thus biased towards popular websites, seem to require more time than the real estate domain where the corpus is randomly picked from yell.com. Figure 7d shows the distribution of processing time over web pages, sorted by processing time. It is worth noting, that these results were achieved with an early prototype where the extraction rules had been implemented with DLV, a far more powerful reasoning language than what would suffice for our purposes.

7 Conclusion

Identifying pagination links with high accuracy is beneficial for many types of automated processing on the web. The approach taken in this paper shows that nearly perfect accuracy is achievable through the use of our flexible block classification framework BER$_y$L. In contrast to previous approaches, BER$_y$L can be easily extended with block specific features. Not only is that essential for high accuracy but also allows us to keep the feature model small. There are two main open issues: Building an optimised version of the current system with sub-second classification time, which we believe is possible if the extraction rules are implemented, e.g., by a first-order rewriting. Another interesting problem would be the further automation of adding new blocks for classification, e.g., by automatic feature selection and gazetteer acquisition.

References

1. Almpanidis, G., Kotropoulos, C., Pitas, I.: Combining text and link analysis for focused crawling - an application for vertical search engines. Inf. Syst. 32(6), 886–908 (2007)
2. Bra, P.D., Post, R.D.J.: Information retrieval in the world-wide web: Making client-based searching feasible. Computer Networks and ISDN Systems 27(2), 183–192 (1994)
3. Chakrabarti, S., Berg, M.V.D., Dom, B.: Focused crawling: a new approach to topic-specific web resource discovery. In: Computer Networks, pp. 1623–1640 (1999)
4. Crescenzi, V., Mecca, G.: Automatic information extraction from large websites. J. ACM 51(5), 731–779 (2004)
5. Cunningham, H., Maynard, D., Bontcheva, K., Tablan, V., Aswani, N., Roberts, I., Gorrell, G., Funk, A., Roberts, A., Damljanovic, D., Heitz, T., Greenwood, M.A., Saggion, H., Petrak, J., Li, Y., Peters, W.: Text Processing with GATE, Version 6 (2011)
6. Diligenti, M., Coetzee, F.M., Lawrence, S., Giles, C.L., Gori, M.: Focused crawling using context graphs. In: VLDB, pp. 527–534 (2000)
7. Fazzinga, B., Flesca, S., Tagarelli, A.: Schema-based web wrapping. Knowledge and Inf. Sys. 26, 127–173 (2011)
8. Hersovici, M., Jacovi, M., Maarek, Y.S., Pelleg, D., Shtalhaim, M., Ur, S.: The shark-search algorithm. an application: tailored web site mapping. Computer Networks and ISDN Systems 30(1-7), 317–326 (1998)
9. Kang, J., Choi, J.: Block classification of a web page by using a combination of multiple classifiers. In: NCM (2008)
10. Lee, C.H., Ken, M.Y., Lai, S.: Stylistic and lexical co-training for web block classification. In: WIDM (2004)
11. Liu, H., Janssen, J., Milios, E.: Using HMM to learn user browsing patterns for focused web crawling. DKE 59(2) (2006)
12. Pant, G., Srinivasan, P.: Learning to crawl: Comparing classification schemes. TOIS 23(4), 430–462 (2005)
13. Pant, G., Srinivasan, P.: Link contexts in classifier-guided topical crawlers. TKDE 18(1), 107–122 (2006)
14. Song, R., Liu, H., Wen, J.-R., Ma, W.-Y.: Learning block importance model for web pages. In: WWW (2004)
15. Srinivasan, P., Menczer, F., Pant, G.: A general evaluation framework for topical crawlers. Inf. Retrieval 8, 417–447 (2005)
16. Wang, J., Chen, C., Wang, C., Pei, J., Bu, J., Guan, Z., Zhang, W.V.: Can we learn a template-independent wrapper for news article extraction from a single training site? In: KDD (2009)
17. Yang, X., Shi, Y.: Learning web page block functions using roles of images. In: ICPCA (2008)
18. Zhai, Y., Liu, B.: Web data extraction based on partial tree alignment. In: WWW (2005)
19. Zheng, S., Song, R., Wen, J.-R., Giles, C.L.: Efficient record-level wrapper induction. In: CIKM (2009)

WebSelF: A Web Scraping Framework

Jakob G. Thomsen[1], Erik Ernst[1], Claus Brabrand[2],
and Michael Schwartzbach[1]

[1] Aarhus University
{gedefar,eernst,mis}@cs.au.dk
[2] IT University of Copenhagen
brabrand@itu.dk

Abstract. We present WebSelF, a framework for web scraping which
models the process of web scraping and decomposes it into four conceptually independent, reusable, and composable constituents. We have validated our framework through a full parameterized implementation that is
flexible enough to capture previous work on web scraping. We conducted
an experiment that evaluated several qualitatively different web scraping
constituents (including previous work and combinations hereof) on about
11,000 HTML pages on daily versions of 17 web sites over a period of more
than one year. Our framework solves three concrete problems with current web scraping and our experimental results indicate that composition
of previous and our new techniques achieve a higher degree of accuracy,
precision and specificity than existing techniques alone.

1   Introduction

The World Wide Web is an enormous source of information, (still) mostly represented as HTML which is designed for presenting information to humans, not
computers. Therefore, automated information extraction from the web (aka.,
web scraping) is difficult. A program for web scraping, called a *web wrapper*,
may be programmed manually [23,25], semi-automatically [14,22,2,11], or automatically [15]. We refer to the survey by Chang et al. [6] for more information.

However, when a web page changes (and similar web pages may have sub-
stantially different structure), the extraction often fails or yields incorrect data
causing programs that depend on the scraping to malfunction. Web wrappers
use *wrapper validation* (aka. wrapper verification) to detect this, typically based
on the extracted text [20,10]. Updating the wrapper to recover is known as *reinduction* [10,12,13,17,8,16], and it is often based on older pages and/or user interaction. Validation and reinduction together constitutes *wrapper maintenance*.

Current approaches suffer from three problems. First, wrapper validation
based solely on the textual contents and structure of the scraped page may be
difficult or inadequate in certain cases. For some pages, it is worth also considering the *context* and *presentation* (i.e., *where* information is physically located
on a page after full rendering and applying stylesheets). Second, with client-side
scripting (e.g., JavaScript and AJAX) and form elements, it becomes useful to
interact with a web page beyond just extracting information. Access to selected

M. Brambilla, T. Tokuda, and R. Tolksdorf (Eds.): ICWE 2012, LNCS 7387, pp. 347–361, 2012.

elements on a page allows for subsequent manipulation of the original document (e.g., pressing buttons, filling in text fields, submitting forms). Third, existing wrapper techniques cannot easily be combined, which makes it hard to reuse the vast amount of work done on selection, reinduction, and validation. There is no general and precise signature definition of the components of the web wrapper, how they interact or what level of automation they exhibit.

This paper presents a framework, WebSelF, that addresses these problems for selecting elements on a web page. WebSelF is characterized and parameterized by four scraping constituent functions, that we call framework functions: one for selecting elements, designated as a *selection function*; one for validating the selected element, designated as a *validation function*; and two for maintaining each of them, designated as *reinduction functions*. WebSelF is novel for three reasons. First, it supports composition and reuse of previously defined validation functions, whereby validation can benefit from not only the textual contents of the selected elements, but also combinations of other dimensions (in particular, context and presentation). Secondly, the selection functions in WebSelF are able to not just extract information, but also subsequently manipulate selected elements in the presence of client-side scripting. Finally, WebSelF has a precise model that explicitly divides the labor into a manual and an automatic part, in which the responsibilities of the four functions are explicitly given. Furthermore the signatures of the four functions are defined, which allows WebSelF to easily wrap and use existing selection, validation and reinduction functions.

We have implemented WebSelF in Java, parameterized by the four framework functions, and used the implementation to author, evaluate, and compare validation functions based on different dimensions (including the influential work of Lerman et al. [10]). The evaluation shows that presentational features of the selected elements are beneficial for validation. Further, it shows that combining existing validation functions (such as the previous approach by Lerman et al.) with other orthogonal dimensions may achieve higher *accuracy*, *precision*, and *specificity* (defined later) than the original approach. The validated elements in our experimental evaluation are selected by real world web wrappers, as most of the selection functions have been harvested from the web where they are used for real web scraping purposes. The evaluation results have high credibility, because every selection has been manually verified. The main contributions of this paper is a framework, WebSelF, for web scraping including:

- a model of the process of web scraping (Section 2) explicitly dividing the labor, by decomposing the process into a *selection function*, a *validation function*, and *reinductions* of both, along with a method of composing validation functions (Section 3);
- a full implementation, parameterized by reusable composable framework functions (available at the WebSelF site: `cs.au.dk/~gedefar/webself`); *and*
- an experimental evaluation and comparison of qualitatively different validation functions (including previous work) based on about 11,000 HTML pages taken from 17 web sites over a period of more than one year (Section 4).

```
<body>                              <body>
<p>ICWE 2012 is to be held         <p>ICWE 2012 will be
in Berlin, Germany.</p> ...         held on July 23-27.</p> ...
</body>                             </body>
```
      (a) A simple web page   (b) A second version of the web page

```
                                    <body>
                                    <p>
<body>                              <img src=".." alt="Group Photo"/>
<p>The ICWE 2012 <a..>program</a>   </p>
is available.</p> ...               <p>The ICWE 2012 conference
</body>                             was a success.</p> ...
```
(c) The third version of the page with an   `</body>`
added **anchor** tag   (d) A fourth version of the web page, where
an image has been added

Fig. 1. Evolution of an example web page from a conference news site over time

2   A Model of the Process of Web Scraping

In this section we introduce the basic structure of our framework by means of a model of the process of web scraping, built from several individual framework functions with a specific interaction. To illustrate the principles, we will use a deliberately simple example and scrape successive evolutions of the "top story" of a conference news site. In WebSelF, a web wrapper consists of a *selection function*, a *validation function* and means for *reinducing* (learning) new versions of both of these functions. As the selection function, the example uses an XPath expression (which is common) with the additional convention that only the *first* element is selected in case the XPath expression matches several elements. For the validation function, the example will use *structural identity* with respect to a DTD[5] in that a selected element is accepted if it conforms to a DTD inferred over the elements selected so far (cf. Bex et al. [4]). The initial DTD is inferred from the first example (which in this example is a p tag containing only text).

Figure 1(a) shows an excerpt from the first version of the web page, and the interesting piece of information is the p tag and its contained text. The initial XPath expression is //p which selects that item in this case.

The next version of the web page is shown in Fig. 1(b). The XPath expression works here by extracting the p tag and the validation function accepts it, as the structure has not changed.

The next version of the web page is shown in Fig. 1(c). The XPath expression still works here, but the validation function rejects the element because an **anchor** tag with a link to the program has been added to the p tag. The framework now asks the user a simple *yes/no* question for whether or not the p tag is the correct element. In this case it is, so a new validation function is reinduced (learned) to allow the new **anchor** tag. The new validation function accepts p tags with an optional **anchor** tag as its child intermixed with the text (remember that the DTD is inferred over the first three versions).

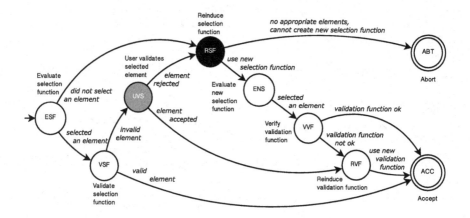

Fig. 2. A model of the process of web scraping

In the next version, shown in figure 1(d), a new p tag with an img tag has been added before the interesting p tag. In this case the selection function selects the first p tag, which does not conform to the previous version of the element. This discrepancy is detected by the validation function, and as it is in fact not the correct element (judged by the user) the XPath expression needs to be *reinduced*, i.e., a new and improved selection function must be constructed. The framework uses the reinduction function for selection functions for this purpose, and this function could consult the user and/or the validation function in order to perform the task. As a result, the XPath expression is updated to select the correct element, e.g., by becoming //p[not(./img)].

The running example illustrates different flows captured by our framework. The general and formal flow between the states of WebSelF is shown in the state diagram in Fig. 2 which shows a model of the web scraping process. Each state has an abbreviated name consisting of three upper-case letters; a nearby explanatory text motivates the choice of letters. Transitions are labeled with a text indicating the decision criterion associated with that transition. One run of the algorithm starts at ESF and ends in a final state—indicated by a double ring—and yields an accepted element from the given page or aborts to indicate that the page does not contain any acceptable elements. At the same time the algorithm maintains the selection function and the validation function, using the provided facilities for reinduction.

The states with a colored background may involve user-interaction and the particular color signifies the level of complexity in the interaction. The state with gray background (UVS) is related to the reinduction of the validation function and is only asking a simple *yes/no* question. In contrast, the state with black background (RSF) is related to the reinduction of the selection function, which may involve the user in a much more complex manner.

For a fully formalized description of WebSelF, where the precise signatures of the involved functions and flow of data and control between the states is

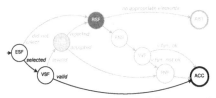

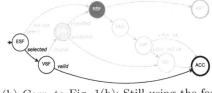

(a) Corresponding to Fig. 1(a): Using the fast path, where everything is okay

(b) Corr. to Fig. 1(b): Still using the fast path

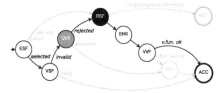

(c) Corr. to Fig. 1(c): Using a not so fast path, where the selection function is correct, but the validation function is not

(d) Corr. to Fig. 1(d): Using the slowest path where the validation function is correct, but the selection function is not

Fig. 3. State model paths corresponding to the example web page evolution

specified, we refer to the accompanying technical report [18]. It contains proofs for a *preservation* and a *progress* property; it also shows in detail how the work by Lerman et al. [10] may be emulated in WebSelF.

In the following we just describe the information flow in terms of our four versions in the running example. Consider the first version of our running example, shown as Fig. 1(a). As the selection function selects an element, we go from the initial state ESF to VSF. The selected element is accepted by the validation function, so we continue directly to the ACC state, without reinducing a new validation function. This path through the state diagram is illustrated by the graph in Fig. 3(a). This is the fast path where everything works smoothly, and hopefully it is also a very typical path. The flow of the second version (Fig. 1(b)) is completely identical to the first version's flow, where it takes the fast path and is likewise shown in Fig. 3(b).

For the third version, an element is likewise selected and so we go to the VSF state. This time, however, the validation function rejects the selected element, so we proceed to the UVS state where the user is asked. The user decides that the element should be accepted, so we go to the RVF state. Since the validation function made an incorrect decision we obtain an improved validation function through reinduction. This path through the state diagram is illustrated by the graph in Fig. 3(c). As a side note, in WebSelF we assume it's always possible to reinduce a validation function, as there is no requirement that the reinduced validation function is improved compared to the previous validation function. In fact the reinduction function is free to return the old validation function in case it is not capable of producing an improved validation function.

Finally, if we run the fourth version we still go to VSF first as an element is selected, but from VSF we go to UVS and then in turn to RSF, because the wrong element was selected, according to both the validation function and the user. The selection function is reinduced as we transition to the ENS state and on to the VVF state. The new element found by the new selection function is accepted by the validation function, so we do not need to reinduce (learn) a new validation function. This is shown in Fig. 3(d).

We have not covered a case where the selection fails entirely, but this could occur if we receive, e.g., an HTTP error 505 (internal error on server). In this case the path taken would be the uppermost path in the state diagram, from ESF to RSF to ABT. Finally, there is a case where both reinductions occur, which is a slight variant of Fig. 3(d).

To sum up, our framework only involves the user when the discrepancy between already learned examples and the new version is too big. What this means will be explained in Sec. 3.2. Moreover, the user is first involved in a simple manner by being asked whether a given selection should be accepted or not. If the blame falls on the validation function it is updated automatically, and only when the selection function is to blame does the framework proceed to involve the user in the more complex task of reinducing (creating) a new selection function. Other approaches [10,20,17] require a set of prelabeled examples to learn from, and they do not support a similar division of labor between a validation function that allows for automatic maintenance and a selection function which may be tailored to embody an arbitrary amount of domain knowledge. Our approach supports this division and our selection and validation functions are composable to utilize arbitrary domain knowledge. We furthermore believe that the precise description of WebSelF can aid in the engineering of web information extraction software.

3 Framework Instances

There are many kinds of selection function and validation function, as well as reinduction functions for either. This section discusses a few of these at an abstract level. An important choice to make is concerned with the environment provided for evaluation of the selection and validation functions. If a full browser is available for rendering the page and running client side code (e.g., JavaScript and AJAX), as opposed to working straight from the HTML source, the validation function can rely on presentational information beyond the contents and structure of the page, e.g., screen coordinates and colors. For generality, we consider below the situation where the pages are rendered in a full browser (our framework implementation directly supports this).

3.1   Selection Functions

A selection function is responsible for choosing a piece of information (i.e. an HTML element, a list of HTML elements, tuples of text, etc.) from a given web page and delivering the *selection result* in a suitable format. It can be anything from trivial to near-impossible to specify the "correct" selection for a web page.

However, a few generic possibilities do exist. In particular, XPath expressions were specifically invented in order to be able to designate elements in an XML tree structure. Also, regular expressions and context free parsers are commonly used to locate specific elements by their content and structure. The work by Lerman et al. [10] utilizes a hierarchy of token classes to select textual elements based on sequences of token types. Finally Kushmerick et al. [9] induce selection functions based on delimiters.

An important property of a selection function is its *robustness*, or its ability to "just keep working" when it is used on evolved versions of a web page with similar but updated content and structure. As with the structure itself, page specific approaches and general computation may be needed to deal with such updates. Myllymaki & Jackson [24] discuss the characteristics of robustness for selection functions based on XPath, but they do not discuss any mechanical way to achieve it. Lately, different mechanical techniques to 'robustify' XPath expressions have been proposed [7,8,16]. Basically all the techniques rewrite the XPath expression into a more robust expression relative to the changes seen in a set of training web pages, and they achieve much better robustness than a corresponding fully specified XPath expression.

Reinduction of selection functions is in general just as hard as inventing them in the first place. For generic selection functions it may be possible to derive the selection function from a history of positive examples; e.g., as it is done by Lerman et al. [10]. This process may be seen as an abstraction process whereby the desired element is described by successively more abstract and inclusive specifications, until it matches all the positive examples. Incrementally building a specification works well for semi-static information where only a part of an element is changing, such as an address or a form field, where the static part of the element can be used as an anchor. If the goal is to extract frequently changing information, such as the *top* news story from a news site, then the selection can benefit from using contextual and/or presentational information, such as the structure of the context (e.g., a highly specific `class/id` attribute or the (x, y) screen coordinates of the elements). Some reinduction approaches [12] support manually specifying a fixed context to search for, others automatically infer it from the history [10]. In general, reinduction of selection functions is likely to require supervision.

3.2   Validation Functions

A validation function validates a selection result by either accepting or rejecting the result from a web page. (In the following discussion of validation functions we will assume for simplicity that the selection result is a single HTML element.) Typically, validation functions utilize textual dimensions of both the selection result along with the original web page when validating, but when the element to be selected changes significantly from time to time, other dimensions might be more effective. It may be more informative to investigate for instance the context (e.g., the tree structure from the grand parent of the selected element). Furthermore, human spectators often rely strongly on the appearance of a web site, and this realization is likewise very useful. For instance, a selection result is likely to be rejected if it appears physically far away from its typical location on the web page.

Validation function *reinduction* is the process whereby an existing validation function is replaced by an updated one that is known to make more appropriate judgments. In WebSelF, as in other approaches [10,20], the validation function is reinduced with respect to a history of selection results. In the theoretic treatment of WebSelF all previous selection results are available, but in a concrete implementation this set can be a too large, so it often suffices to only use the selection results that the validation function wrongfully rejected.

In general, validation functions can be more generic than selection functions because they must primarily flag the occurrence of anomalies. It is our experience that a validation function can often use a generic algorithm customized by a number of parameters, and reinduction then amounts to adjusting those parameters so that the validation function responds more favorably to a given selection history.

One issue to consider in connection with validation function reinduction is whether the new validation function should learn to recognize all examples in the given history. We may wish to suppress the consequences of processing exceptional web pages, also known as *outliers*. The problem is that a validation function may become overly permissive, because a few outliers has taught it to tolerate almost anything. It may be better to reject (or ask for explicit user confirmation in) a few unusual cases, and then retain high selectivity. One example of a validation reinduction function which does not learn to recognize all examples in order to suppress outliers is the one from Lerman et al. [10], as it only includes the examples in the history that are statistically significant.

It is possible to create *composite* validation functions based on existing validation functions. This is particularly interesting as we are able to logically combine qualitatively different (and complementary) validation function strategies; ones that work according to *content, structure, presentation,* and even *context.* If we, for instance, want to extract the top news story from a news site, we might have to combine looking for a styled heading (structure and presentation) placed close to the top of the page (presentation).

Since a validation function returns a boolean result, we can easily compose validation functions to achieve any *propositional logic* formula, ϕ, over basic validation functions, $Q \in \mathcal{Q}_{\text{BASIC}}$:

$$\phi \quad : \quad true \mid false \mid Q \in \mathcal{Q}_{\text{BASIC}} \mid \neg\phi \mid \phi \wedge \phi \mid \phi \vee \phi$$

Reinduction of a composite validation function can be done in many ways, but often it is done by delegating the reinduction to its failing constituents (according to its constituent validation functions). Negation needs special treatment though. Say for instance that $\neg\phi$ has wrongly rejected an element a, which means that ϕ accepted a. As $\neg\phi$ is reinduced, ϕ should be reinduced to learn to reject a

which it used to accept. Hence as ϕ gradually becomes more permissive when reinduced, $\neg\phi$ will gradually become more restrictive. We will see in Sect. 4.3 that negation can be very useful, despite its somewhat counter-intuitive nature. All of this is supported by our framework.

4 Experimental Validation

Our hypothesis is that the flexibility and composability of the validation part of WebSelF leads to an improvement in accuracy, precision and specificity (defined in Sect. 4.2). We have therefore created a concrete implementation of the framework in Java to test this hypothesis. The implementation includes selection functions using regular expressions [1], XPath expressions, and it includes a full browser in order to let client-side computation take place and provide presentational information about the given web page. Furthermore automatic reinduction of validation functions and composition of validation functions as described in Sect. 3.2 are supported by the implementation. We have used this implementation to perform a substantial experiment which is described in more detail below. For details on the implementation, data set and results we refer to the project homepage at `cs.au.dk/~gedefar/webself`.

4.1 Experimental Setup

In order to evaluate WebSelF in a realistic setting, we collected 30 XPath expressions used as *selection functions*, where most of them were sufficiently successful to be published on the Web. Some of these XPath expressions were complete, concrete paths from the root to the target, while other expressions were more robust paths, such as the expression `//a[starts-with(., 'Next')]`, which selects the next button on the Yahoo Web Shop (by searching for any link starting with "Next"). These more robust expressions used the more advanced operators of XPath, like wildcards, descendant axes, etc. In order to do a proper comparison we created robust versions of the fully concrete paths, and used FireBug[1] to create fully concrete versions of the robust ones. The robust versions were crafted using only knowledge of the first web page version and was guided by the findings of Myllymaki & Jackson [24], meaning that the crafted expressions typically used descendant axis and attribute filters.

For the purposes of our experiment, we normalize all XPath expressions to have the same weight, by letting them return the first selected element if more than one is selected. To evaluate the validation functions directly we fix the selection functions, such that they are not reinduced during the experiment. In total we ended up with 60 XPath expressions, 30 fully specified and 30 robustified.

We have constructed 24 qualitatively different *validation functions* that validates textual, structural, context and presentational properties of the selected element. Eight of these validation functions use a combination of other validation

---

[1] Available from `http://getfirebug.com`.

validation function	dimension	response	reinduction
Q_{Random}	N/A	random yes/no	N/A
Q_{LMN}	content	text matches pattern	learn token patterns
Q_{DTD}	structure	valid by DTD	infer DTD
Q_{BOX}	presentation	within a rectangle	learn enclosing rectangle
Q_{DTD3}	context	valid by DTD	infer DTD of ancestor
$Q_{BOX} \wedge Q_{LMN}$	composite	conjunction	Reinduce failing validation function
$Q_{BOX} \wedge Q_{LMN} \wedge Q_{DTD3}$	composite	conjunction	
$\neg Q_{LMN}$	composite	negation	
$Q_{BOX} \wedge \neg Q_{LMN}$	composite	conjunction, negation	

Fig. 4. The nine described validation functions

functions, such as a conjunction of presentation and content validation functions. In this paper we have included the results from nine of them (see Sec. 4.3). The remaining results can be found on the project web page. This section is devoted to describe these nine validation functions.

The nine validation functions are summed up in the table of Fig. 4, where the first column states the name of the validation function or its formula if it is a compositional validation function; the second gives the dimension (content, structure, presentation, or composite) of the element, which the validation function relies on; the third gives abstractly what an element is accepted according to; and finally the fourth describes how the reinduction is done, which is of course related to how an element is accepted.

The first five validation functions are basic validation functions that rely on qualitatively different dimensions. Q_{Random} flips a coin to decide whether an element is accepted or not. Q_{LMN} is the validation function introduced by Lerman et al. [10] and it is based upon the textual content of the selected element. Specifically an element is accepted if the text tokens of the selected element is accepted by a pattern learned in the reinduction step. The used pattern is the statistically most significant pattern over the history of examples. For details we refer to Lerman et al. [10]. Q_{DTD} accepts an element if the HTML structure of the element is accepted by an DTD, which is inferred in the reinduction step. For the DTD inference we use the tool by Bex et al. [4]. Q_{BOX} accepts the selected element if the physical position of the selected element is within a rectangle. The rectangle is constructed in the reinduction step, where it infers the smallest enclosing rectangle, that contains all positions in the history. Q_{DTD3} is similar to Q_{DTD}, except the DTD is inferred from the context of the selected element, namely the great grand parent.

The last four validation functions are composite, as described in Sect. 3.2. $Q_{BOX} \wedge Q_{LMN} \wedge Q_{DTD3}$ really showcase the flexibility of our framework as it uses three basic validation functions that are based on three different dimensions of the selected element.

The XPath expressions harvested data from a total of 17 web sites which exhibit considerable diversity, including a TV guide, a blog, an image repository, price listings, webshops, download sites, search results, and news sites[2]. With the 60 XPath expressions we thus have an average of more than three XPath expressions per site. For each of these sites, we have systematically collected daily versions for a period of one year (from the 24/04 2010 to 1/5 2011), and manually provided a "perfect history" which indicates for each XPath expression whether it selected the correct element. In total 19,664 elements are selected by the selection functions, where 15,843 (81%) are correct selections and 3,821 (19%) are incorrect selections. This data is the starting point of our experiment.

4.2   Evaluation Metrics

When the selection function yields a particular element, there are four outcomes when evaluating validation functions: where the validation function q as well as the human oracle O accept that choice (true positive, TP); where q accepts and O rejects the choice (false positive, FP); where q rejects and O accepts the choice (false negative, FN); and where both reject it (true negative, TN).

There is an inherent asymmetry between FP and FN. Since the user never sees an element accepted by the validation function, FP may be *dangerous* (the scraping program continues with bad data without discovering it) whereas FN is merely *annoying* to the user as it will ask him on an element that is really ok. Thus, it is generally safer for a validation function to answer "too much negative" rather than "too much positive". We will use standard pattern recognition evaluation metrics [20] for evaluating our validation functions, focusing on the ones that involve false positives (**FP**, shown in bold below):

$$accuracy = \frac{TP+TN}{TP+TN+FN+\mathbf{FP}}$$

$$precision = \frac{TP}{TP+\mathbf{FP}}$$

$$specificity = \frac{TN}{TN+\mathbf{FP}} \quad \textit{(aka. negative recall)}$$

The *accuracy* measure quantifies "how often q is right"; *precision* is a metric for "how often q is right, when it makes a positive prediction"; and *specificity* quantifies "how often q is right, when the answer is actually negative". (The term *specificity* comes from medical diagnosis; in information extraction, it is often referred to as *negative recall*.)

4.3   Results

Figure 5 shows a graphic depiction of the accumulated results of the nine validation functions applied and reinduced during the year's worth of data. For each validation function, each of the four outcomes (TP, FP, TN, FN) is depicted as a sphere whose three-dimensional volume is proportional to the number of elements in that category. The evaluation metrics are indicated as **P** for precision, **S** for specificity, and **A** for accuracy.

---

[2] We refer to the project homepage for more information.

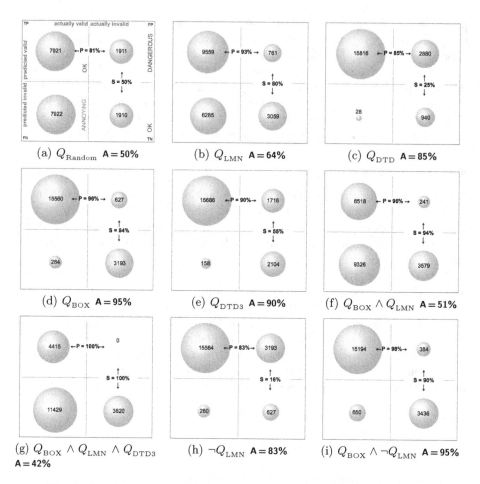

Fig. 5. Results of using validation functions with different characteristics

The first figure (Fig. 5(a)) shows the random validation function Q_{Random} and not surprisingly it scores 50% in accuracy. Note that in 81% of the cases where it accepts the element it was correct, just because correctly selected elements are common. This figure serves as a baseline for the performance of the rest of the validation functions.

The next figure (Fig. 5(b)) depicts Q_{LMN}. The accuracy is relatively low because it is too restrictive, i.e., rejects too often. This is seen by the relatively low amount of false positives (761) and high number of false negatives (6,285). The latter is caused by having frequently changing content, such as news articles.

Figure 5(c) shows the result for Q_{DTD}. This validation function is too permissive as the number of false positives is high. There are several reasons for this: Many of the elements that are selected are leaves in the HTML tree, such as an anchor tag. If the XPath expression only selects anchor tags it can be hard to distinguish a valid element from an invalid one, as there is no internal structure to inspect. A good example is the previous mentioned XPath expression (//a[starts-with(.,'Next')]). Most of the time this XPath expression selects the right element, but once in a while an advertisement for http://nextwarehouse.com/ would show up on the site, and that link would be selected instead. This could not be detected by the validation function, as both anchor tags were anchor tags containing only text.

The following figure (Fig. 5(d)) shows the results of Q_{BOX}. Compared to the previous two validation functions it appears to be in the middle, with regard to false positives and false negatives (presumably since screen coordinates are predictably stable). The number of false positives is mainly caused by one of the XPath expressions, whose purpose is to select a row in a table. The expression uses the row number for the selection, but because the table changes frequently, the correct row jumps up and down in the table, while the selected row is in the same spot in the table throughout the experiment. Hence the presentational features of the selected row is not sufficient to distinguish a correct selection from a wrong selection and therefore the validation function accepts too many selections.

Figure 5(e) depicts the results of Q_{DTD3}. Compared to Q_{DTD} it performs better in all three metrics and this indicates that the contextual dimension is a better guideline for structural validation functions. Still though Q_{DTD3} has a high number of false positives compared to other validation functions.

The next four figures, Fig. 5(f–i) show the different composite validation functions. In Fig. 5(f) we can see that a conjunction of validation functions is, not surprisingly, generally more restrictive than each of its operands(Fig. 5(c,e)), yielding fewer false positives, but at the expense of producing a lot more false negatives. Also, both precision and specificity are higher whereas accuracy suffers from the many false negatives which are also likely to annoy the user. The even more restrictive validation function (Fig. 5(g)) achieves no false positives at all; however, it is at the expense of a very large number of false negatives. In the last two compositional validation functions, Fig. 5(h,i), we have shown the results of using a negation and a negation inside a conjunction. Not surprisingly, using the negation alone on a too restrictive validation function such as Lerman et al., yields a too permissive validation function(Fig. 5(h)). Interestingly, if we take the conjunction of this negated validation function and Q_{BOX}, Fig. 5(i), we get a validation function that performs better than its constituents and in general achieves a high accuracy, a low number of false positives, and a relatively low number of false negatives. Again, like Q_{BOX}, the main source of false positives is the XPath expression using the row number for the selection. If we were to remove that web site from the results, the precision and specificity would become 99.8% resp. 99%. In other words, WebSelF enables significantly improved results in terms of the most important metrics.

We have experimented with disjunction, and performed outlier disqualification (avoiding reinduction on abnormal elements), but none of these validation functions seem to be as promising as either Q_{BOX} nor $Q_{\text{BOX}} \wedge \neg Q_{\text{LMN}}$.

5   Related Work

We have already discussed several pieces of related work, so in this section we focus on a missing perspective, which is the large number of related approaches that would fit very well as the basis for the parameters of WebSelF, namely selection functions, validation functions, or reinduction functions: Kushmerick et al. [9] induce selection functions by finding landmarks in the HTML text. Kistler & Marais [19] uses a markup algebra combining both textual and structural features for selection functions. Cohen & Fan [3] induces selection functions by learning page-independent heuristics and combine them with user interaction. Kushmerick [20] uses textual features of the extracted information for validation. Lerman et al. [10] induce selection functions and validation functions by learning textual patterns and as mentioned in Sect. 2, WebSelF subsumes their approach. The ANDES system [23] uses XPath and XSLT to make selections. SCRAP [8], SG-WRAP [11] and SG-WRAM [12] utilize schemas of the output to guide the induction of selection functions. Liu & Ling [22] extract a conceptual model of the web page upon which the selection is done. Mohapatra et al. [13] induce delimiter based selection functions for a series of web pages with fine grained time resolution. Lingam & Sebastian [21] uses a visual interface to label examples, from which they induces selection and validation functions based on different heuristics. Finally, Dalvi et al. [7] and Parameswaran [16] use a tree edit distance to induce selection functions and validation functions.

6   Conclusion

We have presented WebSelF, a web selection framework that enables the use of existing techniques for selection and validation of selection results, as well as reinducing both of those functions with a carefully minimized amount of assistance from a human being. We have furthermore shown how to compose validation functions based on propositional logic, whereby the validation in WebSelF can benefit from using several dimensions of the selection result. Moreover, we have implemented the framework and performed a substantial experiment involving 11.000 web pages from several diverse web sites over a period of more than one year, based on selection functions successful enough to be published on the web. The experiment shows how validation functions can focus on very different dimensions of the selection result, including contents, structure, and presentation. It also illustrates how the extraction behavior can be tailored according to the needs of the situation. For instance, we may accept an increase in the number of false negatives in order to make sure that we spot almost all false positives, etc. The experiment also shows that by composing several validation functions it is possible to perform better than each of the constituents, and that it is possible to perform better than the previous approach by Lerman et al. [10]. In summary, WebSelF provides a well-understood platform for the exploitation of a large space of possibilities in the choice and combination of selection functions, validation functions, and reinduction.

Acknowledgments. We thank Kristina Lerman for quickly responding to our numerous questions regarding their implementation, Mathias Schwarz for constructive comments on an earlier version of the paper and the anonymous reviewers for valuable feedback.

References

1. Brabrand, Thomsen: Typed and unambiguous pattern matching on strings using regular expressions. In: Proc. of PPDP (2010)
2. Cohen: Recognizing structure in web pages using similarity queries. In: AAAI/IAAI. AAAI (1999)
3. Cohen, Fan: Learning page-independent heuristics for extracting data from web pages. CN 31(11-16) (1999)
4. Bex, et al.: Inference of concise DTDs from XML data. In: Proc. of VLDB (2006)
5. Bray, et al.: DTD: Document type definition. World Wide Web Consortium (November 1996), http://www.w3.org/TR/xml/#sec-prolog-dtd
6. Chang, et al.: A survey of web information extraction systems. TKDE (2006)
7. Dalvi, et al.: Robust web extraction: an approach based on a probabilistic tree-edit model. In: Proc. of SIGMOD (2009)
8. Fazzinga, et al.: Schema-based web wrapping. In: KAIS (2009)
9. Kushmerick, et al.: Wrapper induction for information extraction. In: IJCAI (1997)
10. Lerman, et al.: Wrapper maintenance: A machine learning approach. JAIR (2003)
11. Meng, et al.: Schema-guided data extraction from the web. JCST 17(4) (2002)
12. Meng, et al.: Schema-guided wrapper maintenance for web-data extraction. In: Proc. of WIDM (2003)
13. Mohapatra, et al.: Efficient wrapper reinduction from dynamic web sources. In: Proc. of WI. IEEE Computer Society (2004)
14. Muslea, et al: Hierarchical wrapper induction for semistructured information sources. AAMAS 4(1) (2001)
15. Nakatoh, et al.: Automatic generation of deep web wrappers based on discovery of repetition. In: Proc. of AIRS (2004)
16. Parameswaran et al.: Optimal schemes for robust web extraction. In: Proc. of VLDB (2011)
17. Raposo et al.: Automatic wrapper maintenance for semi-structured web sources using results from previous queries. In: Proc. of SAC (2005)
18. Thomsen et al.: WebSelf: A web selection framework. Tech. report, Computer Science. Aarhus University (2012)
19. Kistler, Marais: Webl - a programming language for the web. CN 30(1-7) (1998)
20. Kushmerick: Wrapper verification. In: WWW (2000)
21. Lingam, Elbaum: Supporting end-users in the creation of dependable web clips. In: WWW (2007)
22. Liu, Ling: A conceptual model and rule-based query language for HTML. In: WWW (2001)
23. Myllymaki: Effective web data extraction with standard XML technologies. CN 39(5) (2002)
24. Myllymaki, Jackson: Robust web data extraction with xml path expressions. IBM Research Report, RJ10245 (2002)
25. Sahuguet, Azavant: Building intelligent web applications using lightweight wrappers. DKE 36(3) (2001)

A Statistical Approach for Efficient Crawling of Rich Internet Applications[*]

Mustafa Emre Dincturk[1,3], Suryakant Choudhary[1,3], Gregor von Bochmann[1,3], Guy-Vincent Jourdan[1,3], and Iosif Viorel Onut[2,3]

[1] EECS, University of Ottawa. 800 King Edward Avenue,
K1N 6N5, Ottawa, ON, Canada
[2] Research and Development, IBM® Security AppScan® Enterprise, IBM,
770 Palladium, Ottawa, ON, Canada
[3] IBM Canada CAS Research
{mdinc075,schou062}@uottawa.ca,
{bochmann,gvj}@eecs.uottawa.ca,
vioonut@ca.ibm.com

Abstract. Modern web technologies, like AJAX result in more responsive and usable web applications, sometimes called Rich Internet Applications (RIAs). Traditional crawling techniques are not sufficient for crawling RIAs. We present a new strategy for crawling RIAs. This new strategy is designed based on the concept of "Model-Based Crawling" introduced in [3] and uses statistics accumulated during the crawl to select what to explore next with a high probability of uncovering some new information. The performance of our strategy is compared with our previous strategy, as well as the classical Breadth-First and Depth-First on two real RIAs and two test RIAs. The results show this new strategy is significantly better than the Breadth-First and the Depth-First strategies (which are widely used to crawl RIAs), and outperforms our previous strategy while being much simpler to implement.

Keywords: Rich Internet Applications, Web Crawling, Web Application Modeling.

1   Introduction

Web applications have been undergoing a significant change in the past decade. Initialy, the web applications were built using simple HTML pages on the client side. Each page had a unique URL to access it. The client (web browser) would send a request for these URLs to the server which in turn would send the corresponding page in response. The client would then entirely replace the previous content with the new information sent by the server.

In the recent years, with the introduction of newer and richer technologies for web application development, web applications have become more useable and interactive. These applications, called Rich Internet Applications (RIAs), changed the traditional web applications in two important aspects: first, client side-scripting languages such as

---

[*] A detailed version can be found at
http://ssrg.eecs.uottawa.ca/docs/ICWE2012_long.pdf

M. Brambilla, T. Tokuda, and R. Tolksdorf (Eds.): ICWE 2012, LNCS 7387, pp. 362–369, 2012.
© Springer-Verlag Berlin Heidelberg 2012

JavaScript have allowed the modification of the web page by updating the Document Object Model (DOM) [5], which represents the client-side "state" of the application. Second, using technologies like AJAX [6] the client can communicate asynchronously with the server, without having the user to wait for the response from the server. In both cases, the URL typically does not change during these client side activities. Consequently, we can now have a quite complex web application addressed by a single URL.

These improvements increased the usability of web applications but on the other hand introduced new challenges. One of the important problems is the difficulty to automatically crawl these websites. Crawling is the process of browsing a web application in a methodical, automated manner or in an orderly fashion. Traditional crawling techniques are not sufficient for RIAs. In traditional web applications, a page is defined by its URL and all the pages reachable from the current page have their URL embedded in the current page. Crawling a traditional web application requires to extract these embedded URLs and traverse them in an effective sequence. But in RIAs, the client-state can also change by executing events which are user actions (or time-outs) that trigger client-side code execution and hence cannot be mapped to a single URL. All these changes mean that traditional crawlers are unable to crawl RIAs, save for a few pages that have distinct URLs.

An important functionality of the web in general is the information it provides. This information can only be made available if the different information sources can be found and indexed. If search engines are not able to crawl websites with new information, they will not be able to index them. Hence a good part of the web in general will be lost. In addition, crawling is also required for any thorough analysis of the web application such as for security and accessibility testing. To our knowledge, none of the current search engines, web application testers and analyzers have the ability to crawl RIAs [1].

In this paper, we introduce a RIA crawling strategy using a statistical model. This strategy is based on the model-based crawling approach introduced in [3] to crawl RIAs efficiently. We evaluate the performances of our statistical model on two real RIAs and two test applications. We further compare our experimental results against other RIA crawling strategies, the Depth-First, the Breadth-First and the Hypercube [3], and we show that the new strategy obtains overall better results.

The paper is organized as follows: In Section 2, we give the basic concepts in RIA crawling. In Section 3, we present the details of the new strategy based on statistical model. In Section 4, we provide experimental results obtained with our prototype. We conclude in Section 5. We omit the related works for space restrictions.

2   Crawling RIAs

A web application can be conceptualized as a Finite State Machine with "states" representing the distinct DOMs that can be reached in the web application and transitions representing event executions. The result of crawling is called a "model" of the application. A model basically contains the states and the possible ways to move from one state to another.

A crawling strategy is an algorithm that decides how the exploration proceeds. In the case of event-based exploration of RIAs, the strategy basically decides which event to explore next. We say that a crawling strategy that is able to find the states of the application early in the crawl is an efficient strategy, since this is the goal of crawling. This is important, since for large RIAs it might not be feasible to wait for the crawler to complete the crawl. In this case, a strategy which discovers a larger portion of the application early on will deliver more data during the alloted time, and thus be more efficient. However, the main problem is that we do not know how the web application has been built and without this prior knowledge of the web application, finding an efficient strategy is difficult.

Primarily motivated by the above goals, we introduced the concept of "Model-Based Crawling" in [3]. Along with that we also introduced a two phase approach. The first phase, "state exploration phase", aims at discovering all the states of the RIA. Once our strategy believes that it has probably found all the reachable states, we proceed to the second phase, the "transition exploration phase" which tries to execute the remaining transitions after state exploration, to confirm that nothing has been overlooked.

In [2], we compiled a list of challenges and assumptions such as state equivalence, user-inputs, server states; which are important to be able to design an efficient crawling strategy and can be handled as separate research efforts.

3   The Probability Strategy

A crawling strategy can be efficient if it is able to predict the results of the event executions with some degree of accuracy. This helps give priority to the events that are more likely to discover new states and hence improve efficiency. Statistics about the past behavior of the event (from different states) can be used to model the future behavior of the event. With this motivation, we introduce a crawling strategy which uses statistical data collected during crawling. The strategy is based on the belief that an event which was often observed to lead to new states in the past will be more likely to lead to new states in the future. We call this new strategy "the Probability strategy".

3.1   Events' Probability of Discovering New States

Let $P(e)$ be the event e's probability of discovering a new state. Remember that the same event "e" can be found in different states (we say that e is "enabled" in these states). The following Bayesian formula, known as the "Rule of Succession" in probability theory, is used to calculate $P(e)$

$$P(e) = \frac{S(e) + p_s}{N(e) + p_n}$$

where

- $N(e)$ is the "execution count" of e, that is, the number of times e has been executed from different states so far.

- S(e) is the "success count" of e, that is, the number of times e discovered a new state out of its N(e) executions.
- p_s and p_n are the terms to represent initial success count and initial execution count respectively. These terms are preset and represent the initial probability of an unexplored event to find a new state.

This Bayesian formula is useful for estimating the probabilities in situations when there are very few observations. To use this formula we assign values to p_s and p_n to set the initial probability. For example, $p_s = 1$ and $p_n = 2$ can be used to set an event's initial probability to 0.5 (note that N(e) = S(e) = 0 initially).

Having Bayesian probability instead of using the "classical" probability, P(e)=S(e)/N(e), with some initial values for P(e), avoids in particular have events that get a probability of 0 because no new state were found at their first execution. With our formula, events never have a probability of 0 (or 1) and can always be picked up after a while.

3.2   Choosing the Next Event to Explore

In this section, we describe the logic that helps the strategy decide which event to explore next. We first introduce the notation and definitions used.

- S denotes the set of already discovered states. Initially S contains the initial state.
- $s_{current}$, represents the current state, the state we are at currently in the application while executing the crawl. $s_{current}$ always refers to one of the states in S.
- For a state s, we define the probability of the state, P(s), as the maximum probability of an unexecuted event in s. If s has no unexecuted events then P(s) = 0
- d(s, s') is the distance from s $\in$ S to s' $\in$ S. It is the length of the shortest path from s to s' in the model of the application discovered so far.

When deciding which event to explore next, the Probability strategy aims to take the action that will maximize the chances of discovering a new state while minimizing the cost (number of event executions). For this reason, starting from the current state $s_{current}$, we search for a state s_{chosen} such that exploring the event with probability P(s_{chosen}) in s_{chosen} achieves this goal.

All the states that still have unexplored events are candidates to be s_{chosen}. However we have to take into account the distance from the $s_{current}$ to the s_{chosen} in addition to the raw probabilities when deciding s_{chosen}. Note that from $s_{current}$ reaching to any other state in S means following a known path (consisting of already explored events). Between two states that are at different distances from $s_{current}$, we may consider reaching the one that is farther away because of its higher probability. However, the time to execute the extra events in this path could actually be used for exploration if the closer state is chosen. To make decisions in such situations we need to balance the cost of executing known events with the higher probability of the farther state.

For our analysis it is necessary to have an estimation of discovering a state by exploring an event from an "average" state in S. For this purpose, we will use the average probability P_{avg} that is defined as follows.

$$P_{avg} = (\Sigma_{s \in S} P(s)) / |S|$$

To select a state that maximizes the probability while minimizing the cost, we need a mechanism that compares two states and decides which is more preferable. Let's say we want to compare s and s'. If both are at the same distance from $s_{current}$ then the one with the higher probability is obviously a better choice. But if the cost of reaching one of the states, is higher than the other, say $d(s_{current}, s) < d(s_{current}, s'))$ then there can be two cases. If $P(s) \geq P(s')$ then s is clearly a better choice. But if $P(s) < P(s')$ then the fact that reaching s' is costlier than reaching s should be reflected in the comparison mechanism. To make up for the difference in the cost, we should allow the exploration of a sequence of $k = d(s_{current}, s') - d(s_{current}, s)$ extra events after executing the event with probability $P(s)$ from s. Thus we use the probability of discovering a new state after executing the event from S and executing k more unexecuted events (each with a probability of P_{avg} to discover new state). This is given by the following formula

$$1 - (1 - P(s))(1 - P_{avg})^{d(s_{current}, s) - d(s_{current}, s')} \tag{1}$$

Now we can compare this value with $P(s')$ and choose the option with higher probability.

Summarizing, the s_{chosen} that we are looking for is the state, $s \in S$ that satisfies the following condition

$\forall s' \in S$

- if $d(s_{current}, s) = d(s_{current}, s')$, $P(s') \leq P(s)$
- if $d(s_{current}, s) < d(s_{current}, s')$, $1 - (1 - P(s))(1 - P_{avg})^{d(s_{current}, s') - d(s_{current}, s)} \geq P(s')$
- if $d(s_{current}, s) > d(s_{current}, s')$, $1 - (1 - P(s'))(1 - P_{avg})^{d(s_{current}, s) - d(s_{current}, s')} < P(s)$

3.3 The Algorithm

In this section we give an algorithm that picks an s_{chosen} from S. The algorithm initializes the variable s_{chosen} to the $s_{current}$ and proceeds in iterations. At iteration i the states at a distance i from the $s_{current}$ are compared against the current s_{chosen}. We check if any of them is more preferable to s_{chosen}.

We optimize the search by exploiting the fact that we do not necessarily need to explore all the states in S to find s_{chosen}. The search can be stopped the moment we detect that it is not possible to find any state further away with a higher probability. This is possible since we take into account the cost of distance while comparing the probability of states. We only need to know P_{best}, the probability of the state with maximum probability in S.

Then the maximum distance that needs to be considered from s_{chosen} (noted as maxDistanceToCheckFrom(s_{chosen})) is the value of smallest d that satisfies

$$1 - (1 - P(s_{chosen}))(1 - P_{avg})^d \geq P_{best} \tag{2}$$

When the left hand side of (2) becomes as large as P_{best} then it is not required to look further since even the states that might have the maximum probability, P_{best}, will not be preferable anymore to s_{chosen} due to the distance factor.

```
Algorithm ChooseStateToExplore
s_chosen := s_current; i := 1; distanceToCheck := maxDistanceToCheckFrom(s_chosen);
while ( i < distanceToCheck) {
    for each s where d(s_current, s) = i {
        if (s is preferable to s_chosen) {
            s_chosen := s;
            distanceToCheck += maxDistanceToCheckFrom(s_chosen);
        }
    }
    i++;
}
return s_chosen;
```

4   Experimental Results

In this section, we evaluate the performance of the Probability strategy on two real
RIAs and two test RIAs. We have used the following metrics for performance
evaluation.

(1) Number of events and resets required to discover all states
(2) Number of events and resets required to explore all transitions

A reset is loading the URL of the application to go back to the initial state. Resets are
typically costlier (in terms of time of execution) than event execution. For simplicity
we have combined the events and resets required for state exploration and transition
exploration into a single cost factor. For this purpose, we have expressed the cost of
resets in terms of number of event execution (the actual value used is application
dependent). We believe that number of events execution is a good metrics for
performance evaluation, since the time to crawl is proportional to the number of
events executed during the crawl.

We compare the performance of our strategy with the Breadth-First and the Depth-
First strategies and our existing Hypercube strategy. We also present, for each
application the optimal number of events executions to explore all the states of the
application. It is important to understand that this optimal value is calculated after the
fact, once the model of the application is obtained. This number is found by an
Asymmetric Traveling Salesman Problem (ATSP) solver [4] on the graph instance
obtained for the application.

In an effort to minimize any influence that may be caused by considering events in
a specific order, the events at each state are randomly ordered for each crawl. Also,
each application is crawled 5 times with each method and the average cost of these 5
runs is used for comparison.

The first real RIA we consider is an AJAX-based periodic table[1]. In total 240 states
and 29034 transitions are identified by our crawler and the reset cost is 8. The second

---

[1] http://code.jalenack.com/periodic
(Local version: http://ssrg.eecs.uottawa.ca/periodic/)

real application considered is Clipmarks[2]. For this experimental study we have used a partial local copy of the website. It consists of 129 states and 10580 transitions and the reset cost is 18. The third application, TestRIA is a test application that we developed using AJAX[3]. It has 39 states and 305 transitions and a reset cost of 2.The fourth application is a demo web application maintained by the IBM® AppScan® Team[4]. We have used the AJAX-fied version of the website. The application has 45 states and 1210 transitions and a reset cost of 2.

4.1   State Exploration

For compactness we have used boxplots: the top of vertical lines show the maximum number required to discover all the states.The lower edge of the box, the line in the box and the higher edge of the box indicate the number required to discover a quarter, half and 3 quarters of all the states in the application, respectively.

For all applications, Probability strategy has performed significantly better than the Breadth-First and the Depth-First strategies. The paper [3] proved the efficiency of the Hypercube strategy compared to the current state of the art commercial products and other research tools. Probability strategy also showed better performance than the Hypercube strategy. The box plots are drawn in logarithmic scale.

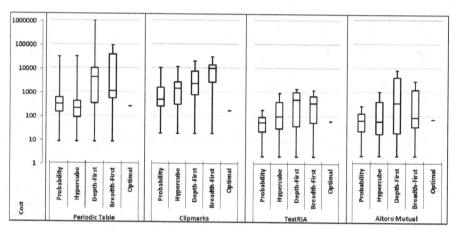

Fig. 1. State exploration statistics (Logarithmic scale)

4.2   Transition Exploration

Table 1 presents the overall cost of crawling. For all applications, the cost required by the Probability strategy is better than or comparable to the Hypercube strategy but it exceeds the Depth-First and the Breadth-First strategies by a significant margin.

---

[2] http://www.clipmarks.com/
   (Local version: http://ssrg.eecs.uottawa.ca/clipmarks/)
[3] http://ssrg.eecs.uottawa.ca/TestRIA/
[4] http://www.altoromutual.com/

Table 1. Transition Exploration Statistics

	Periodic Table	Clipmarks	TestRIA	Altoro Mutual
Probability	31403	9717	979	2526
Hypercube	31810	11233	996	2542
Depth-First	983582	19128	1345	7693
Breadth-First	181924	28710	1324	3744

5   Conclusion

We have presented a new crawling strategy based on the idea of model-based crawling introduced in [3]. Experimental results show that this strategy outperforms the standard crawling strategies by a significant margin. Further, it also outperforms the Hypercube strategy in most cases and it performs comparably in the least favorable example, while being very much simpler to understand and to implement. This makes Probability a good choice for general purpose crawling. When compared to the optimal solution, there is still some room for improvement. However, the optimal solution is calculated after the website model is known, and thus can only be used as a benchmark, not to actually crawl an unknown web application.

Acknowledgments. This work is supported in part by IBM and the Natural Science and Engineering Research Council of Canada.

Disclaimer. The views expressed in this article are the sole responsibility of the authors and do not necessarily reflect those of IBM.

Trademarks. IBM, Rational and AppScan are trademarks or registered trademarks of International Business Machines Corp., registered in many jurisdictions worldwide. Other product and service names might be trademarks of IBM or other companies. A current list of IBM trademarks is available on the Web at "Copyright and trademark information" at www.ibm.com/legal/copytrade.shtml.

References

1. Bau, J., Bursztein, E., Gupta, D., Mitchell, J.C.: State of the Art: Automated Black-Box Web Application Vulnerability Testing. In: Proc. IEEE Symposium on Security and Privacy (2010)
2. Benjamin, K., von Bochmann, G., Jourdan, G.V., Onut, I.V.: Some Modeling Challenges when Testing Rich Internet Applications for Security. In: First International Workshop on Modeling and Detection of Vulnerabilities, Paris, France (2010)
3. Benjamin, K., von Bochmann, G., Dincturk, M.E., Jourdan, G.-V., Onut, I.V.: A Strategy for Efficient Crawling of Rich Internet Applications. In: Auer, S., Díaz, O., Papadopoulos, G.A. (eds.) ICWE 2011. LNCS, vol. 6757, pp. 74–89. Springer, Heidelberg (2011)
4. Carpento, G., Dell'amico, M., Toth, P.: Exact solution of large-scale, asymmetric traveling salesman problems. ACM Trans. Math. Softw. 21(4) (1995)
5. W3C. Document Object Model, DOM (2005), http://www.w3.org/DOM/
6. Garrett, J.J.: Adaptive Path (2005),
   http://www.adaptivepath.com/publications/essays/archives/
   000385.php

Recording and Replaying Navigations
on AJAX Web Sites

Alberto Bartoli, Eric Medvet, and Marco Mauri

DI³ - University of Trieste
Via Valerio 10, Trieste, Italy
bartoli.alberto@units.it

Abstract. Recording and replaying user navigations greatly simplifies the testing process of web applications and, consequently, greatly contributes to improving usability, robustness and assurance of these applications. Implementing such replaying functionalities with modern web technologies such as AJAX is very hard: the GUI may change dynamically as a result of a myriad of different events beyond the control of the replaying machinery and even locating a given GUI element across different executions may be impossible.

In this work we propose a tool that overcomes these problems and is able to handle real-world web sites based on AJAX technology. Recording occurs automatically, i.e., the user navigates with a normal browser and need not take any specific action. Replaying a previously recorded trace occurs programmatically, based on several heuristics that make the tool robust with respect to DOM variance while at the same time maintaining the ability to detect whether replaying has become impossible—perhaps because the target web site has changed too much since the recording. The entire procedure is fully transparent to the target web site. We also describe the use of our tool on several web applications including Facebook, Amazon and others.

1 Introduction

The ability to record and replay GUI navigation sequences has become an essential component of testing procedures for modern software [11]. The need for incorporating similar procedures in web applications is becoming more and more urgent, given the richness of their user interfaces and their ever more stringent requirements in terms of usability, robustness and assurance [9]. Unfortunately, modern web technologies such as AJAX make programmatic interaction with client-side GUIs very hard, due to the stateful and highly dynamic nature of the DOM that determines the actual GUI appearance. Client-side code constructs the DOM and manipulates it as a result of a myriad of different events, that may be triggered by user actions but also by asynchronous interactions between the browser and the server. Indeed, even the seemingly trivial task of identifying the elements in a DOM that may affect navigation is actually very challenging and is still partly unsolved [2,6]. Repeating the same sequence of user actions against

M. Brambilla, T. Tokuda, and R. Tolksdorf (Eds.): ICWE 2012, LNCS 7387, pp. 370–377, 2012.
© Springer-Verlag Berlin Heidelberg 2012

the same initial DOM, moreover, typically results in a different DOM: attributes of individual elements may change across different executions, for example if they include a form of session identifier, and the very same DOM structure may change because the server usually serves different contents at different times. The complexity of replaying a browser session is magnified further by the fact that, in practice, HTML elements usually do not have any form of identity that persists across browsing sessions. It follows that finding programmatically the "same" HTML element accessed in a previous session may be very challenging. Indeed, replaying a browsing session may even be impossible, for example because the web application at the target web site has changed between the registration and the attempted replay.

In this work we propose a method and a tool for recording and replaying traces of user interactions with web applications, which may be of great help in a number of testing activities as pointed out above. Key properties of our contribution are: (i) the creation of a trace is fully automatic: the user merely navigates into the target web site without taking any specific action or issuing any dedicated command; (ii) the process is fully transparent to the target web application, that need not be modified in any way; (iii) the replaying algorithm is highly robust to DOM variance, while at the same time maintaining the ability to notify the user in cases the replay has become impossible to perform—for example because the target web application has changed too much between the record and the replay. We are not aware of any similar tool with all these properties. The tool that implements our method is able to cope with real-world web applications based on AJAX technology and is able to record and replay such actions as login and file upload. These actions are key components of the workflow of many web applications but are notoriously difficult to handle programmatically and are often missing from web analysis tools such as crawlers and vulnerability scanners [3].

2   Related Work

A tool for recording and replaying traces of web application navigations is proposed in [8]. The proposed approach requires that the user explicitly marks every action to be recorded, by right clicking on the desired web element and then choosing the event to register from a menu presented by an instrumented web browser. This approach is manual and, it seems fair to say, quite cumbersome to use. Our proposal, in contrast, is entirely automatic because the user need not take any specific action during the recording process.

Recording and replaying functionalities are an essential component of the approach to web application testing proposed in [9]. Recording is done by replacing dynamically the handler of each event in the page with a handler that merely records its activation and then invokes the original handler. This approach allows recording only events for which the page author has defined handlers using the so called version 0 of the DOM. This technique of defining method handlers is long deprecated and many modern web application no longer use it.

Our approach is radically different in the sense that, essentially, it does not place any requirement on the DOM and, in particular, it does not attempt to discover the event-handler relationships defined in the page being recorded. As a technical but important detail, we also remark that the cited work cannot handle multi-page web applications, which in many cases prevent the handling of the login step. Similar comments apply to [4], except that in this case multi-page web site are supported.

Concerning the replaying process, the method for searching a target element proposed in [9] implicitly assumes that the replay will occur without any content variation. While our heuristics allow identifying the correct element, the approach in [9] would often select other elements during the replay.

The problem of determining whether two serialized DOM trees represent the same page is essential in [5,6,7,10]. The goal of the cited works is to define a distance between two DOM trees and then compare that distance against a threshold in order to detect if the two DOM trees represent the same page. In contrast, in this work we aim at locating a given element across different DOM trees.

3   System Architecture

Our system consists of two separate applications: the *trace recorder*, that records the actions executed by the user during a browsing session, and the *trace replayer*, that replays a browsing session previously recorded by the trace recorder. The system is fully *transparent* to both the user and the target web site. That is, the user navigates with a normal browser and need not take any specific action for recording, and the target web site need not be modified in any way. A fundamental characteristic of both or our tools is the use of a real browser (Firefox), which is very important to ensure compatibility with real-world web applications and to provide the user with a familiar interface. The trace replayer reads the data previously saved in a trace and pilots the browser programmatically, so as to replay the user actions on the target web site automatically.

3.1   Trace Recorder Architecture

The trace recorder consists of: (a) a web application that we developed and that we call *Observer*; (b) a *proxy*; and (c) a browser.

The Observer is composed of a server side code (Observer-S) and a client-side code executed by the browser (Observer-C). Observer-C records all the DOM events generated by the user and periodically sends a description of these events to the Observer-S, that saves the corresponding descriptions into a file—the *trace*.

The proxy, placed in between the browser and the target web site, performs two actions: (i) injects the Observer-C code into all the pages sent to the browser; and (ii) redirects part of the web traffic so as to enable communication between Observer-C and Observer-S without violating the *same origin policy* implemented by modern browsers.

The browser fetches our JavaScript code injected by the proxy—i.e., Observer-C—and executes this code locally. The results produced by Observer-C are sent to Observer-S through the URL /GWT-Observer. The proxy is configured so as to reroute any traffic to /GWT-Observer toward the server in our control that actually executes the Observer-S code. In other words, the browser is tricked into believing that Observer-C is fetched from the target web site and communicates with that site. This fairly complex structuring allows circumventing the *same origin policy (SOP)* implemented by modern browsers, which would prevent any communication from Observer-C to a server in our control [1].

Our tool is able to handle also encrypted https traffic by configuring the proxy to act as a man in the middle between the browser and the target web application.

A trace contains a sequence of *event descriptions*, each of them consists of: (i) type of the DOM event (e.g. click, wheel, etc.); (ii) time at which the event occurred; (iii) description of the target element of the event. The description of the target element contains its tag name, e.g. span or div, its text content, its x and y positions and the possible values of the id, name, src, and type attributes.

We also defined, in addition to those defined by the DOM standard, two *synthetic* event types, write and select, to represents respectively the typing of a text inside an input field and the selection of a choice from a drop-down list as a more compact representation of sequences of events that have actually occurred.

3.2   Trace Replayer Architecture

The goal of the trace replayer is to read the trace created by the trace recorder and reproduce the registered events using the browser. The reproduction of the trace is performed by the trace replayer driving the browser, through Webdriver[1], a browser automation framework that enables to manipulate a real browser programmatically.

We introduce a distinction between *relevant* and *irrelevant* events. A relevant event is any event whose replay is essential to properly replay the entire trace, while replaying an irrelevant one is not essential to properly replay the trace. The trace recorder registers events that could be irrelevant because whether a given event is relevant depends on the events that follow that event. For example, events generated for selecting a text field inside a form are irrelevant, because the subsequent event of typing inside that field implies the selection of the text field itself.

The trace replayer preprocesses the trace as follows: (i) filter out all the irrelevant events from the trace; (ii) shorten the trace by introducing *synthetic events* wherever possible.

After preprocessing, the trace is replayed according to the following algorithm: for each event E in the sequence S, search the associated target element T'_E in the

---

[1] http://seleniumhq.org/projects/webdriver

opened web page; if T'_E is found, replay the event using WebDriver; otherwise, repeat the search for a predefined amount of times, waiting for a fixed amount of time (half a second) after each attempt. This waiting heuristics copes with the case in which the searched element is created dynamically by JavaScript code. If this repeated search fails, trace replayer simply aborts the replay signaling the error.

Often, between the registration and the replay the content of the web page changes in more or less substantial way. Furthermore the only way to uniquely identify an element inside a document is optional (the *id* attribute) and in the vast majority of cases this attribute is not present, so a simple search for an element with identical content to the one in the trace will fail.

We attack this crucial problem with a series of heuristics and decide which one to use based on the element T_E to be found, as explained below. Each heuristic execution can lead to a false negative (the element exists in the page but the heuristic has not found it) as well as to a false positive (the found element is not the correct one, which may or may not exist in the page). In our experiments, described in the next section, we have not encountered any false positive or false negative. As future work, we plan to execute a broader quantitative analysis by systematically labeling a large dataset. Our heuristics are as follows:

findElementBySrc. This heuristic, used for searching media element, retrieves the first element T'_E that has the same tag name of T_E and the same value for the attribute `src`.

This heuristic could cause a false positive result if there are more media elements, in the analyzed web page, distinguishable between them only for the position relative to the page itself.

findElementByInput. This heuristic, used for searching form inputs, retrieves the first element T'_E that represents the same type of form input of T_E and has the same value for the attributes `id` and/or `name`. If none of these attributes are presents in T_E or if no element with those attribute values is found, then this heuristic compares the text content of the form inputs.

This heuristic should not be capable to generate false positives because the values of `id` are unique within a single page while those of `name` are unique within a single form. The heuristic can generate false negatives if the value of the attributes varies between different replays.

findElementByGrid. This heuristic is based on the position of the searched element T_E; it retrieves the first element T'_E that has the same tag name and whose coordinate $(x_{T'_E}, y_{T'_E})$ are similar to those of T_E.

This heuristic can generate false negatives if the position of the searched element varies too much between different replays. It can generate false positives if there is another element with the same tag name and similar coordinates that precedes, in document order, the searched element.

findElementByGridAndText. This heuristic is very similar to findElementByGrid, except that the retrieved element T'_E has also the same text content of T_E.

This heuristic can generate erroneous results in the same conditions of the previous one.

4   Experiments

We tested our tool to verify its ability to work on real web applications. Each experiment consisted of the registration of a trace on a web application and multiple replays of such trace to verify the repeatability of the reproduction. Table 1 is a summary of our experiments: it shows a line for each web application and the number of events in the corresponding registered trace. The table also shows the number of events, computed after the preprocessing of the trace.

Table 1. Summary of our experiments

Site name	# of pages	# of events click	write	select
Amazon	10	7	2	0
Facebook	14	9	4	0
Google Groups	25	23	1	0
Stack Overflow	14	12	1	0
Wacko Picko	34	23	10	0
WIVET	44	29	13	1

Amazon. We registered a trace simulating the search of some products and then the addition of the desired product to the "shopping cart". In detail, we performed a search using the keyword "tablet", selected a specific model and added it to the cart. After that we performed another search using the keyword "stereo", selected a specific model and added it to the cart.

The most notable example of page variations was the search result pages: the products displayed changed between the replays. The trace replayer can withstand this type of variation thanks to the **findElementByGridAnd-Text** heuristic. We replayed this trace several times without encountering any error.

Facebook. We registered a trace simulating a typical user interaction with the social network: (i) login; (ii) checking for new messages; (iii) adding a new event to the calendar; (iv) logout. We could perform the replays without any error. The only peculiar, but correct, behavior was the creation of several duplicated events on the Facebook calendar; this a further example of the resilience of our heuristics to page variations.

Another peculiarity of this web applications is the use of a session ID as the value of the id attribute of the login button. The trace replayer can cope with this kind of variation thanks to the fact that the **findElementByInput** searches by text if it cannot find the right element searching by its id.

Google Groups. We registered a trace containing the navigations on various discussion threads chosen at random, all pertaining to the "Google Web Toolkit" group of this web application, including the use of all the links that change the display mode of the discussions.

This was the web application that displayed the more pronounced page variations: for each replay the list of posts and topic displayed changed with the additions of new contents. All the searches in this web application was performed by the **findElementByGridAndText** heuristic.

We could perform the replays without any error.

Stack Overflow. We registered a trace containing the search of various topic, the navigation of user information and the FAQ section of the web application. Like the previous web application all the searches in this one was performed by the **findElementByGridAndText** heuristic. We could perform the replays without any error.

WackoPicko. WackoPicko is a web application used to test web application vulnerability scanners [3]. It consists in a fake image shop applications that allow users to upload, comment and purchase images.

We created a trace containing the following actions: (i) login; (ii) addition of a comment to an existing image; (iii) search of an image; (iv) purchase of an image; (v) upload of an image; (vi) logout.

Another particular aspect of this trace is the presence of both a login and an upload file steps. Many of the work cited in Section 2 are not able to perform these two actions. We could perform the replays without any error and the majority of searches was performed by the **findElementBySrc** and **findElementByInput** heuristics.

WIVET. WIVET is a benchmarking project for analyzing web link extractors. It consists in a series of pages containing links in ways that are increasingly difficult to find for automated tools. We recorded a trace containing the activation of all of the links with the exception of those involving flash applets and those using the mouse hover event as a trigger to activate the links.

This web application is almost entirely static so the various replays have not encountered any page variation. We could perform the replays without any error.

5   Conclusions

The ability to record and replay sequences of user interactions with web applications is very useful in functional testing, security testing and usability testing. We have presented a novel approach to this problem and described a tool that implements our approach. The approach is suitable for modern web applications, made up of highly dynamic contents and abundant use of AJAX technology. The tool does not require any change or configuration on the web application to be monitored, is completely non intrusive, very easy to use and supports https connections. As discussed in the related work section, the tool overcomes several limitations of earlier proposals.

Our method and tool are useful to improve web application testing by reducing the time needed to thoroughly test the web application. We plan to execute a broader quantitative analysis of our approach on a larger dataset.

Acknowledgments. This work is partly supported by eMaze[2].

---

[2] http://www.emaze.net

References

1. Same origin policy, http://www.w3.org/Security/wiki/Same_Origin_Policy
2. Bai, X., Cambazoglu, B.B., Junqueira, F.P.: Discovering urls through user feedback. In: Proceedings of the 20th ACM International Conference on Information and Knowledge Management, CIKM 2011, pp. 77–86. ACM, New York (2011), http://doi.acm.org/10.1145/2063576.2063592
3. Doupé, A., Cova, M., Vigna, G.: Why Johnny Can't Pentest: An Analysis of Black-Box Web Vulnerability Scanners. In: Kreibich, C., Jahnke, M. (eds.) DIMVA 2010. LNCS, vol. 6201, pp. 111–131. Springer, Heidelberg (2010), http://dx.doi.org/10.1007/978-3-642-14215-4_7, 10.1007/978-3-642-14215-4_7
4. Álvarez, M., Pan, A., Raposo, J., Hidalgo, J.: Crawling Web Pages with Support for Client-Side Dynamism. In: Yu, J.X., Kitsuregawa, M., Leong, H.V. (eds.) WAIM 2006. LNCS, vol. 4016, pp. 252–262. Springer, Heidelberg (2006), http://dx.doi.org/10.1007/11775300_22, 10.1007/11775300_22
5. Medvet, E., Kirda, E., Kruegel, C.: Visual-similarity-based phishing detection. In: Proceedings of the 4th International Conference on Security and Privacy in Communication Networks, SecureComm 2008, pp. 22:1–22:6. ACM, New York (2008), http://doi.acm.org/10.1145/1460877.1460905
6. Mesbah, A., Bozdag, E., van Deursen, A.: Crawling ajax by inferring user interface state changes. In: Eighth International Conference on Web Engineering, ICWE 2008, pp. 122–134 (July 2008)
7. Mesbah, A., van Deursen, A.: Invariant-based automatic testing of ajax user interfaces. In: Proceedings of the 31st International Conference on Software Engineering, ICSE 2009, pp. 210–220. IEEE Computer Society, Washington, DC (2009), http://dx.doi.org/10.1109/ICSE.2009.5070522
8. Montoto, P., Pan, A., Raposo, J., Bellas, F., López, J.: Automating Navigation Sequences in AJAX Websites. In: Gaedke, M., Grossniklaus, M., Díaz, O. (eds.) ICWE 2009. LNCS, vol. 5648, pp. 166–180. Springer, Heidelberg (2009), http://dx.doi.org/10.1007/978-3-642-02818-2_12, 10.1007/978-3-642-02818-2_12
9. Pattabiraman, K., Zorn, B.: Dodom: Leveraging dom invariants for web 2.0 application robustness testing. In: 2010 IEEE 21st International Symposium on Software Reliability Engineering (ISSRE), pp. 191–200 (November 2010)
10. Roest, D., Mesbah, A., van Deursen, A.: Regression Testing Ajax Applications: Coping with Dynamism. In: 2010 Third International Conference on Software Testing, Verification and Validation (ICST), pp. 127–136. IEEE (April 2010), http://dx.doi.org/10.1109/ICST.2010.59
11. Xie, Q., Memon, A.M.: Designing and comparing automated test oracles for GUI-based software applications. ACM Trans. Softw. Eng. Methodol. 16(1), 4+ (2007), http://dx.doi.org/10.1145/1189748.1189752

Leveraging User Modeling on the Social Web with Linked Data

Fabian Abel, Claudia Hauff, Geert-Jan Houben, and Ke Tao

Web Information Systems, Delft University of Technology
{f.abel,c.hauff,g.j.p.houben,k.tao}@tudelft.nl

Abstract. Social Web applications such as Twitter and Flickr are widely used services that generate large volumes of usage data. The challenge of modeling the use and the users of such Social Web services based on their data has received a lot of attention in recent years. In this paper, we go a step further and investigate how the Linked Open Data (LOD) cloud can be leveraged as additional knowledge source in user modeling processes that exploit user data from the Social Web. Specifically, we introduce a user modeling framework that utilizes semantic background knowledge from LOD and evaluate it in the area of point of interest (POI) recommendations. For this purpose, we infer user preferences in POIs based on the users' behavior observed on Twitter and Flickr, combined with referable evidence from the Web of Data. We compare strategies that aggregate knowledge from two LOD sources: GeoNames and DBpedia. The evaluation validates the advantages of our approach; we show that the user modeling quality improves when LOD-based background information is included in the process.

1 Introduction

The Social Web is a gold mine for researchers and developers of user modeling techniques who investigate how user traces such as clicks, ratings, shared resources or textual contributions can be transformed into representations that are beneficial for a given application. For example, the status messages (so-called *tweets*) that people post on Twitter[1] can be exploited to feature personalized website recommendations or news recommendations [1,2]. To apply user modeling in a given application context such as a news recommendation service, it is essential to understand the semantics of Twitter messages. Rowe et al. [3] propose to exploit contextual information in order to clarify the semantics of tweets. In some instances, background information is required in order to utilize user data more effectively. Linked Data principles allow for publishing background information in such a way that the data can be readily consumed by applications[2]. Today, the Linked Open Data (LOD) cloud already provides a great variety of information that can support various applications [4], including expert

---

[1] http://twitter.com

[2] http://www.w3.org/DesignIssues/LinkedData.html

M. Brambilla, T. Tokuda, and R. Tolksdorf (Eds.): ICWE 2012, LNCS 7387, pp. 378–385, 2012.
© Springer-Verlag Berlin Heidelberg 2012

finding [5], semantic enrichment of tweets [3], and a rule-based framework for user modeling [6]. Yet, there are, to the best of our knowledge, no research studies that investigate to what extent LOD is beneficial for user modeling processes that analyze user behavior observed on the Social Web.

It should be stressed, that connecting user data with information from the LOD cloud is a challenging task. While the semantics of linked data are well described and facts can easily be retrieved by means of RDF statements, user data on the Social Web often lacks well-defined semantics. Consider Twitter messages as an example: it is easy to extract meta-data such as the creator or creation time of a tweet, but it is challenging to automatically infer the semantic meaning of a tweet. Recently, researchers have begun to make use of named entity recognition services such as OpenCalais[3] and DBpedia Spotlight[4] to infer the topics of Twitter messages, e.g. [2,7].

Understanding the semantics of user data leads to interesting applications such as the profiling of places [7]. Apart from inferring the main location of Twitter users [8], semantic enrichment is also helpful for user modeling and particularly for deducing user interests from Social Web streams [2]. In this paper, we go beyond the aforementioned works and investigate whether background knowledge from the LOD cloud further improves user modeling effectiveness. We analyze our user modeling framework in the context of geographic recommender systems which recommend points of interest (POIs) to users. We explore how Twitter and Flickr can be utilized as user data sources and investigate how background information from GeoNames[5] and DBpedia[6] can be exploited to improve user modeling and consequently the performance of the recommender systems.

The main contributions of our work are as follows: (i) a user modeling framework that exploits the Linked Open Data cloud, (ii) a showcase in which we apply the framework to recommending POIs, and (iii) the evaluation of our methods based on a large Flickr and Twitter dataset which shows the benefits of considering LOD.

2   User Modeling on the Social Web with Linked Data

We now introduce the core building blocks of our user modeling framework. They allow us to exploit Social Web data and knowledge gathered from the LOD cloud to translate user interests into semantic concepts. An overview of our framework is shown in Figure 1. It derives user interest profiles which consist of a set of weighted concepts (each concept is identified by a URI). The concepts are typically dependent on the domain of the application that is requesting user profiles. The weight associated with each concept indicates the intensity of the user's interest in the concept: the higher the weight, the higher the inferred interest. Our

---

[3] http://www.opencalais.com

[4] http://dbpedia.org/spotlight

[5] http://geonames.org

[6] http://dbpedia.org

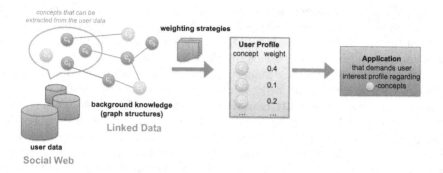

Fig. 1. Overview of the user modeling framework and its three main dimensions: (1) user data sources (what user data to exploit), (2) background knowledge (how to exploit the background knowledge) and (3) weighting strategies (how to weigh the concepts of interests)

framework allows for the creation of various user modeling strategies. Here, we first analyze three design dimensions in detail, namely (i) user data, (ii) background knowledge, and (iii) weighting strategies (see Figure 1). Then, we employ our framework in the domain of geospatial-centric user modeling.

User Data. Our framework provides methods for collecting a user's data from different Social Web streams including her Twitter stream and her resource sharing activities on platforms such as Flickr. As part of the framework's semantic enrichment process, meta-data and semantics are extracted from the observed user activities, the latter being achieved via the named entity recognition service DBpedia Spotlight. Extracted concepts are mapped to the corresponding RDF resources (URIs) in the LOD cloud. The framework can thus represent user activities via the meta-data and via the RDF resources that are related to a user activity. For example, a Twitter message such as "Enjoying the view from the Eiffel Tower" can be represented via information about the application from which the user posted the message and via the semantic concept that can be extracted from the message, namely *http://dbpedia.org/resource/Eiffel_Tower*.

Background Knowledge. Given the concepts extracted from the user data, our framework then acquires background information about the concepts. By following the corresponding URIs, RDF statements are collected to gain a better understanding of a user's interests in concepts that matter to the application that requests the user profile. Lets consider the concept graph example depicted in Figure 1. An application may only be interested in a user's preferences wrt. concepts c_1, c_2 and c_3. Based on the semantic enrichment of the user data, our framework can detect that the user was directly concerned with c_1. By exploiting background information and in particular by following the URIs in the LOD cloud, our framework can infer that the user was also concerned with

Table 1. Examples of (RDF) graph patterns that can be applied to relate a concept c_m, which can directly be extracted from the user data, to a concept of interest c

pattern	description
1.$\textcircled{c}$	*direct mention:* a concept of interest c is directly mentioned in the user data
2.$\textcircled{c_m}\!\!-\!\!\textcircled{c}$	*indirect mention I:* a concept c_m is mentioned that occurs in an RDF statement with the concept of interest c; possible RDF graph patterns: (a) $\{c_m\ p\ c\}$ and (b) $\{c\ p\ c_m\}$
3.$\textcircled{c_m}\!\!-\!\!\textcircled{c_x}\!\!-\!\!\textcircled{c}$	*indirect mention II:* a concept c_m is mentioned that is related to the concept of interest c via another concept c_x; possible RDF graph patterns: (a) $\{c_m\ p_1\ c_x.\ c\ p_2\ c_x\}$, (b) $\{c_m\ p_1\ c_x.\ c_x\ p_2\ c\}$, (c) $\{c_x\ p_1\ c_m.\ c\ p_2\ c_x\}$, (d) $\{c_x\ p_1\ c_m.\ c_x\ p_2\ c\}$

concepts that are related to the concepts that matter for the given application. For instance, the user may have mentioned c_4 which is directly related to c_2 or she may have mentioned c_5 which is indirectly related to c_3.

Different graph patterns (which can be formulated by means of SPARQL queries) can therefore yield different policies for the kind of background knowledge that should be considered in the user profile construction process. Table 1 lists the different graph patterns we analyze in this work. They range from (1) direct mentions of concepts of interests to (3) patterns that relate a mentioned concept c_m with a concept of interest c via another concept c_x. For example, (3.a) describes a situation where c_m and c share the same property value c_x.

Weighting Strategies. Our proposed user modeling framework features different strategies for weighting the concepts of interests for which relations can be discovered according to the aforementioned graph patterns. The basic strategy counts the number of occurrences of a concept c_m, which is related to c via some graph pattern, in the user's data stream to determine the weight associated with c. The weights in a user profile are then normalized so that the sum of the weights is equal to 1.

Geospatial-Centric User Modeling. In this work, the actual application that we evaluate our framework on can be described as follows: *Given a set of POIs and a user* u, *a user modeling strategy has to assign to each POI* p *a weight that reflects to what extent* u *is interested in* p.

We rely Twitter and Flickr as *user data* sources and consider only location-related concepts. From the Twitter stream, we extract the semantic concepts (DBpedia URIs) that are related to places (*http://dbpedia.org/ontology/Place*). In the case of Flickr, we employ an approach that estimates the geographic location of images [11]. The extracted geographic concepts are then utilized to create the geo-related interest profile. Considering these two main Social Web platforms, we have three options of user data sources when creating a user modeling strategy: (1) Twitter, (2) Flickr, (3) Twitter *and* Flickr.

We obtain background information (RDF statements) about the geospatial concepts that are extracted from the user data and about the points of interests for which the application demands user preferences from DBpedia. For relating the concepts from the user data with the POIs, we utilize particularly the following three graph patterns (see Table 1): (1) direct mentions, (2.a) indirect mentions I, and (3.a) indirect mentions II where a mentioned concept c_m and a POI share the same property value.

To assign a preference score to a POI, we apply the occurrence-based weighting strategy. Thus, we count the number of user activities (represented via the extracted semantic concepts) which match a graph pattern that is employed by the user modeling strategy.

Overall, we thus have $3 \times 3 = 9$ different geospatial-centric user modeling strategies *um*: (i) *um(Flickr, direct mentions)*, (ii) *um(Flickr, indirect mentions I)*, etc. Moreover, we experiment with combining different strategies such as *mix(um(Flickr, direct mentions)* and *um(Flickr, indirect mentions I))* where the preference score is defined as harmonic mean of the scores computed by the individual user modeling strategies.

3   Evaluation of Geospatial-Centric User Modeling

In this section, we evaluate the effectiveness of user modeling strategies that are featured in our user modeling framework. We measure the quality of the different user modeling strategies in inferring user preferences for POIs and investigate the following research questions:

1. How does the source of user data influence the quality of predicting user preferences?
2. How does the inclusion of background knowledge from the LOD cloud impact the user modeling quality?
3. Which (combinations of) user modeling strategies yield the highest effectiveness?

3.1   Experimental Setup: Recommending Points of Interests

To answer the research questions above, we test our user modeling strategies in the context of a recommender system that recommends POIs to a user. Given a user u and a candidate set of POIs such as museums or other tourist attractions, the recommender provides a ranking of POIs so that those POIs which are most relevant to u appear at the top of the ranking. The actual recommender algorithm thus orders the POIs according to the preference scores in u's profile which is derived by a user modeling strategy. The recommendation quality thus solely depends on the quality of the user modeling process.

To investigate to what extent user information from more than one Social Web portal can support the recommendation of POIs, we identified 394 users who have an account on Flickr *and* Twitter. We accumulated eleven months worth of user activities on both streams. On Flickr, these users uploaded a total of $833,441$ images, 16.8% of which are geo-tagged. Based on the tags and title terms we were able to derive a location estimate for $473,129$ of the remaining $693,456$ images that had not been geo-tagged. Details of the approach can be found in [11]. To translate a given (or estimated) latitude/longitude into a DBpedia POI, we relied on the *findNearbyWikipedia* web service[7]. With this approach we were able to identify one or more DBpedia entries within a radius of 10km for a total of $588,092$ images (70.6%). On Twitter, the 394 users posted a total of 2,489,088 tweets. For approximately 11% of the tweets we were able to extract geospatial DBpedia concepts.

We rely on precision, recall, and F-measure (within the top k) to quantify the recommender quality. For user modeling and evaluation purposes we split our dataset as follows: we derived user models based on the first 9 months of user activity and evaluated the models on the final two months of the logged user activities. A POI is considered to be relevant for a user u if the POI is spatially closest to a location where the user took a Flickr photo or if the POI was directly mentioned in a tweet that the user posted within these two months. The split resulted in 9916 candidate POIs of which, on average, 59.35 were considered to be relevant for a given user.

3.2   Results

User Data Sources. When comparing the impact different user-data sources (i.e. utilizing Twitter or Flickr or a combination of both) have on the user modeling quality and subsequently the recommendation quality, our results[8] show that Twitter alone is a more valuable source for creating user profiles that feature preferences in POIs than Flickr alone. However, using both Twitter and Flickr as sources for creating user profiles yields the highest effectiveness, indicating that the two user data sources complement each other to some extent, i.e. Twitter-based profiles provide user preferences which cannot be inferred from Flickr activities and vice versa.

Background Knowledge. Table 2 illustrates the effect of each strategy for exploiting background knowledge in order to relate the concepts, which are extracted from the Twitter *and* Flickr activities, to the POIs. While there is no significant difference in performance between the strategy that considers merely *direct mentions* and the strategy that considers merely *indirect mentions I*, we observe that *indirect mentions II*, which relates mentioned concepts and POIs via shared property values, clearly yields the best performance in terms of the precision, recall, and F-measure within the top 10 and top 20 results.

The results presented in Table 2 also reveal that the combination of different graph patterns for inferring the user preferences in POIs further enhances the

---

[7] http://www.geonames.org/export/wikipedia-webservice.html
[8] Due to space constraints, detailed results are omitted.

Table 2. Overview of the different strategies for integrating background knowledge. Twitter *and* Flickr are used in combination as user data source.

strategy	P@10	R@10	F@10	P@20	R@20	F@20
core strategies:						
direct mentions	0.715	0.260	0.412	0.580	0.179	0.298
indirect mentions I	0.699	0.268	0.426	0.566	0.185	0.308
indirect mentions II	**0.820**	**0.312**	**0.475**	**0.727**	**0.436**	**0.569**
combined strategies:						
direct & indirect mentions I	0.733	0.216	0.360	0.608	0.287	0.416
direct & indirect mentions II	0.836	0.333	0.4975	0.747	0.466	0.596
indirect mentions I + II	0.830	0.325	0.489	0.739	0.456	0.587
direct & indirect mentions I + II	**0.839**	**0.337**	0.502	**0.751**	**0.473**	**0.603**

quality of the user modeling and recommendation process. When considering the combination of direct mentions and background knowledge derived from graph patterns of the LOD cloud (indirect mentions I + II), we achieve the highest effectiveness across all evaluation measures: $P@10 = 0.84$, $R@10 = 0.34$, and $F@10 = 0.50$ respectively (last row in Table 2). In comparison with the *direct mention* strategy, which does not exploit RDF statements from the LOD cloud, the $F@20$ performance has more than doubled. Thus, we conclude that taking background knowledge obtained from the LOD cloud into account can significantly improve the effectiveness of user modeling on the Social Web.

Furthermore, we can answer the research questions raised at the beginning of this section as follows. For the task of recommending POIs, it turns out that (1) the aggregation of Twitter and Flickr user data yields the best user modeling performance and that (2) the user modeling quality increases when more background information from the LOD cloud is included. Finally, (3) the best performance is achieved by combining the different graph patterns for acquiring background information and inferring user preferences.

4   Conclusions

In this paper, we proposed a framework for enriching user modeling on the Social Web with information from the Linked Open Data cloud. Our framework monitors user activities on Social Web platforms such as Twitter and Flickr, infers the semantic meaning of user activities and provides strategies for gathering background information from the Web of Data to generate semantically meaningful user profiles that support a given application. We showcased and evaluated our framework in the context of a geospatial recommender system where the core challenge lies in deducing user preferences for POIs. To account for this, we also presented a method that allows for the semantic enrichment of Flickr pictures by (i) estimating the geographical location where a picture was taken and by (ii) exploiting GeoNames in order to identify related DBpedia concepts.

Our evaluation showed the effectiveness of our user modeling framework. Based on a large Twitter and Flickr dataset of more than 2.4 million tweets and 800 thousand Flickr pictures that we obtained by monitoring 394 users over a period of nearly a year, we revealed that the aggregation of user data from both Social Web platforms is beneficial for inferring user preferences. Taking advantage of background information derived from the LOD cloud led to substantial improvements of the baseline user modeling effectiveness.

Acknowledgements. The research leading to these results has received funding from the European Union Seventh Framework Programme (FP7/2007-2013) under grant agreement no ICT 257831 (ImREAL project).

References

1. Chen, J., Nairn, R., Nelson, L., Bernstein, M., Chi, E.: Short and tweet: experiments on recommending content from information streams. In: Proc. of the 28th Int. Conf. on Human Factors in Computing Systems(CHI), pp. 1185–1194. ACM (2010)
2. Abel, F., Gao, Q., Houben, G.J., Tao, K.: Analyzing User Modeling on Twitter for Personalized News Recommendations. In: Konstan, J.A., Conejo, R., Marzo, J.L., Oliver, N. (eds.) UMAP 2011. LNCS, vol. 6787, pp. 1–12. Springer, Heidelberg (2011)
3. Rowe, M., Stankovic, M.: Aligning Tweets with Events: Automation via Semantics. The Semantic Web Journal, Special Issue on Interoperability, Usability, Applicability (2011)
4. Bizer, C., Heath, T., Berners-Lee, T.: Linked data - the story so far. Int. Journal on Semantic Web and Information Systems (IJSWIS) 5(3), 1–22 (2009)
5. Stankovic, M., Wagner, C., Jovanovic, J., Laublet, P.: Looking for Experts? What can Linked Data do for You? In: Workshop on Linked Data on the Web (LDOW), Raleigh, USA (2010)
6. Leonardi, E., Abel, F., Heckmann, D., Herder, E., Hidders, J., Houben, G.-J.: A Flexible Rule-Based Method for Interlinking, Integrating, and Enriching User Data. In: Benatallah, B., Casati, F., Kappel, G., Rossi, G. (eds.) ICWE 2010. LNCS, vol. 6189, pp. 322–336. Springer, Heidelberg (2010)
7. Cano, A.E., Varga, A., Ciravegna, F.: Volatile Classification of Point of Interests based on Social Activity Streams. In: Workshop on Social Data on the Web (SDoW), Bonn, Germany (2011)
8. Hecht, B., Hong, L., Suh, B., Chi, E.H.: Tweets from Justin Bieber's Heart: The Dynamics of the "Location" Field in User Profiles. In: Proc. of Int. Conf. on Human Factors in Computing Systems (CHI), Vancouver, BC, Canada. ACM (2011)
9. Golbeck, J., Hansen, D.L.: Computing Political Preference among Twitter Followers. In: Proc. of Int. Conf. on Human Factors in Computing Systems (CHI), Vancouver, BC, Canada. ACM (2011)
10. Pennacchiotti, M., Popescu, A.M.: A Machine Learning Approach to Twitter User Classification. In: Proc. of the 5th Int. AAAI Conf. on Weblogs and Social Media (ICWSM), Barcelona, Spain. AAAI Press (2011)
11. Hauff, C., Houben, G.-J.: Geo-Location Estimation of Flickr Images: Social Web Based Enrichment. In: Baeza-Yates, R., de Vries, A.P., Zaragoza, H., Cambazoglu, B.B., Murdock, V., Lempel, R., Silvestri, F. (eds.) ECIR 2012. LNCS, vol. 7224, pp. 85–96. Springer, Heidelberg (2012)

ViP2P: Efficient XML Management in DHT Networks

Konstantinos Karanasos[1], Asterios Katsifodimos[1],
Ioana Manolescu[1], and Spyros Zoupanos[2]

[1] Inria Saclay–Île de France and LRI, Université Paris Sud-11
[2] Max-Planck Institut für Informatik, Saarbrücken, Germany
`firstname.lastname@inria.fr`

Abstract. We consider the problem of efficiently sharing large volumes of XML data based on distributed hash table overlay networks. Over the last three years, we have built ViP2P (standing for *Vi*ews in *Peer-to-Peer*), a platform for the distributed, parallel dissemination of XML data among peers. At the core of ViP2P stand *distributed materialized XML views*, defined as XML queries, filled in with data published anywhere in the network, and exploited to efficiently answer queries issued by any network peer. ViP2P is one of the very few *fully implemented* P2P platforms for XML sharing, deployed on *hundreds of peers in a WAN*. This paper describes the system architecture and modules, and the engineering lessons learned. We show experimental results, showing that our choices, outperf related systems by orders of magnitude in terms of data volumes, network size and data dissemination throughput.

Keywords: P2P, XML, DHT, distributed views.

1 Introduction

We consider the large-scale management of distributed XML data in a *peer-to-peer* (P2P) setting. To provide users with *precise and complete* answers to their requests for information, we assume that the requests are formulated by means of a structured query language, and that the system must return complete results. That is, if somewhere in the distributed peer network, an answer to a given query exists, the system will find it and include it in the query result. Thus, we consider P2P XML data management based on a structured peer-to-peer network, more specifically, a distributed hash table (or DHT, in short).

In this setting, users may formulate two kinds of information requests. First, they may want to *subscribe to interesting data anywhere in the network*, that were published before or after the subscription is recorded in the system. We need to ensure that results are eventually returned as soon as possible, following the publication of a matching data source. Second, users may formulate *ad-hoc (snapshot)* queries, by which they just seek to obtain as fast as possible the results which have already been published in the network.

M. Brambilla, T. Tokuda, and R. Tolksdorf (Eds.): ICWE 2012, LNCS 7387, pp. 386–394, 2012.

The challenges raised by a DHT-based XML data management platform are: (*i*) building a *distributed resource catalog*, enabling data producers and consumers to "meet" in an information sharing space; such a catalog is needed both for subscription and ad-hoc queries; (*ii*) efficiently distributing the data of the network to consumers that have subscribed to it, and; (*iii*) providing *efficient distributed query evaluation algorithms* for answering ad-hoc queries fast.

Over the last three years, we have invested more than 6 man-years building the ViP2P[1] platform to address these challenges. Importantly, ViP2P uses *subscriptions as views*: results of long-running subscription queries are stored by the subscriber peers and re-used to answer subsequent ad-hoc queries.

A critical engineering issue when deploying XML data management applications on a DHT is the division of tasks between the DHT and the upper layers. In ViP2P, we chose to load the DHT layer *as little as possible*, and keep the heavy-weight query processing operations in the data management layer and outside the DHT. This has enabled us to build and efficiently deploy an important-size system (70.000 lines of Java code), which we show scales on up to 250 computers in a WAN, and hundreds of GBs of XML data.

Several DHT-based XML data management platforms [3,9,11] are only concerned with *locating* in the P2P networks the documents relevant for a query. All the peers which may hold results then locally evaluate the query, leading to high query traffic and peer overload. In contrast, as in [1,2,6,8], ViP2P answers queries over a global XML database distributed in a P2P network.

In this paper, we make the following contributions. (*i*) We present a scalable, end-to-end architecture of one of the very few DHT-based XML sharing platforms actually implemented. From a system engineering perspective, we believe this is a useful addition to the corpus of existing DHT-based XML data management literature which has focused more on indexing and filtering algorithms, and less on system aspects. (*ii*) We present an experimental study of XML dissemination to DHT-based subscriptions, show which network parameters impact its performance, and demonstrate that ViP2P outperforms competitor systems by orders of magnitude in terms of published data volumes and throughput.

In the sequel, Section 2 presents an overview of the platform and Section 3 the architecture of a ViP2P peer. Section 4 experimentally demonstrate the platform scalability; many more experiments can be found in [4]. We then conclude.

2   Platform Overview

XML data flows in ViP2P can be summarized as follows. XML documents are *published* independently and autonomously by any peer. Peers can also formulate *subscriptions*, or long-running queries, potentially matching documents published before, or after the subscriptions. The results of each subscription query are *stored* at the peer defining the subscription, and the definition of it is *indexed* in the peer network. Finally, peers can ask *ad-hoc queries*, which are answered in a snapshot fashion (based on the data available in the network so far) by

---

[1] http://vip2p.saclay.inria.fr

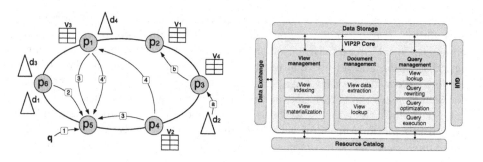

Fig. 1. System overview (left); Architecture of a ViP2P peer (right)

exploiting the existing subscriptions, which can be seen as *materialized views*. In this Section, we detail the overall process via an example.

A sample ViP2P instance over six peers is depicted in Figure 1 (left). In the Figure, XML documents are denoted by triangles, whereas views are denoted by tables, hinting to the fact that they contain sets of tuples.

For ease of explanation, we make the following naming conventions for the remainder of this paper: *publisher* is a peer which publishes an XML document, *consumer* is a peer which defines a subscription and stores its results (or, equivalently, the respective materialized view) and *query peer* is a peer which poses an *ad-hoc* query. Clearly, a peer can play any subset of these roles simultaneously.

View Publication. A ViP2P view is a *long-running subscription query* that any peer can freely define. In the sequel, we will refer to long-running subscription queries as *materialized views* or just *views*. The *definition* (i.e., the actual query) of each newly created view is indexed in the DHT network. For instance, assume peer p_2 in Figure 1 (left) publishes the view v_1, defined by the XPath query $//bibliography//book[contains(.,'Databases')]$. The view requires all the books items from a bibliography containing the word 'Databases'. ViP2P indexes v_1 by inserting in the DHT the following three (key, value) pairs: $(bibliography, v_1@p_2)$, $(book, v_1@p_2)$ and $('Databases', v_1@p_2)$. Here, $v_1@p_2$ encapsulates the structured query defining v_1, and a pointer to the concrete database at peer p_2 where v_1 data is stored. As will be shown below, all existing and future documents that can affect v_1, *push* the corresponding data to its database.

Peers look up views in the DHT in two situations: when publishing documents, and when issuing ad-hoc queries. We detail this below.

Document Publication. When publishing a document, each peer is in charge of identifying the views within the whole network to which its document may contribute. For instance, in Figure 1 left (step a), peer p_3 publishes the document d_2. Peer p_3 extracts from d_2 all distinct element names and all keywords. For each such element name or keyword k, p_3 looks up in the DHT for view definitions associated to k. Assume that document d_2 contains data matching the view v_1 as it contains the element names *bibliography* and *book*, as well as the word $'Databases'$, thus p_3, learns about the existence of v_1 (step b). In the publication example above, p_3 extracts from d_2 the results matching v_1; from now on, we will use the notation $v_1(d_2)$ to designate such results. Peer p_3 sends $v_1(d_2)$ to p_2 (step c), which adds them to the database storing v_1 data.

Ad-Hoc Query Answering. ViP2P peers may pose *ad-hoc queries*, which must be evaluated immediately. To evaluate such queries, a ViP2P peer looks up in the network for views which may be used to answer it. For instance, assume the query $q = //bibliography//book[contains(., 'Databases')]//author$ is issued at peer p_5 (step 1, in Figure 1, left). To process q, p_5 looks up the keys *bibliography*, *book*, *'Databases'* and *author* in the DHT, and retrieves a set of view definitions, v_1, v_2 and v_3 (step 2). Observe that q can be rewritten as $v_1//author$; therefore, p_5 can answer q just by retrieving and extracting q's results out of v_1. Alternatively, assume that q can also be rewritten by joining views v_2 and v_3 as ViP2P can combine *several* views to rewrite a query [4]. In that case, p_5 can retrieve the views v_2 and v_3 (step 3) and join them to evaluate q. However, the whole content of both views has to be shipped to p_5 to evaluate the query q. Instead, v_2 can be shipped to peer p_1, joined locally with v_3 at p_1 (step 4), who will send the query results to the query peer (step 4'), avoiding extraneous data transfers.

3   ViP2P Peer Architecture

Figure 1 (right) outlines the architecture of a ViP2P peer. In this Section, we introduce the auxiliary modules on which every peer relies, and then move to the main modules, which are included in the *ViP2P Core* box of Figure 1.

Resource Catalog provides the underlying DHT layer used to keep peers connected, and to index and lookup views. It employs the FreePastry DHT, which is an open-source implementation of the Pastry overlay network [10]. It provides efficient request routing, deterministic object location, and load balancing.

Data Exchange module is responsible *for all data transfers* and relies on Java RMI. Experience with FreePastry has shown that Pastry-routed inter-peer communications quickly become the bottleneck when sending important volumes of data [1]. Instead, we use RMI (with our own (de)serialization methods, properly controlling concurrency at the sender and receiver side etc.) to send larger messages containing view tuples, when views are materialized and queried.

Data Storage Within each peer, view tuples are efficiently stored into a native store that we built using the BerkeleyDB^2 library. It allows storing, retrieving and sorting entries, with transactional guarantees for concurrent operations.

The VIP2P GUI enables publishing views, documents and evaluating queries. We now describe the core modules.

Document Management determines to which views the peer's documents may contribute data, and extracts and sends this data to the appropriate consumers.

---

^{2} http://www.oracle.com/technetwork/database/berkeleydb/

- **View definition lookup.** When a new document is published by a peer, this module looks up in the DHT for view definitions to which the document may contribute data. The result is a superset of view definitions of the views that the document might contribute data to. These definitions are then passed to the *view data extraction* module.

- **View data extraction.** Given a list of view definitions, this module at a publisher peer extracts from the document the tuples matching each view, and ships them, in a parallel fashion, to the corresponding consumers. The view data extractor is capable of simultaneously matching several views on a given document, thus extracting the corresponding tuples at a single document traversal.

View Management. This module handles view indexing and materialization.

- **View indexing.** This module implements the view indexing process. In this context, a given algorithm for extracting (key, value) pairs out of a view definition is termed a *view indexing strategy* [4]. In our experiments, the most efficient is the *Label Indexing (LI)* strategy, indexing a view v by each v node label (element or attribute name, or word).

- **View materialization.** The *view materialization* module receives tuples from remote publishers and stores them in the respective BerkeleyDB database. In a large scale, real-world scenario, thousands of documents might be contributing data to a single view. To avoid overload on its incoming data transfers, this module implements a back-pressure *tuple-send/receive protocol* which informs the publisher when the consumer is overloaded, so that the publisher waits until the consumer is ready to accept new tuples.

Query Management comprises the following modules for query evaluation.

- **View lookup.** This module, given a query, performs a lookup in the DHT network retrieving the view definitions that may be used to rewrite the query. Depending on the indexing strategy (mentioned earlier in this Section), this module uses a different *view lookup* method.

- **Query rewriting.** Given a query and a set of view definitions, this module produces a logical plan which, evaluated on some views, produces exactly the results required by the query (algorithm detailed in [7]).

- **Query optimization.** This module receives a logical plan that is output by the *query rewriting* module, and translates it to an optimized physical plan. The optimization concerns both the logical (join reordering, push selections/projections etc.) and physical (dictating the exact flow of data during query execution) level.

- **Query execution.** This module provides a set of physical operators which can be executed by any ViP2P peer, implementing the standard iterator-based execution model. Since ViP2P is a distributed application, operators can be deployed to peers and executed in a distributed manner. The query optimization module is the one to decide the parts of a physical plan that every peer executes.

4   Experimental Results

We now present a set of experiments studying ViP2P performance, carried on the Grid5000 infrastructure[3]. Due to space limitations, we only report here on our main findings; many more experiments are described in [4].

In our experiments, we used synthetic "product catalog" documents of controllable size (more details can be found in [4]). First, all views are created and indexed. Then, on a signal sent to all publishers, these peers start publishing all their documents as fast as possible. This is a "flash crowd" scenario, aiming at stress-testing our system. Queries are posed and processed after all the views are filled with data. Section 4.1 examines view materialization, while Section 4.2 studies the performance of the query execution engine.

4.1   View Materialization in Large Networks

We present three materialization experiments; many more can be found in [4].

Experiment 1: One Publisher, Varying Data Size, 64 Consumers. In this experiment we study how materialization time is affected when the total size of published data is increased. We use one publisher holding all the data in the network. The size of the published data varies from 64MBs to 1024MBs.

Each of the 64 consumers holds one view of the form $//catalog//camera_{K\ cont}$ where K varies according to the peer that holds the view. For example, the first consumer holds the view $//catalog//camera_{1\ cont}$, the second holds the view $//catalog//camera_{2\ cont}$ etc. This way, from each document the publisher extracts 64 tuples, each of which is sent to a different consumer. All the content of the documents is absorbed by the 64 views.

We run two variations of the same experiment: (i) one for sequential tuple sending where a publisher sends the tuples to their corresponding consumers one after the other, and (ii) one for parallel tuple sending, where a publisher ships the tuples to their corresponding consumers simultaneously. The graph at left in Figure 2 shows, as expected, that the materialization time increases linearly with the size of data published in the network in both cases. It also shows that the materialization time in the case of parallel tuple sending is considerably shorter (about 3000 sec. instead of 11500 sec. for absorbing 1024MBs of data).

Experiment 2: 64 Publishers, Varying Data Size, One Consumer. We now focus on the impact of the number of (simultaneous) publishers on the capacity of absorbing the data into a single view. The published data size varies from 64MBs to 3.2GBs, and is equally distributed to 64 publishers. All the published data ends up in one view. Similarly to Experiment 1, we test 2 modes of tuple-receiving concurrency: (i) sequential tuple receiving and; (ii) parallel tuple receiving.

Figure 2 (center) depicts the materialization time as the size of the published data increases. We observe that the materialization time increases proportionally to the size of published data in both sequential and parallel tuple receiving

---

[3] https://www.grid5000.fr

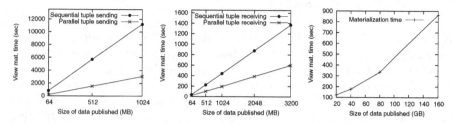

Fig. 2. Experiment 1: one publisher, varying size of data, 64 consumers (left); Experiment 2: 64 publishers, varying data size, one consumer (center); Experiment 3: publishing varying size of data in 50 groups of 5 peers each (right).

modes. Also, parallel tuple receiving reduces the view materialization time by more than 50% (600 sec. instead of about 1400 sec. to absorb 3.2GBs of data).

From the two graphs (left, center) in Figure 2, we conclude that it is faster for the network to absorb data using one consumer and many publishers rather than many consumers and one publisher since it is slow for a peer to extract all the available data by itself and ship them to the consumers.

Experiment 3: Community Publishing. A "community publishing" setting is the closest to real world scenarios: a large and complex environment, with many publishers and many consumers. We use a network of 250 peers, each of which holds the same number of 1MB documents. We logically divide the network into 50 groups of 5 publishers and one consumer each. The data of all publishers in a group is of interest *only* to the consumer of that group. The total amount of data published (and shipped to the views) varies from 20GBs to 160GBs.

Figure 2 (right) shows that the materialization time grows linearly with the published data size. This experiment demonstrates the good scalability properties of ViP2P as the data volume increases. Moreover, it shows that ViP2P exploits many parallelization opportunities in such "community publishing" scenarios when extracting, sending, receiving and storing view tuples. Here we report on sharing up to 160 GB of data over up to 250 peers with a throughput of 238 MB/s while KadoP [1] scaled up to 1 GB of data over 50 peers with a throughput of 0.33 MB/s and psiX [9] used 262 MBs of data and 11 computers.

4.2 Query Engine Evaluation

In this Section, we investigate the query processing performance as the data size increases. We use 20 publisher peers, two of which are also consumers, while another publisher is a query peer. The query peer and the two consumers are located in three different French cities. The number of published documents varies from 20 to 500; all documents contribute to the views.

The document used in this experiment is the same as in the previous experiments with a slight difference: its root element *catalog* has only one child, named *camera*. The views defined in the network are the following:

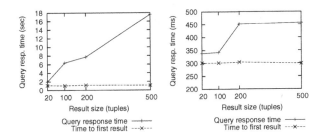

Fig. 3. Query execution time vs. number of result tuples for q_1 (left) and q_2 (right)

- v_1 is $//catalog_{ID}//camera_{ID}//description_{ID,cont}$
- v_2 is $//catalog_{ID}//camera_{ID}//\{description_{ID},\ price_{ID,val},\ specs_{ID,cont}\}$

Each document contributes a tuple to each view. The tuples of v_1 are large in size, since the *description* element is the largest element in our documents. A v_2 tuple is quite smaller since it does not store the full camera descriptions. We use two queries: q_1 asks for the *description*$_{cont}$, *specs*$_{cont}$ and *price*$_{val}$ of each *camera*. To evaluate q_1, ViP2P joins the views v_1 and v_2. Observe that q_1 returns full XML elements, and in particular, product descriptions, which are voluminous in our data set. Therefore, q_1 returns roughly all the published data (from 10MB in 20 tuples, to 250MB in 500 tuples). q_2 requires the *description*$_{ID}$, *specs*$_{ID}$ and *price*$_{ID}$ of each *camera*. It is very similar to q_1 with but it can be answered based on v_2 *only*. The returned data is much smaller since there are only IDs and no XML elements: from 2KB in 20 tuples, to 40KB in 500 tuples.

Figure 3 shows the query response time and the time to get the first result for the two queries. The low selectivity query q_1 in Figure 3 (left) takes longer than q_2 (right), due to the larger data transfers and the necessary view join. The time to first result is always constant for both q_1 and q_2 and does not depend on the result size. For q_1, a hash join is used to combine v_1 and v_2, and thus no tuple is output before the view v_2 has been built into the buckets of the hash join. This is done around one second in the case of q_1 and about 300 ms for q_2.

The ViP2P query processing engine scales quite linearly answering queries in a wide-area network. The fact that ViP2P rewrites queries into logical plans which are then passed to an optimizer, enables it to take advantage of known optimization techniques used in XML and/or distributed databases.

5   Conclusion and Perspectives

We have presented the ViP2P platform for building and maintaining structured materialized views, and processing queries using the views in a DHT network. Our experiments show that ViP2P outperforms similar systems by several orders of magnitude, in particular for the data publication throughput and the overall volume of data published. Many more experiments are described in our technical report [4]. We currently investigate a distributed version of our automatic view selection algorithm [5]. We also consider multiple-level subscriptions, where some views could be filled with data based on lower-level views.

Acknowledgements.   We experimented on Grid'5000 (https://www.grid 5000.fr). We thank A. Tilea, J. Camacho-Rodríguez, A. Roatis, V. Mishra and J. Leblay for their help. This work was partially supported by ANR 08-DEFIS-004.

References

1. Abiteboul, S., Manolescu, I., Polyzotis, N., Preda, N., Sun, C.: XML processing in DHT networks. In: ICDE (2008)
2. Bonifati, A., Cuzzocrea, A.: Storing and retrieving XPath fragments in structured P2P networks. Data Knowl. Eng. 59(2) (2006)
3. Galanis, L., Wang, Y., Jeffery, S.R., DeWitt, D.J.: Locating Data Sources in Large Distributed Systems. In: VLDB (2003)
4. Karanasos, K., Katsifodimos, A., Manolescu, I., Zoupanos, S.: The ViP2P Platform: Views in P2P. Research Report N° 7812 (November 2011)
5. Katsifodimos, A., Manolescu, I., Vassalos, V.: Materialized View Selection for XQuery Workloads. In: SIGMOD (to appear, 2012)
6. Lillis, K., Pitoura, E.: Cooperative XPath caching. In: SIGMOD (2008)
7. Manolescu, I., Karanasos, K., Vassalos, V., Zoupanos, S.: Efficient XQuery rewriting using multiple views. In: ICDE (2011)
8. Miliaraki, I., Kaoudi, Z., Koubarakis, M.: XML Data Dissemination Using Automata on Top of Structured Overlay Networks. In: WWW (2008)
9. Rao, P.R., Moon, B.: Locating XML documents in a peer-to-peer network using distributed hash tables. IEEE TKDE 21 (2009)
10. Rowstron, A., Druschel, P.: Pastry: Scalable, distributed object location and routing for large-scale peer-to-peer systems. In: ICDSP (November 2001)
11. Skobeltsyn, G., Hauswirth, M., Aberer, K.: Efficient Processing of XPath Queries with Structured Overlay Networks. In: Meersman, R., Tari, Z. (eds.) CoopIS/DOA/ODBASE 2005. LNCS, vol. 3761, pp. 1243–1260. Springer, Heidelberg (2005)

Online Change Estimation Models for Dynamic Web Resources[*]

A Case-Study of RSS Feed Refresh Strategies

Roxana Horincar, Bernd Amann, and Thierry Artières

LIP6 - University Pierre et Marie Curie, Paris, France
{roxana.horincar,bernd.amann,thierry.artieres}@lip6.fr

Abstract. Modern web 2.0 applications have transformed the Internet into an interactive, dynamic and alive information space. Personal weblogs, commercial web sites, news portals and social media applications generate highly dynamic information streams which have to be propagated to millions of users. This article focuses on the problem of estimating the publication frequency of highly dynamic web resources. We illustrate the importance of developing efficient *online* estimation techniques for improving the refresh strategies of RSS feed aggregators like Google Reader [8], Datasift [7] or Roses [11]. We study the temporal publication characteristics of a large collection of real world RSS feeds and we define and evaluate several online estimation methods in cohesion with different refresh strategies. We show the benefit of using periodical source publication patterns for change estimation and we highlight the challenges imposed by the application context.

1 Introduction

Understanding how web resources evolve in time is important for conceiving tools designed to ease the interaction between people and dynamic web content published by online newspapers, commercial web sites, social networks and collaborative web sites like Wikipedia. Most of these information sources can only be accessed via standard pull-based web protocols (HTTP) and estimating the degree of information change during a given time period is crucial for developing efficient refresh strategies.

Modern web sites, such as online newspapers or social media sites, publish their stream of changes in form of light-weight RSS/Atom feeds for reducing the communication cost between servers and clients. Technically speaking, an RSS feed is a standard XML document containing a list of time-stamped text descriptions including links to the corresponding web pages. The size of this list is generally limited to a constant value, where the publication of a new item usually removes the oldest one in the corresponding window. From the user's point of view, RSS documents are perceived as a stream of items pushed to their screen.

---

[*] The authors acknowledge the support of the French Agence Nationale de la Recherche (ANR), under grant CARTEC (ANR-07-MDCO-016)

M. Brambilla, T. Tokuda, and R. Tolksdorf (Eds.): ICWE 2012, LNCS 7387, pp. 395–410, 2012.

However, when considering the underlying communication protocol, there is no distinction between RSS feeds and other web resources. Both kinds of resources have to be refreshed by using the standard pull-based HTTP protocol where changes can only be detected by explicitly contacting the server.

As any web resource, RSS feeds evolve independently of their clients which must take their refresh decisions by estimating the change frequencies [1, 17]. In this paper, we focus on the problem of estimating the change frequency of dynamic web data. Our first goal is to improve the refresh strategies of RSS aggregators, but other web data processing systems like web crawlers or web data warehouses may as well benefit from the techniques presented in this article. The main challenges we address are:

Rapidly changing publication behavior : Event-related feed sources like topic based news feeds or social media feeds (Twitter) may suddenly change their publication frequency related to a particular event (e.g. twitter hashtag). This data dynamics leads to the necessity of continually updating the publication frequency estimation, using online estimation techniques.

Incomplete knowledge : Another challenge is the limited access bandwidth due to standard web politeness policies and limited computing, network and storage resources. Estimators then have to deal with incomplete knowledge about the data change history, not knowing how often, how much and when exactly a source produces new information items.

Irregular estimation intervals : In many web applications, data sources are not refreshed in regular time intervals. The exact access moment is generally decided by a refresh strategy, usually conceived to optimize certain quality measures within a minimum cost. Irregular refresh periods also make the estimation process more challenging.

Our main contributions are:

- an analysis of general characteristics with a focus on the temporal dimension of real RSS feed sources using data collected over four weeks from more than 2500 RSS feeds,
- two online estimation methods that correspond to different RSS publication activity models and
- an experimental evaluation of the online estimation methods in cohesion with different refresh strategies and an analysis of their effectiveness on sources with different publication behavior.

The rest of this paper is organized as follows. Section 2 gives a short survey of related work on refresh strategies and parameter estimation for web data. In section 3 we describe the problem and benefits of online change estimation in the context of web data refresh strategies. Section 4 proposes two ways to model the publication activity of a source and introduces some methods for updating these publication models online. Section 5 analysis the temporal characteristics of two collections of real RSS feed sources. Section 6 exposes the experimental results obtained by evaluating the proposed online estimation methods in conjunction with different refresh strategies. Conclusions and future work are presented in section 7.

2   Related Work

The problem of efficiently refreshing dynamic web information is largely studied in the context of web pages [4–6, 12–14] and RSS feed [11, 16, 17]. The majority of these strategies are based on the widely accepted assumption that web resources follow a Poisson process [15] characterized by a change rate parameter $\lambda(t)$ which can be estimated by observing the change history of a web page.

Considering $\lambda(t) = \lambda$ to be constant corresponds to a *homogeneous* (opposed to *non-homogeneous*) Poisson process which represents a stateless and time-independent random process where events occur with the same probability (rate) λ at every time point. It has been shown that this model is appropriate for a time granularity of at least one month [4–6]. On the other hand, for time granularities shorter than a month, researchers have shown that the homogeneous Poisson model is no longer suited [2, 9].

Offline refresh strategies [4, 5, 16, 17] assume that the change frequency of web pages or posting rates of web streams is known a-priori. They usually use average values measured beforehand or learnt during an initial learning phase with access to a complete changing history. This assumption is sufficient for a low frequency refresh activities where each web resource is refreshed rarely (like in web search engines) and the update frequency can be averaged over long time periods [4, 5, 16, 17].

Reference [6] presents several change (frequency) estimators for web pages, assuming an incomplete change history with irregular refresh frequencies. They show that a Web crawler could achieve 35% improvement in "freshness" simply by adopting their estimator. However, their analysis is based on the hypothesis that the date of the last change or the existence of a change on a web page are known in advance for estimation.

Based on the previous observations, [16] uses a periodic (inhomogeneous) Poisson model with a daily periodicity within a RSS feeds scenario. Similarly, [12] presents an empirical study of two *online refresh strategies* that use a curve-fitting over a generative model method and conservative bounds to dynamically adjust refresh parameters.

In the context of information filtering (also referred to as publish/subscribe), a user subscribes to the system to receive notifications whenever certain events of interest take place (e.g., when a document that corresponds to a certain filtering condition becomes available). In order to estimate the probability that a node has published new information relevant to a user's subscription, [18, 19] use time series prediction techniques for approximate information filtering. Our work uses a similar approach in a different context.

3   Refresh Strategies and Online Change Estimation

Large-scale web applications like web search engines, web archives, web data warehouses, publish-subscribe systems and news aggregators have to collect information from a large number of dynamic web resources. In order to accomplish this task efficiently, these systems are generally based on *refresh strategies* for deciding when to refresh each source in order to maximize one or several quality criteria under limited resources.

Refresh decisions are based on appropriate source *publication models* for making predictions. There exist various publication models. Content-independent models [6] estimate the probability that a source has changed at least once or n times at some time instant t, whereas content-dependent models [12] might include some heuristics for estimating the importance of change between two versions. We consider in this article the case of a RSS aggregator node which is subscribed to a collection of sources. Let t_0 represent the last time instant when source s has been refreshed by the aggregator. We define a *divergence* function $Div(s, t, t_0)$ estimating the total number of new items published by the source s in the time period $(t_0, t]$. Obviously the quality (preciseness) of this estimation is important for the quality of the corresponding refresh strategy [4, 5].

A traditional way for estimating divergence is to define the behavior of a source s as a stochastic (Poisson) process which can be characterized by time dependent *publication frequency* variable $\lambda(s, t)$ that measures the number of items published by source s at time instant t. Divergence can then be defined as an integral of publication frequency $\lambda(s, t)$ over time:

$$Div(s, t, t_0) = \int_{t_0}^{t} \lambda(s, x)dx \qquad (1)$$

In practice, refresh strategies use a discrete time dimension, where time periods are divided into time units of fixed size and divergence is defined by a sum of divergence estimations for the intervals (see section 4).

Online and offline change estimation: The general refreshing process illustrated in figure 1 is accomplished by (1) the *refresh strategy* which *uses* the publication model for estimating the divergence and the next refreshing time moment of each source and (2) the *change estimator* which generates and updates the publication model. In an *offline scenario* the change estimator module does not exist. The refresh strategy uses a precomputed publication model which is updated offline (independently of the refresh process). *Online estimation* interleaves both tasks and each new observation (obtained by a refresh) is used immediately for updating the publication model.

Why online change estimation is important: Keeping the estimated publication frequency of a source constant over a long period of time can represent an important source of errors if the source publication activity changes in time.

Fig. 1. Online estimation

This is illustrated in figure 2 showing the evolution of the real and the estimated divergence of a source during a day. Figure 2 compares (for a given source) the real divergence values (red curve) with the estimated values using a constant publication frequency (offline estimated divergence as the green curve) and the estimated values using an adaptive publication frequency (online estimated divergence as the blue curve). In both curves, the source is refreshed in regular time intervals which resets the divergence values to 0. The green estimated divergence function presented in figure 2 increases with a constant slope because it is based on a constant publication frequency (previously learnt in an offline manner and not updated afterwards). Differently from this case, the blue estimated divergence function in figure 2 is computed based on a publication frequency that continuously adapts its value in time (online estimation), converging to a zero publication frequency when the source does not publish anything and increasing as the source starts publishing. The estimation obviously is better in average in the second case.

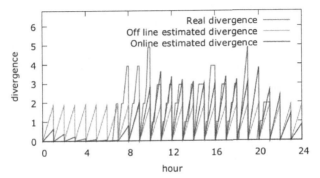

Fig. 2. Real vs. estimated divergence

4   Online Change Estimation for RSS Feeds

Our approach for estimating the change rate of RSS feeds is strongly inspired from standard results in time series analysis [3]. These techniques are used to predict future time series values based on past observations and are usually based on the hypothesis that both observations and predictions are done at equally spaced time intervals. In our particular case, the observations are made at the moment of a refresh, which is decided by the refresh strategy used by the crawler [11]. This makes the prediction process less precise than in the case of classical time series model usage.

We base our online estimation methods on observations of the number of occurred changes, i.e. new items published by a feed. In the particular case of working with RSS feeds, we could have chosen to use the specific RSS field $< pubDate >$ in order to find out exactly the publication date of each item. Nevertheless, we prefer to ignore this attribute for two reasons. First, [10] reports that this information ($< pubDate >$) is missing in about 20% of items. Second, ignoring this particular kind of metadata keeps our estimation methods generic and adaptable for other kinds of data (e.g. web pages).

4.1 Single Variable Publication Model

Estimating Divergence: Our first publication model represents the publication frequency of a source s at time t by a single variable, $\lambda(s,t)$. Let T_r represent the time instant of the rth refresh of s and $\lambda^r = \lambda(s, T_r)$ be the change rate of source s estimated at time instant T_r. Then the divergence of s at time instant $T \in [T_r, T_{r+1})$ can be simply estimated by the following formula:

$$Div^{est}(s, T, T_r) = (T - T_r) \cdot \lambda^r$$

Updating Frequency Estimation: Let $x^{r+1} = Div(s, T_{r+1}, T_r)$ be the number of new items published since the last refresh at T_r and observed at T_{r+1}. The newly estimated value of the publication frequency is obtained by single-exponentially smoothing the new observation with the previous estimation:

$$\lambda^{r+1} = \alpha \cdot \frac{x^{r+1}}{(T_{r+1} - T_r)} + (1 - \alpha) \cdot \lambda^r$$

This estimation method relies on all previous observations, with exponentially decaying weights, parameter $\alpha \in [0, 1]$ representing the smoothing constant.

4.2 Periodic Publication Model

Our second estimation model of publication is based on the hypothesis of periodicity. In this case, the publication frequency of a source is described as a periodic function with some (constant) period Δ_T: $\lambda(s,t) = \lambda(s, t + \Delta_T)$.

We use a *discrete* representation of the publication frequency as a table $P(s)$ of n values, each corresponding to a time slot $[t_i, t_{i+1})$, $i \in \{0, ...n - 1\}$. Each time slot is of constant size $t_{i+1} - t_i = \Delta_T/n$. We will call $P(s)$ the publication model of s. Then $\lambda_i(s,t)$ corresponds to the $(i+1)^{th}$ value in $P(s)$ where $(t \bmod \Delta_T) \in [t_i, t_{i+1})$ (i is the time slot covering t). In the following we denote by λ_i the average publication rate of source s during time slot i. In our experiments (section 6) we use a daily publication model where $\Delta_T = 24$ hours, $n = 24$ time slots of 1 hour each.

Estimating Divergence: Let T_r represent the time instant of the rth refresh of s and $P_r(s) = \{\lambda_i^r\}$, $i \in \{0, ...n - 1\}$ be the publication model of s estimated at time instant T_r. Then the expected divergence of s at time instant $T \in [T_r, T_{r+1})$ can be estimated by the following formula where i corresponds to the time slot containing T_r and there are $k + 1 = (\lceil T \rceil - \lfloor T_r \rfloor) \cdot n/\Delta_T$ time slots "covered" by the interval $[T_r, T)$ (the definitions are illustrated in figure 3):

$$Div^{est}(s, T, T_r) = \int_{T_r}^{T} \lambda_j^r(s, t) \, dt =$$

$$= \lambda_i^r(t_{i+1} - T_r) + \Delta_T/n \cdot \sum_{j=i+1}^{i+k-1} \lambda_{(j \bmod n)}^r + \lambda_{i+k}^r(T - t_{i+k})$$

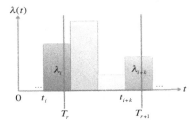

Fig. 3. Periodic publication model

Updating Frequency Estimation: Suppose that the aggregator refreshed some source s at some time moments T_r and T_{r+1} that correspond to time slots i and $i + k$. At T_{r+1}, the aggregator fetches $x^{r+1} = Div(s, T_{r+1}, T_r)$ new items published since the last refresh at T_r. The intuitive idea of the model update is to distribute the last observed items x^{r+1} in the time interval $[T_r, T_{r+1})$. This distribution is done *proportionally* to the expected divergence $Div_{r+1}^{est} = Div^{est}(s, T_{r+1}, T_r)$ estimated using the values of λ_j^r that correspond to the time interval $[T_r, T_{r+1})$. We compute λ_j^{r+1} as the newly predicted value of λ_j that corresponds to time slot j as follows:

$$\lambda_j^{r+1} = \begin{cases} \alpha \cdot \frac{\lambda_j^r}{Div_{r+1}^{est}} \cdot x^{r+1} + (1 - \alpha) \cdot \lambda_j^r \text{ if } j \in \{i, ...i + k\} \\ \lambda_j^r \qquad\qquad\qquad\qquad\qquad\qquad \textbf{otherwise} \end{cases}$$

where $\alpha \in [0, 1]$ represents a smoothing parameter that is used to give more or less weight to recent observations. This reestimation formula corresponds to a maximum likelihood estimate of the publication frequencies λ_j based on the observation x^{r+1} at iteration $r + 1$, smoothed with the estimates at previous iteration r.

5   Dataset Description

In order to better understand the change estimation problem, we studied a collection of real world RSS feeds focusing on their temporal dimension. We used two different datasets: dataset 1 was obtained from crawling a list of feeds [10] harvested from major RSS directories, portals and search engines (such as syndic8.com, Google Reader, feedmil.com, completeRSS.com etc.) and dataset 2 was acquired from a manually chosen list of RSS news feeds of different online newspaper websites, both French (such as Le Monde, Le Figaro, AFP) and international (such as CNN, New York Times, Euro News). We selected 1658 RSS crawled feeds from dataset 1 and 963 RSS news feeds from dataset 2 that had at least one posting within the four-week period between 14 March - 10 April 2011.

Publication Activity: In figure 4 we show the distribution of feeds for various activity classes defined by different posting rates for the two different datasets. The distributions show that feeds with very slow publication activity are predominant, while roughly 20% of the feeds publish more than 10 items daily.

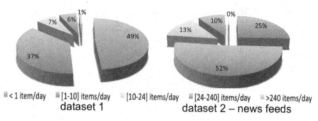

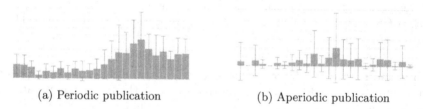

■ < 1 item/day ■ [1-10] items/day ▪ [10-24] items/day ■ [24-240] items/day ▫ >240 items/day
dataset 1   dataset 2 – news feeds

Fig. 4. Feeds per activity class

It has been shown in [10] that whereas the number of productive feeds is quite small, they are the ones that produce most of the items: 17% of RSS/Atom feeds produce 97% of the items.

Feed Periodicity: It is widely accepted that the past change represents a good predictor of future change. This works well especially for those types of feeds that have a foreseeable publication activity, for example, feeds that publish daily the same number of items. In this sense, measurements on real data done in [16] show that most of the daily posting rates of feed sources are stable, at least for their dataset, within the 3-month period they used for their experiments. But there are also feeds whose publication behavior vary in time, both in the number of daily published items and in the shape of publication activity.

In order to detect changes in publication frequency, for each hour (time slot i) of a day, we logged the number of items published by a feed and then computed the *mean* μ_i and the *standard deviation* σ_i on the entire period. We consider that a small *coefficient of variation CV* value is representative for periodic feed sources.

$$CV = \frac{1}{24} \sum_{i=0}^{23} \frac{\sigma_i}{\mu_i} \qquad \text{where } \mu_i \neq 0$$

When the mean values are close to zero, the coefficient of variation becomes sensitive to small changes in the means and inappropriate for testing sources with a low publication activity. Testing for $CV \leq 1$, we discovered that periodic sources represent 20% of the sources in our datasets that publish more than 10 items per day and 50% of the sources that publish more than 48 items per day. As an example, in figures 5a and 5b we represented the average (pink bars) and the standard

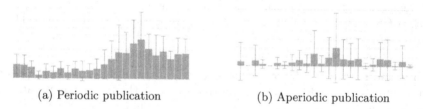

(a) Periodic publication   (b) Aperiodic publication

Fig. 5. Periodic and aperiodic publication behavior

deviation (vertical lines) of the number of published items at different time slots, one for each hour of the day, for a periodic and an aperiodic feed.

Publication Shape: We also studied the feed collection looking for different "shapes" in the daily publication activity. The shape of a daily publication model highly depends on what happens "behind the curtains" of each feed. Some feeds may be generated by human activity, while others may be based on some automatic publication process. We classified the feeds in three different categories, as shown in figure 6: feeds that have peaks, usually generated by an automatic publication robot, that have a uniform publication activity, such as in the case of a news aggregator and those that exhibit waves, following the regular daily schedule of a human activity. This classification has been obtained by using a shape discovery heuristic that uses two thresholds, inferior and superior to the average number of items published during an hour, to distinguish between hours with insignificant, average or very high publication activity.

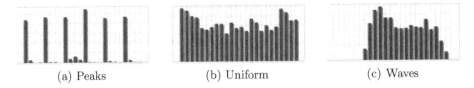

(a) Peaks   (b) Uniform   (c) Waves

Fig. 6. Publication shapes: peaks, uniform and waves

In figure 7 we show the distribution of feeds for various activity classes and publication shapes for dataset 1 (similar results were obtained for dataset 2). The distributions show that feeds with very slow publication activity tend to publish more with peaks, the uniform pattern is very much present in feeds with very high publication activity while the wave shape appears in feeds with low, medium and high publication frequencies.

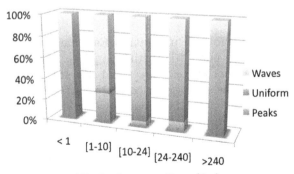

Fig. 7. Feeds per publication shape and activity class - dataset 1

6   Experimental Evaluation

In this section, we evaluate the performance of our online estimation methods in cohesion with different refresh strategies based on real RSS feeds data collected during a four-week period (see section 5).

Setup: We focused our interest on feeds with a relatively high publication activity. For our experiments, we selected (using the shape discovery heuristic) three subsets of 10 feed sources each, representative for the three publication shapes, having a publishing activity of at least 10 items per day.

We emulated the source publication activity by constructing a cycle-based environment, where a cycle corresponds to a time unit of duration 10 minutes. Furthermore, we worked with a normalized source publication, i.e. instead of publishing x items during a time slot, we consider that a source publishes x/N items, where N represents the total number of items published by the source during that entire day. Working this way, we focused ourselves on estimating the shape of a source publication activity and we avoided the influence of any strong fluctuation in terms of total number of items published daily.

Choosing the optimal value of the smoothing parameter α depends on the type of the source, on the refresh frequency and on the level of convergence of the source publication model. In each case, we chose an experimentally found value of α such that it minimizes the divergence errors, usually using values in the interval $[0.01 - 0.2]$.

6.1   Online Estimation Evaluation

In order to evaluate the online estimation techniques presented in section 4, we applied an *uniformly distributed random* refresh strategy, in which the refreshes are done at irregular intervals of time that are uniformly distributed around a fixed average value. For example, when we say that a source is refreshed on average every 1 hour, that means that it can be refreshed within the interval 10 minutes - 2 hours. We put all sources in the same initial conditions, initializing their publication models at 0 and started the evaluation after an initial warm up period.

Robustness of the Periodic Publication Estimation: In order to test the robustness of our periodic publication estimation, how it acts to sudden changes in the publication behavior of the sources and how it is influenced by the refresh frequency used by the strategy, we created an artificial source. We concatenated publication activities from three sources with different types of publication shapes: 16 weeks of uniform, followed by 16 weeks of peaks and followed by 16 weeks of waves.

Experiments were done using the *uniformly distributed random* strategy that refreshed the source every 1 hour and every 24 hours on average. We logged the estimated daily publication models at the end of each week. We also defined the "real" daily publication model as an average done on the 7 days of source publication activity previous to the measurement moment. In figure 8 we present

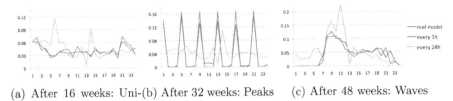

(a) After 16 weeks: Uni-(b) After 32 weeks: Peaks   (c) After 48 weeks: Waves
form

Fig. 8. Daily publication model: real vs. estimated model

in detail the real and estimated daily publication models of the artificial source just before each change in the publication behavior, i.e. at the end of 16th, 32nd and 48th week (time moments circled and marked with vertical blue lines in figure 9). Furthermore, we compute the 24-dimensional Euclidean (2-norm) distance between the real and the estimated daily publication models after each week and present it in figure 9.

Experiments shown in figures 8 and 9 prove the bad influence a small refresh frequency can have on the quality of the estimation process. Convergence speed of the publication estimations are shown in figure 9: while the estimated daily publication model obtained with a refresh done every 1 hour on average converges rapidly towards the real model, the estimated model obtained with a refresh done every 24 hours oscillates and diverges in time.

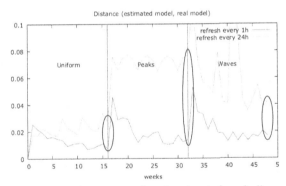

Fig. 9. Distance between real and estimated periodic model

Online Estimation Quality: At each cycle t, we computed the root mean squared error of the estimated divergence (defined in section 3) for all sources $s_i \in S$, separately for the periodic and for the single variable publication model, as follows:

$$divErr = \sqrt{\frac{1}{|S|} \cdot \sum_{s_i \in S} (Div(s_i, t, t_0)^{real} - Div(s_i, t, t_0)^{est})^2} \qquad (2)$$

Results are presented in figure 10, separately for the three types of sources with different publication shapes: peaks, uniform and waves. Each point represents the average of the root mean squared divergence errors computed during the simulation, that were obtained for different refresh frequencies. The values used for the refresh frequencies are shown in hours and they range from a refresh done every 30 minutes to every 24 hours on average.

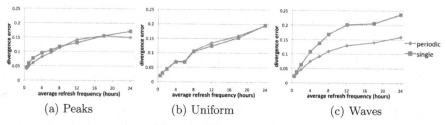

(a) Peaks   (b) Uniform   (c) Waves

Fig. 10. Divergence error

Experiments show clearly that in the case of waves, the periodic estimation obtains better results than the single variable one in terms of minimal divergence error. Since it is more precise, it estimates better the wavy source publication behavior, no matter how often the sources are refreshed and thus, how often the publication model is updated. In the case of peaks, the difference between the two publication estimations is less striking. When the sources are refreshed often and therefore the learnt periodic publication model is precise, the periodic estimation obtains smaller divergence errors. As the sources are refreshed less frequently, the single variable estimation becomes as good as the periodic one; this happens for two reasons: first, the periodic model becomes less accurate and thus it diminishes its performance and second, our feed sources exhibit their peaks at very regular intervals, e.g. every 4 hours, as shown in figure 6a, and this advantages the single variable publication model for refresh frequencies larger than the average interval in between peaks. As for the uniform sources, both single and periodic publication estimations perform similarly, with the observation that the single variable publication model should be preferred because it is much more simple to use and update. The feeds concerned by this case, that publish in a uniform manner, represent 57% of the feeds with high publication rate (more than 1 item published per hour), as we observed on our real feeds datasets (section 5).

6.2   Integration of Online Estimation with 2Steps Refresh Strategy

We also integrated and tested the cohesion between our online estimation techniques with the optimal *2steps* refresh strategy introduced in [11], whose efficient results highly depend on the quality of the used publication models.

In order to better understand the following, we briefly introduce some further notions. A RSS feed is represented by a limited number of items available at some time instant, called a *publication window* of size W_s. We call a source *saturated* if the total number of new items published since its last refresh time reaches the capacity of the publication window W_s. After the saturation point, if the source is still not refreshed, the aggregator node starts to lose items, since the arrival of new items will replace items that have not been read yet by the aggregator.

It is important to mention that we ignored the saturation problem when updating the publication models, but for the evaluation of the *2steps* refresh strategy we considered that sources have a publication window of $W_s = 20$ items. We chose to do that in order to help the online estimation by giving it unbiased information as input, but one must be aware that saturation can not be avoided in real world RSS feed aggregation systems.

As before, we evaluate the online estimation quality by measuring the divergence error (equation 2). The results obtained for the sources having different publication shapes are similar with those obtained when testing with the uniformly distributed refresh strategy (see figure 10).

Furthermore, we test the effectiveness of the *2steps* refresh strategy in terms of feed completeness and window freshness (quality measures defined in [11]), in the cases where the strategy uses *offline* information on the publication model of the sources and publication models estimated with the online estimation techniques presented here (*periodic* and *single variable* publication estimation). The results obtained for the feed completeness and window freshness are presented in figures 11 and 12.

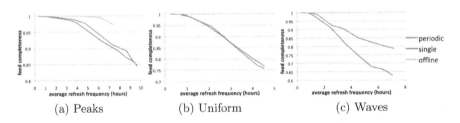

(a) Peaks   (b) Uniform   (c) Waves

Fig. 11. Feed Completeness

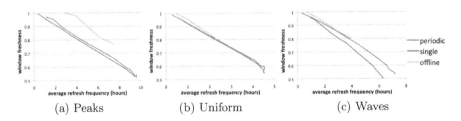

(a) Peaks   (b) Uniform   (c) Waves

Fig. 12. Window Freshness

When sources are refreshed very frequently (big bandwidth), both periodic and single variable publication estimation give very good results in terms of feed completeness and window freshness, no matter the source publication shapes. Frequent refreshes alone assure high scores for quality measures and besides that, good convergence for both periodic and single variable publication models. In the case of peaks, when the aggregator refreshes rarely, sources become saturated very often and the *2steps* strategy focuses itself on refreshing those saturated ones. Predicting when a source publishes $W_s = 20$ items in the case of sources with regular peaks works well both with the periodic and the single variable publication model, because in this case the precision offered by the periodic model (that knows exactly at which point in time each item was published) is useless. All these make that both periodic and single variable publication estimation give similar results in terms of feed completeness and window freshness for the peaks in case of rare refreshes. When sources are refreshed more often and there are less saturated sources, periodic publication estimation give better results. In the case of wavy publication behavior, periodic estimation outperforms the single variable one because of the information accuracy it provides, no matter how often the sources are refreshed. In this case it is the most clear how the preciseness of the information on which a refresh strategy is based influences its performances. For the uniform sources, the same conclusion as for the uniformly distributed random strategy holds. Because results are similar and especially because the single variable publication model is far more easy to use and update, this last one should be used.

6.3   Discussion

Experimental results illustrate the high cohesion between the correctness of the decisions made by a refresh strategy and the publication model used together with the quality of the estimation process. It has been shown that the refresh frequency used by the strategy has an important influence on the quality of the estimation process. Furthermore, saturation has a highly negative impact: if refreshes are not done often enough and items are lost, the estimation process uses inaccurate data for updating the model. In this case, a possible solution is the separation of the estimation from the refresh process of the crawling module, thus separating the bandwidth resources needed for the two processes.

When the refresh strategy has strong constraints in terms of bandwidth usage, online estimation does not represent a reliable solution. One alternative solution is then to allocate separate bandwidth for learning a publication profile (offline scenario) and then to use the precomputed model to refresh the sources, without updating it. This gives good results for feeds (or queries on feeds) that do not change their publication behavior in time, but it is not advisable to be used for specific queries that are very dynamic. Moreover, several such learning periods may be repeated to update periodically the source publication profiles. Since a refresh strategy is based on a publication model and the estimation of the publication model depends on the bandwidth allocated by the refresh strategy, finding the optimal balance between the two represents a challenge.

7   Conclusion

In this paper we have investigated problems related to an RSS aggregator that retrieves information from multiple RSS feed sources automatically. In particular, we have proposed and studied two online estimation methods that correspond to two different models of the source publication activity. We tested the online estimation methods in cohesion with different refresh strategies. We compared these methods for different publication activity shapes and we highlighted the challenges imposed by the application context. In addition, we studied the characteristics of real world RSS feeds datasets focusing on the temporal dimension.

We consider several directions for future work. First, we plan to add other learning components for estimating the total number of items published during a day. Also, we want to integrate an algorithm that adjusts dynamically the value of the smoothing parameter α to the optimal value that assures minimal estimation errors. Finally, for reducing estimation cost, we intend to introduce clustering techniques for grouping source feeds with similar publication activities.

References

1. Adam, G., Bouras, C., Poulopoulos, V.: Utilizing RSS Feeds for Crawling the Web. In: 2009 Fourth International Conference on Internet and Web Applications and Services, pp. 211–216. IEEE (2009)
2. Brewington, B.E., Cybenko, G.: How dynamic is the web? Computer Networks 33(1-6), 257–276 (2000)
3. Chatfield, C.: The Analysis of Time Series: An Introduction. CRC Press (2004)
4. Cho, J., Garcia-Molina, H.: Synchronizing a database to improve freshness. SIGMOD Rec. 29(2), 117–128 (2000)
5. Cho, J., Garcia-Molina, H.: Effective page refresh policies for web crawlers. ACM Trans. Database Syst. 28(4), 390–426 (2003)
6. Cho, J., Garcia-Molina, H.: Estimating frequency of change. ACM Trans. Internet Technol. 3(3), 256–290 (2003)
7. Datasift, http://datasift.com/
8. Google reader, http://www.google.com/reader
9. Gruhl, D., Guha, R.V., Liben-Nowell, D., Tomkins, A.: Information diffusion through blogspace. In: Feldman, S.I., Uretsky, M., Najork, M., Wills, C.E. (eds.) WWW, pp. 491–501. ACM (2004)
10. Hmedeh, Z., Vouzoukidou, N., Travers, N., Christophides, V., du Mouza, C., Scholl, M.: Characterizing Web Syndication Behavior and Content. In: Bouguettaya, A., Hauswirth, M., Liu, L. (eds.) WISE 2011. LNCS, vol. 6997, pp. 29–42. Springer, Heidelberg (2011)
11. Horincar, R., Amann, B., Artières, T.: Best-Effort Refresh Strategies for Content-Based RSS Feed Aggregation. In: Chen, L., Triantafillou, P., Suel, T. (eds.) WISE 2010. LNCS, vol. 6488, pp. 262–270. Springer, Heidelberg (2010)
12. Olston, C., Pandey, S.: Recrawl scheduling based on information longevity. In: WWW 2008: Proceeding of the 17th International Conference on World Wide Web, pp. 437–446. ACM, New York (2008)
13. Olston, C., Widom, J.: Best-effort cache synchronization with source cooperation. In: SIGMOD 2002: Proceedings of the 2002 ACM SIGMOD International Conference on Management of Data, pp. 73–84. ACM, New York (2002)

14. Pandey, S., Olston, C.: User-centric web crawling. In: WWW 2005: Proceedings of the 14th International Conference on World Wide Web, pp. 401–411. ACM, New York (2005)
15. Saporta, G.: Probabilités, analyse des données et statistique. Technip (2006)
16. Sia, K.C., Cho, J., Cho, H.-K.: Efficient monitoring algorithm for fast news alerts. IEEE Trans. on Knowl. and Data Eng. 19(7), 950–961 (2007)
17. Sia, K.C., Cho, J., Hino, K., Chi, Y., Zhu, S., Tseng, B.L.: Monitoring rss feeds based on user browsing pattern. In: Proceedings of the International Conference on Weblogs and Social Media, Boulder Colorado, pp. 161–168 (March 2007)
18. Zimmer, C., Tryfonopoulos, C., Berberich, K., Koubarakis, M., Weikum, G.: Approximate Information Filtering in Peer-to-Peer Networks. In: Bailey, J., Maier, D., Schewe, K.-D., Thalheim, B., Wang, X.S. (eds.) WISE 2008. LNCS, vol. 5175, pp. 6–19. Springer, Heidelberg (2008)
19. Zimmer, C., Tryfonopoulos, C., Berberich, K., Weikum, G., Koubarakis, M.: Node behavior prediction for large-scale approximate information filtering. In: 1st International Workshop on Large Scale Distributed Systems for Information Retrieval, LSDS-IR 2007 (2007)

Active Learning of Expressive Linkage Rules for the Web of Data

Robert Isele, Anja Jentzsch, and Christian Bizer

Freie Universität Berlin, Web-based Systems Group
Garystr. 21, 14195 Berlin, Germany
mail@robertisele.com, mail@anjajentzsch.de, chris@bizer.de

Abstract. The amount of data that is available as Linked Data on the Web has grown rapidly over the last years. However, the linkage between data sources remains sparse as setting RDF links means effort for the data publishers. Many existing methods for generating these links rely on explicit linkage rules which specify the conditions which must hold true for two entities in order to be interlinked. As writing good linkage rules by hand is a non-trivial problem, the burden to generate links between data sources is still high. In order to reduce the effort and required expertise to write linkage rules, we present an approach which combines genetic programming and active learning for the interactive generation of expressive linkage rules. Our approach automates the generation of a linkage rule and only requires the user to confirm or decline a number of example links. The algorithm minimizes user involvement by selecting example links which yield a high information gain. The proposed approach has been implemented in the Silk Link Discovery Framework. Within our experiments, the algorithm was capable of finding linkage rules with a full F1-measure by asking the user to confirm or decline a maximum amount of 20 links.

1   Introduction

The central idea of Linked Data is to extend the Web with a global data space by making data accessible according to the Linked Data best practices [7] and by setting RDF links between data sources. While the amount of data that is accessible as Linked Data has grown significantly over the last years, most data sources are still not sufficiently interlinked[1]. In order to help data publishers to set RDF links pointing into other data sources, several link discovery tools have been developed. These tools compare entities in different Linked Data sources based on user-provided linkage rules which specify the conditions that must hold true for two entities in order to be interlinked. Writing good linkage rules by hand is a non-trivial problem as the rule author needs to have detailed knowledge about the structure of the data sets to be interlinked.

In this paper, we present an approach to learn linkage rules interactively using active learning and genetic programming. It learns a linkage rule by asking

---

[1] http://lod-cloud.net/state/ (09/19/2011)

M. Brambilla, T. Tokuda, and R. Tolksdorf (Eds.): ICWE 2012, LNCS 7387, pp. 411–418, 2012.

the user to confirm or reject example links which are actively selected by the algorithm. Our approach lowers the required level of expertise as the task of generating the linkage rule is automated while the user only has to verify a set of example links. User involvement is minimized by only selecting the links with the highest information gain. Within our experiments, the algorithm was capable of finding linkage rules with a full F1-measure by asking the user to confirm or decline a maximum amount of 20 links. The algorithm chooses which properties to compare together with distance measures, aggregation functions, thresholds and data transformations to normalize data prior to comparison. Although in this paper we focus on interlinking data sources in the Web of Data, our approach is not limited to that use case and can be applied to entity matching in other areas - such as in the context of relational databases - as well.

This paper makes the following contributions to the state of the art:

1. We are the first to apply an approach that combines genetic programming and active learning to the problem of learning linkage rules for generating RDF links in the context of the Web of Data.
2. The learned rules are more expressive than the linkage rules learned in previous work on entity matching as our algorithm combines different similarity measures nonlinearly and also determines the data translations that should be employed to normalize data prior to comparison.
3. We have implemented the proposed approach in the Silk Link Discovery Framework which is available under the terms of the Apache License.

This paper is organized as follows: Section 2 introduces our linkage rule representation. Section 3 describes the proposed active learning method. Section 4 presents the experimental evaluation. Finally, Section 5 discusses related work.

2   Linkage Rules

We represent a linkage rule as a tree built from 4 basic operators:

Property Operator: Creates a set of values to be used for comparison by retrieving all values of a specific property of the entity.

Transformation Operator: Transforms the input values of a single entity according to a specific data transformation function. Examples of common transformation functions include case normalization, tokenization and concatenation of the values of multiple operators. Multiple transformation operators can be nested in order to apply a sequence of transformations.

Comparison Operator: Evaluates the similarity between the values of two input operators according to a specific distance measure, such as Levenshtein, Jaccard, or geographic distance. Allowed input operators are property operators and transformation operators. A threshold specifies the maximum distance.

Aggregation Operator: Aggregates the similarity values from multiple operators into a single value according to a specific aggregation function. Aggregation functions such as the weighted average may take weights into account. Aggregation operators can be nested in order to create nonlinear hierarchies.

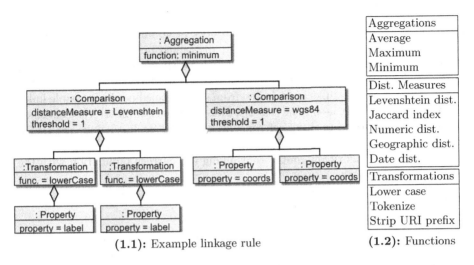

(1.1): Example linkage rule

(1.2): Functions

Our approach is independent of any specific aggregation functions, distance measures or data transformations. Table 1.2 shows the set of functions which has been used by us in all experiments[2].

3   Learning Workflow

The main idea of our approach is to evolve a population of linkage rules iteratively while building a set of reference links. Figure 1 summarizes the three steps which are involved in each iteration:

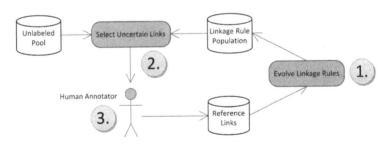

Fig. 1. Learning Workflow

(1) A genetic programming algorithm evolves a population of linkage rules. It starts with an initial population of candidate solutions which is iteratively evolved by applying genetic operators. The population is evolved until either a maximum number of iterations is reached or a linkage rule has been found which covers all reference links. As in most use cases there are either no or only a small number of reference links available, the purpose of the subsequent steps is to add additional links to the set of reference links.

---

[2] The details about the functions are provided in the Silk user manual on the website

(**2**) The active learning algorithm selects the example links to be labeled by the user. Links are selected according to a query by committee (QBC) strategy: As the linkage rules in the population are all trained on the current reference links they represent competing hypotheses. By selecting the links for which most linkage rules disagree, the contribution of the user confirming or declining the link is maximized. The links are selected from an unlabeled pool of possible links.

(**3**) A human expert labels the selected links as correct or incorrect. Confirmed links are added to the positive reference link set and declined links are added to the negative reference link set. After the human expert labeled the provided links, the genetic algorithm continues evolving the current population with the updated reference links.

3.1   Evolving Linkage Rules

The initial population is build by generating random linkage rules. In order to reduce the search space, we employ a simple algorithm by only selecting property pairs which hold similar values.

Starting with the current population, the genetic algorithm breeds a new population by evolving selected individuals using the genetic operations crossover and mutation. A detailed description of the algorithm as well as the specific crossover and mutation operators that are used is found in [8]. The individuals are selected from the population based on two functions: The *fitness function* and the *selection method*. The purpose of the *fitness function* is to assign a value to each individual which indicates how close the given individual is to the desired solution. In order to make the algorithm more robust against unbalanced reference link sets, we use *Matthews correlation coefficient* (MCC) as fitness measure. Based on the fitness of each individual, the *selection method* selects the individuals to be evolved. As selection method we chose tournament selection as it has been shown to produce strong results in a variety of GP systems [10] and is easy to parallelize.

The algorithm iteratively evolves the population until either a linkage rule has been found which covers all reference links or a configured maximum number of iterations is reached.

3.2   Selecting Uncertain Links

This section describes how the initial unlabeled pool is generated from which the links are selected for manual evaluation according to the query strategy.

Building the Unlabeled Pool. The overall goal of the learning algorithm is to create a linkage rule which is able to label all possible entity pairs as matches or non-matches with high confidence. The number of possible entity pairs can be very high for large data sets and usually far exceeds the number of actual matches. For this reason we use an indexing approach to build a sample which does not include definitive non-matches.

Given two data sets A and B, the initial unlabeled pool $\mathcal{U} \subset A \times B$ is built according to the following sampling process: The sampling starts by querying for all entities in both data sets. Instead of retrieving all entities at once, a stream of entities is generated for each data set. For each property in the streamed entities, all values are indexed according to the following schema:

1. All values are normalized by removing all punctuation and converting all characters to lower case.
2. The normalized values are tokenized.
3. A set of indices is assigned to each token. The indices are generated so that tokens within an edit distance of 1 share at least one index. The MultiBlock blocking algorithm is used to generate the index [9].
4. The indices of all tokens of a value are merged. If in total more than 5 indices have been assigned to a value, 5 indices are randomly selected while discarding the remaining indices.

Now all pairs of entities which have been assigned the same index are added to the unlabeled pool until a configured maximum size is reached.

Query Strategy. The purpose of the query strategy is to select links which are to be labeled by a human expert as correct or incorrect. In order to minimize the number of links to be verified by the user the algorithm selects the links from the unlabeled pool for which the linkage rules in the current population disagree the most. To measure the disagreement with respect to a link l, we use the vote entropy:

$$d(l) = H\left(\frac{v(l)}{|P|}\right) \quad \text{with } H(p) = -p \cdot log(p) - (1-p) \cdot log(1-p)$$

With $v(l)$ denoting the number of linkage rules which confirm the link and $|P|$ the size of the population. The rationale here is that if the percentage of linkage rules which confirm the link approaches 50%, half of the linkage rules are implicitly upvoted or downvoted by the user by confirming or declining the given link. The links with the highest vote entropy are returned for evaluation by the user.

4 Evaluation

4.1 Experiment Setup

All experiments have been run 10 times with 2 fold cross-validation. For each experiment, we provide the averaged results with respect to the training data set as well as the validation data set together with the standard deviation. All experiments have been run on a 3GHz Intel(R) Core i7 CPU with 4 cores while the Java heap space has been restricted to 1GB. Table 1 lists the parameters which have been used in all experiments.

Table 1. Parameters

Parameter	Value	Parameter	Value
Population size	500	Probability of Mutation	25%
Maximum generations	50	Stop Condition	MCC = 1.0
Selection method	Tournament selection	Unlabeled Pool size $|\mathcal{U}|$	10,000
Tournament size	5	Query Size $|\mathcal{U}_q|$	5

4.2 Experiment 1: Comparison with Related Work

In order to show the competitiveness of the genetic programming algorithm that is used to evolve the populations within our approach, we compare the algorithm to the state-of-the-art genetic programming algorithm presented by Carvalho et. al. in [4]. One data set commonly used for evaluating different record deduplication approaches is *Cora*. The Cora data set contains citations to research papers from the Cora Computer Science research paper search engine. Table 2.1 summarizes the cross validation results. The learned linkage rules compared by title, author and venue. Figure 2.2 shows an example of a learned linkage rule. On average, our approach achieved an F-measure of 96.9% against the training set and 93.6% against the validation set and needed less than 5 minutes to perform all 50 iterations on the test machine. For the same data set, Carvalho et. al. report an F-measure of 90.0% against the training set and 91.0% against the validation set [4].

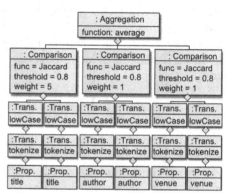

Iter.	Time	Train. F1 (σ)	Val. F1 (σ)
1	4.0	0.896 (0.022)	0.896 (0.021)
10	31.1	0.956 (0.013)	0.954 (0.015)
20	71.4	0.964 (0.008)	0.960 (0.010)
30	132.5	0.965 (0.007)	0.962 (0.007)
40	217.6	0.968 (0.004)	0.945 (0.036)
50	271.1	0.969 (0.003)	0.936 (0.056)
Ref.	-	0.900 (0.010)	0.910 (0.010)

(2.1): Experiment 1. The last row contains the best results of Carvalho et. al.

(2.2): Example linkage rule

4.3 Experiment 2: Active Learning

In this experiments we evaluated that the presented approach is able to learn a linkage rule with minimal user interaction using an easy to understand example from the media domain: Interlinking movies from LinkedMDB[3] with the corresponding entry in DBpedia about the same movie. For evaluation we used a manually created set of 100 positive and 100 negative reference links.

First we evaluated the capability to learn a linkage rule from reference links. Table 2.1 shows the averaged results of all runs. In all runs, the learning algorithm needed no more than 12 iterations in order to achieve the full F-measure.

Next we evaluated if our active learning approach is able to build a reference link set interactively. For this, we started with an empty reference link set and in each iteration let a user manually confirm and decline 5 links which have been selected by the algorithm. We repeated the experiment 3 times and averaged the

---

[3] http://linkedmdb.org/

Iter.	Time in s (σ)	Train. F1 (σ)	Val. F1 (σ)
1	5.9 (0.1)	0.968 (0.005)	0.968 (0.005)
10	19.6 (4.0)	0.995 (0.005)	0.995 (0.005)
12	20.9 (5.3)	1.000 (0.000)	1.000 (0.000)

(2.1): Experiment 2: Passive learning

Iter.	Links	Train. F1	Val. F1
1	5	1.00	0.65
2	10	1.00	0.97
3	15	1.00	0.99
4	20	1.00	1.00

(2.2): Experiment 2: Active l.

results. Table 2.2 shows results for each iteration. For each iteration it shows the F-measure based on the manually confirmed links (Training F1) and on the full reference link set (Validation F1). The second column shows the links which have been evaluated by the user. The results show that after querying 10 links from the user, the learning algorithm already learned a linkage rule which achieves a F-measure of 97 % when compared with the reference links.

4.4 Experiment 3: Large Scale Active Learning

In this experiment we show that the presented approach is able to scale to large data sets. At the time of writing, DBpedia contains 323,257 settlements while LinkedGeoData contains 560,123 settlements. The execution of the learned linkage rules generates over 70,000 links. While for passive learning the learning only needs to take the provided reference links into account, active learning also needs to take the pool of unlabeled data into account which in this example amounts to over 180 billion pairs. In order to evaluate the learned linkage rules we used a manually collected set of 100 positive and 100 negative reference links.

Iter.	Time (σ)	Train. F1 (σ)	Val. F1 (σ)
1	2.6s (1.0)	0.984 (0.025)	0.932 (0.059)
10	3.8s (2.1)	0.996 (0.007)	0.932 (0.059)
20	3.9s (2.3)	0.998 (0.004)	0.964 (0.032)
25	4.0s (2.4)	1.000 (0.000)	1.000 (0.000)

(2.1): Experiment 3: Passive learning

Iter.	Links	Time	Train. F1	Val. F1
1	5	7.3s	1.00	0.98
2	10	15.6s	1.00	1.00

(2.2): Experiment 3: Active learning

Table 2.1 summarizes the cross validation results for passive learning. Table 2.2 shows results for each iteration in an active learning setting. The runtimes only include the time needed by the algorithm itself and not the time needed by the human to label the examples.

In all three runs, the algorithm managed to learn a linkage rule with full F-measure after the second iteration. In the first iteration it missed the case that two entities with the same name may in fact relate to different cities. In the second iteration it managed to include this rare case in the proposed example links.

5   Related Work

Genetic Programming. To the best of our knowledge, genetic programming for learning linkage rules has only been applied by Carvalho et. al. so far [3,2,4].

Their approach uses genetic programming to learn how to combine a set of pre-supplied pairs of the form `<attribute, similarity function>` (e.g. `<name, Jaro>`) into a linkage rule. Their approach is very expressive although it cannot express data transformations. On the downside, using mathematical functions to combine the similarity measures does not fit any commonly used linkage rule model [6] and leads to complex and difficult to understand linkage rules. We are not aware of any previous application of genetic programming to learn linkage rules in the context of Linked Data other than our own work [8].

Active Learning. While the majority of the approaches targeted at learning linkage rules use supervised learning, some approaches based on active learning have been proposed: Arasu et. al. propose a scalable active learning approach for entity matching by introducing the assumption of *monotonicity of precision* [1]. While they show that their approach can scale to large data sets, it is only able to learn simple linear or boolean classifiers, while our approach is capable of learning expressive linkage rules which include nonlinear aggregation hierarchies and data transformations. The only approach which combines genetic programming and active learning to learn rules for record deduplication known to us has been proposed by Freitas et. al. [5]. It is based on the genetic programming approach by Carvalho et. al. mentioned earlier and thus shares its limitations as described in the previous Section.

References

1. Arasu, A., Götz, M., Kaushik, R.: On active learning of record matching packages. In: Proceedings of the 2010 International Conference on Management of Data, SIGMOD 2010, pp. 783–794. ACM, New York (2010)
2. Carvalho, M., Laender, A., Gonçalves, M., da Silva, A.: Replica identification using genetic programming. In: Proceedings of the 2008 ACM Symposium on Applied Computing, pp. 1801–1806. ACM (2008)
3. de Carvalho, M.G., Gonçalves, M.A., Laender, A.H.F., da Silva, A.S.: Learning to deduplicate. In: Proceedings of the 6th ACM/IEEE-CS Joint Conference on Digital Libraries, JCDL 2006, pp. 41–50. ACM, New York (2006)
4. de Carvalho, M.G., Laender, A.H.F., Goncalves, M.A., da Silva, A.S.: A genetic programming approach to record deduplication. IEEE Transactions on Knowledge and Data Engineering 99(preprints) (2010)
5. de Freitas, J., Pappa, G., da Silva, A., Gonçalves, M., Moura, E., Veloso, A., Laender, A., de Carvalho, M.: Active learning genetic programming for record deduplication. In: Evolutionary Computation (CEC), pp. 1–8. IEEE (2010)
6. Euzenat, J., Shvaiko, P.: Ontology matching. Springer (2007)
7. Heath, T., Bizer, C.: Linked data: Evolving the web into a global data space. Synthesis Lectures on the Semantic Web: Theory and Technology 1(1), 1–136 (2011)
8. Isele, R., Bizer, C.: Learning linkage rules using genetic programming. In: 6th International Workshop on Ontology Matching, Bonn, Germany (2011)
9. Isele, R., Jentzsch, A., Bizer, C.: Efficient multidimensional blocking for link discovery without losing recall. In: 14th International Workshop on the Web and Databases (WebDB 2011), Athens (2011)
10. Koza, J., Keane, M., Streeter, M., Mydlowec, W., Yu, J., Lanza, G.: Genetic programming IV: Routine human-competitive machine intelligence. Springer (2005)

Extracting Navigational Models from Struts-Based Web Applications*

Roberto Rodríguez-Echeverría, José María Conejero, Pedro J. Clemente,
María Dolores Villalobos, and Fernando Sánchez-Figueroa

University of Extremadura (Spain),
Quercus Software Engineering Group
{rre,chemacm,pjclemente,mvillalofy,fernando}@unex.es
http://quercusseg.unex.es

Abstract. Nowadays, there is a current trend in software industry to modernize traditional Web Applications (WAs) to Rich Internet Applications (RIAs). In this context, Model Driven (MD) Web Engineering approaches have been extended with new modeling primitives to obtain the benefits provided by RIA features. However, during the last decade, widespread language-specific Web frameworks have supported actual Web system development. In this paper we present a MD modernization process to obtain RIAs from legacy WAs based on such frameworks. MD techniques reduce complexity and improve reusability of the process. Being navigational information of upmost importance for the modernization process of a Web application, the paper is focused on presenting the metamodel defined to extract navigational information from the legacy system, the models obtained and the projection of these models to a particular MD Web Engineering methodology.

Keywords: Web Models Transformations, Software Modernization, RIA.

1 Introduction

Rich Internet Applications have emerged as the most promising platform for Web 2.0 development combining the lightweight distribution architecture of the Web with the interface interactivity and computation power of desktop applications [10]. To take advantages of these new capabilities, there is a current trend in the industry to perform a modernization of their legacy WA to produce RIA counterparts. This trend is, even, more evident with the transition to the forthcoming HTML5 that implements natively most of these features gaining momentum.

In this context, Model Driven Web Engineering (MDWE) approaches [13] have been extended with new modeling primitives to obtain the benefits provided by RIA features [5][9]. This way, introducing RIA features in legacy WA

---

* Work funded by Spanish Contract MIGRARIA - TIN2011-27340 at Ministerio de Ciencia e Innovación and Gobierno de Extremadura (GR-10129) and European Regional Development Fund (ERDF).

M. Brambilla, T. Tokuda, and R. Tolksdorf (Eds.): ICWE 2012, LNCS 7387, pp. 419–420, 2012.

developed using models becomes a feasible task as it has been shown in [14][12]. However, during the last decade, widespread language-specific Web frameworks (e.g. Struts[1]) have supported the actual developments of these WAs, neglecting the benefits provided by model driven approaches. These frameworks are often tied to the programming-language level, making maintenance and moderniza- tion processes a difficult task. Traditionally, these modernization processes have been performed in an ad-hoc manner, resulting in very expensive and error-prone projects.

This work is part of a larger research project, called MIGRARIA[2], where a systematic and semi-automatic process to modernize legacy non-model-based data-driven WAs into RIAs has been defined. The modernization process out- lined before comprises a series of complex challenges so we try to provide the engineer with a systematic method and a partially automated toolkit. One of the leading ideas of this project is to use model driven techniques and tools to deal with the complexity of extraction and interpretation processes [11]. In this paper we focus on the navigational information of the legacy system, being of upmost importance for a WA.

The rest of the paper is structured as follows. In Section 2 an illustrative example is depicted. Section 3 introduces our approach to extract navigational models from a Struts-based legacy WA. The related work is discussed in Section 4. Finally, main conclusions and future work are outlined in Section 5.

2   Illustrative Example

The Agenda[3] system is one of the projects used within the MIGRARIA project. The main goal of this system is to manage the student agenda in a university faculty. Agenda is an example of data-driven WA since the Web layer of the system mainly consists of a CRUD client that interacts with the underlying information system. Several frameworks and Java stack technologies for WAs have been used in the development of the system, e.g. Struts for the Web layer.

Figure 1 shows a snapshot of the system. This part corresponds to the pro- fessor management process within the administrator session and includes all the CRUD operations related to the professor data entity resulting in different nav- igational flows that start (depart from) and finish (arrive to) in the same page (*page01*). This part of the system is representative enough to be an example of the most common navigational flows used in the system. Observe in the fig- ure that the page containing the list of professors (Display action) is marked as *page01*, the professor sign in page (Creation action) is marked as *page02* and the removing and updating page (Remove and Update actions) as *page03*. We have also identified the navigational flows between these pages in order to be referenced in subsequent sections. The example contains 5 different navigational flows identified as: *p01-p02* flow (*page01 Create Professor* link), *p02-p01* flow

---

[1] http://struts.apache.org/

[2] http://www.unex.es/eweb/migraria

[3] http://www.unex.es/eweb/migraria/cs/agenda

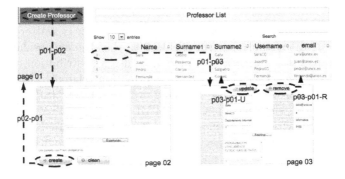

Fig. 1. Pages and flows of the illustrative example

(*Page02 create* button), *p01-p03* flow (*page01* list item links), *p03-p01-U* flow (*page03* update button), and *p03-p01-R* flow (*page03* remove button).

3   The Approach

The main goal of this work consists of the extraction of navigational models from WAs developed with MVC-based Web Frameworks. Figure 2 describes the main steps of our model driven reengineering process. As previously shown, for practical purposes, Struts has been selected as the reference Web Framework for this work.

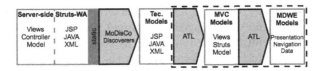

Fig. 2. Model Driven Reengineering

As input, our process takes the source code of a Struts-based WA to perform a static analysis. First of all, MoDisCo [2] discoverers are used to generate models directly from the source code (text-to-model transformation). We then use these models to produce a representation of the WA on a higher level of abstraction conformed to our MVC (Struts) metamodel. This transformation is specified by the definition of ATL Rules (not detailed in this work). On this stage, we build a MVC (Struts) model that collects all the interaction flows (and the elements involved) defined on the Web layer, generating a comprehensive view of the navigational concern. So an intermediate model representation of the WA is produced before generating a concrete conceptual representation according to a MDWE approach [13]. Following the main elements and activities involved in the last section of our process are detailed (dashed line at figure 2).

3.1 Locating Navigation Information

In MVC Web Frameworks, the navigational information is scattered throughout the views and the controller specification so that the encapsulation of this information into a software artifact (model) is also a contribution of our work. So we need to locate and extract all the information related to every request-response mapping process and the elements involved. Every JSP is analyzed to locate every request, that may appear as HTML links or as HTML form actions. The source of extraction for request parameters differs: actual action method source code or ActionForm, respectively. Front Controller configuration is also analyzed. The Struts framework allows defining several requests for each action. These requests can be forwarded to a JSP or to a different action (concatenating actions). And regarding actions, it is necessary to know their methods in order to identify possible process flows of a request (different responses). Moreover, we also analyze the operations related with the poppulation of data to the selected view.

Navigation Paths in the Case Study. Regarding our running example, Table 1 shows the information to be extracted from the ActionMappings and their relationships with the navigational flows described in Section 2. As the example denotes, it is common practice to write Actions that both navigate to a page and handle forms submitted from that page. Its general form is to hard code the mapping decision, depending on the value of a request parameter, inside the execute method of the Action and to use a single ActionMapping in struts-config.xml to configure it [4]. Two of the three ActionMappings considered follow that pattern. Both, *createProfessor* and *ProfessorDetail* response in a different way to the same request with different parameters. On the other hand, if the request does not contain data (page01 as source) they forward to *page02* and *page03* respectively, whilst forward and returns to *page01* if the form contains data, processing previously the operation with the data contained in the form. ActionMapping *ProfessorDetail* may be considered a special type of this pattern: one action responses to three different requests. The first ActionMapping is related with the request of the action that generates *page01* (the source of this request is out of the scope of the example considered).

Table 1. Navigation information in the ActionMapping instances considered

Page	Page Name	Request	Action	Forward	Nav. Path
		No data	ProfessorList	P01	
01	ProfessorList	No data	CreateProfessor	P02	p01-p02
	ProfessorList	No data	ProfessorDetail	P03	p01-p03
02	CreateProfessor	Form	CreateProfessor	P01	p02-p01
03	ProfessorDetail	Form update	ProfessorDetail	P01	p03-p01U
	ProfessorDetail	Form delete	ProfessorDetail	P01	p03-p01R

3.2   MVC Metamodel

To represent the information extracted from the legacy system, an Ecore meta-model has been defined, named the Struts navigation metamodel. It allows spec-ifying the elements of the Struts framework but also their relationships in order to define the different navigational flows. Figure 3 shows an excerpt of the Struts metamodel (simplified view).

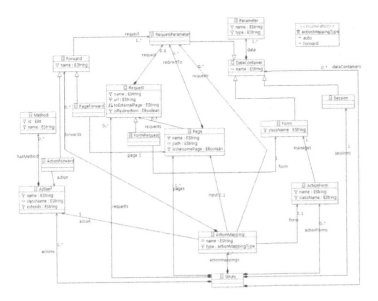

Fig. 3. Struts Navigation Metamodel

The entities defined in our Struts metamodel try to represent the three fun-damental components of the MVC pattern and their relationships. The Model component is represented by the Parameter class referencing actual data enti-ties from the data model. Data transmission is represented by DataContainer hierarchy, which defines convenient subclasses for representing request param-eters, form fields and session data. The View component is represented by the Page class. The View-Controller relation is mainly represented by the Request class. The Controller component is represented by the ActionMapping, Action and Method classes. The Controller-View relation is represented by the Forward classes.

Due to space limitation, we have not included the figure presenting the Struts model of the illustrative example nor its explanation[4].

---

[4] The interested reader may refer to the online material of this work, see footnote 3

3.3   Projection to a MDWE Approach

To exemplify the projection process, Object-Oriented Hypermedia (OOH) [6] has been selected as final representation. OOH has been recently extended to RIA [7], so it fulfills one of our main requirements. In this work, just navigational model is considered. Table 2 summarizes the fundamental mappings defined between Struts elements and OOH navigational elements. Those mappings have been implemented by means of ATL rules.

Table 2. Struts-OOH mapping overview

Struts	OOH
Struts	Navigational Model
Page Request/Form	Navigational Class
Request Parameters, ActionForm fields	Navigational Attribute
ActionMapping/ActionForward	Service Association
ActionMapping/PageForward	Traversal Association

It is worth noting that the way OOH defines navigation is structurally and semantically different from the viewpoint of Struts. Basically, OOH defines concrete views of data model entities as navigation nodes (navigational classes). And it then links those nodes by means of navigational associations, which may be node-to-node navigation (traversal association) or mediated by a business logic invocation (service association). Precisely, we focus on that differentiation in the projection example presented herein as figure 4 illustrates. On the one hand, *p01-p02* flow is finally represented as a traversal association instance, meanwhile a service association instance captures *p02-p01* flow. As stated before, both flows are processed by the same ActionMapping; however, each of them is forwarded to a different Struts element: the former to a page, and the latter to an action. We have used that difference to select one or another navigational association type. On the other hand, *page01* and *page02* are directly translated into corresponding navigational class instances. *Page02*, by example, is populated with the navigational attributes corresponding to the form fields of *request02*.

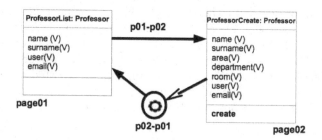

Fig. 4. OOH Navigational Model

4   Related Work

Web Application information extraction has been performed by reverse engineering techniques [8]. Although those approaches obtain similar results to those presented herein, we consider they follow an alternative strategy that we also consider to follow in the MIGRARIA project.

Although our intention is to use Architecture Driven Modernization (ADM) [15] as the reference framework to define our modernization process, we have declined to use Knowledge Discovery Metamodel (KDM) because of its complexity and lack of definition for user interface representation. In that sense, MoDisco [2] is a generic, extensible and open source approach for software modernization that makes an intensive use of MDD principles and techniques which could be used as base to implement ADM. Our work presents a specialization of the framework defined by MoDisco to be applied in concrete modernization scenarios from legacy WAs into RIAs.

Framework-Specific Modeling Language (FSML) [1] is a DSL to support the development of framework-based applications. FSML has been applied successfully to migrate a WA from Struts to JSF. But it is a migration proposal defined at a low-level of abstraction and, then, it does not align with our goals.

In [3] the authors introduce a process to extract models from Struts systems by means of DSLs to generate a JavaServer Faces version of the system. Note that the goals of this work and ours are slightly different. The former proposes a modernization of a system based on a Web framework to a system based on a different framework whilst our work presents a modernization to a RIA.

5   Conclusions and Future Work

The context of this work is established by the MIGRARIA project, an approach for systematic WA-to-RIA model driven modernization. In this paper, we have specially focused on extracting navigational models from Struts-based Web Applications. By means of a running example we have detailed the main activities (locate, represent, transform) and artifacts (code, metamodel, model, transformation rules) related to the extraction process. The process is lead by different model driven artifacts that allows to define a systematic and reusable process. We have also specified our own Struts metamodel to define intermediate navigation models that remain independent of any MDWE approach. Those intermediate models may be eventually projected to the selected approach by means of model transformations.

As main lines for future work on navigation extraction we consider the following: (1) refining and validating the approach with a larger set of case studies; (2) extending the approach to support uniformly a set of MVC-based Web frameworks; (3) complementing the approach with WARE strategies; and (4) defining a comprehensive tool chain to assist the whole extraction process.

References

1. Antkiewicz, M., Czarnecki, K.: Framework-Specific Modeling Languages; Examples and Algorithms. Technical Report 2007, Electrical & Computer Engineering, University of Waterloo, Waterloo (2007)
2. Bruneliere, H., Cabot, J., Jouault, F.: MoDisco: A Generic And Extensible Framework For Model Driven Reverse Engineering. In: IEEE/ACM International Conference on Automated Software Engineering, pp. 1–2 (2010)
3. Cánovas Izquierdo, J.L., Molina, J.G.: A Domain Specific Language for Extracting Models in Software Modernization. In: Paige, R.F., Hartman, A., Rensink, A. (eds.) ECMDA-FA 2009. LNCS, vol. 5562, pp. 82–97. Springer, Heidelberg (2009)
4. Dudney, B., Lehr, J.: Jakarta Pitfalls: Time-Saving Solutions for Struts, Ant, JUnit, and Cactus (Java Open Source Library). Wiley (2003)
5. Fraternali, P., Comai, S., Bozzon, A., Carughi, G.T.: Engineering rich internet applications with a model-driven approach. ACM Transactions on the Web 4(2), 1–47 (2010)
6. Gomez, J., Cachero, C., Pastor, O.: Conceptual modeling of device-independent Web applications. IEEE Multimedia 8(2), 26–39 (2001)
7. Meliá, S., Gómez, J., Pérez, S., Díaz, O.: Architectural and Technological Variability in Rich Internet Applications. IEEE Internet Computing 14(3), 24–32 (2010)
8. Patel, R., Coenen, F., Martin, R., Archer, L.: Reverse Engineering of Web Applications: A Technical Review. Technical Report July 2007, University of Liverpool Department of Computer Science, Liverpool (2007)
9. Pérez, S., Díaz, O., Meliá, S., Gómez, J.: Facing Interaction-Rich RIAs: The Orchestration Model. In: 2008 Eighth International Conference on Web Engineering, pp. 24–37 (July 2008)
10. Preciado, J.C., Linaje, M., Sanchez, F., Comai, S.: Necessity of methodologies to model Rich Internet Applications. In: Seventh IEEE International Symposium on Web Site Evolution (2005)
11. Rodríguez-Echeverría, R., Conejero, J.M., Clemente, P.J., Preciado, J.C., Sánchez-Figueroa, F.: Modernization of Legacy Web Applications into Rich Internet Applications. In: Harth, A., Koch, N. (eds.) ICWE 2011. LNCS, vol. 7059, pp. 236–250. Springer, Heidelberg (2012)
12. Rodríguez-Echeverría, R., Conejero, J.M., Linaje, M., Preciado, J.C., Sánchez-Figueroa, F.: Re-engineering legacy Web applications into Rich Internet Applications. In: 10th International Conference on Web Engineering (2010)
13. Rossi, G., Pastor, O., Schwabe, D., Olsina, L.: Web Engineering: Modelling and Implementing Web Applications (Human-Computer Interaction Series) (October 2007)
14. Rossi, G., Urbieta, M., Ginzburg, J., Distante, D., Garrido, A.: Refactoring to Rich Internet Applications. A Model-Driven Approach. In: 2008 Eighth International Conference on Web Engineering, pp. 1–12 (July 2008)
15. Ulrich, W.: Modernization Standards Roadmap, pp. 46–64 (2010)

Towards a Method for Unsupervised Web Information Extraction[*]

Hassan A. Sleiman and Rafael Corchuelo

Universidad de Sevilla, ETSI Informática,
Avda. Reina Mercedes, s/n, Sevilla E-41012
{hassansleiman,corchu}@us.es

Abstract. The literature provides a variety of techniques to build the information extractors on which some data integration systems rely. Information extraction techniques are usually based on extraction rules that require maintenance and adaptation if web sources change. We present our preliminary steps towards an unsupervised information extraction technique that searches web documents for shared patterns and fragments them until finding the relevant information that should be extracted. Experimental results on 1230 real-web documents demonstrate that our system performs fast and achieves promising results.

Keywords: Web Information Extraction, Unsupervised Technique.

1 Introduction

The Web is a huge and still growing information repository. Web information is usually embedded into HTML tags and buried in other contents that are not relevant for a particular purpose. Business processes that require structured information, need to extract and structure the information they require from HTML documents. Information extractors are usually used for this purpose and can be broadly classified into two types: Those that work on free text, including blogs and news documents [1], and those that work on semi-structured documents such as search results and web documents with detailed information about some items [2]. Our work fits within the second category.

Information extractors are usually based on rules. These rules can be hand-crafted, learnt using semi-supervised techniques that require the user to provide some annotated training documents [3,4], or unsupervised techniques that learn extraction rules for all the information they consider as relevant inside some training documents [5,6]. Rule-based information extractors need to be maintained or even rewritten if the web source on which they were trained changes [7].

[*] This work was supported by the European Commission (FEDER), the Spanish and the Andalusian R&D&I programmes (grants TIN2007-64119, P07-TIC-2602, P08-TIC-4100, TIN2008-04718-E, TIN2010-21744, TIN2010-09809-E, TIN2010-10811-E, and TIN2010-09988-E).

M. Brambilla, T. Tokuda, and R. Tolksdorf (Eds.): ICWE 2012, LNCS 7387, pp. 427–430, 2012.
© Springer-Verlag Berlin Heidelberg 2012

This has motivated researchers to work on a new group of unsupervised information extractors that are not based on extraction rules [8,9], but on a number of hypothesis that have proven to perform well on many web sources.

In this paper, we report on our preliminary ideas on an unsupervised information extractor based on the hypothesis that web documents, generated by the same server-side template, share string patterns that are irrelevant.

2   System Overview

Our proposal takes two or more web documents, and searches for shared patterns amongst them of size $s = max$ down to $s = min$, where $max \geq min \geq 1$. When a shared pattern sp is found, the text of each document is partitioned to create 3 groups: prefixes, suffixes, and separators. Prefixes contain the text fragment from the beginning of each text until the start of the first occurrence of sp in this text; suffixes contain the text fragment from the end of the last occurrence of sp in each text to the end of this text, and separators include each separating text between every two consecutive occurrences of sp inside each text.

Now that we have created three groups of text, the algorithm tries to search for a shared pattern of the the same size s between the components of each group. If a group shares a string pattern, it is partitioned again; if not, s is

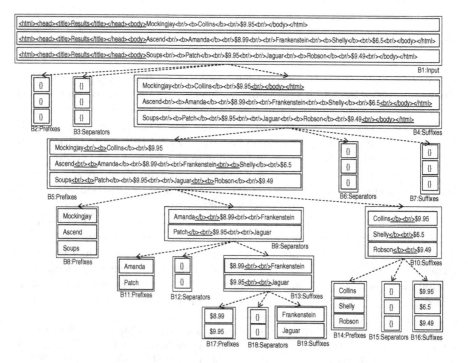

Fig. 1. An example of how our proposal works

decreased, as long as $s \geq min$, and the algorithm starts again its shared pattern search on this group. When $s = min$ and no shared patterns are found, the proposal considers that the remaining non-empty text fragments inside each group can be considered as relevant text that should be extracted. The search for shared patterns is performed using a modified version of Knuth-Morris-Pratt's algorithm [10] in which all the occurrences of a string sequence are detected without overlapping.

Figure 1 illustrates an example on how our proposal works. Strings are tokenised in a scheme of two types HTML tags or #PCDATA. The proposal takes the first block $B1$ that contains three sample web documents, $max = 10$, and $min = 1$ as input. It searches for a shared pattern of $size = 10$ tokens between the three documents in $B1$. Since none is found, the algorithm continues decreasing $size$ to 9, then 8, until it finds a shared pattern of $size = 7$ tokens ($< html >< head >< title > Results < /title >< /head >< body >$) between the three strings in $B1$. Then, it creates prefixes $B2$, suffixes $B4$ and separators $B3$. $B2$ and $B3$ are discarded since they are empty. The algorithm now searches for patterns of $size = 7$ inside $B4$, but since no shared pattern of the given size is found in $B4$, $size$ now changes to $6, 5, 4, 3$. It finds a pattern of $size = 3$ in $B4$ ($< br/ >< /body >< /html >$), partitions it into the prefixes $B5$, suffixes $B7$ and separators $B6$. It searches for shared patterns of the same size in the $B7$. Since the strings in $B7$ do not contain a shared pattern of $size = 3$, $size$ is decreased and the algorithm finds the shared pattern of $size = 2$ ($< br/ >< b >$) between the strings in $B7$. It partitions $B7$ and creates the prefixes $B8$, suffixes $B10$ and separators $B9$. Since strings inside $B8$ do not share a pattern of $size \in [2, min]$, then $B8$ is added to the output. It now repeats the previous steps on $B9$ and $B10$ until finding blocks whose strings do not share any pattern, which are added to the output. The output of this example is a list of blocks that contain $B8$, $B11$, $B17$, $B19$, $B14$, and $B16$. Empty blocks like $B12$ and $B15$ are discarded. According to our experience, max and min can be automatically determined by considering max as 5% the size of the smallest input document, and min as 1.

3   Experimental Results

We implemented a prototype and tested it on a collection of 41 datasets from different web sites. These web sites belong to the following categories: books, cars, conferences, doctors, jobs, movies, real estates, and sports. These categories were randomly sampled from The Open Directory sub-categories, and the web sites inside each category were randomly selected from the best ranked web sites between December 2010 and March 2011 according to Google's search engine. We annotated in each dataset the relevant information and then each string item extracted by our proposal was considered as a true positive (tp), false negative (fn), or false positive (fn). We are interested in measuring precision $P = \frac{tp}{tp+fp}$, recall $R = \frac{tp}{tp+fn}$ and the extraction time of our proposal.

Table 1. Comparison between our proposal, RoadRunner, and FiVaTech

	Precision	Recall	Time (seconds)
RoadRunner [5]	0.312	0.323	0.014
FiVaTech [6]	0.800	0.904	0.348
Our proposal	0.958	0.980	0.0310

We used our collection of datasets to compare our proposal to RoadRunner [5] and to FiVaTech [6], cf. Table 1. Note that our proposal achieves a better recall and precision than both techniques. Although the extraction time archived by our proposal is higher than that one archived by RoadRunner, they both are very close to 0 and the difference between them is insignificant.

4   Conclusions

We have presented an abstract of our preliminary steps towards a totally unsupervised web information extraction technique. It builds on a simple heuristic that has proven to work well in many real-world web documents since it can achieve high precision and recall while requiring very little time. In future, we plan on studying its complexity, comparing it to other well-known techniques in the literature, to create extraction rules that can be reused, and to label the information extracted semantically.

References

1. Turmo, J., Ageno, A., Català, N.: Adaptive information extraction. ACM Comput. Surv. 38(2) (2006)
2. Chang, C.H., Kayed, M., Girgis, M.R., Shaalan, K.F.: A survey of web information extraction systems. IEEE Trans. Knowl. Data Eng. 18(10), 1411–1428 (2006)
3. Kushmerick, N., Weld, D.S., Doorenbos, R.B.: Wrapper induction for information extraction. IJCAI (1), 729–737 (1997)
4. Hsu, C.N., Dung, M.T.: Generating finite-state transducers for semi-structured data extraction from the Web. Inf. Syst. 23(8), 521–538 (1998)
5. Crescenzi, V., Mecca, G., Merialdo, P.: RoadRunner: Towards automatic data extraction from large web sites. In: VLDB, pp. 109–118 (2001)
6. Kayed, M., Chang, C.H.: FiVaTech: Page-level web data extraction from template pages. IEEE Trans. Knowl. Data Eng. 22(2), 249–263 (2010)
7. Chidlovskii, B., Roustant, B., Brette, M.: Documentum ECI self-repairing wrappers: performance analysis. In: SIGMOD Conference, pp. 708–717 (2006)
8. Álvarez, M., Pan, A., Raposo, J., Bellas, F., Cacheda, F.: Extracting lists of data records from semi-structured web pages. Data Knowl. Eng. 64(2), 491–509 (2008)
9. Elmeleegy, H., Madhavan, J., Halevy, A.Y.: Harvesting relational tables from lists on the Web. PVLDB 2(1), 1078–1089 (2009)
10. Knuth, D.E., Morris Jr., J.H., Pratt, V.R.: Fast pattern matching in strings. SIAM J. Comput. 6(2), 323–350 (1977)

Web-Based Tool Integration:
A Web Augmentation Approach

Oscar Díaz[1], Josune De Sosa[2], Cristóbal Arellano[1], and Salvador Trujillo[2]

[1] ONEKIN Group, University of the Basque Country (UPV/EHU), Spain
{oscar.diaz,cristobal.arellano}@ehu.es
[2] IKERLAN Research Centre, Mondragon, Spain
{jdesosa,strujillo}@ikerlan.es

Abstract. Desktop tools are steadily being turned into web applications. Tool integration then becomes a question of website integration. This work uses Web Augmentation techniques for this purpose. An integration layer is deployed on top of the existing Web-based tools that augments the rendering of those tools for the integration experience. Layers are specified through a statechart-like DSL and transformed into JavaScript.

1 Introduction

Tool integration is a matter of reducing *"accidental complexity"* due to the different semantics brought by each tool. Tools might differ on the data format, user-interface conventions, use of common functions, the process flow, etc [3]. Tool integration can be achieved on three different levels: the data source level, the business logic level, and the user interface (UI) level [4]. UI integration has two significant benefits: *(i)* existing applications' UIs can be reused, and *(ii)* users already familiar with existing UIs do not have to learn how to work with new ones. So far, UI integration has been investigated at the component level where a bright new integration application is constructed from existing components [1]. However, tools are not components but full-fledged web applications. Portlets can fit this scenario but they impose a heavy footprint on both the tool provider and the tool consumer (i.e. the tool integrator) [2]. This certainly hinders the openness and self-serviceness of the solution.

This work's research question is whether the use of Web Augmentation (WA) techniques can provide an alternative balance between expressiveness and self-serviceness. Rather than sophisticated and expressive solutions such as those of portlets or UI components, WA introduces a lightweight solution based on the front-end. WA is to the Web what *Augmented Reality* is to the physical world: layering relevant content/layout/navigation over the existing Web to customize the user experience. This is achieved through *JavaScript* using browser weavers (e.g. *Greasemonkey*). However, WA is hindered by being programming intensive and prone to malware. As a result, we resort to Domain-Specific Languages (DSLs) as a way to abstract away from the implementation details, ease user participation, and promote openness. We introduce *CORSET*, a DSL for Web-based tool integration based on process flows.

M. Brambilla, T. Tokuda, and R. Tolksdorf (Eds.): ICWE 2012, LNCS 7387, pp. 431–434, 2012.

2   The Running Example

The tools to be integrated include: *Jazz Rational Team Concert*[1] (hereafter, just *Jazz*) to be used for the management of the software development lifecycle, and *LucidChart*[2], a tool for model design. Figure 1(a) outlines the process flow between *Jazz* and *LucidChart*. First, the user opens *Jazz* to check the workload. Task *24* has been assigned: *"design the xml schema"*. This task involves the design of a UML class diagram. This requires to move to a different tool: *LucidChart*. Once created, the UML diagram is assigned a permalink. This permalink is to be shared with the rest of the *Jazz* community. To this end, the user goes back to task *24* in *Jazz*. Finally, the user copy&paste the permalink as an artefact associated to the *Jazz* task. In this scenario, the integration functionality is in the user's head: no support is given to sustain neither the control flow (e.g. when to navigate from *Jazz* to *LucidChart*, and vice versa) nor the data flow (e.g. the diagram permalink that flows between the websites). This is the very purpose of *CORSET*. Figure1(b) introduces a *CORSET* layer to sustain the

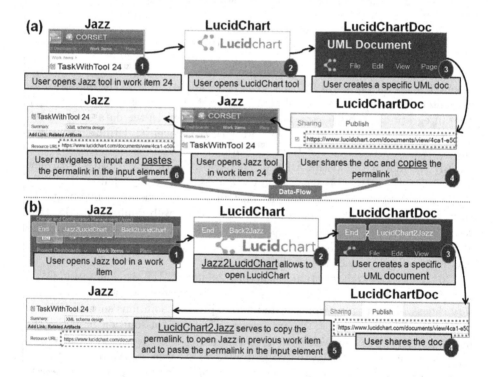

Fig. 1. Integrating the websites of *Jazz* and *LucidChart*. (a) The process expands along the two websites. (b) A CORSET layer is interspersed to support this integration.

---

[1] https://jazz.net/projects/rational-team-concert/
[2] http://www.lucidchart.com/

sample scenario. The *Jazz* website is augmented with three additional buttons: *Jazz2LucidChart*, *Back2LucidChart* and *End*. The former serves to seamless navigate to *LucidChart* the very first time (creating a bright new UML diagram) whereas *Back2LucidChart* handles posterior visits. Likewise, the *LucidChart* website now exhibits two new buttons. *Back2Jazz* serves to navigate back to the departing state at *Jazz*. Unlike the previous case, this navigation is contextual in the sense that navigation is parameterized by the permalink of the current *LucidChart* artefact. It is worth noticing that at any moment the user can move away from these two tools, and browses other web applications. At any moment, users can finalize the process by clicking the *End* button.

3   CORSET

CORSET uses statecharts to describe the integration scenario. Figure 2 shows the *CORSET* expression for the running scenario. This diagram is transformed into a JavaScript program. A process-based UI-centric approach to tool integration entails a control flow, a data flow and the UI augmentations.

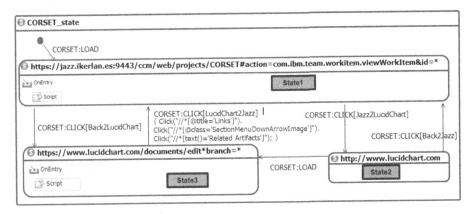

Fig. 2. *CORSET* expression for the running scenario

Control Flow. It is captured through statecharts: a state is characterized by a URL pattern that identifies the set of pages that participate in accomplishing a given task; a transition normally implies moving between websites. For our running example, we have three simple states, one for *Jazz* (*https://jazz.ikerlan.es:9443/ccm/web/projects/CORSET...* see Figure 2) and two for *LucidChart* (*https://www.lucidchart.com/documents/edit...* and *www.lucidchart.com*). A transition has an *event*, a *condition* and a *target* state. *Events* denote abstractions of happenings which are meaningful for the integration purpose. They are signalled by *CORSET* and abstracted from low-level DOM events. So far, two event types are considered: *CLICK*, that denotes pushing a *CORSET* button, and *LOAD*, that is an abstraction of the DOM load event. This event is risen by *CORSET* when a tool loads an UI that matches a state of the *CORSET* at hand. Finally, an action denotes a *CORSET Script*. These scripts describe actions to be enacted in the target tool as a result of this transition. For instance, moving from *State3* in *LucidChart* to *State1* in *Jazz* requires the previous "internal navigation" of three clicks till the right UI is reached (see Figure 2 where the "Click" action mimics user clicks)

Dataflow. Some transitions might be turned into contextual links, i.e. links that carry data from the source to the target. Broadly, we have to mimic copy&paste as conducted by the user. Hence, CORSET offers a high-level "copy" and "paste" operation, and uses state variables as the clipboard. This is part of the CORSET script (not shown in the figure). For instance, the script *Copy("XPath expression").Into($stateVariable)* keeps in the state variable the output of evaluating the XPath.

UI Integration Augmentation. A *CORSET* expression also has a rendering counterpart: *the buttons*. Buttons are automatically generated from transitions. Button placement is based on the assumption that the place that holds some data of interests (the data being extracted) coincides with the place where the control flow should be governed. If no such data exists, buttons are inserted in the upper left of the window. This heuristic permits the *CORSET* engine to automatically generate the UI.

4   Conclusions

We investigate Web Augmentation techniques for tool integration. By using a DSL, we strive to shelter users from JavaScript and describe the integration declaratively as statecharts. A must follow-on is to conduct usability studies among the tool users to assess whether *CORSET* expressiveness fulfils their requirements.

References

1. Daniel, F., Soi, S., Tranquillini, S., Casati, F., Heng, C., Yan, L.: From People to Services to UI: Distributed Orchestration of User Interfaces. In: Hull, R., Mendling, J., Tai, S. (eds.) BPM 2010. LNCS, vol. 6336, pp. 310–326. Springer, Heidelberg (2010)
2. Díaz, O., Rodriguez, J.: Portlets as Web Components: an Introduction. Journal of Universal Computer Sciences (JUCS) 10(4), 454–472 (2004)
3. Thomas, I., Nejmeh, B.: Definitions of Tool Integration for Environments. IEEE Software 9(2), 29–35 (1992), http://dx.doi.org/10.1109/52.120599
4. Westermann, U., Jain, R.: Toward a Common Event Model for Multimedia Applications. IEEE MultiMedia 14(1), 19–29 (2007)

Clustering Visually Similar Web Page Elements for Structured Web Data Extraction

Tomas Grigalis[1], Lukas Radvilavičius[1], Antanas Čenys[1],
and Juozas Gordevičius[2]

[1] Vilnius Gediminas Technical University, Lithuania
{tomas.grigalis,lukas.radvilavicius,antanas.cenys}@vgtu.lt
[2] Vilnius University Institute of Mathematics and Informatics, Lithuania
juozas.gordevicius@mii.vu.lt

Abstract. We propose a novel approach for extraction of structured web data called ClustVX. It clusters visually similar web page elements by exploiting their visual formatting and structural features. Clusters are then used to derive extraction rules. The experimental evaluation results of ClustVX system on three publicly available benchmark data sets outperform state-of-the-art structured data extraction systems.

1 Introduction

Automatic extraction of structured data from web pages is one of the key challenges for the Web search engines to advance into a more expressive semantic level. However, current algorithmic approaches often fail to achieve satisfactory performance in real-world application scenarios due to abundant structurally complicated and dynamic WEB 2.0 pages.

Information extraction systems can be broadly divided into supervised and unsupervised categories. Supervised learning approaches, such as Lixto [1], require some manual human effort to derive the extraction rules, while automated information extraction systems [2,3,4,5] work automatically and need no manual intervention. In this work we focus on the latter as we believe that only fully automatic systems can be applied for web-scale data extraction.

Thus we present a novel stuctured web data extraction system, ClustVX, which is fully automatic, scalable, and domain independent. ClustVX is based on two fundamental observations. First, vast amount of information on the Web is presented using fixed templates and filled with data from underlying databases. For example, Fig. 1(a) shows three Data Records (DRs) representing information about three digital cameras in an online store. The three DRs are listed according to some unknown to us style template and the information comes from a database. This also means, that each DR has almost the same Xpath (tag path from root node in HTML tree to particular web page element), where only a few node numbers differs. Second, although the templates and underlying data differ from site to site, humans understand it easily by analyzing repeating visual patterns on a given Web page [6]. We hypothesize, that the data which

M. Brambilla, T. Tokuda, and R. Tolksdorf (Eds.): ICWE 2012, LNCS 7387, pp. 435–438, 2012.

has the same semantic meaning is visualized using the same style. For example in Fig. 1(a) prices are brown red and bold, title is green and bold, text "Online Price" is grey.

ClustVX exploits both of these two observations by representing each web page element with a combination of its Xpath and visual features such as font, color and etc. For each visible web page element we encode this combination into the string called Xstring. Clustering Xstrings allows us to identify visually similar elements, which are located in the same region of a web page and in turn have same semantic meaning. See Fig. 1(b) where price elements are clustered together according to their Xstring. Subsequent data extraction leads to a machine readable structured data that is shown in Fig. 1(c).

| Samsung ES80 | Fujifilm FinePix T300 | Vivitar ViviCam F529 |
| $84.95 Online Price | $174.95 Online Price | $84.95 Online Price |

(a) An example of three digital cameras (Data Records) in a web page

Xstring:	htmlbodydivdiva-Verdana,FF6600;400
$84.95	/html/body/div[1]/div[3]/a
$174.95	/html/body/div[2]/div[3]/a
$84.95	/html/body/div[3]/div[3]/a

(b) A cluster with visually similar price elements

Image 1	Samsung ES80	$84.95	Online Price
Image 2	Fujifilm FinePix T300	$174.95	Online Price
Image 3	Vivitar ViviCam F529	$84.95	Online Price

(c) Desired extraction result

Fig. 1. An example of structured web data extraction using ClustVX

2   The Proposed Approach

The ClustVX processes a given Web page in the following steps:

1. A web page is retrieved and rendered in a contemporary web browser. This is very importand step, since web browser handles all WEB 2.0 features, such as client-side scripting, AJAX requets and etc. All visual styling information from HTML source code and CSS files is also processed by the browser.
2. All HTML text formatting tags, such as $<b>$, $<em>$, are removed from a web page. This is done to enhance clustering accuracy.

Table 1. The details of three public benchmark data sets used for ClustVX evaluation

Data Set	TBDW [7]	ViNTs-2 [8]	Alvarez [2]
Sites	51	102	200
Pages per site	5	11	1
AVG records	21	24	18
Total records	1052	2489	3557

3. An Xstring representation is generated for each visible web page text element. As we see in Fig. 1(b) Xstring consists of a) tag names from Xpath b) visual features of that element (font style, color, weight, etc.). Structural features (string of tag names) identifies position in HTML document. Visual features, which are obtained from web browsers API, enhance understanding of semantic similarity between web page elements.

4. All visible web page elements are clustered according to their Xstring. Resulting clusters contain only semantically similar web page elements. In Fig. 1(b) we see a cluster of price elements that all have the exaclty same Xstring and therefore belong to the same cluster.

5. Extraction of structured data. This process is based on two observations about DR representation in a web page. First, a group of DRs are usually rendered in a contiguous region of a web page [5] and are visually similar. Second, a group of DRs are formed by some child subtrees and at some level have same parent node [5]. Thus, by calculating longest common prefix of Xpaths from each cluster , we can find the exact locations of DRs groups (Data Regions) in a page. For a simple example, consider the Fig. 1(b), where Xpaths of clustered price elements are located. First, we find the longest common prefix (/html/body) of these clustered Xpaths. The prefix leads us to the particular region of a web page, where DRs are located. Then, the longest common suffix (/div[3]/a) is items' path in the DR. The Xpath substring between prefix and suffix (/div[*]) is used to segment Data Region into DRs. All clusters that have the same longest common Xpath prefix represent one particular Data Region. There may exist many Data Regions in one page and ClustVX locates them all.

3   Experimental Evaluation

We evaluate ClustVX using the three publicly available benchmark data sets containing in total of 7098 DRs from 353 different template web sites. See Tab. 1 for details. These data sets contain web pages retrieved from different web sites. Each web page contains DRs, which should be extracted. To evaluate ClustVX we take only one web page per site because all pages in one site use the same template.

We compare the evaluation results of ClustVX system to these state-of-the-art automatic structured data extraction systems: M. Alvarez et. al. [2], G-STM

Table 2. Experimental evaluation results of ClustVX system compared to other state-of-the-art methods

Data Set	TBDW				VINTS-2			Alvarez	
System	ClustVX	G-STM	DEPTA	FiVaTech	ClustVX	G-STM	DEPTA	ClustVX	Alvarez
Precision	**99.81%**	99.80%	99.50%	97.00%	**98.57%**	98.50%	95.10%	**98.20%**	97.90%
Recall	**99.52%**	96.60%	85.30%	97.40%	**98.51%**	96.70%	83.90%	**99.69%**	98.30%

[3], FiVaTech [4] and DEPTA [5]. Since none of these systems are available to download, we use the evaluation results reported in corresponding publications. As shown in Tab. 2, where best results are marked in bold, ClustVX consistently outperforms other approaches.

4 Conclusions and Research Directions

We have introduced a novel approach, ClustVX, to extraction of structured data from web pages. It uses structural as well as visual features of web page elements to discover the structure of underlying data. Evaluation on three publicly available benchmark data sets demonstrated, that the method consistently achieves very high quality in terms of precision and recall and outperforms other approaches.

Our future work will focus on evaluation of ClustVX on contemporary real-world web pages that are full of Java Scripts and are dynamic. The existing benchmark data sets lack features introduced by Web 2.0, such as, AJAX. Although we stipulate that ClustVX is invariant to these advanced features, a proper dataset is necessary to prove its applicability in real-world settings.

References

1. Baumgartner, R., Flesca, S., Gottlob, G.: Visual web information extraction with lixto. In: Proc. VLDB, pp. 119–128 (2001)
2. Álvarez, M., Pan, A., Raposo, E.A.: Extracting lists of data records from semi-structured web pages. Data & Know. Engineering 64(2), 491–509 (2008)
3. Jindal, N., Liu, B.: A generalized tree matching algorithm considering nested lists for web data extraction. In: The SIAM Int. Conf. on Data Mining, pp. 930–941 (2010)
4. Kayed, M., Chang, C.: Fivatech: Page-level web data extraction from template pages. IEEE Trans. on Know. & Data Engineering 22(2), 249–263 (2010)
5. Zhai, Y., Liu, B.: Web data extraction based on partial tree alignment. In: Proc. WWW, pp. 76–85. ACM (2005)
6. Miao, G., Tatemura, J., Hsiung, W., Sawires, A., Moser, L.: Extracting data records from the web using tag path clustering. In: Proc. WWW, pp. 981–990. ACM (2009)
7. Yamada, Y., Craswell, N., Nakatoh, T., Hirokawa, S.: Testbed for information extraction from deep web. In: Proc. WWW, pp. 346–347. ACM (2004)
8. Zhao, H., Meng, W., Wu, Z., Raghavan, V., Yu, C.: Fully automatic wrapper generation for search engines. In: Proc. WWW, pp. 66–75. ACM (2005)

Improving Toponym Extraction
and Disambiguation Using Feedback Loop

Mena B. Habib and Maurice van Keulen

Faculty of EEMCS, University of Twente, Enschede, The Netherlands
{m.b.habib,m.vankeulen}@ewi.utwente.nl

Abstract. This paper addresses two problems with toponym extraction and disambiguation. First, almost no existing works examine the extraction and disambiguation interdependency. Second, existing disambiguation techniques mostly take as input extracted toponyms without considering the uncertainty and imperfection of the extraction process.

It is the aim of this paper to investigate both avenues and to show that explicit handling of the uncertainty of annotation has much potential for making both extraction and disambiguation more robust.

1 Introduction

Toponyms are names used to refer to locations without having to mention the actual geographic coordinates. The process of *toponym extraction* aims to identify location names in natural text.

Toponym disambiguation is the task of determining which real location is referred to by a certain instance of a name. Toponyms, as with named entities in general, are highly ambiguous. For example, according to GeoNames[1], the toponym "Paris" refers to more than sixty different geographic places around the world besides the capital of France. Another source of ambiguousness is that some toponyms are common English words.

A general principle in our work is our conviction that toponyms extraction and disambiguation are highly dependent. In previous work [1], we studied not only the positive and negative effect of the extraction process on the disambiguation process, but also the potential of using the result of disambiguation to improve extraction. We called this potential for mutual improvement, the *reinforcement effect* (see Figure 1).

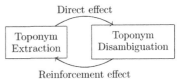

Fig. 1. The reinforcement effect between the toponym extraction and disambiguation processes

In general, we concluded that many of the observed problems are caused by an improper treatment of the inherent ambiguities. Natural language has the innate property that it is multiply interpretable. Therefore, none of the processes in information extraction should be 'all-or-nothing'. In other words,

---

[1] www.geonames.org

M. Brambilla, T. Tokuda, and R. Tolksdorf (Eds.): ICWE 2012, LNCS 7387, pp. 439–443, 2012
© Springer-Verlag Berlin Heidelberg 2012

all steps, including entity recognition, should produce *possible* alternatives with associated likelihoods and dependencies.

Our Contributions. In this paper, we focus on this principle. We turned to statistical approaches for toponym extraction. The advantage of statistical techniques for extraction is that they provide alternatives for annotations along with confidence probabilities. The probabilities proved to be useful in enhancing the disambiguation process. We believe that there is much potential in making the inherent uncertainty in information extraction explicit in this way.

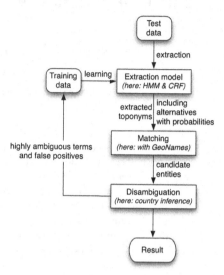

Furthermore, extraction models are inherently imperfect and generate imprecise confidences. We were able to use the disambiguation result for increasing the confidence of true toponyms and reducing the confidence of false positives.

Fig. 2. General approach

This enhancement of extraction improves as a consequence the disambiguation (the aforementioned reinforcement effect). This process can be repeated iteratively, without any human interference, as long as there is improvement in the extraction and disambiguation.

2   Our Approach

The task we focus on is to extract toponyms from EuroCottage holiday home descriptions[2] and use them to infer the country where the holiday property is located. We use this country inference task as a representative example of disambiguating extracted toponyms.

We propose an entity extraction and disambiguation approach based on uncertain annotations. The general approach illustrated in Figure 2 has the following steps:

1. Prepare training data by manually annotating named entities.
2. Use the training data to build a statistical extraction model.
3. Apply the extraction model on test data and training data.
4. Match the extracted named entities against one or more gazetteers.
5. Use the toponym entity candidates for the disambiguation process.
6. Evaluate the extraction and disambiguation results for the training data. Use a list of highly ambiguous named entities and false positives that affect the disambiguation results to re-train the extraction model.

---

[2] www.eurocottage.com

7. The steps from 2 to 6 are repeated automatically until there is no improvement any more in either the extraction or the disambiguation.

Toponym Extraction. For toponym extraction, we developed two statistical named entity extraction modules[3], one based on Hidden Markov Models (HMM) and one based on Conditional Ramdom Fields (CRF).

The goal of HMM [2] is to find the optimal tag sequence (in our case, whether the word is assigned to toponym tag or not) $T = t_1, t_2, t_3, ..., t_n$ for a given word sequence $W = w_1, w_2, w_3 ..., w_n$ that maximizes $P(T \mid W)$.

Conditional Random Fields (CRF) can model overlapping, non-independent features [3]. Here we used a linear chain CRF, the simplest model of CRF.

Extraction Modes of Operation. We used the extraction models to retrieve sets of annotations in two ways:

- **First-Best:** In this method, we only consider the first most likely set of annotations that maximize the probability $P(T \mid W)$ for the whole text. This method does not assign a probability for each individual annotation, but only to the whole retrieved set of annotations.
- **N-Best:** This method returns a top-25 of possible alternative hypotheses for terms annotations in order of their estimated likelihoods $p(t_i|w_i)$. The confidence scores are assumed to be conditional probabilities of the annotation given an input token.

Toponym Disambiguation. For the toponym disambiguation task, we only select those toponyms annotated by the extraction models that match a reference in GeoNames. We furthermore use an adapted version of the clustering approach of [1] to disambiguate to which entity an extracted toponym actually refers.

Handling Uncertainty of Annotations. Instead of giving equal contibution to all toponyms, we take the uncertainty in the extraction process into account to include the confidence of the extracted toponyms. In this way terms which are more likely to be toponyms have a higher contribution in determining the country of the document than less likely ones.

Improving Certainty of Extraction. In despite of the abovementioned improvement, the extraction probabilities are not accurate and reliable all the time. Some extraction models retrieve some false positive toponyms with high confidence probabilities. This is where we take advantage of the reinforcement effect. To be more precise. We introduce another class in the extraction model called 'highly ambiguous' and annotate those terms in the training set with this class that the disambiguation process finds more than τ countries for documents that contain this term. The extraction model is subsequently re-trained and the whole process is repeated without any human interference as long as there is improvement in extraction and disambiguation process for the training set. The intention is that the extraction model learns to avoid prediction of terms to be toponyms when they appear to confuse the disambiguation process.

---

[3] We made use of the *lingpipe* toolkit for development: `http://alias-i.com/lingpipe`

3   Experimental Results

Here we present the results of experiments with the presented methods of extraction and disambiguation applied to a collection of holiday properties descriptions. The data set consists of 1579 property descriptions for which we constructed a ground truth by manually annotating all toponyms.

Experiment 1: Effect of Extraction with Confidence Probabilities. Table 1 shows the percentage of holiday home descriptions for which the correct country was successfully inferred. We can see that the **N-Best** method outperforms the **First-Best** method for both HMM and CRF models. This supports our claim that dealing with alternatives along with their confidences yields better results.

Table 1. Effectiveness of the disambiguation process for First-Best and N-Best methods in the extraction phase

	HMM	CRF
First-Best	62.59%	62.84%
N-Best	68.95%	68.19%

Table 2. Effectiveness of the disambiguation after iteration of refinement

	HMM	CRF
No Filtering	68.95%	68.19%
1st Iteration	73.28%	68.44%

Table 3. Effectiveness of the extraction process after iteration of refinement

	HMM			CRF		
	Pre.	Rec.	F1	Pre.	Rec.	F1
No Filtering	0.3584	0.8517	0.5045	0.6969	0.7136	0.7051
1st Iteration	0.7667	0.5987	0.6724	0.6989	0.7131	0.7059

Experiment 2: Effect of Extraction Certainty Enhancement. Tables 2 and 3 show the effectiveness of the disambiguation and the extraction processes respectively before and after one iteration of refinement. We can see an improvement in HMM extraction and disambiguation results. The initial HMM results showed a high recall rate with a low precision. In spite of this, our approach managed to improve precision through iteration of refinement. The refinement process is based on removing highly ambiguous toponyms resulting in a slight decrease in recall and an increase in precision. In contrast, CRF started with high precision which could not be improved by the refinement process.

4   Conclusion and Future Work

Named entity extraction and disambiguation are inherently imperfect processes that moreover depend on each other. The aim of this paper is to examine and make use of this dependency for the purpose of improving the disambiguation by iteratively enhancing the effectiveness of extraction, and vice versa.

We examined how handling the uncertainty of extraction influences the effectiveness of disambiguation, and reciprocally, how the result of disambiguation can be used to improve the effectiveness of extraction. The extraction models are automatically retrained after discovering highly ambiguous false positives among the extracted toponyms. This process improves the precision of the extraction.

References

1. Habib, M.B., van Keulen, M.: Named entity extraction and disambiguation: The reinforcement effect. In: Proc. of MUD 2011, Seatle, USA, pp. 9–16 (2011)
2. Ekbal, A., Bandyopadhyay, S.: A Hidden Markov Model Based Named Entity Recognition System: Bengali and Hindi as Case Studies. In: Ghosh, A., De, R.K., Pal, S.K. (eds.) PReMI 2007. LNCS, vol. 4815, pp. 545–552. Springer, Heidelberg (2007)
3. Wallach, H.: Conditional random fields: An introduction. Technical Report MS-CIS-04-21, University of Pennsylvania (2004)

GeForMTjs: A JavaScript Library Based on a Domain Specific Language for Multi-touch Gestures

Dietrich Kammer, Dana Henkens, and Rainer Groh

Fakultät Informatik
Professur Mediengestaltung
Technische Universität Dresden
01062 Dresden
dietrich.kammer@tu-dresden.de, dana.henkens@googlemail.com

Abstract. This paper presents GeForMTjs, a library which features an abstract way of representing multi-touch gestures. A domain specific language for multi-touch gestures, Gesture Formalization for Multi-touch (GeForMT), is adapted to the needs of web development. Web standards are addressed and mouse input is incorporated as well. A short overview of related work shows that a formal abstraction of multi-touch gestures is missing in the web context. A brief example illustrates the seven processing steps of the library.

Keywords: Gestures, Multi-touch, CSS, JavaScript, Web standards.

1   Introduction

Multi-touch interaction is currently almost ubiquitous with web browsers on mobile devices. Although a set of standard navigational gestures are used throughout these browsers, a great potential for more complex gestural interaction remains to be researched. The web events working group of the W3C is currently developing a standard to integrate multi-touch and pen input in web sites. The official recommendation is due in August 2012 [1]. However, few of the currently available web libraries assist the programmer in the definition of application specific multi-touch gestures.

This paper contributes an implementation of a domain specific language (DSL) for multi-touch gestures in JavaScript. It is more powerful than relying on fixed gesture events or raw touch data. The short, concise, and self-explanatory syntax is graspable for both developers and designers. Providing gesture definition and recognition in a library should help web programmers to design and test novel interaction concepts.

2   Related Work

Most web applications on mobile devices use standard gestures and seek to emulate native multi-touch concepts available on each platform. Examples are jQuery Mobile [2], the Dojo-plugin dojox.mobile [3], and Sencha Touch [4]. WKTouch [5] focuses object manipulation, where gestures and actions are implicitly assigned to objects. Jester [6] provides a library of common standard gestures. Representations of gestures on a higher abstraction level are investigated by researchers such as Kin et al. [7],

M. Brambilla, T. Tokuda, and R. Tolksdorf (Eds.): ICWE 2012, LNCS 7387, pp. 444–447, 2012.

Khandkar and Maurer [8], and Kammer et al. [9]. Currently, these approaches are not available on the web. Libraries such as Moousture [10] are rather limited in expressing complex multi-touch gestures. A greater freedom and ease to design gestures can result in better and more powerful multi-touch interfaces in the future.

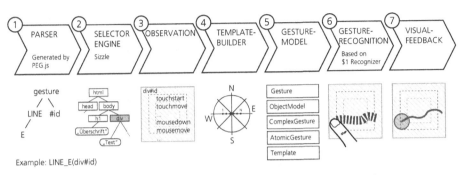

Fig. 1. Library components and processing steps of GeForMTjs

3   Gesture Library GeForMTjs

GeForMTjs relies on web standards to make touch data available in the web browser. Seven components are responsible for registering and processing gestures (see Fig. 1).

Step 1: The Gesture Formalization for Multi-touch (GeForMT) by [9] provides a DSL for multi-touch gestures defined by a context-free grammar. GeForMT features atomic gestures, which describe the form or path of a gesture and operators to describe the temporal progression of gesture strokes. Complex gestures are defined by combining atomic gestures. A GeForMT expression is validated by the Parser and split into syntactical units. PEG.js is used to generate a concrete parser implementation (http://pegjs.majda.cz/, last access: 05/09/2012), which is based on the parsing expression grammar formalism [11].

Step 2: The Selector Engine checks selectors contained in the gesture description for focus definition and returns corresponding nodes of the DOM tree. For the concrete implementation, Sizzle (http://sizzlejs.com/, last access: 05/09/2012) is used.

Step 3: The Observation module registers mouse and touch events for these elements. Mouse events are emulated as single touch gestures by dispatching appropriate touch events (cp. [12, 13]). To detect gesture input on content or structure elements (e.g. div) as well as on underlying parent elements of the DOM tree (e.g. html), the bubbling strategy of events is adopted. The programmer can define a contiguity interval to allow the specification of gestures that require the user to lift all fingers from the multi-touch display, e.g. a double-tap.

Step 4: The Template Builder converts formal parameters of the parsed expressions into a computable data structure containing ordered coordinates.

Step 5: Results of Parser and Transformation are stored in the Gesture Model.

Step 6: Based on these templates, Gesture Recognition is performed. Wobbrock et al.'s $1-Recognizer [14] has a good balance between recognition rate, memory

Fig. 2. Sample web page using GeForMTjs

requirements, and tolerance and is suitable for a JavaScript implementation. A key advantage is the minimal effort used for feature extraction at runtime. Wobbrock et al.'s algorithm is adapted according to the specification of GeForMT including sequentially and simultaneously performed gesture paths, as well as gestures that are continuously recognized. In these cases, the steps of classification are processed in repetition.

Step 7: Visual feedback is provided and application specific event handlers are called for recognized gestures on their corresponding DOM elements. Gestures strokes and contacts are visualized on two separate overlaying canvas elements, which are excluded from event processing. Sequential gesture paths are considered in the feedback visualization as well. The gesture expression illustrated in Fig. 1 defines a line drawn to the east on a div element. The definition is embedded in JavaScript code and is registered with the API of GeForMTjs as follows:

```
GeForMT.addGesture ({
    identifier: "swipe",          // unique identifier
    expr: "LINE_E(div#id)",       // GeForMT expression
    online: true,                 // continuous/discrete recognition
    handler: function(e) { … } // gesture specific event handler
});
```

GeForMTjs can be seen in action in a test environment[1] demonstrating example gesture sets and a sample web page[2] (see Fig. 2), which substitutes access keys with stroke shortcuts to access menu entries. Browser functions can be accessed by gestures as well, for example browsing through the history or bookmarks. If a gesture cannot be recognized, a short information is displayed as a layer on top of the website, which indicates how to access the help page.

4   Conclusions and Future Work

The library presented in this paper is based on a DSL for multi-touch gestures. It complies with web standards to reap the benefits of platform-independent, web-based

---

[1] http://vi-c.de/geformtjs/testbench/
[2] http://vi-c.de/geformtjs/sample/

development. GeForMTjs supports different interaction techniques by generalizing mouse, touch, and pen input. Extensions like the browser plugin npTUIOClient and MagicTouch [12] working with the TUIO protocol [15] are considered as well for more hardware independence. However, further performance tests and web browser compliance must be tested and ensured. An important issue is the visualization of feedback and feed-forward, which reveals available gestures in an application. Another interesting possibility is the combination of GeForMT with a UI library. Combining GeForMT with other DSLs or adding extensions might make it feasible to address other modalities such as speech, spatial gestures, or video processing.

References

1. Brubeck, M., Moon, S., Schepers, D.: Touch Events version 1, http://www.w3.org/TR/touch-events/ (last access: September 05, 2012)
2. jQuery: jQuery Mobile, http://jquerymobile.com/ (last access: September 05, 2012)
3. Dojo: Dojo Mobile, http://dojotoolkit.org/features/mobile (last access: September 05, 2012)
4. Sencha: Mobile JavaScript Framework for HTML5 Web App Development I Sencha Touch, http://www.sencha.com/products/touch (last access: September 05, 2012)
5. Gibson, A.: WKTouch, https://github.com/alexgibson/WKTouch (last access: September 05, 2012)
6. Seaward, S.: Jester, https://github.com/plainview/Jester (last access: September 05, 2012)
7. Kin, K., Hartmann, B., DeRose, T., Agrawala, M.: Proton: Multitouch Gestures as Regular Expressions. ACM, Austin (to appear, 2012)
8. Khandkar, S., Maurer, F.: A Domain Specific Language to Define Gestures for Multi-Touch Applications. In: Rossi, M., Tolvanen, J.-P., Sprinkle, J., Und Kelly, S (hrsg.) Proceedings of the 10th Workshop on Domain-Specific Modeling (DSM 2010), Aalto University School of Economics, B-120, Aalto-Print (2010)
9. Kammer, D., Wojdziak, J., Keck, M., Groh, R., Taranko, S.: Towards a formalization of multi-touch gestures. In: ACM International Conference on Interactive Tabletops and Surfaces. S.49–S.58. ACM, New York (2010)
10. Sibt-e-Hassan, Z.: Moousture, http://maxpert.github.com/moousture/ (last access: September 05, 2012)
11. Ford, B.: Parsing expression grammars. In: Proceedings of the 31st ACM SIGPLAN-SIGACT Symposium on Principles of Programming Languages, pp. S.111–122. ACM Press (2004)
12. Smus, B.: MagicTouch, https://github.com/borismus/MagicTouch (last access: September 05, 2012)
13. Carstensen, B.: Phantom Limb I Vodori Blog, http://www.vodori.com/blog/phantom-limb.html
14. Wobbrock, J.O., Wilson, A.D., Li, Y.: Gestures without libraries, toolkits or training: a $1 recognizer for user interface prototypes. In: Proceedings of the 20th Annual ACM Symposium on User Interface Software and Technology, pp. S.159–S.168. ACM, New York (2007)
15. Kaltenbrunner, M., Bovermann, T., Bencina, R., Costanza, E.: TUIO: A Protocol for Table-Top Tangible User Interfaces. In: Gehalten auf der 6th International Workshop on Gesture in Human-Computer Interaction and Simulation, Vannes, France Mai 18 (2005)

SemaKoDE: Hybrid System for Knowledge Discovery in Sensor-Based Smart Environments

Stefan Negru

Faculty of Computer Science A. I. Cuza University of Iasi, Romania
stefan.negru@info.uaic.ro

Abstract. This article describes a conceptual hybrid architecture for a knowledge discovery system, able to automatically annotate, reason, classify and operate with sensor data. The adoption of semantic web technologies to enrich sensor and link data represents an adequate methodology that facilitates the processes of reasoning, classification and other types of automation. We discussed a system deployment scenario in the context of e-health.

Keywords: Knowledge Discovery System, Sensors, Linked Data.

1 Introduction

The ubiquity of sensors and sensor networks brought opportunities regarding software applications in areas like smart environments, ambient management, disaster prediction and management, adaptability to climate change, security, support systems, infrastructures management etc.

Recent work has raised the idea to combine the sensor data with web technologies in order to design future services and applications. This vision is related to the aim of ubiquitous computing, as well as the proposal of "Internet of Things" [6].

We envision and design a conceptual hybrid knowledge discovery system, able to automatically annotate, reason, classify and operate with sensor data. Although several similar sensor network systems exist [8,5], our system proposal also takes into consideration additional factors like evaluation and re-usability of the discovered knowledge in different contexts, thus making it available to other services and applications.

2 System Architecture

The SemaKoDE (**Sema**ntic **K**nowledge **D**iscovery **E**nvironment) system consists of two main components: the first one is similar to a classical KDD system [7], and provides an established and well researched base for identifying patterns or models in data. The second component takes advantage of semantic

M. Brambilla, T. Tokuda, and R. Tolksdorf (Eds.): ICWE 2012, LNCS 7387, pp. 448–451, 2012.

web technologies which facilitate the reusing and sharing of information, within the system and with other systems. Our system is divided into the following layers: **Knowledge Base Layer, Network Management Layer, Database Layer, Discovery Layer, Application Layer** (Fig. 1).

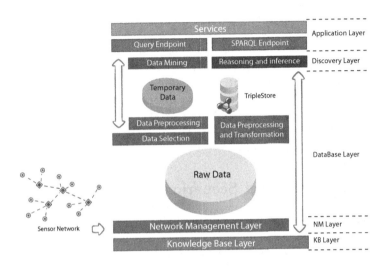

Fig. 1. SemaKoDE System Architecture

Knowledge Base Layer. This layer contains the axioms defining the classes and relations in the ontology along with the logic operations which are used to perform inferences – the TBox [1,4].

Network Management Layer. The main responsibility of the Network Management Layer is to facilitate collecting data for the Database Layer and also to manage the functions related to the interaction between multiple sensors. Other aspects, such as network hierarchy and clustering of sensor, nodes are also done at this layer.

Database Layer. Data Selection and Data Preprocessing sub-layers correspond to two of the steps from the KDD process [2]. The Data Preprocessing and Transformation sub-layer handles similar functions but, in addition, offers support for semantically annotating sensor data and storing this data into a triple store [11] (ABox [1,4]).

Discovery Layer. The Discovery Layer encapsulates both data mining [7] and reasoning algorithms as presented in [1,4], used for knowledge discovery. Although the types of algorithms have roughly the same purpose, we believe that patterns/models obtained via data mining and the inferred information via reasoning provide slightly different results. Thereby, we want to integrate them into the Application layer in order to improve the discovery process accuracy and the knowledge quality. Regarding evaluating the knowledge quality, we take into consideration methods for evaluating triple-stores [9,3], or the ontology quality [10].

Application Layer. The top level layer handles the data interpretation (extracting knowledge) and data integration too. As the KDD process operates with user predefined goals, this layer also provides a user interface which handles the user interaction, as we need to represent the discovered knowledge in an easy to understand manner.

Considering the query endpoints, two methods are to be explored. One in which we **keep the current structure** (Fig.1) with the two query endpoints (classical query service and SPARQL endpoint), the integration being done via several services, and one in which the **two query endpoints are unified** into a single service, using a future SPARQL extension. Next versions of the SemaKoDE system will incorporate predictive capabilities, via extensions implemented at the Application Layer.

3   System Deployment Scenario

In order to illustrate SemaKoDE usefulness and versatility, we imagine a scenario centered around hospital building environment. The hospital maintains a patient database (that stores diseases, disease symptoms, disabilities, patient rooms etc). The hospital building has several spatially distributed sensors, that monitor the environment. SemaKoDE system will act as a bridge linking the data between the database and sensor network in order to extend the overall knowledge about this environment. For example, certain environmental factors (detected via the sensor network) might cause the patient health status to aggravate, depending on the disease (Disease Ontology – http://www.disease-ontology.org/).

In case of major event (hazard) such as a fire, the system will make use of its knowledge discovery capabilities. First it confirms the fire is real, by linking data

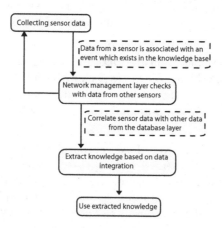

Fig. 2. SemaKoDE Main Processes

from various sensors from the sensor network and deploying the fire sprinklers. Operations are done by the Network Management layer as represented in Fig. 2. After confirming the fire, the system proceeds to provide a list of patients located near the fire, having a high risk factor (e.g. patients that have certain disabilities or have trouble breathing and can not evacuate themselves). The predictive capabilities of the system come in handy in providing a fire spreading pattern.

4   Conclusions and Future Work

This paper presented SemaKoDE, a hybrid system used for knowledge discovery in sensor-based smart environments. Our system proposal combines traditional knowledge discovery, based on data mining, with ontology based knowledge discovery, in order to create not only a well optimized KDS, but also a system able to share and reuse data. Our further direction of research is focused on developing, testing and improving such a system, in order to constantly perfect the way it can collect, process and operate with sensor data, with the purpose of using it in real world scenarios, similar with those presented in this paper.

Acknowledgements. This work was supported by the European Social Fund in Romania, under the responsibility of the Managing Authority for the Sectorial Operational Program for Human Resources Development 2007-2013 [grant POSDRU/107/1.5/S/78342].

References

1. Baader, F., et al.: The Description Logic Handbook. Cambridge University Press (2007)
2. Fayyad, U., et al.: From data mining to knowledge discovery: an overview. AI Magazine, 37–54 (1996)
3. Guo, Y., Pan, Z., Heflin, J.: An Evaluation of Knowledge Base Systems for Large OWL Datasets. In: McIlraith, S.A., Plexousakis, D., van Harmelen, F. (eds.) ISWC 2004. LNCS, vol. 3298, pp. 274–288. Springer, Heidelberg (2004)
4. Harmelen, F.V., et al.: Handbook of knowledge representation. Elsevier (2008)
5. Huang, V., Javed, M.K.: Semantic sensor information description and processing. In: 2nd International Conference on Sensor Technologies and Applications, pp. 456–461. IEEE (2008)
6. International Telecommunication Union: ITU Internet Report 2005: The Internet of Things (2005)
7. Leondes, C.T.: Knowledge-based systems: techniques and applications. Academic Press (2000)
8. Moraru, A., et al.: Using semantic annotation for knowledge extraction from geographically distributed and heterogeneous sensor data. In: 4th SensorKDD. ACM (2010)
9. Rohloff, K., Dean, M., Emmons, I., Ryder, D., Sumner, J.: An Evaluation of Triple-Store Technologies for Large Data Stores. In: Meersman, R., Tari, Z. (eds.) OTM-WS 2007, Part II. LNCS, vol. 4806, pp. 1105–1114. Springer, Heidelberg (2007)
10. Stvilia, B.: A model for ontology quality evaluation. First Monday (2007)
11. Yeh, C., Lin, R.: Design and Implementation of an RDF Triple Store. In: Proceedings of the 1st Workshop of DATF. Academia Sinica (2002)

WebREd: A Model-Driven Tool for Web Requirements Specification and Optimization

José Alfonso Aguilar Calderon[1], Irene Garrigós[2], Sven Casteleyn[3], and Jose-Norberto Mazón[2]

[1] Señales y Sistemas (SESIS)
Universidad Autónoma de Sinaloa, México
ja.aguilar@maz.uasnet.mx
[2] Department of Software and Computing Systems (DLSI)
University of Alicante, Spain
{igarrigos,jnmazon}@dlsi.ua.es
[3] Departamento de Sistemas Informáticos y Computación
Universitat Politècnica de València, Spain
sven.casteleyn@upv.es

Abstract. In this paper we present the WebREd-Tool, a set of Eclipse plugins that have been developed to assist the designer in the early phases of a Web application development process. With the WebREd-Tool, the designer can specify the Web application requirements by using the *i** goal-oriented framework. The WebREd-Tool assists the designer to compare different configurations of functional requirements, while balancing and optimizing non-functional requirements. The underlying algorithm to support this is based on the Pareto efficiency, but to help the designer to better assess and compare each configuration, the WebREd-Tool is also able to visualize each configurations using a radar-chart.

Keywords: Web Engineering, Requirements Engineering, Softgoal Optimization.

1 Introduction

Although there are many methods for the development of Web applications, only a select few offer methodological support for the requirements engineering phase, and only one, namely NDT, also provides dedicated tool support, as reviewed in [1]. Nevertheless, the complexity and dynamic nature of Web applications demand the development of methods and tools to support the Web designer in performing the requirements analysis phase. Furthermore, solutions that take into account both functional (FR) and non-functional (NFR) requirements from the beginning of the development process are needed, in order to assure that the final product corresponds qualitatively to the users expectations.

In this work, we describe our efforts to build a set of Eclipse plugins called WebREd-Tool[1] to meet these needs. The WebREd-Tool enables the analysis and

---

[1] http://code.google.com/p/webred/

M. Brambilla, T. Tokuda, and R. Tolksdorf (Eds.): ICWE 2012, LNCS 7387, pp. 452–455, 2012.

specification of the Web application requirements by using the i^* framework and helps designers to improve the quality of the Web application perceived by users by assisting them in prioritizing and making tradeoffs between NFRs, based on the Pareto efficiency algorithm. To better assess and compare different configuration, the WebREd-Tool allows to visualize them by means of radar charts. Although this work was perceived in the context of the A-OOH method [2], it is in fact a stand-alone, independent approach that can thus be used in any Web engineering method.

2 Web Requirements Modeling with i* and Pareto Efficiency

The i^* modeling framework is a goal-oriented requirements engineering (GORE) technique that incorporates social analysis by modeling the relationships between different actors. The basis of i^* is that the actors depend on each other to reach their goals successfully, to perform their tasks and to obtain the necessary resources to do so. In order to model NFRs, i^* provides softgoals which allow designer to systematically explore various design alternatives for the software system. In our previous work, the basic i^* model was adapted for the Web Engineering domain by combining it with the Web requirements classification proposed in [3]. A metamodel has defined for including requirements typically encountered in Web applications, such as service, navigational, content, personalization and layout requirements (see [2] for details).

Given an extensive i^* requirement model, the designer faces the choice which FR to implement, given time and cost constraints, so that maximum perceived user satisfaction is achieved. In other words, the aim is to balance and optimize NFRs to help the designer achieve a *good* configuration of implemented FRs: a trade-off that takes into account the priorities among NFRs and, given this priority, ensures there is no better solution. To do this, we extended our proposal with the Pareto efficiency algorithm [4], which is particularly useful when there are multiple competing and conflicting objectives that need to be balanced. Applied to the problem of optimizing NFRs, a configuration of FRs that is in the Pareto front is a solution where it is not possible to improve the satisfaction of any NFR without reducing another NFR. The set of Pareto front configurations can subsequently be used to make a well-informed decision about which requirements configuration is an optimal balance between NFRs. For a more detailed explanation of the Pareto algorithm we refer the reader to our previous work [5].

3 WebREd-Tool

The WebREd-Tool is developed by combining a set of technologies such as EMF (Eclipse Modeling Framework) and GMF (Graphical Modeling Framework) both part of the Eclipse Modeling Project (EMP)[2] and J2EE in the context of the Model-Driven Development (MDD).

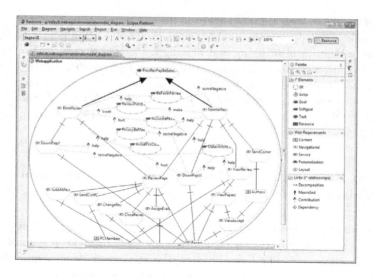

Fig. 1. WebREd-Tool implemented in Eclipse

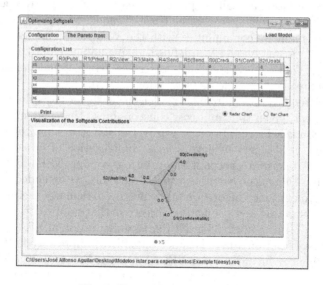

Fig. 2. ParetoVisualizationTool

The tool development consists of three main parts. The first one consists on the implementation of the adapted i^* modeling framework for the Web domain. This adaptation was made by defining a EMF metamodel and creating a specific class for each type of component of the i^* framework. In the second part, the meta-model was used within the GMF to create a graphical editor (see Figure 1). With the graphical editor, the designer can specify the Web application requirements in

---

[2] http://www.eclipse.org/modeling

a graphical environment using the i^* components such as goals, tasks, softgoals, decomposition, means-end and contribution links and the Web requirements types including service, navigational, content, personalization and layout. The tool-box is shown on the right side of Figure 1, including the aforementioned modeling elements. The third part is the implementation of the Pareto algorithm and, based on it, the visualization of requirement configurations. The implementation was carried out by using the J2EE and the EMF core classes to create the so-called Pareto Visualization Tool (see Figure 2) which works as follows: first, the softgoals that the designer wants to optimize are extracted from the i^* requirements model, then the algorithm is executed and a list of Pareto front configurations (see top of the Figure 2) are presented to the designer. From the list, the designer can select the configuration that better satisfies the softgoal(s) to optimize. To do this, the tool offers a graphical representation of each configuration by using a radar chart (see the bottom of the Figure 2) in order to help the designer with the selection of the optimal configuration.

4   Conclusions

A tool called WebREd-Tool has presented in this demo paper. This tool supports designers in both specifying Web requirements with i^* and optimizing the softgoals by means of the Pareto algorithm (including a visual representation based on radar charts). The WebREd-Tool is stand-alone, and can thus be deployed for the requirements engineering phase of any existing Web engineering method.

Acknowledgments. This work has been partially supported by: Universidad Autónoma de Sinaloa (Mexico) and MANTRA (GVC) from the University of Alicante. Sven Casteleyn is supported by an EC Marie Curie Intra-European Fellowship (IEF) for Career Development, FP7-PEOPLE-2009-IEF, N 254383.

References

1. Aguilar, J.A., Garrigós, I., Mazón, J.N., Trujillo, J.: Web Engineering approaches for requirement analysis- A Systematic Literature Review. In: Web Information Systems and Technologies (WEBIST), vol. 2, pp. 187–190. SciTePress Digital Library, Valencia (2010)
2. Aguilar, J.A., Garrigós, I., Mazón, J.N., Trujillo, J.: An MDA Approach for Goal-oriented Requirement Analysis in Web Engineering. Journal of Universal Computer Science (JUCS) 16(17), 2475–2494 (2010)
3. Escalona, M.J., Koch, N.: Requirements Engineering for Web Applications - A Comparative Study. Journal of Web Engineering 2(3), 193–212 (2004)
4. Szidarovszky, F., Gershon, M.E., Duckstein, L.: Techniques for Multiobjective Decision Making in Systems Management. Elsevier (1986)
5. Aguilar, J.A., Garrigós, I., Mazón, J.N.: A Goal-Oriented Approach for Optimizing Non-functional Requirements in Web Applications. In: ER Workshops, Web Information Systems Modeling (WISM), pp. 14–23 (2011)

Answering Fuzzy Preference Queries over Data Web Services

Soumaya Amdouni[1], Mahmoud Barhamgi[1], Djamal Benslimane[1],
Allel Hadjali[2], Karim Benouaret[1], and Rim Faiz[3]

[1] LIRIS Laboratory, Claude Bernard Lyon1 University 69622 Villeurbanne, France
[2] Enssat, University of Rennes 1 22305, Lannion, France
[3] University of Carthage-IHEC 2016 Carthage, Tunisia
[4] {samdouni,barhamgi,dbenslim,benouaret}@liris.cnrs.fr,
hadjali@enssat.fr, Rim.Faiz@ihec.rnu.tn

Abstract. This paper describes a system that supports preference query answering over a set of data Web services. The proposed system is capable to rank-order the query results in the presence of fuzzy preferences. To do so, we provide different software components organized into two main modules. The first module provides the top-k service compositions. It is mainly based on (*i*) query rewriting techniques to generate relevant services and compositions, (*ii*) fuzzy dominance relationship to rank both individual and composite services. The second module adopts a fuzzy database approach to provide a graded service composition execution engine ranking returned data results.

1 Introduction

Mashups are situational applications that join data sources to better meet the information needs of Web users. Typically, the access to data sources is carried out through Web services. This type of services is known as Data-as-a-Service [4]. Due to the Web dynamic nature, building mashups at Web scale triggers the need to set up an effective service composition framework that would identify the most relevant services, compose them, and rank the constantly-changing data items accessed by services with respect to user's preferences. In this work, we adopt a flexible approach to model preferences based on fuzzy sets theory [6].

Example. Consider a Web user planning to buy a new apartment. The user would like to find an apartment with an affordable price and located near to

Table 1. Available Web Services

Service	Functionality	Constraints
$S_1(\$c, ?s, ?t, ?r, ?a)$	Returns the schools s along with their tuition fees t, reputation r and addresses a in a given country c	$t=cheap$, $r=high$
$S_2(\$c, ?s, ?t, ?r, ?a)$		$t=expensive$, $r=good$
$S_3(\$a, ?ap, ?p)$	Returns the apartments for sale ap, their prices p at a given address a	$p=affordable$
$S_4(\$a, ?ap, ?p)$		$p=expensive$

M. Brambilla, T. Tokuda, and R. Tolksdorf (Eds.): ICWE 2012, LNCS 7387, pp. 456–460, 2012.
© Springer-Verlag Berlin Heidelberg 2012

high schools with cheap tuition fees and good reputation. A such query Q is described in SPARQL language as in Figure1. Many online data sources (e.g., apartments.com) provide the pricing information of a large set of apartments available for sale. Other yellow-pages provide various information about schools (including their locations, fees, and reputations). Assume that these information are provided by the services in Table1. Input and output parameters are proceeded by "$" and "?" respectively.

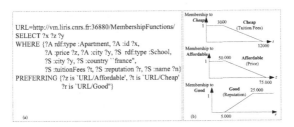

Fig. 1. (a)SPARQL query Q, (b) the associated membership functions

Challenges. Answering the fuzzy query Q over data services raises the following two main challenges:(1) *Computing the best service compositions answering the fuzzy preference queries.* This challenge necessitates to understand the semantics of the published services, to retain the most relevant services that better satisfy the user's preferences and to generate the best k compositions that satisfy the query. (2) *Ranking the results of fuzzy preference queries.* Data returned from the services invocations may partially satisfy the fuzzy preferences of the query. It is then important for a given service composition to rank-order results it may return to express how good results they are.

2   System Overview

Our system is composed of the following two modules:

2.1   Top-K Web Service Compositions

The Top-k service compositions module is provided to compute the best k compositions that answer the user query. The processing of this component is shown in window (a) Figure 2. We briefly describe below its different components, more details are provided in [1,2].

Query Rewriting. The component *RDF Query Rewriter* is provided to identify the relevant services that match all or parts of the user query. It exploits the semantic descriptions of services given in the form of SPARQL queries.

Fuzzy Constraints Matching. The *Fuzzy Constraint Matcher* component is used to compute the matching degrees between the fuzzy preference constraints of the query and the fuzzy service constraints for each relevant service. Four distinct Fuzzy Constraints Matching Methods are used and implemented to associate to each relevant service 4 degrees. Such degrees express to what extent a fuzzy service constraint matches a fuzzy query constraint.

Services Ranking. Our proposed *Services Ranker* component uses a fuzzy dominance to express the extent to which a matching degree dominates another one and associates fuzzy score with individual service.

In this step, we propose a fuzzy dominating score (FDS) for individual services. An FDS of a service S indicates the average extent to which S dominates a set of services, those answering the same subquery. Moreover, it associates fuzzy score with a composition. The score of a composition is computed as an aggregation of the scores of its services.

Top-k Compositions. This component is provided to efficiently generate the compositions that better answer a fuzzy preference query. Instead of generating all possible compositions, we compute their scores and return the top-k compositions, we provide an optimization technique that eliminates some relevant services for which we are sure that if they are composed with other ones, the obtained compositions are not in the top-k.

2.2   Query Results Ranking

The results returned by a composition may be large which may cause the users to miss the ones that are most relevant to their prefrences. We propose a fuzzy database approach to rank data returned by service composition execution [3]. Each relation R obtained from a service invocation is extended to include a new column noted *grade* that expresses to what degree a tuple t of R satisfies the fuzzy predicates and graded relation is noted by R^g. The graded relations are orchestrated using a graded relational algebra.

Formally speaking, assuming a fuzzy predicates set $FP = P_1 \wedge P_2 \wedge ... \wedge P_d$, where P_i, $i = 1...d$, is a fuzzy predicate (such that x is "cheap"...) and $\wedge$ stands for the conjunction connector. Window (b) in Figure 2 shows how the user can edit and test different fuzzy terms. A service composition execution plan is displayed on window (c). Generated service composition execution plan is expressed in terms of graded relational algebraic operators which are an adaptation of relational algebraic operators to the graded relations. The following set of graded operators are defined.

- *The Graded Invocation $Invoke^g(S, t^g_{in}, O^g)$*: Let S be a service, t^g_{in} the graded input tuple with which S is invoked, O^g the graded output, and $S.O$ be the output of S. The $Invoke^g$ computes $g_1(t_i) = \top(\mu_{P_1(t_i)}, \mu_{P_2(t_i)}, ..., \mu_{P_n(t_i)})$ where $\top$ is a t-norm operator and μ_{P_i} the membership function associated with P_i. Our system implements the following t-norms: *Zadeh, Probabilistic,* and *Lukasiewicz*.
- *Graded Join:* $\infty^g(I^g_1, I^g_2)$, where I^g_1 and I^g_2 are two graded data sets. The grade of an outputted tuple is given by: $g(\infty^g(t, t')) = \top(g(t), g(t'))$ where $\top$ is a t-norm, and t and t' are tuples from I^g_1 and I^g_2 respectively.

- *Graded Projection* $\prod_A^g$. The projection is an operation that selects specified attributes $A=\{a_1, a_2, ...\}$ from a results set. The grade of an outputted tuple t is: $g(t) = \perp (g(t_1'), .., g(t_i'), .., g(t_n'))$ where $t = \prod_A(t_i')_{i=1:n}$ and $\perp$ is the co-norm corresponding to the t-norm $\top$ used in the graded join.
- *Graded Union* $\cup^g$. The grade of an outputted tuple t is:
  $g(t) = \perp (g(t_1'), .., g(t_i'), .., g(t_n'))$, where $t_i' = t$ and $i = 1 : n$

The *Ranking aware Execution Engine* implements the defined operators and the final ranked results are displayed in window (d).

3   Demo Highlights

The demo will show all of the components in figure 2. To illustrate the robustness of our approach in different settings, we apply our scenario on a set of 200 different data services, accessing a synthetic dataset containing information about a consequent data objects of the real-estate application domain.

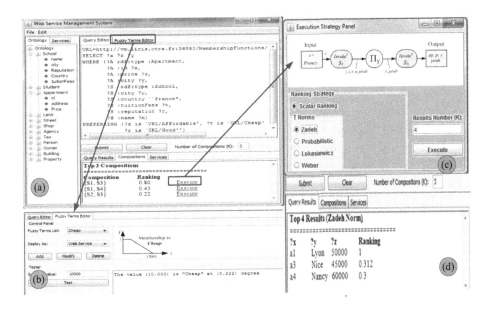

Fig. 2. Demo - Compositions and Results Ranking

References

1. Barhamgi, M., Benslimane, D., Medjahed, B.: A query rewriting approach for web service composition. IEEE T. Services Computing 3(3), 206–222 (2010)
2. Benouaret, K., Benslimane, D., HadjAli, A., Barhamgi, M.: Fudocs: A web service composition system based on fuzzy dominance for preference query answering. PVLDB 4(11), 1430–1433 (2011)

3. Bosc, P., Buckles, B.B., Petry, F.E., Pivert, O.: Fuzzy Databases, vol. 3, pp. 403–468. Kluwer Academic Publishers (1999)
4. Carey, M.J.: Soa what? IEEE Computer 41(3), 92–94 (2008)
5. Dubois, D., Prade, H.: Beyond min agregation in multicriteria decision: (ordered) weighted mean, discri-min, leximin, pp. 181–192. K.A.P (1997)
6. Zadeh, L.A.: Fuzzy sets. Information and Control 8(3), 338–353 (1965)

UsiWSC: Framework for Supporting an Interactive Web Service Composition*

Mohamed Boukhebouze, Waldemar P. Ferreira Neto,
Erbin Lim, and Philippe Thiran

PReCISE Research Center, University of Namur, 5000, Belgium
{mboukheb,waldemar.neto,erbin.lim,philippe.thiran}@fundp.ac.be

Abstract. In this paper, we propose the UsiWSC framework for designing, deploying and executing Web service compositions with user interactions. The UsiWSC design relies on an extension of the BPEL standard: UI-BPEL. The extension supports the derivation of user interfaces as well as executable compositions for different user contexts. The UsiWSC execution requires the coordination of the control and data flows between web services and user interfaces.

Keywords: Interactive Web Service Composition, BPEL, User Interface, User Interaction.

1 Introduction

A Web service composition is the process that orchestrates or choreographs a set of Web services in order to implement a business process [8]. This mechanism is used to fulfill the user request that a single Web service cannot satisfy [8]. Several initiatives have been adopted to provide languages that allow the description of Web service composition execution. Nowadays, WS-BPEL (BPEL for short) [7] has become the *de facto* standard in the industry [8]. This standard is intended to express a composition process in a fully automated way. As such, users are not able to interact with the Web services until the end of the process execution: they cannot provide input to a Web service at runtime, they cannot cancel the process execution, nor they can see some intermediary output from a Web service. However, many Web service composition scenarios require user interactions [6].

In this work, we propose the UsiWSC framework (Usable uSer Interface for Web Service Composition) that supports the design, the deployment and the execution of an interactive Web service composition. **At design time**, an interactive composition is defined based on an UI-BPEL extension [2] that supports the specification of user roles and the different types of user interactions. **At deployment time**, abstract user interfaces and BPEL are derived from UI-BPEL. Abstract user interfaces (AUI) and BPEL are not intended to be executed: they

---

* Research supported by la Wallonie.

M. Brambilla, T. Tokuda, and R. Tolksdorf (Eds.): ICWE 2012, LNCS 7387, pp. 461–464, 2012.
© Springer-Verlag Berlin Heidelberg 2012

are independent of any user context and can therefore be adapted for different use cases. **At runtime**, user contexts are used for providing concrete user interfaces (CUI) and executable BPEL.

UsiWSC is part of several initiatives to enhance BPEL with user interactions. An example of such an initiative is ActiveBPEL for People [1]. The ActiveBPEL for People framework describes an interactive WSC based on an extension of BPEL called BPEL4People [6]. BPEL4People introduces a new type of BPEL activity to specify user tasks. ActiveBPEL for People framework also supports the generation of user interfaces according to user task parameters. Another initiative is BPEL4UI [3]. This framework relies on an extension of BPEL in which *Partner Links* can be used to connect BPEL activities and user interfaces. User interfaces are developed separately from the composition. UsiWSC differs from these main initiatives in that (1) UI-BPEL of UsiWSC supports the user event interaction (a process can be cancelled by the user at any time of the composition); and (2) UsiWSC enables the generation of user interfaces adapted to the user contexts.

The rest of the paper is organized as follows. Section 2 describes the UsiWSC architecture by focusing on its main software components. Section 3 presents the online demonstration scenario that is based on a simple purchase order process.

2   UsiWSC Architecture

The UsiWSC architecture is presented in Figure 1. The figure shows the major software components (namely, the UI-BPEL designer, the transformation tools and the UI manager) and their interactions. Software components are classified according to two different views: the abstraction level (abstract or concrete) and the modeling object (user interface or Web service composition).

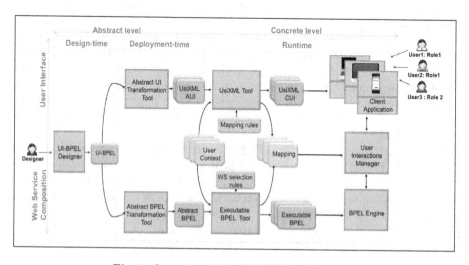

Fig. 1. Overview of the UsiWSC Architecture

2.1   UI-BPEL Designer

The UI-BPEL Designer is a tool that supports the design of a UI-BPEL process. This tool is developed as an Eclipse plug-in based on the Eclipse BPEL Designer [4]. The UI-BPEL specification enables the description of different user interactions by introducing new BPEL elements [2]: (1) a new set of BPEL activities (*DataInputUI, DataOutputUI, DataSelectionUI*) to express different user data interactions; (2) a new type of BPEL events (*InteractionEventUI*) to express the interaction event; (3) an extension of the BPEL's *Pick* and *Scope* activities that supports the new *InteractionEventUI*; (4) a new activity attribute *UserRole* that specifies the role that is assigned to a data interaction activity.

2.2   Transformation Tools

From an UI-BPEL process, the UsiWSC framework derives both a valid BPEL and the related user interfaces, first at an abstract level, and then at a concrete level. The user interfaces are described as AUI and CUI by using the UsiXML language [5] while the abstract and executable BPEL are compliant with the BPEL specification [7]. UsiXML has been chosen due to its good expressiveness to describe the different facets of user interfaces. In addition, UsiXML is in the process of being standardized by W3C.

The abstract UI transformation tool generates an AUI for each UI-BPEL role directly from an UI-BPEL process. The generated AUI describes UI independently to any user context (user preference, user device or user environment). As such, the transformation rules apply for each role and each UI-BPEL user interactions for converting them into a set of abstract UsiXML compounds (e.g. output abstract compounds, and output abstract compounds). CUI are obtained from the AUI by applying a UsiXML transformation tool. For each abstract compound, the UsiXML transformation tool creates a concrete compound based on the user context. For instance, an output abstract compound can be transformed into a label, which is expressed in the user preference language. The UsiXML transformation tool also keeps track of the transformations so that mappings can be defined between the executable BPEL and the different CUI as explained below.

The abstract BPEL transformation tool derives an abstract BPEL from the UI-BPEL. The generated abstract BPEL describes the control flow of the composition independently to any concrete Web service. Moreover, the abstract BPEL transforms each user interaction to an invocation of a particular Web service, namely the UI Manager (Section 2.3). An executable BPEL can then be generated by selecting component Web services that are involved in the composition. This selection is based on the user context and a set of predefined Web service selection rules. Note that, the Web service selection is not in the scope of this demonstration.

2.3   UI Manager

The UI manager routes data between the executable BPEL and its CUI. The routing is derived from the mappings that are automatically generated from the UsiXML transformation tool. When an executable BPEL process invokes the UI manager, the UI manager relies on the mappings between the related UI-BPEL interactions and the CUI compounds for specifying the related CUI. This CUI is displayed as a final user interface to a client application. When the user interaction is completed (e.g., data input are provided by the user), the UI manager sends the user interaction result (user data or event) to the BPEL engine.

3   Demonstration

The scenario used in the demonstration is a simple purchase order process which involves different users with different roles and contexts of use. Though simple, the demonstration scenario outlines the main features of the UsiWSC framework: (1) user interactions modeling with the UI-BPEL editor (e.g. the shipper is manually selected by an administrator (data selection)); (2) multi-role and multi-context user interfaces generation as well as an executable BPEL process generation; and (3) runtime coordination between the WSC and its UI in multi-context (different user devices). The demonstration video is available at: http://webapps.fundp.ac.be/usiwsc/index.html & http://www.youtube.com/watch?v=_py7E9zqqg4

References

1. Active-Endpoint: ActiveBPEL 4 People (2007), http://www.activebpel.org/samples/samples-4/ActiveBPELforPeople/doc/index.html
2. Boukhebouze, M., Neto, W.P.F., Erbin, L.: Yet Another BPEL Extension for User Interactions. In: De Troyer, O., Bauzer Medeiros, C., Billen, R., Hallot, P., Simitsis, A., Van Mingroot, H. (eds.) ER Workshops 2011. LNCS, vol. 6999, pp. 24–33. Springer, Heidelberg (2011)
3. Daniel, F., Soi, S., Tranquillini, S., Casati, F., Heng, C., Yan, L.: From People to Services to UI: Distributed Orchestration of User Interfaces. In: Hull, R., Mendling, J., Tai, S. (eds.) BPM 2010. LNCS, vol. 6336, pp. 310–326. Springer, Heidelberg (2010)
4. Eclipse-Fundation: Eclipse bpel designer (2011), http://www.eclipse.org/bpel/
5. ITEA2: UsiXML Project (2009), http://www.usixml.eu
6. Kloppmann, M., Koenig, D., Leymann, F., Pfau, G., Rickayzen, A., von Riegen, C., Schmidt, P., Trickovic, I.: Ws-bpel extension for people–bpel4people. Joint White Paper, IBM and SAP (2005)
7. OASI: Web Services Business Process Execution Language(BPEL) 2.0. wsbpel-specification-draft-01 (2007)
8. Zeng, L., Benatallah, B., Ngu, A.H.H., Dumas, M., Kalagnanam, J., Chang, H.: Qos-aware middleware for web services composition. IEEE Trans. Softw. Eng. 30, 311–327 (2004)

Sticklet: An End-User Client-Side Augmentation-Based Mashup Tool

Oscar Díaz and Cristóbal Arellano

ONEKIN Research Group, University of the Basque Country (UPV/EHU),
San Sebastián, Spain
{oscar.diaz,cristobal.arellano}@ehu.es
http://www.onekin.org/

Abstract. A critical aspect of mashup tools for end users is to come up with an intuitive metaphor. *Sticklet* is an augmentation-based mashup tool that conceives websites as *walls* where you can fix *HTML* fragments (*sticky notes*) from other websites. *Notes* are contextualized to the hosting website, i.e. location, parameter passing and layout should be harmonized to those of the website. A set of declarative constructs are available to declaratively specify complex *sticky notes*. *Sticklet* is realized as an internal DSL in *JavaScript* that capitalizes on browser weavers (e.g. *Greasemonkey* (*GM*)). Being full-fledged *GM* scripts, *Sticklet* benefits from the sharing repositories (e.g. *www.userscripts.org*) or management utilities (e.g. activation, installation, edition) available for *GM*.

1 Motivation

We address a special kind of mashuping known as Web augmentation [2]. Web Augmentation is to the Web what Augmented Reality is to the physical world: layering relevant content/layout/navigation over the existing Web to customize the user experience. For instance, when rendering a book at *Amazon*, it could be useful to know the prices/comments for this book at other online bookshops, or to directly check if this book is available at your library, all without leaving *Amazon*. Traditionally, this is achieved through *JavaScript (JS)* using browser weavers (e.g. *Greasemonkey*). To date, over 43 million of downloads of *Greasemonkey* scripts ground the vitality of this movement. However, these efforts are hindered by being programming intensive and prone to malware. We strive to open Web Augmentation to users other than *JS* programmers. To this end, we developed *Sticklet*, an internal DSL in *JavaScript* which targets *JS*-ignorant users. Users are expected to be computer-literate (e.g. able to write an *Excel* formula).

2 Sticklet

The lifecycle of a *Sticklet* expression (hereafter referred to as a "sticklet") includes three main stages: definition, deployment and enactment.

Definition. *Sticklet* conceives the Web as a *wall* to be decorated with *stickers* (i.e. *HTML* fragments *dynamically* obtained from other websites). The pair *(wall,*

M. Brambilla, T. Tokuda, and R. Tolksdorf (Eds.): ICWE 2012, LNCS 7387, pp. 405–400, 2012.

```
1  Metadata(<><![CDATA[
2  // ==UserScript==
3  // ...
4  // @onekin:sticklet
5  // ==/UserScript==
6  ]]></>);
7  StickletBox([
8    Sticklet("Price At BookByte for $isbn").
9    WhenOnWall("*.amazon.com/*").
10     SelectBrick("assisted").ExtractContent("assisted").As("$isbn").
11     InlayLever("link").At("after","$isbn").
12     OnTriggeringLeverBy("click").
13     LoadNote("http://www.bookbyte.com/product.aspx?isbn=$isbn").
14     SelectBrick("assisted").ExtractContent("assisted").As("$price").
15     StickNote("Price At BookByte: $price")]);
```

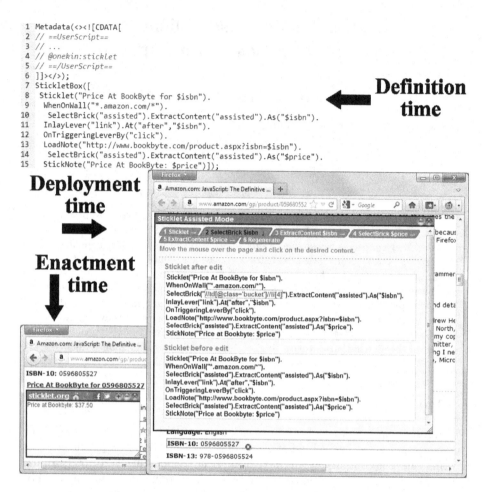

Fig. 1. *Sticklet* lifecycle: definition, deployment and enactment

sticker) conforms an augmentation unit, i.e. a ***sticklet***. Consider fixing *stickers* in *Amazon* with the prices of the current book at other online bookshops. This is a popular *JS* script known as *BookBurro* which accounts for over 900 lines of *JS* code[1]. The *sticklet* counterpart is shown in Figure 1. The constructs of the DSL include: *walls*, *bricks*, *notes* and *levers*. **Walls** (line 9) can be regarded as "views" upon existing websites. A *wall* comprises those websites whose URLs match a given regular expression (*WhenOnWall* clause). The scope of the *sticklet* is defined by its *wall* as well as the existence of some *bricks*. For our sample problem, the *wall* expands along those *Amazon* pages that hold an *ISBN brick*. **Bricks** (lines 10 & 14). They are named nodes upon *HTML* documents which are worth singularizing for either data extraction, scoping or layering purposes. A *brick* holds (1) an *XPath* to pinpoint the node (*SelectBrick* clause), (2) a

---

[1] *BookBurro* is available at http://userscripts.org/scripts/source/1859.user.js

regular expression to extract the node's content (*ExtractContent* clause), and (3), the *brick*'s name (*As* clause). **Notes** (line 15) are expressions that combine text and *bricks* (*StickNote* clause). *Bricks* can be obtained from the *wall* as well as from URL-addressable services (*LoadNote* clause, line 13). For the sample problem, a request is made to *BookByte* where URL parameters are obtained from previously extracted *bricks* (e.g. *$isbn*). The outcome is used to pinpoint a new *brick: $price*. Finally, *bricks* from different sources are used to conform the *note* (*StickNote* clause). *Notes* might be readily stuck as soon as the user enters the *wall* or displayed on demand by acting on a *lever*. **Levers** (line 11) permit to obtain *notes* on demand. *Levers* are named after the *sticklet* (e.g. *"Price At BookByte for $isbn"*) where the *brick* content is resolved at runtime. *Levers* are positioned according to *bricks*. For our sample problem, a *lever* (realized as a *link*) is inlayed *after* the brick *$isbn*. On acting upon the *lever* (in this example through a "click"), a URL-addressable service is enacted. For our sample case, on clicking, the *BookByte* request is conducted; next, the book price is obtained and finally, the *note* is rendered.

Deployment. Being Sticklet an internal DSL, *sticklets* do behave as traditional *Greasemonkey* (*GM*) scripts, e.g. the file extension is .user.js. Hence, *sticklets'* deployment is achieved in the very same way as *GM* scripts: drag&drop on *Firefox*. However, unlike *GM* scripts, *sticklets* postpone the definition of some of its clauses till deployment time. Specifically, "assisted-valued" clauses are resolved at deployment time through the help of the *Sticklet* engine. Specifically, *XPath* and regular expressions are heuristically obtained by interacting with the user. *Sticklet* intersperses a grid-like structure on top of the current *DOM* tree. As the user moves the cursor around the screen, the *DOM* node under the current cursor location is highlighted. By clicking, the user feeds the *XPath* inferring algorithm with the selected node as an example, while *Sticklet* highlights all the nodes that fulfilled the extraction pattern generated so far. This process is iterated till the desired nodes are selected. The process ends by re-generating the *sticklet* but now fully resolved and ready for enactment.

Enactment. *Sticklets* are automatically executed by *GM* when on the *wall*. Pages are augmented with the *sticklet* supplement as soon as they are loaded and lever triggered. Besides *GM* itself, this requires the previous installation of the *Sticklet* engine[2]. Over 20 *sticklets* are available at *http://userscripts.org/users/Sticklet*.

3   Related Work

Platypus is a Visual Programming Tool [4]. It obtains full-fledged *JavaScript* code for *Greasemonkey* using a graphical toolbar. Users directly act upon the current page through the *Platypus* toolbar to obtain the *GM* script. *Platypus* is a neat tool for its purpose: changing a web page based on the page itself. On the downside, visual tools might restrict the expressiveness to facilitate

---

[2] `https://addons.mozilla.org/addon/Sticklet/`

code generation (e.g. in *Platypus*, no page other than the current page can be accessed).

Chickenfoot illustrates the API approach [1]. An API introduces some abstractions that shelters users from how these abstractions are implemented *but without leaving the hosting language*. *Chickenfoot* is more expressive than *Sticklet*. *Sticklet* just focuses on a special kind of customization: augmentation. But this limited focus permits to come up with a self-contained, domain-oriented vocabulary, and to stick to this vocabulary. Unlike *APIs*, DSLs have to do without resorting to the underlying language. *Sticklets* can only contain *Sticklet* terms. No general *JS* sentences are permitted. Although this limits expressivity, it brings understandability and trustworthiness ("malware free by construction").

MashMaker illustrates a hybrid approach [3]. A distinctive aspect is that programmers and end-user asynchronously collaborate to come up with the augmentation. A *MashMaker* project encompasses three artefacts: the data extractor (graphically defined), the augmentation widget (which is separately coded in *JavaScript*), and the so-called "mashup" (graphically defined). The "mashup" links the two previous artefacts so that the widget is fed from the extractor. A library of widgets is made available by programmers to end users. This introduces two actors during augmentation: widget programmers and end-user "linkers". By contrast, *Sticklet* relies on a single user.

4   Conclusions

We introduce *Sticklet*, a textual DSL for Web Augmentation. *Sticklet* is based on *JS* but limits *JS* generality for the sake of learnability and understandability. First evidences indicate that users with no *JS* background can easily build their own *sticklets*, and, not less important, understand someone else's *sticklets*, hence promoting sharing and collaboration.

References

1. Bolin, M., Webber, M., Rha, P., Wilson, T., Miller, R.C.: Automation and Customization of Rendered Web Pages. In: Proceedings of the 18th Annual ACM Symposium on User Interface Software and Technology, Seattle, USA, pp. 163–172 (October 2005)
2. Bouvin, N.O.: Unifying Strategies for Web augmentation. In: Proceedings of the 10th ACM Conference on Hypertext and Hypermedia, Darmstadt, Germany, pp. 91–100 (February 1999)
3. Ennals, R., Brewer, E.A., Garofalakis, M.N., Shadle, M., Gandhi, P.: Intel Mash Maker: Join the Web. SIGMOD Record 36, 27–33 (2007)
4. Turner, S.R.: Platypus (2005), http://platypus.mozdev.org

NDT-Suite: A Model-Based Suite for the Application of NDT

Julián Alberto García-García[1], Manuel Alba Ortega[1],
Laura García-Borgoñon[1,2], and Maria Jose Escalona[1]

[1] IWT2 Research Group. University of Seville, Sevilla, Spain
[2] Aragon Technological Institute. Zaragoza, Spain.
{julian.garcia,manuel.alba}@iwt2.org,
laurag@ita.es, mjescalona@us.es

Abstract. In general, a methodology needs to be empowered by appropriate tool support. Despite MDE paradigm does not result friendly enough in enterprise environments, particularly, the application of transformations among models may become complex, monotonous and very expensive if there are no software tools automating the process. In this context, this research paper presents NDT-Suite. Nowadays, NDT-Suite is composed by a wide set of free Java tools which gives support to enterprises that are using NDT (Navigational Development Techniques) methodology in their projects. All of them support different aspects in NDT usage: quality assurance, exit generation or code checking, among others. These seeds set the environment for NDT usage for both research and practical use.

Keywords: Model-Driven Web Engineering, Model-Based Suite, Tools, Practical Experiences, NDT.

1   Introduction

The Model Driven Engineering paradigm (MDE) in general, and the Model-Driven Web Engineering (MDWE) in particular, came up in order to tackle the complexity of platforms and the inability of third generation languages to relief this complexity. This new paradigm intends to increase automation during the life cycle of software development and works, as primary form of expression, with definitions of models and transformation rules among these models by entailing the production of other models. In addition, if suitable tools are defined, this process could even be automatic.

However, MDWE is not easy to be applied in enterprise environments since it does not result too friendly for development teams. Concepts such as models, metamodels, transformations or QVT, among others, are not common notations in the enterprise environment and they seem too abstract and complex.

For this reason, this research paper presents how NDT [1] (Navigational Development Techniques) addresses this challenge with the aim of involving the enterprise with the power of MDE. NDT is a methodological proposal included within MDE that provides support to all phases of software life cycle: feasibility study,

M. Brambilla, T. Tokuda, and R. Tolksdorf (Eds.): ICWE 2012, LNCS 7387, pp. 469–472, 2012.
© Springer-Verlag Berlin Heidelberg 2012

requirements, analysis, design, implementation, testing and maintenance phases. For each development phase, NDT defines a set of metamodels and proposes a set of QVT transformations that enables to get one phase results from the previous one.

This paper is structured as follows. After this introduction, Section 2 presents the suite of tools for NDT. Finally, in Section 3 the final conclusions are expounded.

2   NDT-Suite

NDT-Suite[1] is a set of free Java tools that facilitates the application of NDT in real projects. With this suite, enterprises can benefit from the advantages of using MDE in their projects.

NDT-Suite works on/with a UML- based tool named Enterprise Architect[2] (EA). To select Enterprise Architect did not result an easy task. In fact, a comparative study developed by our research group and the Andalusian Regional Government concluded that this was the tool that offered the best value for money. Furthermore, EA offers several important advantages, such as the possibility of defining profiles or tools for document management by drawing UML diagrams, for instance, which have been very relevant to carry out our work.

Currently, the suite of NDT is composed by the following tools:

- NDT-Profile: it is the main tool for NDT usage. This tool is composed by a set of UML-profiles which were developed for each metamodel of NDT. These UML-profiles were defined in Enterprise Architect. With this, NDT-Profile offers the chance of gathering all the artifacts that define NDT easily and quickly, as they are integrated within the tool Enterprise Architect. Figure 1 shows a perspective of NDT-Profile.. Area (a) shows a diagram associated with the information storage requirements. Area (b) shows the package where these requirements are stored. With NDT-Profile, all NDT artifacts can be graphically specified. Area (c) shows the toolbox related to these requirements. It offers the possibility of collecting all the artifacts that define NDT in an easy and quick manner.

- NDT-Driver: it is one of the main tools of NDT methodology. It is completely based on NDT-Profile and implements a set of automated procedures so as to carry out each of the QVT transformations defined in NDT. It generates the analysis models from requirements, the design models from the analysis and the tests models from requirements. In addition, NDT-Driver allows obtaining the model requirements from the requirements collected within the feasibility study phase of the project. Moreover, NDT-Driver can be used in projects using both, a sequential life cycle and an evolutionary life cycle. Once transformations to perform have been selected, models to generate can be chosen.

- NDT-Quality [2]: it is a tool that automates most of the methodological review of a project developed with NDT-Profile. It checks both, the quality of using NDT methodology in each phase of software life cycle and the quality of traceability of MDE rules of NDT. It also provides a report in different formats describing the inconsistencies appeared during the review.

---

[1] NDT-Suite available from http://www.iwt2.org
[2] Enterprise Architect available from http://www.sparxsystems.com

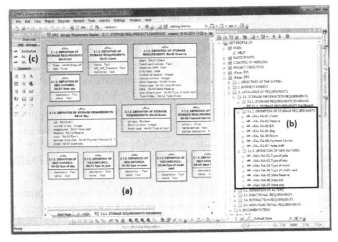

Fig. 1. A NDT-Profile Perspective

- NDT-Prototypes: it is a tool that generates a set of XHTML prototypes from the navigation models described in the analysis phase in a project developed with NDT-Profile. This tool is not related to the test phase, although it gives very good support for requirements validation.
- NDT-Glossary: it is a tool in its suite offered by NDT which uses the model-driven paradigm to generate a glossary from the requirements model. This tool allows engineers to gather and define the more relevant and critical concepts to the system. Furthermore, the use of a common glossary reduces the risk of misunderstandings and facilitates communication between users and analysts.
- NDT-Counter: This tool provides a measure of effort required to develop a project. This measurement is based on the use case technique [3].
- NDT-Report: it is a tool to generate PDF documents from NDT-Profile.

The demo of [8] shows how to use NDT-Quality to validate the requirements phase which has been specified using NDT-Profile, how to use NDT-Driver for generating the different models of the analysis phase the from requirements phase, and finally how to use NDT-Prototypes to generate XHTML prototypes.

3   Conclusions

The application of MDE becomes complex, monotonous and very expensive if there are no software tools automating the process. To meet this need, NDT has defined a set of supporting tools called NDT-Suite. In the last ten years, NDT and NDT-Suite were used in a high number of real projects. In fact, NDT-Suite is currently being used in several projects developed by different companies, either public or privates, big or small. On the one hand, public companies such as the Andalusian Regional Cultural Ministry, the Andalusian Regional Health Ministry, among others, are using NDT and NDT-Suite. Private ICT companies in Andalusia also are using NDT in some of theirs projects.

The main advantage of NDT-Suite is that it reduces the cost of ensuring the quality and traceability of the deliverables carried out during the project development phases (requirements, analysis, design, etc.). It also reduces the cost of deliverables from one phase because they are obtained from other deliverables of the previous phase, through MDE rules. On the other hand, we are working on how to extend NDT to provide support in the implementation phase of a Web project. Only few Web engineering methods support the systematic development of Web applications with a mature CASE tool. Thus, some methodologies like OO-H methods [4] with Visual-WADE[3] and WebML [5], WebRatio[4], OOWS[6] with Olivanova[5] or UWE[7] with UWE4JSF[6] are some specific solution that offer code generation in a MDE context.

Acknowledgement. This research has been supported by Tempros project (TIN2010-20057-C03-02) and Red CaSA (TIN 2010-12312-E) of the Ministerio de Ciencia e Innovación, Spain and NDTQ-Framework project of the Junta de Andalucia, Spain (TIC-5789).

References

1. Escalona, M.J., Aragón, G.: NDT. A Model-driven Approach for Web requirements. IEEE Transaction on Software Engineering 34(3) (2008)
2. Escalona, M.J., Gutiérrez, J.J., Pérez-Pérez, M., Molina, A., Martínez-Force, E., Domínguez-Mayo, F.J.: Measuring the Quality of Model-Driven Projects with NDT-Quality. In: Information System Development, vol. 1, ch. 26, pp. 307–317. Science Business Media, LLC 2009, USA (2011) ISBN/ISSN: 978-1-4419-7355-9
3. Karner, G.: Resource Estimation for Objectory Projects. Objective Systems SF AB (1993)
4. Gómez, J., Cachero, C., Pastor, O.: On Conceptual Modeling of Device-Independent Web Applications: Towards a Web-Engineering Approach. IEEE Multimedia 8(2), 26–39 (2001)
5. Ceri, S., et al.: Designing Data-Intensive Web Applications. Morgan Kaufmann, San Francisco (2002)
6. Fons, J., Pelechano, V., Albert, M., Pastor, Ó.: Development of Web Applications from Web Enhanced Conceptual Schemas. In: Song, I.-Y., Liddle, S.W., Ling, T.-W., Scheuermann, P. (eds.) ER 2003. LNCS, vol. 2813, pp. 232–245. Springer, Heidelberg (2003)
7. Koch, N.: Software Engineering for Adaptive Hypermedia Applications. Ph. Thesis, FAST Reihe Softwaretechnik, vol. (12). Uni-Druck Publishing Company, Munich, Germany (2001)
8. IWT2. Video demonstration of NDT-Suite available from canal youtube of IWT2 Research Group,
   http://www.youtube.com/watch?v=uLDrqz9t690&feature=plcp

---

[3] http://www.visualwade.com/
[4] http://www.webratio.com
[5] http://www.care-t.com
[6] http://uwe.pst.ifi.lmu.de/toolUWE4JSF.html

Enriching Web Applications with Collaboration Support Using Dependency Injection

Matthias Heinrich[1], Franz Josef Grüneberger[1],
Thomas Springer[2], and Martin Gaedke[3]

[1] SAP Research, Germany
{matthias.heinrich,franz.josef.grueneberger}@sap.com
[2] Dresden University of Technology, Germany
thomas.springer@tu-dresden.de
[3] Chemnitz University of Technology, Germany
martin.gaedke@cs.tu-chemnitz.de

Abstract. Web-based collaboration tools such as Google Docs are pervasive in our daily lives since they have proven to efficiently support joint work of distributed teams. Nevertheless, the development of web-based groupware systems is a time-consuming and costly task because developers either have to become familiar with specific groupware libraries or are asked to re-implement concurrency control services (i.e. document synchronization, conflict resolution). Therefore, we propose a dependency injection mechanism using declarative annotations to incorporate concurrency control services into web applications. Instead of adopting comprehensive libraries or implementing application-specific components, synchronization capabilities are integrated in a lightweight and rapid fashion. To validate the approach, we enriched the widely-adopted Knockout framework with dependency injection facilities and transformed two Knockout-based applications into collaborative ones.

1 Introduction

In the course of the Web 2.0 movement, numerous collaborative web applications such as Google Docs or EtherPad have emerged and were rapidly adopted. In contrast to single-user web applications, the development of collaborative web applications requires additional services such as document synchronization and conflict resolution. While the document synchronization is in charge of reconciling all documents copies, the conflict resolution mechanism handles conflicts emerging when multiple users simultaneously change the very same document artifacts. To incorporate concurrency control services (i.e. document synchronization, conflict resolution), developers either have to learn new Application Programming Interfaces (APIs) or are asked to implement the required functionality themselves. Both traditional approaches are time-consuming and costly. Therefore, we propose to annotate existing single-user applications with dependency injection tags which can, in contrast to traditional approaches, considerably ease the task of integrating groupware-specific features. Thus, the groupware development efficiency can eventually be increased.

M. Brambilla, T. Tokuda, and R. Tolksdorf (Eds.): ICWE 2012, LNCS 7387, pp. 473–476, 2012.
© Springer-Verlag Berlin Heidelberg 2012

The rest of this paper is organized as follows: Section 2 discusses related work. Section 3 describes the system architecture, the workflow to inject collaboration services as well as the demo applications and Section 4 exhibits conclusions.

2   Related Work

In this section, we expose a number of approaches promising to rapidly integrate concurrency control services in web applications.

The generic transformation approach [1] aims to enhance existing single-user web applications with shared editing capabilities exploiting the so-called Generic Collaboration Infrastructure (GCI). The GCI allows recording, propagating and replaying arbitrary Document Object Model (DOM) manipulations among all sites. In contrast to our approach, the GCI cannot synchronize web applications leveraging a separate JavaScript data model (e.g. Knockout-based applications).

Apache Wave [2] is a full-fledged collaboration framework facilitating concurrency control and allowing to either create *extensions* or *client applications*. While extensions are defined adopting a specific XML syntax, client applications are built using a Java or Python API. Therefore, Apache Wave is dedicated to develop widgets or applications from scratch rather than enriching existing ones.

ShareJS [3] and OpenCoWeb [4] are two JavaScript libraries supplying concurrency control services. Including document objects in the synchronization procedure requires various API calls (e.g. object registration, value propagation or callback implementation). In comparison to our compact dependency injection syntax, the libraries expose a verbose binding language entailing cumbersome and scattered code changes.

3   System Architecture and Demonstration

Dependency Injection (DI) has proven to be an efficient means to eliminate boilerplate code and thus, it has been adopted in numerous development toolkits (e.g. the Java Enterprise Edition 6 or the Eclipse e4 framework). We leverage DI in order to furnish a lightweight integration approach capable of speeding up the incorporation of concurrency control services in web applications. In this section, we present the devised collaboration architecture and the enhanced Knockout[1] framework [5] which has been enriched with DI facilities.

The system architecture materializing the approach of concurrency control injection is depicted in Figure 1(a). The shown sync server connects numerous clients and provides a sync service that is based on the prevalent concurrency control algorithm called Operational Transformation (OT) [6]. All clients exhibit a stack encompassing Knockout components (the UI and the View-Model) as well as synchronization components (the Knockout Adapter and the OT Engine). The OT Engine is in charge of sending out local changes, receiving remote changes

---

[1] We chose to enrich the Knockout framework because of its massive developer adoption (e.g. Knockout 2 reached 110 000 downloads in 3 months).

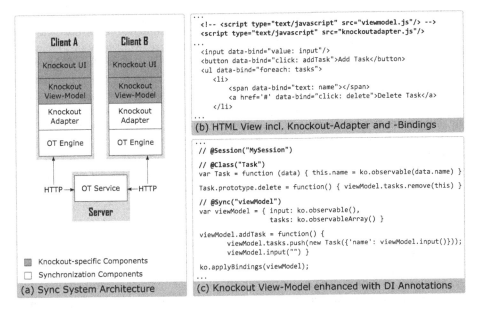

Fig. 1. System architecture and minimal dependency injection example

and incorporating all those modifications in a dedicated OT data model. The associated Knockout Adapter links the OT model with the View-Model (VM), i.e. VM changes are propagated to the OT model and vice versa.

To introduce the workflow enriching Knockout applications with concurrency control support, we use a minimal example where multiple users can simultaneously edit a list of tasks. Figure 1(b) depicts an excerpt of an HTML page representing the Knockout UI. The main HTML elements are the input element to enter the task name, a button to add the new task and a list showing all tasks accompanied by a delete button. Additionally, Knockout-specific `data-bind` expressions establish data-bindings to the VM. Our UI enhancements, highlighted using bold text, are limited to the replacement of the original Knockout VM (encapsulated in the `<!-- / -->` tags) with our "knockoutadapter.js" script. This script contains the generic sync adapter as well as the parser logic which allows to locate and eventually to replace DI annotations with the actual source code carrying out the synchronization. Moreover, the script imports an application-specific configuration to specify the file name of the VM, the VM elements that should be excluded from the sync, etc. The VM associated to the HTML view is illustrated in Figure 1(c) whereas changes to the original VM are reflected once again in bold text. The complete set of DI annotations encompasses @Session, @Class and @Sync annotations which are always accommodated in comments to prevent JavaScript errors. The @Session annotation enables session management by exploiting the Session-ID argument (e.g. "MySession"). The @Sync annotation specifies the model that should by synchronized among all clients. In our example, the `input` property and the `tasks` array are part of the sync model. Note that Knockout VMs can comprise three types of observable objects (properties, computed properties and arrays) which all supply a notification mechanism capable of informing subscribers about changes. This notification mechanism is exploited to record local changes which are eventually propagated. Besides recording changes, remote edits have to be replayed locally. Therefore, the last annotation @Class marks object constructors allowing the sync mechanism to re-create objects (e.g. a `Task`) using the appropriate constructor function.

To validate our approach, we implemented the proposed architecture on top of the OT platform SAP Gravity [7] and the widely-adopted Knockout framework. In the validation we included two Knockout-based to-do applications. While TodoMVC [8] is a ready-for-use single-user application, our MyTodoApp was developed from scratch. Both applications were enhanced with DI annotations injecting concurrency control services and eventually could support collaborative work. The results are exposed on our demo page `http://vsr.informatik.tu-chemnitz.de/demo/DI/`.

4   Conclusion

In this paper, we presented an approach to add concurrency control support by means of dependency injection. In contrast to adopting verbose programming libraries, the proposed approach exposes an easy-to-learn and compact syntax. Thus developers are empowered to efficiently program new collaborative applications or to rapidly migrate existing single-user applications to collaborative applications. Even though the Knockout framework was exclusively enriched with dependency injection facilities, the approach could be transferred to other JavaScript libraries exhibiting a separation of the view and the data model. Moreover, we noted that besides concurrency control, workspace awareness is another essential collaboration service exposing what other users are doing in the shared space. Thus, injecting awareness services is a challenging research question we will try to tackle in future work.

References

1. Heinrich, M., Lehmann, F., Springer, T., Gaedke, M.: Exploiting single-user web applications for shared editing: a generic transformation approach. In: WWW, pp. 1057–1066 (2012)
2. Apache Software Foundation: Apache Wave (2011),
   http://incubator.apache.org/wave/
3. Gentle, J.: ShareJS – Concurrent editing in your app. (2012),
   http://sharejs.org/
4. The Dojo Foundation: OpenCoWeb Framework (2012), http://opencoweb.org/
5. Sanderson, S.: Knockout: Home (2012), http://knockoutjs.com/
6. Ellis, C.A., Gibbs, S.J.: Concurrency Control in Groupware Systems. In: SIGMOD Conference, pp. 399–407 (1989)
7. Rickayzen, A.: Simple way to model processes in the Web (2011),
   http://www.sdn.sap.com/irj/scn/weblogs?blog=/pub/wlg/25360
8. Osmani, A., Boushley, A., Sorhus, S.: TodoMVC (2012),
   http://addyosmani.github.com/todomvc/

XFormsDB: A Declarative Web Application Framework

Markku Laine, Denis Shestakov, and Petri Vuorimaa

Department of Media Technology, Aalto University
P.O. Box 15500, FI-00076 Aalto, Finland
{markku.laine,denis.shestakov,petri.vuorimaa}@aalto.fi

Abstract. Most Web applications utilize a three-tier architecture, in which the presentation, application logic, and data management are implemented as separate tiers. The disadvantage of this popular approach is that it usually requires expertise in multiple programming languages and paradigms as well as data models used in each tier. A single expert rarely masters all the technologies involved. In this demonstration, we give an overview of the XFormsDB framework that allows developers to implement entire Web applications using only markup languages. The framework is based on the XForms markup language and our server-side extensions. We demonstrate the functionality of the framework using a simple blog application as an example.

Keywords: Web Framework, Web Application, Web Development, Declarative Language, XForms, XFormsDB.

1   Introduction

Highly interactive data-driven Web applications enrich the Web user experience. However, their development is complex because developers need not only to know multiple systems, frameworks, best practices, and languages, but also to deal with their conceptual dissimilarities [1]. Indeed, both imperative (e.g., Java and JavaScript) and declarative (e.g., CSS, HTML, and SQL) languages are often used together when implementing Web applications.

To provide support for complete Web application development (i.e., client-side and server-side application logic, client-server communication, and interaction), the client-side (presentation tier) and server-side (logic and data tiers) programming can be done under a single model. This architectural approach simplifies the development process, and particularly reduces the skill set required from a developer. For instance, Google Web Toolkit (GWT)[1] realizes a server-side approach, in which a general-purpose programming language (i.e., object-oriented imperative Java) is used to author not only the server-side application logic but also a Web application user interface. Similarly, a client-side programming language (e.g., XForms [2]) can be extended with server-side functionalities to cover all three tiers of a Web application. An extensive comparison of frameworks realizing different *tier-expanding* architectural approaches can be found in [3].

---

[1] Google Web Toolkit (GWT), http://developers.google.com/web-toolkit/

M. Brambilla, T. Tokuda, and R. Tolksdorf (Eds.): ICWE 2012, LNCS 7387, pp. 477–480, 2012.
© Springer-Verlag Berlin Heidelberg 2012

In this demonstration, we overview XFormsDB [4], a tier-expanding Web application framework based on the XForms markup language and our server-side extensions. We describe and demonstrate its functionality by showcasing a full-fledged Web application utilizing the framework.

The advantages of the XFormsDB framework are as follows. First, as the XML data model is used on all three tiers, developers can avoid complex mappings between different data models. Second, at a minimum, developers only need to learn one markup language (i.e., XHTML 2.0) and few XForms server-side extensions. Third, all the core languages are declarative, and thus are more preferable to people with limited programming skills (particularly, to Web user interface developers, who are already familiar with declarative XHTML and CSS) [5]. Fourth, the framework is extensible: on the presentation tier, JavaScript can add animations and interactivity; on the logic tier, XQuery extension functions can extend server-side application logic; and on the data tier, XQuery can complement the more limited XPath language.

2   XFormsDB: Language and Framework Implementation

The standard XForms [2] offers only client-side functionality. Our XFormsDB markup language extends XForms with common server-side and database-related functionalities, allowing developers to implement all three tiers (i.e., presentation, logic, and data) of a Web application using only markup languages. The design of XFormsDB addresses the following general requirements of a Web application: *persistent storage*; *error handling*; *session management and security*; *modularity*; *state maintenance*; *authentication, authorization, and access control*; *uniform syntax and processing model*; and *extensible architecture* [4].

Listing 1 illustrates an example of the XFormsDB extension syntax[2]. This code snippet can be included into the `head` part of an XHTML document to provide an inclusion and authorization functionality.

```
<xformsdb:include resource="../xinc/meta.xinc"/>
<xformsdb:secview>
  <xforms:model>
    <xforms:load resource="../login.xformsdb"
      ev:event="xforms-ready"/>
  </xforms:model>
</xformsdb:secview>
<xformsdb:secview roles="admin">...
</xformsdb:secview>
```

Listing 1. XFormsDB code example

---

[2] For space and readability reasons, the source code (available at `http://tinyurl.com/xformsdb-blog-sc`) may differ from the code snippets shown in Listings 1-4.

As a Proof-of-Concept, we implemented the XFormsDB framework, a generic platform for developing and hosting Web applications based on the XForms markup language and our server-side extensions. The architecture of the framework is given in [4] and the framework itself is available at `http://code.google.com/p/xformsdb/`.

3   XFormsDB: Demo Description

Next, we showcase XFormsDB with a simple blog application. The application and its source code are available at `http://testbed.tml.hut.fi/blog` and `http://tinyurl.com/xformsdb-blog-sc`, respectively. The blog application has two main user interfaces, one for end users and the other for administrators. The user interfaces look and feel like any other modern Web application, i.e., they give a fast response to user inputs and remain responsive while submitted requests are being processed on the server side.

The internal architecture of the application separates the code on each Web page into the three logical tiers: data, logic, and presentation. We walk through, step by step, how a query is defined and submitted to a server, and then executed against the data stored in a database. The example continues by showing how the query result is sent back to the client, and finally ends up being displayed in the user interface.

Data Tier. The database stores published blog posts and comments in a single XML document (`blog.xml`). The hierarchical document structure has three levels: the `root` element followed by a series of blog `post` child elements, each including `comment` elements. All `post` and `comment` elements have unique identifiers. Listing 2 shows an XPath expression, which selects one blog post—defined by an external variable *$id*—and extracts its comments from the database.

Logic Tier. We divide the code responsible for the application logic between the client and the server on each Web page. We define the client-side application logic using standard XForms, whereas our XForms extensions are responsible for the application logic on the server side. Listing 3 shows a *query* command, which uses the XPath expression of Listing 2. The code snippet in Listing 4 submits the *query* command to the server, where it is securely executed against the `blog.xml` document stored in the database. For triggering the submission, the standard XForms `send` action is used. After a successful submission, the *query* result extracted from the database is stored in an XForms `instance` element, whose original content is replaced with the extracted data.

Presentation Tier. The blog user interface controls (e.g., input and output) are bound to the data in XForms `instance` elements. The user interfaces are updated every time the data in XForms `instance` elements changes, such as in the case when *query* results are received from the server.

```
/root/blog/posts/post[ @id = $id ]/comments
```

Listing 2. XPath expression to extract the comments of a selected blog post

```
<xformsdb:instance id="select-and-update-comments">
  <xformsdb:query datasrc="exist-db" doc="blog.xml">
    <xformsdb:expression resource=
      "xpath/select_and_update_comments.xpath" />
    <xformsdb:xmlns prefix="xformsdb"
      uri="http://www.tml.tkk.fi/2007/xformsdb" />
    <xformsdb:var name="id" />
  </xformsdb:query>
</xformsdb:instance>
```

Listing 3. Definition of a *query* command

```
<xformsdb:submission id="sub-select-comments"
  replace="instance" instance="comments"
  requestinstance="select-and-update-comments"
  expressiontype="select">
  <xforms:action ev:event="xforms-submit-done">...
  </xforms:action>
  <xforms:action ev:event="xformsdb-request-error">...
  </xforms:action>
</xformsdb:submission>
```

Listing 4. Definition of a *query* command submission

4   Conclusions

In this demonstration, we overviewed XFormsDB, a comprehensive Web application framework based on the XForms markup language and our server-side extensions. We demonstrated the functionality of the framework using a simple blog application as an example. The application looks and feels like any modern Web application. In addition, it runs on all modern Web browsers.

References

1. Mikkonen, T., Taivalsaari, A.: Web Applications — Spaghetti Code for the 21st Century. Technical Report SMLI TR-2007-166, Sun Microsystems (2007)
2. Boyer, J.: XForms 1.1. W3C Recommendation, http://www.w3.org/TR/xforms/
3. Laine, M., Shestakov, D., Litvinova, E., Vuorimaa, P.: Toward Unified Web Application Development. IEEE IT Professional 13(5), 30–36 (2011)
4. Laine, M., Shestakov, D., Vuorimaa, P.: Extending XForms with Server-Side Functionality. In: 27th ACM Symposium on Applied Computing (SAC 2012), pp. 688–695. ACM, New York (2012)
5. Schmitz, P.: The SMIL 2.0 Timing and Synchronization Model — Using Time in Documents. Technical Report MSR-TR-2001-01, Microsoft Research (2001)

A Framework for Service Discovery Based on Structural Similarity and Quality Satisfaction

Fernando Lemos[1], Ahmed Gater[1], Daniela Grigori[2], and Mokrane Bouzeghoub[1]

[1] Versailles University, 45 Av. des États Unis 78000 Versailles, France
{fernando.lemos,ahmed.gater,mokrane.bouzeghoub}@prism.uvsq.fr
[2] Paris-Dauphine Univ., Pl. Maréchal de Lattre de Tassigny 75775 Paris, France
daniela.grigori@dauphine.fr

Abstract. The increasing number of published web services rendered the searching for a service within repositories a critical issue in many application domains. Recent approaches resorted to service structure and to preferences over quality attributes to reduce selectivity rate. In this paper, we present *S-MatchMaker*, a tool for service discovery based on both service structure and quality preferences. The tool implements several algorithms that can be coupled in different ways to provide a personalized solution for service discovery.

Keywords: Web service discovery, QoS, process model matching.

1   Introduction

The increasing number of published web services rendered searching for a specific service within repositories a critical issue for the success of service computing in general. On the functional aspect, recent approaches [1,2] invited users to detail their requirements by specifying a process model (PM) describing the structure of the requested service, and thus PM matchmaking techniques were necessary to find the services best matching the query. On the non-functional aspect, one way to discriminate between structurally similar services is to consider non-functional requirements such as quality preferences (e.g., response time) [3,4].

In previous works, we provided to the service discovery problem a number of contributions based on the PM specification of the service and on quality preferences [2,5,6,7]. These contributions are composed of (i) two heuristics to reduce the execution time of PM matchmaking, which is NP-complete, and (ii) a set of metrics from classic and fuzzy logics to evaluate structural similarity and quality preference satisfaction. In our approaches, services have their behavior represented by a PM graph adorned with QoS annotations, which can be also defined at the activity level. The user query is also a PM graph complemented with a set of selection clauses, which are defined either as required (hard preferences) or preferred criteria (soft preferences). The service discovery is seen as a matching process between the user query PM and a target PM. These contributions have been implemented to forge a flexible tool, called *S-MatchMaker*, capable of coupling different approaches for personalizing service discovery based on structural and quality aspects, as it will be described in the following sections.

M. Brambilla, T. Tokuda, and R. Tolksdorf (Eds.): ICWE 2012, LNCS 7387, pp. 481–485, 2012.
© Springer-Verlag Berlin Heidelberg 2012

2 Architecture

The modules of S-MatchMaker, depicted in Figure 1, are executed as follows:

First, input query and target PMs, described in OWL-S or BPEL (the two most used languages for describing service composition), are parsed into our abstract graph model [2,5] by the *Parser* module. Next, *Service PM Matchmaking* module finds a mapping between query and target graphs based on the name and input/output similarities between activities. An optional heuristic based on graph summarization can be used to reduce the matchmaking time [8].

At the same time, the *Hard Preference Evaluation* module evaluates the satisfaction degrees of hard preferences when each pair of activity is matched (activity preferences) and when a mapping of two graphs is discovered (process preferences). A mapping is discarded whenever it disrespect a hard preference [5,7]. After that, the *Soft Preference Evaluation* module evaluates the satisfaction degrees of soft preferences.

The *Structural Similarity Metric* calculates the structural similarity degree from the mapping between query and target graphs. Four metrics were implemented: one is the sum of the mapping dissimilarities [2], another is based on linguistic quantifiers [6] and two others are based on bipolar conditions [7].

The *Preference Satisfaction Metric* aggregates the satisfaction degrees of hard and soft preferences. Three methods were implemented: one is the weighted average of satisfaction degrees [5], another is based on linguistic quantifiers [6] and the last one is based on a bipolar condition [7].

Then, the *Degree Aggregation* module provides four methods to aggregate structural similarity and preference satisfaction degrees: weighted average of structural similarity and preference satisfaction [5], min-combination of structural and preference degrees [6] and two other based on bipolar conditions [7].

Finally, the mapping and the similarity degree based on structural similarity and preference satisfaction for each query and its potential targets are returned.

The S-MatchMaker tools is very extensible: developers can use its API to create new parsers, matchmaking algorithms, similarity metrics, etc., and attach them to the tool. A Web interface offering less functionalities can be found at http://infosystems.prism.uvsq.fr:8080/WebMatchMaker.

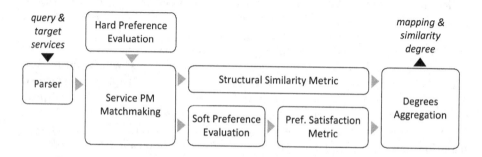

Fig. 1. S-MatchMaker architecture

3   Using S-MatchMaker

A typical session with S-MatchMaker is depicted in Figure 2. It starts with the
user loading the service repository over which one or more queries will be posed

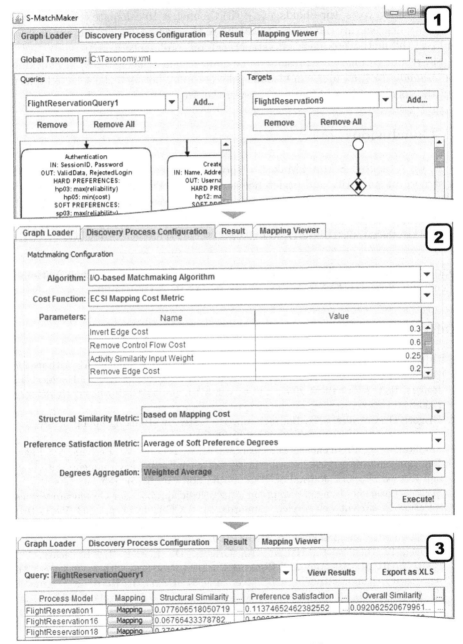

Fig. 2. A session with S-MatchMaker

(step 1). Through a BPMN[1] representation of the service PM, user can analyze the query/target structure and its preference/quality annotations.

In step 2, the user configures the discovery process by selecting: (i) the matchmaking algorithm to be executed (either the default I/O-based algorithm or the algorithm with the summarization heuristic) and defining its specific parameters (edit operation costs, thresholds, etc.); (ii) the metric to calculate the structural similarity degree; (iii) the metric to calculate the preference satisfaction degree; and (iv) the method to aggregate structural and preference degrees.

The results by query are presented in a dedicated interface (step 3). By clicking the *Mapping* button, user can visualize the mapping between the selected query and the corresponding potential target in the *Mapping Viewer* tab.

4   Conclusions

Here, we presented S-MatchMaker, a tool for service discovery process based on structural similarity and preference satisfaction. The tool features a graphical interface to load service PMs, configure the discovery process and visualize the results. Its modular architecture can be adapted to other service discovery approaches based on structural similarity and/or preference satisfaction.

Acknowledgment. This work has received support from the French National Agency for Research (ANR) on the reference ANR-08-CORD-009.

References

1. Dijkman, R., Dumas, M., García-Bañuelos, L.: Graph Matching Algorithms for Business Process Model Similarity Search. In: Dayal, U., Eder, J., Koehler, J., Reijers, H.A. (eds.) BPM 2009. LNCS, vol. 5701, pp. 48–63. Springer, Heidelberg (2009)
2. Grigori, D., Corrales, J.C., Bouzeghoub, M., Gater, A.: Ranking bpel processes for service discovery. IEEE TSC 3, 178–192 (2010)
3. Mokhtar, S.B., Preuveneers, D., Georgantas, N., Issarny, V., Berbers, Y.: Easy: Efficient semantic service discovery in pervasive computing environments with QoS and context support. Journal of Systems and Software 81(5), 785–808 (2008)
4. Şora, I., Lazăr, G., Lung, S.: Mapping a fuzzy logic approach for QoS-aware service selection on current web service standards. In: ICCC-CONTI, pp. 553–558 (2010)
5. Lemos, F., Gater, A., Grigori, D., Bouzeghoub, M.: Adding preferences to semantic process model matchmaking. In: GAOC (2011)
6. Abbaci, K., Lemos, F., Hadjali, A., Grigori, D., Liétard, L., Rocacher, D., Bouzeghoub, M.: Selecting and Ranking Business Processes with Preferences: An Approach Based on Fuzzy Sets. In: Meersman, R., Dillon, T., Herrero, P., Kumar, A., Reichert, M., Qing, L., Ooi, B.-C., Damiani, E., Schmidt, D.C., White, J., Hauswirth, M., Hitzler, P., Mohania, M. (eds.) OTM 2011, Part I. LNCS, vol. 7044, pp. 38–55. Springer, Heidelberg (2011)

---

[1] http://www.bpmn.org

7. Abbaci, K., Lemos, F., Hadjali, A., Grigori, D., Liétard, L., Rocacher, D., Bouzeghoub, M.: A bipolar approach to the handling of user preferences in business processes retrieval. In: IPMU (to appear, 2012)
8. Gater, A., Grigori, D., Bouzeghoub, M.: Complex mapping discovery for semantic process model alignment. In: iiWAS, pp. 317–324 (2010)

WebTribe: Dynamic Community Analysis from Online Forums

Damien Leprovost[1], Lylia Abrouk[1], and David Gross-Amblard[2]

[1] Le2i CNRS Lab, University of Bourgogne, Dijon, France
`firstname.lastname@u-bourgogne.fr`
[2] IRISA, University of Rennes I, France

Abstract. In this demonstration we present WEBTRIBE, a tool for community discovery based on the analysis of large discussion forums or e-mail repositories[1]. In this tool, communications are tracked in real time, analyzed according to a reference ontology, and a summary of users' activity is built in an incremental way. The demonstration will illustrate how communities are identified and updated depending on the semantics and structure of communications between users.

1 Introduction

Discussion forums constitute a well-known advertising tool for companies, as they attract existing and potential customers on the company's website, give product insights, and show the company openness and activity. In this context, the *community manager* is an emerging role in such companies. Typically, the community manager, aside the traditional task of moderating forums and managing topics, has to monitor the forum activity, report on existing sub-communities, identify expert users and opinion leaders for specific targeting (advertising, special offers, ...). But due to the exploding rate of forum contributions, monitoring tools are needed to assist the manager.

In this demonstration we will present WEBTRIBE, a system that allows community managers to perform these tasks on various kind of forums or public e-mails archives in a scalable and incremental way. Our model encompasses every type of user communications (forums, tweets, emails, ...), as soon as a specific wrapper is provided (we give such a wrapper for a specific healthcare company forum). Several analysis axes can be considered in forum analysis: users connections and posting rates, citations (replies) between users, and post content. Existing methods usually rely for the latter on term frequencies, a method that allows to give a rough overview of the forum activity. In WEBTRIBE, we enable the community manager to be active, by giving a controlled term vocabulary in the form of a target ontology. It also allows reasoning within the ontology: a user posting terms (concepts) such as *ventricle*, *aorta* or *vena cava* will be identified as a *heart* expert, while this term never appears explicitly in the user's posts.

---

[1] An earlier version of this demo has already been presented at the French conference BDA 2011, which has informal proceedings and does not retain any copyright.

M. Brambilla, T. Tokuda, and R. Tolksdorf (Eds.): ICWE 2012, LNCS 7387, pp. 486–489, 2012.

Concept analysis allows a real-time interpretation of the evolution of communities. This demonstration proposal is organized as follows. After briefly presenting the related work, we present our model (Section 2) and detail the architecture of the WEBTRIBE system (Section 3) along with the scenario of our demonstration.

Related Work. The importance of comment activity on blogs was the subject of several studies [5]. Previous works have focused on highlighting the structure of discussions within new articles, in order to determine popular topics, conflicts of opinion [7,3,1], or relational implications between users [2,6]. In these works, ontologies are not used to structure the vocabulary or refine the analysis. Dedicated ontologies like SIOC[2] exist for structuring forums. Our approach is complementary, as it allows a community manager to analyze external forums with a specific ontology (say a brand product), different from the forum's SIOC. Moreover, there are still numerous forums without such SIOC structurations. The model underlying this demo was detailed in our previous work [4].

2   Model and Architecture

Figure 1 shows an example of communications in a healthcare forum, where Alice, Joey and Bob discuss. In order to finely define the axis of the forum semantic analysis, we rely on a domain or generic ontology, as uses in Figure 3, which describes concepts with their subconcept relation (we restrict our attention to structural relations like is-a, part-of, sort-of, etc.). Choosing a target ontology enables a flexible forum exploration: a generic ontology like WordNet for a forum overview, a specific, e.g. brand product ontology for a specific tracking of topics.

Given a post, we identify its author (according to the forum API or syntactic rules of the Web page). The set of concepts occurring in the post is computed by stemming the post and removing stop-words, and by comparison with the (stemmed terms of the) ontology (for example, terms `arm` and `shoulder` in Figure 1 are identified as relevant concepts). During posts analysis, the running *user profile* for each user is computed, as the sum of concepts occurrences in

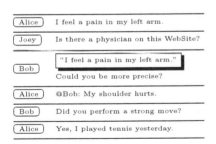

Fig. 1. Posts in a forum

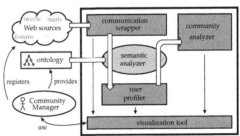

Fig. 2. WEBTRIBE architecture

---

[2] http://www.sioc-project.org/, 2012.

the ontology. Figure 3 shows the profile of a user who used once the concept `shoulder`, 16 times `humerus` and 8 times `biceps`. Interpreting such profiles can be tedious, due to the huge potential number of concepts. In order to overcome this difficulty, we build a *user abstract* by saturating the following rules:

Relevance. If a concept occurrence, relatively to the other concepts, is smaller than the relevance threshold $\delta_{relevance}$, the concept is discarded in the abstract. This limits the impact of terms used occasionally, and favor long-term interests.

Coverage. If almost all subconcepts of a concept c are covered (non-zero occurrence), the concept c itself receives the average occurrence. The fraction of covered concepts required is controlled by the $\delta_{coverage}$ threshold. This models the fact that a user, talking significantly about `biceps`, `humerus` and `triceps`, should indeed be considered as talking about `arm`, with the corresponding strength.

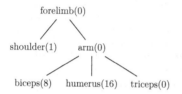 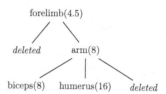

Fig. 3. User profile   **Fig. 4.** User abstract

Observe that we do not rely on a tf-idf computation for concepts detection because we want to perform generalization. Choosing the value of these thresholds depends on the ontology and the forum pace, and is managed for now by a manual tuning. As an example recall the profile of Figure 3. For $\delta_{coverage} = 0.66$ and $\delta_{relevance} = 1/24$, the resulting *abstract* appears in Figure 4.

Finally, the *forum abstract* is computed in a similar way: we sum the abstract of all users and only apply the relevance threshold. Communities are then identified by the top k concepts with the largest occurrence (each community is identified by a unique concept). Users may belong to several communities, proportionally to their concepts occurrence in their abstract. For example, if *arm* and *shoulder* turn out to be the two communities of the system (the top 2 concepts), the user of Figure 4 belongs to the first community with score 8, and does not belong to the second.

We enrich the previous analysis by taking into account the context of communication. there are several technical or textual conventions for answering a given post. For emails or tweets the user who is answered to is explicitly given. For purely web systems, classical patterns are to start the answer to user u with "@u", or to cite the answered message. In Figure 1, the first post of Bob explicitely cites Alice's post, hence the `arm` concept is propagated in Bob's post. The second post of Bob is an implicit answer to the previous post: we then propagate the previous `shoulder` concept into Bob's post. Figure 2 presents the general WebTribe architecture.

3 Demo Scenario

Our 10mn demo considers a community manager taking over the health section of the USA Today forum[3]. We will illustrate the following functionalities, available as a video at `http://www.damien-leprovost.fr/webtribe`:

1. **Source registration, Ontology selection** The manager selects the forum URL and a target ontology (as an OWL file or a subtree of WordNet, given a root concept).

2. **Visualization.** During the entire demonstration, the whole activity can be monitored. For example, as the target forum is analyzed on the fly, a specific window allows seeing the forum with ontology concepts highlighted. Given a community, both its main topic and users can be displayed. For a user, her/his main manipulated topics and possible related communities are listed.

3. **Forum health status.** A global indicator of the community is given, that measures its global health: number of users, covered topics, activity rate, . . .

4. **Alert system.** A simple alert language allows to monitor the activity at the post / user / community level, to warn the community manager of any interesting event (for example, the first use of the name of a disease).

5. **Multiple forum analysis.** Finally, the system can also perform the analysis of several sources, with the same workflow. It allows comparisons, in order to detect similar communities, potential new users, and login equivalences.

References

1. Amer-Yahia, S., Lakshmanan, L., Yu, C.: Socialscope: Enabling information discovery on social content sites. In: Conference on Innovative Data Systems Research (CIDR) (September 2009), `http://arxiv.org/abs/0909.2058`
2. De Choudhury, M., Mason, W.A., Hofman, J.M., Watts, D.J.: Inferring relevant social networks from interpersonal communication. In: International Conference on World Wide Web (WWW), pp. 301–310. ACM, New York (2010)
3. Gloor, P.A., Zhao, Y.: Analyzing actors and their discussion topics by semantic social network analysis. In: Conference on Information Visualization, pp. 130–135 (2006)
4. Leprovost, D., Abrouk, L., Gross-Amblard, D.: Discovering implicit communities in web forums through ontologies. Web Intelligence and Agent Systems: An International Journal 10, 93–103 (2011)
5. Menchen-Trevino, E.: Blogger motivations: Power, pull, and positive feedback. Internet Research 6.0 (2005)
6. Mitrović, M., Paltoglou, G., Tadić, B.: Quantitative analysis of bloggers' collective behavior powered by emotions. Journal of Statistical Mechanics: Theory and Experiment 2011(02), P02005 (2011)
7. Schuth, A., Marx, M., de Rijke, M.: Extracting the discussion structure in comments on news-articles. In: ACM International Workshop on Web Information and Data Management (WIDM), pp. 97–104. ACM, New York (2007)

---

[3] `http://yourlife.usatoday.com/health/`, 2011.

MIGROS: A Model-Driven Transformation Approach of the User Experience of Legacy Applications

Luca Mainetti, Roberto Paiano, and Andrea Pandurino

GSA Lab, University of Salento, Via Monteroni, 73100 Lecce, Italy
{luca.mainetti,roberto.paiano,andrea.pandurino}@unisalento.it

Abstract. Model-driven engineering is a promising approach for the modernization of legacy applications, but there are still many issues to address, especially to obtain automatic refactoring of the User Experience (UX) of existing applications applying modern interaction paradigms as Rich Internet Application (RIA). The MIGROS tool tries to solve the hurdles for the model-driven modernization of the UX of legacy application (as implemented in Cobol CICS, Visual Basic, Power Builder, etc.). It is designed upon a set of well-known methods in the web engineering field. It is implemented as a set of Eclipse plug-ins that support reverse engineering and model transformation exploiting the OMG Architecture-Driven Modernization (ADM) technology.

1   Introduction

According to a 2003 report by the Aberdeen Group, investment in Legacy Applications (LAs), which account for upwards of 70% of enterprise business operations, consumes as much as 80% of software budgets. In a 2006 report, Gartner suggests that organizations need a wholesale re-architecting of the application platform, and conclude that "CIOs and their IT executives must complete enterprise platform migration by 2009." Even if the current economic crisis reduced IT budgets and slowed down the process, in the next future many organizations will start LA's modernization projects. Currently, many tools are available to convert legacy languages to new ones (e.g. from Cobol to Java). They mainly focus on the business logic and the server side of LAs. We observe a lack of approaches specifically intended to migrate the client side. To overcome this limitation, here we present a demo of the MIGROS tool chain that developers can use to automatically modernize the client side of LAs. Thanks to its MDE approach, MIGROS allows developers to refactor the User Experience (UX) of LAs during the modernization journey, taking the opportunities offered by novel interaction paradigms (i.e. RIA). MIGROS is deployed as a set of Eclipse plug-ins that support reverse engineering and model transformation adopting well-known methods in the web engineering field, and exploiting the OMG ADM technology.

Section 2 reports on key related works. Section 3 gives an overview of the MIGROS tool chain architecture and shows an example of its user interface. Finally, section 4 draws conclusions and sketches future steps.

M. Brambilla, T. Tokuda, and R. Tolksdorf (Eds.): ICWE 2012, LNCS 7387, pp. 490–493, 2012.
© Springer-Verlag Berlin Heidelberg 2012

2   Related Work on RIA Modeling and Generation Approaches

Other authors have proposed the use of Model Driven Architectures to evolve web systems [4], and RIAs to unleash superior user interaction [2]. In general, existing methods lack in connecting re-design artifacts with UX requirements. If complex LAs are evolved to web systems, often the presentation layer is migrated to a RIA whereas the business logic and data are offered through a SOA [1]. At the same time the OMG's ADM Task Force (omg.adm.org) is proposing a set of modernization standards to facilitate the exchange of existing systems meta-data for various modernization tools. The OMG's Knowledge Discovery Meta-model (ISO/IEC 19506) provides a comprehensive view of application structure and data, but does not represent directly the UX, even if it is open to exchange meta-data form other models. Many RIA design methods are actually available (readers can look to [3] for a complete survey). The Object Oriented Hypermedia Design Method (OOHDM) proposes a model process for requirements modeling, conceptual modeling, navigation design, interface design, and implementation. WebML for RIAs extends the WebML method considering a well-defined separation between the client side and the server side, and a better definition of the application interface. The Rich Internet Application User eXperience (RUX) method defines the interface of an application through four levels: concepts and tasks, abstract interface, concrete interface, and final interface. UML-based Web Engineering (UWE) exploits an UML profile and integrates RUX method to provide a specification of a rich web system. OOH4RIA is a model-driven approach to design a complete RIA for the GWT framework. OOWS is an approach to develop web applications in an OO modeling oriented software development environment. ADRIA is an UML-based method for designing RIAs departing from the results of an object-oriented analysis. Internet Application Modeling Language (IAML) aims to provide modeling support for all of the fundamental concepts of RIAs using ECA rules, ER diagrams, and UML diagrams. Very often the same research groups that proposed design methods, also released tools to model, fast prototype, and generate web systems and RIAs. Some of these are very strictly related to our work as they use similar approaches and architectures: WebTE, WebRatio, MVC-Webflow, UWE4JSF, MagicUWE, RUX-Tool, and OIDE. Whereas these approaches provide support for abstracting existing RIA technologies and to generate rich web systems, they lack in bridging the fluid nature of the user interaction in RIAs to the design. So, only partially they can be used to transform the UX of LAs to RIAs preventing interface flaws. To meet this challenge, we proposed the use of Rich-IDM [5] and the MIGROS tools as a restructuring bridge between a flat reverse engineering of legacy user interfaces and a structured forward engineering of the presentation layer of RIAs.

3   Tool Chain for Automatic Transformation

The MIGROS tools exploit the OMG's ADM framework. Whereas other research groups (as those at Microsoft's and IBM's laboratories) are working on tools for the server side of existing LAs adopting horizontal transformations (paths 1 and 2 of Fig.

1a) or vertical ones (path 3 of Fig. 1a), we focused our attention on a tool chain to refactor the UX of the existing solution. Following the path 4 of Fig. 1a: (i) we represent the UX of the source code using an extension (WAE+) of the Conallen's UML stereotypes [3]; (ii) we abstract and re-design the UX employing the Rich-IDM primitives, which give the opportunity to add knowledge on UX requirements and communication; and (iii) we map the Rich-IDM primitives to RUX elements, which have the advantage of being mechanically mappable to the target client technology (enabling a generative approach). To refactor the UX, we mainly lever on the following Rich-IDM primitives: *RIA-Page Element*, an atomic fragment of RIA page, which displays contents and links as directly mapped from LA's database; *UX Core*, a connected composition of page elements, which communicates the semantic nucleus of what is offered to the user at a given moment; *Context View*, a set of UX Cores, which maintains navigational context, orientation, organic, and fluid transition between the cores.

Fig. 1b draws the generation process – made up of three phases – of the MIGROS tool chain (domain and application levels) and the supporting technology (lower level). Following the diagram from left to right, in the Knowledge Extraction phase two *Knowledge Extractor* tools (implemented as Modisco Code2Model plug-ins) obtain an OWL domain knowledge model from the LA's database and a WAE+ application model from the LA's user interface. In the Knowledge Recomposition phase, the *Knowledge Recomposer* tool (written as ATL Model2Model rules) transforms the UX

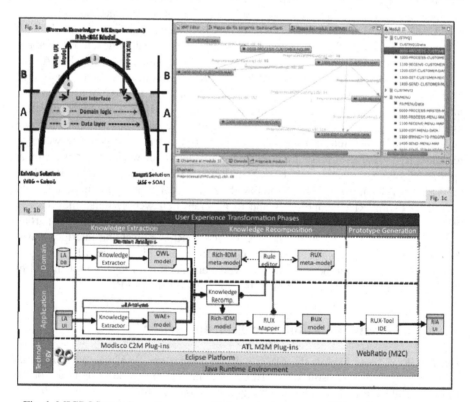

Fig. 1. MIGROS transformation process (1a), generation process (1b), and screenshot (1c)

of the LA representing it as an OWL-encoded Rich-IDM model. To do this, the Knowledge Recomposer uses all the concepts discovered from the database and from the logical and physical user interface of the source LA. Moreover, through a *Rule Editor*, the Knowledge Recomposer allows an UX expert to manually improve the obtained Rich-IDM model in order to better bridge the smooth nature of the user interaction in RIAs, applying usability principles. Then, through a RUX Mapper tool, the Rich-IDM model is converted to a RUX Abstract Interface model. In this step also, the UX designer can use the Rule Editor to obtain the better mapping between Rich-IDM primitives and RUX elements. Finally, in the *Prototype Generation* phase, starting from the RUX Abstract Interface model and using the RUX-Tool IDE, and the WebRatio M2C generator, a RIA prototype of the LA's user interface can be automatically obtained. Fig. 1c shows a screenshot of the Knowledge Extractor tool. Demonstrators of MIGROS tools are available at www.migrosproject.unisalento.it.

4   Conclusions and Future Work

The proposed demonstration illustrates MIGROS, a tool chain based on the Eclipse platform for the model-driven modernization of the user interface of LAs. The demonstration shows how an intensive use of knowledge extraction and model transformation can help developers to automatically re-factor the UX of LAs. The originality of our approach lies in the ability to connect the transformed user interface model to UX requirements, adopting the Rich-IDM method we presented at the 13th IEEE Symposium on Web Systems Evolution. Currently we are working on a large-scale industrial innovation project, which goal is to migrate a complex LA (VB6 + Cobol) to a RIA (JSF + SOA). In the future, we will extend the tool chain to accept input from other LA's client technologies than VB6 (e.g. Cobol CICS or PowerBuilder).

Acknowledgments. This research has been partially supported by the GPS Italian funded DM29255 MIGROS project and Data Management S.p.A.

References

1. Bhallamudi, P., Tilley, S., Sinha, A.: Migrating a Web-based application to a service-based system - an experience report. In: Proceedings of the 11th IEEE International Symposium on Web Systems Evolution, WSE 2009, pp. 71–74. IEEE, NY (2009)
2. Brambilla, M., Preciado, J.C., Linaje, M., Sanchez-Figueroa, F.: Business Process -based Conceptual Design of Rich Internet Applications. In: Proceedings of the 8th International Conference on Web Engineering, ICWE 2008, pp. 155–161. IEEE, NY (2008)
3. Casteleyn, S., Daniel, F., Dolog, P., Matera, M.: Engineering Web Applications. In: Carey, M.J., Ceri, S. (eds.), pp. 978–973. Springer (2009) ISBN 978-3-540-92200-1
4. Feng, C., Hongji, Y., Hong, Z., Bing, Q., Huifang, D.: Web-based system evolution in model driven architecture. In: Proceedings of the 10th IEEE International Symposium on Web Systems Evolution, WSE 2008, pp. 69–72. IEEE, NY (2008)
5. Pandurino, A., Bolchini, D., Mainetti, L., Paiano, R.: Rich-IDM: Extending IDM to Model Rich Internet Applications. In: Proceedings of the ACM 12th Information Integration and Web-based Applications & Services Conf., iiWAS 2010, pp. 145–152 (November 2010)

Crowdsourced Web Site Evaluation
with CrowdStudy

Michael Nebeling[1], Maximilian Speicher,
Michael Grossniklaus[2], and Moira C. Norrie[1]

[1] Institute of Information Systems, ETH Zurich
CH-8092 Zurich, Switzerland
[2] Computer Science Department, Portland State University
Portland, OR 97201, United States of America
{nebeling,norrie}@inf.ethz.ch, speichem@student.ethz.ch,
grossniklaus@cs.pdx.edu

Abstract. Many different automatic usability evaluation tools have been specifically developed for web sites and web-based services, but they usually cannot replace user testing. At the same time, traditional usability evaluation methods can be both expensive and time consuming. We will demonstrate CrowdStudy, a toolkit for crowdsourced testing of web interfaces that allows, not only to efficiently recruit larger amounts of test users, but also to evaluate web sites under many different conditions.

Keywords: Web usability, web site evaluation, crowdsourcing.

1 Introduction

Usability evaluation is an important topic in user interface design practice and research. Many different methods have been specifically developed for web sites [1], while the most prominent example is still user testing [2]. Existing techniques for remote usability evaluation use a range of different user activity tracking methods [3,4], but are frequently restricted to either server or client-side logging, which limits the kinds of information they can collect. Even worse is the fact that none of them specifically take the context of use into account. In contrast to previous approaches, our solution for web site evaluation integrates a simple notion of context-awareness, which is necessary to cater for the increased diversity of devices nowadays used for web browsing. Another shortcoming of existing usability evaluation tools is that essential tasks, such as subject recruitment including qualification tests, and many key aspects of remote usability testing, such as task distribution within or between subjects, are typically not even considered. Our solution is designed to integrate with existing crowdsourcing services such as Amazon Mechanical Turk[1], where requesters may, not only recruit a larger group of users in a short amount of time, but also control the

---

[1] http://mturk.com

M. Brambilla, T. Tokuda, and R. Tolksdorf (Eds.): ICWE 2012, LNCS 7387, pp. 494–497, 2012.

conditions for each worker to be able to participate. This generally makes it a viable platform for conducting different kinds of online user studies [5], but has so far not been considered in existing usability evaluation tools.

In this paper, we present CrowdStudy, a web site evaluation toolkit that can be easily integrated with existing sites for remote usability testing and can also leverage services such as Mechanical Turk to advertise and facilitate online studies with the help of new users. CrowdStudy evolved out of our previous work on crowdsourcing web site adaptations for different devices [6], where it was first built to enable user evaluations for a specific set of tasks. However, we have now built several mechanisms into CrowdStudy that allow it to be configured with different metrics as well as different tasks to support a range of evaluation scenarios. As one example, we will show how CrowdStudy was used for evaluations on mobile touch phones, which is a new important scenario that poses a number of interesting challenges.

We start by presenting CrowdStudy in Section 2. This is followed by a description of our demo in Section 3 and concluding remarks.

2   CrowdStudy

CrowdStudy is designed to integrate with the typical client/server infrastructure of web applications. It introduces additional components for user activity tracking on the client-side and a context engine as well as data logging and crowdsourcing components on the server-side. Figure 1 shows the CrowdStudy architecture. Below we describe how each component contributes to supporting remote usability evaluations.

First note that clients can either be "normal" web site users or workers specifically recruited using crowdsourcing services. CrowdStudy can be configured with

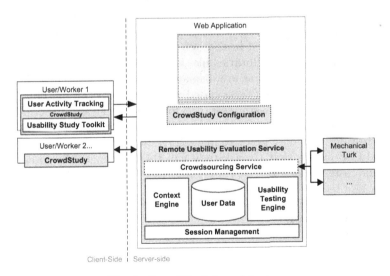

Fig. 1. CrowdStudy's architecture

multiple sets of tasks which are then distributed to users. Tasks may require that other tasks are completed first as well as user qualification in terms of the user's knowledge or skills based on a questionnaire or the client device characteristics based on programmatic checks. Each task may involve one or several web site components as well as navigation between pages. Using client-side scripting, some aspects of a task may be automated to allow users to focus on specific activities. For example, we provide tools that can automatically scroll to a component of interest and annotate and highlight certain parts that require interaction and attention of users. CrowdStudy then automatically tracks the user actions in terms of user interface events fired by the interaction components and also captures the context in terms of the screen size, window size and position in the page. The collected data is first buffered and cached locally before it is sent to the server-side at suitable intervals.

Looking at the server-side extensions, the first is a configuration for Crowd-Study and the second the CrowdStudy service which contains the usability testing engine responsible for assigning and distributing tasks to participants. We have built simple administrative tools for managing and running studies as well as evaluation tools for browsing and analysing the results generated by Crowd-Study. The analysis tools of CrowdStudy range from a simple response viewer that displays questionnaire data submitted by participants to a more advanced log analyser that allows evaluators to browse and visualise the data based on a combination of criteria. For example, CrowdStudy can visualise the touch data aggregated from several smartphone users to see how they interacted with the web site, e.g. where they have mis-clicked links and how much they had to zoom to counteract. CrowdStudy automatically takes care of the necessary user session management and stores all collected information in a database. Finally, as part of the crowdsourcing service component, we have implemented an interface to Mechanical Turk that can be used for recruiting external, paid crowd workers using Amazon's service. Other services could be integrated in the same way.

While most existing frameworks are proxy-based, our solution only requires that CrowdStudy is embedded in the web site using a single line of code similar to including JavaScript libraries like jQuery. User tasks may be based on simple textual descriptions that are displayed in an instruction box. Moreover, CrowdStudy supports custom tasks based on client-side scripting, but also provides a set of pre-defined task classes, e.g. for clicking certain links, navigating to parts of the page or reading text paragraphs and answering questions. In this case, the test designer only needs to mark corresponding web site elements with additional CSS classes that CrowdStudy will then automatically interpret and compile into a test scenario.

3   Demonstration

Our demonstration of CrowdStudy is based on a study we conducted for the Wikipedia web site. CrowdStudy was embedded in an example article and configured with the tasks shown in Figure 2 to assess the usability for smartphones

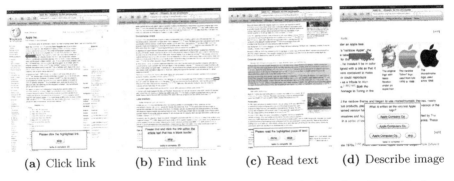

(a) Click link   (b) Find link   (c) Read text   (d) Describe image

Fig. 2. Set of tasks used in the evaluation of Wikipedia based on CrowdStudy

and tablets. Wikipedia was chosen for the test scenario since it provides both a desktop and mobile version with different layouts and features. We performed simple A/B testing by letting CrowdStudy assign one of the layouts to each participant and collected the data from 84 participants using a wide range of mobile devices and also different browsers.

CrowdStudy provided valuable insight into how users interact with such a text-heavy web page in terms of the optimal font size for reading, preferred device orientation with respect to different tasks (landscape was generally preferred on tablets and often used for reading on smartphones, where the other tasks were preferably done in portrait mode) as well as how they made use of multi-touch gestures for zooming and navigating within the page.

Acknowledgements. This work was supported by the SNF under research grant 200021_121847. Michael Grossniklaus, who contributed the integration with Mechanical Turk, is funded by the SNF under grant PA00P2_131452.

References

1. Matera, M., Rizzo, F., Carughi, G.: Web Usability: Principles and Evaluation Methods. Web Engineering (2006)
2. Insfran, E., Fernandez, A.: A Systematic Review of Usability Evaluation in Web Development. In: Hartmann, S., Zhou, X., Kirchberg, M. (eds.) WISE 2008. LNCS, vol. 5176, pp. 81–91. Springer, Heidelberg (2008)
3. Atterer, R., Wnuk, M., Schmidt, A.: Knowing the User's Every Move – User Activity Tracking for Website Usability Evaluation and Implicit Interaction. In: Proc. WWW (2006)
4. Hong, J.I., Heer, J., Waterson, S., Landay, J.A.: WebQuilt: A Proxy-based Approach to Remote Web Usability Testing. TOIS 19(3) (2001)
5. Kittur, A., Chi, E.H., Suh, B.: Crowdsourcing User Studies With Mechanical Turk. In: Proc. CHI (2008)
6. Nebeling, M., Norrie, M.C.: Tools and Architectural Support for Crowdsourced Adaptation of Web Interfaces. In: Auer, S., Díaz, O., Papadopoulos, G.A. (eds.) ICWE 2011. LNCS, vol. 6757, pp. 243–257. Springer, Heidelberg (2011)

Web Service Composition Reuse
through Shared Process Fragment Libraries

David Schumm, Dimitrios Dentsas, Michael Hahn,
Dimka Karastoyanova, Frank Leymann, and Mirko Sonntag

Institute of Architecture of Application Systems, University of Stuttgart,
Universitätsstraße 38, 70569 Stuttgart, Germany
{schumm,karastoyanova,leymann,sonntag}@iaas.uni-stuttgart.de

Abstract. More and more application functionality is provided for use over corporate and public networks. Standardized technology stacks, like Web services, provide abstraction from the internal implementation. Coarse-grained units of Web service composition logic can be made reusable by capturing it as 'process fragment'. Such fragments can be shared over the Web to simplify and accelerate development of process-based service compositions. In this demonstration, we present a framework consisting of an Eclipse-based process design environment that is integrated with a Web-based process fragment library. The framework enables extracting process fragments, publishing and sharing them on the Web, as well as search, retrieval, and their reuse in a given process. Process fragments can be shared with others using a Web frontend or through a plug-in within the process design environment which is building on Web service technology.

Keywords: Process Reuse, Service Composition, Web Services, BPEL, Process Fragments.

1   Reuse of Web Service Compositions

The main principles in service-oriented applications are providing componentized functionality via stable interfaces abstracting from the implementation details and realizing loose coupling for improved flexibility. Web services are often used as the technology for abstractly describing the service interfaces of components (using WSDL[1]) and for composing them in Web service compositions (using BPEL[2]). Web service compositions allow for the definition of complex orchestration logic and integration of simple and complex application functions that are exposed as Web services. Reusability is one of the main principles of SOA, which however has not been completely realized by existing systems for the purposes of reusing coarse-grained units of service compositions, so-called 'process fragments'. A *process fragment* is a connected process structure, which can either be modeled from scratch

---

[1] http://www.w3.org/TR/wsdl
[2] http://www.oasis-open.org/committees/
tc_home.php?wg_abbrev=wsbpel

M. Brambilla, T. Tokuda, and R. Tolksdorf (Eds.): ICWE 2012, LNCS 7387, pp. 498–501, 2012.

or extracted from a given process. Note that in the field of Web services the terms 'process', 'service composition', and 'service orchestration' are used synonymously. Thus, a process fragment can also be understood as coarse-grained unit of service composition logic. Examples of such fragments have already been presented in [1], where we also discussed the benefits of having multiple process fragment libraries, which can be used to *store* such service composition units and to *share* them between partners in order to ease the creation of service compositions. In this demonstration, we will present a complete and integrated framework, enabling reuse and sharing of Web service compositions over the Web. As platform for process design we rely on a prototype for simulation workflows[3] developed in our institute, see also [2]. As platform for fragment sharing we build on the Fragmento library [3] – a repository that provides version management and further functions to support the work with fragments. The integration is mainly achieved through Web service technology, an OSGi-based Eclipse plug-in, and process design environment extensions.

2   Framework Walkthrough

There are four key components in the framework (Figure 1): (i) multiple deployments of the Fragmento Library[4] and underlying database, which account for versioned process fragment management; (ii) Fragmento's Web interface, which is not part of the demonstration, allows users to share and reuse process fragments over the Web without a tight integration, using just a common Web client; (iii) the Process Design Environment, which is based on the open source tool Eclipse BPEL Designer[5]; and (iv) an Eclipse plug-in that tightly integrates Fragmento with the design environment. The plug-in connects to the Fragmento library via its Web service interfaces (through generated code skeletons in Java). The plug-in is made available within Eclipse as 'View' so that it can be easily positioned between the other graphical components of the design environment.

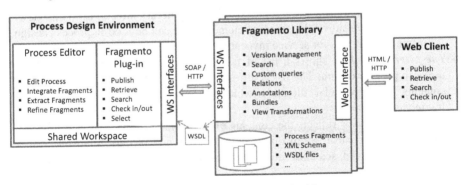

Fig. 1. Overview of the Integration Architecture

---

[3] http://www.iaas.uni-stuttgart.de/
   forschung/projects/simtech/index.php
[4] http://www.iaas.uni-stuttgart.de/
   forschung/projects/fragmento/start.htm
[5] http://eclipse.org/bpel/

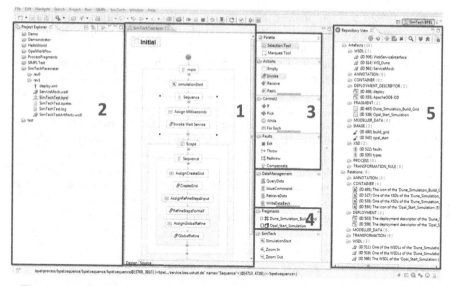

Fig. 2. Main Graphical Components of the Process Design Environment's User Interface

Figure 2 shows the user interface of the process design environment, which is structured into multiple graphical components that can be flexibly arranged:

1. *The editor pane* displays the model of a process or fragment graphically. The user can select process logic and extract and store it locally as fragment. Furthermore, it is possible to insert a fragment into a process by a simple drag-and-drop operation.
2. *The project explorer* shows all files relevant for process design – models of processes and process fragments, deployment descriptors, graphical files (e.g. icons), XML Schema and WSDL interface descriptions. Fragments extracted from a process can be published to a connected fragment library directly from this view.
3. *The editor palette* shows the standard elements that can be used in process design, for instance, activities for service invocation or loop controls.
4. *The fragment palette* shows a list of fragments which are currently selected for usage in process design. The list is refreshed on demand. It is assembled based on contents in a particular directory which is populated by previously exported fragments.
5. *The repository view* reflects the contents of a selected process fragment library in form of a tree control. From this view, processes and process fragments can be published, retrieved, searched, checked in and out, and selected for inclusion in the fragment palette.

3   Demonstration

With the help of examples we will demonstrate the main steps of the approach, namely extraction, publishing, retrieval, selection, and finally integration of process fragments, explained in the following.

Process Fragment Extraction. The editor pane allows the user to select a structured activity, e.g. a BPEL <flow> activity containing several variable assignment and service invocation activities. A right-click on this structure shows a context menu allowing for process fragment extraction. When this function is selected, a connected process fragment is determined, based on the selected activities. A new process file is generated, containing only the fragment and all required variables, XML Schema, and WSDL information of the involved services and information of the process interface related to the fragment. The extracted fragment is opened in a new tab to prepare it for sharing, e.g. placeholders can be added.

Process Fragment Publishing. Publishing of extracted fragments can be directly triggered from within the project explorer by selecting the files generated during fragment extraction. These files can be passed to the Fragmento plug-in by selecting a function in the extended context menu. The plug-in then prepares a set of SOAP messages, each containing a file belonging to the fragment. Based on identifiers returned by Fragmento, interrelations between the artifacts are then created through sending further SOAP messages to Fragmento, i.e. a fragment 'bundle' is defined.

Process Fragment Selection and Retrieval. To be able to select and retrieve fragments using the process design environment or the Web client, a fragment library needs to be chosen, either in the Eclipse plug-in (i.e. using the repository view) by pointing to a WSDL location of a Fragmento deployment or by entering the URL in the Web browser (i.e. using the Web client). In Eclipse the whole contents available in the library are downloaded after connecting to the library. Further work is made on a local copy that is refreshed on demand. Search can be made in Eclipse and in the Web client using keywords, contained text, etc. A fragment can be made available for reuse in the fragment palette through an export function in the repository toolbar. The newest version is chosen by default, but also older versions can be selected. All files of selected fragments are copied to a directory which is shared with the process design environment. Multiple fragments can be added to the palette that way.

Process Fragment Integration. After manual refresh of the fragment palette all exported fragments are shown by their name (and icon if specified). In this palette a fragment can be selected for integration. A click on a location of an opened process defines the place where the fragment should be integrated. During integration, the activities in the fragment are added to that location in the process, the WSDLs and XML Schemas are added to the project, and deployment descriptors are merged.

References

1. Schumm, D., Karastoyanova, D., Kopp, O., Leymann, F., Sonntag, M., Strauch, S.: Process Fragment Libraries for Easier and Faster Development of Process-based Applications. Journal of Systems Integration 2(1), 39–55 (2011)
2. Sonntag, M., Karastoyanova, D.: Next Generation Interactive Scientific Experimenting Based On The Workflow Technology. In: Proceedings of the 21st IASTED International Conference on Modeling and Simulation, MS 2010 (2010)
3. Schumm, D., Karastoyanova, D., Leymann, F., Strauch, S.: Fragmento: Advanced Process Fragment Library. In: Proceedings of the 19th International Conference on Information Systems Development (ISD 2010). Springer (2010)

Engineering the Evaluation Approach to Fit Different Web Project and Organization Needs

Luis Olsina

GIDIS_Web, Engineering School at Universidad Nacional de La Pampa, Argentina
olsinal@ing.unlpam.edu.ar

Abstract. Web applications, among other software entities, and their quality evaluation has been the subject of abundant research; however, open issues still remain. This tutorial discusses a *general measurement and evaluation approach* which is based on both a quality modeling framework and strategies. An evaluation strategy is in turn grounded on three principles namely: a conceptual framework, a well-established process, and methods/tools. The illustrated evaluation approach allows instantiating evaluation strategies –reusing these three principles- to engineering different organization-level information needs.

1 Introduction

Measurement, evaluation, analysis and recommendation are support processes to primary web engineering processes, i.e. by giving support to deal with information needs at different project or organizational levels. In addition, quality is one out of four main dependent variables for managing web projects. For each engineered project, and independently of the development/maintenance lifecycle adopted, levels of quality for its entities and attributes should be agreed, specified, measured and evaluated for analyzing and improving them. To assure repeatability and consistency of results for better analysis and decision making, it is necessary to have a well-defined yet customizable evaluation approach.

This tutorial discusses a *general measurement and evaluation (M&E) approach* which is based on two main pillars, namely: i) a *quality modeling framework*; and ii) *M&E strategies*, which in turn are grounded on three principles viz. a *M&E conceptual framework*, a *well-established M&E process*, and *evaluation methods and tools*. The *M&E conceptual framework* capability should be built on a robust terminological base, e.g. an ontology, which explicitly and formally specifies the main concepts, properties, relationships, and constraints for the M&E domain, as well as their grouping into components. This principle ensures terminological uniformity among the other capabilities and thus the consistency of results. The second principle is the *M&E process* [1], which describes what to do, by specifying the activities to be planned and executed, their inputs and outputs, roles, interdependencies, among other aspects. A well-established M&E process not only facilitates the understanding and communication among stakeholders but also ensures repeatability and reproducibility in the implementation of the activities. Lastly, *methods and tools*, which enable to

M. Brambilla, T. Tokuda, and R. Tolksdorf (Eds.): ICWE 2012, LNCS 7387, pp. 502–503, 2012.

perform and automate the activities' descriptions. Methods are allocated in a flexible way to perform the specified activities and usually automated by tools.

This general M&E approach can be adapted to fit different organizational levels and information needs for different quality focuses regarding entities categories such as resource, product, system, system in use, etc. in a flexible yet structured manner.

The development of this tutorial makes use of both theoretical and practical background. From the practical point of view, so far, we have developed two M&E strategies, namely: GOCAME (*Goal-Oriented Context-Aware Measurement and Evaluation*) [3], and SIQinU (*Strategy for understanding and Improving Quality in Use*) [2], which the latter was used in a testing industry case. These strategies can be instantiated regarding the quality modeling framework and specific information needs.

2   Learning Objectives

To summarize, the main tutorial learning objectives are: 1) Review background concepts such as *information need*, *quality* and *entity category*; *quality models*, and *strategies* regarding the M&E process, conceptual framework, method/tool; 2) Get insight on how the quality modeling framework can be instantiated in a purposeful way not only for understanding but also for improvement, using for this end the customized strategy. The learning aim is to see that many different strategies can be instantiated from the same quality modeling framework, regarding different information needs and organizational levels; and 3) Understand how a concrete strategy for improving a web application (e.g. its external quality and quality in use) can be used, while excerpts of a real case study are illustrated.

References

1. Becker, P., Lew, P., Olsina, L.: Specifying Process Views for a Measurement, Evaluation and Improvement Strategy. Advances in Software Engineering Journal 2012, 28 (2012), http://www.hindawi.com/journals/ase/contents/
2. Lew, P., Olsina, L., Becker, P., Zhang, L.: An Integrated Strategy to Understand and Manage Quality in Use for Web Applications. Requirements Engineering Journal 16(3), 1–32 (2011)
3. Olsina, L., Lew, P., Dieser, A., Rivera, B.: Using Web Quality Models and a Strategy for Purpose-Oriented Evaluations. Journal of Web Engineering 10(4), 316–352 (2011)

Epidemic Intelligence:
For the Crowd, by the Crowd

Avaré Stewart and Ernesto Diaz

L3S Research Center,
Appelstrasse 4, 30167 Hannover, Germany
{stewart,diaz}@L3S.de
http://www.L3S.de

Abstract. Event Based Epidemic Intelligence (e-EI) encompasses activities related to early warnings and their assessments as part of the outbreak investigation task. Recently, modern disease surveillance systems have started to also monitor social media streams, with the objective of improving their timeliness in detecting disease outbreaks, and producing warnings against potential public health threats.

In this tutorial we show how social media analysis can be exploited for two important stages of e-EI, namely: (i) Early Outbreak Detection, and (ii) Outbreak Analysis and Control. We discuss techniques and methods for detecting health-related events from unstructured text and outline approaches, as well as the challenges faced in social media-based surveillance. In particular, we will show how using Twitter can help us to find early cases of an outbreak, as well as, understand the potential causes of contamination and spread from the perspective of the field practitioners.

1 Introduction

Social Media streams, such as Twitter and other real-time media are now seen as a valuable source of temporally and spacially relevant information. Applications that rely upon social media streams include trend detection [6, 10]; and intelligence gathering for applications such as: natural disaster detection [7, 9] or flu outbreak tracking [1–3, 8].

In this tutorial, we focus on the application of social media streams for Event-Based Epidemic Intelligence (e-EI). e-EI encompasses activities related to early warnings and their assessment as part of the outbreak investigation task. The tutorial is divided into two parts, in each, we take up an important aspect of e-EI. In Part I: Early Outbreak Detection, we discuss both supervised and unsupervised techniques for detecting health-related events from unstructured text. We also outline the approaches for detecting relevant disease-reporting entities; such as affected organisms, medical condition, location and temporal mentions and address the problem of disambigating semantic relations which contain these entities. Next we discuss the approaches and challenges of generating early warnings from relevant semantic relations, for domain experts [4].

M. Brambilla, T. Tokuda, and R. Tolksdorf (Eds.): ICWE 2012, LNCS 7387, pp. 504–505, 2012.
© Springer-Verlag Berlin Heidelberg 2012

In Part II: Outbreak Analysis and Control, we focus on two types of support for helping domain experts with the problem of information overload when assessing the risk associated with system generated warnings; namely, ranking of early warning alerts [5] and appropriate visualization services. As a case study, we show how using Twitter can help us to find early cases of an outbreak, as well as, understand the potential causes of contamination and spread from the perspective of the field practitioners. Throughout the tutorial, we present practical lessons that have been learned within the context of the M-Eco project (http://www.meco-project.eu/) and numerous results from field practitioners assessments; finally we conclude with an outlook for the domain of e-EI.

Acknowledgments. This work was funded, in part, by the European Commission Seventh Framework Program (FP7/2007-2013) under grant agreement No.247829 for the M-Eco Medical Ecosystem Project.

References

1. Aramaki, E., Maskawa, S., Morita, M.: Twitter catches the flu: Detecting influenza epidemics using twitter. In: Proceedings of EMNLP 2011 (2011)
2. Collier, N., Son, N.T., Nguyen, N.M.: Omg u got flu? analysis of shared health messages for bio-surveillance. CoRR abs/1110.3089 (2011)
3. Culotta, A.: Towards detecting influenza epidemics by analyzing twitter messages. In: Proceedings of the First Workshop on Social Media Analytics, SOMA 2010 (2010)
4. Diaz, E., Stewart, A.: Tracking twitter for epidemic intelligence. case study: Ehec/hus outbreak in germany. In: ACM Conference on Web Science 2012 (2012)
5. Diaz, E., Stewart, A., Valasco, E., Denecke, K.: Towards personalized learning to rank for epidemic intelligence based on social media streams. In: Proceeding of the World Wide Web 2012 (2012)
6. Mathioudakis, M., Koudas, N.: Twittermonitor: trend detection over the twitter stream. In: Proceedings of SIGMOD 2010 (2010)
7. Sakaki, T., Okazaki, M., Matsuo, Y.: Earthquake shakes twitter users: real-time event detection by social sensors. In: Proceedings of WWW 2010 (2010)
8. Szomszor, M., Kostkova, P., Louis, C.S.: Twitter informatics: Tracking and understanding public reaction during the 2009 swine flu pandemic. In: Proceedings of WI-IAT 2011 (2011)
9. Vieweg, S., Hughes, A.L., Starbird, K., Palen, L.: Microblogging during two natural hazards events: what twitter may contribute to situational awareness. In: Proceedings of CHI 2010 (2010)
10. Yang, J., Leskovec, J.: Patterns of temporal variation in online media. In: Proceedings of WSDM 2011 (2011)

An Introduction to SPARQL
and Queries over Linked Data

Olaf Hartig

Humboldt-Universität zu Berlin
hartig@informatik.hu-berlin.de

Abstract. Nowadays, more and more datasets are published on the Web adhering to the Linked Data principles. Our tutorial provides a beginners' introduction on how to query this data using the query language SPARQL.

1 Motivation

Since the Linked Data principles have been proposed in 2006 [1], a grass-roots movement started to publish and interlink multiple open databases on the Web based on these principles [2]. Today an increasing number of data publishers such as the BBC, Thomson Reuters, The New York Times, the Library of Congress, and the UK government adopt this practice. This ongoing effort resulted in bootstrapping the Web of Linked Data which, today, comprises billions of statements including millions of links between datasets. The published datasets include data about books, movies, music, radio and television programs, reviews, scientific publications, genes, proteins, medicine, clinical trials, geographic locations, people, companies, statistical and census data, etc.

The availability of this data, including the existence of data-level connections between datasets, presents exciting opportunities for the next generation of Web-based applications. As a consequence, consuming Linked Data is a highly relevant topic in the context of Web engineering.

2 Topics

Our introductory tutorial aims to provide participants with an understanding of one of the basic aspects of Linked Data consumption, that is, querying Linked Data. The tutorial consists of three main parts.

Part 1: The RDF Data Model and Linked Data. In the first part, we briefly introduce the concept of Linked Data and its underlying data model, RDF [3].

The idea of Linked Data is based on four principles [1]. These principles require to identify an entity as well as provide access to a structured data representation of it, via a single HTTP scheme based URI. Hence, resolving such a URI via the HTTP protocol yields data about the entity identified by the URI. This data should be represented using the Resource Description Framework (RDF). RDF is a generic data model that represents data using triples of the form (subject, predicate, object). Each element of such an RDF triple can be a URI or a local identifier for unnamed entities; objects can

M. Brambilla, T. Tokuda, and R. Tolksdorf (Eds.): ICWE 2012, LNCS 7387, pp. 506–507, 2012.

also be a literal. A set of RDF triples is called an RDF graph. Furthermore, the Linked Data principles require that the provided RDF data includes *data links* pointing to data from other data sources on the Web. A data link is an RDF triple where the subject is a URI in the namespace of one data source and the object is a URI in the namespace of another source. By connecting data from different sources via such links a single, globally distributed dataspace emerges.

Part 2: The SPARQL Query Language.   The second and largest part provides a comprehensive introduction to SPARQL [4], the de facto query language for RDF.

SPARQL is based on RDF graph patterns and subgraph matching: The basic building block for SPARQL queries is called *basic graph pattern* (BGP). A BGP is a set of triple patterns which are RDF triples that may contain query variables at the subject, predicate, and object position. More complex query patterns are unions of pattern, optional patterns, filter expressions, etc. Query results in SPARQL are defined based on graph pattern matching: Each element of the result is a set of variable bindings that, basically, represents a matching subgraph in the queried RDF graph.

Part 3: Querying Multiple Linked Datasets.   In the third part of the tutorial, we discuss several approaches for executing SPARQL queries over multiple, interlinked datasets. These approaches can be classified in three categories: data warehousing, query federation, and Linked Data query processing [5].

Data warehousing is an approach where data is collected and copied into a central database. Queries are executed over this central database.

The query federation approach is based on distributing the processing of queries to query services provided by Linked Data publishers. A mediator analyzes and decomposes the user query into several sub-queries. These sub-queries are distributed to the query services which, then, execute these sub-queries and return the results.

Linked Data query processing approaches evaluate queries over the Web of Linked Data by relying only on the Linked Data principles. The prevalent example of a Linked Data query processing approach is link traversal based query execution. The idea of this approach is to intertwine the traversal of data links with the construction of the query result and, thus, to integrate the discovery of data into the query execution process [6].

References

1. Berners-Lee, T.: Linked Data (2006), http://w3.org/DesignIssues/LinkedData
2. Bizer, C., Heath, T., Berners-Lee, T.: Linked Data – The Story So Far. Journal on Semantic Web and Information Systems 5(3) (2009)
3. Klyne, G., Carroll, J.J.: Resource Description Framework (RDF): Concepts and Abstract Syntax. W3C Recommendation (February 2004)
4. Prud'hommeaux, E., Seaborne, A.: SPARQL Query Language for RDF. W3C Recommendation (January 2008)
5. Hartig, O., Langegger, A.: A Database Perspective on Consuming Linked Data on the Web. Datenbank-Spektrum 10(2) (2010)
6. Hartig, O., Freytag, J.C.: Foundations of Traversal Based Query Execution over Linked Data. In: Proceedings of the 23rd ACM Conference on Hypertext and Social Media (2012)

Natural Language Processing for the Web

Silvia Quarteroni

Dipartimento di Elettronica e Informazione - Politecnico di Milano
Via Ponzio, 34/5 - 20133 Milan, Italy
quarteroni@elet.polimi.it

Abstract. The Web offers a wealth of unstructured textual data that is not readily processable using computational resources both because of its format and owing to the ambiguity of natural language. The Natural Language Processing for the Web tutorial focuses on challenging and interesting aspects dealing with natural language Web applications. The audience is introduced to Natural Language Processing as a discipline in order to acquire a basic knowledge of its different methods, particularly statistical, and evaluation metrics. State-of-the-art applications of natural language research will then be discussed in detail, including information extraction from the social Web and Web crawling with particular focus on question answering systems and natural language data service querying.

1 Summary

The Web offers huge amounts of unstructured textual data that are not readily processable using computational resources. Indeed, the ambiguity of natural language is the main obstacle to its understanding by computers. However, dialogue with artificial intelligences has been a human goal since the Turing test and the first conversational machines appeared in the 1960s, with ELIZA the Rogerian psychotherapist [3].

Fifty years later, we have designed machines able to win TV game shows such as *Jeopardy!* by giving more correct answers to complicated questions than the all-time top participants [1]; we are able to search the Web via spoken interfaces using our smartphone thanks to billion-word phonetic models [2] and we can make sense of user-contributed data thanks to tagging and what is called the "social Web".

The Natural Language Processing for the Web tutorial illustrates the fundamental building blocks of Natural Language Processing (NLP), with particular attention to statistical models. Furthermore, state-of-the-art applications such as open-domain Web question answering and natural language data service querying are described in higher detail.

Part I: Introduction to Natural Language Processing. This section of the tutorial provides the audience with the main motivations underlying NLP research, which joins aspects of Information Retrieval, Linguistics and Statistics.

M. Brambilla, T. Tokuda, and R. Tolksdorf (Eds.): ICWE 2012, LNCS 7387, pp. 508–509, 2012.
© Springer-Verlag Berlin Heidelberg 2012

Motivations and Definitions. We define NLP and its main challenges and opportunities; a brief history of NLP with examples from concrete applications is provided.

Levels of Natural Language Understanding. The syntactic, semantic and pragmatic levels of interpretation of textual documents are explained. We discuss syntactic tasks, e.g. Part-of-Speech tagging, shallow parsing and deep syntactic parsing; semantic tasks, including word sense disambiguation, semantic role labeling and recognizing textual entailment; pragmatic and discourse tasks, including anaphora, ellipsis and co-reference resolution.

Methods. Rule-based and Machine learning approaches to NLP are introduced, along with fundamental algorithms for textual classification and sequence labeling. Generative and discriminative models are discussed, including Naïve Bayes, Hidden Markov Models, Support Vector Machines, Conditional Random Fields.

Evaluation. Quantitative assessment of NLP methods include measuring Precision, Recall, F1-measure, Mean Reciprocal Rank, all of which are discussed.

Part II: Applications of Natural Language Processing. This section of the tutorial outlines a few key application of NLP of particular interest to the Web Engineering community. The technology required to convert a natural language query into an "exact" query suitable for an information retrieval engine or a Web service collection is briefly discussed with examples from ongoing research.

Overview of Natural Language Applications. The most widespread applications of NLP include Information Extraction, Machine Translation, Automatic Summarization, Opinion Mining/Sentiment Analysis, Text categorization, (Spoken) Dialogue Systems.

Question Answering. The aim of a Question Answering (QA) system is to reply to queries in natural language with concise answers – not just relevant documents. We illustrate the main components and phases of a QA system: question processing, document retrieval and answer extraction. Advanced QA techniques such as answer re-ranking, interactive and personalized QA are also discussed.

Querying Data Services. Data services allow users to access structured information via Web APIs; however, their interfaces are generally cumbersome for the end-user. We discuss how such a limitation can be overcome by outlining techniques converting queries in natural language into Web Service "logical" queries.

References

1. Ferrucci, D.A.: Introduction to this is watson. IBM Journal of Research and Development 56(3.4), 36–45 (2012)
2. Franz, A., Milch, B.: Searching the web by voice. In: Proceedings of the 19th International Conference on Computational Linguistics, vol. 2, pp. 1–5. Association for Computational Linguistics (2002)
3. Weizenbaum, J.: Eliza - a computer program for the study of natural language communication between man and machine. Commun. ACM 9(1), 36–45 (1966)

The Web of Data for E-Commerce in Brief

Martin Hepp

Universität der Bundeswehr München
E-Business and Web Science Research Group
Werner-Heisenberg-Weg 39, 85577 Neubiberg, Germany
mhepp@computer.org

Abstract. The GoodRelations ontology (http://purl.org/goodrelations/) is one huge success story of applying Semantic Web technology to business challenges. In this tutorial, we will (1) give a comprehensive overview and hands-on training on the conceptual structures of the GoodRelations ontology, including patterns for ownership and demand, (2) present the full tool chain for producing and consuming GoodRelations-related data, (3) explain the long-term vision of linked open commerce, (4) describe the main challenges for future research in the field, and (5) discuss advanced topics, like access control, identity and authentication (e.g. with WebID); micropayment services (like Payswarm), and data management issues from the publisher and consumer perspective.

Keywords: GoodRelations, schema.org, Semantic Web, eCommerce, eBusiness, Search Engines, RDFa, Microdata.

1   Overview

The GoodRelations ontology [1,2] is one of the very few OWL DL ontologies that have reached Web-scale adoption and are officially supported by major Web search engine like Google and Yahoo. GoodRelations has been implemented by major technology vendors (e.g. OpenLink Software), retailers (e.g. Bestbuy), and manufacturers (e.g. Volkswagen). In essence, GoodRelations is an industry-neutral conceptual model for representing commerce-related information that fits the needs of various stages of value chains, ranging from raw materials over manufacturing and retail to after-sales support and disposal. While GoodRelations is available in a representation based on the W3C stack for the Semantic Web vision, namely the OWL DL ontology language and the RDF data model, it can be used in arbitrary syntactical formats, including RDFa, Microdata, RDF/XML, Turtle, NTriples, dataRSS, JSON-LD, GData, or OData [3]. The GoodRelations conceptual model can be used for various purposes, namely exposing ecommerce information on the Web in a way that is easily accessible for search engines ("Semantic SEO", see [4]), browser extensions, and novel mobile applications, or for integrating product and offer information from heterogeneous sources, e.g. in data warehouses or for data quality management.

M. Brambilla, T. Tokuda, and R. Tolksdorf (Eds.): ICWE 2012, LNCS 7387, pp. 510–511, 2012.
© Springer-Verlag Berlin Heidelberg 2012

2   GoodRelations and the Semantic Web Vision

One key distinction that sets GoodRelations apart from most other Web ontologies is the fact that it is stable and mature and accompanied by a comprehensive documentation and tool-chain. As a rough estimate of effort we can say that GoodRelations has so far consumed at least ten person-years of development and documentation work, and that maintaining the comprehensive documentation and supporting the GoodRelations community of adopters account for at least 75 % of all effort, whereas the core ontology coding was a relatively moderate task.

GoodRelations is fully compatible with the state of the art of Semantic Web and Linked Data engineering and will work even in very sophisticated environments, e.g. where complete OWL DL reasoning is required. On the other hand GoodRelations does not critically depend on a state-of-the art Semantic Web infrastructure. In fact, GoodRelations data can be processed in any graph-based environment that follows the Entity-Attribute-Value paradigm [cf. 5].

3   Tutorial Outline

In this tutorial, participants will learn how to use the GoodRelations ontology to augment Web shops and other Web applications with metadata on business entities, products and services, prices, warranty, shop locations, terms and conditions, etc. This includes a comprehensive overview and hands-on training on the conceptual structures of the GoodRelations ontology including patterns for ownership and demand, an introduction to the tool-chain for producing and consuming GoodRelations-related data, and an outlook into the long-term vision of linked open commerce. We will also cover advanced topics, like access control, identity and authentication (e.g. with WebID); micropayment services (like Payswarm), and data management issues from the publisher and consumer perspective. The tutorial materials will be available from http://wiki.goodrelations-vocabulary.org/Events/ICWE2012.

Acknowledgments. The work on this paper and the ICWE 2012 tutorial have been been supported by the German Federal Ministry of Research (BMBF) by a grant under the KMU Innovativ program as part of the Intelligent Match project (FKZ 01IS10022B).

References

1. http://purl.org/goodrelations/
2. Hepp, M.: GoodRelations: An Ontology for Describing Products and Services Offers on the Web. In: Gangemi, A., Euzenat, J. (eds.) EKAW 2008. LNCS (LNAI), vol. 5268, pp. 329–346. Springer, Heidelberg (2008)
3. http://www.ebusiness-unibw.org/wiki/Syntaxes4GoodRelations
4. http://wiki.goodrelations-vocabulary.org/GoodRelations_for_Semantic_SEO
5. Dinu, V., Nadkarni, P.: Guidelines for the effective use of entity–attribute–value modeling for biomedical databases. International Journal of Medical Informatics 76(11-12), 769–779 (2007)

Author Index